State Laughter

State Laughter

Stalinism, Populism, and Origins of Soviet Culture

EVGENY DOBRENKO
and
NATALIA JONSSON-SKRADOL

UNIVERSITY PRESS

Great Clarendon Street, Oxford, OX2 6DP,
United Kingdom

Oxford University Press is a department of the University of Oxford.
It furthers the University's objective of excellence in research, scholarship,
and education by publishing worldwide. Oxford is a registered trade mark of
Oxford University Press in the UK and in certain other countries

© Evgeny Dobrenko and Natalia Jonsson-Skradol 2022

The moral rights of the authors have been asserted

First Edition published in 2022

Impression: 1

All rights reserved. No part of this publication may be reproduced, stored in
a retrieval system, or transmitted, in any form or by any means, without the
prior permission in writing of Oxford University Press, or as expressly permitted
by law, by licence or under terms agreed with the appropriate reprographics
rights organization. Enquiries concerning reproduction outside the scope of the
above should be sent to the Rights Department, Oxford University Press, at the
address above

You must not circulate this work in any other form
and you must impose this same condition on any acquirer

Published in the United States of America by Oxford University Press
198 Madison Avenue, New York, NY 10016, United States of America

British Library Cataloguing in Publication Data

Data available

Library of Congress Control Number: 2021944925

ISBN 978-0-19-884041-1

DOI: 10.1093/oso/9780198840411.001.0001

Printed and bound by
CPI Group (UK) Ltd, Croydon, CR0 4YY

Links to third party websites are provided by Oxford in good faith and
for information only. Oxford disclaims any responsibility for the materials
contained in any third party website referenced in this work.

For Liudmila Nedialkova.

ED.

For Olga Skradol and Nick Jonsson.

NJS.

Mankind, which in Homer's time was an object of amusement for the Olympian gods, now is one for itself. Its self-alienation has reached such a degree that it can experience its own destruction as an aesthetic pleasure of the first order.

> Walter Benjamin, *The Work of Art in the Age of Mechanical Reproduction*

Table of Contents

List of Illustrations   xi

   Introduction   1

1. The Stalinist World of Laughter: The Fate of the Comic in a Tragic Age   18
2. A Killer Wit: Laughter in Stalinist Official Discourse   68
3. The Funny War: Laughing at the Front in World War Two   115
4. "One Might Think It Is a Ward in a Madhouse": Late Stalinism, the Early Cold War, and Caricature   152
5. The Gogols and the Shchedrins: Lessons in "Positive Satire"   211
6. The Soviet Bestiary: Genealogy of the Stalinist Fable   250
7. The Merry Adventures of Stalin's Peasants: Kolkhoz *Commedia dell'arte*   285
8. "A Total Racket": Vaudeville for the New People   325
9. Metalaughter: Populism and the Stalinist Musical Comedy   361

Bibliography   399
Index   417

List of Illustrations

Fig. 1. Caricature by Boris Efimov, text by Boris Laskin. *Literaturnaia gazeta*, May 1, 1951.   154

Fig. 2. Caricature by Boris Efimov. *Literaturnaia gazeta*, January 30, 1951.   155

Fig. 3. Caricature by Boris Efimov. *Literaturnaia gazeta*, August 4, 1951.   156

Fig. 4. Caricature by Boris Efimov. *Literaturnaia gazeta*, April 5, 1950.   157

Fig. 5. Caricature by Boris Efimov. *Literaturnaia gazeta*, December 4, 1948.   158

Fig. 6. Montage cartoon by A. Zhitomirskii. © Vladimir Zhitomirskii. *Literaturnaia gazeta*, November 30, 1949.   159

Fig. 7. Caricature by B. Efimov. *Literaturnaia gazeta*, November 26, 1947.   160

Fig. 8. Montage cartoon by A. Zhitomirskii. © Vladimir Zhitomirskii. *Izvestiia*, March 27, 1952.   161

Fig. 9. Montage cartoon by A. Zhitomirskii. © Vladimir Zhitomirskii. *Literaturnaia gazeta*, October 1, 1947.   162

Fig. 10. Cartoon reprinted from the Czech newspaper *Rude Pravo*. *Literaturnaia gazeta*, February 23, 1952.   163

Fig. 11. Caricature by Boris Efimov. *Literaturnaia gazeta*, November 4, 1950.   166

Fig. 12. Caricature by the Kukryniksy, *Pravda*, October 1, 1947.   171

Fig. 13. Montage cartoon by A. Zhitomirskii. © Vladimir Zhitomirskii. *Literaturnaia gazeta*, March 24, 1948.   172

Fig. 14. Boris Efimov. Illustration to the satirical piece by D. Zaslavskii "The Trial of Lynch-Medina" in the collection *Cavemen in America* (Moscow, 1951).   184

Fig. 15. Boris Efimov. Illustration to the satirical piece by D. Zaslavskii "How Mr. Acheson Flogged Himself" in the collection *Cavemen in America* (Moscow, 1951).   186

Fig. 16. Boris Efimov. Illustration to the satirical piece by D. Zaslavskii "Acheson overthrows...Karl Marx" in the collection *Cavemen in America* (Moscow, 1951).   188

Introduction

In 1989, in the heyday of perestroika, the American publisher Andrews & McMeel published a book about Soviet humor that included caricatures from the principal Soviet satirical magazine, *Krokodil*. The book had two introductions. One was by *Krokodil*'s editor-in-chief, Aleksei P'ianov, and the second was penned by the famous historian of animation and caricature, Charles Solomon. Solomon's text opened with a short overview of how the Soviet Union was perceived in the West, through Cold War films from Hollywood:

> That anyone could compile an anthology of Soviet cartoons will surprise many Americans. In the United States, the USSR is usually depicted as either a bleak, grey land where gloomy peasant women sweep the sidewalks, or a sinister conspiracy of a country bristling with missiles, spies, and aging generals in medal-encrusted uniforms. In both scenarios, the graphic arts are restricted to garish, "heroic" murals on the walls of tractor factories.[1]

What kind of laughter could there be in a country like that?

P'ianov's introduction, a showcase of perestroika rhetoric (glasnost', cooperation, trust), was, in a way, an answer to that question. Soviet people, it says, are full of optimism, as attested by the astronomical print-runs of the country's principal satirical magazine. Make laughter, not war, P'ianov urged his American reader.

As we shall see, the external, almost cartoonish projection of Soviet laughter did not, alas, stray far from the perspective usually adopted within the country itself. Of all aesthetic categories, the comic has the least obvious connection with Stalinism. It is much easier to associate the Stalinist aesthetic with the heroic, the monumental, the sublime, even the tragic. For most of those familiar with Socialist Realism as the official Soviet art, there is nothing more boring, more helplessly gloomy, and further removed from laughter and merriment. The very words "Soviet laughter" usually made one think of the same old anti-Soviet jokes and Aesopian language, the same old Soviet (read: anti-Soviet) satire, intellectuals giving someone the finger on the sly—the Sovietologists' favorite subjects. The names that came to mind would be those of Mikhail Bulgakov, Mikhail

---

[1] *Soviet Humor*, p. 3.

Zoshchenko, Nikolai Erdman, Il'ia Il'f and Evgenii Petrov—satirists of the first Soviet decades, whose names are well known and whose works are still much loved today. Some readers might think of examples of the more radical humor of the absurd, for example Daniil Kharms. Yet others might be more familiar with the names associated with the late Soviet decades: Vladimir Voinovich, Venichka Erofeev—all dissidents, all printed in *tamizdat* and read at home, behind closed doors and drawn curtains.

There is no shortage of works on Soviet satire and satirists, humor and humorists. In this book, we approach the topic from a completely different perspective. Rather than turning our attention to the dissident and the original, the talented and the disruptive authors, texts and styles, we will be talking about what constituted the fabric of state-sanctioned humor, where individual voices were lost in the multitude of constantly recycled patterns. Here, we are interested in the transformations that the comic underwent in the unique political and aesthetic context of Stalinism, the role it played, and the genres in which it was manifest. The names of the authors and artists who interest us here are next to unknown to anyone except a very narrow circle of experts. But back in the day, the satirical features and sketches [*fel'etony*] by Leonid Lench, Semen Narin'iani, Grigorii Ryklin, and Ivan Riabov were devoured by millions of Soviet readers. Those same readers also went to theaters to see the vaudevilles of Valentin Kataev, Anatolii Sofronov, Vladimir Dykhovichnyi, and Moris Slobodskoi, and to the movies—to laugh at the comedies of Ivan Pyr'ev and Konstantin Iudin. In their daily newspapers they sought out the cartoons of Boris Efimov, Mikhail Cheremnykh, Boris Prorokov, and the Kukryniksy trio. These cartoons, film and theater comedies, satirical features and sketches filled the pages of the popular press and the screens and stages of the vast country. The comic genres were favored by a mass audience looking for light reading and enjoyable performances. The print runs for *Krokodil* peaked at 7 million copies (by way of comparison, *Pravda*, the country's principal newspaper, held the record at 10 million).

Here, the comic is to be understood as an aesthetic dimension of the things that were supposed to be considered funny.

It seems appropriate to preface an analysis of this phenomenon with a kind of meta-joke. A boss is telling his subordinates a joke. Everyone cracks up, except for one person who does not laugh at all. The boss asks, "Why aren't you laughing?" Whereupon the employee responds, "Because I'm quitting tomorrow." One might say that the non-laugher in this story is the only one really laughing, because, being no longer afraid of the boss, this person can laugh not at the silly joke, but at the boss. This non-laugher has been the object of a huge body of works (both in the USSR/Russia and in the West) about the liberating and anti-establishment power of Soviet laughter and satire. In order to break out of the endless rhetorical circle of, and about, subversive laughter, we suggest a complete change of perspective and focus our attention, first of all, on the boss's joke, and second, on the laughter of all the other employees, less fortunate than the non-laugher because they will not be quitting the next day.

The boss's laughter is the laughter sanctioned by the state, and this is exactly what we call here "state laughter." It is in all senses a phenomenon that is yet to be fully explored. It lacked sophistication, relying as it did on the masses' tastes and an undeveloped sense of humor. It was associated less with the great satirists and humorists mentioned above, and much more with characters like Grandfather Shchukar', a hapless peasant in Mikhail Sholokhov's *Virgin Soil Upturned* (*Podniataia tselina*, 1932, 1959), and satirists like Sergei Mikhalkov. It violates all possible stereotypes of the comic.

First of all, it is not funny, as it relies on endless repetitions of the same templates.

Second, it does not conform to the stereotypical (Bakhtinian) perception of the social function of collective laughter—as always anti-totalitarian, always democratic, a tool for a destruction of hierarchies and fear—but instead decidedly contradicts this perception. The phenomenon of state laughter shows that laughter can be a most efficient instrument of intimidation, a way to anchor the hierarchy, a powerful tool of totalitarian normalization and control. We are interested in the nature and functions of the comic in Stalinism that made it into such an efficient tool. If we want to understand the Stalinist subject, we can only do so if we understand the mental profile of the person who laughs at Grandfather Shchukar', who is captivated by the merriment in Ivan Pyr'ev's kolkhoz comedy *The Swineherd and the Shepherd* (*Svinarka i pastukh*, 1941), who is filled with the sense of Soviet national pride when looking at the Kukryniksy's caricatures, and who is moved to tears by the "warm humor" of Fedor Reshetnikov's paintings.

The ideal Stalinist subject was only partly a product of social engineering. To a much larger extent this figure was the result of efforts to make the utopian Marxist project correspond to the "human material" at hand—with the state of the "human material" being the defining factor. The Bolsheviks, guided by the ideology of Marxism, were not known for "kowtowing to the people" (*narodopoklonstvo*), to use their own words. But Lenin knew very well that there were lines that could not be crossed. He defined the link between populism and authority very clearly: "We can only rule when we correctly express what the people are conscious of. Without this the communist party will not be able to lead the proletariat, and the proletariat will not be able to lead the masses, and the whole machinery will fall apart."[2] In other words, if the authorities do not express the consciousness of the masses, the "machinery" stops working, which is why the authorities must function as a "machinery for encoding the flow of the masses'

---

[2] Lenin, "Politicheskii otchet," p. 112.

desires."[3] Seen from this perspective, Stalinist culture must be understood as a meeting point between the sublime and the mass-oriented, the sacral and the profane, the high and the low. It is a true "carnival of power."

The oxymoronic nature of Socialist Realism was a derivative of the political functions of Stalinist art, wherein the authorities created an image of themselves that intended to legitimize them in the eyes of the masses. This image was created concomitantly with the image of the masses themselves, who were now supposed to self-identify in accordance with the image created "from above," just as the concept of "the Soviet people" was a political and ideological construct. This self-identification could only be achieved if the desired product, the image of the masses as they should be, was produced by Soviet art. Laughter as a foundation of "popular culture" was one of the key instruments in the production of "the people." Only when seeing their own reflection in the mirror could "the masses" materialize as "the people," a supreme sovereign that legitimizes the regime. Because of this, the reflected image of the masses could not be allowed to arise spontaneously, but had to be the object of the "incessant care of the party." The Soviet mirror was not a single, simple mirror, but rather more like a maze of mirrors. If there were just one mirror, it would be possible to turn away from it, which is why the system of Socialist Realism did not leave any escape routes and reflected into all possible autonomous niches, including "folk culture." Because the image of the people was an obligatory component of the image of power, it was a constructed image of themselves that the Soviet subjects saw in the mirrors of Socialist Realism.

After the revolution, the creation of this image was part of the "civilizing mission" assumed by the intelligentsia. Revolutionary culture had looked at its object "from the outside" and found it to be quite comical. Hence the wealth of satirical characters created in the 1920s. Stalinism was much more preoccupied with retaining power than with the construction of a utopia, as it replaced the communist project with a nation-building one. In the national construction, popular culture took priority. Consequently, national aspects acquired increasing importance, and appeals to national traditions and sacralized conventions of style and genre became more and more demonstrative. The object of laughter turned into a subject. Socialist Realism internalized the position of the laughing masses. As it stopped laughing *at* them, it now laughed *with* them, until it ultimately replaced them completely and started laughing *instead* of them. This is how populism (and popular spirit—*narodnost'*) became the *modus operandi* of the Stalinist culture.

As a result, Stalinist state laughter acquired a completely new nature. Il'ia Kalinin suggested that in discussing Soviet cultural and political practices,

---

[3] Nadtochii, "Drug," p. 115.

laughter as labor and laughter as commodity should be distinguished from each other. In the West, laughter and merriment are commodities in the marketplace of entertainment, a means to extract revenues. Consequently, those who are involved in the production of laughter are alienated from their labor and the final product. "In contradistinction to this bourgeois industry," Kalinin writes, "Soviet laughter was not a commodity, and it functioned exactly like Soviet (collective) labor. This means that laughter was not part of the marketplace where it was produced, bought and sold. Instead, as collective labor, it was not so much a product as a process in the course of which the collective was produced."[4] It was not by chance that the venue where Stalin pronounced his words about how "life has become merrier" was his speech at a congress of shock workers, glorifying their enthusiastic labor.[5]

These efforts directed towards the creation of a nation-building canon and the celebration of new labor relations should not mislead us into thinking that the society was approaching a period of stabilization. Stalinism is nothing but civil war frozen in political institutions, ideological postulates, and multiple artifacts, and each of its gestures is charged with violence.

Only after the Soviet era had ended did its place in history become clearer, as a special (catch-up) version of modernity and a society in transition from a patriarchal to an industrial order. In the wake of the revolution, famine, the civil war, and political repressions, the thin layer of Russian urban culture was almost completely destroyed. The urban centers were not able to resist the powerful archaization coming from the erstwhile peasants who were flooding cities in the course of accelerated industrialization and urbanization. Soviet society was becoming more and more archaic just as it was becoming more and more modern. This is why the Soviet person became a transitional figure—half urban, half rural. The related crisis of identity reached epidemic proportions. Even though this process was made more complex by the need for a collective correction of behavior and a (re)construction of one's own biography for many people,[6] it was still grounded in a psychology of marginalized individuals who, in the words of the poet Osip Mandelstam, had been "knocked out of their own biographies like balls from billiard pockets."[7]

A marginalized personality is an ideal comic figure. It creates comic situations and expresses itself through them. There is a huge body of works of comedy that center on characters marginalized by the Soviet order (the better-known authors include Zoshchenko and Bulgakov, Platonov and Mayakovsky, Kataev and Olesha, Erdman and the co-authors Il'f and Petrov, but there are many more). However, in these works the comically liminal characters were shown as if from the outside, critically; they were laughed at. The perspective of Socialist Realist

---

[4] Kalinin, "Nam smekh," p. 120. [5] Stalin, I. "Rech' 17 noiabria," p. 89.
[6] See Fitzpatrick, *Tear off the Masks!* [7] Mandelstam, *Slovo*, pp. 74–5.

culture was quite different. Not only was it very sensitive to the mass taste of semi-urbanized peasants; essentially, it became simultaneously a product and an expression of this taste, a real mirror of the Soviet people's consciousness, a mirror that reflected, among other things, their laughter. It is well known that how people laugh and what they laugh at reflects their level of cultural awareness, their sensitivity, the depth of their perception, the level of their intellectual development, and their type of wit. This is where an exploration of state laughter is helpful, as it allows us to analyze this phenomenon from the inside (the side of the people who were *laughing together*), rather than from the outside (the side of those who were *laughing at* these people).

Our starting point is the conviction that, as a social phenomenon, laughter cannot be understood except in the context of social, historical, and, if necessary, political parameters. This is especially true of periods of national construction, which is exactly what Stalinism was—the era when the Soviet nation was born. To quote the prominent Russian philologist and cultural historian of Ancient Rus, Dmitrii Likhachev,

> laughter is defined by one's environment, by the views and opinions that are prevalent in this environment. Laughter demands the company of like-minded people. This is why the type of laughter, its character, cannot be changed easily. It is as bound to tradition as folklore is, and it is ruled by inertia to the same extent. It strives towards a fixed pattern in the representation of the world. Then it is easier to understand laughter, and it is easier to laugh. Laughing people are akin to "conspirators" who know the code of laughter. This is why laughter is subject to an immense power of inertia. This power of inertia creates whole "epochs of laughter," its own anti-worlds, its traditional culture of laughter.[8]

As we will see, contrary to the common perception of Stalinist culture as "numbingly serious," it was, in fact, an "epoch of laughter" that produced its own (anti-) world. If we gain an understanding of what was supposed to be laughed at in this world, and what was not, we will come close to understanding the "code" of Stalinist laughter—and the Stalinist subject. For this to happen, we need to re-examine critically some stereotypes that have been widely accepted both in the USSR/Russia and in the West and that for decades shaped research on the topic.

The first stereotypical belief is that because it is a natural expression of a spontaneous emotion, laughter cannot be controlled and is thus "a moment of awakening of the "natural" behavior, spontaneous and uncalculated, that otherwise remains repressed in the process of socialization."[9] As the history of the twentieth century shows, not only is direct control of laughter possible, but so are

---

[8] Likhachev et al., *Smekhovoi mir*, p. 204.   [9] Vershina and Mikhailiuk, "Smekh," p. 128.

the practices of manipulation that replaced such direct control. These practices proved highly effective in overcoming people's "'natural' behavior, spontaneous and uncalculated."

Second, there is the erroneous assumption that laughter by its nature defies coercion, that it "cannot be prescribed, as it is the breaking of a prohibition."[10] In fact, as we will show, laughter can work perfectly as an instrument of prohibition, and a much more efficient one, too, than purely repressive measures.

Then there is the oft-repeated claim that laughter by its very nature is anti-totalitarian. This belief is often supported by references to the favorite genre of most authors writing about Soviet laughter: political jokes. According to the proponents of this view, the Soviet "laughing culture" was the "reverse side of the totalitarian era," laughter was "corroding the totalitarian ideology, affirming the superior value of individuality over the collective idiocy," and the "epic scope of the political jokes shows that totalitarianism was not only ugly and terrifying, but also ridiculous."[11] It is still all too often assumed that laughter is "in its essence nothing other than a sign of rebellious behavior; it cannot be anything else."[12] But in fact the Soviet culture of laughter was not at all a reverse side of the totalitarian era. The opposite is true: the façade of that era was Aleksandrov's and Pyr'ev's comedies, Dunaevskii's merry songs and marches, and the jubilant crowds at mass sports parades. In Stalinism the main function of laughter was to consolidate behavioral norms and to train individuals in state-sanctioned behavioral and social roles.

This last point links with the more general myth of the democratic and revolutionary nature of laughter, wherein it is seen as a natural force undermining the social hierarchy. This, essentially, was the basis of Bakhtin's theory of the carnival. Before Bakhtin the same thought was formulated by Alexander Herzen: "It is true that laughter has something revolutionary about it... One never laughs in a church and in a palace—at least not openly. Serfs are deprived of the right to smile in the presence of landowners. Only equals laugh in each other's company."[13] If this were true, then a world in which there was a shortage of "equals" would die of boredom. The carnival is not the norm but an exception from the regular routine of the social order, to the extent that Giorgio Agamben suggested that it be seen as an instance of the state of exception.[14] If so, then we should acknowledge that even though laughter and the comic continue to reside in the normalized social order, this order is inevitably based on inequality. The most common form of the comic is a clever person laughing at someone they consider stupid, while two "equally" clever people understand each other as they laugh with each other, preferring irony to direct jokes and laughter. In a semi-urbanized

---

[10] Vladimir Mikushevich cited in Stolovich, p. 261.
[11] Stolovich, *Filosofiia*, pp. 290, 128.
[12] Kozintsev, "Smekh i antipovedenie," p. 168.
[13] Herzen, <O pis'me>, p. 190.
[14] Agamben, *State of Exception*.

society, irony is unlikely to be the preferred style of humor. Researchers often regard the kind of laughter that might be characteristic of it as unworthy of scholarly interest. However, if we want to understand the formation of subjectivity in a society like the USSR under Stalin without falling into the trap of equating all laughter with anti-totalitarian impulses, this is exactly the kind of laughter we should be looking at.

The belief in the democratic, uncontrollable nature of an empowering laughter that liberates one from the shackles of fear, destroys ideological and religious dogmatism, undermines necrotic social structures and hierarchies is essentially reductive, as it limits any discussion of the subject to analysis of ridicule and satire directed at power structures. This approach does not in any way advance the understanding of the political functions and the social nature of the special kind of the comic that emerged from a prohibition on unrestrained laughter and served both to legitimize the regime and to strengthen the culture of resentment. This kind of the comic was to be found in the leading "official" satirical magazine *Krokodil*, which was printed in many millions of copies. It was promoted by early Soviet poets like Dem'ian Bednyi, whose raw and quite vulgar style was loved by many. It inspired the writers of the exceptionally popular satirical features in the 1930s newspapers that were virtually indistinguishable from each other. It drew hundreds of thousands to "artistic recitals" after the war, when Sergei Mikhalkov's satirical fables on predictably familiar and "safe" topics were read from the stage. It guided the pencils in the hands of caricature artists such as the Kukryniksy and Boris Efimov, who tirelessly satirized foreign enemies and entertained generations of grateful Soviet newspaper readers. Needless to say, the films that applied the thickest layer of glossy varnish to Soviet reality were the exceptionally popular comedies, from *The Rich Bride* (*Bogataia nevesta*) and *Volga-Volga* (both 1938; dir. Ivan Pyr'ev and Grigorii Aleksandrov, respectively) to *The Shining Path* (*Svetlyi put'*, 1940; dir. Grigorii Aleksandrov) and *The Kuban Cossacks* (*Kubanskie kazaki*, 1949; dir. Ivan Pyr'ev). All these products of Soviet popular culture were genuinely loved by millions of people, and this evidence does not support the claim that Bakhtin's concept of the carnival can explain all, or most, of the manifestations of laughter and humor in the Soviet context.

Yet for many years Bakhtin's concept of the carnival was the pinnacle of the Soviet theory of laughter. It provided the moral foundation for the narrative of a heroic struggle of the dissident "culture of laughter" (a culture that was, according to Bakhtin, deeply populist) against the "numbing seriousness" of Stalinism. This take on Soviet history was much favored by both Sovietologists and the Soviet intelligentsia. Today, however, it would be enough to change the predicates in the scheme described by Bakhtin, replacing the dogmas of Stalinism with the nationalistic rhetoric of conservatism and state-supported religiosity in order to understand that we are dealing here not with an opposition of people versus regime, but with an opposition of liberalism versus populist (popular, patriarchal, semi-peasant) culture. This latter force may be associated with the patriotic zeal of today's Russian regime, or the orthodox spirit of the paternalistic omnipresent State, the Russian Orthodox Church, or Islamist moralizing that promotes medieval or archaic values in the modern society. The opposition of "liberalism" to "populist culture" and the accompanying rhetoric always follows a model of archaic anti-liberalism that is set by the respective regime and religious obscurantists.

Bakhtin could not imagine a "carnival" with an inner content of fear and jubilation, the language of which would be pompous mockery and spiteful satire directed at everything and everyone outside the borders of one's own territory, with the external world dissolving in the acid of resentment. Yesterday, as today, this "carnival of power" was and is a tool not of liberation but of intimidation. After the spasms of the twentieth century, popular culture can no longer be seen as opposition to unfreedom. As a social phenomenon, popular culture that spans generations should be examined together with its political equivalent—populism, which is grounded in a patriarchal culture, that is, the broken culture of yesterday's peasants. In this sense the main manifestations of popular culture are perceived as a direct challenge to liberalism and modernity that favor not shallow satire, but deep irony of the kind that is equally alien to both Soviet and post-Soviet official laughter. Being a product of doubt, of a weakening or complete loss of faith, or of a downright rejection of the fundamental tenets of a system, it is such deep irony that stands in true opposition to the archaic popular culture.

More and more cultural historians who are working on the topic of the comic now insist on the necessity of studying the changing cultural and political attitudes to laughter, shifts in the understanding of laughter and wit. They share the conviction that researchers must overcome the transcultural and nonhistorical perspective on laughter and humor that dominated the field for far too long.[15] As Stephen Halliwell says, "there is a price to be paid for dissociating psychology from history. And it is too high a price where laughter is concerned,"[16] considering the important role that forms of the comic play in human cultures and political regimes. It is surprising that this call for a change in perspective has yet to find a wider following among the scholarly community, as the idea itself is not new. Some thirty years ago, one of the founders of the new cultural history, Peter Burke, wrote:

> in the last thirty years we have seen a number of remarkable histories of topics which had not previously been thought to possess a history, for example, childhood, death, madness, the climate, smells, dirt and cleanliness, gestures, the body, femininity, reading, speaking, and even silence. What had previously

---

[15] See Bremmer and Roodenburg, "Introduction," p. 3, as well as Rüger, "Laughter and War."
[16] Halliwell, *Greek Laughter*, p. viii.

been considered as unchanging is now viewed as a "cultural construction," subject to variation over time as well as in space.[17]

Even though laughter is absent from this list, it is not just a legitimate topic of new cultural history, but an essential one. It cannot be analyzed ahistorically, since in different social and political environments it performs not just different (and sometimes opposing) functions, but it also radically changes its nature, texture, and forms.

This is why our starting premise is that laughter is culture-specific and historically defined. Indeed, the last decades have brought with them some first-rate scholarship on the cultural and intellectual history of laughter.[18] For the authors of these works, laughter, humor, satire, and caricature are not just prisms through which to research emotions, corporality, visual and verbal imagery, language and everyday life. They also see varieties of the comic as key factors of the political culture in which they were rooted in time and in space, whose national and historical dimensions cannot be reduced to general theories.

Hence another emerging trend in studies of laughter and humor—an interest in political aspects of the comic. It was first brought to the fore when the poststructuralists turned to the topic of laughter. In their pioneering work on Kafka, Gilles Deleuze and Félix Guattari showed, to quote Anca Parvulescu's pithy remark, that it is because "everything is laughter" that "everything is political."[19] This exposed some aspects of laughter that are not at all funny. One of the best works on the cultural and intellectual history of laughter published in the last two decades is Anca Parvulescu's monograph *Laughter: Notes on a Passion*. "It is important to note at the outset," writes Parvulescu in its opening pages, "that to talk about the laughing twentieth century is not to propose an alternative to the century of horrors, war, and genocide. In fact, in the twentieth century, laughter was often imagined as a way into horror."[20] The book marked a turning point in our understanding of laughter.

With the recognition of the existence of laughter not *at* a political regime, but *of* the regime itself, more and more analytical works exploring this topic began to appear. Studies in the sociology of Soviet laughter saw light,[21] followed by several collections on "official Soviet laughter"[22] and comparative studies of "sanctioned humor" in various dictatorships. In 2018 and 2019 three monographs were published on the subject of state-appropriated Soviet laughter. However, all three of them deal with issues that, though related, are outside the scope of our

---

[17] Burke, "Overture," p. 3.
[18] See Gantar, *The Pleasure*; Gatrell, *City*; Halliwell, *Greek Laughter*; Beard, *Laughter*.
[19] Parvulescu, "Kafka's Laughter," p. 4.   [20] Parvulescu, *Laughter*.
[21] Dmitriev, *Sotsiologiia*; Tsipursky, *Socialist Fun*.
[22] Narskii, *Ot velikogo*; Oushakine and Ioffe, *Totalitarian Laughter*; see also the special section on state laughter in *Novoe literaturnoe obozrenie*, 121, no. 3 (2013).

analysis here. Art historian Annie Gérin looks at the comic in early Soviet satire (1920s); John Etty (also an art historian) is mostly interested in the history of *Krokodil* during Khrushchev's "Thaw," while historian Jonathan Waterlow talks about the mechanics of anti-Soviet humor.[23] The appearance of these studies signals an emergence of scholarly interest in the place of the comic in dictatorships, where the comic is not just an element of counter-culture but is an instrument of the dictatorship itself.

Dmitrii Likhachev used the expression "state laughter" when describing the culture of the comic in Russia under Ivan the Terrible and Peter the Great. He did not explain this concept, possibly because he did not consider it central to the "Laughing World of Ancient Rus," and since he put it in quotation marks, one can assume that for him this was nothing more than an expressive turn of phrase.[24] Likhachev spoke of a "comic stereotype."[25] His main premise was that any stylistic distinctions in ancient Russian literature were only genre-related, not based on individual styles.[26] This principle was key to his interpretation of the poetics of old Russian literature, and a logical conclusion from it was that "state laughter" could only be genre-related, too.

As the role of individuality in Socialist Realism was growing less and less significant, and the role of state laughter in the "laughing world" of Stalinism increased, the dominance of genre over authorial style became more and more obvious. The main manifestations of comic genres in Stalinism are almost completely deprived of the individual dimension. In the 1920s one could distinguish between the humor of Mikhail Bulgakov and that of Iurii Olesha, between the comic devices of Vladimir Mayakovsky and those favored by Dem'ian Bednyi. In Stalinism it no longer mattered who was the writer of this or that satirical text in a newspaper (Leonid Lench or Semion Narin'iani), the author of a satirical play (Nikolai Virta or Andrei Makaenok), or the artist who drew a caricature (Mikhail Cheremnykh or Iulii Ganf). This is why we focus on the nature of the comic itself in the specific historical and social conditions of Stalinism and on the particularities of its functioning across a variety of genres. This explains why the book is a study in cultural history and an analysis of genres.

The forms and genres of the comic that are addressed in this book not only enable us to look inside the machinery of Stalinist art, but also bring us to an understanding of the Stalinist subject in ways that have so far remained unexplored. In following these untrodden paths, we confront important aspects of the Stalinist regime that are otherwise hidden on the central thoroughfares of political and social history.

In this book we not only introduce new and often unexpected primary sources, but also attempt to suggest new strategies for working with cultural texts. Since

---

[23] See Dobrenko, "Grustnaia istoriia."
[25] Ibid., p. 59.
[24] Likhachev et al., *Smekhovoi mir*, p. 57.
[26] See Likhachev, *Poetika* and *Razvitie*.

there are few scholarly studies on the subject that we can use for our analysis, chapter 1 of the book is a theoretical one, in which the different theories of laughter and the comic are explored at length and where the key concepts used in the monograph are explained. Our attention here is focused on the aesthetic of a radically popular culture that is based on an adaptation of ideology to the level of a population, half of which came from the peasantry and had a traditional folkloric sense of the comic. The development of this aesthetic resulted in the comic becoming a tool of the Soviet political and artistic project. This tool was then used to ensure that the people internalized the required political and ideological principles. While in the 1920s any satirical representation of the new order was considered to be counter-revolutionary, Stalinism brought with it a new concept and practice—"positive satire." Works of "positive satire" were exercises in "criticism and self-criticism," ridiculing "errors" and "faults" in a way that did not undermine the regime but rather strengthened it. Such works became an efficient method of manipulating the objects of ridicule, channeling any sentiments of dissatisfaction the population might experience in a direction preferred by the authorities. A connection between the comic and the heroic was of primary importance, the heroic being the dominant mode of Stalinist culture. This satire did not in any way run counter to the heroic master narrative; in fact, it actively contributed to the development of the master narrative. We try to formulate analytical models to provide an alternative to the still dominant concept of the Bakhtinian carnival, which is supposed to always be in opposition to power, always undermining the hierarchy. The radical carnival of Stalinism was the exact opposite of this: it strengthened the existing hierarchy, increased class barriers and gaps between social groups, and provided an additional legitimacy to the laws, prohibitions, and restrictions that were in place. It was a carnival of fear and jubilation. Understanding it allows us to come closer to understanding certain national and historical particularities of Soviet laughter, and thus of Soviet subjectivity.

In chapter 2 the comic is examined as an element of the ritual of terror. Its central claim is that contrary to the seemingly obvious lawlessness of Stalinist rule, the true tragedy was that, in fact, Stalinism was a triumph of law taken to the extreme. Almost every word, every action, and every form of interaction fell into the realm of law, either as crime or as a manifestation of law-abiding behavior. Insofar as laughter was a handy instrument for dividing both those who laughed and those who were laughed at into groups, it was an integral element of this special type of ever-present, ever-alert law. The differences between these groups were clear-cut: there were the chosen ones and the outsiders; those who behaved themselves and those who broke written and unwritten rules alike. This chapter also shows how a transformation of the contexts in which laughter was allowed and encouraged at public events during the Great Terror reflected an evolution of the Stalinist grand narrative. Jokes in the *Short Course of the History of the*

Communist Party of the Soviet Union (Bolsheviks), in Stalin's speeches, and in the speeches of the General Prosecutor Andrei Vyshinskii during the show trials of the late 1930s are analyzed as elements of a special kind of training that shaped the people's shared understanding of right and wrong, truth and lie, friends and enemies.

This shared understanding proved to be vital during the war, which is the subject of chapter 3. The Great Patriotic War was not only a period of great suffering, but also a time of laughter. Front-line newspapers regularly featured comic stories, caricature flourished, and the print runs of satirical pamphlets were higher than before and after the war. There was a greater than ever variety of genres, levels of linguistic sophistication, degrees of complexity, and range of rhetorical devices. Some of the more popular realizations of the comic during the war included the "TASS Windows," Aleksandr Tvardovskii's poem *Vasilii Terkin*, Moris Slobodskoi's adaptation of Jaroslav Hašek's *The Good Soldier Švejk*, the satirical representations of the enemy in Il'ia Erenburg's wartime features, and memorable couplets with always masterfully crafted verses by Samuil Marshak put to music and performed at the front, but this was by no means all. There was a clear target for ridicule, and there was no limit in how far one could go. Sometimes comic works created at the time are seen as characteristic examples of a typically Soviet type of humor, though it would be just as true to say that this was the time in which state laughter came closest to its national (Russian), and thus European, roots. In this chapter we look at the texts and genres mentioned above and analyze the superimposition of the "Russian," "Soviet," "Stalinist" and "European" elements in humor and satire in the context of the Great Patriotic War. This humor was equally a return to the past and a modeling of the future, and as such, it is a key element for an understanding of Soviet discourse in general. Vasilii Terkin was a typical Soviet soldier, combining the features of a prerevolutionary Russian holy fool with the fearlessness of a hero of European folk tales. In the same way, the exceptional efficiency of the fiercely satirical TASS posters was due largely to the use of traditional forms of visual entertainment (going back to the motifs of cheap wood prints popular at Russian village fairs) and their appeal to principles absorbed by many members of their target audience during their pre-Soviet childhood religious education. The same holds true for the satirical and comic devices used for the purposes of war propaganda in the other genres analyzed in this chapter.

The Great Patriotic War was followed by the Cold War, during which the image of the enemy was shaped over a relatively short time—and for decades to come. Chapter 4 is dedicated to two aspects of this image—visual and verbal. In its first part we look at post-war Soviet caricatures satirizing events and political figures on the international scene. Political caricature occupied a much more central place in the Soviet press than in the media of other countries. Somewhat unexpectedly, we discover that the art of caricature was the one genre that was most organic to Stalinism. Traditional devices of caricature (typification, exaggeration, animalization, the use of external markers to express the object's inner essence, and a belief in the predictability of a character's actions once this character has been assigned to a particular type) were key to the propagandistic practices of Stalinism across genres. Our focus on the presentation of external (Western) enemies exposes some key features of how the Soviet population saw the world. There was, for example, a distinction between what the alleged enemies seemed to do and what they were doing in reality; the insistence that the Soviet reader of news should understand reported events not as incidents, but as references to precedents; an underlying assumption that events on the international political stage were best understood as episodes in a comic strip—an interpretation which in itself produced a certain type of meaning and demanded a certain kind of interpretation; a view of Western politicians not as state officials and individual persons, but as types. We also introduce the concept of an ideological hieroglyphic sign. In the second part of the same chapter, we discuss verbal caricature. It made use of the same tools and tropes as its visual counterpart, which is why caricature acquired new forms in Soviet propaganda poetry and theatrical works of the time, expressing the spirit of bravura and resentment. The sardonic laughter of the kind that was practiced in Stalinist post-war satire was grounded in discursive strategies that in the era of social networks and hybrid wars has come to be called political trolling—an intentional and malicious offense against the ethics of communication that is expressed in various forms of aggressive, mocking, and insulting behavior. Modern trolling is new only insofar as it is practiced through a new medium, but the toxic atmosphere out of which it grew was a product of the heyday of the Stalinist Cold War.

The topic of satire is continued in chapter 5, in which satire in the Soviet theater is explored. Although it starts with an overview of Soviet satirical plays of the 1930s, the emphasis is on the post-war years, the heyday of the so-called "theory of conflictlessness." Somewhat counter-intuitively, this era of "satirophobia" was the time when hundreds of satirical plays were produced. They are examples of a unique sub-genre: "conflictless" satire. Our analysis clarifies the particularities of a system whose main function was to create more and more ingenious ways to enforce a repetition of patterns of behavior and communication sanctioned by the state. The main function of this type of playwriting was the constant affirmation of the regime's foundations. As such, it became a unique instrument of social mobilization (in the form of "criticism and self-criticism") at a time when there were no far-ranging purges, and a reminder of the possibility of terror returning "on a low heat" without making the threat explicit. At the same time, as this form of satire exhibited certain social vices that allowed for communal ridicule, these vices were relegated to the past, considered to have been overcome, "outlived." Hence the constant allusions (disguised, but easily recognizable) to the terror of the late 1930s; hence the constant parodying of the methods of management or professional relationships that were now considered condemnable. Between these two points of reference a distinct Soviet sub-genre developed, with petty conmen and scoundrels, mysteries and exposures, elements of vaudeville and gender mix-ups. It was no longer about enemies of the regime, but about unscrupulous bureaucrats; no longer about saboteurs and spies, but about careless workers and fashion-obsessed wives of functionaries. The main function of these plays was to relieve the real or potential mass dissatisfaction through entertainment, while also maintaining the existence of satire sponsored from above. The dramatic works examined in this chapter are a kind of meta-satire—a satire of satire, and as such, they are a unique invention of Stalinism.

An understanding of the types of allegory favored by a certain political regime can explain a lot about its nature. In Stalin's Russia, fables were exceptionally popular as a special literary allegorical genre that brought together satirical comedy and moralizing. Chapter 6 looks at the transformation of the comical allegorical vocabulary from the late 1920s (Dem'ian Bednyi) to the mid-1950s (Sergei Mikhalkov) via a less known "proletarian-kolkhoz" fable-writer of the 1930s, Ivan Batrak. Changes in the kind of allegorical images were reflective of how the relationship between the authorities (the state ideology) and its ideal consumer transformed over time. Our attention will be focused on a transition from the brutal laughter of early Bednyi to the conventional, fixed, and predictable imagery in Mikhalkov's post-war fables. Bednyi transformed complex political ideas and ideological postulates into farce, the language of his characters often reduced to simple noise—exclamations and shouts, names turning into nicknames, interactions between people mutating into exchanges of insults. Ivan Batrak was representative of a whole generation of producers of texts in popular genres that emerged when the novelty of the post-revolutionary years started to give way to the established reality of new regulations, images, and associations. Devoid of distinct features, his texts are worthy of attention mainly as markers of a transition to a new vocabulary of state-sanctioned satire. Mikhalkov's fables were populated by officials rather than animals, their language a bureaucratic jargon rather than a string of unintelligible sounds, the place of ridiculous enemies taken by employees of state institutions who were supposed to be funny simply because they made mistakes. We are dealing here with a transition from the primitive alphabet of a newly established regime to a rather complex system of "hieroglyphic writing" a generation later, when a literate, correctly educated reader, who was the consumer of the state-sponsored satire, was supposed to be able to react to relatively large blocks of implied satirical references.

Following the period of collectivization, it became essential to create works that would show how much better the life of Soviet peasants-turned kolkhoz members had become. Kolkhoz comedy quickly became popular on both stage and screen after it first appeared in the 1930s. Its farcical humor, mostly borrowed from situational comedy, was not particularly complex, and the plots usually revolved around how kolkhoz labor and everyday life were intertwined. The ideological message conveyed by these works was also very straightforward: those who work well live well; those who have developed a communist attitude to labor achieve a higher social status; those who are loyal in love are happy, and so on. The personal and the collective always go hand in hand, which is why a hard-working young man who never tires of setting work records always earns the love of a lovely girl, while the lazybones is left with nothing, and in the end there is always a wedding. These plays depict a harmonious reality, and the advantages of the Soviet regime are undeniable. The plot templates used in the kolkhoz comedy followed motives that were familiar from fairytales and the popular forms of entertainment traditionally found at village fairs. An examination of the Sovietization of these genres of low mass culture allows us to understand how thoroughly the Marxist ideology was adapted to the peasant masses' tastes and horizon of expectations, and why it was so efficient. The normalization of the kolkhoz reality resulted in the creation of stereotypical characters, situations, and devices—a true kolkhoz *commedia dell'arte*, which is analyzed in chapter 7.

In chapter 8 we look at a genre that was usually called "lyrical comedy," but which was essentially a Soviet version of vaudeville that shared many traits with kolkhoz comedy, although it was also a genre in its own right. It was not just a matter of these works being set in an urban rather than village environment. They depicted a distinct slice of urban culture, where the urban lifestyle overlapped with the traditional habits of workers' suburbs. The heroes and audiences of these plays and films were erstwhile peasants and current residents of Stalin's cities. From the late 1930s until the 1960s, the names of Valentin Kataev, Vladimir Dykhovichnyi and Moris Slobodskoi, Tsezar' Solodar', Viktor Gusev, Konstantin Iudin, and many others became firmly associated with this distinctly Soviet form of "soft" humor. This humor was more refined than that of the kolkhoz comedy. It also contained significantly fewer ideological imperatives than was obligatory in almost any other Soviet genre. Here, the characters were in love (or else were searching for love), found friends, became disappointed or inspired, went through periods of lack of confidence, or else had the course of their lives disturbed by contingencies. The events of these plays were (to some extent) funny and (sometimes) touching. The plays touched on what it means to be human. At least that is the impression one gets until the existentialist foundation of the character types and plot templates is exposed, when the public merges with the private and the functional with the personal. In the Soviet vaudevilles, characters in love were workers, engineers, and doctors to exactly the same extent as they were attractive men and women; their disappointments were caused not by the vagaries of blind fate, but by stubborn bureaucrats; stupidity was ridiculed because it was the main characteristic of people who were stuck in the past; any uncertainty and confusion was resolved once the correct, socially sanctioned order of things was restored and the characters returned to their normal state, started behaving in accordance with their designated functions. Mistakes were personified, virtues were equally distributed between all the dramatic personae, and emotions acquired a clear cause and purpose. This lack of distinction between the collective and the private, function and character, social role and natural disposition is at the basis not only of the Soviet vaudeville but also of the Soviet idea of what it means to be human. Looking at the seemingly inane, shallow humor of the Stalinist "lyrical comedy," this chapter seeks to solve the complex and little studied problem of a functionalist understanding of private life in the Stalinist (and broader—Soviet) world.

Chapter 9, the last chapter of the book, discusses meta-laughter. We turn to the most popular musical comedies of the Stalinist era, comedies whose subject was Soviet laughter itself. This self-reflection emphasizes the important place occupied by laughter in the Stalinist order, where official discourse and low culture were closely interrelated. Their synthesis gave birth to one of the main principles of Socialist Realism—that of popular spirit, which made it possible for the authorities to create the image of the People as the highest legitimizing instance of the authorities themselves. This ideological *perpetuum mobile* was the most essential trait of the culture of Stalinism.

Chapters 1, 5, 7, and 9 were written by Evgeny Dobrenko (and translated by Natalia Jonsson-Skradol); chapters 2, 3, 6, and 8 were written by Natalia Jonsson-Skradol. Chapter 4 is co-authored.

1
The Stalinist World of Laughter
The Fate of the Comic in a Tragic Age

> He who has laughter on his side has no need of proof.
> Theodor Adorno, *Minima Moralia*

The Aesthetics of "Radical Populism": Political Dimensions

No other aesthetic category has attracted more attention from the philosophers and theorists of art than the comic—from Aristotle to Kant, from Hobbes to Hegel, from Schlegel to Schelling, from Schopenhauer to Kierkegaard, from Jean Paul to Bergson, from Nietzsche to Freud and Jung. Major Soviet intellectuals and literary scholars have also written about laughter: Iurii Tynianov and Boris Eikhenbaum, Viktor Shklovskii and Vladimir Propp, Lev Vygotskii and Ol′ga Freidenberg, Mikhail Bakhtin and Dmitrii Likhachev, Elezar Meletinskii and Aron Gurevich, Sergei Averintsev and Iurii Lotman.[1] Neither the heroic nor the tragic nor the sublime has been the subject of such an intense interest—a fact for which one possible explanation is that the comic is a challenge to theoretical discourse as such. In a way, it is theoretical seriousness estranged. By exposing the comic in similarities and differences, in alogical statements, grotesque and ironic tropes and devices, philosophers subject their own work to analysis and criticism; they engage in meta-descriptions, directing their analytical and ironic glance at themselves.

---

[1] Russian formalists, too, showed a consistent interest in the question of the comic. Boris Eikhenbaum's first work after the revolution, "Kak sdelana 'Shinel′' Gogolia", saw light in 1918; in 1921 Iurii Tynianov's "Dostoevskii i Gogol′ (k teorii parodii)" was published; A. L. Slonimskii's *Tekhnika komicheskogo u Gogolia* appeared in 1923, followed a year later by V. V. Gippius's *Gogol′*. Viktor Shklovskii's writings and OPOIAZ collections on Zoshchenko and Babel also belong to this category. The second wave of interest in the comic in the USSR was triggered by the political campaign of 1952, when the call for a revival of satire was sounded. The books that were published in the wake of the campaign include: Ermilov, *Nekotorye voprosy*; El′sberg, *Nasledie*; Frolov, *Sovetskaia komediia*; Borev, *O komicheskom*. In addition, there was El′sberg's critical collection *Voprosy teorii satiry* (1957) and numerous articles (see, e.g., Vykhodtsev and Ershov, "Smelee razrabatyvat′"; Pavlovskii, "Satira"; Ershov, "Nekotorye voprosy"; Dikii, "Geroika i satira"; Kalacheva, "Chto zhe takoe"; Kogan, "V chem sila," and many others).

Finally, the third stream of publications followed the appearance of Bakhtin's book on Rabelais (1965). This last group includes: Borev, *Komicheskoe*; Kiselev, *Problemy*; Propp, *Problemy*; Likhachev et al., *Smekhovoi mir*; Luk, *Iumor*; Nikolaev, *Satira Shchedrina*; Nikolaev, *Satira Gogolia*; Vishnevskaia, *Komediia*, and others.

But just as it has attracted the interest of theoreticians more than any other aesthetic category, it has also proved to be the one most resistant to theorizing. A huge number of works on laughter are devoted to fruitless classifications of principles and devices of the comic, introducing endless typologies based on a range of criteria, often boring and shallow systematizations, definitions, and identifications. Or else they establish varieties that are often far-fetched and contrived, invented by adroit analysts with the exclusive purpose of assigning every single example taken from real-life situations and every artistic image to an appropriate taxonomic category.

In 1956, there were eighty theories of laughter.[2] A quarter of a century later, the number reached two hundred (including variations on the original ones).[3] It would make sense to assume that another thirty years later there would be more than three hundred such theories. These theories themselves are in need of classifications, and they can be sub-divided into psychoanalytic, cognitive, physiological, communicational, structural, formal, and so on. For all their differences, what they have in common is that their subject is usually laughter as such. Much less frequently, it would be national laughter, and it is only in rare cases that these theories turn to historical modifications of the comic. The usual staple references in the discussions not focused on a particular historical period or national context are Harpagon and Don Quixote, Khlestakov and Tartuffe, Falstaff and Figaro. Examples are borrowed liberally from Aristophanes and Lucian, Grimmelshausen, Rabelais, Sterne, Cervantes, Shakespeare, Molière, Swift, Heine, Daudet, Gogol and Saltykov-Shchedrin, Mayakovsky, and Il'f and Petrov. But the problem with the majority of studies of this last type is that when the comic is analyzed from this perspective, it is deprived of any social and historical dimension. However, the comic (and laughter) is not only social but also socially and historically specific. The Romance medieval comic is different from the Germanic medieval comic, but there are even more differences between the comic of Old Russia and that of medieval Western Europe. The comic of the pre-Petrine era is different from the comic of nineteenth-century Russia. In each period, laughter in an aristocratic salon would be different from laughter on the market square. Laughter is a phenomenon that is not only national, but civilizational.

Lev Pumpianskii, a theorist close to Bakhtin and a brilliant scholar of the comic, once perceptively remarked:

> It is obvious that the essence of comedy is painless condemnation, that is, a fictitious condemnation, which is a phenomenon as fully aesthetic as the fictitious dignity of history is in tragedy. It is for this reason that the birth of comedy

---

[2] For a survey, see Berger, *Laughter*, pp. 1–31.   [3] See Holland, *Laughing*, pp. 115, 117.

is a proof of the completely fictitious, that is, deeply aesthetic, truly ingenious character of culture. Which is why only those few civilizations that had a particularly profound historical sense created comedies.[4]

Clearly, Stalinism, which gave birth to its own aesthetic version of laughter (here, we understand the comic as an aesthetic dimension of laughter), was one of such civilizations and the birthplace of an original culture of laughter.

In so far as Stalinist culture was populist, our subject here is the meeting point of historical and social laughter. The reader will not find here classifications, typologies, or general discussions of the nature of the comic. Such discussions, whatever varieties of them there may exist, are similar in that they try to explain why something is funny, but not why something *is not funny*; how that which is funny "is made," but not how that which is *not funny* is made; how laughter undermines power structures, but not how it *strengthens* them and becomes *a pillar of power*. These points, thus far disregarded by scholarship, are at the center of this book.

Unsurprisingly, Bakhtin's book on Rabelais, which was the first to connect laughter and "popular culture," provided new perspectives for a reading of cultural texts and offered tools for decoding behavioral codes of the past. Unlike his predecessors, who were engaged in developing typologies of laughter and offering psychological theories explaining it, Bakhtin placed laughter in a sociological and historical context, and thus discovered a new dimension of popular culture. However, whatever few studies of the world of Soviet laughter have been done since then have primarily been based on a non-critical reception of the Bakhtinian theory. It is not that Stalinist culture was completely ignored, but it was interpreted from a simplified anti-Soviet perspective as a quasi-heroic epic narrative rendered in heavy-handed officialese, where "comic culture" simply had no place.[5] The Bakhtinian theory of the carnival lent itself perfectly to such a reading, strengthening the image of the heroic struggle of the dissident "comic culture" with the "dreary seriousness" of Stalinist dogmatic postulations and state violence. This vision has been shared by Sovietologists and Soviet intelligentsia alike, even though, as we will see, in practice Stalinist culture was anything but bleakly serious.

According to Bakhtin, the function of carnival was to destroy (even if temporarily) "all-powerful socio-hierarchical relationships":

---

[4] Pumpianskii, "Gogol'," p. 258.
[5] We should mention, however, some works of the past decades where "political laughter" is regarded not only as a subversive phenomenon, but as an element of political manipulation: Billington, *The Social History*; Stallybrass and White, *The Politics*; Faulkner, *Sociology*; Powell, *Humor*; Mulkay, *On Humor*; Palmer, *Taking Humor*; Corbeill, *Controlling Laughter*.

The laws, prohibitions and restrictions that determine the system and order of ordinary, that is, non-carnival, life are suspended during carnival; what is suspended first of all is hierarchical structure and all the forms of terror, reverence, piety and etiquette connected with it—that is, everything resulting from socio-hierarchical inequality or any other form of inequality among people (including age). All *distance* between people is suspended, and a special carnival category goes into effect: *free and familiar contact among people*. This is a very important aspect of a carnival sense of the world. People who in life are separated by impenetrable hierarchical barriers enter into the free familiar contact of the carnival square.[6]

For Bakhtin, laughter was authentic only when it was subversive. But the "popular culture of the comic" he described does not allow us to understand the phenomenon of "totalitarian laughter."

The difference between totalitarian laughter (or what we will call here "state laughter") and subversive laughter is about the same as the difference between the Stalinist kolkhoz musical *The Kuban Cossacks* and an anti-Soviet joke: both are part of the Soviet culture of the comic, but they do not have much in common beyond that. What Stalinism offered its audience had all the external features of a carnival: the masses rejoicing on (former) market squares, defeating bureaucrats. But this is where the similarities with the Bakhtinian carnival ended. The Bakhtinian theory does not allow for a "carnival" the main goal of which was a *strengthening* of the social hierarchy, *upholding* social distances and class barriers, *legitimizing* existing laws, prohibitions, and restrictions—a "carnival" at the core of which was fear as well as jubilation.[7]

Bakhtin's theory of the "culture of popular laughter" is based on a sharp juxtaposition between low and high culture. In Soviet aesthetics, this division of culture into "official" and "popular" was a common premise, based as it was on the "Leninist theory of two cultures." Quotations from Lenin's "Critical Remarks on the National Question" (*Kriticheskie zametki po natsional'nomu voprosu*, 1913) were memorized by Soviet school pupils:

The elements of democratic and socialist culture are present, if only in rudimentary form, in every national culture, since in *every* nation there are toiling and exploited masses.... But every nation also possesses a bourgeois culture (and most nations a reactionary and clerical culture as well) in the form, not merely of "elements," but of the dominant culture.... There are two nations in every modern nation.... There are two national cultures in every national culture.[8]

---

[6] Bakhtin, *Problems*, p. 123. Italics in the original. [7] See Ryklin, *Prostranstva*.
[8] Lenin, "Kriticheskie zametki," pp. 120–1, 129.

Remarkably, the Bakhtinian division into two cultures could fit both the official and the dissident Soviet cultural model: one could read anti-Soviet allusions into it, and Bakhtin could be classified as a fighter against Soviet orthodoxy.

When the Rabelais book is taken as a reflection of the era of terror, scholars usually point out that it was a special form of response to a particular political situation:

> The serious aspects of class culture...are official and authoritarian; they are combined with violence, prohibitions, limitations, and always contain an element of fear and of intimidation...Laughter, on the other hand, overcomes fear, for it knows no inhibitions, no limitations. Power, repression and authority never speak in the language of laughter.[9]

It is hard to believe that these reflections on laughter (especially those sections that go beyond the Middle Ages and set claim to a more general validity) were written in Stalin's Russia, in a cultural and aesthetic environment that was simply bursting with never-ending collective joy, beaming with smiles, and overflowing with happiness, where, according to Stalin's dictum, "life has become merrier." *In the Stalinist (class) culture laughter was a channel and a legitimizing mechanism of violence, prohibitions, and limitations. It was a tool of intimidation. Power, repression, and authority, which gave voice to, and was sanctified by, "the carnival world view of" the "popular" (that is, patriarchal) culture, the culture of yesterday's peasants, spoke to those peasants, and for them, in the language of laughter.*

However, of utmost importance (in the context of the question considered here) is the juxtaposition Bakhtin introduced between the feudal-state-religious culture of the late Middle Ages, on the one hand, and the "certain, indestructible, nonofficial nature" and the "radical popular character" of Rabelais, on the other. Except that it was not the medieval carnival that had a "radical popular character." The medieval carnival had its limits, and was constrained by temporal conventions. *A regime that does not set itself off from "popular culture" but rather incorporates it and adapts itself to it becomes radically popular. Stalinism and Socialist Realist art were examples of such a model.*

Bakhtin's categorical opposition of the two cultures in the Middle Ages cannot be directly translated into the opposition between official and popular cultures in the modern era that brought with it "the revolt of the masses" (José Ortega y Gasset), radical populism, and mass societies (be they fascist, Nazi, or Stalinist). It is not about a changed principle of legitimacy. In the Middle Ages, the source of the legitimacy of power was God, but the modern era, the time of radical democratization and the deification of "the People," does not need God. "The

---

[9] Bakhtin, *Rabelais*, p. 90.

People" become the source and ultimate source of power and terror, ideologically shaped and politically institutionalized by the regime. As an expression of the ultimate will, "the People" equal God. As "the People" are the only object of veneration, there is no reason for them to fear divine wrath. To quote Mikhail Ryklin's perceptive observation, this is an atheism of terror, which has collective bodies as its foundation and which includes God in its own self as the people. It is "the atheism of the new religion that can nourish the life of a society based on violence."[10]

Once the replacement of God by the masses is used as a legitimization of a political regime, art acquires a completely new foundation. In this sense, Socialist Realism is much more "radically popular" than medieval carnival, which was defined by "temporal limits" and was restrained by strict spatial borders. Not so the "popular culture" in Ivan Pyr'ev's *The Swineherd and the Shepherd* or the "carnival" in Grigorii Aleksandrov's *Volga-Volga*. There, no restrictions in either space or time were applicable; the masses were celebrating in every corner of the country, from North to South (Pyr'ev) and from East to West (Aleksandrov). *Stalinism not only instrumentalized and incorporated low culture, not only oriented itself at the horizon of expectations of yesterday's peasants. It also raised the culture and aesthetics of a patriarchal society to the level of state policy, attributed to them ideological weight, aesthetic materiality and social acoustics—it medialized, institutionalized, utilized, historicized, and endlessly reproduced the features traditionally associated with low culture. In other words, Socialist Realism created the legitimizing political subject itself: "the popular masses." In its radical character such a practice simply cannot be compared to medieval carnival.*

Bakhtin's ideas used to be read as a subversive allusion to Stalinism, a "popular" challenge to Stalinist officialdom. Boris Groys responded to this reading of Bakhtin in his essay "The Totalitarian Nature of Carnival," the 1989 German original of which carried an even more provocative title: "A Carnival of Cruelty: Bakhtin's 'Aesthetic Justification' of Stalinism." Groys formulated the main objections to Bakhtin's ideas from the viewpoint of a kind of "postmodern humanism." According to him, the political implications of Bakhtin's thought make it obvious that the philosopher cannot by any means be considered "a consistently anti-totalitarian thinker." In fact, the opposite is true: he was one of those engaged in "an aesthetic justification of the era." "Bakhtin's carnival is terrible—God forbid one should end up in it," Groys says. It denies personal sovereignty; it celebrates the death of individuality; it rejoices at the "victory of the purely material, of the corporeal over everything transcendent, ideal, individually immortal." In this carnival,

---

[10] Ryklin, *Terrorologiki*, p. 214.

the popular and the cosmic, the "corporeal" idiocy celebrate victory over the painful convulsions of a suffering individual, who is seen as ridiculous in his lonely helplessness. Carnival laughter is born out of a primitive belief in the people being qualitatively, materially greater than an individual, and in the world being greater than the people, which is none other than the belief in a totalitarian truth.... In carnival, an individual has no chances except to recognize its own demise as a positively valuable entity.[11]

Having stated that "Bakhtin's goal was by no means a democratic critique of the Revolution and Stalinist terror, but their theoretical justification," Groys concluded his fulminations by saying that Bakhtin's theory reproduces "the atmosphere of Stalinist terror, with its unrealistic encomia and vilifications, and with its constantly random crownings and dethronements, which had an undoubtedly carnivalesque character."[12]

The consolidated chorus of critical responses to Groys from the side of Bakhtinian scholars did not, however, address the main weakness of his position. What matters is not whether or not Bakhtin was a "crypto-Stalinist" in his theory of the carnival[13] (Groys's whole essay is about this, even though he usually seeks to avoid moral evaluations). Of much greater importance is the fact that Bakhtin's theory just *did not fit* the pattern of Stalinist culture and *cannot* be used to describe this culture because Bakhtin's theory of ambivalent laughter, based on oppositions that never overlap, cannot provide tools for a description of the culture of a mass society in which laughter (and broader—"popular culture") long became part of the official culture. Had Stalinist culture been based on that split between "low" and "official" culture that Bakhtin postulates, it would not have been able to perform its functions. Bakhtin's theory disregards the most prominent feature of Stalinism. It would never allow us to understand the true role of Dunaevskii's songs, Aleksandrov's films, the always happy sports parades, the optimistic Soviet poetry inspired by raree-shows (nothing could be further away from "dreary seriousness"!)—everything that surrounded Bakhtin just as he was working on his theory. It is as if he did not hear, did not see, did not know everything that permeated daily life in his own time. *His theory is astonishing not because it "reflects" Stalinism, as Groys claims, but for the opposite reason: by being completely blind, deaf, and unreceptive to Stalinism.*

Since Bakhtin's book appeared, discussions about the "carnivalesque" in the culture of Russia in the twentieth century have never stopped. Some claim that the carnivalesque reached its highest point in the Silver Age, with its interest in

---

[11] Groys, "Totalitarizm," pp. 78–80. [12] Ibid., p. 79.
[13] A comprehensive analysis of the ethical aspects of Bakhtin's theory of the carnival in the context of Stalinist terror can be found in the dissertation by Simons, *Carnival*.

harlequinade, eccentric slapstick comedy, and the "low" genres.[14] Others are convinced that its heyday was in the 1920s and revolutionary culture.[15] But everyone agrees that Stalinism marked a demise of the carnivalesque. This last claim, however, is a fallacy, based as it is on seeing Socialist Realism as a celebration of the "officialese," whereby Stalinist art is associated with heroic and monumental genres patterned on classic forms, and its populist nature is completely ignored. In fact, Stalinist art did not just cater to the mass taste of yesterday's peasants and their understanding of "the beautiful." It was also a response to this mass demand for a particular kind of aesthetic production that corresponded to the consumers' horizon of expectations. A typical assessment of Stalinist culture goes like this:

> According to the laws of the carnivalesque, the "official" and "unofficial" spheres of life have equal rights and differ only in the time and space to which they are assigned. In the Soviet Union in the 1930s, however, they became almost completely mutually exclusive. Besides, the very artistic movement that had been most conducive to the renaissance of the carnival in Russia came to be marginalized and ostracized.[16]

Seen from this perspective, Socialist Realism is nothing more than an ideological chewing gum, boring didacticism, far from the true tastes of "a simple man," and is forced upon the consumer. This is how Socialist Realism was regarded in Western Sovietology as well as Soviet dissident literary studies in those rare moments when the scholars allowed themselves to be distracted from their research on Pushkin, Blok, and Pasternak long enough to glance contemptuously at lame Socialist Realist "artistic production." Or, as a variation on the same, an allegedly "real mass taste" was juxtaposed to a didactic "pressure from above." As ever, Boris Groys offers the most lucid and radical version of this view:

> The 1930s and 1940s in the Soviet Union were anything but the time of a free and unrestrained demonstration of true mass taste, a taste that in reality no doubt veered towards Hollywood comedy, jazz, novels about "a beautiful life," etc., but not towards the Socialist Realism called upon to educate the masses and hence primarily scaring them off by its bossy tone and its lack of any entertainment value, the gap between it and real life being no less significant than in the case of Malevich's *Black Square*.[17]

But Socialist Realism by no means shunned Hollywood comedy (what else were the most popular films directed by Aleksandrov, Pyr'ev, or Iudin?), nor did it

---

[14] See Gasparov, *Literaturnye leitmotivy*, p. 4.
[15] See Khimich, "Karnavalizatsiia."
[16] Gus'kov, *Ot karnavala*, p. 23.
[17] Groys, *Utopiia*, p. 15.

reject easily memorizable music and jazz (how would one otherwise classify omnipresent Dunaevskii's songs or highly popular Utesov's band?), and it was most certainly not opposed to novels from "a beautiful life" (Soviet "varnishing literature" knew no equal when it came to stories of "a beautiful life"). But it is more than that: "Socialist Realist populism" such as this was not some marginal version of a "showcase" (official) Socialist Realism, and the directors Aleksandrov and Pyr'ev, composers Dunaevskii and Zakharov, poets Isakovskii and Tvardovskii, writers Nikolaeva and Koptiaeva, actors Zharov and Chirkov, and actresses Orlova and Ladynina were all recipients of numerous Stalin Prizes. The populist version of Socialist Realism they were creating was an integral part of "showcase" (official) Socialist Realism. As Maria Chegodaeva reminds us, Fedor Reshetnikov's painting *Low Marks Again* (*Opiat' dvoika*, 1952) was popularized and no less reproduced than Fedor Shurpin's monumental *Morning of Our Motherland* (*Utro nashei Rodiny*, 1949).[18] The two types of Socialist Realism were created by the same authors, with Konstantin Simonov, for example, working simultaneously on the poems "Wait for Me" and "Kill Him!" Quite often, one would be hard pressed to separate the different elements in the same work, as is, for example, the case with the Vasil'ev Brothers' film *Chapaev* (1934) and Sergei Eisenstein's *Aleksandr Nevskii* (1938), Aleksandr Tvardovskii's poem *Vasilii Terkin* (written over the years of the Great Patriotic War), Mikhail Sholokhov's novel *Virgin Soil Upturned* or Shostakovich and Kornilov's *Song of the Counterplan* (*Pesnia o vstrechnom*, 1932). In none of these instances was Socialist Realism just a didactic exercise. The "truly popular spirit" it propagated was the flip side of "bourgeois mass culture." Both undoubtedly "belonged to the people," except that, while in the latter case "the people" were solely consumers, when it came to the "popular" version of Socialist Realism, they were also an object to be constructed. The difference is vital.

Juxtaposing "the taste of the masses" with official culture gives birth to yet another myth, according to which the great masters of Soviet art were not party to the production of Socialist Realism (as the latter supposedly belonged exclusively to the category of "mass culture"). This position was very well formulated by Chegodaeva:

---

[18] Chegodaeva, "Massovaia kul'tura," p. 119. Chegodaeva is mistaken when she says that Reshetnikov's *Low Marks Again* was awarded the Stalin Prize. In fact, Reshetnikov received the prize in 1949 for two other paintings—*Generalissimo of the Soviet Union, I. V. Stalin* and *Arrived for a Holiday*. These are two clear examples of the "celebratory" and "populist" kinds of Socialist Realism, which emphasizes even more the identical status of these two sub-genres. It would be more correct to speak but of a difference in the subjects depicted, as despite all the generic differences (a formal portrait versus a comical family scene), both paintings are stylistically quite similar and correspond to all Socialist Realist conventions. Interestingly, the overall print run of postcards reproducing *Arrived for a Holiday* (1948) was more than 13 million copies, which is more than the print run of any other postcard ever printed in the Soviet Union.

Nine tenths of totalitarian Stalinist literature were "mass culture." Under the sobriquet of "Socialist Realism" it was promoted as the pinnacle of world culture transcending time and national contexts. Zakharov's light jocular song to Isakovskii's words, "And how could I know why he keeps winking," performed by the Pyatnitsky Russian Folk Chorus, schooled Shostakovich and Prokof′ev in the art of music composition. Possessed by powerless rage, the Association of Arts of Revolutionary Russia, in charge of the Academy of the Arts and presiding over all the visual arts, was tearing Van Gogh and Cezanne from the museum walls.[19]

The problem, however, is that Shostakovich and Prokof′ev, Eisenstein and Vertov, and Zholtovsky and Shchusev were creating exemplary works of Stalinist culture.

The other side of the intelligentsia's "elitist" mythology was their "folk" mythology, to which the Bakhtinian theory of the culture of laughter undoubtedly belonged. All these interpretations were united in perceiving Socialist Realist art as something boring, "serious," a series of dogmas that, in Groys's words, was "scaring people off by its bossy tone," from which jokes, puns, sparkles of laughter, everything reminiscent of the free language of *lubok* and popular comedy shows were banished. Censors and editors were intent on driving away the popular voice in a consequential, stubborn fashion, and they were pretty good at their job. "Yes," Neia Zorkaia claimed,

> in the victorious masses' state, state ideology was fixated on annihilating the popular voice. Together with the legacy of "the shameful and disgraceful decade in the history of the Russian intelligentsia," as the "Russian Silver Age" was referred to in Soviet historiography, the folk culture, the *lubok* culture of the same period was being discarded.[20]

But folk culture being ineradicable,

> *lubok* (in a broad sense) quietly penetrated, Trojan-horse style, the triumphant aesthetics of "Socialist Realism." Structurally and poetically, the film *Chapaev* is a replica of a traditional Russian robber ballad. Ivan Pyr′ev's musical "kolkhoz comedies" were in the tradition of folk slapstick comedies, slightly seasoned with references to socialist competition and agricultural abundance in the real-life conditions of the early 1930s famine, which was especially deadly in Ukraine, where the comedy *Rich Bride* was set.[21]

Maya Turovskaya wrote about fairytale elements in Pyr′ev's films, too.[22]

---

[19] Chegodaeva, "Massovaia kul′tura," p. 125.
[20] Zorkaia, "Ot *Maksima*," p. 210.
[21] Ibid.
[22] Turovskaia, *Zuby*.

It is the starting premise in such accounts of Stalinism that is highly problematic. Arguing against the common claim that "nine tenths of totalitarian Stalinist literature was 'mass culture'," these scholars present the opposite thesis, where "low culture" penetrated the official Stalinist cultural paradigm "Trojan-horse style." What emerges is a distorted perspective, where the total folklorization of Soviet art under Gorky's guidance in the 1930s, the "popular spirit" of Socialist Realism, the fight against formalism (which was the real "Trojan horse" in Socialist Realism), the orientation toward the stylistic conventions of a more traditional "realism," and other similar phenomena are nothing but "accidents." But the Soviet kolkhoz poem was composed in the tradition of rhymed popular poetry,[23] while the "popular spirit" was dominant in both literature (suffice it to mention the discussion on Mayakovsky, in the course of which it emerged that "the best, most talented poet of the Soviet era" had no heirs) and cinema (beginning with Boris Shumiatskii's "cinema of millions"). In the later, distorted interpretation, favored in the circles of Soviet intelligentsia, "high" ("elitist") Stalinist culture repressed "low" culture. But in reality, the opposite was true. The composer Shostakovich, the film director Eisenstein, and the poet Pasternak were barely tolerated guests (against their own will) in Socialist Realism; at the same time, the author of popular chorus songs Zakharov, the director of cinematic fairytales Pyr'ev, and the writer of easily remembered songs Isakovskii were at home in it. Doctor Zhivago was an unwelcome visitor, but Vasilii Terkin and Grandpa Shchukar' were the hosts.

There is no doubt that Stalinism's special kind of laughter came from the masses, as did its terror. This laughter was "popular" to exactly the same degree to which it was totalitarian, in so far as it was one of the practices of terror. The power, functioning as "a machine for encoding the flow of the masses' desires,"[24] institutionalizes and politically instrumentalizes these desires, bestows upon them an aesthetic and ideological shape, and maintains them. In this sense, Socialist Realism is a *radically popular* culture, and it is only the inertia of the interpretive mythology promoted by the intelligentsia (dissidents, Sovietologists, emigrants) that has positioned it as a culture imposed from above, in which the true masters supposedly did not have to "engage" and which they did not have to "consume," and which was supposedly very far removed from the true public taste.

The masses were not mere participants, but active partners (if not accomplices) in the creation of Stalinist culture. This is why Socialist Realism can be seen as a matrix of the Soviet mass political unconscious: it allows one to understand the aesthetic dimension of this unconscious, too. Socialist Realism is that very "popular culture" of the modern era that should be examined not within the traditional

---

[23] See Dobrenko, "Raeshnyi kommunizm."   [24] Nadtochii, "Drug," p. 115.

opposition of "popular" versus "official," but through the categories of "radically popular spirit," that is, outside of this traditional juxtaposition. In the Middle Ages and the Renaissance, as described by Bakhtin, "popular culture" was, indeed, opposed to the official one, but in modernity it became a remnant of patriarchy, a battlefield where collectivist peasant culture was fighting advancing modernization and its emphasis on individualism and intellectualism.

"Russian Laughter" and the National Origins of the Stalinist "Popular Spirit"

Of key importance in Bakhtin's theory of the carnival is the concept of ambivalence, with death and rebirth evoked side by side. However, as Marina Riumina justly observed,

> demise, death, denial, destruction, etc., are absolute and real, while the birth of something new, rebirth, life, blossoming, etc., are relative and ephemeral.... Even more precisely, "ambivalence" presupposes the reality of denial, negation, destruction, death, etc., while everything positive, affirmative, the ideas of rebirth, life, etc., merely appear to be there.[25]

Nothing of the kind can be said of the Stalinist carnival, where the forces of destruction and death were never associated with the Soviet world, but only with external or internal enemies (fascists, "warmongers," and the like). These forces were never equal to "the forces of good." At the core of this kind of carnival is a transformed religiosity nourished by a clear differentiation between the positive and the negative and a denial of any kind of ambivalence.[26]

Unsurprisingly, the main debates around Bakhtin's concept of the carnival concerned its religious interpretations. There are justifiable reasons to doubt not only the theoretical but also the historical foundations of Bakhtin's model. In summarizing these reasons, Riumina notes that, according to Bakhtin,

> in Medieval Europe, Christianity and the official culture based on it could not have emerged from popular visions of the world. This premise, however, is wrong. It is well known that Christianity in the Middle Ages permeated all spheres of people's lives, from the most mundane daily chores to holidays, from peace to war, always and across all social strata.[27]

---

[25] Riumina, *Estetika*, p. 220.
[26] Cf.: "A carnival world view, for all its blasphemous nature, is the other side of true religiosity, as there is no blasphemy without faith" (Shchukin, "Dukh karnavala," p. 102). On the other hand: "The realm of religion and the realm of laughter are mutually exclusive" (Propp, *Problemy*, p. 26).
[27] Riumina, *Estetika*, p. 213.

This explains why it is possible to consider the carnival as a practice that is not church-related, but never as a practice which is beyond religion. Herein lies also the answer to the question concerning the nature of Soviet carnival. To assume that there were spheres within the Stalinist world that belonged to the realm of some ideal, "pure popular culture"—uncontaminated by Soviet ideology, remaining deeply anti-Soviet, dissident, and subversive, producing parodies of the Stalinist order—would be akin to contemplating the possibility of a medieval person being "beyond religion."

This religious aspect is important to an understanding of the specificity of "Russian laughter," of which Soviet laughter is one particular (though radical) instance. At the same time, clearly, parallels between the carnival and Christianity in an atheist state had some distinct features.

First of all, laughter in Orthodox Christianity is seen as an unequivocally negative phenomenon: laughter is sinful. In Russia, a laughing devil, a blasphemous fiend was called a "jester." Hence the moral injunction against laughter in Russia, apparent in some of the popular old proverbs: "laughter and giggles lead to sin," "where there is sin, there is laughter," "where laughter resides, sin is not far," "much laughter, much sin," "laughter leads to sin," and so forth.

Only one aspect of laughter—the "liberating" one—is traditionally emphasized. In his article "Bakhtin and the Russian Attitude to Laughter," Sergei Averintsev speaks of "a calm enjoyment of what is allowed." In response, Aleksandr Kozintsev remarked that this formula is "an oxymoron in its very essence. Even if the place of laughter in a particular culture is widely recognized, even if its context is thoroughly institutionalized, even then, the act of laughter itself, sudden and negativist in its very essence, is predicated upon overcoming some internal prohibition."[28] It may, however, be a good idea to consider a situation in which laughter itself is a form of prohibition.

In his critical reading of Bakhtin, Averintsev noted that laughter is "a transition...from a certain unfreedom to a certain freedom." He made sure to explain: "a transition to freedom is by definition not the same as freedom, as being 'in' freedom. Laughter is not freedom, but liberation."[29]

Averintsev did not operate with the same categories as Chernyshevskii, who, writing in the nineteenth century about the "sublime" and "noble" nature of people who understand humor, differentiated between wise men and simple men. However, the sociological background of their arguments is the same: a simple man is less free than a wise man; a culture that is oriented to "simple men" (that is, yesterday's peasants) and which at the same time seeks to affirm its place in a patriarchal (and thus unfree) society undergoing a transition to modernization, is doomed to reproduce characters like Grandpa Shchukar' and endless

---

[28] Kozintsev, "Smekh," p. 153.   [29] Averintsev, "Bakhtin, smekh."

"swineherds and shepherds." This culture was assigned the task of mass producing these characters and situations, thus proving that *laughter is related not only to freedom but also to unfreedom.*

Averintsev formulates this thought with reference to religious premises: "The Christian conviction that Christ never laughed is rather logical and convincing from the point of view of the philosophy of laughter. In a place of absolute freedom, laughter is not possible because it is superfluous." Following up on this statement, we can say that in a place of an absolute unfreedom (which was exactly what Stalinist Russia was), laughter is not only possible but essential. More than that: the culture of unfreedom is permeated with laughter.

Addressing the degree of freedom in laughter brought Averintsev to question the very foundation of the theory of Bakhtin, who wrote:

> It was understood that fear never lurks behind laughter (which does not build stakes) and that hypocrisy and lies never laugh but wear a serious mask. Laughter created no dogmas and could not become authoritarian; it did not convey fear but a feeling of strength. It was linked with the procreating act, with birth, renewal, fertility, abundance. Laughter was also related to food and drink and the people's earthly immortality, and finally it was related to the future of things to come and was to clear the way for them.[30]

Commenting on these "principles of creed" that Bakhtin "puts forth in a tone that leaves no place for arguments to the contrary," Averintsev agrees that, indeed,

> it is not the function of laughter to create dogmas, but when it comes to *imposing* by force whatever opinions and ideas, conceptions and ideals may be incomprehensible or not sufficiently comprehensible, that is, those very "dogmas," when it comes to terrorizing those who hesitate by means of what the French call *peur du ridicule*—this is very characteristic of laughter, and any form of authoritarianism makes use of it quite readily. Laughter can make anybody shut up, much like a gag..."Violence never lurks behind laughter." What a strangely categorical statement for Bakhtin to make!...There are so many examples of the opposite that trying to choose the most striking ones can prove exhausting.

Turning to the monumental figure of Ivan the Terrible as a "carnivalizer," Averintsev concludes: "at the origin of any 'carnivalization' there is blood." Finally, he directly invokes Soviet history:

---

[30] Bakhtin, *Rabelais*, p. 95.

As is well known, Ivan the Terrible was an example for Stalin, and the Stalinist regime could not have functioned without its own "carnival," without playing with ambivalent figures of the popular imagination, without the Grobian enthusiasm of the press, without the precisely calculated psychological effect of the endless and unpredictable turns of the wheel of fortune. Even much earlier, in the 1920s, those court sessions against God at Komsomol meetings—what were they, if not a carnival?[31]

The connection between laughter and fear had been noted long before that. It was through this connection that Nietzsche explained the nature of laughter. His irrational interpretation of the comic is based on a vision of laughter emerging out of the atavistic nature of fear:

> If one considers that man was for many hundreds of thousands of years an animal in the highest degree liable to fear and that everything sudden and unexpected bade him to prepare to fight and perhaps to die; that even later on, indeed, in social relationships all security depended on the expected and traditional in opinion and action; then one cannot be surprised if, whenever something sudden and unexpected in word and deed happens without occasioning danger or injury, man becomes wanton, passes over into the opposite of fear: the anxious, crouching creature springs up, greatly expands—man laughs. This transition from momentary anxiety to short-lived exuberance is called the *comic*.[32]

The modern Russian philosopher Leonid Karasev makes the following observation concerning Bakhtin: "Fear [as] the only emotion that can compete as an equal to laughter [is] ... the implicit argument in all of Bakhtin's analytical constructions; his conception of laughter is first of all a response to the question posed by an era of fear and terror: laughter against fear."[33]

Such are common statements on the connection between laughter and fear. But laughter can also be a tool of intimidation. This is what state laughter is about. Just as fear and terror do, laughter belongs to "popular culture."

Bakhtin's claims about laughter being a liberation from social prohibitions should be examined in the context of reality. Such a liberation was temporary and, most importantly, it was sanctioned from above, built into the very fabric of social prohibitions. As Dmitrii Likhachev wrote, in Russia something being funny does not preclude its being terrifying.[34] Iurii Lotman expanded on this idea, writing about how the West European carnival was defined by the formula "funny—hence not scary," because laughter allowed one to step beyond the

---

[31] Averintsev, "Bakhtin, smekh," 11–12.
[32] Nietzsche, *Human*, p. 169.
[33] Karasev, *Filosofiia smekha*, p. 189.
[34] Likhachev et al., *Smekhovoi mir*.

restrictions of the medieval world, with its victimization to social and religious "fears" (prohibitions). In Russian laughter, however, the principle is "funny *and* scary." Play does not lead one beyond existing reality as such; rather, it allows for glimpsing into its hidden layers, into spheres where, were one to reside "seriously," death would be inevitable. Which is why play in this context is always simultaneously both funny and dangerous.[35] This brings us closer to an understanding of the distinct nature of "Russian laughter."

After Dmitrii Likhachev and Aleksandr Panchenko's *The World of Laughter in Ancient Rus* (*Smekhovoi mir drevnei Rusi*, 1976) was published, Iurii Lotman and Boris Uspenskii in their critical review of the book argued, among other things, against Likhachev and Panchenko's thesis that in ancient Russia there existed a "world of laughter" and a "culture of laughter" compatible with those in the West. Most importantly, they claimed that the phenomena that were characteristic of ancient Russia and which the book described were not expressions of a particular kind of "laughter"; that is, they were not "universal" and "ambivalent" enough, and did not transcend the limits prescribed by the church, by religion.[36] Seen from this perspective, there can be no doubt that Stalinism did indeed have a "culture of laughter." This, however, was a very particular kind of laughter, grounded in a "popular culture" that is not to be understood as a (neo-)folkish model of some "traditional way of life" or as a composite construction of putative "national characteristics" (kindness, warmth, generosity, and other similar virtues). Rather, it implied an accumulation of a variety of aesthetic preferences and horizons of expectations in the sphere of the arts, including political culture, which is to a great extent defined by both historical remnants of traditional patriarchy and elitist complexes that had been instilled in the people (anti-Westernism, statism, and nativism).

Bakhtin idealized laughter, seeing it as an exclusively affirmative, positive force, a means of promoting freedom and victory over oppression and fear. He imagined a laughter devoid of ridicule. But in so far as any parody contains an element of ridicule, his popular carnival laughter is a utopia.

In making its characters appear so insignificant, satire affirms an "authoritative irrefutability of the truth"[37] and of the social world order, just like writings in praise of heroes. "In practice, satire takes the model of a heroic individual as a pertinent spiritual social ideal, but realizes this model in an 'unheroic' situation of present-day life."[38] This is why satire is the genre most natural to the heroic-epic world of Stalinism. This world left no space for either irony or humor. After all, irony is the flip side of tragedy. Unlike the authoritarian orientation of satire, irony is always highly individualized. Tragedy and irony are equally infrequent guests in Stalinist culture. The same can be said of humor. Socialist Realist laughter is

---

[35] Lotman, "Gogol'," p. 692.   [36] Lotman and Uspenskii, "Novye aspekty," pp. 155–6.
[37] Tiupa, *Khudozhestvennost'*, p. 114.   [38] Ibid., p. 116.

almost always informed by ridicule. It is especially obvious in sarcasm, this reversed reflection of romanticism. Sarcasm, mockery, caricature—such are the products of romanticism decaying in the era of Socialist Realism.

Socialist Realism, the ruins of "revolutionary romanticism," left emptiness where the revolutionary romantic and tragic culture used to be. Now there was merely a scorched desert that, akin to the dead alkaline land marking a dried seabed with its patches of salt, filled up with acid, bitter, mean sarcasm directed at the world outside. But it was not just the orientation toward ritualized heroic narratives that determined the domination of these twins (satire and sarcasm) in Socialist Realism. There were also more profound reasons for this, inherent in the very nature of "Russian laughter."

The Marquis de Custine, who was not particularly interested in the religious aspects of life in Russia, thought that laughter and merriment were infrequent guests in Russian society not because of people's extreme religiosity, but because "empty amusements are those alone permitted in Russia."[39] The French visitor added: "All courts are deficient in life and gaiety; but at that of Petersburg, one has not even the permission to be weary" (605). The forced joviality that permeated the spirit of high society (when people laughed not because it was *allowed*, but because they *had to*) was conducive, according to de Custine, to a development of "mockery and mean ridicule." "the most ordinary humor of mind [in this country]," he wrote, "is melancholy, disguised by irony; in the salons especially. There, more than elsewhere, it is necessary to dissimulate sadness; hence the sneering sarcastic tone of language, and those efforts in conversation, painful both to the speaker and the listener" (474).

In de Custine's opinion, the most distinct feature of Russian laughter is its maliciousness: "Like a vicious snake, the Russian wit is the most caustic in the world. Ridicule is the powerless consolation of the repressed; this is where the peasant finds satisfaction, just as the nobleman's finesse is in sarcasm. Irony and imitation are the only natural talents I detected in the Russians" (189). And then: "Only comedians, sycophants, or drunkards laugh in Russia" (217). This similarity between the laughter of "high" and "low" society makes it obvious that these are traits of "national laughter." Later witnesses confirm this. Dostoevsky once made a shrewd observation: "If you want to examine a man and know his soul, then don't delve into how he keeps silent, or how he speaks, or how he weeps, or even how he is stirred by the noblest ideas; you'd best look at him when he laughs."[40]

So, how does the Russian laugh? Here are Somerset Maugham's notes on Russians laughing, made during his visit to the country in 1917:

---

[39] de Custine, p. 108. Further references to this work are given with page in parentheses.
[40] Dostoevsky, *Podrostok*, p. 175.

When a Russian laughs he laughs at people and not with them; and so the objects of his humour are the vapours of hysterical women, the ridiculous clothes of the provincial, the antics of the inebriated. You cannot laugh with him, for his laughter is a little ill-mannered. The humour of Dostoievsky is the humour of a bar-loafer who ties a tin to a dog's tail.[41]

The similarities in the impressions of two observant foreigners are significant. Maugham, who described the "laughing habits" of Russians belonging not to the upper social classes, but to the lower, and not in the "stable" era of Tsar Nicholas I, but during the Revolution, came to the same conclusion as de Custine concerning the main characteristics of "Russian laughter." It was mean (and often malicious), he said; it was laughter *at*, not *with*; undeveloped, primitive, and in poor taste, it was plebeian laughter. Remarkably, both men were sensitive to the social aspects of the nation's laughter.

The origins of the sociology of laughter in Russia go back to Chernyshevskii. In an era long before modern political correctness, he made a direct connection between humor, satire, and the level of an individual's development. In his opinion, those whose intellectual and emotional development was more advanced are more sensitive to humor, while those with a lower level of development prefer satire and farce.[42]

Socialist Realism, which aspired to satisfy mass taste, was insensitive to humor. In the peasant country, mass taste was undeveloped, "a little ill-mannered," to quote Maugham. Yesterday's peasant was laughing at Grandpa Shchukar'; yesterday's audience of slapstick shows was looking for buffoonery, crude theatrics; yesterday's consumer of *lubok* prints and "bar-loafers" wanted caricature. Their world is that of simple physics, cheap tricks. Humor as a product of sophisticated intellectual games is not just foreign to them; it is *inaccessible*.

Yet another aspect of ridicule concerns it being essentially a form of self-affirmation. In Chernyshevskii's opinion,

> when I laugh at a fool, I feel that I understand his stupidity, I understand why he is stupid, I understand what he should be so as not to be a fool. Consequently, at this moment I see myself as significantly superior to him. The comic awakens a sense of self-worth in us.[43]

But in order to feel one's superiority over the derided fool, the fool's level must be *lower* than that of the one laughing. Clearly, the lower the level of the one laughing is, the lower (*even* lower!) the level of the one being mocked has to be. When the

---

[41] Maugham, *The Partial View*, p. 129.
[42] Chernyshevskii, "Vozvyshennoe," pp. 190–1.
[43] Ibid., pp. 193–4.

person laughing is at a critically low level, the object of his laughter becomes a half-idiot peasant. All these considerations bring us back to the topic of "Russian laughter," whose strongest element is the need for self-affirmation as a nation through dumbing down, satirizing, and caricaturing the Other.

Valentin Khalizev sees as one of the main achievements of Russian classical literature that it "condemned and denounced the arrogantly cold and cynically mocking kinds of laughter."[44] But if we remind ourselves that there has never been a literature that has "mocked," for example, the "little man" or whatever its national history holds sacred, it becomes all the more obvious that such "arrogantly cold and cynically mocking kinds of laughter" were very prominent in the culture of laughter under Stalin. Even the Soviet "victorious laughter" with its arrogantly imperialist undertones had precursors in Russian nineteenth-century literature, and not just in marginal works, but in its very "core of values," from Pushkin's poem "To the Slanderers of Russia" (*Klevetnikam Rossii*, 1831) to Dostoevsky's *A Writer's Diary* (*Dnevnik pisatelia*, 1873–81), both of which radiate contempt and mockery of the West and celebrate Orthodox and imperialist arrogance. "Soviet laughter" is the direct heir of Russian laughter.

As an anti-intellectual culture, contemptuous of the intelligentsia, Bakhtin's "popular culture of laughter" is a stranger to irony and humor. We may want to remember the characteristic open hostility that Stalinism manifested toward "humor devoid of ideological principles" ("*bezydeinyi iumor*"). Like many similar attitudes, this position was not directly formulated in the culture itself, but found its final expression in post-Soviet Stalinist and nationalist ("red-brown") journalism. Vil'iam Pokhlebkin was an especially prominent exponent of this genre. In his apologetic book about Stalin, *The Great Pseudonym* (*Velikii psevdonim*, 1998), he engaged at length with the topic that interests us here:

> Humor, snickers, giggles and chuckles—the simple Russian folk have always associated them with buffoonery and clowning, and have always regarded such "funnymen" as deranged [*iurodivye*]. Hence, for the most part they not only refused to take such people seriously, but also sensed—as did educated people, too—something unseemly, unpleasant, or shocking in these deranged actions. On the occasions when laughter and the comic did make their way into the popular milieu, they were always associated with vulgarity, with deficiency, with something damaged or underdeveloped.[45]

---

[44] Khalizev, *Tsennostnye orientatsii*, p. 355. See especially the chapter "Smeiushchiisia chelovek" for an analysis of laughter in Russian nineteenth-century literature.

[45] Pokhlebkin, *Velikii psevdonim*, pp. 64–5. Further references to this edition are given with page numbers in parentheses.

At the same time,

> a revolutionary prefers angry, vicious, annihilating *satire*, not trite and flimsy intelligentsia giggling.... Lenin and Stalin lashed out at any attempts to replace or substitute crushing, murderously sharp satire with giggly, small-scale, shallow "humor." Neither the Russian people, nor its proletarian, serious party (unlike those puppet-like ones) needed this sort of "activity." "Funnymen" are particularly numerous among members of the Bund and Trotskyites. Their psychology and national character made them inclined, even in political arguments, not so much to argue substance as to try to "get to" their Bolshevik opponents with "witty" but superficial remarks in order to avoid the essence of the problem and resort to obvious sophisms.... The Russian people needed serious, strict, firm leaders. (66)

But Pokhlebkin did not stop at the history of Bolshevism. He plumbed the depths of national history and Russian literature, claiming that

> in Russia, among the Russian people, who in the ninth century imbibed Greek culture through religion, "sneering" is considered one of the most negative features of human nature. Hence, it is despised as "buffoonery" and "tomfoolery," as a sign of a lack of seriousness and of underdevelopment. (65)

And only in the twentieth century, according to Pokhlebkin, did this "traditional way of life" fall victim to corrupting foreign influences. In Russian literature,

> cheap buffoons emerge, and works of Western humorists are translated... In Soviet times "home-grown" "foreign professional funnymen of Jewish extraction" appear—Il'ia Il'f, Leonid Lench [pseudonym of Russian writer Leonid Popov], Mikhail Zoshchenko [sic], not to mention the "small potatoes," "amateur gigglers"—Dykhovichnyi, Slobodskoi, Raikin and their present-day followers.
>
> The Russian national character has always liked annihilating satire, sharp, pointed, and ruthless, like that found in Saltykov-Shchedrin's writings, not those giggles and chuckles. "Toothless" (in fact *vulgar*) humor has never been part of Russian national culture, nor of Russian character, nor of Russian historic conditions. Giggles and chuckles are an exclusively southern phenomenon, a result of a history of insouciance. (65)

These speculations are significant in that they make a direct connection between the Stalinist "annihilating," "sharp," "pointed," "ruthless," "strict" laughter with the "national culture" understood in nationalistic terms. The author's comic ignorance and crass antisemitism allowed him to make an argument for this connection in the most direct form possible. Such zeal shuns any kind of irony, and "Soviet laughter" did not allow for irony. As Andrei Sinyavsky wrote in *What Is Socialist Realism* (1957), "*Irony* is the faithful companion of unbelief and *doubt*; it vanishes as soon as a faith that does not tolerate sacrilege appears."[46] We can add that it disappears, too, whenever there is a claim to possessing the totality of knowledge, as was the case with Stalinism and its later derivatives.

Such is Socialist Realism—an enemy of irony, but a welcome environment for satire and sarcasm based on "knowledge" and "ideals." It is worth noting that Soviet aesthetics never developed a discourse appropriate for a discussion of the subject so alien to it. Those rare instances when Soviet critics tried to discuss irony were themselves prime targets for irony, as the following statement shows: "Irony has first and foremost a broad social significance; it must be at a high ideological level, must protect the vital interests of social progress and address the interests and questions that occupy the society."[47]

After the Carnival: "The Favorite Weapon"

De-carnivalization, which is a feature of modernity as such, found its most complete expression in satire. Bakhtin had no sympathy at all for satire, viewing it as a manifestation of the decline of ambivalent popular laughter. Satire does not signal "a demise of the popular culture of laughter," but is in itself only one kind of laughter (ridicule, mockery, derision). Stalinism radically de-carnivalized "popular culture," exposing a form of indirect aggression inherent in it and turning it into "an instrumental activity of laughter," as Iu. Artemova put it so well.[48] It is true that satire is rarely merry (funny). More often than not it is rather gloomy, being grounded in a skeptical attitude to the world; it is cheerless, being a form of moralizing; it is anti-carnivalesque, being devoid of any ambivalence. Satire is less funny also because it is connected not to "popular culture" but to personal self-identification, which is characterized by an ironic rather than comic perception of the world.

As an aesthetic form, satire demands immense personal freedom. In this sense, state laughter is no more similar to satire than Sergei Mikhalkov is to Gogol. This, by the way, explains why in Soviet culture an otherwise universal rule, so precisely formulated by Lev Pumpianskii, did not work: "A tragic poet can be (and usually is) an ideal figure of a nation, but a comic poet can never perform this role."[49] This is not the case in Stalinism, in which one of the most prominent *comediographers* is also the author of the state anthem.

The official Soviet doctrine, with its political instrumentalization of art, viewed laughter almost exclusively as "the weapon of satire" (and classified all other kinds

---

[46] Terts, "Chto takoe," p. 433. [47] Makarian, *O satire*, p. 170.
[48] Quoted in Kozintsev, *Chelovek*, pp. 220–1. [49] Pumpianskii, "Gogol'," p. 266.

of laughter as "devoid of ideological principles" and "meaningless giggles"). In fact, satire turned into a universal instrument of "realistic reflection of life." If life itself, according to the well-known Soviet formula, is a never-ending "process of the fight of everything new and advanced against everything that belongs to the past," then satire, as defined by Vladimir Ermilov, is the most adequate form of a reflection of life: "The fight of all things new and advanced with everything old and outdated is the content of Soviet satirical comedy in all possible cases and varieties."[50]

Unsurprisingly, comedy here was implicitly understood as satire, with humor being only a stage to be passed through. The true, big target demands satire and nothing else: "Humor covers the whole broad range of forms of the comic, reaching its highest, most profound and incisive expression in satire."[51] This was the opinion not only of Soviet critics but also of literary scholars such as Vladimir Propp, who regarded humor (and comic sub-genres in general) only as a repository of devices to be used for satire: "Uses of the comic are the means, satire is the end."[52] In this sense, Soviet comedy and satire can be compared to the process of making cheese (satire) from milk (comedy), where lyrical (non-satirical) comedy is a kind of whey. Vaudeville and lyrical comedy became the flip side of Stalinist satire, filling the gaps in mass demand that could not remain vacant when there was less demand for satire.

Vladimir Frolov's book *On Soviet Comedy* (*O sovetskoi komedii*, 1954), which summarized the experience and theory of Stalinist comedy, opened with the following words:

> Laughter *deals a deadly blow* to those phenomena of our life that belong to the past.... A theater play without *unmasking*, without merry or *angry* laughter cannot be considered comedy.... Satire, living humor, are the *weapons* of comedy. Laughter is *ruthless* to everything that deserves to be *exposed*.... In realistic comedy, laughter is a merry but *cruel unmasker*. (Italics added throughout)[53]

The very choices of words show how comedy was understood in Stalinism: it deals a deadly blow, unmasks, exposes; laughter is a weapon of satire, and satire is a weapon in fighting for communism, and so on.

Unsurprisingly, Soviet satirists became suspiciously similar to state security officers:

> In the Soviet society, bearers of certain vices very rarely act openly; they do whatever they do on the sly, they adapt, they wear masks. A satirist is called upon to expose all kinds of tricks of fake people, to show the "new" devices and means

---

[50] Ermilov, *Nekotorye voprosy*, p. 41. [51] El'sberg, *Nasledie*, p. 186.
[52] Propp, *Problemy*, p. 188. [53] Frolov, *Sovetskaia komediia*, p. 3.

they use as disguise; he must have the qualities of a skilled scout who can detect evil under any cover.[54]

Considering that the 1952 campaign aimed at promoting satire was a preparation for the purges that Stalin was planning for the highest echelons of power, it is not surprising that the instrumentalization of the genre reached its climax at that time. Here it was directly associated with such concepts as vigilance, agents, and enemies in disguise. Critic Iakov El'sberg opened his book on satire (1954) with the following statement:

> The Soviet people must remember that we are surrounded by capitalist countries who send their agents to us, that our enemies are skilled in disguising themselves.... Living and acting in our midst are fake, disintegrating people, champions of foreign, hostile views, bourgeois turncoats, and enemies in disguise.[55]

The list of targets worthy of ridicule makes the political dimension obvious: one should be alert to the presence of "bureaucrats, pen pushers, privileged darlings, careerists, those who silence criticism from below, breachers of socialist law," as well as to that of "hoodwinkers, all those hindering the improvement and perfection of the state apparatus, those who stand in the way of satisfying the working people's needs and providing for their welfare, those who cannot keep a state secret, those who are careless in affairs of the state, scatterbrains, slanderers" (6–7).

Satirists had to be always aware of the potential unintended political consequences of everything they did. On the one hand, "satirists have no right to represent the bureaucrat as a more or less harmless type. For the Soviet people, bureaucrats are 'sworn enemies of the party'"[56] (23), but, on the other hand, a too-offensive depiction of a bureaucrat was no less politically suspicious, because, according to El'sberg, "if a writer who criticizes some problems in our life and in our everyday affairs loses the sense of proportion, he will forget our achievements, will betray the truth of life and history; such criticism will turn into slander" (86).

The rebirth and demise of satire and specific topics for a satirical representation were always directly dependent upon the mobilizational agenda of the regime. This is why El'sberg was right when he wrote that the demand for Gogols and Shchedrins was not just a passing literary fad: "One of the most important tasks that the party has assigned literature is the creation of significant satirical works, of

---

[54] Novichenko, "Zametki."
[55] El'sberg, Nasledie, pp. 5–6. Further references to this work are given with page numbers in parentheses.
[56] This enclosed quote is from Malenkov's report to the Twentieth Party Congress.

interesting, striking generic satirical types that can contribute to the promotion and strengthening of political alertness" (192). In the transitional period from 1952 through 1954, when the critic was working on his monograph on the heritage of Gogol and Shchedrin and Soviet satire, his style and vocabulary displayed a mixture of Stalinist threats and injunctions to alertness combined with post-Stalinist rhetoric of a new "collective leadership":

> The weakening of the historical role of the popular masses, the vestiges of bourgeois-nationalistic prejudices, the personality cult, detachment from life, doctrinarism, dogmatism, the exaggeration of undeserved authority and veneration of it—all these and other hostile and mistaken views and characteristics should be targeted by the arrows of satire. (30)

State laughter is a very important link in the functioning of the Soviet political and aesthetic project—a link often overlooked by traditional Sovietology. A prominent example is Michael Heller's "The Clown and the Commissar." According to Heller, in order to survive under Stalin, a writer had to

> accept the Soviet regime as a co-author. This is where the uniqueness of Soviet literature lies. The books written by Soviet authors are written by them in co-authorship with the regime.... There is only one genre where this is not the case: satire. Satire remains the only genre that Soviet literature is unable to digest, to cope with. Satire cannot be fixed by censorship, as it is ambiguous in its very essence. Even a censor specializing in hidden meanings cannot eviscerate it: it is an embodiment of subtext, all of it. Satire cannot say "yes" without ceasing to be itself. An object of satire cannot be its co-author. A commissar would not be willing to don a clown's hat.[57]

This is how the heroic image of satire so dear to emigrants was born: "The clown, the only free man in the Soviet Union, continues to laugh at the commissar.... Today buffoonery is an act of heroism. Satirical literature has become heroic literature, having rejected a co-author whose power seemed unlimited" (225). Sovietology saw this genre as a real mirror of Soviet life: "Satire, the grotesque, caricature, and buffoonery are the most suitable means of conveying the grotesque, caricatured Soviet reality. The distorted mirror of satire precisely and clearly reflects the distorted, abnormal reality of the society" (224–5).

These pronouncements are a good summary of the logic of the Sovietological approach to satire. According to this logic, *only anti-Soviet* texts can be

---

[57] Heller, "Kloun," p. 223. Further references to this edition are given with page numbers in parentheses.

called satirical: Heller quotes Evgenii Zamiatin and Mikhail Bulgakov, Andrei Platonov and Mikhail Zoshchenko, Nikolai Erdman and Iurii Olesha—up to Andrei Sinyavsky and Arkadii Belinkov, Alexander Solzhenitsyn and Vladimir Maksimov, Vladimir Voinovich and Georgii Vladimov, Venedikt Erofeev and Aleksandr Zinov'ev. Paradoxically, toward the end of his essay, Heller comes to the same conclusion for which he ridiculed those who argued in the 1920s that satire had no right to exist: "Soviet satire" for him is just as much of an oxymoron as it had been for them.

This one-sided approach, which has not yet been overcome, does not take into consideration the fact that, like Eisenstein's Ivan the Terrible, the commissar was quite willing to don a clown's cap. More than that: it was when wearing such a cap that the commissar was most efficient, as it granted him full control over the mirror and allowed him to make sure the mirror reflected exactly the picture of Soviet reality he needed, one the masses were likely to comprehend and with which they could identify. Soviet literature did not just "digest and cope with" satire—it also manufactured huge amounts of it. Of course, it was a special kind of satire. It performed specific functions, while remaining accessible to the Soviet readers and audience and loved by them. Such was *state laughter*, unrecognized.

Ironically, the heroic presentation of the same narrative that was favored by Sovietological and emigrant criticism reproduced the Soviet discourse on the subject. Clearly, the literature of this kind did not so much "reflect...the true face" of reality as create the reality itself, as well as its image, as well as the subjects who were constructed in the process of "consuming" that image and who received their own "face" through self-identification with it.

Once we remember that in Socialist Realism the legitimizing subject itself ("the popular masses") was created through the comic, through manipulation by laughter, it becomes clear that by no means are we dealing here with a marginal phenomenon, simply "an instance of literary production." Satire was an important element of dynamics and transgression within the Soviet ideological model. And in this sense the genre was quite far from the mimetism that Soviet aesthetics ascribed to it, coming as it did from "the Leninist theory of reflection," according to which the comic in literature and the arts is a *reflection* of the comic in life. From this point of view "the enemies of the new, the socially and aesthetically negative forces themselves contain the objective foundation for being ridiculed in satire. An enemy being comic is his Achilles's heel."[58]

In fact, however, the cause and effect relationship went the other way round: *by turning a certain phenomenon into the comic, Soviet satire marked it as hostile.* Generally speaking, a figure was designated as comic based on the political agenda

---

[58] Borev, *O komicheskom*, p. 53.

of the moment (on a particular day it could be "a bureaucrat," the next day "a petit bourgeois," the day after that a "rootless cosmopolitan," and then it could be a foppish "hipster" (*stiliaga*), etc.). Reprehensible features of the past were marked the same way.

Actually, satire is always about the past:

> The zest of satire comes from its targeting of the outdated, the decomposing, the dying, the remnants of what we do not want in our social life. It comes from our profound belief in our victory over everything that belongs to the past... [T]he Soviet satirist juxtapos[es] poetic images of the new sort of people to the disgusting features of the scum of the past.[59]

Indeed, that which Soviet satire ridicules and rejects *today* is always the image of power as it was *yesterday*. It is not that the past is ridiculous, but that whatever is ridiculous is associated with the past. An image or figure that is supposed to be replaced is satirized and thus in a certain way annihilated, eradicated simply by virtue of being placed in the past.

This partly explains why Soviet theoreticians of the comic (from Bakhtin and Propp to El'sberg and Ermilov) loved so much the quotation from early Marx about how "history is thorough and goes through many phases when taking an old form of life to the grave. The last phase of a world-historical form is its *comedy*.... Why is the course of history like this? So that humanity should part with its past *cheerfully*."[60] With reference to state laughter, this thought should be reformulated: in accordance with the political agenda, in order to ensure its own survival and adaptability to constant changes, power must update its own image from time to time. However, in order to appear natural, not to damage the regime's legitimacy, and not to be perceived as political manipulation, this process is accompanied by a populist image shift, which is performed by means of traditional satirical devices.

On the one hand, satire is based on a personification of evil (just as a prude hypocrite is embodied in Tartuffe, and a Soviet bureaucrat in Byvalov from Aleksandrov's *Volga-Volga*). A satirical type has a name, which makes it possible to individualize, to personalize a social phenomenon—to talk about a bureaucrat, maybe about bureaucratism, but never about bureaucracy. On the other hand, a comic type (not an individual) is static, generic, its depiction almost always focused on one prominent feature of character that is accentuated and frequently exaggerated. This is what differentiates it from psychologized and dynamic tragic characters for whom there was no place in the heroic culture of Stalinism.

---

[59] El'sberg, *Nasledie*, pp. 63, 89.   [60] Marx, "Contribution," p. 179 (italics in the original).

Victorious Laughter: The Origins of "Positive Satire"

Stalinism was an era of epic heroic narratives, an era that Soviet aesthetics celebrated as even more authentically heroic than that of the epos of antiquity:

> It is only now, in the age of socialism, and not in the past, that the true unity of an internal impetus and an external will has been achieved. This unity is richer, more profound than the one supposedly accessible to a mythological hero.... A truly Soviet person is always *a statesman*; however modest his function might be. His intrinsic unity of the personal and the social, of passion and duty makes him—and allows him to—act always as a representative of the interests of the "substantial whole," an advocate of these interests, a fighter for their victory.
>
> This is why Soviet art has an unlimited supply of potential heroes. The people of our time possess the kind of characteristics and perform the kind of deeds that respond to the main requirement of heroic art, of art about heroes and for heroes.
>
> ...We have every right to call our age heroic.[61]

In such a world there was simply no place for humor. The only adequate form of laughter was "victorious laughter," either joyful and jubilant or else directed against all the "remnants of the past" that were swarming around the stage of the great heroic drama being acted out in the Soviet state.

In *1984* Orwell painted a picture of an even more glorious future than the one in which his central character lives. In this future, the novel's O'Brien says, "there will be no laughter, except for the laugh of triumph over a defeated enemy." This is the kind of laughter Mikhail Kol'tsov spoke about in his speech at the First All-Union Congress of Soviet Writers: "The proletariat is the last class, and in the history of classes it will be the last to laugh."[62] But in so far as all class actions of the proletariat in Stalinism were appropriated by the state, this class could just as well be defined as bureaucratic, and its laughter—state laughter—cannot be understood without turning to the origins of the Soviet utopian project.

A leading theoretician of proletarian culture, Aleksandr Bogdanov, who devoted an essay to the subject of laughter, took the expression "victorious laughter" quite literally. In his opinion, laughter was only possible as an expression of a winner's superiority over those who, or that which, have/has been defeated, that is, "excluded from the social network." The subject of laughter is a group, whether large or small; the object is an enemy or prey; the content is a feeling of superiority. This is how it has always been, "along the axis of history, from the primeval and crude forms of laughter to the most civilized and subdued ones."[63]

---

[61] Gus, "Sovremennye kollizii," pp. 88, 89.   [62] Kol'tsov, "Rech'," p. 223.
[63] Bogdanov, "Taina," p. 178. Further references to this edition are given with page numbers in parentheses.

Bogdanov claimed that "empathy and feelings of social affiliation repress the comic, and laughter is possible only when these emotions are absent or else when they temporarily fade." The "social feeling" of the opposite kind is much more important: "Laughter is social.... Its social nature connects those who laugh together in a shared emotion. More than that: the most fertile ground for laughter is hostility, a state of conflict.... Laughter is a powerful, brutal weapon in social struggle" (177).

Anatolii Lunacharskii, who was close to Bogdanov, had a special interest in laughter and wrote a great deal about it. Tracing the evolution of his views on the subject, we should especially note the emphasis on the social, political function of laughter. As early as 1925, Lunacharskii wrote that "laughter is a sign of victory.... We have a great reserve of strength in us, since laughter is a sign of strength."[64]

Lunacharskii's reflections on laughter expressed his aspiration to combine the political functionality of laughter with his understanding of it as a "force coming from the people." On the one hand, the only justification he could find for laughter in the new state was in its being a kind of a "sanitary worker" in conditions when the defeated class

> keeps ensnaring you with thousands of poisonous webs coming from all directions, some of its tentacles making its way right into your brain, into your very heart. Like other hydras, it might come back to life. These webs must be torn out, they must be annihilated.... There is an agent that can do this, a means of disinfection that drives away all this vermin: laughter, the great sanitary worker.
> (3, 77)

But, on the other hand, the efficiency of this weapon, according to Lunacharskii, is directly dependent upon it becoming a true weapon of the people. And here he attributes the greatest importance to that very "force coming from the people" in an almost carnivalesque version:

> Long live the jesters of its majesty the proletariat! In the past jesters, playing their antics, may have been telling the truth to the tsars, but they still remained slaves. The proletarian jesters will be the workers' brothers, their beloved, joyful, smartly dressed, lively, talented, sharp-eyed, eloquent advisers. (3, 78)

As the years passed, however, Lunacharskii became more and more interested in satire, relinquishing his egalitarian utopia of "popular laughter." And not only that; in his interpretation, laughter was too social to accommodate humor. In his

---

[64] Lunacharskii, "Budem," p. 76. Further references to this edition are given with volume and page numbers in parentheses.

article "On Satire" (1930) he is a fierce advocate of satire, claiming that it is actually a form of self-criticism. Naturally, he realized that

> it is also possible that there will be instances of all kinds of bullying mockery disguised as self-criticism, even some behavior with a bit of a counter-revolutionary flavor encroaching upon the very essence of the Soviet power, etc. In this respect, censorship should be armed really well. Any counter-revolutionary attempts masquerading as free satire must be swept aside. This is true. But, on the other hand, we must master the freedom of true self-criticism, also in the sphere of the theater. *Down with the suppression of self-criticism on the theater stage*! (Italics in the original) (8, 186)

In fact, Lunacharskii was making a plea for allowing satire within a certain framework, and in this he was more flexible than those who at the time were calling for a complete ban on satire.

For Lunacharskii, laughter was almost exclusively mockery. In this sense, he can be considered a theoretician of that secondary, inauthentic laughter that Bakhtin so disliked. Lunacharskii thought of laughter in class terms and only in the categories of social domination: "the one who laughs is aware of his superiority over the one he subjects to mockery; he is looking to expose his adversary's weaknesses....Contemptuous laughter turns into a steel weapon, inflicting extremely deep wounds that never heal" (8, 535–7).

This topic seemed so important to Lunacharskii that he tried to integrate this "denunciatory trend" (*oblichitel'noe napravlenie*) into the nascent theory of Socialist Realism. While Gorky demanded "revolutionary romanticism" and stood up against attempts to "slander Soviet reality," associating the critical zeal of literature exclusively with its past ("critical realism"), Lunacharskii's paper "Socialist Realism" for the second plenum of the Organizational Committee of the Union of Soviet Writers in February 1933, shortly before his death, addressed the importance of "forms of negative realism." He made a direct reference to satire: "We must use caricature, satire, and sarcasm to attack the enemy, to disorganize him, to humiliate him—if we can—in his own eyes, and in any case—in our eyes, to dethrone his sacredness, to show how ridiculous he is" (8, 500).

Lunacharskii's evolution becomes clearer when considered against the background of the endless 1920s debates about laughter in the conditions of the new regime. Advocates of revolutionary ideology and proletarian austerity played a prominent role in those discussions. Mikhail Kuzmin wrote in his article "Through History in Seven-League Boots," published in the magazine *Zhizn' iskusstva* in June 1920:

> Following the victory, in the time of construction, satire must become quieter, even fall completely silent. Who are we raising this whip against? Whipping

defeated enemies is not generous, and annihilating enemies who haven't been broken yet means diminishing the significance of victory. As to using satire to depict the surrounding reality, even if there are faults—doesn't this mean tripping up those engaged in productive labor?[65]

Satirists themselves, too, demanded a rejection of the petit bourgeois "vaudeville" variety of laughter. For example, Vladimir Mass wholeheartedly attacked what was then being called "empty entertainment" and the "theater of smiles." "The modern theater," he wrote in 1922, "needs laughter...as a weapon of social discipline."[66]

The choice between the merriment of cheap cabarets and social satire was decided in favor of the latter. But this satire inevitably met with resistance on the part of censorship. Iakov Shafir, the author of the 1923 *Krasnaia Pechat'* article "Why Can't We Laugh?," asked: "Why have the humor pages that always played such an important role in newspapers fallen into decay?" Of course, Shafir continued, there is not just the NEPman and the priest—there is also the Soviet bureaucrat, but "unfortunately, so far our press hasn't proven brave enough to address most decisively this topic that is of central concern to Soviet power."[67]

Laughter has become impossible because the authors of satirical pieces in newspapers "don't dare" write about Soviet bureaucrats. Only "the sores of the past" (priests and NEPmen) can be ridiculed. Besides, it was at just this time, the mid-1920s, that the debates about bureaucracy acquired a distinctly political tone, with Stalin's opponents accusing him specifically of a bureaucratic degeneration of the party. Shafir saw a solution in allowing censorship bodies to establish a limit on what was allowed:

> Insofar as a satirical *fel'eton* serves primarily to expose something undesirable, one must pay particularly careful attention to make sure the job of helping the Soviet authorities in their struggle against abuse doesn't instead undermine the foundations of the Soviet state. It is no easy task to know exactly where a criticism of particular individuals stops and where a criticism of the regime begins.... Nobody apart from the leading party organs should be allowed to provide guidance on this.[68]

Shafir's appeal opened a discussion about the satirical newspaper *fel'eton*. The first person to respond to Shafir was Nikolai Krynetskii, who in his article "About Red Laughter" asked, "Who could even think of laughing when hungry?" in the civil war era. He went on: "The war, the revolution, hunger, struggle, a decline in production, unemployment...hardly inclined anyone to laugh." So, "laughter died away for a time."[69]

---

[65] Kuzmin, "Skorokhody."   [65] Mass, "Smekh," p. 9.   [67] Shafir, "Pochemu," pp. 6–7.
[68] Ibid., p. 8.   [69] Krynetskii, "O krasnom," p. 8.

It was not about the past, however, but about the future. "Laughter has not had in revolutionary Soviet Russia the kind of significance it had in the pre-revolutionary press, as a means of fighting against, for example, bureaucracy, and will never have it again," Krynetskii claimed. "Do we need satirical newspaper pieces?" he asked rhetorically, and gave an unambiguous answer: "Of course not. The pre-revolutionary press had no choice but to do this.... Angry laughter was its only weapon. The laughter of the liberal pre-revolutionary press was a measurement of its helplessness against absolutist tsarism."[70]

But now things were different:

> Does our revolutionary press need that kind of laughter now in the struggle against the bureaucracy of our Soviet institutions and Soviet bureaucrats? The answer is clear: it doesn't. The press can at any moment publish any exposé, and appropriate measures will be taken against the all-too-confident bureaucrats. Bureaucratism is completely inappropriate as a topic for a satirical newspaper piece in its own right.

His argumentation is worth dwelling upon: "Insignificant, petty bureaucratism does not make anyone laugh at all, because of its pettiness.... As to ridiculing more significant kinds of bureaucratism, those that border on the criminal and sometimes actually are criminal, this would inevitably provoke the anger of the masses, and the results would be quite unfortunate." Krynetskii's conclusion sounds like a verdict: "There are no appropriate conditions for the development of the genre of newspaper satire."[71]

This was the background of the discussion about satire that broke out in 1925. (In practice, discussions about laughter were always discussions about satire.) This discussion reflected a conflict between literature and the authorities that had long been in the making: on the one hand, the accumulated dissatisfaction with censorship, and, on the other, the branding of any critique of the regime as counter-revolutionary. The discussion was taking place in the pages of the magazines and newspapers *The Life of Art* (*Zhizn' iskusstva*), *Soviet Art* (*Sovetskoe iskusstvo*), *Art for the Workers* (*Iskusstvo trudiashchimsia*), *The New Spectator* (*Novyi zritel'*), and *Evening Moscow* (*Vecherniaia Moskva*).[72] Its central figure was the critic Vladimir Blium, who suggested an alternative to the use of satire: whenever Soviet society is "plagued" by anything, "the comrade artists have at their disposal, just as all the other Soviet citizens do, *direct, organized* channels both of state and social construction and of eliminating any undesirable turns, mistakes and any particular faults and distortions."[73]

---

[70] Ibid., pp. 9–10.   [71] Ibid., p. 10.
[72] For a detailed survey of this discussion, see Mikulášek, *Puti*, pp. 59–62.
[73] Blium, "Po linii," p. 49.

Blium understood such "direct, organized channels" in a literal way. In one of his articles he explained how faults should be rectified "at a different level":

> Remember... that you are *a citizen*, damn it. So, write a letter to a newspaper about a cheating cooperative member, go to the cooperative's general meeting, where you will be elected to the supervision committee, apply to the RKI [the Workers' and Peasants' Inspectorate] and to the GKK [the State Supervision Committee], and so forth. But beware of "creative generalizations," as their results will only gladden the heart of anyone who is abroad.[74]

This radical version of life-building, allowing for only institutionalized criticism, categorically refused to accept what was at the very core of traditional satire: "creative generalization" and "typification."

But Blium went even further, denying the right to any criticism whatsoever. In the article "Concerning Soviet Satire," he writes:

> It goes without saying that now, after October, when the state has become "ours," these [satirical] devices are no good. To engage in mockery, thus "shaking the foundations" of the proletarian state, or to ridicule the first, maybe uncertain and "awkward" steps of the new Soviet society, is unwise and improvident, to say the least.[75]

The time had come, he said, for the satirist to renounce the satirical mission. In light of the changes in the social situation, the goals of so-called Soviet satire are becoming vastly narrower. From now on, the target of satire is not social but individual; indeed, the satirist is now becoming a "moralist." The only things left for "Soviet satire" to depict are the "accidental grimaces" of reality. Any "Soviet satirist" who has not yet understood this is falling prey to counter-revolutionary feelings and slandering the new way of life.

Another critic, Vladimir Veshnev, occupied a position close to Blium's. According to Veshnev, Soviet satire would only become possible when the socialist regime had been fully and irrevocably established. Since "our present social period... is characterized by carrying within itself a conscious and voluntary self-denial for the sake of the future of the society," there is simply no room for satire in it. Reality itself "disarms the satirist by its voluntary self-denial, depriving him of any serious points of application for organic criticism that could have any lasting artistic value whatsoever."[76]

Yet another author, Vladimir Mass, responded thus to Blium's "nihilism":

---

[74] Blium, "'Prochev'," p. 9.   [75] Blium, "K voprosu," pp. 2–3.   [76] Veshnev, p. 95.

Satire is important and significant precisely because it does not allow for falling behind, for resting on one's laurels with a smug grin of satisfaction (*samodovol'no oblizyvaias'*); it brings our consciousness to life and stirs it up, pushes and drives it forward... To regard every instance of satire as "a shaking of the foundations" is to demonstrate that same exaggerated suspicion that comes quite close to shallow arrogance and narrow bureaucratic thinking.

And then:

> Laughter is the best broom to sweep clean and brush away all the outdated, rotten, and vulgar things that still remain in our mores and in our everyday life. But what we need is not just laughter, "pure laughter," entertaining and all-conciliatory. What we need is tendentious laughter, with a definite social orientation, laughter directed at the old in the name of the new. *We need Soviet satire.*[77]

The next discussion on the topic took place in 1929–30,[78] against the background of a political demand for criticism as Stalin was crushing any sort of opposition. This discussion was much more predictable. Once again, Blium was a central figure, but this time the outcome was obvious, as it was virtually a dispute between Stalin and Gorky. Having decimated "the right opposition" and made an abrupt turn to the left, Stalin declared a grand campaign for "criticism and self-criticism," which was to accompany the usual round of purges. Gorky, who did not accept this slogan, demanded that an emphasis be put on "our achievements." In his correspondence with Gorky, Stalin admonished the writer who, once extremely critical of the Bolsheviks in his *Untimely Thoughts*, had now become their passionate supporter:

> We cannot do without self-criticism. By no means can we do without it, Aleksei Maksimovich. Without it, we would be headed towards stagnation, a decay of the apparatus, a growth of bureaucratism, destruction of the creative impetus of the working class. Of course, self-criticism gives material to our enemies. You are quite right about that. But it also provides material for (and a push to) our movement forward, for a release of the constructive energy of the working people, for the development of competition, for the work teams that are setting records, and the like.
> The negative aspect is balanced and *out*balanced by the positive one.[79]

---

[77] Mass, "O sovetskoi satire."
[78] For a detailed overview of these debates, see Mikulášek, *Puti*, pp. 105–9.
[79] Stalin, "Pis'mo," p. 173. English translation: Stalin, "Letter."

Later, in 1934, Gorky would formulate his own position in the most straightforward manner possible: "Satire is a sure sign of a society being ill: in a healthy society, whose core is whole and not broken, which is grounded in a unified, scientifically justified and organically flexible ideology, satire cannot find anything to feed upon."[80] For the moment, however, that was the position upheld by one of the leading theater critics, Vladimir Blium writing under the pseudonym "Sadko," and, simultaneously, by Blium as a leading theater censor writing under his own name. This latter participant of the debate called the very expression "Soviet satire" meaningless,[81] since satire is always an enemy of the existing regime, and, in a proletarian state, fighting the regime is criminal. Whatever must be eradicated in this state is dealt with not by satire but by the militia, courthouses, public prosecution, and state security agencies. In such conditions satire could cause only harm.

Blium was speaking up against the "idealized" view itself of satire, according to which it supposedly educates or reshapes someone and thus can be regarded as a means of a social cure: "All our social experience can teach us that satire has never helped to correct anyone or anything." On the contrary, it "has always been a trenchant weapon of class struggle." Hence the conclusion: "A continuation of the tradition of pre-revolutionary satire against the state structures and society is becoming a direct blow against *our* state structures and *our* society. This is merciless dialectics, and there is nothing anyone can do about it."[82]

Blium's theory was panned in the same newspaper by the joint forces of G. Iakubovskii, M. Rogi, and the editorial board itself, in an editorial article. It was in the course of this discussion that the idea of "positive satire" was formulated for the first time. Defending the right to satire against Blium's accusations, Rogi warned that

> satire should not be used to snap the young sprouts, to tear down the fruit of the Soviet regime, nor even less to burrow under its roots. Here, too, we should mention the party, the professional unions, and the voluntary associations. Satire, if it is truly Soviet, cannot just bypass these bodies and organizations and not show their positive role, their fight against the infamous remnants [of the past] in our state system and in our society. Otherwise what we will have is truly one-sided satire—misleading, distracting, and causing unwarranted panic.[83]

---

[80] Gorky, "O zhenshchine," p. 195.
[81] Later, at a discussion of satire at the Polytechnical Museum in January 1930, Blium claimed that the concept of "a Soviet satirist" contains an irreconcilable contradiction, being as incongruous as "a Soviet banker" or "a Soviet landowner." Kol′tsov, Mayakovsky, Zozulia, and Ryklin disagreed with him (see "Nuzhna li nam sovetskaia satira").
[82] Ibid.   [83] Rogi, "Puti."

In other words, it was time for "positive satire." In the article "The Present Day of Soviet Popular Entertainment [*estrada*]," Osaf Litovskii spoke about this directly: "We cannot have only negative satire; there must be positive satire, too. The genre of satire must include moments of poignant pathos."[84]

The editorial entitled "On the Directions of Soviet Satire" concluded this discussion by demanding "serious satire" since "so-called empty giggling, telling anecdotes, laughter for the sake of laughter—none of this, of course, can be applied to Soviet satire in any manner whatsoever. It has nothing in common with that world of spiritual idleness."[85]

As it happened, members of the Russian Association of Proletarian Writers (RAPP) were the ones who stood up to defend Soviet satire. Advocates of the idea of a "proletarian satire," they had no doubts about this: "Satire is a weapon of the *revolutionary* class, which exposes the true face of its *class enemy*."[86] Their orientation toward classic examples ("learning from the classics"), their fight against "idealistic romanticism" ("Down with Schiller!"), and, finally, the slogan of "tearing off the masks" made them natural supporters of satire. It was in the critical writings of RAPP members that the very concept of "varnishing" was introduced.

As they viewed classic literature as an example to be imitated, RAPP leaders demanded that proletarian writers "study" in such a way that would enable them to develop their own "method" based on "the technique of the classics":

> The gap between criticism and the social-political regime, the impossibility of finding in reality the means to fight the negative aspects of this very reality: all this was a peculiarity of Russian satire—of Gogol, Griboedov, and Saltykov-Shchedrin.... The subjective intentions of a proletarian satirist coincide with the objective course of the developing socialist construction. While for a satirist of the past the reality he was targeting was the threatening present, and his ideal was an ephemeral future, for satire in the October Revolution era the field is open for fighting for the present, and thus—for the future against the past, which still possesses a strong will to survive and to resist.[87]

While for the classics the present was dark and the future was abstract, for Soviet satirists, on the contrary, everything dark remained in the past, and all the good things were happening in the present and in the future.

After RAPP had been dissolved, satire became a target of criticism yet again. Thus, in 1932 Boris Alpers, following in the steps of Ermilov and Blium, insisted:

---

[84] Litovskii, "Segodnia."   [85] "O putiakh."   [86] Senin, "Za proletarskuiu."
[87] Boichevskii, "Puti," p. 143.

In cases when the object of... ridicule is the world of the past... these traditions ["the traditions of Russian derunciatory comedy"] can still be used by a playwright. However, when the author uses the same weapon to approach phenomena of the new life in construction, what the audience sees on stage is a distorted face of reality, twisted by an ugly grimace.[88]

The kind of satire that RAPP leaders were defending was wholly directed toward the past ("remnants") and, in fact, it had no future. Appropriation of the classics played an important role here, and the question of pre-revolutionary satire, which was raised in nearly every intervention on the subject, the use of the "classical heritage" by all parties, played a key role in the justification of the new role of comic genres (primarily satire) in the conditions of the Soviet regime. In fact, it was a matter of the direction, limits, and functions of criticism (inside) the regime.

On the one hand, Soviet historians of literature proudly claimed that "Russia is the true motherland of great denunciatory comedy and social satire."[89] On the other hand, as early as May 1927, S. Gusev wrote in *Izvestiia*: "Unfortunately, we still lack our own Soviet Gogols and Saltykovs who would be capable of castigating our faults with the same force."[90] Exactly a quarter of a century later, at the very end of the Stalin era, *Pravda* confirmed: Gogols and Shchedrins had still failed to appear.[91]

What Soviet satire actually came to be was, indeed, directly connected to "the classical heritage." Except that this heritage was not that of the nineteenth century, but of the eighteenth. German Andreev observed in his comparison of Soviet and pre-Soviet satire: "Soviet satire assumed that the highest moral categories are defined by the Soviet criminal code. As to Russian satire, its point of reference was not the criminal code but moral and religious considerations."[92] This is true of the nineteenth-century satire, but Soviet satire had no connection at all with it. The true origins of the latter, Andreev claimed, are in the eighteenth century. Extending Sinyavsky's claim that Socialist Realism is classicism more than realism, Andreev compared Soviet satire to the pre-Pushkin era:

---

[88] Alpers, "Zhanr."   [89] Frolov, "Ob osobennostiakh," p. 45.
[90] Gusev, "Predely kritiki." We should note that already in the 1920s the canonization of Gogol and Saltykov-Shchedrin was well under way. See Moeller-Sally, *Gogol's*, as well as Elina, *Literaturnaia kritika*, pp. 114–21.
[91] The appeal in *Pravda* marked the beginning of a discussion of the problem of tradition and innovation in Soviet satire, which opened with El'sberg's article "Klassiki russkoi satiry" (1952). See also the articles by Gural'nik, "Russkaia"; Kirpotin, "Satira"; Keren, "Vyzhigat'," as well as V. Ermilov's articles which were then republished in his book *Nekotorye voprosy teorii sovetskoi dramaturgii*. But El'sberg's numerous articles remained in the center of the debate: "Za boevuiu"; "Velikie traditsii"; "Nasledie Gogolia i Shchedrina i sovetskaia dramaturgiia"—and there were more. He then collected these articles for a monograph on tradition and innovation in Soviet satire (*Nasledie...*). These publications were followed by a whole range of works on the influence of Shchedrin on Gorky, Mayakovsky, and Dem'ian Bednyi. See Ozmitel', *Sovetskaia satira*, p. 25.
[92] Andreev, "O satire," p. 191.

What the satire of the 18th century shares with Soviet satire is the transference of sins onto the past: "Before 'mother Catherine' life was bad, but now we can fight this." Dobroliubov wrote: "In the satirical works of Catherine's time...the thought [is expressed] that these faults and defects come only from the disarray of past epochs, that they are remnants of the past, and that now finally time has come to eradicate them; now there are new, quite propitious conditions for life." This is Dobroliubov writing about today's Soviet satire!

Furthermore, the 18th century Russian satirist was working in full cooperation with the government. There is a very interesting quotation from Dobroliubov about this, too: "The Russian satirist of the 18th century...set out bravely to chastise everything that was already relegated to the backstage by all kinds of reforms already in effect or else the ones that were in planning. But he didn't touch the things that really needed improvement—not for the sake of the state reforms, but for the welfare of the people."...Such are the predecessors of Soviet satire.[93]

However, the Soviet theory of the comic insisted (even in the 1980s!) that "Soviet satire is path-breaking.... It has become—unlike the satire of previous eras—not a weapon destroying the society that brought it into being, but a weapon consolidating it."[94] The positive and affirmative zeal of the satire of the Soviet Gogols and Shchedrins had little to do with the classics:

> Classical comedy condemned the foundations of an exploitative regime. It was *demolishing criticism*, ridiculing and exposing the exploitational nature of the ruling classes.... In our socialist society, which is free from class-related antagonistic tensions, the function of criticism has become qualitatively different. In our society criticism and self-criticism are aimed at affirming the ideas of communism, at strengthening the foundations of the socialist order.[95]

Besides, the very ideal that Soviet satire was affirming had already been realized in Soviet reality, so that, in fact, Soviet satire had nothing to affirm; it did not know a gap between the ideal and the real: "As Soviet satirists affirm the foundations of our reality, they deny everything that undermines these foundations, everything that prevents their development and consolidation. This is what dramatically distinguishes Soviet satire from the satire of the past."[96]

This is why this unheard-of *mimetic satire* was based on a certain idea of "realistic comedy" that was supposedly promoted by Belinskii, Chernyshevskii, and "revolutionary democratic criticism,"[97] calling for "typical living characters,"

---

[93] Ibid., pp. 193–4.   [94] Moldavskii, *Tovarishch*, p. 6.
[95] Frolov, *O sovetskoi komedii*, pp. 35–6.   [96] Belova, "Nam Gogoli," p. 60.
[97] See Dzeverin, *Problema*.

"truthfulness and historical concreteness."[98] The only thing left for satire to do in the Soviet reality was to reflect "the beautiful." Hence it is not surprising that, contrary to the very nature of the genre, Soviet satire is optimistic. It might well have been true that "the impossibility of giving concrete expression to a force that could defeat evil and falsehood sometimes made dark, tragic tones appear in the intrinsically optimistic satire of great Russian writers,"[99] but, needless to say, such "tones" were not to be heard in state laughter.

One of the leading RAPP theoreticians, Isaac Nusinov, formulated the new approach to satire in the best way possible.[100] He understood the goals of satire exclusively in class terms. Seeing it as "a weapon of class struggle," he acknowledged just three functions of satire in the Soviet conditions: (1) "the young class attacks the old order"; (2) "the avant-garde of the young class must overcome the resistance of backward members in its own ranks"; and (3) "the new hegemonic class is striving to re-educate its fellow travellers from other social groups" (39).

"As the proletariat grows stronger, there is less and less chance for the possibility of a mismatch between its ideal and reality," which is why Nusinov insisted that there was simply no room left for satire. But it is not only proletarian satire that is impossible. According to Nusinov, proletarian humor is not possible, either, because "humorous laughter is permeated with sympathy, condescension, and indiscriminate forgiveness, at times slipping into petty-bourgeois self-consolation." Clearly, it was an inappropriate means for advancing "class struggle" (43).

"Proletarian literature will not create classics of satire and humor" (43). "Only on its native soil" can satire "produce good fruit," such soil for it being the petty-bourgeois milieu of fellow travelers, never a proletarian context. But "as a writer from the ranks of fellow travellers opens himself to proletarian ideology, to the tasks of proletarian struggle and construction, the zeal of creation, the zeal of creative struggle will replace satirical laughter in his works" (40).

Nusinov's predictions came true. The advent of the 1930s marked the rapid transformation of satire and humor into state laughter.

Later, when RAPP's slogan of "tearing off the masks" (which could not be applicable to Soviet reality) became a target of criticism, satire lost whatever "principled advocates" there had been to defend it (satirists themselves excluded, of course). For years to come it remained without any defense whatsoever, up until 1952, when *Pravda* demanded "Soviet Gogols and Shchedrins." The last battle in the defense of satire was led at the First Congress of Soviet Writers by Mikhail Kol'tsov:

---

[98] Frolov, *O sovetskoi komedii*, pp. 11–14, 25.   [99] Ibid.
[100] Nusinov, "Voprosy zhanra." Further references to this work are given with page and volume numbers indicated in parentheses.

Quite a few times we've heard voices in newspaper discussions claiming that satire in our present situation is unnecessary, that its role is deceptive, that it is meaningless.... But one does not even need to be a Soviet writer, it is enough to be a contemporary with eyes and ears, somebody sensitive to our time, in order to understand how completely mistaken and lightweight this claim is.[101]

But what kind of satire was it?!

Vladimir Kirshon, one of the former leaders of the RAPP and a playwright popular at the time, in his report to the Congress was already out to develop the idea of "a new type of comedy—a comedy of positive characters," which in practice made the question of satire irrelevant. According to him, it was the time for laughter that would transpose the present into the past and declare it defeated. Faced with this "victorious laughter," which is anything but castigating, satire recedes and is replaced by "refreshing lyrical comedy" in which there are no conflicts. Conveniently, by the end of the 1920s two sub-genres had emerged in Soviet comedy: satire and vaudeville. The former included Gorky's *Slovotekov, the Workaholic* (*Rabotiaga Slovotekov*, 1919–20), Mayakovsky's *Bedbug* (*Klop*, 1929) and *Bathhouse* (*Bania*, 1930), Boris Romashov's *Flying Cake* (*Vozdushnyi pirog*, 1925), Aleksandr Bezymenskii's *Shot* (*Vystrel*, 1929), Leonid Leonov's *The Taming of Badadoshkin* (*Ukroshchenie Badadoshkina*, 1929), Erdman's *Mandate* (*Mandat*, 1924), plays by Bulgakov, and other works. Representative comedies of the household-vaudeville type were Aleksei Tolstoi's *Factory of Youth* (*Fabrika molodosti*, 1927) and *Wonders Never Cease* (*Chudesa v reshete*, 1926), Valentin Kataev's *Squaring the Circle* (*Kvadratura kruga*, 1927), Vasilii Shkvarkin's *Harmful Element* (*Vrednyi element*, 1926) and *Swindler* (*Shuler*, 1929), and others.[102] This second type (in its Soviet variety which will be explained in chapters 7 and 8) would dominate in the 1930s. Satire raised its head briefly during the war, but it was stifled again in 1946 by a series of ideological decrees and in particular by the bullying of Zoshchenko—until the demand for Soviet Gogols and Shchedrins was voiced in 1952.

However, by that time satire had been hit so hard that even after Stalin's death one could read the following:

Can we be sure that...the ridicule of a certain phenomenon will with absolute certainty bring the viewer or the reader to the right conclusion? Isn't it better, without trying to be too clever, to show the example one should follow in their behavior, a character one should seek to imitate? Wouldn't it make more sense to paint directly—in a clear, expressive, striking fashion—the images of the best Soviet people?[103]

[101] Kol'tsov, "Rech'," pp. 127–8.
[102] See Boguslavskii, "Bor'ba."
[103] Malovichko, "Pogovorim."

Ridiculing such recipes of "satirical mockery," Vladlen Bakhnov predicted the following for Soviet satire in the twenty-first century:

> I think by that time the satirical genre will grow significantly due to its merging with other genres such as eulogy, the panegyric, and the ode. We can even imagine that the broader community will call on the satirists of the future to be bolder and more critical in revealing the positive aspects of our life.[104]

Harmonizing Laughter: A Dialectics of "Positive Satire"

All theories of the comic agree that the comic is based on a juxtaposition—between the ugly and the beautiful (Aristotle), the low and the sublime (Kant), the false and the true (Hegel), the incongruous and the meaningful (Jean-Paul, Schopenhauer), determination and randomness (Schelling), an image and an idea (Fischer), the automatic and the living (Bergson), the truly valuable and that which just aspires to be valuable (Chernyshevskii), necessity and freedom, the great and the paltry, and so on. Soviet aesthetics was no different in this respect. As Iurii Borev concluded, "the comic is a juxtaposition of the socially perceived, the socially significant mismatch (between the ends and the means, form and content, action and circumstances, an essence and its demonstration, an individual's claims and what the individual truly is, and so on)."[105]

The problem, however, is that in Stalinism, "the comic as a means of exposing contradictions" is faced with a major obstacle: the epic world of Socialist Realism seeks to reach a stage of harmony, never to expose juxtapositions or contradictions. In such conditions true comic production is impossible, but *at the very same time* there must be a constant simulation of it to maintain the populist spirit and optimism that are obligatory elements of Socialist Realism. We are thus dealing here with the essentially oxymoronic phenomenon of *harmonizing laughter*, which nourished a great variety of endless dialectic exercises. We will examine this dialectics here at greater length.

The 1930s were the time when the principles of "life-affirming" state laughter and "positive satire" were introduced. What Kirshon presented merely in general terms in 1934 became dogma just a few years later.[106] Thus, according to Evgeniia Zhurbina, in Soviet literature "the unmasking spirit of satire has penetrated deeply into the 'peaceful' literary genres. A properly Soviet satirist must attune his lyre to

---

[104] Bakhnov, "Otvety."   [105] Borev, *O komicheskom*, pp. 60–1.
[106] The idea of "positive comedy" found support among authoritative critics such as Iu. Iuzovskii, S. Tsimbal, and others (see, e.g., *Rabochii i teatr*, no. 12 (1934)).

'sublime sounds,' if he wants his satire to remain realistic."[107] This interpenetration of the lyric and the comic, according to Zhurbina, completely reformed the latter:

> Only now, before our very eyes, is satire beginning to come to life in the full range and fullness of lyrical tones. The kind of satire that is emerging here is unheard of, it is unknown in world history: a satire that contains no indissoluble residues of bile, bitterness, and irony.[108]

Only by attuning their "lyres" to those "sublime sounds" could Soviet satirists be "at the level necessary to achieve their goals":

> A lyrically-enthusiastic attitude to our reality becomes the bridge which helps these writers move over to the path of a new, Soviet satire.... Only thanks to the powerful wave of anger and hatred, the powerful wave of life-affirming lyrical emotionality, has it become possible to solve the problem of developing a Soviet kind of satire.[109]

This "Soviet kind of satire" was free from "critical zeal and a sense of indignation"; instead, it was "filled with a cloudless, bright lyrical mood." In the world of this "cloudless, bright lyrical mood" there is no room for satire as such. This mood inspires the Soviet "lyrical comedies" on stage and on screen, as well as kolkhoz plays and novels.

Zhurbina claimed that "Soviet literature in general is developing under the slogan of 'unmasking' on a scale previously unknown in world literature. It has a rich experience of 'tearing off all kinds of masks'."[110] Needless to say, the "masks" were being "torn off" the face of the past. Things were quite different when it came to talking about the present day:

> The life-affirming emotionality must penetrate every element of the Soviet practice of unmasking without reducing the power of the unmasking attack, but simply by putting it against a new, contrasting background—that of joy, energy, inner calm, and confidence.[111]

This practice of unmasking inspired by "energy" and "joy" marked a rejection of the passionate zeal of accusatory satire in favor of lyrical emotionality. Ridding satire of its old "nutrient medium" of "indissoluble residues of bile, bitterness, and irony" meant doing away with the critical essence and core passion that made satire satire. For Zhurbina, these forms of criticism are simply "old wineskins" that

---

[107] Zhurbina, "Zametki," p. 247. [108] Ibid., p. 248. [109] Ibid., pp. 248–9.
[110] Zhurbina, "O mere," p. 128. [111] Ibid., p. 129.

cannot contain the "new wine" of joy, optimism, and enthusiasm. "Anger, contempt, sarcasm, bitterness, and indignation" were rejected as bourgeois categories inapplicable to Soviet art. It is hardly surprising that these intellectual balancing acts resulted in reckoning satire to be a *lyrical*(!) genre of literature. Now, lyrical undertones and intonations, lyrical pathos formed the emotional background of "positive satire," creating a new foundation for satire as such. "A lyrically enthusiastic, lyrically emotional attitude to our reality," the critic claimed, "has replaced the traditional satirical bile and become a nutrient medium for a new, optimistic kind of satire."[112] In fact, this was the first definitive formulation of what later would come to be called the *theory of conflictlessness*, the first time the recipe for the "pink varnish" of Soviet literature was offered.

This theory was soon extended to drama. Mikhail Gus, whom we already quoted above, published the article "Modern Collisions" (1940), in which he claimed there were two types of plots that were most characteristic of the time: plots of discovery and plots of achievement. "The nature of these plots," Gus wrote, "is that the conflict in them is between the new and that which is even newer."[113] Viktor Gusev, a popular "lyrical comedy" playwright of the 1930s, complained in his article "Thoughts on the Hero" that he was sick of plays in which people suffer.[114]

Predictably, satire had completely disappeared from the public arena by the second half of the 1930s. The genre now only survived in museum form—for example, in new translations of canonical classical texts such as Juvenal's *Satires* (Academia, 1937) and Martial's *Selected Epigrams* (State Literary Publishing House, 1937). One of the few examples of modern satire was a collection of satirical essays by Il'f and Petrov about, of course, America. The theater stage was dominated by the "positive comedy," that is, comedies without any negative characters. Kolkhoz comedy was flourishing, as were the kolkhoz novel and kolkhoz poem. Satire was reserved almost exclusively for political caricature and journalism depicting internal and external enemies.

After the war, in order to justify the return to the previous course following the ideological decrees of 1946, Vladimir Ermilov refurbished Chernyshevskii's slogan into "The Beautiful is Our Life." This remained the motto of Soviet art until the declaration in *Pravda* that "playwriting is falling behind," accompanied by a warning that the "conflictless" strategy is harmful and the demand for Soviet Gogols and Shchedrins. Until then, little was being written about the comic. Whenever there was talk about "comedy," satire was automatically implied, with the concept of "satire" understood accordingly. "We are living in a socialist country and are confidently advancing towards communism," Boris Gorbatov reflected in *Novyi Mir* in 1949:

[112] Ibid.   [113] Gus, "Sovremennye," p. 93.   [114] Gusev, "Mysli."

Hence, our satire can and must be life-affirming and positive.... This is why our humor includes the genre of the "positive newspaper satire," which was not known to humorists of the past at all; this is why our satire and humor are not just critical, but also empowering, solidifying our truth, our way of life, and our ideals.

Dissatisfied with the books of certain satirists (who remain nameless), Gorbatov complains that their world looks "strange": "there are no Stakhanovites, no working people, no factory life at all in this world."[115]

The return to satire in April 1952, driven by Stalin's political considerations, was rather abrupt, as there had not been much happening that would have allowed one to predict this development of events just a few months previously, when the "theory of conflictlessness" was still in full swing, affirmed by writers and critics alike. Thus, at a meeting of Moscow playwrights on the topic "Conflict in the Modern Theatre" on January 11, 1952, Konstantin Finn talked about a special type of "quiet conflict." According to him, since there were "no 'freaks' in our life, no clashes between the clever and the stupid, [playwrights] have to look for conflict where there might be struggle, but without it being a matter of 'survival,' without there being instances of who 'drove whom away,' without somebody 'making use of his official position'." Finn declared: "I am an advocate of quiet conflict. I personally (again, not based on my own experience, but on the experience of world drama) see that quiet conflict is the most interesting kind of conflict."[116]

However, once the reason for "playwriting falling behind" was named, the search began for those who were to blame for creating the harmful "theory of conflictlessness." It was no easy task, as one had to condemn this theory "in a conflictless way," with as few casualties as possible, without exaggerating the harm it had done to Soviet art (and this alone made it clear what kind of Gogols and Shchedrins were needed).

The theory of conflictlessness itself was then declared almost an act of political sabotage. Ermilov and El'sberg, both masters of such formulations, competed with each other in wittily formulated political accusations: "The theory of conflictlessness in art is practically destined to atrophy the political wakefulness of our artists" (Ermilov);[117] "All these mistaken views led to complacency, lack of vigilance, and atrophy of political wakefulness, playing in the hands of varnishers and control freaks, bureaucrats, and gawkers" (El'sberg).[118]

Finally, the party supposedly guilty of having launched the "conflictless campaign" was presented to the public. It was the orthodox Stalinist writer Nikolai Virta, whose review of the feature film *The Country Doctor* (*Sel'skii vrach*, 1951;

---

[115] Gorbatov, "O sovetskoi satire."
[116] Quoted in Frolov, *O sovetskoi komedii*, p. 270.
[117] Ermilov, *Nekotorye voprosy*, p. 8.
[118] El'sberg, *Nasledie Gogolia*, p. 20.

dir. Sergei Gerasimov) entitled "A Work of Great Realist Truth" was published on January 16, 1952 (thus, supposedly, the "theory" in question was born just a few months before the campaign against it). In the review, Virta wrote that

> there does not seem to be any visible, obvious conflict in life any more, any clashes of forces, ideas and concepts. If such conflicts do arise, then this happens in conditions that are not at all typical for our country. But if a conflict begins to acquire a typical character, it is solved by the mighty interference of our party, of the vast masses of the people, of everything new and positive, everything that is incessantly moving forward... Conflicts have been qualitatively transformed, because the life-affirming force of everything that is young, healthy, and blossoming, which defines our present society, puts a stop to the spread of anything that is becoming obsolete.

Virta was happy to witness "the smooth, crystal-clear flow of the great current of our life" as he saw it in *The Country Doctor*. Hence his conclusion:

> In the film *The Country Doctor* the screenwriter M. Smirnova and the director S. Gerasimov proved beyond any doubt that creating works of art where there are no antagonistic conflicts, but just episodes of real-life clashes between modern people, clashes that are, so to say, "bloodless"... is quite possible, and not only possible but logical, and that this is the path that our dramatic art will be following.

However, Virta did not distort the message of the film. The screenwriter Smirnova herself published an article in the same newspaper on October 22, 1952, under the title "The Truth Is in the Typical," where she developed her views of the typical as what was most common:

> Whenever I start working on something new, I am reminded of my search for the typical in defining the topic for the screenplay of the film *The Country Doctor*.
> ...There might still be careerist teachers, angry and ignorant people, but they are not typical of what our Soviet teachers are—teachers called upon to educate the members of a new society.
> What a terrifying slander I would have uttered against hundreds of thousands of honest workers, who have given their very soul to this noble and difficult cause! What lies I would have been telling, had I focussed on some singular cases instead of reflecting the truth, that is, the typical.

A typical "little man" is transformed by Smirnova into a completely average object, as she strives to represent everything that is average:

I'll take a very average MTS [machine-tractor station] somewhere in the midlands of our Motherland, where the soil has been farmed for so long it is now thin.... I can see our hero out in the fields. He is of average height, covered in dust, a grey cap on his greyish hair, wearing a more than unpretentious jacket, his face in no way remarkable—there are millions of such faces. And then we discover that this person is a treasure of knowledge, that he possesses an amazing spiritual power and a beautiful mind, as well as management talent. But he is just a person like many others. He is the people.

It is a whole aesthetic program that is formulated here: if *the people* are an embodiment of everything average, then realistic art must choose stereotypical representation as its strategy. In fact, a depiction of such an object cannot be unconventional. For example, satire, which naturally gravitates to exaggeration of certain traits, is not only out of place here but aesthetically impossible.

These "advocates of the theory of a disappearance of conflicts, like Manilovs without a care in the world, idealized life, closed their eyes to flaws, to fighting them," thus "doing a disservice to art, doing away with conflicts and realistic art, its true and active power." They were declared "a rearguard"—of formalists: "[Both they and the formalists] have been busy annihilating the genre of realistic comedy, working on this task with just the same enthusiasm."[119]

Liberated from formalism and the demands of the "theory of conflictlessness," comedy (satire) remained, however, constrained by the familiar dialectics even after 1952, as it struggled to find the right mix of pink and black, symbolically speaking: "Soviet satire is a stranger to mockery, empty giggling and sneering at daily Soviet life and Soviet order. Like all other genres of Soviet art, it keeps its distance from both the indiscriminately pink balm of varnishers and the tar-black smear of ill-wishers."[120] In everyday life, the middle ground between these two "balms and smears" was dictated by party directives, but in public discourse, finding a solution to the problem was taking a long time. Then it became clear that comedy had to represent both principles, with positive characters being absolutely necessary to balance out the negative ones.

The presence of an obligatory positive hero side by side with a negative one was dictated by the very essence of Soviet comedy, its populist and cheerful nature. Supposedly, the playwrights needed the positive heroes "to show the best characteristics of the people living today. At the same time, these heroes evoke laughter and smiles."[121] In fact, these were the heroes of "lyrical comedies," already familiar to the audience, characters who may be depicted in a humorous manner, but whose comic nature is "positive, because it is inseparable from the optimism that permeates the people's life."[122] According to the Soviet theory of the comic,

---

[119] Frolov, *O sovetskoi komedii*, p. 28.
[120] Borev, *O komicheskom*, p. 112.
[121] Frolov, *O sovetskoi komedii*, p. 37.
[122] Ibid.

"Soviet realist comedy does not seek to subject Soviet people to mindless, mocking laughter. Its goals are noble."[123]

But there is an element of seriousness at the core of this "noble comedy": "A playwright should not get carried away writing for comic effect at the expense of the message of a particular work."[124] In other words, Soviet comedy should avoid slipping into vaudeville of the "variety-show" type; in it, "merriment is an organic development of the ideological principles governing its content, and it should not eclipse the content, should not become a goal in itself."[125]

But none of these recipes were appropriate for satire. The project was to create a kind of hybrid of satire and lyrical comedy. Accordingly, the theory of "positive satire" was to undergo but a partial fixing. This question was addressed by most participants of the discussion of satirical comedy organized on April 8, 1953 by the Executive Board of the Union of Soviet Writers along with representative Moscow writers and critics. Evgenii Surkov called for an obligatory juxtaposition of "two socially different characters" in satirical comedy. "A struggle can be efficient and can influence the audience only when the positive character wins, having overcome impediments and affirmed his rightness in action."[126] As it turns out, after the call for Soviet Gogols and Shchedrins,

> the significance of positive heroes in Soviet comedy has increased. Their appearance is a response to an insistent demand of our Soviet life, which contains endless manifestations of the beautiful and where not a single bureaucrat, not a single fool or vulgar character exists alone, isolated from society. No, such people all live among wonderful Soviet people; our social norms are there fighting against them, influencing them, and they themselves, in their turn, may exercise some influence on certain people that are not particularly stable. And such a negative character is asking to become a hero of comedy! But not alone, by himself: he must be there together with those who expose him.[127]

Thus a step forward was made, away from "positive comedy": "Experience has shown that comedy with positive characters only, without negative figures, is a meaningless contrivance."[128] However, the new direction was by no means straightforward, for neither critics or playwrights and directors. Director Aleksei Popov responded to *Pravda*'s appeal in 1952 by writing that "in our dramatic art we cannot create comedy built on negative types only without distorting the overall picture of the distribution of forces in our reality."[129]

This is where the theory of "realistic comedy" came in handy yet again. Even though "Soviet satire furiously exposes the negative and pernicious phenomena in

---

[123] Ibid.   [124] Ibid.   [125] Ibid., p. 38.
[126] Surkov, "Ne po tomu puti."   [127] Frolov, *Zhanry*, p. 207.
[128] Frolov, *O sovetskoi komedii*, pp. 8–9.   [129] Popov, "Za komediiu!," p. 12.

our life," its "lofty and noble goal" is incompatible with "the exaggeratedly hyperbolic depiction of negative characters." The best type of comedy is now "comedy that depicts unmediated clashes between positive and negative characters, exposes people with evil inclinations acting in *a positive environment*, an environment governed by principles of Soviet, socialist life."[130]

"Positive characters" were a sign of this sort of "positive environment." Comedy offers a more or less broad picture of reality, encompasses a more or less broad range of people. And since this is *Soviet* reality and a range of *Soviet* people, a creator of such comedy would be hard pressed to do without positive types. Otherwise the end product might be a "satire" of the kind satirized so sharply by S. Shevtsov in his "List of Dramatic Personae of One Supposedly Satirical Play":

> Father—scoundrel
> Son—idiot
> Daughter—halfwit
> Mother—slanderer
> Older brother—ruthless bureaucrat
> Younger brother—obviously retarded
> Son-in-law—bigamist
> Grandfather—turncoat
> Grandmother—miser
> Nephew—hipster
> Grandsons and granddaughters—all spoiled brats
> Antip the street sweeper—amoral type
> Daria the milkwoman—scandalmonger
> Fools, good-for-nothings and ignoramuses also make an appearance in the play.[131]

Of course, Soviet satire did not exist just to paint this horror picture. This is why "conversations about creating a satirical comedy, a novel or a poem that would only depict negative characters lack any justification."[132]

In such a context, references to Gogol and Shchedrin, whose works featured exclusively negative characters, became meaningless. This is why Ermilov and El'sberg, responding to *Pravda*'s appeal to produce "Gogols and Shchedrins," set about painting the classic authors as Soviet satirists. Thus, Ermilov wrote of Gogol's "affirmative laughter": "The unbreakable connection between love and hate, denial not in the name of denial but in the name of affirmation—these are the classical Gogolean traditions. Gogol introduced the concept of enthusiastic

---

[130] Frolov, *O sovetskoi komedii*, pp. 42–3.   [131] Dzeverin, *Problema*, p. 219.
[132] Ershov, *Sovetskaia satiricheskaia literatura*, p. 33.

laughter, positive laughter into aesthetics."[133] According to Ermilov, an artist's goal is to depict the struggle between the old and the new, and criticism of the old "is only necessary insofar as it is vital for defeating that which belongs to the past." Thus, Gogol's satire was declared "affirmative" and "positive."

Ermilov, a leading literary critic of Stalin's era, showed himself to be a real expert of such dialectics, easily reconciling the irreconcilable: "The author of Soviet satirical comedy does not know the difficulty that Gogol was facing: the absence of a typical environment, of an action field for a positive hero" (22). To avoid the impression that this was an appeal for a return to the "theory of conflictlessness," Ermilov hastened to add: "It is essential to depict the *struggle* with negative phenomena as a characteristic feature of our reality, and not just to represent negative phenomena by themselves" (32).

The word "struggle" suggests a conflict. A neutralization mechanism is switched on at once: as it turns out, a positive hero has a "forward-looking nature." He must "guide" the plot. Otherwise, if the plot is "guided" by a negative character, there is a "distortion of proportions," and "a ridiculous freak show" is passed off as "the Soviet social environment" (34–5). A reader of the book on "Gogol's tradition" might be tempted to ask: So how did Gogol make it work without any positive heroes? Ermilov had a response ready:

> In *The Inspector General* Gogol could not depict a conflict with the negative characters. The characters Gogol created were in conflict with a positive ideal of a new, progressive Russia, but in the comedy itself the conflict between the old and the new was not depicted directly. In Soviet satirical comedy this very conflict, this very opposition between the new and progressive versus the old and outdated, is what determines the course of a play, its passion, its content. This explains why positive heroes confronting negative characters directly is characteristic of Soviet comedy. (38)

These statements left unresolved the question of how "Gogol's tradition" was relevant to Soviet satire.

Ermilov addressed in the same unorthodox way every other issue that he touched upon, using the full range of dialectical oppositions, in attempting to explain the specific nature of Soviet satire. Ridicule is important in satire? But "a love of good without a hatred of evil is not love but a Manilov-like softness" (6), and "the more we love our motherland—the motherland of socialism, ... the more forceful, the more ruthless we should be in *removing everything negative, rotten, and stagnating from our life, everything that hinders our progress. We should mercilessly insult, persecute, and annihilate every kind of evil*" (7). Can the slogan

---

[133] Ermilov, *Nekotorye voprosy*, p. 10. Further references to this edition are given with page numbers in parentheses.

"The Beautiful is Our Life" be regarded as a justification for varnishing? Not at all: "From the point of view of materialist aesthetics, and especially from the point of view of the aesthetics of Socialist Realism, the beautiful is struggle, it is creative work!" (47).

Soviet aesthetics demonstrated miracles of such dialectic acrobatics, turning concepts upside down. Thus, it was claimed that since "a typical character is always an expression of a certain natural order of life," a negative type "is a negative reflection of the invincibility of the power of the new in our reality, the invincibility of our progress towards communism."[134]

In other words, *the negative is the positive*. And the other way round: "We can say that the negating power of Socialist Realism has increased in the same proportion as its life-affirming power. And Soviet comedy should by no means renounce its characteristic feature—negation."[135] Unsurprisingly, the "fundamental question of the theory of Soviet satire" turned out to be the question concerning... "the heroic positive character."[136] In 1953 El'sberg claimed that "one of the most important questions pertaining to the sphere of the arts... concerns the distribution of dark and light colors on the satirical canvas, deciding what the proportion of negative and positive characters should be."[137] Just thirteen years later, Leonid Ershov demanded from satire nothing less than heroic narratives: "Our satire needs not just a progressive ideal, a positive example, but a heroic character."[138]

Not that the critics completely ignored the difference between heroic and satirical narratives: "We wouldn't look in comedy for that lofty heroic spirit that constitutes the pathos of tragedy. But this is by no means to say that satirical exposure in Soviet comedy is devoid of a passion for affirmation, that it cannot paint attractive images."[139] Demanding that satire create "attractive images" was not at all paradoxical. Clearly, "Soviet comedy cannot limit itself only to condemnation, mockery and a criticism of negative phenomena, to a depiction of negative characters only—unless it wants to go against the key requirements of Soviet art. A positive hero is necessary, as is the affirmation of positive principles."[140]

But even the presence of positive heroes embodying "positive principles" in satirical comedy could not save authors from political accusations. They were blamed for "distorting the truth of life," since they were expected to always make sure that the positive characters were at the foreground, always "the leading, advancing force in a conflict,"[141] and that they were more numerous than those being satirized. This approach gained the upper hand way back in the 1920s, when critics detected in Bezymenskii's *The Shot* "a ratio between positive and negative

---

[134] Burov, "Smekh–oruzhie," p. 20. [135] Ibid., p. 18. [136] Kiselev, *Problemy*, p. 141.
[137] El'sberg, "Otritsatel'noe," p. 59. [138] Ershov, *Sovetskaia satiricheskaia proza*, p. 297.
[139] Starinkevich, "Nasushchnye problemy," p. 159. [140] Malovichko, "Pogovorim," p. 117.
[141] Ermilov, *Nekotorye voprosy*, p. 41.

aspects among the working class, the party members" that "distorts the real proportions of life."[142] The distortion was not only quantitative but also qualitative, since "the weak and inexpressive nature of positive characters, or even more so their total absence, allows a negative phenomenon to spread, meeting hardly any resistance at all."[143]

We are dealing here with a truly oxymoronic aesthetics that demands the impossible:

> Soviet satire, however threatening, however mercilessly targeting people's faults, cannot exist without an ideal, without the affirmation of a positive principle. Its zeal must contain a positive, beautiful ideal....A Soviet playwright, while ridiculing the remnants of capitalism in the consciousness of our people, cannot disregard the truly beautiful, truly advanced phenomena in Soviet life. A writer of comedies thus faces the challenge of depicting the sublime in comedy.[144]

And another example of the same: "Monumentalism in comedic art is all about a lofty wholeness of characters. An actor on stage constructs his actions in accordance with the logic of a character's behavior, he thinks everything through, feels it, from which a natural and truthful kind of the comic [sic] emerges."[145]

These truly radical demands for a heroic satirical narrative, for comic monumentalism, for the sublime in comedy, for the wholeness of comedic characters, are all examples of the radical Stalinist "impossible aesthetic."[146] One of the main problems in assessing the phenomenon of state laughter lies in the non-differentiation of concepts. Just as art in Socialist Realism is not quite art, satire in state laughter is not quite satire, and humor is not quite humor. If we succeed in clarifying their specificity and exposing these differences, we will consider our task accomplished.

---

[142] Fedoseev, "*Vystrel*," p. 248.   [143] Surov, "Nashi," p. 309.
[144] Frolov, *O sovetskoi komedii*, pp. 34–6.   [145] Ibid., p. 67.
[146] See Robin, *Socialist Realism*.

2
A Killer Wit

Laughter in Stalinist Official Discourse

> I am not only
> Witty in myself, but the cause that wit is
> In other men.
>
> William Shakespeare, *Henry IV*

After the turbulent years of the revolution, Stalinism brought with it a victory of law—or rather, of legislatorial practices. In a kind of mirror reflection of Émile Benveniste's conclusion that "in Indo-European languages the words which are used to utter the law are related to the verb 'to speak',"[1] Stalinism was based on the conviction that everything uttered was related to law—either as crime, or as a legislative act. By "legislative act" we mean an expression of the principles of social order in a broad sense, without the restriction of strictly legal frameworks. In Stalinism, as noted by Igal Halfin, a historian who is particularly sensitive to the discursive dimension of the time, "jurisprudence had no specific arena, no carefully delineated area of application."[2] In the Stalinist system, where everyday behavior, a carelessly blurted-out word, and even thoughts could be classified as criminal offenses, legislatorial practices had a dual function: on the one hand, they played an important role in disciplining citizens everywhere and at any time, and, on the other, they were supposed to be a confirmation of the democratic nature of the Soviet regime. This was a regime in which the norms regulating the interactions between the state and its citizens were determined with the immediate participation of citizens themselves, in various contexts and at all levels.

This dual function of legislatorial practices demanded an appropriate linguistic framing of a qualitatively new kind. Apparently State Prosecutor Andrei Vyshinskii felt this on an intuitive level, too, when he expressed concern that his classical legal training might not be sufficient to adequately articulate his attitude to the defendants at the Moscow show trials. "I cannot find the words in my vocabulary!" he exclaimed in despair.[3] But the prosecutor underestimated himself. He found the necessary words, and, if the transcripts published in the newspapers

---

[1] See Bourdieu, *Language*, p. 41.   [2] Halfin, *Stalinist Confessions*, p. 14.
[3] Vyshinskii, *Sudebnye rechi*, p. 384.

are any indication, the audience often greeted those words with laughter. Michel Foucault recommended that researchers of political systems "try to fixate power at the extreme of its exercise, where it is always less legal in character"[4]—and in a courtroom where a death sentence is about to be pronounced, there are few things further removed from the core of formal law than laughter.

We can characterize the laughter that appears in the transcripts of formal events as "politically correct." Our starting point here is the conviction that it was this laughter that legitimized the division into "insiders" and "outsiders" that was so fundamental to Stalinism. In so far as the former category was synonymous with innocence and the latter with guilt, and to the extent that this synonymity had legal consequences, laughter should be regarded as an integral part of the legal discourse of Stalinism. Transformations of the contexts in which laughter was heard (or registered in the transcripts of the events in question) reflect an evolution of the very foundations of the Stalinist master-narrative. The issue of authenticity of the transcripts and the notes accompanying them is but of secondary importance here, since what we are concerned with is what place laughter, and humor, were supposed to occupy in that particular context, under those circumstances.

The Beginning of the Plot

We begin with several speeches given by Stalin at key party events. The first ones are "The Opposition Bloc in the CPSU(b): Theses for the Fifteenth All-Union Conference of the CPSU(b)"[5] and "The Social-Democratic Deviation in our Party: Report Delivered at the Fifteenth All-Union Conference of the CPSU(b)" from the autumn of 1926.[6] These relatively early texts are crucial for an analysis of Stalinist rhetoric, since the criteria for distinguishing between friends and enemies were announced in them with more precision and at greater length than at earlier party forums. Judging by the significant number of notes indicating "Italics mine. I. S.," the leader carefully edited the text of his report on "the social-democratic deviation" before its publication in the newspapers; thus it is safe to say that the laughter of the public is noted wherever and whenever he considered it appropriate and necessary, regardless of whether or not it actually was heard at the actual event, on the actual day. Apparently he deemed it appropriate and necessary primarily when the internal party opposition was mentioned, and above all

---

[4] Foucault, "Two Lectures," p. 97.
[5] Stalin, "Ob oppozitsionnom bloke," pp. 214–33. English translation: Stalin, "The Opposition Bloc." We provide references throughout to the available English translations of Stalin's texts discussed here, but our use of them has been freely modified in the interest of greater precision.
[6] Stalin, "O sotsial-demokraticheskom uklone." English translation: Stalin, "The Social-Democratic Deviation."

Trotsky, the author of "a wonderful and musical, completely useless" work, the reference being to Trotsky's book *Towards Socialism or Towards Capitalism?* (*K sotsializmu ili k kapitalizmu?*, 1925). Stalin quotes the "confused" party comrade often and readily, framing his quotes with comments on Trotsky's awkward style:

> "As a system of revolutionary action, Leninism presupposes a revolutionary sense developed through reflection and experience, which in the social realm is equivalent to muscular sensation in physical labor."[7]
> Leninism as a "muscular sensation in physical labor." Isn't it new, and original, and deep? Did you understand any of this? (*Laughter*).[8]

Trotsky's letter from September 1926 concerning the presumed results of the rivalry inside the party is mockingly mentioned by Stalin in his "Reply to the Discussion on the Report" as "almost a prophecy of a purely Marxist kind, foreseeing something whole two months in advance. (*Laughter*),... [which], of course,... contains some exaggerations. (*Laughter*)."[9] Having quoted a few other excerpts where comrade Trotsky allowed "some exaggerations," the speaker comes to the conclusion that, "if we disregard these exaggerations that comrade Trotsky allowed in his document, there will be nothing left of his forecast, in fact. (*Laughter*)."

Trotsky's attempts at a scientific presentation are supposed to be mocked because the philosophy of Stalinism presumed that truth is on the side of simplicity, with complex formulations being ridiculous at best, and suspicious and potentially criminal at worst.[10] Trotsky had ventured here into a domain that was to be understood as accessible only to Stalin: forecasts, knowledge of the future. There is some logic in this principle: as only the nation's leader had the right to determine policy at any given moment, whether with regard to the past, the present, or the future, all other forecasts and analyzes were inherently wrong and could only be laughed at. This is exactly what the audience's reaction was to Stalin's extended metaphor based on a quotation from Zinov'ev:

> Comrade Zinov'ev boasted a while ago that he can press his ear to the ground (*Laughter*), and when he presses it to the ground, he hears the footsteps of history. It may well be so. But one should still acknowledge that comrade Zinov'ev, though able to press his ear to the ground and hear the footsteps of history, sometimes fails to hear certain "trifles." (*Syrtsov*: "He was listening with

---

[7] The quote is from Trotsky's text *Novyi kurs*, p. 47.
[8] Stalin, "O sotsial-demokraticheskom uklone," p. 276.
[9] Stalin, "Zakliuchitel'noe slovo"; English translation: Stalin, "Reply to the Discussion."
[10] See, e.g., Bogdanov, *Vox populi*, in particular pp. 58–63 (chapter "O prostote i pravde"), as well as Halfin, *Stalinist Confessions*, p. 4 [Introduction] and Kozlova, "Uproshchenie."

only one ear.") It is quite possible that the opposition can, indeed, press its ears to the ground and hear wonderful things, such as the footsteps of history. But one must also acknowledge that, while being able to hear wonderful things, it was not able to hear one "trifle," namely, that the party has long since turned its back on the opposition, and the opposition has remained stranded since then. This they didn't hear. (*Voices*: "Exactly!"). So, what follows from this? What follows is that the opposition apparently is having trouble with its ears. (*Laughter*). Hence my advice: comrades from the opposition, get your ears cured! (*A prolonged, thunderous ovation. The conference members stand as comrade Stalin leaves the stage*).[11]

True to the principle that everything written and said by anyone other than by the supreme lawgiver and creator of meaning can only reveal its true sense in the master's interpretation, the Soviet leader does not just quote leaders of the opposition—he actually *represents* them, in the almost theatrical sense of *making present* a particular image that would otherwise be restricted to an act of writing (as with Trotsky), or to a casual remark (as with Zinov'ev). In this, he is a worthy heir of his historical model, Ivan the Terrible, who was known for his love of comic effects in interactions with his adversaries. The despotic monarch understood, too, the comic potential of repeated quotations reproduced with exaggerated precision, copying his addressee's style and embodying his voice, whether in writing or in personal contact.[12] Inevitably, this *re-presentation* results in a comic effect, as the quoted words are transferred from one medium to another, to a different contextual, temporal, and situational framework. Besides, a metaphor or a turn of phrase used once and then extended into a whole passage, a thesis, acquires a further comic flavor.

The examples above show how two completely opposite styles—Trotsky's pseudoscientific, pompous rhetoric and Zinov'ev's entirely too "common" images—turn out to be equally ridiculous in Stalin's representation. As a matter of fact, what exactly the leader's political adversaries were saying, and how they were formulating it, is not that important. The comic effect in this case is not a result of the form or content of the actual original statements, but rather is achieved by exaggerating or magnifying certain details when these pronouncements are reproduced.

Stalin performs what discourse theorists Frank Burton and Pat Carlen (with reference to Jacques Lacan) call "unauthorized reading," not only because, in a parody of the democratic principle of allowing political opponents to voice their opinion, he almost literally re-creates the authors of the words he quotes, but also because at the moment of doing so he himself is *un-authorized*: he is not a ruler

---

[11] Stalin, "Zakliuchitel'noe slovo," p. 356.   [12] Likhachev et al., *Smekhovoi mir*, pp. 33–43.

but a jester. The implicit assumption is that only as a jester can he adequately quote the ridiculous words of the enemies—and here, too, the parallels with Ivan the Terrible are evident. Only a jester who is also a ruler can assume the voice of anyone at all, exaggerating the meaning and the tone, intentionally overdoing it, celebrating the *un-authorized* reading. This role of mocking quotations in rhetorical and ideological gestures of inclusion and exclusion in totalitarian regimes is at least as important as their solemn and routinely evoked double—the obligatory references to a limited number of "sanctified" texts and voices. The style and the general tone of the oppositionists' rhetoric is also supposedly ridiculous because they are a sign of these individuals being estranged from the collective—that is, from the commonly accepted way of expressing one's thoughts and their interpretation.

This is why the opposition is accused first of all of being stubborn and disregarding the will of the majority. This is their fatal mistake, a mistake referred to as an objective category, something clear both to Stalin and to simple workers, and even, it would seem, to the oppositionists themselves, who nevertheless persist in being wrong, rejecting the friendly advice to soften somewhat the formulation of their blatantly incorrect suggestion of a political reform:

> The oppositionists said they were going to mention in the first paragraph of their "statement" that they are not going to change their opinion, that it's not just that they are going to remain in their old position, but they are going to remain "completely" in it. We tried to convince the oppositionists not to insist on this. Why? For two reasons. First of all, because if they, having renounced the fractionalist principle, have also renounced the theory and practice of the freedom of fractions, having split from... "the workers' opposition."... it means that they have renounced not only the fractionalist methods of struggle, but also some political positions. Can one still claim after this that the oppositionist bloc remains "completely" loyal to its mistaken views, to its ideological position? Of course not. Secondly, we told the oppositionists they would be at a disadvantage if they shout from the roofs that they, the oppositionists, are going to remain loyal, even "completely," to their old positions, because then the workers would have every reason to say: "it means the oppositionists are looking to pick a fight, it means the thrashing we gave them was not enough, it means they are in for more." (*Laughter; shouts*: "Exactly!").[13]

The contrast between the formal context of the event and the rather vulgar allusion to a "thrashing" might indeed be seen as funny—at least for some of the audience. It is possible that an identification mechanism is activated here: people laugh because they recognize themselves in their leader's speech; the

---

[13] Stalin, "O sotsial-demokraticheskom uklone," pp. 239–40.

supreme power gives its blessing to the language of the common people as an alternative to the dangerously complicated style of the enemies:

> Me, sinful as I am, I am somewhat suspicious when it comes to this matter (*Laughter*) and I must say that such speculations, unfortunately, do not correspond to reality at all.[14]

Such was Stalin's sarcastic response to "some people's" speculations that "Comrade Trotsky has really renounced, or else this book shows that he is trying to renounce, some of his basic mistakes."[15]

In general, sarcastic remarks concerning the oppositionists' inability to acknowledge and correct their own mistakes was a tried and true way to trigger the audience's laughter:

> Comrade Trotsky further mentioned that I replaced an imprecise and wrong formulation of the question concerning the victory of socialism in one country, the one given in my book *Foundations of Leninism* of 1924, with a different formulation, one more precise and accurate. It appears that comrade Trotsky is not happy about it. Why, for what reason, he didn't specify. What harm can there be in my changing a wrong formulation and replacing it with a correct one? I do not by any means consider myself free from sin. I think the party can only profit from having a mistake made by this or that comrade acknowledged and corrected by him. What is it, exactly, that comrade Trotsky is trying to say by emphasizing this fact? Could it be that he wants to follow a positive example and, finally, to set about correcting his own numerous mistakes? (*Applause; laughter*). Well, I am ready to help him with this, if my help is needed, ready to push and help him. (*Applause; laughter*).[16]

This passage is clearly a parody of the principle of comradely mutual help, of the style of a party discussion as such. Hence the crudely sarcastic suggestion that the former comrade-in-arms should be "pushed" to correct his mistakes: "it appears that...", "could it be that...", "if my help is needed." Hence also the questions directed at the audience, ostensibly an invitation to express their opinions concerning the matter being discussed, but in fact—a command to be on the right side. Laughter as a response to a suggestive question as proof of a joke being understood, and understood correctly, is a common signal confirming the establishment of rapport between the speaker and the audience, which originates in a ritual gesture signaling the willingness to accept the rules of behavior in the given

---

[14] Ibid., p. 274.   [15] Ibid.   [16] Stalin, "Zakliuchitel'noe slovo," pp. 348–9.

system. Those who laugh know who is right and who is wrong, for whom mistakes are the foundation of a useful experience, and in whose case they are criminal.

Mistakes are likely to lead to undesirable consequences, for which the powerful ruler finds powerful images:

> Wherein lay the strength of Zinov'ev's group?
>
> It was its determined struggle against the foundations of Trotskyism. But once Zinov'ev's group renounced its policy of fighting Trotskyism, it emasculated itself, as it were, deprived itself of strength.
>
> Wherein lay the strength of Trotsky's group?
>
> It was its determined struggle against the mistakes of Zinov'ev and Kamenev in October 1917 and against their repetition in the present. But once this group renounced its policy of fighting the Zinov'ev-Kamenev deviation, it emasculated itself, it deprived itself of its strength.
>
> What we have here is a doubled strength of the emasculated. (*Laughter; long applause*). Clearly, nothing but embarrassment could result from that.[17]

The implication is that all these enemies were no fools: everyone understood what was right and what wrong, and if someone was determined to cling to false views, they did so only because they had dark motives, and were completely aware of the fact that their views were wrong. This is an expression of the ultimate skepticism formulated by Peter Sloterdijk and quoted by Žižek: "They know perfectly well what they are doing, but still, they are doing it."[18] Except that, unlike Žižek's skeptical subject, the stubborn enemies of Stalinism are not sceptics but tragic victims of their own crime, not only in a juridical sense but also in a religious-expiatory one. In order to affirm the truth, these people are prepared to stand on the side of the "lie"—and to be punished for it. Laughter is the first stage in the punishment of these stubborn enemies who are willing to make such a comic appearance in front of the audience: with a poorly hearing ear pressed to the ground, or else emasculated, deprived of all energy.

Stalinist discourse can be defined as "saturated":[19] the ideological apparatus functions based on the premise that fixed meanings occupy the whole space of language—hence the endless reproduction of previously tested formulations. This "saturation" of which Žižek speaks explains a particularity of the language of Stalinism that Roland Barthes noticed many years ago. In his essay on political writing the French critic remarked that "in the Stalinist world...there are no

---

[17] Stalin, "O sotsial-demokraticheskom uklone," pp. 243–4.
[18] Žižek, *The Sublime Object*, p. 33.
[19] See, e.g., Žižek on the "semantically saturated space [of discourse]" (*In Defense*) and also Halfin, "The Bolsheviks' Gallows Laughter," p. 261, on "the semantic field [that] was completely saturated."

more words without values attached to them."[20] The ideal language of Stalinism is a situation impossible in principle, when the *langue* generated in accordance with the party line finds its direct realization in the *parole* of carefully constrained everyday practices. But as this ideal is unrealizable in reality, there are constant mistakes made in the "grammar" of this language, generating again and again meanings that do not comply with the rules, that contradict the rules. As intentional mistakes, the instances of these meanings are punishable by law; as offenses against the style and semantics of the language of power, they are ridiculous. This is why defining the ridiculous at the highest level was the first, and necessary, step toward defining the judicial goals of the new society. But in order for a particular reaction to the alleged presence of enemies to become automatic, the comic nature of their thoughts, actions, and words must be emphasized all the time. At the same time, in so far as the very existence of ideological enemies is supposed to be associated with offenses against the rules of totalitarian grammar, the leader himself needs to talk about them in a comic mode—after all, it is only through his talking about them, indirectly, that the broad masses could find out who the enemies are and how to recognize them.

In Stalin's speeches the mistaken, confused, literally ridiculous logic and rhetoric of the oppositionists is contrasted with the pedantically consistent logic of those who know the truth and who can point to the incongruities in the roles played by the members of the opposition. Laughter seems to be deemed especially requisite whenever there are direct references to the roles played, or to the actors' inability to perform the very roles adequately, as when, for example, Stalin offers several pieces of advice to the opposition:

It is time to understand that one cannot be a revolutionary and an internationalist when in a state of war with our party, which is the vanguard of the Communist International.   (*Applause*).

It is time to understand, that, once they declared a war on the Communist International, they stopped being revolutionaries and internationalists.

(*Applause*).

It is time to understand that the oppositionists are neither revolutionaries nor internationalists, but windbags left over from the revolution and from internationalism.   (*Applause*).

It is time to understand that they are not revolutionaries of deed, but revolutionaries of shrill phrases and of filmstrips.   (*Laughter; applause*).

It is time to understand that they are not revolutionaries of deed, but revolutionaries on film only [*kino-revoliutsionery*].   (*Laughter; applause*).[21]

---

[20] Barthes, *Writing*, p. 24.   [21] Stalin, "Zakliuchitel'noe slovo," p. 332.

Frank Burton and Pat Carlen noted that in official discourse, the purpose of which is to establish certain general, standard forms of behavior,

> ... actor-subjects within the text have to be construed as recognizable subjects tailored to specific discursive strategies.... Articulation is achieved by the continuity of the egos formed in Official Discourse with those formed outside. The text's structure functions to achieve this continuity of subjectivity as a form of ideological productivity.[22]

The "continuity of subjectivity" of the masses is valuable for an authoritarian regime, in so far as it guarantees the predictability of the collective subject. The representation of others' voices by means of the voice of the omnipotent ruler guarantees that they are included in the collective perception of reality as an inevitable and necessary part of the shared experience; taking apart the ridiculous behavior of the enemies-to-be in this consistent, logical manner ensures that the types are recognizable. Hence the comparison with "revolutionaries on film only": these were a kind of virtual heroes, figures from a comic strip, ridiculous exactly because they are predictable and one-dimensional; an analysis of their actions leaves a pleasant sense of control over the events, as one can know well in advance what they are going to do—and laugh about it.

Remarkably, it is implied that all the actions of the oppositionists are merely an unserious game ("cinematic revolutionaries"), while on the other hand it is exactly this lack of seriousness that makes these actions criminal. To laugh, then, means to recognize the ridiculous (=criminal) under the guise of the serious (=politically reliable); to laugh means to accuse someone of concealing the truth—one of the most horrible crimes in those years. By the same token, confused thinking is to be mocked: in an ideology where simplicity equals truth, any type of confusion is to be considered incompatible with the honest way of life.

Stalin's speech culminates in a disclosure of the true nature of the oppositionists. Their masks—pompous formulations of their political declarations or impressive-sounding titles—are torn off, and in the classical carnivalesque tradition, a powerful, intelligent man is brought down to the lowest level of the social hierarchy:

> Plainly speaking, Kamenev has assumed the role of, so to say, a street-cleaner for Trotsky (*Laughter*), cleaning the way for him. Of course it is sad to see the Director of the Lenin Institute in the role of a street-cleaner for Trotsky, not because the work of a street-sweeper is something bad, but because Kamenev,

---

[22] Burton and Carlen, *Official Discourse*, p. 45.

undoubtedly a person with professional qualifications, I think, could have found a job of a higher professional level.   (*Laughter*).[23]

Kamenev being "exposed" as a street-cleaner triggers the audience's laughter, as it would trigger the laughter of preschool children. The infantilization of the public in totalitarian societies has been discussed in scholarship more than once.[24] These ideal listeners and viewers would always be happy to laugh at the ridiculous heroes in films and comic strips, or else at how some comrades, like, for example, comrade Zinov'ev, have funny things going on in their heads while engaging in "tricks":

> Here lies the solution to the secret of Zinov'ev's exercises concerning how our party "forgets" the international goals of our revolution.
> Here lies the solution to the secret of Zinov'ev's tricks, the mishmash and the mess in his thinking.
> And Zinov'ev has the modesty to present all this incredible mishmash, this ramble and mess in his own head as if it were the "real" revolutionary spirit, the internationalist spirit of the oppositional bloc.
> Isn't it all ridiculous, comrades?[25]

Zinov'ev is ridiculous in a childish kind of way, both because he turns out to be a child feeling lost in the world of adults, trying to make "all this incredible mishmash, this ramble and mess in his own head" appear as "the "real" revolutionary spirit," and because this invitation to laugh ("Isn't it all ridiculous, comrades?") puts the "comrades" themselves in the position of children to whom a grown-up explains who is good, who is bad, and what one should laugh at.

The starting point of the leader's argumentation in this case, just as in the other excerpts from the same event quoted above, implies a principle that is foundational to Stalinist discourse (and totalitarian discourse in general): if simplicity and truth are inseparable, then the truth, however crude, is on the side of those not afraid to speak clearly and simply and of those always ready to laugh. Hence, the latter are transformed from mere participants of events to accomplices in a campaign that has the goal of tearing off the cunning enemies' masks.

It is possible, of course, that the audience's laughter might be evoked simply by unpretentious mockery, but in the context of the general policy of revealing the enemies' true nature and punishing them accordingly, it is reasonable to suppose

---

[23] Stalin, "Zakliuchitel'noe slovo," p. 317.
[24] See, e.g., Erren, *Selbstkritik*, referred to in Griesse, "Soviet Subjectivities," p. 622; Gentile, *Educazione*, referred to in Golino, *Parola di Duce*; Naiman, "Discourse," p. 304.
[25] Stalin, "Zakliuchitel'noe slovo," pp. 331–2.

that this laughter is to a great degree indicative of a release of tension that may well have been tied to a sense of an unclear threat, an inability to understand the motives behind the enemies' actions. This laughter signals, or at least accompanies, the pleasure brought about by the realization that the mystery of an enemy threat has been solved, that the sense of wholeness and clarity is there, again, and that the world has become simple, clear, and safe—just as children like to see the world.

As he reveals the true meaning of the words and deeds of the oppositionists, Stalin appears as an author of *fiction*—and not only because from the late 1920s onwards the language of law and the actions of related authorities were becoming more and more dependent on made-up narratives, but also in the original meaning of *fingere* as shaping, bestowing a structure upon something.[26] Here, another term with a multiple meaning might prove useful. In the examples quoted above Stalin's images set down the foundations of *plotting* in a way that was to define the developments of the next decade. *Plotting* in the legal sense of a "conspiracy" is, without a doubt, a key judicial fantasy of Stalinism. As to the second meaning of the word *plot* ("the structure of a narrative"), its connection with foundational legal discourse may be less obvious, but it is there, and it is important.

The suggestive questions in the examples quoted above lead the audience to accept a form of narrative that is unequivocally defined by the speaker, thus shaping the audience's consciousness of events in a very specific way. Laughter in this context is nothing but a signal confirming that the message was received and understood correctly. Thus, the meaning of the narrative is generated by the very dynamic of the story, its movement toward the climax.[27] By revealing the essence of the oppositionists, by retelling their story in a way that fit the needs of the present moment, Stalin creates the matrix of an ideally predictable plot, which, in accordance with the rules of the genre, arrives at a resolution that gives the audience the satisfaction it needs—and the audience acknowledges it by laughing. For the moment, the plot of this narrative is rather short and relatively simple; the jesters and jugglers who had been presenting themselves as masters of theory and action are put to shame. Those who had claimed they were big and important turn out to be small and pitiful, and each time this happens, laughter is a confirmation of how this fact is rooted in the people's consciousness. A few years later, both meanings of plotting will collapse into one: invented stories with plots involving conspiracies will become equivalent to conspiratorial plots themselves. But the mechanism will still be the same as the one activated by Stalin at the end of the

---

[26] On the importance of this particular meaning of *fingere* for an interpretation of historically significant texts and historical accounts see, e.g., Davis, *Fiction*, p. 3 [Introduction].

[27] Brooks defines plotting as "that which makes a plot 'move forward,' and makes us read forward, seeking in the unfolding of the narrative a line of intention and portent of design that hold the promise of progress toward meaning" (Brooks, *Reading*, p. xiii).

1920s: the promise of a revelation at the end of a story will be kept, every mystery will be solved, every secret will be disclosed. Turned ridiculous, the enemies fulfil their function in Stalin's version of history as an embodiment of absolute evil that will be defeated by the powers of the good.

Funny Activists

On December 11, 1937, Stalin presented a report to the pre-election meeting of the Stalin Election District of Moscow, which was held in the Bolshoi Theater.[28] In it, he drew his audience's attention particularly to the legal mechanism that promised to become a reliable tool in differentiating loyal servants of the people from those who had not yet fully absorbed the ideals of socialist democracy. We hear Stalin quote folk proverbs quite freely when making his point, to the great amusement of the audience (here as elsewhere, the style of the original is preserved):

> For 4 or 5 years, that is, until the new elections, a deputy feels himself completely free, independent of the people, of those who elected him. He can switch camps, he can turn from a right road to a wrong one, he can become entangled in undignified affairs, he can perform any somersaults he wants—he is independent.
> Can such a situation be considered normal? Absolutely not, comrades. Our Constitution made provisions for this as it passed the law that allows voters to recall their deputies in case they start being funny [*esli oni nachinaiut fintit'*], if they get off track, if they forget about their dependence on the people, on the voters.
> This is a wonderful law, comrades. A deputy should remember that he serves the people, that he is the people's representative in the Supreme Council, and that he must behave himself in accordance with this line, where he's been given a task by the people. If he has left the straight road—the voters are entitled to demand new elections, and they can give him a ride on a black horse.   (*Laughter, applause*).[29]

Stylistic shifts in Stalin's language, the mixture of official rhetoric (Constitution, people, voters, deputies, law, the Supreme Council) with ostentatiously colloquial expressions ("to give somebody a ride on a black horse," that is, to blackball someone in anonymous voting) predictably trigger outbursts of laughter. Here

---

[28] Stalin, "Rech' na predvybornom sobranii." English translation: Stalin, "Speech Delivered."
[29] Stalin, "Rech' na predvybornom sobranii," p. 241.

Stalin sounds like a benign father, using clear images to explain democratic institutions to the common people, images with which these people would be familiar.

But here is another excerpt from the same speech, where the humor is already much cruder, in a typically Stalinist style, but where the transcripts still record laughter:

> Can we say that all candidate deputies are people of this kind [that is, dedicated to serving the people, body and soul]? I wouldn't say so. There are all kinds of people in the world, and they do all kinds of things. There are people about whom you can't say what they are, whether they are good or bad, courageous or cowardly, whether somebody will go for the people the whole way, or whether he'll be on the side of the people's enemies. There are such people and such activists. And among us, among the Bolsheviks, there are such people. As you know it yourselves, comrades, it is a small flock that doesn't have a black sheep. (*Laughter, applause*). It was about people of this undefined type, about people who are political drones rather than political activists, about people of this undefined, shapeless type [*neopredelennogo, neoformlennogo tipa*] that the great Russian writer Gogol remarked quite spot-on: "There are these people," he says, "undefined, neither this nor that, you can never quite understand what they are, neither here nor there." (*Merriment, applause*). There is another, also rather accurate, folk expression for such people: "who knows what this guy is, neither fish nor flesh" (*Exclamations of approval, applause*), "neither fish nor fowl." (*Exclamations of approval, applause*).[30]

Stylistically, an old, time-tested rhetorical device is applied here. Vernacular expressions combined with repeated hints at being in a tight-knit group, "between us" ("can we say that...", "and among us, among the Bolsheviks," "you know it yourselves," "folk expression") invite the audience to engage in a friendly conversation whose participants laugh readily and often. On a less obvious level, what is exemplified here is obsessive (with a multiple repetition of proverbs on the same topic) "collectivization of speech,"[31] which is supposedly a sign of a democratization of law in society, where the masses can and should define both the starting point and the sphere of the application of law—on condition that they remain absolutely anonymous. The anonymity of the masses represented by a sovereign is an integral feature of revolutionary terror. It is evoked by Robespierre when, trying to save the bloody revolution, he repeatedly uses the impersonal formula *on veut* in one of his last speeches. It is also discussed by Merleau-Ponty who speaks about the function of hearsay (*on-dit*) as a rhetorical figure in the

---

[30] Ibid., p. 242.   [31] Ryklin, *Terrorologiki*, p. 200.

mechanics of Stalinist show trials.[32] The invitation to laugh at easily recognizable proverbs and popular expressions is a manifestation of the same principle of collective anonymity: one can laugh at these turns of phrase exactly because these are jokes without an author; their origin is lost in time. It is the voice of the people that one hears when the great leader speaks.

A maximum degree of the saturation of language with words and turns of phrase with fixed meanings is achieved at moments when, on the one hand, any production of ambiguity is likely to be punishable, while on the other, there is a necessity for an unequivocal, strict codification of fixed criteria for a definition of "right" relative to "wrong," "those who belong" relative to "those who don't." In a situation wherein the regime's reaction to anything not previously tested by use is severe, the practice of quoting only what has been already said or written guarantees a greater security for the speaker or the writer, whoever (s)he might be. The Stalinist universe, which defined itself as a victory of democracy, was dominated by a kind of "circular citationality," when the broad masses were expected to cite the leader,[33] while the leader cited the broad masses. The former was a guarantee of security (though not always completely reliable), the latter—a legitimization technique for the maintenance of power.

As he again and again quotes writers and proverbs to illustrate various points of law, the speaker stresses that the law is there to give a formal definition to something that the people in their wisdom have always known: some traits of human personality are *objectively* objectionable. But what previously had been merely an object of ridicule becomes a point of the application of law in the era of great achievements, when universal dedication to the common cause is an indispensable condition of moving toward a better society. A direct interdependence between the ridiculous and the punishable is asserted the moment the audience in the hall is invited to laugh at whomever a law may be targeted at; at the same time, the law is referred to as just an administratively necessary measure to legitimize popular wisdom. The leader of the Soviet state does not speak in his own name, but simply gives voice to the will of the people; at the same time, his audience is identified not as a group of individual agents, but as an anonymous, collective laughing body. It is through laughter that anonymity is pushed to the foreground as a legitimizing move.[34]

---

[32] Merleau-Ponty, *Humanism*, p. 26: "In a trial of this kind [a show-trial], where in principle all documents are missing, we are left with the things that were said, and ... all [the accusations] inevitably rest at the level of hearsay [*on-dit*]."

[33] The practice of citations here is to be understood not only in the obvious meaning of direct quotations, obligatory in any official statement, scholarly publication, and the like, but in the broader sense of turning the leader's key pronouncements into a basis for the creation of supposedly authentic products of folk culture, a definition of the goals for collective labor and individual "work on oneself," and so forth.

[34] On the anonymity of collective laughter as a legitimizing technique see, e.g., Skradol, "Laughing," esp. p. 33.

In both the case of the speaker ceaselessly appealing to folk wisdom and that of the constantly laughing audience, language becomes not so much a means of conveying information as one of affirming one's place in the matrix of social relations, empty speech more reminiscent of an exchange of signals than meaningful communication. The individual traits of the speaker and the audience are as undefined as the individual traits of those who, apparently, are not in the audience and against whom the law under discussion is targeted. There is no reference to actual individuals, but only to "all kinds of people" who do "all kinds of things," to "such activists," "people of this undefined, shapeless type," "people who are political drones rather than political activists." This vagueness of definitions as a key feature of rhetoric brings this "empty speech" closer to the language of law, in so far as law always retains its status only for as long as there is a distance between, on the one hand, concrete events and individuals, and, on the other, law as a set of universally applicable rules and criteria for a determination of punishment. As Stalin refuses to speak in his own voice, as he relies on "the Russian writer Gogol" or on "another, also rather accurate, folk expression" to convey his thoughts, both he and his audience supposedly bow down to the voice of the law.

The traditional medium of law is writing. Here it is appropriate to mention again that, despite the fact that Stalin himself authored relatively few texts,[35] official propaganda traditionally pictured him as immersed in writing.[36] However, here, as in almost all other similar "dialogs" between Stalin and his audience, it is in "empty" speech that law manifests itself. The contradiction is only an apparent one: even Stalin's oral pronouncements have the status of law, which will then find its practical application at political trials, only to be put down in writing a bit later, in an alternative history of the party. This legalistic nature of the language can also serve as a justification of the awkwardness of the dictator's speech, in which, on the one hand, fixed general formulas abound, expressions characteristic of legal language, and, on the other, Stalin clearly tries to sound as "folksy," as "colloquial" as possible; it is between these two poles that laughter is generated. Laughter, then, is not only a predictable reaction but the only admissible reaction that fixates the logical chain: being ridiculous is followed by being punished. The concentrated performative power of totalitarian speech is thus expressed in its ability to have an immediate effect—just like law, because "the most rigorously rationalized law is never anything more than an act of social magic which works."[37] Magic—and law—work only if the pronunciation of specific words brings about immediate consequences. The words of a person invested with supreme power must bring about an immediate reaction from the audience. Both the laughter and the calls to annihilate the enemies are first of all

---

[35] Dobrenko, "Mezhdu istoriei."
[36] Cf. Podoroga, "Golos," p. 109, referred to in Dobrenko, "Mezhdu istoriei," p. 639.
[37] Bourdieu, *Language*, p. 42.

affirmations of a collective identity, a confirmation of belonging to the camp of those on the side of truth.

At the same time, the object of laughter can remain rather vague. What is ridiculous is the absence of determination as a general quality, uncertainty as such ("all kinds of people in the world, they do all kinds of things"; "people of this undefined, shapeless type" about people who are "political drones rather than political activists"). This lack of precision—or, in a more negative formulation, ambiguity—as a quality associated with borderline illegal behavior in the Stalinist system has been discussed by researchers in various contexts.[38] But in addition to its place in the purely Stalinist understanding of the binary "clarity/ambiguity" structure, ambiguity is also a traditional part of potentially humorous situations. Igal Halfin's argument that in Stalinism, the absence of true humor was a direct consequence of ambiguity being banished from political discourse is true. All these "people of this undefined, shapeless type" were supposed to be ridiculous because of their uncertain—ambiguous—nature. This kind of associative connection replaced "the principle of analogy," the status of which in the Soviet legal system had been debated for many years by that point.[39]

Halfin himself comes to the same conclusion when he writes:

> The Soviet justice system could turn anyone into a counterrevolutionary, but this transformation was wrought not only by mechanisms of power but also by systems of meaning that were understood, if not fully shared, by those who populated the Stalinist universe. In this connection, verisimilitude could be more important than veracity.[40]

The usual tools of collective marking such as proverbs used to illustrate points of law were especially useful for determining verisimilitude, which could be established easily at the level of general categories. Verisimilitude as a generalizing principle is more convenient than veracity for defining the collective identity of both friends and enemies, as there is no need for a specific examination of each particular case. At the same time, transforming people into types pre-defined by specific frameworks can produce a comic effect, just as popular jokes addressing stereotypical qualities ascribed to a certain group are commonly perceived as funny.[41] This is where jokes that are not particularly sophisticated come close to

---

[38] See Mark Steinberg's *Proletarian Imagination* on how this elimination of ambiguity was a project of modernity in general. Cf. also Natalia Kozlova's article mentioned above, as well as Orlova, "Rozhdenie," p. 311.

[39] On the principle of analogy in Soviet and pre-Soviet judicial discourse, when a certain action could be deemed punishable if it was analogous to what law defined as a crime, see Solomon, *Soviet Criminal Justice*, p. 31.

[40] Halfin, *Stalinist Confessions*, p. 131.

[41] A typical analysis of jokes, divided into groups, can be found in Raskin, *Semantic Mechanisms*.

generalizations at the opposite semantic pole—the penal code of a totalitarian system.

The examples below refer to an instance when Stalin's humor targeted not internal but external enemies. In his report to the Extraordinary Eighth All-Union Congress of the Soviets on November 23, 1936, which dealt with the project of the new Soviet Constitution, Stalin directed most of his mocking comparisons at foreign adversaries of socialism, taking his literary reference this time from the figure of a bureaucrat in Saltykov-Shchedrin's satirical texts:

> In one of his stories the great Russian writer Shchedrin gives the type of a petty bureaucrat, very limited and stupid, but, for all that, incredibly self-confident and zealous. Once this bureaucrat has ensured that there is total "order and quiet" in the area for which he is "responsible," once he has exterminated thousands of residents and burnt dozens of cities, this bureaucrat looks around and notices America somewhere on the horizon, a country that, of course, is but little known, but where there are, as it turns out, some freedoms that only confuse the people, and where there are various methods for running the country. The bureaucrat notices America and becomes annoyed: what kind of a country is it, where has it come from, on what basis does it exist? (*General laughter, applause*). Of course it was discovered [*otkryta*, which also means "opened"] by chance a few centuries ago, but can it not be "closed" [*zakryta*] again, so that it is never heard of again? (*General laughter*). And having said this, he declares his decision: "Close America!" (*General laughter*).[42]

This passage is one example of the many performative speech acts in Stalin's interventions, which abounded especially when they were aimed at evoking an immediate reaction from the public. Stalin is literally performing a scene based on an episode from classic literature, acting a double role: he is both a caricatured version of a generalized type of the enemy of the Soviet state, and a bureaucrat (a traditional target of mockery in the 1930s). At the same time, he never stops being the top bureaucrat—the leader of the state, who also retains the power to "open" and "close" anything he feels like. As he is acting out the scene from Saltykov-Shchedrin, Stalin is also playing himself. The play principle is important here, the implication being that a person who can *play* "a petty bureaucrat, very limited and stupid," who can invite the audience to laugh at this grotesque figure, simply cannot be like that himself.

Stylistically, Stalin's jokes are not particularly sophisticated; the monotony and predictability of images in his speeches have been commented upon by researchers more than once.[43] In light of this, it becomes all the more interesting that he was in

---

[42] Stalin, "O proekte," p. 132. English translation: Stalin, "On the Draft."
[43] Barmin, *Sokoly*, p. 307; Vaiskopf, *Pisatel'*.

the habit of alluding to Russian classical writers and popular fables. Elsewhere I discuss this as appealing to the infantile sensibilities of the audience, the recognizability of images from distant childhood, images from popular collective cultural memory.[44] Here we can also add that quotations from popular literary works are similar to proverbs in that they, too, are more or less commonly known language formulas, recognizable regardless of the context and referring to a shared collective knowledge. It is exactly the implicit claim to shared knowledge here that provides the basis for the division into "the insiders" and "the outsiders"—an element of the legislative function of language that is inevitably accompanied by laughter. "Those who belong" cannot be petty bureaucrats, cannot demand absurd decisions, cannot be ridiculous; only "those who don't" can have all these qualities.

Katerina Clark notes that in Bakhtin's theory, laughter in social interactions and symbolically charged spaces (that is, the kind of laughter that Bakhtin would define as carnivalesque) is used in order to "render external" everything that is perceived as strange and unfamiliar.[45] This exteriority can be defined by markers of genre (Saltykov-Shchedrin's ridiculous hero), or by markers of place and political sympathies (like the unfortunate, misguided foreign critics who refuse to see the true value of the new Soviet constitution)—but the exteriority will always be there. In the Stalinist context, this model is a fundamental feature of the ideology. As long as a certain referent becomes part of the Soviet political discourse, it automatically implies being in possession of an exclusive knowledge, which in its turn implies that the rival party manifests a complete ignorance and misunderstanding of the subject, regardless of what the subject may be; the enemy, thus, is "exterior" to the community of those who share true knowledge. The enemies are ridiculous because they do not understand that the Soviet Union cannot simply be "closed," that this new country is part of an objective reality that cannot be changed by imperialists with limited thinking. They are ridiculous because they fail to understand they can neither create nor destroy this new reality—just as they cannot formulate, or even just understand, the laws of this new reality.

This misunderstanding of Soviet laws by enemies, or rather, their misinterpretation of the Soviet Constitution, made the audience laugh in November 1936. If the newspaper reports are any indication at all, Stalin's speech was constantly interrupted by outbursts of laughter, and what the public found especially funny were his mocking references to the criticism of the project of the new constitution that appeared in the international—fascist as well as liberal—press:

> This journal just says outright that the project of the Constitution is an empty promise, a deception, a "Potemkin village." It makes the straightforward claim

---

[44] Skradol, "Laughing," p. 37.
[45] Clark, "M. M. Bakhtin," p. 285; with reference to Bakhtin, "Formy vremeni," pp. 309–10.

that the USSR is not a state, that the USSR is "nothing but a precisely definable geographical concept" (*General laughter*), and hence the Soviet constitution cannot be recognized as a valid constitution.

The first signs of responses in the press to the project of the Constitution were expressed by a certain tendency—to hush up the project of the Constitution... One could say that hushing up is not criticism. But it is not true.... The method of silencing down, as a special form of ignoring something, is also a form of criticism; even though it may be silly and ridiculous, it is still a form of criticism. (*General laughter, applause*).

The second group of critics accepts that the project of the Constitution actually exists in nature, but they believe the project is of no special interest since it is, in fact, not a draft of a constitution at all, but just a piece of paper, an empty promise, a special manoeuvre designed to deceive people. To this they add that the USSR could never be expected to produce a better project, since the USSR itself it not a state but simply a geographical concept (*General laughter*), and since it is not a state, its constitution cannot be a real constitution.

What can one say about these, if I may call them that, critics? If they interpret extending the foundation of the dictatorship of the proletariat and turning this dictatorship into a more flexible, and hence more powerful, system of governmental regulation of the society not as a strengthening of the dictatorship of the proletariat, but as a weakening of it or even as giving up on it altogether, then we might ask if these gentlemen have any idea at all of what the dictatorship of the proletariat is. If a legal expression of the victory of socialism, a legal expression of the successes of industrialization, collectivization and democratization is seen by them as a "right turn," then we might ask if these gentlemen have any idea at all what the difference between right and left is. (*General laughter, applause*).

The allusion to Stalin's favorite writer, Gogol,[46] from whose writings the motif of left-right confusion comes, is not openly declared this time. What is important is not the source but the insistent repetition of suggestive questions ("if these gentlemen have any idea"), on which the audience is invited to concentrate and which triggers the ritualistic laughter. The laughter here is a response to tautology, to an almost verbatim repetition of both suggestive questions and a rhetorical figure ("the USSR is simply a geographical concept"). Such repetitions are elements of a ritualistic action, when certain verbal formulations, similarly to magic incantations, are repeated until the desired response has been obtained, until the required reaction has been internalized.

Roland Barthes's remark that the language of Marxism is essentially a language that assumes knowledge finds confirmation here in a somewhat generalized and

---

[46] On Stalin's love of Gogol, see Moeller-Sally, "'Klassicheskoe nasledie'."

simplified form. Instead of an absolute, abstract knowledge of the laws of the world and nature, which, according to Barthes, is postulated by the philosophy of Marxism, Stalinist rhetoric assumes that the people should be party to some specific form of privileged knowledge: only the Soviet people can really know the essence of the Constitution. Since an assumption of this knowledge functions on a principle of exclusion, those who are deprived of this knowledge are excluded from the group of the select few. An integral part of developing the right understanding of these newly acquired values and practices seems to be a celebration of the ideological enemies' misunderstanding of them. Hence the mocking "if these gentlemen have any idea...", and a laughing—or rather, mocking—attitude to the world (let us remember that the phrase comes from Bakhtin) contribute to the construction of the Soviet picture of the world.

A special value of collective laughter as a response to the affirmation of knowledge against ignorance is that the orator is not obligated to find argumentation for his position. Thus it is unnecessary to explain what exactly the mistake made by the enemies of the Soviet order is—it is enough to convey their position through images that leave no doubt about the ridiculous and pitiful state of ignorance the other side is in. By representing ideological adversaries in such an unflattering light, the leader engages in "the articulation of knowledge," the ultimate products of which, according to Burton and Carlen, are "official discourses on law and order."[47] We should stress here that we are not talking about actual "knowledge," but only about its articulation, of which the invitations to laugh at the ignorant are an integral part.

When the performative potential of the letter of the law is secondary in significance to the citizens' "correct"—that is, politically reliable—perception of the very fact that law exists, the style of the "articulation of knowledge" becomes particularly important. The weaker the factual force of law as such is, the more important is the status of the one allowed to "articulate knowledge." The greatest freedom in this law-positing practice is enjoyed by the one who is allowed to laugh himself and amuse others while discussing law because he himself is outside of the sphere of its application—that is, according to Foucault's famous definition, the sovereign himself.[48] This extralegal position allows Stalin the sovereign to do what is completely impossible for other participants in the discursive situation: he has the exclusive right to define what kind of knowledge and understanding of the law separates friends from enemies. At the same time, there is no necessity for him to explain the criteria by which this separation is performed. The simple act of pointing to some natural right or knowledge, or else to the opposite—being doomed to ignorance—suffices. Stalin's right to make jokes extends to all spheres of knowledge covered by the sovereign right of judgment, from the childish

---

[47] Burton and Carlen, *Official Discourse*, p. 34.
[48] Foucault, *The Abnormal*, session of January 29, 1975.

inability to distinguish between left and right to the difficulty of distinguishing a "geographic concept" from a legal and democratic state.

In general, consolidating a community on the basis of a "knowledge versus ignorance" opposition is akin to many other totalitarian practices, which modern political philosophy sometimes defines as *obscene*. For Slavoj Žižek this obscenity of power is fundamental to the structure of totalitarian consciousness itself, the very thing that makes it so hard to resist the spell of oppressive regimes. Importantly, this kind of obscenity has nothing to do with the obscenity in the usual, colloquial sense of the term. Its meaning is closer to the dictionary meaning of "abhorrent to morality or virtue," in the sense of substituting the true meaning of actions, events with a false one, using a referent to cover up an essentially different phenomenon—in this case, using law to cover up the total absence of legal order. If we extend Mikhail Ryklin's observation on the horror of bureaucracy from the viewpoint of philosophy, this is the obscenity of revolution. Ryklin remarks that the logic of a revolution is "a victory of unwritten law over written law, so that unwritten law restores its power in violence and incorporates its logic in Terror."[49] The "unwritten" means not just spoken; it also means implied, just hinted at by the reference to a surface—like a shared secret that one merely alludes to in public, in the presence of the knowledgeable few, who then laugh with the satisfaction of their knowledge. Such is, for example, the true meaning of the Soviet Constitution, when it is enough to pose the rhetorical question about whether "these gentlemen have any idea" to make the audience laugh, thus confirming that the "gentlemen" in fact have no idea at all, while the laughing spectators are confident they themselves do.

A further investigation of this might reveal a completely new dimension, until now virtually neglected by scholarship, of the Soviet campaign of comprehensive aestheticization. This aestheticization refers not to the gigantic architectural constructions and visually bold mass performances, not to an aestheticization of politics as a spectacle in the spirit of Benjamin and Debord, but rather to the production of certain types of discursive pleasures.[50] Considering the privileged status of oral speech and collective discursive practices in the political context of Stalinism,[51] laughter sanctioned by power was one of the most frequent of such "pleasures"—and, from a functional point of view, it was one of the most important ones.

For the production of this type of "discursive pleasures," the constant presence of an external enemy is necessary. An external enemy is an image of an absolutely foreign body, with respect to which all the roles of political subjects within the "in"

---

[49] Ryklin, *Prostranstva*, p. 32.
[50] My use of "discursive pleasures" is inspired by the "narrative pleasures" that Elana Gomel speaks of in her analysis of the textual practices used by Nazi ideologists to attract the readers of popular literature. See Gomel, "Aliens Among Us," p. 127.
[51] Murašov, "Schrift."

society are formulated. What matters is not so much what this enemy actually does, but the very fact of its existence—even if this existence is largely imaginary and postulated by talking about it, or else hinted at by means of mocking remarks. The more absurd the attitude of external (ignorant) enemies toward the socialist law seems, the more natural is the "correct" perception of the legal foundations of the socialist state. Here, laughter has a double function: it produces both the external enemy—or, rather, its ridiculous traits—and the attitude toward this enemy.

A Funny Hunger Strike

The figure of the dictator and that of an external enemy realize diametrically opposed manifestations of being outside the law.[52] While the former is outside the law to the extent that he has the right to model both the law itself and the attitude to it, the latter may, and must, be ridiculed as someone doomed to both ignorance of the law and to punishment by it. Between these two forms of being outside the law there are internal enemies, those who cannot claim ignorance as a mitigating circumstance—after all, as noted above, there were no fools in the Stalinist universe.

For the participants of the plenum of the RCP(b) Central Committee that took place in Moscow from February 23 to March 5 of 1937, it was obvious that Nikolai Bukharin, a prominent Bolshevik from the "Old Guard," was no fool, either.[53] Bukharin's alleged numerous crimes and the hunger strike he had declared were at the center of the discussions at the plenum, but from the point of view of the Central Committee members, his hunger strike was feigned, which is why Bukharin's ex-comrades laughed a lot and with apparent enjoyment during the sessions. The following excerpts from the transcripts help illustrate the general tone of the interactions:

KABAKOV: I am not talking about using this hunger strike to scare us. Bukharin would never go on a hunger strike. (*Budennyi*: He said he went on a hunger strike from midnight and until the next morning, that is, he fasted the whole night.) (*Laugher in the room.*) It is unlikely that somebody on a hunger strike would drink 5 glasses of water in 50 minutes.[54]

---

[52] In *Abnormal* Foucault discusses the similarities between the sovereign and the monster as the most extreme examples of figures that are beyond the law. In this sense, an external enemy is a monster doomed to living outside the sphere of the law.

[53] "Materialy fevral'sko-martovskogo Plenuma."

[54] "Materialy fevral'sko-martovskogo Plenuma," the morning session of February 25, 1937 (issues 8–9, pp. 9–10).

MOLOTOV: It has been 2 days since he declared his hunger strike, and here he is, saying: I have been on a hunger strike for 4 days now. Why doesn't he at least read his own letter? What a comedian, what an actor Bukharin is. A cheap provincial actor. Who is he trying to move? It is nothing but a cheap actor's trick. A comedy of a hunger strike. Is this how revolutionaries declare a hunger strike? This Bukharin is a counterrevolutionary. (*Stalin*: Has anyone counted how many days he has been on this hunger strike now?) They say on the first day he was on a hunger strike for 40 days and 40 nights, then on the second day he was on a hunger strike for 40 days and 40 nights, and on and on it went; every day it was 40 days and 40 nights. This is Bukharin's comedy of a hunger strike. We all grew scared, we were really desperate. And then the hunger strike was over. He is not on a hunger strike, he is just an actor, but a very minor actor, of course, an actor with ridiculous roles, but still an actor.... Comrades, this whole hunger strike is a comic occurrence in our party. This is what everybody will be saying: there was this comic occurrence in the party with Bukharin's hunger strike. This is Bukharin's role, which he finally reached by crawling. But this is not art for art's sake, this is all for the sake of fighting our party. (*Voices*: True.).[55]

ZHUKOV:[56] And how do you [Bukharin] repay the Central Committee for its long-suffering with all your loathsome deeds? You declare a "hunger strike." Viacheslav Mikhailovich [Molotov] was right when he said future generations would be laughing at Bukharin, who would go on a hunger strike every night between 12 p.m. and 10 a.m.! (*Laughter*.) Shame on you. Trotsky himself is still using [such tricks], and all the world's bourgeois press of all kinds is always full of news about how this miserable fascist is complaining about his heart disease, his liver, his spleen, his gallbladder, and I don't even know what organs are absent from these lists. (*Laughter*).[57]

In contradistinction to the examples we analyzed earlier, here the object of ridicule himself has the right of voice—which is the reason he is laughed at, especially when it is about his hunger strike. In the logic of terror, Bukharin's hunger strike is genuinely ridiculous because it marks a completely mistaken assessment of the situation on his part. As we know from the classical theory of the comic, what causes laughter is an instance of *incongruity* (in behavior, words, or the general situation). There is a disparity between the way things actually are (that is, that his fate had been decided long before he even suspected there was something wrong) and his behavior in response. It has been argued that incongruity is the essence of

---

[55] Ibid., p. 25.
[56] Ivan Zhukov was at that time one of the Deputy People's Commissars. He was arrested in June 1937 and executed in October 1937.
[57] "Materialy fevral'sko-martovskogo Plenuma," the evening session of February 25, 1937 (issues 4–5, p. 22).

humor, and it is possible that for some of those present in the room, the situation was genuinely humorous. Bukharin quite simply does not realize that his life no longer belongs to him. He does not realize that the validity of the fundamental law whose existence he assumes, the law affirming the power of an individual to have control over his life, has been suspended, and that it has been replaced with what the Italian philosopher Giorgio Agamben defines as "the force of law," that is, pure violence, for which there are (as yet) no words in language. This lack of words in language must be understood literally, so that the behavior of the participants in the new ritual is mostly non-verbal—for example, laughter. It is laughter that turns all the people in the room into accomplices engaged in a political campaign, training them in a disciplined performance of their roles. Involved as they are in the production of language formulas, they must not say anything on their own behalf, but just repeat, again and again, what has already been approved by the whole group as a correct perception of the situation and the right kind of behavior. In so far as laughter in this case signals unconditional approval, it is not surprising that each burst of laughter is followed by the participants repeating, again and again, the words that triggered the laughter in the first place, as if emphasizing that they are, indeed, unquestionably funny ("a comic occurrence in our party"; "there was this comic occurrence in the party with Bukharin's hunger strike"; "future generations would be laughing at Bukharin..."). In this way the words "hunger strike" themselves acquire a grotesque flavor, as do the counting of the hours and days of "the hunger strike" and the number of glasses of water Bukharin must have drunk.

While the Soviet dictator at each one of his public appearances articulates an (as yet) unwritten law, his victims do their best to try to express adequately their understanding of this law—though not always successfully. As Bukharin suggests a solution that, he thinks, might be most acceptable from the point of view of the Central Committee members, he makes his former comrades laugh even more:

BUKHARIN: I cannot shoot myself, because otherwise people will say that I committed suicide to damage the party; but if I die, as it were, from an illness, what will you lose? (*Laughter. Voices*: Blackmail! *Voroshilov*: How mean! Curse that tongue of yours! What a mean thing to say. Think about what it is you are saying.) But please understand how hard it is for me to live. (*Stalin*: And is it any easier for us? *Voroshilov*: Just think: "I will not shoot myself, I will die instead").[58]

It is a common, and justified, conviction that in Stalinism human life was hardly worth anything. However, paradoxical as it might sound, one could also claim that

[58] Ibid., p. 24.

in the Stalinist universe human life was actually more precious than before, having become a means of communication between state power and its subjects. This is why it was unimaginable that there might be someone who would decide to refuse food of his own free will, and not to follow the will of the party; the very thought that it might be possible was to be regarded as ridiculous. The language of communication between the power apparatus and the citizens covered all manifestations of the citizens' physical existence, and much of it was body language. In this system, there could be no death "by natural causes"—the only admissible cause of death could be a decision of the party.

We can neither prove nor reject a claim that "the laughing crowd" (to use Bakhtin's famous expression) at the plenum was necessarily conscious of the fact that they were preparing their victim for sacrifice. One of the paradoxes of Stalinist terror was that even—or especially—in the rooms where the fate of the most prominent citizens was decided, nothing was "for real." Thus, Bukharin's hunger strike, his threats to commit suicide, his pleading with his comrades that he be allowed to "die, as it were, from an illness" are rejected as the tricks of a "cheap provincial actor." At the same time, the torturer poses as the one who is suffering ("And is it any easier for us?"), and the slow and sadistic murder is presented as a comradely attempt to discover the truth so as to facilitate a fair legal investigation, should one become necessary.

Scholars of cultural history frequently reference the Bakhtinian carnival whenever laughter in politically charged situations is involved. Carnival, however, is a performance where what at first glance appears to be a murder turns out to be but a prelude to a merry drinking party, where torture turns into a dance, and where none of the participants of supposedly "official ceremonies" are what they seem to be. Without engaging in debates for or against the application of the term "carnival" to Stalinist realities, one might possibly regard the events at the 1937 February–March plenum as "an upside-down carnival," similarly to Bakhtin's succinct definition of the nature of carnival as "an upside-down world" ("le monde à l'envers"):[59] what at first seems to be merely an informal discussion of certain mistakes committed by a comrade (albeit a former one) from the same party fraction at a certain point turns into a bloody drama, a session in a court of law without law. Soviet humor had already undergone the transformation discussed by Igal Halfin: innocent friendly jokes had turned into wicked mockery and accusations of hiding one's true face; the language of carnival became the voice of the "force of law."[60]

It is well-known that Bakhtin emphasized the liberating function of laughter, claiming that "violence knows no laughter," for which his analysis has been

---

[59] Bakhtin, *Problems*, p. 122.   [60] Halfin, "The Bolsheviks' Gallows Laughter," p. 258.

subjected subsequently to justified criticism.[61] Looking closely at laughter in the Stalinist political (anti-)carnival should make it possible to see laughter as *both* liberating *and* disciplining. The obviously mocking laughter of the Central Committee members can be seen as liberating in the sense that the system in the name of which these people speak (or rather, laugh) can simply ignore the traditional judicial and moral law that "encumbers" human life with unnecessary significance beyond simple physical existence and the satisfaction of immediate physiological needs. A living human body must eat, drink, and sleep; a human body that refuses to do so, that threatens to put an end to its very existence, is ridiculous because it appeals to a symbolic significance of daily actions that has been abolished by the carnival logic, with its celebration of pure physicality. Totalitarian law coincides with physiological laws; any manifestation of disagreement or doubt is a criminal offense and equally an offense against nature, and, as such, it is countered by laughter, mocking injunctions to "think what you are saying," and is classified as "blackmail" and "a mean thing." On the other hand, life reduced to physiology inevitably becomes a focus of the application of supreme power that is not restricted by law, and laughter becomes possible as a channel for transmitting the will of this power. It is precisely after the shared outburst of laughter that the participants of the plenum offer their "interpretations" of Bukharin's plan to commit suicide. Thus, politicized laughter is a reminder of the complete subjection of one's own will and one's own body to the interests of power—which was equally applicable to those who laughed and those who were the objects of laughter.

The only theoretical engagement we are aware of with the laughter recorded at this meeting is that which appears in Slavoj Žižek's article "When the Party Commits Suicide."[62] Žižek quotes an episode of Kafka's *The Trial* wherein the judge asks K. what his occupation is, whereupon K.'s straightforward and factual response (that he is a bank clerk) is met with a fit of hysterical laughter from those present. This classic, truly "Kafkaesque" scene illustrates a core element of a situation with potentially far-reaching legal consequences, where traditional structures of law are suspended ("the state of exception"), namely, an inevitable gap in the way newly introduced legal and paralegal practices are perceived by the different parties involved. This gap remains there until these practices have acquired a fixed legal status—that is, throughout the de facto existence of the state of exception. The laughter of those who at a given moment find themselves on the side of power signals their conviction that the opposite party ascribes to the events in question a meaning different from that desired by the masters.

---

[61] Bakhtin, *Estetika*, p. 338. Boris Groys noted that the cruelty of Bakhtinian carnival should not be underestimated: "God forbid one should end up in it," writes the philosopher ("Mezhdu Stalinym," p. 95; in German: Groys, "Grausamer Karneval"). See also Eco, "The Frames," p. 3.

[62] Žižek, "When the Party," p. 31.

One of the paradoxes of Stalinism was that, on the one hand, any politically colored statement was potentially dangerous, but, on the other, both the state and the judicial system demanded that citizens perpetually engage themselves and affirm their engagement in affairs of the state through oral participation—for the sole reason that a spoken word can be easily distorted or misquoted depending on the needs of a particular moment. Bukharin calls on the plenum's participants to pay attention to the problematic nature of the oral testimonies of party comrades: "Please understand the psychology of people today," he pleads. "They smell with their noses what it is they should say."[63] Naturally, his plea is greeted with laughter: the hint at any comprehensive control over thoughts and actions is dismissed by what is supposed to be perceived as a manifestation of spontaneous feelings. The absence of law as the main regulating principle, on the one hand, and the premise of unlimited democracy, on the other, combine to imply, quite literally, that each subject of power is willing to dedicate his or her whole being to the construction of discursive practices that replace the law. Jurij Murašov speaks of an "acoustical and phonetical presence" that was to be constantly sustained and reaffirmed by servants of the Stalinist regime.[64] Words could always be used against the one who uttered them, but absolute silence, too, was no less dangerous: it was perceived, almost automatically, as a sign of hidden motives. Non-verbal expressions of presence and agreement were much more reliable, as they allowed one to turn into a mediator for practices that replaced the actual law.

The officially proclaimed unlimited freedom implied (in theory) that any citizen had the right to say anything he or she wanted to at any moment, thus realizing the main democratic principle. However, the additional implication brought into this principle—that any word could potentially be either a piece of evidence, or a witness' testimony—turned it into parody. This dangerously exaggerated performativity of spoken pronouncements is exactly what Bukharin is trying to make the Central Committee members aware of. The Stalinist state of exception, however, did not leave him much chance of success. No matter how much Carl Schmitt's classical definition of the sovereign being "the one who decides on the exception"[65] might have been applicable to Soviet reality in practice, Stalin's sovereign decision never made itself known as such. The Stalinist sovereign system needed a great number of intermediaries to speak the will of sovereign power in their own voices. Their participation in the practices that replaced the law was essential, which allows us to draw yet another parallel with Kafka's works, where, according to Walter Benjamin, the assistants of bureaucrats and legal clerks were precisely the ones who played the leading roles.[66] Quite often the participation

---

[63] "Materialy fevral'sko-martovskogo Plenuma," the evening session of February 23, 1937 (issues 4–5, pp. 33; 31).
[64] Murašov, "Schrift," p. 90.   [65] Schmitt, *Political Theology*, p. 4.
[66] Benjamin, "Franz Kafka," pp. 116–17.

of Stalinist "assistants" in paralegal practices manifested itself in synchronized expressions of emotions—for example, in collective laughter, which both guaranteed the joy of feeling part of the same "right" cause and relieved the individual of the need to articulate his or her personal position.

Articulation of one's personal position on any matter was potentially dangerous anyway, as the argumentation of any point of view implied some kind of logical foundation—and there was only one person, the bearer of supreme power, who possessed the exclusive right to the kind of logic required in the new reality. This is why the Central Committee members laugh merrily whenever Bukharin tries to point out obvious contradictions in the testimonies of "witnesses" concerning the individuals supposedly targeted by him and his alleged accomplices, with whom he had supposedly shared secret plans to assassinate the top leaders of the state:

BUKHARIN: At the pre-trial face-to-face interrogation [witness Kulikov] stated that I instructed him to act against Kaganovich..., but in his written testimony he claims that I gave him instructions to act against Stalin. Please, comrades, tell me,... if somebody, even in the old days, accused somebody else of conspiring against a certain person, and then a day later accused the very same individual of conspiring against another person—how would it have been classified? (*Ezhov*:[67] This is a lawyer's trick of twisting evidence. Why do you need to do that?)... He even gave this example that he knows you, that you, too, had worked as a tanner, that the right wing supposedly hates you especially, and so on. (*A voice*: As if this were of any importance. *Laughter*).

The shared merry laughter of the participants of the plenum in response to the supposition that maybe, just maybe, the lack of consistency in the "testimonies of witnesses" concerning specific individuals is reason enough to cast doubt on the fairness of the accusation itself clearly shows that the bloodthirsty Soviet carnival with its rapid change of social roles extended well beyond the transformations of yesterday's "tanner" into tomorrow's party leader. The carnivalesque substitutions encompassed the very core of state regulations, including criminal law and related procedures—so much so that there was nothing at all strange about one potential victim of a murder plot being substituted for another, retroactively.

In Stalinist discourse, virtually all personal names and position-defining nouns are empty of meaning unless defined by a specific context. Stalinism turns the absence of concrete referents into a general rule. Any words traditionally used to determine and define individuality become simply markers of roles that need to be performed at certain moments for certain purposes; specific names of specific

---

[67] Nikolai Yezhov, a senior party official, at that time—Chairman of the Central Commission for Party Control.

people have no importance. Even more important are the social and political functions associated with these roles. Much like in a carnival, in Stalinist terror there must be a murderer and a victim, and who fulfils these functions is just a matter of chance—and the needs of the moment. The two most famous pronouncements of Stalin—"nobody is irreplaceable" and "the cadres decide everything"—can be brought together here: anybody can become anything. The word "cadre" here should be understood in its etymological meaning pointed out by Žižek ("square," "without fault").[68] Like any other process of production, the production of laws requires cadres in order to achieve its goal and fulfil its functions. These functions can be varied, and they can change rather quickly. The only thing that can be considered ridiculous here is a supposition that someone could find these speedy transformations surprising—the transformations themselves are at the core of the regime.

It is because of this fundamental difference in the assessment of what is happening that, as it appears, from Bukharin's perspective his former comrades laugh at the most inappropriate moments:

BUKHARIN: You have it easy talking about me. So what do you have to lose? Because, if I'm a saboteur, a son of a bitch and so on, why should you have pity on me? I don't want anything, I'm just telling you what I think and what I'm going through. If this is somehow connected to even the smallest possible political damage, then of course I will do whatever you tell me to do. (*Laughter*). Why are you laughing? There is absolutely nothing funny about it.

Having decided to accept the role assigned to him—that of a "saboteur" and "son of a bitch"—Bukharin persists in making the same mistake: he tries to follow through the logical implications of this role that his former comrades have defined for him. He is unable to see that the moment he tries to detect a logic in the chain of events, real and postulated, this logic slips away from him. He does not recognize the special nature of logic in the Stalinist system of meaning allocation. Unlike in most other legal procedures, where an actual narrative of events (a sequence of actions or offenses) is what provides the basis to the particular application of a law, in the Stalinist system, judicial (and all other) meanings are determined ad hoc—as they would be in any state of exception. While normally a joke is something that disrupts the flow of logic, in Stalinist discourse humor is triggered by attempts to realize in practice ("proceed to execution") that which has just been defined verbally, disregarding the fact that the speed with which significations and meanings change dooms these attempts to failure—and makes them simply ridiculous.

[68] Žižek, *In Defense*, p. 229.

One question that must always arise in this context concerns the agent of change: who has the right to decide when and how roles undergo a transformation, when and why a certain "cadre" assumes a specific function, and where and how events and words acquire one meaning or another? Giorgio Agamben talks about the state of exception as a system where the presence of a legal referent is implied by the very gesture of its temporal suspension.[69] But the philosopher does not offer the parameters for defining who has the right *to imply*. In the state of exception, the right "just to imply" defines true power to a much greater extent than the right to speak. Halfin writes about the brutal struggle among party members over the exclusive right to "the only correct" use of certain words[70]—but no less brutal was the internal fighting over the right to imply the status of the main markers of political and judicial discourse. Non-verbal articulations of emotions, and laughter among them, signal being party to this undeclared right to an understanding of the true meaning of "that which is implied." However, this understanding cannot be expressed in words, as the true meaning of "that which is implied" changes on the dictator's whim, of which it is a continuation. In such a context, laughter is automatically directed against the person who exhibits a dangerous tendency to doubt the right of the other party "to imply"—and looking for logic in this case is equal to doubting.

Bukharin's having started his hunger strike at midnight also makes the members of the Central Committee laugh. Apparently they are strangers to the symbolic meaning of midnight as a new beginning, a moment of transformation, which Bukharin tries to point out:

SHKIRIATOV:[71] What can be more hostile, more counterrevolutionary than these actions of Bukharin's! In his letter he writes that he declared his hunger strike at 12 midnight. (*Stalin*: So his hunger strike began at night. *Laughter. A voice*: After dinner).

RYKOV:[72] What I have written down in my notes here is that Bukharin's hunger strike is an anti-Soviet act, a completely inadmissible means of putting pressure upon the Central Committee. And I personally have my doubts as to how sincere he is in that note to the Central Committee. Because if one wants to die, why announce this in advance to the Central Committee of the Party? (*General laughter. A voice*: Well put. *Voroshilov*: This means going out with a bang. *Petrovskii*: Not with a bang, but with a scandal. *A voice*: A delayed suicide).

---

[69] Agamben, *Potentialities*, p. 161.   [70] Halfin, *Stalinist Confessions*, p. 382 (endnote 186).
[71] Matvei Shiriatov, a member of the Committee for Party Control.
[72] Aleksei Rykov, at that time People's Commissar of Communications. He was arrested, charged, and executed simultaneously with Bukharin, shortly after the Plenum.

IKRAMOV:[73] Declaring a hunger strike—well, comrades, this is a system of real blackmail and petty marauding. (*Laughter*). Here, I want to draw a parallel: observant Muslims fast with a slightly stronger devotion than Bukharin, who declared here this hunger strike of his. (*Laughter*). I think they at least do not eat from dawn to sunset... (*Laughter*), while Bukharin, on the contrary, does not eat from sunset to dawn. (*Laughter*).

The striving of Stalinism for a concrete understanding of metaphors manifests itself here, too. Traditional practices of defining one's status from the point of view of the law lose their significance, as their symbolism is not appropriate for the new era. The merry servants of the regime celebrate an annihilation of all previous conventions, including key metaphors and symbols. Laughter in such a case is a completely predictable reaction to the previously acceptable metaphors and symbols having been reduced to their literal meaning, now realized in their utmost concreteness through multiple repetitions with very minor variations ("he declared his hunger strike at 12 midnight... He said he went on a hunger strike from midnight and until the next morning, that is, he fasted the whole night... after dinner... he does not eat from sunset to dawn"). Since the declared moment of the beginning of the hunger strike is deprived of its symbolic significance, suicide itself as an expression of protest becomes an action that causes "general laughter," a poor attempt "to go out with a bang," even "with a scandal," "a delayed suicide."

The significance of the 1937 plenum is not only that it sealed the tragic fate of Bukharin and other "old guard" Bolsheviks; on a less obvious level, it was also one of the most decisive moments in establishing the Kafkaesque essence of Stalinist judicial discourse. "Kafkaesque" here is to be understood in the sense outlined by Mikhail Ryklin: that which has a stable meaning to one person seems nonsense to others; that which incorporates existential horror for one person is perceived by others as a joke—and justly so, since any joke is based on a shifting of meaning. Since Stalinist practices of articulating law implied a constant shifting of meaning-producing referents, their humorous potential was virtually unlimited. The insistent repetition of the same was the main strategy for shifting the initial meaning, until words ended up referring to ideas that were practically their opposite. The repetitions triggered laughter, but, by the same token, they made one want to repeat what had triggered laughter in the first place, as a confirmation and consolidation of the "correct" point of view. This circular, self-sufficient production of meaning was the basis of the production of Stalinist law and the application of this law in practice.

---

[73] Akmal' Ikramov, Secretary of the Central Asian Bureau of the Party. He was arrested in September 1937 and executed in March 1938.

The Monster of Wit

The actual, though undeclared, author of laws in the Stalinist society was Stalin himself, with "assistants" and "mediators" playing important roles during events behind closed doors, such as party plenums. But at the heyday of terror, laws and verdicts alike were voiced by the State Prosecutor, Andrei Vyshinskii. In his performances, the numerous imprecations and mockeries with which he interspersed his accusatory speeches were simultaneously jokes (since the audiences were willing to laugh at them, if the transcripts are any indication) and death verdicts (since the butts of the prosecutor's jokes rarely survived).

The examples from the published transcripts of the court proceedings that we analyze here are not always accompanied by the remark "laughter," since for inexplicable reasons, only one of the transcripts actually featured such remarks. The excerpts have been selected on the basis of the same stylistic principle: all of them contain insults and mocking remarks, which, just like the mockery of Bukharin above, should be analyzed in the context of the regime's legitimizing practices. Until now, the nature of insults as speech acts, integrated into the rhetoric of the production of law, has remained practically unexplored, even though no analysis of the official discourse of Stalinism can claim to be comprehensive without taking account of the function of imprecations and insults coming from men of law.

Quite often these insults and mocking remarks took the form of a pedantic, uncompromising interrogation of defendants and witnesses. However, the demonstrative fixation on the truth could acquire quite grotesque features. The following exchange between Vyshinskii and two defendants at the trial of the "Anti-Soviet Trotskyist Center" in January 1937 is representative:[74]

VYSHINSKII: So what did Sedov say to you?
SHESTOV: At that time he just handed me—not letters, but, as we had agreed before that, a pair of boots.
VYSHINSKII: So you didn't receive letters, but boots?
SHESTOV: Yes. But I knew there were letters in them. There was a letter sealed into each of the boots. And he said the envelopes would be marked. One was marked "P"—that meant it was for Piatakov, and the other one was marked "M"—that meant it was for Muralov.
VYSHINSKII: Did you pass the letter on to Piatakov?
SHESTOV: I gave him the letter marked "P".
VYSHINSKII: And the other letter?
SHESTOV: The other letter, marked "M", I gave to Muralov.

---

[74] *Protsess Antisovetskogo Trotskistskogo Tsentra*, p. 27.

VYSHINSKII: Defendant Muralov, did you receive the letter?
MURALOV: I did.
VYSHINSKII: With or without the boot? (*Laughter in the room.*)

There are variations upon this rhetorical device, such as repeating the same word over and over, a word allegedly taken from the statements of the defendants themselves, until its meaning is so transformed that the word itself nearly turns into a piece of evidence, as in the following excerpt:

> Zinov'ev said: "We embarked upon a carefully thought through and deeply conspiratorial plot, we considered ourselves Marxists and, remembering the slogan 'an uprising is an art,' we changed it to fit our purposes, claiming that 'a conspiracy against the party, against Stalin, is an art.'" Here are the masters of this "art," sitting in the prisoners' dock. I wouldn't call them superb masters. Rather low-grade masters they are! But they still succeeded in realizing their base intentions. So, what was it, this "art" of theirs?[75]

In Vyshinskii's speeches multiple repetitions and exaggerated details, with their hypnotizing effect, sometimes replaced factual procedural rhetoric. In the example above, the boot as a central element of the accusation is supposedly proof that the letter had (or had not) been opened before it was delivered to the addressee—but it is actually lampooned as a ridiculous technique for transferring secret messages. In the other example, the word "art" loses the impact of a revolutionary slogan after multiple repetitions and instead emphasizes the criminal absurdity of the defendants' actions. The subject of the interrogation is made a subject of ridicule, the multiple reproduction of details of the file and of the defendants' words practically turns into interpretation, quantity becomes quality, speculations are transformed into proofs, and insults acquire the weight of judicially significant statements; the simple repetition of certain words produces a new level of meaning where some individuals, and more broadly, certain forms of life in the new socialist society, are declared inherently funny, unfit for the new life, and thus— criminal.

Vyshinskii never tires of emphasizing comic traits or features in the character and behavior of the defendants. He shares with his audience a story of how Trotsky was busy "recruiting ecstatic people," calls on the defendants to "give up on this ridiculous comedy" and finally reveal "their real faces, completely." Without worrying too much about the factual evidence, he puts the stress on the moral characteristics of a defendant ("Here is Rataichik, either a German or a Polish spy, but definitely a spy, and, as befits him, a liar, a deceiver, and a

---

[75] Vyshinskii, *Sudebnye rechi*, p. 381.

scoundrel"), habitually turning direct quotations from the evidence supplied by witnesses and defendants into puns:

> So he, this Rataichik, with all his wonderful qualities revealed by the investigators and the court, becomes Piatakov's closest assistant, in charge of the chemical industry. A wonderful chemist! [a pun on the slang meaning, "rogue," of the Russian word "chemist"]. (*Agitation in the court hall*). Piatakov knew who he was choosing. As they say, the ball comes to the player. Rataichik tries to approach higher officials. He stays silent on the motives behind his actions and does not make such phoney declarations as, I guess, Arnold said once, confessing that he was tormented by "the striving to approach the higher strata of society."
> <div align="right">(<i>Laughter, movement in the hall</i>).</div>

In one of his speeches, Vyshinskii calls the defendants "former people."[76] It may well be that he used this phrase only once, but it was rather common in the late 1930s, appropriately reflecting the status of the victims from the point of view of the Stalinist judicial system. Researchers have often commented on the "inhuman" qualities that were ascribed to the "enemies of the people" in Stalinist courtrooms,[77] and when the prosecutor invites his audience to make sure, yet again, that the prisoners' dock is occupied by "liars and jesters, contemptible pygmies, pugs, and dirty mongrels who dared to attack an elephant,"[78] his words are fully in conformance with the general direction of Stalinist judicial rhetoric.

"Former people"—the expression itself hints at something monstrous. Those who were defined by the Stalinist system as enemies were, indeed, monsters, in so far as being outside the law is, at least according to Michel Foucault, one of the main characteristics of a monster.[79] For the philosopher, monsters are people whose "being outside the law" is defined by the fact that they have been perceived as deformed creatures from the moment of their birth. The monstrosity of the enemies of the Soviet system was less apparent, and it made sense that the guardians of the law had to work hard to ensure that the monsters' true essence was revealed, so that the law-abiding citizens could enjoy themselves while laughing at the failed spies and saboteurs.

The laughter of the public acknowledges the nature of the defendants as an incorporation of the most anomalous, deformed personal qualities, which run against law and nature itself, thus legitimizing the verdict, which becomes not just an expression of "the will of the people" but the only possible way to eliminate deformities of human nature, all those "wonderful qualities" that could be "revealed" only through the joint efforts of "investigators and the court." The

---

[76] Ibid., p. 370. [77] See, e.g., Brossat, "Le bestiaire"; Orlova, "Rozhdenie"; Weis, "Parazity."
[78] Vyshinskii, *Sudebnye rechi*, p. 373.
[79] Foucault, *The Abnormal*, session of January 22, 1975.

motif of correcting everything that runs contrary to the laws of nature will later find its full expression in the *History of the CPSU (Short Course)*, which will be our topic in the concluding section of this chapter.

The discursive practices of Stalinist trials show that this principle of "monster production" is not only valid with respect to metaphysical constructions in texts but also applicable to cases in which inherently different styles clash in situations when the performative effect of words is especially powerful. From the point of view of the habitual norms of courtroom discourse, the leading Soviet lawyer himself spoke in a language that was quite "monstrous," combining as it did the primitive vulgarity of obscene curses with the full legal authority to bestow punishment suitable for the most serious crimes. When Vyshinskii mocks the "foreign policy" program of these people, adding that "for this 'program' alone our Soviet people will string up the traitors at the very first gate! And they will deserve it!", the insistent ironic repetition of the key word ("program") and the use of the common colloquial "string up at the very first gate" suggest that the prosecutor was counting on the laughter of the audience. Indeed, this phrase could have been a not-too-funny joke—except that the execution (the "stringing up") of the defendants happened for real.

This realization of jokes in real life annihilates the carnival aspect of Stalinist courtroom performances. Giorgio Agamben writes that "what offends in the insult is... a pure experience of language, and not a reference to the world."[80] In other words, an insult cannot be argued against because it is self-sufficient—just as a joke cannot be argued against. For this very reason, it was impossible to prove the absurdity of the accusations at the Stalinist trials. These accusations were not grounded in factual evidence and reliable witnesses; hermetically closed against the external world, they were simply facts of language that brought about results in real life (or death)—something that was true of the rhetoric of Stalinism in general.[81]

To say that Vyshinskii's language, just as the language of Stalinist law in general, is a language of insults to the same extent that it is a language of rude jokes aiming to provoke the audience's laughter is to point to its fundamental stylistic and performative features. This language is close to *name-calling* in its primary meaning of attaching a name to someone, forming a subject as an actor in interpersonal communication. Scholarly literature on the theory and practice of jurisprudence usually regards insults as examples of legally punishable speech acts. Additionally, one of the leading theorists of the judicial status of speech acts,

---

[80] Agamben, "Friendship," p. 4.
[81] Aleksandr Etkind warns scholars of Stalinism against an excessive fascination with an analysis of rhetorical models, reminding them that "the revolution, hunger, torture and the camps were not language games" (Etkind, "'Odno vremia'," p. 49). To this we can reply that quite often "language games" were the foundation that made it possible to introduce the practices of torture and imprisonment in the camps on an unprecedented scale.

Judith Butler, notes that offensive language in general exposes the "volatility of one's 'place' within the community of speakers" and hints at the possibility that one may be relocated to "a place [that is] no place,"[82] thus suggesting that the functional arena of insults can be extended beyond legally punishable practices. Vyshinskii's mocking remarks, repeated over and over again by the chief representative of supreme judicial power in the strictly ordered context of show trials, fixate the civil and judicial status of the accused—and not only theirs. "Names" are given not just to the victims, but also to the figures mentioned in the context of the evidence given as part of the court proceedings. Thus, Kamenev's foreword to an edition of Machiavelli's writings becomes proof of his anti-socialist inclinations, and the classical political theorist is not spared mockery: "So this Machiavelli, for Kamenev, is a dialectician! This inveterate scoundrel turns out to be a dialectician!"[83] The indignation of the State Prosecutor is so great that he turns to the judge with an appeal to "consider this book part of the factual evidence in this case." Referring to Stanislav Rataichik, former head of the High Commission for Chemical Industry, the State Prosecutor calls him "a wonderful chemist [*khimik*]," the profession becoming a pun on the Russian colloquial word "*khimichit'*" (fiddle around, cheat). Once again, the very fact of emphasized repetition becomes a strategy for turning a neutral definition/name into mockery, thence to insult, then into criminal evidence.

What triggers laughter here is not so much the new definition itself as its application to a specific person in a specific case. Laughter is generated by the fact of the substitution itself. Someone becomes "a chemist" or "a dialectician," and their being "a chemist" or "a dialectician" is no longer a reference to their profession or the school of philosophy they represent, but a definition of that particular person as a grotesque figure. The grotesque effect is even stronger when the mocking insults come from someone whose office invests them with the power to be the voice of the law.

As the formal language of law and the language of anonymous street violence merge together, curses and insults in the speech of the State Prosecutor become nothing more than the principle of absolute democracy taken to the absurd. It is a principle that implies that there should be no obstacles, no border between the voice of the masses and its formal expression. The use of primitive curses in the courtroom runs against the conventions of judicial discourse to exactly the same extent as the audience's laughter in this context; this is why a combination of cursing and laughter, mutually legitimizing each other, played an important role in demolishing previously acceptable interactions between representatives of power and the masses.

---

[82] Butler, *Excitable Speech*, p. 4.   [83] Vyshinskii, *Sudebnye rechi*, p. 386.

Paradoxically, it is here that the language of Stalinist law incorporates a principle of liberal jurisprudence, even though the essence of the self-sufficient production of meanings is different in the two contexts. This principle is analyzed by Peter Goodrich, who points out that the liberal tradition of law postulates that a lawyer in a courtroom should develop a kind of amnesia with respect to the outside world; he is called upon to relate to the letter of the law in constructing and presenting his argument.[84] The theory of jurisprudence that Goodrich examines postulates an obligation on the part of representatives of law in a courtroom to measure their decisions and the very course of their thoughts against the letter of the law. The communicative potential of judicial language is thus supposed to be limited contextually—by the facts under consideration, and stylistically—by the letter of the law and regulations of the courtroom ritual. Vyshinskii's speeches illustrate an amnesia that works in the opposite direction, when what is forgotten is, on the one hand, the selective and highly formalized letter of the law, and, on the other, the factual basis of evidence. The repetitions of specific concepts, divorcing neutral definitions from their primary meanings and turning them into mocking insults, exemplify the workings of this "amnesia" in two spheres: it is not only in the mind of the speaker but also in the collective perception of an audience required to respond to these rhetorical figures in a certain way.

In its self-sufficiency Vyshinskii's language is reflective of the core tendencies of the language of Stalinism as such. The further this language is removed from legal language (if legal language is to be understood as being based on the logic of persuasion and appealing to facts), the closer it is to the language of jokes. In both cases there is a strong element of incompatibility, incongruity, which is often achieved through multiple repetitions and quotations out of context; in both cases a de-metaphorization of conventional definitions plays an important role; and in both cases achieving a particular effect at a given moment takes priority over reference to the facts of the external world. In both cases one can speak of a certain "state of exception" in language, when the habitual principles of organization and production of significations have been put on hold; audiences are expected to laugh in recognition of this shift.

The Sense of an Ending

One of the great achievements of Stalinism was that it gave people the satisfaction of witnessing a narrative develop according to all the conventions of an exciting plot line. Following a series of fatal battles between good and evil, the forces of evil are annihilated, the noble heroes celebrate victory, and the audience—citizens of

---

[84] Goodrich, "Of Law."

the state—can enjoy the special feeling of satisfaction that, as Frank Kermode tells us, is granted by the resolution at the end of a story. The victory over the internal enemies of the Soviet regime is the main motif of the book that was to become the foundation of the Soviet image of the world: the *History of the All-Union Communist Party (Bolsheviks): Short Course* (*Istoriia Vsesoiuznoi Kommunisticheskoi Partii (Bol'shevikov): Kratkii kurs*, 1938). This text is truly epic, in terms both of the events it recounts (considering their importance to Soviet society) and of the structural and narrative level. Between the endlessly complex beginning of the plot and its end, culminating in the glorious victory over the enemies, there is a consistently developing story line, with each event having a momentous significance for the narrative as a whole; and its agents of good have truly superhuman qualities. The author of the *Short Course* states unequivocally: "The history of the development of the inner life of our party is a history of struggle and defeat of opportunistic groups inside the party—the 'economists,' the Mensheviks, the Trotskyites, the Bukharinites, the national deviators."[85] Laughter (or rather mockery, sarcasm, and irony) was an integral part of celebrating the victory over the enemy. Tested during the enemies' lifetime, these rhetorical tools remained useful in the narrative of the events after the enemies' deaths.

Since it was impossible to add the remark "laughter in the hall," the tone of ridicule and mockery had to come across differently in the book than it would in the transcripts published in newspapers. Thus, for example, quotation marks (even when the words in question were not supposed to be quotations) acquired a special significance in the *Short Course*—they literally turned into a part of the plot. Quotation marks abound in the text, especially in the chapters describing the first years of the Soviet power—there, they are used almost as frequently as full stops and commas. The readers learn about "the so-called 'military opposition,' [which] united a significant number of former 'left communists'" in 1918; they discover that at party congresses oppositionists "brought... examples from 'practice'," that "'leftist communists' hide their true nature behind 'leftist' phrases," and read about the participants of a party congress who "rejected the views of an antiparty group of 'democratic centralism,'... which was advocating an unrestricted 'collegiality' and irresponsibility in the management of industry"—and there is no end to such examples.

Scholars have already written on the function of quotation marks in the written discourse of Stalinism. Svetlana Boym says that "everything that appeared in quotation marks in the criticism of the Stalin era was meant to be an insult; it parodied the words of the invisible enemy that was everywhere"; Galina Orlova in her analysis of the evolution of the concept of "saboteur" speaks of the

---

[85] *Istoriia Vsesoiuznoi Kommunisticheskoi Partii*, p. 4. English edition: *History of the Communist Party*. For ease of reading, and since the numerous quotations given here are representative of the tone of the book in general, specific page references will be omitted in this section.

"imprisonment [of concepts] within ironic quotation marks, demonstrating that the particular construct was foreign to the language of power."[86] Just as in the examples of spoken insults and mockery of the victims of show trials, here, too, the stubborn repetition of concepts thus parodied gradually replaces any other kind of definition of political actors ("various oppositional 'leaders'"), movements ("'economists'," "'new opposition'," "'democratic neutralists'," "so-called 'workers' opposition'"), events and actions ("'leftist' shouters...'claimed' that...," "direct capitulators...worshipped the 'might' of capitalism," supporters of Bukharin developed their "'theory' with a 'new' slogan"), so that the ironic charge turns into an integral part of the definitions themselves.

It is a distinctive feature of definitions in quotation marks (or inverted commas) that they imply both the citationality that was so fundamental to Stalinism (cf. the practice of "circular citationality" mentioned above) and mockery, turning factual or fictitious definitions and statements into their opposite. Two poles come together in these quotation marks/inverted commas: the absolute plus and the absolute minus, the canonized and the buffoonish. This is hardly surprising, as both rhetorical devices are grounded in the same principle: establishing fixed associations with particular names. Likewise, purely structural elements are also important in achieving the desired effect. Thus, in quoting canonized authors, and first of all Lenin and Stalin, it was customary to enclose whole sentences in quotation marks. The quoting of relatively long fragments of the original texts emphasized the coherence of the general narrative ("Lenin...wrote: 'Kamenev and Zinov'ev *betrayed* to Rodzianko and Kerenskii the decision of the Central Committee of their Party on insurrection'"; "Lenin pointed out that 'Bukharin and Trotsky actually *helped* German imperialism and *hindered* the growth of the German revolution'"; "Lenin advised that the party needed to be 'purged of rascals, of bureaucratic, dishonest or wavering Communists, and of Mensheviks who have repainted their "façade" but who have remained Mensheviks at heart'"; "Comrade Stalin said: 'Either we create a real worker and peasant—primarily a peasant—army, strictly disciplined army, and defend the Republic, or we perish'"; "In his speeches comrade Stalin stressed that 'it is the duty of the party *to bury Trotskyism as an ideological trend*'"). However, when quotations are from texts authored by enemies and rivals, the general rule of thumb seems to have been to cite in inverted commas only certain words, and only rarely whole statements. In this latter case the emphasis is not on the meaning of the statements, but on establishing firm associations with particular words, which end up sounding not quite serious simply because they are repeated so frequently—but also in inverted commas:

---

[86] Boym, "Paradoxes," p. 830; also Orlova, "Rozhdenie," pp. 311–12.

> *"In the interests of the world revolution,"* "left" *communists wrote in their statement, "we consider it expedient to accept the possibility of losing Soviet power, which is now becoming purely formal."*
>
> At that time the real cause of this anti-Party behavior of Trotsky and the "left communists" was not yet clear to the Party. But the recent trial of the Anti-Soviet "Bloc of Rights and Trotskyites" (at the beginning of 1938) has now revealed that Bukharin and the group of "left communists" he headed, along with Trotsky and the "left" Socialist-Revolutionaries, were at that time secretly conspiring against the Soviet Government. Now it is known that Bukharin, Trotsky and their fellow-conspirators had determined to wreck the Peace of Brest-Litovsk, arrest V. I. Lenin, J. V. Stalin and Yu. M. Sverdlov, assassinate them, and form a new government consisting of Bukharinites, Trotskyites and "left socialist-revolutionaries." [italics mine.—NJS].

The stronger the element of belittling ridicule and sarcasm conveyed by the insistent use of quotation marks, the clearer the contrast with the monstrous essence of the phenomenon that the text's author explains at a subsequent point in the narrative. Thus, it came to light that

> all the petty-bourgeois parties, which styled themselves "revolutionary" and "socialist" parties in order to deceive the people—the Socialist-Revolutionaries, Mensheviks, Anarchists and nationalists—became counter-revolutionary parties even before the October Socialist Revolution, and later turned into agents of foreign bourgeois espionage services, into a gang of spies, wreckers, diversionists, assassins and traitors to the country,

and

> the "left" phraseology of the "left communists" served to camouflage their defense of the kulaks, idlers and profiteers who were opposed to discipline and hostile to the state regulation of economic life, to accounting and control.

The explanations of the mocking nicknames given to the enemies are purely functional. They mark the second stage in the creation of a system of meanings after the use of inverted commas has already affirmed a firm associative link between certain people and certain actions: they are unworthy and deserving of ridicule. Humor, thus, can be seen as an intermediate stage between perceiving some people as those who "do not quite belong" and the urge to see them as incorrigible criminals.

From the perspective of usage, diminutive forms and expressions of contempt are similar to the use of inverted commas. Here, too, contrast plays an important role, be it the contrast between the ambitions of cunning enemies and their actual impotence, or between their unworthy nature and the noble spirit of the party and the people. "Those petty oppositional groups" that interfered with the work of the party, the "rascals" of which the party should have purged itself long before, Trotsky's "slanderous little book," the "bunch of deserters" whose only goal is to slow down the movement to socialism—all these are ridiculous against the background of the great achievements of the Party and the people. Predictably, "not for a moment was the Party shaken by this handful of deserters. The Central Committee of the Party contemptuously branded them as deserters from the revolution and accomplices of the bourgeoisie, and proceeded with its work." Even more importantly, the only result of the sinister traitors' activity seems to be an infusion of even more energy to the builders of communism: an attempt at an alternative demonstration on an anniversary of the Revolution, organized by "these satellites and their patrons," shamefully failed when they were "overwhelmed by the general demonstration and swept off the streets." The pitiful attempts of "Zinov'ev and Kamenev, driven to the wall" to justify themselves are followed by the laconic and victorious statement: "The 14th Party Congress opened in December 1925." Having "approved the annihilation of the Bukharin-Trotsky gang, ... the Soviet people ... proceed with their work," which happens to be "preparations for the elections to the USSR Supreme Council."

Let us note that the ease with which the party and the people proceed from annihilating hated enemies to the next item on their agenda—the preparation of congresses and elections and working on other building blocks for the better future—is reminiscent of the elements of classical comedy, where key moments of the plot are based on a similar combination of the heroic and the exaggeratedly mundane. Tellingly, the culmination of the struggle between, on the one hand, the heroic people and the party, and, on the other, their determined enemies, is announced by an introduction of classic images and "celebrated hero[es]" that were characters "in the system of mythology of the ancient Greeks." Granted, these were epic rather than comic figures. A comic charge (probably not intentional) is only apparent in the contrast between the rhetoric of most of the text and its end, between the vulgar swearing and the heroic passion.

In a text like this one, heroic passion was indispensable. It celebrated the exclusion of enemies from life as such. For as long as the narrative follows the tricks of living enemies, there is less passion and more mockery. It makes sense to suggest that this dynamic might be connected to the logic of superior knowledge as a political category in Stalinism: as long as the enemies are alive, both quotation marks and mocking remarks emphasize the difference in the understanding of the events by those who see the truth, who see the end of the plot in its beginning, and those who are doomed to ignorance. The one in charge of inverted commas and mocking nicknames knows the future; he knows which characters in the drama show their authentic selves right at the beginning of the story, and which ones are just intent on deceiving the audience, be they of "the so-called workers' opposition," "the so-called new opposition," or "the so-called platform of the 83." At the end, the implication is that whatever may have remained hidden previously has now become obvious to all. These hints at the superior knowledge of the whole "plot," regardless of the specific situation, are what distinguishes the *Short Course* from the examples of verbal interactions analyzed above, wherein the mockery of political and ideological adversaries was based, as a rule, on a lack of knowledge, or a misunderstanding, of a particular expression of new legal or procedural norms and practices of behavior in the new society. This fundamental text of Stalinism does not address the question of knowledge or ignorance as such; situations and dates succeed each other, but those who are wrong are always wrong and hence always ridiculous, and those who know are always right and always have the right to make jokes and to laugh. At the same time, the one who has the right to make jokes (in this case—the author and teller of the epic himself) can ridicule and mock the others exactly because he himself is beyond the story, beyond history. He has the exclusive right to see and understand the essence of all events on a historical scale, to detect the logic that guarantees inverted commas will one day turn into a death verdict.

The author of the *Short Course* explains to his readers the difference between true and false knowledge in the Soviet society via the category of "substance": "Mastering the Marxist-Leninist theory does not at all mean learning all its formulas and conclusions by heart and hanging on to their every letter. To master the Marxist-Leninist theory we must first of all learn to distinguish between the letter and the substance of it." Apparently "political freaks" and "crass ignoramuses" cling to the letter of the classical Marxist theory while ignoring its spirit. Like any exaggeratedly literal understanding of words and phenomena, this approach is ridiculous, and true Stalinists, who have a healthy sense of humor, know it. In the general context of Stalinism, the presence or absence of a sense of humor had far-reaching consequences. After all, if the true understanding of fundamental categories could and had to be grounded not in strict definitions, but in some elusive ability to understand the essence of phenomena, then laws, too, should not be applied literally, but only in accordance with their essence, which is revealed to those who have the right knowledge—and a sense of humor.

In the Stalinist epic, enemies are ridiculous not only because they are deprived of knowledge but also because their attempts to imitate the possession of the "right" kind of knowledge are doomed. This is why "the Menshevik 'theory of permanent revolution'" could only be called "a Marxist theory" by enemies determined to mock the very essence of Marxism; this is why the assorted enemies of the party line were nothing but "political freaks," "White Guard insects" and "contemptible pygmies,... [who] apparently flattered themselves—just for a laugh—that they were the masters of the country" and whose "'theory of a weakening of the class-struggle'" could only be defined as "farcical."

The comic situation of these "former people" is further intensified by the fact that they imitate not only true communists, so as to be considered as such themselves, but also sometimes, in the confusion of their mangled thinking, end up imitating themselves. The reader learns about the "satellites and their patrons," "freaks *like*... [X]," "downright capitulators *like*... [Y]," about an "anti-Party bloc which *resembled* the notorious Menshevik August Bloc" [italics mine.—NJS]. The function of the numerous qualifiers "like," "akin to," "similar to," "resembling," and so forth is close to that of ironic inverted commas: a fake, a mistaken identity is ridiculous not only in comparison to the genuine and the authentic but also with respect to itself and to other manifestations of wrong opinions and ideologically doubtful positions.

This inability to understand the true nature of things, the lack of capacity to discern the true value of things, turns all the enemies' actions, including the most mundane ones, into buffoonery—at least, that is the impression one gets from reading the *Short Course*. These people do not occupy a professional position, but "sit" in a certain organization, like "the Trotskyite Piatakov"; they do not submit political statements, but "stick out their heads"; they "make a sortie," "get sucked down deep into the anti-Soviet bog," perform "all kinds of dirty tricks," "concoct... ridiculous theories"—and do all this only so that they can, like evil spirits, "at 'an appropriate moment' crawl back to the political stage and walk all over the nation as its 'rulers'." Even when it would appear at first glance that these people's behavior is no different from that of others, for example, when they present reasonably comprehensible reports at party events, "the party" (personified by its leaders and the author of the *Short Course* himself) needs only look at them to see that "the hollow speeches of these gentlemen were in reality meant for their supporters outside the congress, to serve as a lesson to them in duplicity, and a call to them not to lay down their arms."

Given such unworthy desires, combined with their strikingly grotesque behavior, it is not surprising that oppositionists constantly "wavered and vacillated in the face of... difficulties." The firm and consistent position of the party is all the more admirable against the background of the chaotic and unpredictable maneuvering of its enemies. The actions of the party leadership are grounded in irrefutable logic, and there are objective results manifesting the fruit of its work. We learn that in 1921,

> nearly 170,000 persons, or about 25 per cent of the total membership, were expelled from the party as a result of the purge. The purge greatly strengthened the party, improved its social composition, increased the confidence of the masses in it, and strengthened its reputation. The party became more unified and better disciplined.

Naturally one did not need to wait long for the results of such active measures:

> In March 1922 the party held its 11th Congress. It was attended by 522 voting delegates, representing 532,000 party members, which was fewer than at the previous congress. There were 155 delegates with no voting rights. The reduction in the membership was due to the party purge, which had already begun.

The trend continued in the following year:

> In April 1923, the party held its 12th Congress.... The congress was attended by 408 voting delegates, representing 386,000 party members. This was fewer than at the previous congress, the reduction being due to the fact that, in the interval, the party purge had continued and had resulted in the expulsion of a considerable percentage of the party membership. There were 417 non-voting candidates.

And this is what the 14th Congress looked like in 1925:

> The congress was attended by 665 delegates with the vote and 641 non-voting delegates, representing 643,000 party members and 445,000 candidate members. This was slightly fewer than at the previous congress. The reduction was due to a partial purge, a purge of the party organizations in universities and offices to which anti-Party elements had gained entrance.

And so on, all the way to the denouement—the show trials. The dark symmetry of the numbers is, of course, full of black humor, which probably was not intentional. In this account the enemies play a parodic role—but here the concept of "parody" is to be understood in its original meaning, as "singing along" or "singing in reverse," alongside the singing "for real."[87] The canonical narrative of Stalinism needs the parody to keep the plot going: against the enemies' grotesque actions, which can be assumed behind the statistics, the victorious march of the new way of life and socialist ideals must impress the readers even more. Behind the creation of both the parodic and the heroic figures there is the same anonymous (but known to everyone), omnipotent author of the epic. He is the only one who sees clearly both the beginning and the end of the plot, as well as the roles of all the characters in the drama; he is the only one whose breadth of vision enables him to see the vital energy leaving the enemies (who grow weaker by the day) and instead nourishing the true Stalinists, who are certain in the truth of their cause. Readers of the *Short Course*, who do not have the special gift, discover only gradually that, as it turns out, the enemies had been doomed from the very beginning; there had

---

[87] Agamben, *Profanations*, pp. 38–9 (with reference to Giulio Cesage Scaligero).

never been any doubt that their evil plans would come to light. Readers are given to understand that the Party can always be relied upon to know who is who, which explains why the Soviet leader could always make jokes at the expense of his political opponents and, at critical moments, make the only correct decision. For example, when many Party members were uncertain about which "deviation" in the Party policy was "worse," comrade Stalin responded by saying: "Both of them are worse, the first deviation and the second one. And if these deviations develop, they may disintegrate and destroy the Party. Fortunately there are forces in our party that can cut off both the first and the second deviation." Unsurprisingly, "the party did indeed defeat and cut off both the 'left' and the right deviation."

But rank-and-file Party members could learn about all this only once the story had been told from the beginning to end. From the standpoint of the construction of narrative this is a completely legitimate move. After all, had there not been something secret that is only revealed as the narrative progresses, the plot itself would not be there, and the denouement would not have performed its main function—it would not have brought the satisfaction from the just punishment of the hypocritical monsters. And the author of the *Short Course*, the omnipotent semi-god, would not have been able to create—and tell—the history of the creation of the new world from the viewpoint of its creator, accompanying it with mocking characterizations of certain characters so that future readers would never forget on whose side the truth is. There would have been none of the sense of victory that accompanies the liberation from the ridiculous and the movement toward the joyful, when enemies have been defeated and court verdicts have pronounced the last word in this breathtakingly exciting story. This movement is the core of this programmatic text of Stalinism. In his analysis of Stalin's frequent use of the binary rhetorical constructions ("question-answer," "cause-effect," "action-result," "offense-punishment") Mikhail Vaiskopf reminds us of the religious education that the Soviet leader received as a young man.[88] It is also possible, however, that in addition to having been trained to build his argument in a certain way, the dictator's stylistic preferences were dictated by his ambition to achieve a complete, comprehensive order in everything, everywhere. Whatever happens by chance (and thus is, by definition, ridiculous) should be excluded from immediate reality, and his subjects should know that each action, word, and thought is not only monitored by the supreme ruler but also part of a general plot that drives the story to its predetermined ending.

Roman Jakobson writes that minor narrative genres reflect the same principles as those underlying epic texts.[89] An analysis of mocking remarks in the *Short Course* confirms this proposition. The structure of the text itself to a great extent reproduces the structure of condensed mini-narratives where events develop in a

---

[88] Vaiskopf, *Pisatel'*, p. 127 and passim.   [89] Jakobson, *Iazyk*, pp. 96–8.

strict order, and where the denouement is not only inevitable but also complete, bringing with it a sense of the restoration of the world that has just escaped a complete catastrophe. Such narratives qualify as what is usually called "anecdotes"—episodes from life laconically summarized to serve as moral tales to those who did not experience them directly, where key elements are emphasized in accordance with the goals of the narrator, and where the interconnection between causes and effects, actions and intentions, is outlined schematically. Such are all the episodes in the *Short Course* that describe the clashes between "the forces of evil" and "the forces of good." The ease with which the schematic narrative network is outlined in the text was guaranteed by the simple fact that at the moment of writing nearly all targets of the authorial sarcasm were dead, and no unexpected changes in the heroes' behavior were to be expected. Well-rehearsed in oral interactions with the then still living victims, particular turns of phrase were now fixed in writing as a necessary element of both the plot (the division into those who belong and those who do not) and the style (producing direct associations with particular names and concepts). But this representation of the "correct" development of relations between the Party and its enemies, which culminated in a just punishment, had to be preceded by a long series of "live training sessions," in which the required reaction of the audience was tested over and over. The laughter of the people present at these events, whether real or only supplied in the written transcripts at a later stage, played an important role in this process. This laughter reflected the changing principles behind the punishment of those who were not loyal or reliable enough: First a reaction to a grotesque type of an unworthy Party member or to inappropriate claims by ideological adversaries, laughter later turned into a harbinger of the coming trials, and finally became the background to the announcement of a death verdict.

* * *

Hayden White claims that "narrative in general, from the folktale to the novel, from the annals to the fully realized 'history,' has to do with the topics of law, legality, legitimacy, or, more generally, *authority*."[90] This statement is all the more justified when applied to an authoritarian narrative, when the oral speech of a dictator introduces the figures of speech that later will become the basis for administering legal justice at the highest level, and finally will remain fixed both as the official version of the past and as guidelines for future developments in the fundamental written text of the regime. The real law of Stalinist society was not contained in its criminal or civil code; its real law was the law of the narrative authored by the dictator, promising satisfaction from mastering what appeared complex, frightening, and confusing—and what turned out to be simply

---

[90] White, "The Value," p. 13.

ridiculous. Events in this story develop with the inevitability and ruthlessness of natural phenomena, whose only master is the creator himself—or, in this case, the dictator. The punishment of traitors by a court decision is only the ultimate manifestation of this supreme law. Unlike laws formulated by people, which are supposed either to prevent crimes from happening or else to punish people for committing them, supreme laws are determined by fate itself; unlike the civil and criminal law that is supposed to be applied individually and on a case-specific basis, supreme laws use absolute categories that define the belonging of social and political actors to particular groups. In the context of the law-positing Stalinist history, the one who laughed was, indeed, the one who laughed last, since only those who had the right to laughter had the right to tell the story.

Igal Halfin claims that "a symptomatic reading of Stalinist language, written and oral, is necessary if we are to understand how texts generated meanings and shaped their subjects."[91] According to the historian, the audience's laughter at the key moments when the nature of those who "belong" and those who do not is determined is one of the "symptoms," as it points to hidden mechanisms in the formation of political subjectivity in Stalinism. Halfin particularly emphasizes the gradual disappearance of polysemy from Stalinist discourse, which led to the transformation of relatively harmless jokes and relatively free laughter at the early 1920s Party forums into refined sarcastic mockery and cruel laughter during the infamous "purges." It would appear, however, that the role of jokes and laughter in the formation of Soviet subjectivity and the Soviet ideology and worldview in the late 1920s and 1930s was more complex; not less importantly, the transformations of humor were directly related to law-positing and legitimizing practices, all the way up to their appearance in the fundamental text of the regime. The examples we have adduced illustrate stages in these transformations of laughter and humor that accompanied the interactions between the supreme power and representatives of "the people" as the power of state terror increased—and as the image of ideal Soviet subjects acquired clearer outlines, with the people mastering the art of when, how, and at what they were supposed to laugh.

---

[91] Halfin, *Stalinist Confessions*, p. 380 (endnote 78).

3

The Funny War

Laughing at the Front in World War Two

> Laughter is the most dangerous thing.
> People have died laughing.
>
> Simon Mawer, The Fall

There is no shortage of studies on humor in times of conflict.[1] World War One demonstrated for the first time in history how a widespread use of printed media for propaganda purposes can influence public opinion on all sides involved. But it was the next great war that provides ample material for analyzing how popular humor in its various guises serviced not just enemies at war but also rival ideologies. In World War One, humor and comedy were used "for the mobilization of morale during the war," with popular comic culture boosting "pragmatic patriotism."[2] Twenty years later, the two main parties involved in the conflict also sought to employ war propaganda to promote and cement as the very foundation of their existence the values each regime held dear, and humor played a special role in these efforts.

In July 1943, at the very first formal meeting of Soviet satirical writers, the First Secretary of the Soviet Writers' Union Aleksandr Fadeev spoke of the great role that satire and humor played "in educating [the readers of army newspapers] in the spirit of Soviet patriotism and hatred of the enemy."[3] At the same meeting, one of the masters of Soviet satire and humor of the time, Samuil Marshak, reminded the participants that, "of course, on the face of it, it was in the first days of the war that our satire emerged, our humor appeared. Until then nobody really understood what kind of war this is and what challenges we are facing."[4] Just as nobody knew exactly what kind of war it was and what was in store, in the summer of 1941 nobody knew yet what kind of humor would emerge in the new conditions—except that it would clearly need to be different from whatever had come before.

---

[1] For a generally comprehensive bibliography on humor in the war, see Mel'nichenko, "Fenomen."
[2] Rüger, "Laughter and War," p. 36, citing Chickering, *Imperial Germany*, p. 136, with reference to Martin Baumeister.
[3] Samoilenko, *Stikhotvornaia satira*, p. 5.
[4] Contribution by Samuil Marshak in "Satira i iumor."

State Laughter: Stalinism, Populism, and Origins of Soviet Culture. Evgeny Dobrenko and Natalia Jonsson-Skradol, Oxford University Press. © Evgeny Dobrenko and Natalia Jonsson-Skradol 2022.
DOI: 10.1093/oso/9780198840411.003.0004

Any discussion of wartime Soviet humor must begin with a reminder that for Soviet citizens, the years of the confrontation with fascism brought with them a relief on the domestic front, "a loosening of control and centralization," with the "policy of 'national agreement'" coming in place of the preceding era of terror.[5] At the Eighteenth Party Congress in March 1939 Stalin assured the delegates that "the edge of our punitive organs and intelligence service is no longer turned to within the country but to without, against external enemies."[6] The Nazis as unequivocally evil external enemies made them a safe target for any form of attack, actual or verbal. The "friend-enemy" dichotomy which had certainly been at the heart of the Soviet world view since the Revolution now acquired clear outlines, and these outlines coincided with those of the state's borders, of language, culture, and tradition. For the first time in a generation, in the midst of unspeakable suffering, the vast country was genuinely laughing together, *with* its heroes and *at* its enemies. Below we will examine two of the most representative instances of "laughing with" and "laughing at," each a distinct mixture of rhetorical devices and traditions, the comic and the tragic: Aleksandr Tvardovskii's poem *Vasilii Terkin* and Il'ia Erenburg's satirical pieces published in Soviet newspapers throughout the four years of the war and that were later compiled into *The War: 1941–1945*.[7]

These two authors, and their works, could not be more different. The popular tone of Tvardovskii's poem embodies an idealized but also down-to-earth version of the Russian-turned-Soviet folk spirit, while the cosmopolitan multilingual Erenburg documents a great war of cultures. Tvardovskii's humor is aimed at arousing sympathy and solidarity; it seeks to touch readers and make them smile in recognition. Erenburg's satire is biting and unrestrained; its aim is not to encourage connection, but rather to illustrate the insurmountable divide between the readers (friends) and the objects of the author's ridicule (enemies). Poles apart in their background and choice of genres, they represent the two extremes of humor that can be "cohesive and divisive... [occupying] all points of the sliding scales between affection and cruelty, wit and buffoonery, expression of the status quo and subversion."[8] Both these extremes are equally in demand during war, whatever the era, whoever the adversaries, and whatever the political regimes they speak for. In the specifically (Stalinist) Soviet context the two authors and the two kinds of humor they represented foregrounded the very elements of communication between the power apparatus and the citizens that remained fundamental throughout the years of the Soviet era. Just as with every other aspect of life, the war made the essential characteristics of "state laughter" much more obvious, outlined their contours with much greater precision.

---

[5] Edele, "Paper Soldiers," p. 93. [6] Weiner, *Making Sense*, p. 54. [7] Erenburg, *Voina*.
[8] Holmanm and Kelly, "Introduction," p. 249.

Vasilii Terkin: The Typical and the Exceptional

In his introduction to an English translation of Tvardovskii's poem, the English novelist Charles Snow recounts the experience of meeting the Russian poet in 1960: "For the first time anywhere, I was being presented with someone who possessed literary fame as Dickens might have known it."[9] Tvardovskii's creation—a simple Russian soldier, charismatic and witty, heroic and devoid of any pretense, cheeky and modest, courageous and open about his weaknesses, uneducated and endowed with a natural wisdom—enjoyed an enormous popularity from the appearance of the first chapter in 1942 and until well after the war. The general consensus among the critics of the time was that his poem *was* the embodiment of the era and of (Russian and/or Soviet) tradition, and that the reason the poem "became an immediate favorite of Soviet readers" was that "it is full of good, truly merry and healthy laughter" and that "it shows a living, typical soldier."[10] Another critic echoed these words when he wrote that "Vasilii Terkin is an embodiment of the enduring typical characteristics of the Soviet man."[11] Yet another was convinced that "exactly in order to turn Vasilii Terkin into a general, popular character, Tvardovskii chose somebody who at first glance does not appear to have any distinct characteristics." But, adds this particular reviewer, "in fact Terkin is a true hero of the spirit, a direct descendant of the favorite characters from Russian folk ballads."[12]

On the face of it, the last two statements contradict each other—is Terkin an embodiment of the "typical characteristics" of a Soviet man, or is he devoid of any special characteristics? Is he a worthy heir of the mighty knights in Russian folk legends, or does his strength lie in being just one of many—very many—fighters at the front? Why is it that being a man without characteristics is a prerequisite for becoming the exponent of characteristics that are supposedly most typical of the citizens of the most advanced society in the world?

This aporia can be resolved at the level of the definition of "the typical" and with reference to one possible interpretation of the category of the comic. Bearing in mind Georgii Malenkov's famous pronouncement made exactly a decade later, in 1952, on the typical being "not what is most common, but what most fully and keenly expresses the essence of a given social force,"[13] it would seem to make sense that one had to be devoid of personal, idiosyncratic characteristics in order to serve as a vessel for some broadly recognizable qualities. Of course, Malenkov's statement contains a double contradiction. First of all, as many scholars have noticed, the supposedly "typical" apparently alluded to something desirable rather than something actually recognizable from real life experience. But in our context

---

[9] Snow, "Introduction," p. 9.   [10] "Satira i iumor," contribution by David Zaslavskii.
[11] Vykhodtsev, "Osobennosti," here p. 167.   [12] Tarasenkov, *Sila*, p. 79.
[13] Malenkov, *Otchetnyi doklad*, p. 115.

it is a different kind of paradox imbedded in the ideology of "the typical Soviet person" that comes to the fore.

Because this "typical" person in the ordinary times of the peaceful construction of socialism needed to be a pure embodiment of an idea (a shock worker, an enlightened communist etc.), it became imperative for these people to be extraordinary—every day, always. A logical implication of the extraordinary having become ordinary is that, when the war brought with it circumstances that were truly exceptional, the norm (that is, the extraordinary) was no longer sufficient. The rules of the game changed, and being "just human" became the quality most called for in wartime propaganda. Now, the emphasis in "the Soviet man" (or "Soviet person") was on the noun, not the adjective.[14] Even though it may be true that "unlike the soldiers of other wars and epochs (for example, unlike Jaroslav Hašek's hero Švejk) Terkin thinks in terms of the state, in historical terms; his path is always that of Soviet power,"[15] this grand historical thinking is not what guides the hero of Tvardovskii's poem in his heroic deeds. He himself offers a joking apology for the lack of sophistication in his manners and turns of phrase when it comes to politically enlightened talks, explaining that he is "a farm lad," but "never mind; / And not much of a graduate. / Shame accordion's left behind; / I could teach you something yet."[16]

Terkin can appreciate the rare moment when he can enjoy a solid routine of "stew—that's first; and porridge then / For every day... fit," because he knows what it is like to lie "Three whole days and nights again / Gut empty, knotted, stomach growling." Yes, it is true that he is a "Russian wonder-man"—but it is also true that he is

> not some hero, celebrated
> In legend and in rhyme,
> But a knight in marching-kit,
> Simple lad, for trials fit,
> And as for fear—he is used to it,
> When sober (which is all the time...).

For all the celebratory reports in the press about the advances of the Soviet Army, he knows how exhausting it can be to spend hours in preparation for an attack and to wait, motionless, whether an enemy shell "is going to biff [him] on the bum." Yes, his will to live is invincible, but the reason he feels "reluctant, if the truth be told / To die now, his feet all wet, / To die so soon—it seems a shame" is that he

---

[14] On this as a general tendency in the Soviet propaganda through literature and the arts, see, e.g., Dobrenko, *Metafora*, p. 219.

[15] Vykhodtsev, "Osobennosti," p. 171.

[16] I have used Jill Higgs's translation of the work as a guide for the English, but have amended it slightly in some instances (*Vasily Tyorkin*).

would like to "get warm again, / And dry his foot-cloths by the stove." Having defeated fascism, the first thing he needs upon entering the enemy territory is a good wash in a bathhouse, when he can finally relax and when the words "front, rear and flanks" no longer refer to the distribution of troops on the ground, but to his body parts. This is a universally recognizable voice of someone who wants to survive, and who looks for the simple comforts of a peaceful, regulated life, rather than the excitement of industrial records and rebuilding the world.

Philosopher Alenka Zupančič writes that comedy is about a clash, "establish[ing] a ... connection between [the] heterogeneous orders" that she defines as "the human" (that is, one's life as a biological being) and "the inhuman" (that is, one's symbolic role).[17] It is in this sense of connecting these two different orders that *Vasilii Terkin* is a work of comedy, even though its narrative follows the profoundly tragic trajectory of the war. As if in confirmation of Socrates's conviction that "the skillful tragic dramatist should also be a comic poet,"[18] the narrator interrupts his own story when it risks becoming too true to the brutal reality of the war:

> For a time I've been forgetting
> Where I am, and when, and who;
> Make a joke of it's the best thing—
> Laugh's the only thing to do.

Taken in their own right, few of the episodes, lines or expressions used in the text are funny except as characteristically colloquial expressions allowed to appear in print in a society where written language otherwise was strongly formalized. Taken together as integral elements of the text, they are parts of a comedy where the human takes over the symbolic and the literal takes over the metaphoric. For Terkin, being "a brave soldier at war" is just one of a number of occupations he is good at, on a par with, for example, being "a welcome guest at parties" or easily "being the best at any job." Just as he himself is a true Russian war hero because he is not extraordinary, he refuses to accord the war an exceptional status. Having taken a German prisoner, he experiences the calm satisfaction that one feels after accomplishing a challenging but by no means out-of-the-ordinary task:

> Oh, it's blissful for a chap
> Returning to his unit, once
> He's fulfilled his mission; back
> Home from dawn reconnaissance.

---

[17] Zupančič, *The Odd One In*, pp. 7–8 (Introduction).
[18] Plato, Symposium, 223d, as quoted in Agamben, *The Use*, p. 257.

The war is ultimately just another kind of work, a routine revolving around "soup until full, tea until sweaty," when it is "a life like any other"—except that this life is at stake at any given moment. Whatever might call for his skills as a handyman, he is proud to conclude that he and his friends

> have made a solid, reliable structure,
> Good not just for war—
> For drinking tea,
> For publishing a wall

—except that it is not tea-drinking they are going to engage in next, but brutal fighting. When a shell lands next to him and his comrades, he manages to save them all, not through a particularly cunning military strategy, but because he quickly comes up with an ingenious solution: "Near the crater where it fell / Terkin turns towards the shell, / And indulges in a pee."

The Soviet critic who wrote about Tvardovskii's poem that "like in folk tales, the characters are... somewhat elevated, idealized" in that they are being able "to turn their hand to anything," was right only in part. Terkin is somebody who knows, quite simply, that work must be done. For him, war is *just another form of work*, as demanding as any other kind of work would be, imposing obligations ("And here we are back at war—at work: / Get ready!"), requiring one's full attention—but also more satisfying, so that other needs are relegated to the background:

> One is likely to even forget hunger
> When the war is going well.
> It's no mean feat: a town in a day,
> In two days—a city.

In this calm willingness to face whatever misfortunes may befall him on his way through the work of war, Terkin, "True to his duty and orders, / The Russian laborer-warrior," is an embodiment of the best qualities of classical Russian folk heroes—such, at least, is the opinion of one of the first reviewers of Tvardovskii's poem. "'We are soldiers' means 'we are masters of our trade'; for a Russian man, these two concepts merge together," critic Vladimir Ermilov writes in one of many reviews of the poem. "A soldier is good at everything; he solves all the riddles, he fixes all the jobs, he overcomes all the difficulties and dangers: such is the soldier in Russian folk tales.... It is a dedicated laborer for whom a war is a continuation of his household."[19] Over a decade later, another analysis of the poem reaches pretty

---

[19] Ermilov, "Russkii voin," p. 2.

much the same conclusion, noting how "Tvardovskii was striving to show us a regular Soviet man, one of the multi-million army of simple and modest laborers of the war."[20] And here is a quote from yet another critical article from around the same time: "Terkin is a Soviet working man. He treats everything as a worker does."[21] We could add here: as *just* a worker.

Vasilii Terkin: "Being" and "Just Being"

The comic thrust of the poem is, at least partly, in this move from "something is X" to "something is *just* X"—from being a complete, recognizable entity in itself to being defined through an exclusion of other (potential) attributes. The Soviet man is *just* a man, dreaming not so much of a momentous victory as of having a wash and changing his foot cloths.

He is praised as a true master in everything he does, but he does not do anything particularly grand: he can *just* take care of household duties, fix a broken clock, sing, dance, and tell stories. He is also a hero, undoubtedly, but his heroism itself is often presented as a result of *just* a stroke of luck rather than of some superior skill or knowledge of special military techniques. More than once the weather itself happens to side with Terkin and his comrades, the cold winter making them rejoice:

> Let the German lord freeze,
> The German lord is not used to it.
> The Russian will be fine—
> He is a simple man.

The one-on-one confrontation between Terkin and the enemy sounds more like *just* a scuffle in a village club after a drink than a heroic battle:

> Jerry deals him such a blow,
> Terkin's jaw has quite a list.
> And then our warrior, without taking aim,
> Wham! Between the eyes his fist,

with Terkin's heroic behavior born as much of fear as of ideological and moral conviction: "in alarm / Such a thumping blow he shoots..."[22]

---

[20] Vykhodtsev, "Osobennosti," p. 167.   [21] Tarasenkov, *Sila*, p. 80.
[22] In this chapter, "Jerry" is chosen as a slang pejorative term to designate German soldiers (cf. the Russian "Фриц").

At first it seems like it would make perfect sense to read the poem as a straightforward example of carnivalesque literature, with its obvious emphasis on the physical rather than the spiritual, the mundane rather than the lofty, the colloquial rather than the elevated. The register throughout the book is a consistently low one, with the protagonist taking off his "underpants" ("*podshtanniki*") in a German bathhouse where "some count's chairs stand / In the dressing room" and sharing details of his physical discomforts with little inhibition. We should also not forget that war itself has a lot in common with carnival, in so far as both signal a suspension of the regular order and an erasure, however temporary, of conventional norms.[23] In war as in carnival, with any systemic order being abolished, the reduction of phenomena to their momentary, literal significance—the bare core—is likely to be experienced in an extreme way, whether as tragedy or as comedy. A fool crowned for a day makes the symbolic attributes of the royal privilege more noticeable, but his rule does not extend beyond the moment and the situation. His is a reign stripped bare of anything but the external signs marking his role at the actual moment in time, lacking the consistency and continuity in which a regulated order should be grounded. Likewise, a soldier at war triumphs over death at any given moment just for that moment, with no promise of the outcome of the next confrontation; laughter and tears are never far apart. However, a straightforward carnivalesque reading of the poem would disregard a crucial particularity of the text that accounts for much of its comic appeal and its popularity: rather than turning an ordered reality upside down, the poem simply incorporates reversals into the regular flow of life.

The way the story of Terkin is told—the style and the vocabulary, the light-hearted, joking references to the prompt transitions from life to death and to the simultaneously fragile and stubborn nature of the human body—does not manifest a carnivalesque reversal, a breaking down of the conventional order, because the emphasis is on all these elements of daily existence in wartime being completely normal. One of the Soviet critics quoted above noted that "the words [from the poem, describing Terkin] to which critics usually refer—'accepts everything as it is'—express a thought shared by all the Soviet people about how in war one must render the surroundings 'habitable,' get used to them, however unsuitable the situation might be for doing this."[24] Another critic reminds the reader that "this [i.e. the war] is not a special world, separate from the rest of the people in our society; rather, these are the very same Soviet people, thrust into the conditions of living in the army, at the front."[25] Tvardovskii himself wrote in a letter to his wife:

---

[23] See, e.g., "these myths of the End of the World implying, as they do in clearer or darker fashion, the re-creation of a new Universe, express the same archaic and extremely widespread idea of the progressive 'degradation' of a Cosmos, necessitating its periodical destruction and re-creation...The essential thing is not the fact of the *End*, but the certainty of a *new beginning*" (Eliade, *Myth*, pp. 60, 75, referred to in Chernus, "War and the Enemy," here p. 339).

[24] Vykhodtsev, "Osobennosti," p. 169.   [25] Tvardovskii, "Kak byl napisan," here p. 238.

"The basic sense of the war is that it has already become a normal state of affairs for the people, that it is not the war that appears to be extraordinary, unimaginable, but its opposite."[26]

It is largely the characters' refusal to grant the man-made catastrophe the status of an emergency that turns the poem into a comic—not just tragic—epic. In and of itself, eating porridge or soup is not touchingly comical, but it becomes so when bombs are landing nearby and a "practical...old man [i.e., a veteran soldier] thought of making a soup / Right there, on the move." Nor is fixing a grandfather clock a particularly remarkable feat, except when accompanied by a narrow miss that is greeted by the old man in the house and his soldier visitor with the equanimity of old acquaintances registering a mildly irritating sound from a neighboring house, so that when

> Again somewhere in the back yard
> A shell struck the frozen ground,
> Neither Vasilii Terkin nor the old soldier
> Bat an eyelid.

The historian George Mosse wrote of the "trivialization of war" and the "domestication of modern war" as defense mechanisms activated when its sufferings might otherwise prove too much to bear. Humor, in Mosse's opinion, is an important tool in this process.[27] Remembering the first version of *Terkin*, the one from the time of the Soviet-Finnish war, Tvardovskii speculated that "the kind of success that "Vasia Terkin" had during the Finnish war can be explained by the need of a soldier's soul to be entertained by something that, even if it does not exactly correspond to the harsh reality of everyday life at the front, it still creates a kind of fairy-tale out of this reality, and not out of some obscure stuff from legends."[28] The same can be said of the final, much more popular version of the poem.

Vasilii Terkin: All Is Well That Ends Well

After reading the introductory sections of the text, the poet's wife wrote him, "you're absolutely right to...make it clear the book will offer a 'tale' of the former peaceful life...this idea that in wartime it's more interesting to hear about the past, and after the war is over, one wants to hear about the war."[29] The events

---

[26] Tvardovskii, *"Ia v svoiu khodil ataku,"* p. 202 (October 30, 1943, AT's letter to his wife).
[27] Mosse, *Fallen Soldiers*, p. 11. Quoted in Purseigle, "Mirroring Societies," p. 323.
[28] Tvardovskii, "Kak byl napisan," p. 236.
[29] Tvardovskii, *"Ia v svoiu khodil ataku,"* p. 149 (December 18, 1942, AT's letter to his wife).

narrated in this sort of tale should not be understood so much as fantastical or wonder-inspiring; they simply belong to a different reality. The genre as such was an integral part of Stalinist propaganda in all its forms, from the 1936 Constitution[30] to the immensely popular comedies of Ivan Pyr'ev and Grigorii Aleksandrov. However, most of the other applications of this generic device lack an important element that is present in narrating the experience of war as a fairy tale. Unlike the film comedies or the Constitution, the utopian tone of which suggests the possibility of an ideal state of being somewhere very close to the actual moment of the narrative (or else in the near future), fairy-tale narratives of wartime experiences point to the past. At war, there is a certain comfort in believing the events one is going through are reminiscent of a fairy tale, in recognizing a connection to the past, to something that has already happened, again and again and again. A fairy tale has a fixed, predictable pattern, and no matter how challenging the trials that the hero must endure, it all ends well.

One can easily see the benefits of translating unbearable events from the present moment into a genre associated with predictable outcomes, in which horrors happen not "for real," but "as if"—as if they had already been reworded, encoded in popular memory as an episode in the long (hi)story of the people. The present enemy might seem particularly ferocious or invincible, but the skilled storyteller reminds us that it is not the first time Russia has been attacked, and that the end has always been the same, when "its enemy—and there've been so many!— / Is flat on his face, paws asunder."

It has been said that comedy is tragedy plus time.[31] Translating current horrific events into a genre associated with collective memory rather than personal direct experience makes it possible to look at the present moment from a different perspective, as if from another—future—point in time, as if it had already happened, and will happen again, and this current experience is just one instance among many and, thus, nothing particularly terrible. Only from a point in the future can one speak of events with additions like "there've been so many!" ("*kakoi po schetu*"), "it used to happen" ("*sluchalos'*"), "more than once" ("*ne raz*"), or "now, as in the old days" ("*chto teper', chto v starinu*"). Horror turns into adventure, and death is merely another experience, when one is more exhausted by the uncomfortable waiting than the moment itself:

> So in age no kindly Fate
> Gave them comfort; no,
> They just stand at Heaven's gate,

---

[30] Schmid, "Konstitutsiia."
[31] The most obvious classical reference here is Marx with his "first as tragedy, then as farce," though see Joshua Clover for an elaboration on the standard reading of Marx's formula, also explored further in this chapter. Clover, "*Genres.*"

> Waiting to go through.
> Just some poles to shelter under,
> Sacks of spuds for stool,
> Clutch of chickens, and a bundle,
> And some lumps of coal.

Only from a future perspective, however imaginary, can one know that the most important "motivational speech" at the most trying of times is simply "don't despair," because "if alive, we won't be dead" and "we'll stick it out. We'll get through." A Soviet critic noted that this motif of the soldier-hero being "able to come out of any difficult situation unscathed," as if he were "under a protective spell,"[32] was a feature of war humor in general.

Much of the humorous charm of Tvardovskii's poem comes from such references to fairy-tale motifs. There is the traditional magic pattern of three, with the hero boasting about how

> Three times they surrounded me,
> And three times I broke free.
> And even though it was worrying
> I stayed safe
> Under a three-layered fire,
> Both slant and straight.

He plans for the undesirable outcome "if the bullet bites for the third time, / This time deadly, wicked"; he reminisces about what it was like to be "Three whole days and nights in an ambush, / Gut empty, knotted, stomach growling." Then there are the traditional folk metaphors for extreme experiences—drinking parties, kissing mother earth:

> Still alive: some satisfaction;
> That's a little jamboree.
> Take a breather, have a bite,
> Smoke and take it easy, see.
> Worse are mortars when they just
> Burst in—that's a jamboree.
> It'll get you more, perhaps,
> You'll kiss mother earth, maybe.
> But just bear this in mind, old chap:
> That's a medium jamboree.

---

[32] Samoilenko, *Stikhotvornaia satira* p. 132.

There is the archaic motif of being approached by death and negotiating the conditions of passing over to the other side. There are even parodies of metaphysical reflections on life and death, with the soldiers speculating on the mind-body dichotomy: "'Now isn't this a weird thing?' / They say, in no hurry. / 'Just the body—that's OK, / But what if it's body and soul?'"

But in a real war people do die, of course. While the narrative and the war it describes are epic in their significance, a defining feature of this epic is that it is composed of short episodes, and any of the single and singular events comprising it brings the most crucial feature of war experience to the fore: unpredictability, so that the momentary is superimposed on the momentous, the private and the seemingly insignificant—on the shared and the communal, and an anecdote—on the story of one's life. Such is the convention of war, and also of a "comic narrative novella" ("*komicheskaia skazovaia novella*"), with its "complete narrative of a single moment" and "attention to an insignificant mundane fact, which is rendered by the hero-narrator as an event."[33] Attributing major significance to a minor event in one's life might be comic, but only if it is not the last thing to happen in this life. Once again, the assignment of a narrative, or any of its parts, to a genre depends on the temporal perspective from which it is viewed, so that the same moment can be read as either completely insignificant or as an instance of redemption. This is why an older soldier's annoyance at having lost his tobacco pouch after he'd lost his family and home is both touchingly comical and deeply tragic:

> What a nuisance.
> All at once:
> Lost my family. Well, OK.
> But now—my 'baccy pouch!

The epic narrative consists of episodic events; hence all the "transitions in the poem from joking to pathos, from some little everyday scene to the description of a heroic deed," which, according to a critic writing about Tvardovskii's poem more than thirty years after it appeared, are "effortless, free."[34]

Part of their being "effortless" and "free" comes from this general "downshifting" of the heroic to the level of the comic, which results in what Freud calls "a *descending* incongruity," when "consciousness is unawares transferred from great things to small"[35]—never, we should note, the other way round. In the poem, the "great thing" of the national catastrophe that is the war, of heroism and courage, of shared effort and sacrifice, is combined with the "small things" that appear to be equally important—the joy of having hot tea at the right moment, the pleasure of

---

[33] Mushchenko, *Poetika skaza*, p. 257.   [34] Tarasenkov, *Sila*, p. 81.
[35] Freud, *Jokes*, p. 146, quoting Spencer, *The Physiology of Laughter* (1860).

being offered a second helping of soup, the satisfaction of being allowed to drink a sip of the alcohol that brings one back to life after having nearly drowned in a frozen river. Of course, a disruption of the epic narrative of one's life can also be occasioned by "small things"—a stray bullet, or failing to hit quite as hard as necessary the enemy soldier one stumbled upon. But small things, too, are exactly what can make an epic narrative comic. A narrative told on a large scale cannot be comic as a whole; only the episodes that it consists of can be. The grand narrative is a progression from being a victim to being a winner; the comic is the incongruous, the unexpected that happens along the way.

One of the characteristics of "state laughter" as an overarching generic principle is its attempt to integrate the comic into the grand narrative of historical progress. But the comic, the truly comic, is by its very definition unpredictable—as unpredictable as whatever might happen at war, when

> Suddenly—a rust-red flash
> From the undergrowth around,
> All churned up. A shell lands: Crash!

Unlike in tragedy, where misfortunes occur because of the intervention of fate, here it is simply because one's "number is up" ("*nomer vyshel*")—just as it happens in life, and especially in life under Stalinism with its random violence. To this, people could relate.

And they did. As the narrator of the poem says with pride, the text is "all in Russian," that is, understandable to all its readers. The heavy reliance of the poem on Russian folk tradition is pointed out by many researchers, even if some of them disagree as to which elements of it are exclusively Russian, and which come from Soviet reality, and to what extent the predominance of the former over the latter or of the latter over the former matters, if at all.[36] Originally with a hero who is a product of collective efforts by many authors (a Soviet researcher mentions over sixty such characters that were conceived by more or less popular Soviet poets and reached different stages of development; another speaks of the poem's hero having "at least seven fathers"[37]), modeled on traditional images of Russian warriors, the poem as a whole was cited as an example of modern *skaz*.[38] Going back to Russian 19th-century literature, the genre of *skaz* has variously been described as a kind of narrative "made up of the actual elements of speech and verbalized emotions" and "a stylized rendering of a kind of meaningless, naïve chatter,"[39] or as a special kind

---

[36] Vykhodtsev, "Osobennosti," pp. 167–171; Matskin, "Kniga," p. 3; Ermilov, "Russkii voin," p. 2.

[37] Samoilenko, *Stikhotvornaia satira*, p. 110; Makarov, *Vospitanie chuvstv*, p. 34. For a discussion of both numerous prototypes and simultaneous versions, see Abranskii, *Smekh sil'nykh*, p. 315.

[38] "Readers are quite familiar with A. Tvardovskii's poem *Vasilii Terkin*, written in the style of a *skaz*, narrated by a battle-seasoned Russian soldier" (*Poeticheskii slovar'*).

[39] Eikhenbaum, "Kak sdelana 'Shinel'.'"

of narration which "makes a word physiologically palpable—the whole narrative becomes a monologue, it is addressed at every reader" and which "draws the reader, rather than the character, into the prose. Herein lies its close connection to humor."[40]

Tvardovskii's poem obviously fits all the criteria, though the principles of *skaz* as a genre in the Soviet context were somewhat different from the classical ones. In the first post-revolutionary years, "the function of the skaz changed in its very essence—*readers became heroes*" and "the subject of skaz became its consumer,"[41] whereupon Socialist Realism encouraged closer and more direct contacts between readers and writers, irrespective of the genre.[42] Now, during the war, the production-consumption chain became even more circular and complex. Whether or not they used to be readers or not in more peaceful times, in the harsh reality of the war many at the front line turned into writers. Professional satirists noted with some surprise that, while the Soviet press "in peaceful times suffered from a lack of humor,... in front newspapers there is always a comic section, or a column, or satirical poems, and the language itself is lively and colorful, and Red Army activists contribute quite a lot."[43] The country's leading satirical journal was receiving thousands of letters with ideas, suggestions, plots, and anecdotes every year,[44] and Tvardovskii himself said later that his own history as the poem's author, if not the history of Terkin as a character, takes its beginning from the moment he started receiving readers' letters as the creator of "the book about a warrior."[45] Many of these letters contained suggestions for Terkin's further adventures at the front and for his future after the war. A reader shared his thoughts on how it might be good to "let Terkin join 'the agricultural front'," offering his help in the preparation of a

> comprehensive brochure with a collection of texts... "Terkin in agriculture"... with illustrations and various chapters and subtitled sections—Terkin on a collective farm, on a cooperative farm, on a dairy farm, in a poultry-house, on tobacco or beetroot plantations, in an orchard, in a vegetable garden, growing watermelons, at a grain elevator, at a fishing facility, and so on and so forth.[46]

In general, people were likely to "assign Terkin the profession they themselves were most familiar with."[47] Others took the liberty of continuing the Terkin story without sharing it with the author. The author did not mind, because, as he himself acknowledged, "*Vasilii Terkin* emerged from that half-folkloric modern 'element' that includes satirical pieces in newspapers and amateur wall

---

[40] Tynianov, *Poetika*, p. 160. [41] Dobrenko, "Russkaia literatura," p. 250.
[42] Drubek-Meyer, "Mass-Message," p. 129.
[43] "Satira i iumor," contribution by David Zaslavskii.
[44] Samoilenko, *Stikhotvornaia satira*, p. 11. [45] Tvardovskii, "Otvet," p. 204.
[46] Tvardovskii, "Kak byl napisan," p. 264. [47] Vykhodtsev, "Osobennosti," p. 169.

newspapers, stand-up comedy, folk verse, joking songs, peep shows, and so forth. Now he himself has generated much similar material in newspapers, popular entertainment, and folk humor. Whence he came, there he returns."[48]

It is probably fair to assume that many of the roles suggested by dedicated readers for Terkin in various areas of post-war "socialist construction" would have made him look quite comical. Comical, but never ridiculous; to be understood and sympathized with, taken as proof of a continuity of tradition, however unpredictable the dark surprises of the war and whatever the future might have in store— such is the function of these war heroes, heirs of the folk tradition and of the great future alike.

It is different for the enemies, who are our next topic.

Erenburg's *War, 1941–1945*: A Question of Trust

A latter-day researcher of World War Two satire noted that "the years of the Great Patriotic War, from the viewpoint of literary history, are justly called the era of journalism,"[49] and it would be no exaggeration to say that the one journalist whose name would have automatically come to mind to anyone who lived through the great war was Il'ia Erenburg. According to at least one account, at a meeting with Soviet writers during the war the Soviet ambassador to London went so far as to say that "'throughout the war there were only two people [in the Soviet Union] whose influence was equally great.' One was Erenburg, and the second one remained unmentioned—apparently the diplomat became terrified of his own idea to compare this second person with anyone whatsoever."[50] Jochen Hellbeck compares Erenburg's influence during the war to that of a prominent figure on the other side of the border: "In terms of his efforts to shape the fighting morale of the Soviet community, Erenburg was comparable to Goebbels and his propagandistic efforts on the German side."[51]

However, in June 1941 it was by no means obvious that Erenburg would have this role in Soviet wartime propaganda. It was almost by chance that this writer with a colorful biography (he had spent years in Europe), whose status in Soviet letters at that time was uncertain, would end up becoming "the country's only ideologue" ("*edinstvennyi ideolog strany*")[52] in the earliest days of the war and continue being the most widely read author until its very end. Unquestionably, he was perfectly qualified for this kind of job, with his "solid basis in world history and culture, a brilliant knowledge of modern politics and European art that the

---

[48] Tvardovskii, "Kak byl napisan," pp. 268–9.
[49] Mel'nichenko, "Fenomen," p. 30, with reference to Morokhin, *Satira*, p. 3.
[50] Frezinskii, *Ob Il'e Erenburge*, pp. 221–2.   [51] Hellbeck, "'The Diaries'," p. 588.
[52] Sarnov, "Shest'desiat let," p. 139.

writer acquired in the 1920s and 1930s while working abroad."[53] A significant proportion of the more than fifteen hundred articles he authored over the course of the four years of the war[54] were satirical pieces, which were especially beloved by his readers—and which will be central to our analysis.

Erenburg must have taken the lead from Gorky's injunction to create documentary satire by making the enemy ("bourgeois" in Gorky) press "speak in facts" ("*govorit' faktami*").[55] The writer's trademark was his reliance on original—or supposedly original—documents, be they the diaries and private correspondence of soldiers and officers (mostly killed, but also POWs), radio broadcasts, or newspaper publications. No one else, on either side of the front lines, surpassed Erenburg in his ability to process so much material, so quickly, and to be so prolific.[56] The Soviet press and subsequent publications on wartime journalism routinely praised Erenburg's rendering of the German primary sources for its "documentary character, ... a special kind of authenticity, the sense of a 'historically concrete' and 'untransformed' truth."[57] Historians of the future were advised well in advance that they would need to "study Erenburg's *fel'etony* carefully" as documents of the era.[58] The writer himself was reported to have refused to call some of his pieces "*fel'etony*" (the word used in Russian for satirical newspaper pieces), because "in a *fel'eton*, according to the laws of the genre, one can make things up, but here everything is completely true, taken from reality. Irrefutable facts and documents. So, why confuse the reader?"[59]

The advantages of relying upon original sources for ridiculing the enemy were obvious. First, it implied that the accounts could be trusted—it was, after all, "the German army talking about itself," to quote the frequent title of Erenburg's public talks, or, in an even more direct style, "Fritzes On Fritzes."[60] Situated somewhere between news and storytelling, satirical pieces of this kind satisfied two essential needs of their readers: the thirst for knowing the true state of things, on the one hand, and, on the other, the desire for stories, for entertainment. At the very heart of this particular kind of documentary satire was a humorous situation wherein primary sources were taken to be reliable in representing a higher, more general reality exactly because they lied in their primary capacity, be they official reports or private diaries. "What is necessary for a description of German heroism," Erenburg wrote, "are a mediocre journalist and a quart of schnapps. Thus, we learn that a certain German pilot shot down three hundred eighty English

---

[53] Morokhin, "Dokument," pp. 76–7, with reference to: Tsurikova, *Utverzhdenie*, p. 8.
[54] Rubashkin, "Erenburg," here p. 32.
[55] Morokhin, "Dokument," p. 76, quoting Gorky, "Kakim dolzhen byt'," p. 386.
[56] Hellbeck, "'The Diaries'." [57] Morokhin, "Dokument," p. 76.
[58] Rubashkin, "Erenburg," p. 34, quoting Matskin, "Pisatel' v stroiu."
[59] Ortenberg, *Iiun'—dekabr'*, p. 58.
[60] "Fritsy o fritsakh." *Krasnaia zvezda*, September 15, 1942. Throughout the chapter, all references to Erenburg's texts are based on Erenburg, *Voina*, but for ease of reading, the endnotes will cite the primary source.

airplanes, that six German soldiers destroyed a whole Serbian division near Scutari, and that three German soldiers surrounded a Soviet battalion."[61] Clearly, the report's German authors included the numbers to add credibility to their communication, making it all the more laughable that none of the events referred to actually took place. The Germans' total disregard for facts, when they "started the war... with hysterical enthusiasm, 'annihilating' the Red Army every day,... 'liquidating' the Soviet air force every day," became the tool of their own demise when people started wondering "how it was possible to 'destroy' for a third or fourth time an air force that had already been 'destroyed' a week before."[62] What is *reported in* the original pieces is not what is *communicated by* these pieces and picked up by the interpreter (Erenburg). The former refers to (falsified) evidence of something that never took place; the latter refers to an acknowledgment that the reports lie.

Time and again, Erenburg emphasizes the discrepancy between the traditional expectations of the genre of newspaper reporting (presentation of facts) and the fact that deceit and misinformation have been perfected to a professional level in Nazi Germany. He writes that

> the German army has special "propaganda squadrons"—"RK."... According to an instruction authored by Goebbels, RKs must engage in "active propaganda," specifically "to break the enemy's will to resistance by disseminating false and demoralizing information..." Within Germany, according to the same instruction, the RK squadrons must "edit facts, transforming them when necessary, in order to strengthen the spirit of the German people." What does "transforming, editing facts" mean? It means, quite simply, to lie. They must lie to their enemies. They must also lie to their own people.[63]

Terkin, we will remember, "could lie for a laugh, / But never lied for lying's sake." The implied difference (*our* side only reports the truth; *they* always lie) is crucial and highlights an issue of primary importance in wartime: how does one know whether to trust propaganda, and whose propaganda to trust? How does one distinguish, if at all, between the information supplied for the enemy's consumption and that which is directed toward one's own people? To put it in yet simpler terms—how does one learn to read propaganda correctly, whatever its nature? After all, both sides publish victorious reports and have inspiring slogans and images that capture one's attention. In practice, of course, Kenneth Burke's vision of propaganda as "applied literature"[64] was equally applicable to either party, which made it all the more important to convince the target audience that there

---

[61] "Lozh'." *Krasnaia zvezda*, August 29, 1941.
[62] "Voina nervov." *Krasnaia zvezda*, September 4, 1941.   [63] "Lozh'."
[64] Burke, "Auscultation," p. 55.

were reports, and there was propaganda; there was information, and there were lies; there was news to be taken as facts and there was wishful thinking disguised as news, to be decoded and exposed as deception.

Thus, Erenburg's documentary satire addresses the question of trust, fundamental to the relationship between a state and its citizens, war or no war. If the genre of a newspaper report or a radio broadcast, with references to dates, figures, and names, is no guarantee of reliability, if what the audience would usually perceive as a "document" (that is, a product of a genre that by its very definition lays claims to truth) is actually just a piece of evidence (of the source's unreliability), then the whole system of orientation in the discursive field of propaganda changes, and the most basic categories outlining the distribution of responsibilities in a well-ordered world are deprived of their meaning. If Erenburg's ironic interpretation of the German reports is much more trusted than the original reports themselves, then "primary" no longer implies "authentic," and it is the Soviet journalist's commentary on the enemy's propaganda machinery that provides true information on how false information is produced by the other camp. "Various departments" in Goebbels's information ministry are said to have carefully outlined duties for "transforming" facts before publication in mass media: "There is one describing atrocities, another collects data of an ethnographic nature, the third one concocts *lubok*-like pieces on the incredible courage of the Germans."[65] Journalists are no longer people whose job is to write short topical pieces, with "German journalists [being] clerks in the propaganda ministry," who "even in peacetime... were wearing a uniform and obeying military discipline."[66] Nor is science any longer what it used to be:

> In 1938 the Nazi journal *Archiv für Biologie und Rassengesellschaft* published an article under the following title: "On the Use of Aerial Bombardments from the Standpoint of Racial Selection and Social Hygiene." The author claimed: "People with a damaged nervous system cannot bear large aerial bombardments. Thus, aerial bombardments will help us detect neurasthenics and remove them from social life..." Now the German press is vehemently protesting against the aerial bombardments of German cities.... We are waiting for an authoritative statement by the journal.... Clearly, these racists must explain to the residents of Essen and other German cities that bombardments are useful because they target neurasthenics. But could it be that the contributors to the respectable publication also fell victim to neurasthenia under the four-ton air bombs?[67]

Sometimes there are discrepancies between the quasi-scientific interpretations of reality within the Nazi scholarly community and fascist politicians:

---

[65] "Lozh'." [66] Ibid. [67] "O pol'ze bombardirovok." *Pravda*, September 22, 1943.

But Aleksandru Randu... determined that Romanians are the master race... "Romania is the cradle of the Aryan race... the only people to have inherited the spirit of the Roman empire." Imagine Hitler reading this! Because he thought that the cradle of the Aryan race is in the boozers of Munich. But no! I am not even talking of Mussolini's exasperation. He was the first to call his beaten divisions "the heirs of the Roman empire." But now it turns out the Romanians are the real "heirs."[68]

Erenburg's *War, 1941-1945*: Knowing What, and How Much

Examples could fill pages and pages, but the ones quoted here are quite representative. Erenburg is careful to reproduce significant parts of the original text in order to demonstrate that whatever ridiculous incongruities there are in the Nazi world view and in the presentation of events by the German mass media, they all come from a faulty perception rooted deep in the enemy's world order. Quite simply, things are not adding up in the Nazi universe: factual reports have nothing to do with facts, scientific research asserts blatantly false claims, government officials are busy making sure that whatever leaves their desks is not true but false, and journalists get drunk before putting pen to paper to write supposedly accurate and inspiring pieces. It is as if they got their "semantic scripts" wrong, which, according to the prominent humor researcher Viktor Raskin, is what happens in a humorous situation.[69] Coming from a completely different tradition, Gilles Deleuze makes a similar point: "You cannot help but laugh when you mix up the codes."[70] Or, shall we add, when your enemy mixes up the codes.

The Germans consistently get their "semantic scripts" wrong and "mix up their codes" also when it comes to private experiences, the daily organization of their own lives. The Soviet readers who see Erenburg's excerpts from the private correspondence and diaries of German soldiers and officers are likely to get the impression that the people on the other side are reading the war in the wrong key, off-beat, missing its pathos and tragedy. For example, the wife of a Rottenführer is devastated that she carelessly exchanged a suitcase for a beautiful armchair, and now that the houses in their Berlin street have been destroyed by allied bombings and she "wants to escape," she must confront the tragic question of "how to pack the linen." "Luckily," Erenburg adds, "she will now be able to swap her husband's civil clothes for a backpack, as her Rottenführer has been killed by the Desna river."[71] In a booklet containing instructions for soldiers sent to the front Erenburg finds "various tips that can come in handy in wartime, for example,

---

[68] "Bednye muzykanty." *Krasnaia zvezda*, July 9, 1941.
[69] Raskin, *Semantic Mechanisms*, quoted in Wepler, "Nabokov's Nomadic Humor," p. 82.
[70] Deleuze, *Desert Islands*, p. 258.   [71] "Moral'." *Pravda*, September 22, 1943.

advice on which wine to drink with fish and which with poultry."[72] The Berlin newspaper *Völkischer Beobachter* supposedly reports that "sacred ideals are burning" in the hearts of soldiers looking forward to the "invasion of the Russian soil"; Erenburg explains, on the basis of the numerous diaries and letters he has read, that this is because "there is a promise of roasted chickens and Iron Crosses."[73] An officer by the name of Fritz Weber carefully records in his diary the progress of his culinary explorations in Soviet territory: "7 July. Managed to get 2 chickens and prepared them, unfortunately, didn't finish...22 July. Slaughtered a pig and dressed it...26. The unit butchered a pig. First-rate meat and bacon...28 July. Had nothing to eat all day." Erenburg then adds: "That is the end of the diary. Two days later Red Army soldiers 'dressed' Fritz Weber."[74] However oblivious the authors of the original lines might have been to it, their testimonies as reproduced by the Soviet journalist might be seen as examples of Menippean satire, which, in Bakhtin's interpretation, is a genre of "last questions," of thresholds and transitions.[75] They themselves may not have realized it, but they were about to cross the threshold into the other world, and the requests and promises made, the questions asked, the anecdotes shared and revealed in a different language to the unintended reader were thus seen in a completely different light.

Terkin, of course, also mixes up the codes, being both a "Russian wonder-man" (*"chudo-chelovek"*) and a joker, a hero and a clown. He is also open about his desire to survive and to live, about the discomforts of hunger and the joys of having a meal at the right time, the concerns of the body often taking precedence over lofty deliberations. But there is an important difference: in his case, neither the desires nor their satisfaction are ever to excess. If he eats, it is just a meal, "Simple, healthy army food." If he wants to enjoy himself, it is just a bath; if he drinks alcohol, it is just a bit. If he fantasizes about a woman, it is always that one special girl he will be looking to impress on that one special evening. If Terkin's longings and pleasures are slightly humorous, it is only because they are those of a living body, and the hero's being in tune with the healthy demands of his body is as natural to him as serving the country at the time of need. Just as the Soviet regime itself is natural and healthy, so, too, is the collective body of those serving it.

Nazi soldiers, on the contrary, know no restraint; the temptations of excess are too great to resist. They recognize no boundaries in the satisfaction of their desires, just as they recognize no borders between states:

As they invaded Paris, Hitler's soldiers marched under the Arc de Triomphe. They

---

[72] "Eshche odnogo." *Pravda*, August 17, 1941.
[73] "Pauki v banke." *Krasnaia zvezda*, September 20, 1941.   [74] Ibid.
[75] Bakhtin, *Problems*, p. 111.

were ordered to shout "Heil!", but they could not do it, their throats blocked by food. It seemed they were blowing into trumpets, but these were no trumpets, but rather Lyon sausages, which the soldiers were hurriedly stuffing into their mouths.[76]

There is a sense of the enemy army being composed of creatures not quite human, a point to which we will come back later. In the meantime, we should just note that in Erenburg's rendering the authors of the original confessions are depicted as unwittingly confirming "a kind of exponential rule for pleasure" whereby anything beyond engaging in two kinds of pleasure at once "becomes perhaps more obsessional than perverse, more baroque than delicate"[77]—and more ridiculous, we might add, as is any kind of self-satisfaction that runs counter to conventional interactions with the world. The Soviet soldier, used to moderation, not in the habit of consuming more than what he needs, never finds himself in this ridiculous position. But the Germans do, like the unfortunate Fritz Weber who, knowing no limits in the consumption of chickens and pigs that do not belong to him in the first place, ends up assuming the role of a chicken/pig himself when he is "dressed" by the soldiers of the Soviet army.

Not having a sense of proportion in satisfying one's own desires leads to being "out of sync" with one's place in the world. This is one of the many reasons the authors and addressees of the lines Erenburg quotes appear not to be able to keep up with reality as it is, not as they would like it to be. Very often they are stuck firmly in the past, like the wife from Berlin who exchanged her suitcase for a cosy armchair at the wrong time, or "the gentlemen from the German information bureau who find it difficult to learn new tricks at their advanced age: they got used to playing at weddings, and now they are merrily fiddling away at funerals."[78] At other times, they would be too caught up in fantasies of conquering the world, so that even as a prisoner, a "melancholic German," is convinced that "in the end, Hitler will win," though he also worries that, after taking the last Russian city, they would have "just one regiment of the whole army [left]. And... there will still be the march into India to do."[79] The victims of megalomaniac fantasies include the all too gullible devotee of Goebbels's propaganda who foresaw himself in Siberia even before crossing the line of the Eastern Front, or the Germans who "are trying to explain to themselves how come the Russians have soldiers, how come the Russians have tanks" and "find themselves lost in explanations, because they've already destroyed the Red Army on paper. And now this 'destroyed army' is driving them westwards."[80] The Rottenführer's wife apparently saw herself as an

---

[76] "Moto-mekh-meshochniki." *Krasnaia zvezda*, August 9, 1941.
[77] Barthes, *The Neutral*, p. 33 (session of March 4, 1978).
[78] "K nim!" *Krasnaia zvezda*, March 26, 1944.
[79] "Orda na Donu." *Krasnaia zvezda*, July 12, 1942.
[80] "14 ianvaria 1943." *Krasnaia zvezda*, January 14, 1943.

embodiment of the ideal German housewife—a loyal partner and the owner of a beautiful flat with nice, fashionable furniture. The young soldier asking his mother for mittens for the victorious march into Siberia just before his whole regiment was obliterated by the Red Army must have over-identified with the image of an invincible German soldier out to conquer the world.

Zupančič speaks of the "relating of the 'universal essences' (characters) to themselves and to other 'universal essences'" that "always succeeds either too much or not enough."[81] In our examples, the "universal essences" of an ideal wife, a brave soldier and a loyal recipient of state propaganda end up being not quite adequate to actual events in real life because these individuals struggle to realize their "essential" symbolic role. Zupančič sees this misjudgment of "either too much or not enough" as the building block of "most comic situations and dialogues."[82] There are, of course, hardly any dialogues in Erenburg's pieces—at least not in the sense of his characters talking to each other. However, his satire is essentially dialogic in that he brings out the absurdity of the enemy's claims, actions, and forms of being in the world by juxtaposing an earlier report with a later one, a newspaper article with what actually happened, a person's intentions with actual events, the name of a department with what it actually does, or the definition of a profession with the duties actually performed by the people in this profession. There is a dialogue between different reports on the same event, and a dialogue between those still in a state of ignorance and those who already know and realize their knowledge has come too late.

This dialogue is, of course, not direct, but mediated. Erenburg "quotes what different fascist newspapers...have to say" concerning the same event, so that "sometimes the content of a [primary] document is shown to contradict human reasoning itself."[83] The Soviet journalist has the privilege of true knowledge, while the Germans must acquire this knowledge the hard way, once what they thought they knew is tested by harsh reality. If the formula of fatal innocence is "they know not what they do," and that of absolute cynicism, as per Peter Sloterdijk (and later Slavoj Žižek), is "they know very well what they do, and still do it," then the enemies in Erenburg's presentation follow the path of "they think they know what they do, and discover the truth only by doing it," which can best be described as the way of the fool. Enemies who are fools deserve being talked about sarcastically, as Erenburg does when he quotes from the broadcast of the German Information Bureau reporting that

> between the Bug and Dniester rivers there were local battles, in the course of which we [i.e., the German army] captured prisoners,

---

[81] Zupančič, *The Odd One In*, pp. 36–7. [82] Ibid.
[83] Morokhin, "Dokument," pp. 76–82, 79.

and then continues:

> One thing is unclear: why are the Russians, stuck at river crossings, drowning in mud and defeated by the German tanks, still advancing dozens of kilometres every day? According to the German Information Bureau, the Russians are stuck. According to the Fritzes, the Russians are advancing. Clearly, the Fritzes know better...[84]

The "Fritzes" are the German soldiers and officers at the front, those actually going through the experience and gaining knowledge the hard way, the Russian attacks having an unmediated effect on their lives, their bodies, and their very existence. Those who started the war confident of a speedy victory have become unrecognizable just a few months later:

> Their hair has gone white from frost. They've forgotten about "the crusade," about signs of racial belonging. They've even forgotten about trophy glass holders. They now prefer warm jackets to Iron Crosses, and even generals dream of belly-warmers rather than of "Great Germany."[85]

A former dedicated reader of Goebbels' victorious reports learns the truth about the position of his army

> from soup. When the Fritz smelled the disgusting stench coming from a bowl of soup, he mumbled a shocked "What is it?" Officers explained: "That's horse meat." But a soldier called Bernhard Schulze replied: "First of all, this is not horse meat, but dog meat. Horse meat is for the gentlemen officers. Second, now it's clear: we've fallen into a frying pan..."[86]

Others are forced to eat cats:

> The Fritzes are no longer listening out for the droning of airplanes. They're more interested in cats meowing. The supermen who used to dream of conquering Europe have switched to cat meat.... They used to think they were a step away from triumph. They used to think they had the world's riches in their greedy hands. Now they are hunting cats and dreaming of crows.[87]

Freezing in cold Russian winters, sniffing the air, or fine-tuning one's hearing to try to detect some unpalatable food replacement—all these ways of relying on one's body as a means of gaining knowledge about the true state of things are

---

[84] "K nim!" [85] "S Novyim Godom!" *Krasnaia zvezda*, January 1, 1942.
[86] "Oblava." *Krasnaia zvezda*, January 17, 1943.   [87] Ibid.

obviously vastly inferior to the ability to analyze, compare, and juxtapose pieces of information. Someone in the former position can be either a hero in a tragedy or a character in a comedy, but whether it is one or the other can only be determined by an interpreter with the privilege of a higher, more general perspective, someone who can compare and contrast, see inconsistencies, and draw general conclusions.

Erenburg's *War, 1941–1945*: A Question of Perspective

Paul Cefalu notes that "typical comic characters are invisible to themselves but visible to the world."[88] In this sense, Erenburg represents "the world," that is, an external point of view that offers a more complete and adequate picture of the behavior of those who are comical for being caught in the repetitive compulsion of their own ideology—or, more often than not, those who *had been* caught in it, as the writers of the private notes and letters he shares with readers are, for the most part, dead at the moment of his writing.[89] Then, the ridiculousness of the forward-looking request for warm mittens for the comfort of the future conqueror of Siberia is magnified against the backdrop of the impending defeat of the German army. So, too, the sentimental tone of the promises of glorious military endeavors in the spring when "birds will start singing, new grass will grow green, brooks will come back to life, and the German army will go on a major offensive" sounds all the more deserving of ridicule when an alternative perspective is proposed: "Undoubtedly, the grass will grow green. But it will grow green on German graves. The Fritzes will not hear the sounds of the brooks."[90]

One of the obvious differences between the representation of "our men" in Tvardovskii's poem and the depiction of the enemy in Erenburg's satirical pieces is the position of the narrator. In *Terkin*, the narrator's voice accompanies the hero and often merges with him. It is in this capacity of an insider that he *makes* jokes; he is the agent of humor even when he risks being a victim of the next, almost inevitable, accident at the front. Erenburg looks at his material from the outside, *finding* the comic in it, even if, or exactly when the material itself is supposed to be read in a completely different key; the documents and people generating the comic effect are not in control of it.[91] Whether the external point of view is simply that of the opposite camp in warfare, or is granted by the passing of time (the act of

---

[88] Cefalu, "What's So Funny," p. 50, quoting Bergson, *Laughter*, p. 17 ("the comic character... becomes invisible to himself while remaining visible to all the world"). Cf. also Avital Ronell: "The stupid cannot see themselves" (*Stupidity*, p. 21).

[89] Cf. this: "To an extent, Erenburg's own citations from the captured diaries already prefigured the death that he wanted his soldiers to inflict on the German enemy, for in most cases (save those diaries and letters that were taken from surviving German POWs) the author was dead" (Hellbeck, "'The Diaries'," p. 593).

[90] "Nastuplenie prodolzhaetsia." *Krasnaia zvezda*, November 27, 1942.

[91] Cf. Freud, *Jokes*, p. 181: "A joke is made, the comic is found."

interpretation taking place by definition at a moment in the future, when a document's author is dead), an external point of view always provides the option of alternative readings. An external observer and interpreter can foreshadow the possibility of what is presented as an event full of epic pathos turning into a farce, as with the coming of spring welcoming either the Germans' victory or their shameful defeat. As we know from Hayden White, "one narrative account may represent a set of events as having the form and meaning of an epic or tragic story, while another may represent the same set of events—with equal plausibility and without doing any violence to the actual record—as describing a farce."[92]

Quite predictably, the mention of the same event being perceived as farce on secondary reading takes us back to Marx's famous pronouncement about tragedy returning as farce. In a recent article on elements of the comic in historical dialectics, Joshua Clover expanded on this classical maxim by suggesting that the mediation of crisis "allows tragedy at one level to return as comedy at a higher level.... Comedy is in this regard not tragedy plus time, exactly. Comedy is tragedy plus scale."[93] In our context, both these elements of turning a past tragic moment into comedy are present: a temporal perspective, as well as a simple change of the optics applied as a consequence of the commentator not being the intended reader of most of the documents he comments on. Much of Erenburg's mockery of the German enemies is based on what was and what is, what is and what will be. Having set out as the snobbish exponents of what they deemed the world's greatest culture, who shared with their diaries reflections on how they could not remember "a single book translated from the Russian, not a single play," convinced they were out to conquer a country having "neither art nor theater," with a "capital...built by Germans [and] schools in large cities...organized by Germans,"[94] they ended up with an existence reduced to the bare essentials, sprayed with cologne and full of lice, hunting cats and crows for food. Having spent lifetimes mocking the "backward" Russian culture, after a few months of war they "are eyeing Russian felt boots with envy. They ask: 'What are they?...' German doesn't even have a word for them.... It's all new to the Germans. It's minus 30, and there they sit in their tiny little shoes. Sitting and crying."[95] Having blindly followed the man they had taken for a prophet, they find themselves with an ideologically bankrupt dictator who "no longer believes in the future. He is greedily hanging on to the past. He is shouting hysterically, 'I spoke... I conquered... I defeated...' Of all the verb tenses he has only one left: the past."[96]

In his study of tropes, Kenneth Burke offers "an over-all ironic formula" that is most certainly applicable to the German army's experience at the Eastern Front, and of which Erenburg makes full use in his sarcastic pieces: "what goes forth as

---

[92] White, *Figural Realism*, p. 28.   [93] Clover, "Genres of the Dialectic," p. 449.
[94] "Orda na Donu."   [95] "Ledianye slezy." *Krasnaia zvezda*, December 9, 1941.
[96] "S Novym Godom!"

A returns as non-A."[97] The formula of "going forth" in one state and returning in another is an adequate description not only of the private experiences of people unfortunate enough to be involved in the Nazi military campaign but of the whole narrative of the war presented by the German side. This is where a change in the optics applied, or a shift in the scale by which things are examined, can produce an effect of parody, and Erenburg successfully exploits this. In accordance with the original meaning of parody as "singing along," accompanying a piece slightly off-key in order to bring forth—and ridicule—certain features of it, Erenburg's "writing along" the events—that is, commenting on them either just as they are taking place, or else shortly after the death of those who recorded them—guarantees that nearly every accident and incident reported by the German side is offered an alternative—mocking—reading. From nursery school teasing to debates in high politics, repeating an adversary's words in a different key, with a different emphasis, has always been the preferred way to ridicule. This is where Erenburg's ability to produce nearly immediate reactions to whatever caught his attention becomes particularly valuable. He does not even need to change much by way of content; all he needs is a shift in tone, a different set of adjectives applied to quotations from the original sources.

This is exactly what he does, for example, when reading the death notices and a personals section in a German newspaper where

> the most exciting section is that of announcements. Eighteen German women notify the readers of the death of their Fritzes. It makes for nice reading. Of course, the Gretchens use poetic turns of phrase.... But then, the death notices are followed by others, much merrier ones: Fritzes and Gretchens are looking for partners. The announcements make it clear that the value of Fritzes has gone up: the "Führer's idea" has significantly decreased the number of breeders in Germany.... Seeing as the Fritzes in Germany are now in limited supply, she [i.e., one of the women seeking a partner] would be prepared to take an invalid. She is offering a shop and 60 thousand marks for a damaged Fritz.[98]

The sarcastic and parodic effect of repeating an original message "off-key" is strengthened by engaging two rather different genres—death notices and personals—in a peculiar dialogue with each other. Men die; men are mourned by their partners; partners of dead men look for new partners—it is as if all these were following each other in fast motion, with the last link in the chain casting a shadow of parody onto the previous ones. First as tragedy, then as farce, with hardly any time elapsing between the two, with just a shift of perspective in reading a document, a change of scale.

[97] Burke, "Four Master Tropes," p. 517.
[98] "Beskorystnye Gretkhen." *Krasnaia zvezda*, October 16, 1942.

Neither does Tvardovskii's hero differentiate between the public and the private, with the site and the time of war being just another place and time for living his life, of which death is as much a part as the knowledge that one is immediately replaced: one dies, another takes his place. Both regimes worked hard to eliminate the distinction between the private and the public, between "man as simply living, having his place in the house, and man as political subject, who has his place in politics," which Giorgio Agamben sees as "the categorical, fundamental feature" of social life.[99] However, in *Terkin* the elimination of this distinction leads to a calm acceptance of the war as just another kind of everyday routine one must live through, when Terkin's being at war is as self-evident as the natural course of his life, as his very presence in the world ("Well, it's war, so here I am"). He is touchingly indifferent to the suddenly accessible comforts of the bourgeois lifestyle, barely noticing "some count's chairs.../ In the dressing room" of the bathhouse where he has the first proper wash upon crossing the border into the enemy's territory. The only mention of money in Tvardovskii's poem is when the Soviet soldiers jokingly ask each other for more hot water ("Come on, add for another pfennig") to wash off the mud from the long road westwards.

For the Nazis, the question of value is different. For them, the issue is not personal worth, so persistent in the Soviet soldier's mind that even at a moment of death one is reported to be jokingly wondering whether he will be accepted in heaven "without a high school certificate." Instead, the question that occupies the enemies, brutal and ruthless in their hatred, is how much things are worth: How many jars of salt pork? How many sausages, fried chickens, expensive fabrics? "They destroyed Paris with sacks [i.e., to put booty in]," Erenburg reports. "From morning till night one command only could be heard: 'Twenty pairs of ladies' tights! Forty silk shirts! Three hundred metres of English covert cloth!'"[100] While the Soviet fighters are confident of their equality in the face of both misfortune and happiness ("From Ivan to Foma, / Dead or alive, / All of us together—it's us, / The people, Russia"), the only equality the Nazis seem to be interested in is one convertible into a monetary equivalent: How much would a new partner be worth? Would there be a discount for an injured one? Like a living illustration (though not living for long, considering most of Erenburg's sources) of Adam Smith's dictum on the innate urge of human beings to "truck, barter, and exchange one thing for another,"[101] they are driven by the most primitive capitalist urges. Even when succumbing to their base instincts, they remain calculating: "Love for them is a mix of cattle barn and stock exchange."[102] In this, they are ridiculous for exactly the same reason they are ridiculous in everything else they do: they refuse to acknowledge that the war has changed the rules. They are

---

[99] Agamben, "Das unheilige Leben," p. 20.   [100] "Moto-mekh-meshochniki."
[101] Smith, *An Inquiry*, p. 25.   [102] "Beskorystnye Gretkhen."

ridiculous in the same way that anyone attempting to keep on conducting regular business during the time of carnival would be.

Erenburg's *War, 1941–1945*: Authenticity and (Self-)Parody

Of course, Erenburg chooses his sources with great care, making sure the satire works and that it is not so much him satirizing, or parodying, the enemy's ideology and its realization as the original voices themselves doing the self-parodying and -satirizing. It has been said that "the perfect comprehension of a phenomenon is its parody,"[103] but with documentary satire, an even better comprehension is achieved by detecting parody in what the phenomenon itself generates. The evidence Erenburg collects from the dead bodies and the prisoners of war works all the more as a parody of the official Nazi ideology for having retained what Bakhtin called, in a completely different context, "the memory of the genre."[104] The genre, in this case, is that of official narrative, and the memory of it comes across in the many inappropriate and confused remnants of it in a variety of private documents and testimonies. Such is, for example, the attempted rational explanation of a thief's behavior Erenburg quotes from a "plaintive letter by an aunt, from whom her nephew, a major in the German army, stole a watch." The considerate and politically aware aunt consoles herself that "this is because of nerves after the Eastern offensive."[105] An officer worried about the fate of the German army in the war dutifully records his schedule, which involves daily executions of Soviet citizens for weeks on end, adding some of his private worries, on which Erenburg comments: "He is so scared that his fear gives him scabies and diarrhoea."[106] A junior officer feels offended by a sergeant-major who did not divide the looted goods fairly: "I personally took only a scarf and a tea-strainer, but then our sergeant-major pilfered them from me and had the cheek to send them to his wife, claiming it was our shared booty."[107] To many of the Soviet readers of the time, the genre that these excerpts would be most reminiscent of is that of *skaz*, though not of the same kind as Tvardovskii's tale of a soldier. Rather than evoking the traditional Russian tales of exploits and adventures, these lines suggest satirical variations on the old genre associated, for the most part, with Mikhail Zoshchenko. This particular type of *skaz* does not seek to bring listeners or readers closer to the narrators, with their colloquial style and mundane preoccupations. Instead, it aims to achieve the opposite effect, emphasizing the abyss between what these narrators believe themselves to be (heroes) and what they actually are (petty thieves seeking easy profit).

---

[103] Agamben, *The Highest Poverty*, p. 5.
[104] Bakhtin, *Problems*, p. 106.
[105] Morokhin, "Dokument," p. 78.
[106] "Nemets." *Krasnaia zvezda*, October 11, 1942.
[107] "Fritsy o fritsakh.".

What makes all of these instances ridiculous and, ultimately, parodic of the original master-narrative of the enemy is not that they testify to the ideology having been abandoned completely by those called upon to translate it into deeds at the front, but exactly the opposite. They prove the inability to keep completely different registers of discourse apart—the headlines in party newspapers on the one hand, and on the other, one's own hygienic habits and intimate health worries; or the Führer's visions versus the misfortune of having one's watch stolen. Situations and objects are assigned incorrect "tags of meaning," like objects in a popular game, so that a heavily charged phrase like "shared booty" is applied to an act of petty theft, and stealing from a relative is explained by a reference to the general geopolitical situation. These are all signs of what Eric Santner calls a "collapse of social space and the rites of institution into the most intimate core of one's being,"[108] which, when observed from the outside, can be either tragic or ridiculous, depending on the observer's position.

"The Germans' diaries are so eloquent that, in my opinion, they do not require any commentaries,"[109] writes Erenburg, convinced that the primary sources will do a good enough job of ridiculing their own authors, their intended recipients, and the greater story that generated them. However, even leaving aside the question of the authenticity of Erenburg's sources, to which we will come back below, the very fact of his treating the diaries, letters, radio broadcasts, and newspaper announcements as evidence and as a tool for exposing the self-parodying potential of the regime changes the nature of this communication. Erenburg's parodic renderings of the content of the dead Nazi soldiers' diaries and letters, which purport to reveal the true meaning of the original documents by establishing a connection—or disconnection—between them and the official narrative, are instances of the Hegelian "absolute recoil," when the reaction to a phenomenon or event is the presupposition of the very existence of the phenomenon or event in the first place.[110] Erenburg's primary sources are "eloquent" only if their Soviet interpreter chooses to cite them and frame them accordingly.

With this in mind, both the "cardinal questions of satire" posed by Soviet researchers two decades after the war, concerning whether that which is ridiculous can be true, and whether that which is true can be ridiculous,[111] must be answered with a definite "yes." More than that: what is ridiculous has more chances of being true, because it discloses the internal mechanics of whatever presents itself as a fluent, consistent narrative, each constituent element of which (in this case—the official ideology, the reports, private testimonials, personal experiences) seems otherwise to fit into the whole quite smoothly. Men at war worried about their digestion, wishing for warmer clothes, and thinking about their partners back at

---

[108] Santner, *My Own Private Germany*, p. xii (Preface).
[109] Erenburg, *Na tsokole*, p. 293 (a letter from October 7, 1941).
[110] See Žižek, *Absolute Recoil*.   [111] Eventov, "M. Gor'kii," p. 204.

144 STATE LAUGHTER

home—put this way, all of it makes perfect sense in the context of the official ideology of either side. Nazi officers worried about their digestion and counting the eggs they had for breakfast before getting on with the killing of Soviet civilians, enemy soldiers asking for mittens well in advance for their march into Siberia, recording their fantasies about how happy their partners will be when they hear about the hangings of Russian women—put this way, the horrors of the system that could generate such incongruities cannot be overlooked. Then, one must respond with a full-hearted laughter that precedes thoughts of vengeance: "There is a need for pamphlets.... These muzzles must be painted in a way that would inspire the desire to shoot them."[112]

Importantly, Erenburg is only able to read the letters, diaries, and propaganda materials "off key" because he is neither the implied nor the intended addressee of these documents. Not being either the wife or the fiancée, an aunt or a parent allows him to step outside the communicational frame presumed by the original texts, where the medium truly is the message, in so far as this medium includes the bodies of dead enemies on whom most of the original documents were found. Erenburg's function here can also be compared to that of a medium, albeit in a different sense, as he takes over the voice and the words of defeated enemies. He can lay claim to being a reliable medium of the enemies' thoughts and wishes because he has a first-hand knowledge of the Germans. Even though he has not met every single one of them in person, he knows them as a type, so that individuals can never surprise him. He knows, for example, why some of the popular positive preconceptions concerning the German nation should be reconsidered. Thus, someone who would generally be regarded as a "pedantic German"[113] performs the most atrocious acts in the Soviet territory. In another piece, the introductory remark "as everybody knows, Germans are tidy" is followed by a summary of the author's personal observations:

> This tidiness becomes quite absurd. In Berlin, in their own flats,... people have their own sugar cans marked "sugar"; light switches are marked "light—[flip] up" (in one's own room!). When a German travels, he carries an umbrella in a special cover, and "Umbrella" is written on the cover. But then the transition from fanatical order to complete chaos is very quick. In the countries they invade, Germans behave like total savages: they break [things], burn [them], slaughter purebred cows, and cut down fruit trees.[114]

Some of the most admirable qualities of these people emphasize all the more how horrifying what they do is: "They are literate. They have the latest models of fountain pens. They analyze their feelings, but these feelings are rubbish. They

---

[112] "Satira i iumor," contribution by Il'ia Erenburg.   [113] "Nemets."   [114] "Voina nervov."

use their 'smart pens' to write down disgusting things, making no mistakes, either."[115]

This is a feature of many of Erenburg's pieces—turning something that would normally be a source of pride for the enemy and a reason for envy on the part of a backward nation like the Russians into a target of ridicule. The "yes, but..." rhetorical device is nothing new, except that here it is accompanied by a complete reversal. It is not just that the Germans are tidy, meticulous and advanced, while also being deeply immoral, evil monsters; it is that the advances in the German civilization only contribute to a delay in their perception of reality, while the proverbial backwardness of the Russians makes them winners in this unequal confrontation. Interestingly, the figure Erenburg describes in the examples quoted above is a typical German city dweller, that is, a character ridiculed just as much by the Nazis themselves, who built their "Blut und Boden" ideology on a return to the roots, to the native soil, to communal dwellings in the country rather than comfortable flats in the city. Those without "smart" pens and who do not necessarily know how to spell will win because they, like Terkin and his comrades and unlike the enemy soldiers, know what felt boots are and are familiar with the relative advantages of tea over alcohol in freezing temperatures, because "spirit warms us, but not like that," just as they know that whatever is "hard for a German is just right for us," and that the only thing one needs to fall asleep at war is a warm army hat, because "at first our nerves / Wouldn't let us sleep without a hat."

Whatever the actual topic of a particular piece, Erenburg makes it clear that his knowledge of "the German" is so accurate that—as paradoxical as it might sound—it should not matter so much whether his documentary satire is based on actual documents. Jochen Hellbeck shows convincingly that it is quite possible that at least some of the Soviet journalist's colorful evidence may have been simply invented.[116] Which is just as well, however, because Erenburg knows *the type*— and comedy is all about types, unlike tragedy, which is singular, comedy is generic.[117] The Soviet reporter is the one who can detect the reflection of the plural in the singular, whether this singular be a killed soldier's diary, or a letter home, or a particular line in an internal Wehrmacht instruction, or a news update in the Nazi media. He is, quite literally, "the subject supposed to know" speaking to those hungry for this knowledge, when "people were looking for an answer to the question of who the invaders were, how one could explain their inhumanity, how their mind works, what their life is like, what moral norms they obey" and it was comforting to believe that "the enemies themselves could provide an answer in their notes."[118] Hence the titles of some of his pieces: "Who They Are" (*Kto oni*); "The German" (*Nemets*); "Fritz the Historian (*Frits-istorik*); "Fritz the

---

[115] "Orda na Donu." [116] Hellbeck, "'The Diaries'," p. 592, fn. 55.
[117] Zupančič, *The Odd One In*, p. 37 and Dolar, "The Comic Mimesis," pp. 584–5 (also with reference to Bergson on this point).
[118] Morokhin, "Dokument," p. 78.

Philosopher" (*Frits-filosof*); "Fritz the Biologist" (*Frits-biolog*); "The Refined Fritz" (*Izyskannyi Frits*); "The Autumn Fritzes" (*Osennie Fritsy*); "Fritz the Writer" (*Frits-literator*).

Erenburg himself acknowledges that he is not quite unbiased in his assessment of the enemy's character. He openly advocates renouncing complexity in descriptions of the other side, arguing that

> war does not allow for any subtleties; it is built on black and white, on heroic self-sacrifice and on crime, on bravery and cowardice, on selfless dedication and on moral turpitude. Whoever might think of complicating the enemy's psychology would be knocking the weapon out of the hands of his own defender.[119]

Such was his response to those who had doubts about the efficacy of an extremely one-sided representation of the Germans, one of them being Zoshchenko, who voiced his concern that "Fritz" being consistently "represented just in one dimension... as a drunkard, an idiot, ... a thief, a marauder" was not convincing because, "even though all of it is true, ... it's not enough."[120]

In at least some versions of the theory of the comic, Erenburg's one-sidedness makes perfect sense, because "a comic character appears in the form of its *einziger Zug*, its 'single trait'."[121] In Erenburg's presentation, each of the Nazi aggressors taken separately, and all of them collectively, are but walking, murdering and marauding "single traits," because "there is little variety among the Fritzes. The Fritz is not complicated. He is not a genius you could spend a lifetime studying. In practice, it is difficult to find a new feature."[122] The invaders are a shapeless mass of "brewers, clerks, pimps, metaphysicians, wheeler-dealers, hangmen, superhumans, sausage-makers, baboons; ... SS-men with skulls on their sleeves; ... grey-green locusts; ... German women who look like drooling hyenas; ... vermin from the 'Adolf Hitler' division, thugs, adjunct professors with the muzzles of toads, quacking and croaking butchers."[123] Whatever variety and spontaneity their behavior may have, it comes from their being closer to animals than to human individuals. They are, of course, consistently compared to animals in the traditional pejorative metaphoric sense,[124] with Erenburg publishing a collection of his satirical pieces titled "In the Fascist Menagerie" and drawing vivid pictures for his readers of how "herds" of the alleged "Kulturträgers... are galloping to brothels,"[125] reminding them that "we must kill them not as people, but as vermin, as

---

[119] "Rol' pisatelia." [120] "Satira i iumor," contribution by Mikhail Zoshchenko.
[121] Zupančič, *The Odd One In*, p. 66, with reference to Benjamin, "Fate and Character," p. 205. Cf. also Weber, "Between Part and Whole," *Paragraph* 32, no. 3 (2009): pp. 382–99.
[122] "Satira i iumor," contribution by Il'ia Erenburg.
[123] Begak, "Kto smeetsia," pp. 161–2, quoting Erenburg's introduction to a collection of his satirical pieces previously published in *Krasnaia zvezda*.
[124] See, e.g., Sarasin, "Die Visualisierung."
[125] "Dnevnik nemetskogo unter-ofitsera." *Krasnaia zvezda*, July 16, 1941.

disgusting poisonous insects. Grey-green lice—this is what Fritzes are, malicious flies disguised as humans"[126] and expressing his conviction that "Nietzsche would be unlikely to recognize these predatory muttons as his followers. The amoral spirit of modern Germany is closer to a cattle barn than to a philosophical system."[127]

Erenburg's *War, 1941–1945*: A Numbers Game

But the comparisons with animals in this case go beyond the long tradition of curses, insults and comic representations.[128] A wild beast, a herd animal or an insect—at least from a commonly shared point of view—exists as a representative of a species rather than as a unique personality; in an animal, the generic can be expected to override the individual. The absence of a clearly defined personality is compensated for by the relative longevity of the species, which, just like the Bakhtinian collective body, cannot die, at least not in the same way a unique individual can. For the grotesque communal body, "death brings nothing to an end," with everything being "renewed in the next generation [and] the events of the grotesque sphere [being] always developed on the boundary dividing one body from the other and, as it were, at their points of intersection. One body offers its death, the other its birth, but they are merged in a two-bodied image."[129]

In an army at the front, there are no births, but there is a continuity in so far as each soldier is expected to persevere in pursuing the cause of those who died before him. The "point of intersection" is not necessarily a point of division between a body associated with birth/life and one associated with death/killing (even if the fact that most of the actual bodies that had gorged on free sausages and fried chicken were dead by the time Erenburg found out about their exploits adds a macabre carnivalesque touch to this behavior). Rather, the boundary dividing the bodies in Bakhtin's interpretation can also be understood as a boundary separating—or connecting—different forms of existence. It is not just about life versus death, indulgence versus abstinence. In the epic of the war that Erenburg draws, the variety of forms of existence is such that it cannot be easily subsumed under the general category of "bodies." The enemies in these presentations are not invincible—they are undead, akin to "what Lacan called 'lamella': it appears indestructible, in its infinite plasticity; it always reassembles itself, able to morph into a multitude of shapes; in it, pure evil animality overlaps with machine-like blind insistence."[130] This is why Erenburg reminds his readers:

---

[126] "Osennie fritsy." *Krasnaia zvezda*, October 10, 1942.   [127] "Velikoe odichanie."
[128] See, e.g., Robert Pfaller: "... in A. W. Schlegel it is already the animal in man on which comedy bases its amusing effects" (Pfaller, "Comedy," p. 268).
[129] Bakhtin, *Rabelais*, p. 322.   [130] Žižek, *In Defense*, p. 53.

One should kill off a hundred Germans, so that a hundred others start thinking. One should kill off a thousand Germans, so that that first hundred start hesitating. One should kill off ten thousand Germans, so that the hundred who started hesitating surrender. It's not stamina, it's not tenacity, it's the German stupidity, the fear of a thief facing punishment.[131]

Not quite mechanical and not quite animal-like, these creatures, "tall and miserable-looking, with square stupid heads, with eyes that appear to be made from muddy glass, stomping and guffawing,"[132] combine both extremes of being non-human. At the boundary where the different forms of life meet, "at the crossing point where automaton infringes upon life and constitutes its core... the comical object springs up, or, more precisely, the springing up of the comical object produces in the first place the very split and redoubling into automaton and life."[133] On the one hand, the bodies that have "the head not of a human, but of an automaton,"[134] "these automatons with girlfriends and guns"[135] are, indeed, "something mechanical encrusted upon the living,"[136] in Henri Bergson's classical definition of the comic. On the other hand, they are at the furthest opposite end from anything mechanical, because they are guided by the intensity of their immediate bodily desires—exactly like animals, or else like Bakhtin's "communal body marked by overwhelming vitality, enhanced appetite, and reproductive desire."[137] Even the rare instances in which the authors of the letters and diaries acknowledge their unenviable role in the events are marked by a realization that they are nothing but a herd of animals: "Marching. Marching. You march like sheep, and you don't know anything about either the situation or the targets. This is wrong."[138] These creatures are horrifying and ridiculous to an equal degree.

At the same time, Erenburg's sarcasm about the unthinking, blind obedience of the Nazi soldiers brings to the fore an important feature of sarcasm itself: often, what is deemed to be most deserving of mockery and ridicule are the very features one recognizes in oneself. Igal Halfin talks about "mirroring" in the interactions between those considered internal enemies of the Soviet regime and their interrogators, and the same could be said of the two warring sides.[139] Regardless of whatever differences there were between the two regimes, they both had the ideological demand to renounce the private in favor of the public and to internalize shared values. Indeed, why is the hero of Tvardovskii's poem—with his friendly advice to "just stop thinking," his conviction that there's no point to

---

[131] "Orda na Donu."
[132] Begak, "Kto smeetsia," pp. 161–2, quoting Erenburg's introduction to a colleciton of his satirical pieces previously published in *Krasnaia zvezda*.
[133] Dolar, "The Comic Mimesis," p. 583.   [134] "Orda na Donu."   [135] "Dnevnik."
[136] Bergson, *Laughter*, p. 34, quoted in Dolar, "The Comic Mimesis," p. 583.
[137] Tihanov, *The Master*, p. 289.   [138] "Dnevnik."
[139] Halfin, *Intimate Enemies*, p. 23 onwards.

"Thinking on one's own," and his habit of cheering up his comrades by reminding them "anyway, lads, don't waste time thinking, / We must hurry to beat the German"—to be laughed *with*, while the Nazi prisoner who brings Erenburg to despair by responding to the question "but what is your personal opinion about it?" with the same indifferent "I have no opinion, I just obey"[140] is to be laughed *at*? Why does Terkin evoke warm sympathy, while Erenburg's descriptions are designed to make the same reader shudder? How is being part of a substance made up of millions of unthinking bodies, closer to being undead than being alive, different from being part of a collective effort fully shared by all those participating in it? How does one mark this difference?

We have already discussed excess as a defining feature of the enemies' behavior. Everything they are, everything they do, is multiplied; a multitude rather than a collective unity, they are bound to invite distrust and resentment. There are no individuals; in descriptions of their behavior, a reference to "every" is hardly complimentary:

> Every German is used to the life of an automaton. He does not reflect, because thinking might disrupt the machinery of the state, as well as his, Fritz's, digestion. He obeys with enthusiasm. He is not just a nutcase; no, he is an ecstatic nutcase, he is an exquisite exemplar of nutcase and a top nutter.[141]

It is never a matter of just one weakness, one fault, one lack, or one abhorrent character flaw; it is always many. Their plurality is that of faceless imitation even when it comes to their art, as is the case when the printings of their songs, which are composed "not for a human voice, but for the barking of hyenas or for the meowing of tomcats in March" and whose "evil kitschy essence, blood-thirsty stupidity is hard to imagine," reach "millions of copies."[142] It is not just that Nazi soldiers and officers do not know how to restrain their own sexual desires, having "set up mating points"; they also engage in a whole range of sexual practices associated with perversion: "they are whoremongers, buggers, sodomites."[143] The contagious diseases carried by "these dirty creatures...lewd and greedy" are made even worse by their carriers' exceedingly repugnant appearance, when they come "with syphilis, with scabies, with slobbery baboon-like muzzles."[144]

Repetition is funny; numerous forms of the comic are based on repetition. But there is a fundamental difference between the Soviet army as a collective composite body that includes millions and millions of individuals, and the enemy army, where each and every person is merely a replica of all the others (at least in the way Erenburg depicts them). The instances of doubling that are jokingly

---

[140] "Velikoe odichanie." [141] Ibid.
[142] "Fashistskie mrakobesy." *Krasnaia zvezda*, June 29, 1941.
[143] "Vystoiat'!" *Krasnaia zvezda*, October 12, 1941. [144] "Beskorystnye Gretkhen."

introduced throughout the text of *Terkin* are suggestive of differences within the seeming sameness, as when "another Terkin" emerges and the comrades argue about which one is the real one, or else when the hero, wounded, feels prompted to protect the honor of his native region when realizing that a fellow fighter is from another area:

> We are not trying to claim other's native land,
> We have our own.
> Are you from Tambov?
> Fine with me.
> Me, I am from Smolensk.

Reminding his readers of Pascal's remark about one face never being funny, while a comparison of two faces can be amusing, Mladen Dolar goes on to "propose an extension of Pascal's adage: one is not funny, two is funny, many is not so funny either."[145] The confusion of the "two Terkins" in the poem, the protagonist's light-hearted chats with people he meets on the paths of the war, the exchanges between him and his comrades always revolve around the "two is funny" principle, with Terkin being "one," and his audience, or dialogue partner(s), being the second participant of the interaction. The enemies, however, always speak on behalf of a multitude and always address the void: their letters read by a wrong person in a wrong key, their inspiring political messages mistranslated into immoral and criminal deeds, their victorious reports exposed as lies on a massive scale. The Soviet hero never repeats himself; each episode is a different adventure, rendering justice to both the repetitive nature of life at the front and to its predictability, with Terkin's wit and ingenuity always winning. The Nazi fighting automatons repeat both themselves and everybody else in everything they do, think about, dream of, or aspire to.

Erenburg tried hard to show there was not much potential for diversity in the presentation of the enemy's nature. It worked, and it helped the readers form the right feelings about the enemy. At the meeting of Soviet satirical writers referred to above, one of the participants said:

> Some people think satire absolutely must be funny, that satire without humor is not funny. I think this is wrong. Il'ia Erenburg's satirical pieces are not funny—it's true. They are not humorous, but sarcastic. It is a very powerful type of angry laughter, and it gives Erenburg's writings the special force that made him such a popular journalist on the battle lines as well as on the home front.[146]

---

[145] Dolar, "The Comic Mimesis," p. 587.
[146] "Satira i iumor," contribution by David Zaslavskii.

However, as the end of the war was drawing near and the writer's epithets for the enemies were growing in intensity and multiplying, the accusations became more and more frequent that Erenburg was encouraging his readers to hate the German people rather than the Nazis.[147] It was time to turn against other enemies, to employ a new range of rhetorical weapons.

---

[147] Frezinskii, *Ob Il'ie Erenburge*, p 223; "Sowjetische Kritiken"; Sarnov, "Shest'desiat let," pp. 139–42; Passet, "Im Zerrspiegel," pp. 17–48.

4

"One Might Think It Is a Ward in a Madhouse"

Late Stalinism, the Early Cold War, and Caricature

> If they [the Russians] ever succeed in bringing to full light their real genius, the world will see, not without some surprise, that it is a genius for caricature.
>
> Astolphe de Custine,
> *Empire of the Tsar*

The Soviet culture of the Cold War required a genre that would be both highly accessible and congruent with a Manichean image of the world. With its combination of sardonic laughter as a key element of the culture of ressentiment and the directness and unpretentiousness of a soldier's humor, caricature satisfied both these requirements.

An Enemy in Pictures

These being the last years of Stalinism, one can look back and say that the postwar period marked the last one of the "dramatic and abrupt shifts" in the representation of the enemy by Stalinist propaganda[1]—a transition from a predominantly internal enemy figure to an external one. These being the first years of the Cold War, one can look forward and say, together with the author of a monograph on the Soviet image of the enemy, that this was the time when the "image of the enemy of the Soviet Union acquired its final shape" for the decades to come.[2] Both these factors were important for satire in general and political caricature in particular, as we will show below. Kam Shapiro notes in his analysis of Carl Schmitt's theory of the political that for Schmitt, the friend-enemy distinction is associated with "a complex dislocation" of the enemies' very being

---

[1] Bonnell, *Iconography*, p. 15 (Introduction). [2] Fateev, *Obraz*.

State Laughter: Stalinism, Populism, and Origins of Soviet Culture. Evgeny Dobrenko and Natalia Jonsson-Skradol, Oxford University Press. © Evgeny Dobrenko and Natalia Jonsson-Skradol 2022.
DOI: 10.1093/oso/9780198840411.003.0005

in the world: their "political identity is divorced not only from normative principles but from habitus; what is suspended...is not merely a set of ideologies (neither legitimacy, legality, religion, nor any set of normative principles) but a 'way of life'."[3] And there is hardly a genre that lends itself better to showing the "dislocation" and "suspension" of a way of life than political caricature, with its free license in overstepping the boundaries of realistic references. It is, thus, understandable why the beginning of the Cold War brought with it "large-scale coordination of political cartoon themes with newsprint propaganda efforts."[4]

Political caricature occupied a central place in the shaping of the Soviet citizens' view of the world in the first decades of the existence of the state, and the leading Soviet caricaturist Boris Efimov was right to claim that "foreign press was obviously baffled by the activity of Soviet satire when *Pravda*—a newspaper of international scale—as well as *Izvestiia* and other Soviet newspapers attributed to caricature the role of an important and valuable political material."[5] In his memoirs, Efimov writes that Stalin not only requested that he draw caricatures to illustrate certain international topics but also was involved in the most minute details of the execution of such orders, including the editing of captions.[6] Anti-Western caricatures were produced in the USSR in industrial quantities. As early as 1949, a US publisher printed a collection of anti-American caricatures from *Krokodil*, where they were thematically divided to reflect the typical rubrics under which they appeared in the Soviet press.[7] As Stephen Norris writes in his article on the leading political caricaturist of the Soviet era: "Efimov's remarkably consistent rendering of the West as the enemy makes his images not just important artifacts of Soviet socialism. To a certain extent, they *were* Soviet socialism"[8] (italics mine—NJS) and helped it define itself with respect to external enemies.

The examples on which the following analysis is based are taken for the most part from *Literaturnaia gazeta*, though references to images that appeared in other central publications are also made. The decision to concentrate on the newspaper of the Union of Soviet Writers is explained by its position more or less in the middle between the publications that concerned themselves primarily with serious political matters (*Pravda*, *Izvestiia*) and the one exclusively satirical magazine *Krokodil*. The status of a "literary" newspaper allowed if not for deviations from the strict party line, then at least for a certain variety in the genres of commentary and the form and subjects of discussion. As we will see below, this was of no marginal importance.

---

[3] Shapiro, *Sovereign Nations*, p. 106.   [4] McKenna, *All the Views*, p. 89.
[5] Efimov, *Osnovy*, p. 44.   [6] See Efimov, *Desiat' desiatiletii*.
[7] Nelson, *Out of the Crocodile's Mouth*.   [8] Norris, "The Sharp Weapon," p. 51.

On the Typical

With there being more caricatures than actual portraits of foreign leaders in the newspapers one can assume that, just like political posters in the early years of the Soviet power, the caricatures on foreign issues often "functioned as a 'who's who' of the capitalist enemy."[9] Thus the readers, and viewers, had a chance to develop associations with the names of Winston Churchill, Ernest Bevin, Mario Scelba, Alcide De Gasperi, Charles de Gaulle, George Marshall, Dwight D. Eisenhower, Trygve Lie, and other central and less central actors on the international political scene (Fig. 1; see also Fig. 4, satirizing members of the Italian government, their heads fastened to the front of a military vehicle driven through Rome by a lazy American officer). Likewise, the audience of the Soviet newspapers was made

Fig. 1. Caricature by Boris Efimov, text by Boris Laskin. *Literaturnaia gazeta*, May 1, 1951.

---

[9] Golubev, "Praktiki," pp. 350–1 (the article covers the pre-war years, but it gives useful background to the established pattern). Cf. also Golubev, "Interwar Europe," p. 131; also Bonnell, *Iconography*, p. 204.

familiar with allegorical representations of the general key categories: what "they" look like and what "their constitution" means (Fig. 5), what the American army is really busy doing (Fig. 2), what their laws are about (Fig. 3). It is not by chance that after the war, *Pravda* presented the publication of a three-volume collected work of Marshak's satirical poems and Kukryniksy's caricatures as a necessary addition to other chronicles of the great war,[10] or that during the Nurnberg trials in November–December 1946, central Soviet newspapers dispatched none other than the leading caricature artists to attend the courtroom sessions and draw portraits of the Nazi criminals.[11]

A caricaturist has a whole range of methods at his or her disposal. There is, of course, the classical device of animalizing the characters depicted, which goes back to the origins of the genre. Of this, there are countless examples in the Soviet press, with Boris Efimov so predictably translating his own drawings into words when he describes the defendants at the Nurnberg trials as "a kind of a ferret...; a bold rat..., a fox-baboon mix; the buffalo-type minister of construction Speer; the

Fig. 2. Caricature by Boris Efimov *Literaturnaia gazeta*, January 30, 1951.

---

[10] *Pravda*, September 6, 1945, a review of Marshak, Samuil. *Chernym po belomu: Stikhi S. Marshaka/ ris. Kukryniksy* (Moscow, 1945).
[11] Efimov, *Rovesnik*, pp. 168–75.

156 STATE LAUGHTER

Fig. 3. Caricature by Boris Efimov. *Literaturnaia gazeta*, August 4, 1951. First frame: volume entitled "Facts on the Atrocities Committed by American Invaders." The word inside the speech bubble: "I–de–ny!" Caption: "Under the weight of facts, or a depiction of Mr Austin trying to deny that Americans commit atrocities in Korea in defiance of the report by the Committee of the International Democratic Federation of Women." Second frame: volumes being trampled entitled "Law"; "Right"; "Justice." Caption: "Federal Judge Conger orders the chairman of the US Communist Party Foster to deposit a security bail of $10,000 before August 6th, otherwise Foster will be arrested." Third frame: The locomotive carries a poster saying "Sunday, August 5th" and a flag inscribed "For Peace!"; the two figures in the front carry a poster "Move Back" and a ribbon inscribed "Forbidden." Caption: "Despite the efforts of Bonn's chancellor Adenauer and his American mate MacCloy, thousands of young fighters for peace are arriving in Berlin as planned."

gigantic gaunt vulture Kaltenbrunner…; Goebbels's big-nosed parrot Fritzsche,"[12] or with countless infectious bugs of capitalism, imperialist spiders, and US army geese[13] adorning the pages of the newspapers, or with Aleksandr Zhitomirskii producing numerous images of politicians and whole political movements in the shape of animals (Figs. 8, 9). The "dislocated" forms of life traditionally feature combinations of the incompatible, when the world is ruled by imperialists who are actually bugs, leading politicians who are clinically mad, or—quite literally—ghosts of the past risen from the dead (Figs. 2, 6). The bugs wear dinner jackets and top hats, dead Nazi leaders reanimated as half-animal, half-skeleton acquire a supernatural ability to guide present-day Western leaders, and it appears that madness is the normal mode of living for all of them. Theirs is

[12] Ibid., pp. 179–80.
[13] See, e.g., the caricature by I. Semenov on September 3, 1949, depicting beetle-like capitalists, the words "Marshall Plan" on their wings, landing on the map of Italy—an allusion to the discovery that some of the crops imported from the US under the Marshall Plan were infected with Colorado beetles.

Fig. 4. Caricature by Boris Efimov. *Literaturnaia gazeta*, April 5, 1950. Text: "Italian authorities commissioned advanced automobile pumps from the USA which they use to disperse workers' demonstrations (From the press)." Caption: "The most advanced automobile pump made in the USA."

a world of disturbingly uncanny interrelationships between the physical and the symbolic, the present and the past, the living and the dead.

Translated from the language of caricature into the mathematics of the world order these drawings both reflected and created, each of these characters appears as equal not to himself as a person with a name and a life, but to an entity beyond him. It may be an alien species, another being, or a social function he happens to embody—but it will always be a reference to a general category. Hannah Arendt identified the tendency to think in types as one of the features of totalitarian consciousness.[14] For caricaturists, the ability to see the typical behind the individual is a professional skill. In this, they had a certain advantage over other creative artists, all of whom, regardless of the genre in which they worked, were expected to understand that people behave in accordance with the roles they have: "A class enemy kills the worker writer, a thief steals, a vulgar person produces more and more vulgarities, a lazy student fails all exams."[15] What better material for caricatures than

---

[14] See Arendt, *The Origins*. [15] Atarov, "18x24," p. 151.

158 STATE LAUGHTER

ИХ «КОНСТИТУЦИЯ»

Fig. 5. Caricature by Boris Efimov. The book's title is "Business." The caption: "Their 'constitution'." *Literaturnaia gazeta*, December 4, 1948.

this fatalistic vision of the world? The senator and the gangster are busy stealing because they are a senator and a gangster (Fig. 1); the spider is covering all of Europe with her spiderweb because she is a spider and does not know any differently, and since Marshall is like a spider (that is since he is made to look like a spider since he is identified as belonging to this species), he does what a spider does, whatever else he may be saying (Fig. 7). Such is the circular logic of cartoons in the service of ideology: one who looks like something or somebody else *is* this something or somebody else, and his character and actions are shaped accordingly.

One of the first Soviet caricature artists summarized thus the general trajectory of the genre in the Soviet Union:

> Together with...explorations of generalized, typical images in caricature, another approach became also prominent. It focused on individualized images expressed through concrete individuals, concrete representatives of this or that social group.[16]

---

[16] Igin (Ginsburg) I., RGALI, fund 2781, file 1, doc.872, pp. 42–4, quoted in Golubev, "'Zverinyi stil'," p. 241.

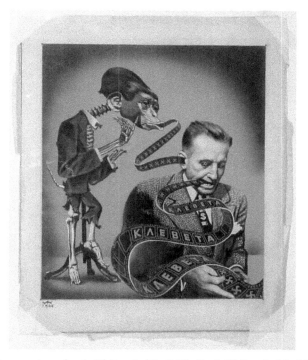

Fig. 6. Montage cartoon by A. Zhitomirskii. © Vladimir Zhitomirskii. *Literaturnaia gazeta*, November 30, 1949. Caption: "A factory of slander 'Goebbels—Johnson & Co.'."

Leaving aside for the moment the question of whether it was justified to see in these creative methods a distinctly Soviet phenomenon, we can note that in this presentation the two approaches to caricature are similar rather than different. In both cases, the emphasis is placed on the general—whether it be a "generalized, typified image," or "this or that group." Just as in the textbook example of the French king as a pear, it is the movement along the scale of the individual/general, from the uniqueness of the self to the generality of a different semantic group (with cross-species taxonomies being among the most frequent ones), that makes an image funny.[17] In Zhitomirskii's montage cartoons (exemplified by Fig. 9), the similarity between a human and an animal is supposed to generate laughter not only because of the conventional associations with humans behaving like animals but also because being made part of an animal species means being refused the right to individuality: "The particularity of a faceless animal is that in it, the natural and the biological come to the fore as something generic, as something

---

[17] See Petrey, "Pears."

Fig. 7. Caricature by B. Efimov. *Literaturnaia gazeta*, November 26, 1947. Title: "A Dollar Spider (To Marshall's Speech in Chicago)." Caption: "Close 'Ties of Civilisation' connect Wall Street with Europe."

that belongs to a category, to a range of similar entities."[18] Then, all of the subject's actions and words turn into a repetition of patterns prescribed by, and for, the laws governing the development of the species. Politicians and military leaders (Fig. 1) may look like satirized images of themselves—but they also look like a group of madmen, and it is their looking like members of the "madmen" category that adds to the ironic impact of the images, especially since the accompanying text announces that this is a "gallery of individuals in their usual, as it were, natural state." Likewise, in I. Semenov's cartoon "American Beetles in Italy" (*Literaturnaia gazeta*, September 3, 1949) satirizing the fact that Colorado beetles were imported into Italy with potatoes delivered from the USA as part of the Marshall Plan, a straightforward depiction of the American imperialists as Colorado beetles could be an insult or a metaphor, or both.[19] It is only once their being like beetles is justified by a kind of behavior that is characteristic of this

---

[18] Iampol'skii, *Demon*, p. 270.
[19] On shared features between caricaturistic and metaphoric likeness, see, e.g., Ross, "Caricature."

Fig. 8. Montage cartoon by A. Zhitomirskii. ©Vladimir Zhitomirskii. *Izvestiia*, March 27, 1952.

particular type of insects that the satirical distortion carries with it a pleasure of discovery of "as" being recognized as "is." In a cartoon reprinted from a Czech satirical publication that appeared in *Literaturnaia gazeta* on February 23, 1952 (Fig. 10), President Truman is funny not just because he is made to look ridiculous, but because he is made part of a line (or category) of unsuccessful aggressors: first Hitler, now Truman. In Kukryniksy's drawing "Team of Warmongers" (*Pravda*, November 7, 1946), the effect of the comic distortion of the appearance of each of the Western leaders sitting on the bandwagon driving into war and death is intensified because they are squashed onto a narrow platform like performers of a wandering circus orchestra. In I. Igin's illustration to a report on accelerated biological military research in the US, published in *Izvestiia* on March 25, 1952, Uncle Sam has given birth to a rat that looks just like him—and there is apparently much they share, as members of the same species, of the same type in terms of behavior and appearance.

The concept of "types" was one of the most semantically loaded notions in the Soviet theoretical-propagandistic discourse of the time. When one of the Soviet masters of ideology declared that "the problem of the typical is always a political problem,"[20] he might just as well be referring to the caricatures that accompanied many a page of international reports of the central newspapers, where specific

---

[20] Malenkov, *Otchetnyi doklad*, p. 115.

Fig. 9. Montage cartoon by A. Zhitomirskii. © Vladimir Zhitomirskii. *Literaturnaia gazeta*, October 1, 1947. The rubric above reads: "Friends." Caption: "Two friends are clearly represented, / Their faces and words are alike. / The moment somebody mentions Churchill, / McNeil cries: 'And Bevin, too!' "

political figures and specific political events were ridiculed through being typified. Not being equal to oneself or belonging to a category that is subsumed within a type larger than the original category or different from it (seeing the general in the particular, the social in the personal, the animal in the human) are well-known traditional conventions of caricature and of the comic in general of which Soviet propaganda made full use. In a synecdochal move, which some consider to be a feature of totalitarian paradigm as such,[21] any form of generalization was welcome in depictions of external enemies: seen from Moscow, they *were* the system they lived in, each of their actions was a transgression of some basic principle of humanity, and each transgression was indicative of the nature of things in their world which obeyed laws different from those governing the life of normal, law-abiding, honest citizens in peace-loving progressive countries. The American Secretary of State George Marshall is deemed to have transgressed international law and, by extension, biological laws; he turns into a spider-like creature (Fig. 7). The American government effectively lost credibility when it violated the laws of common sense by proclaiming a study of Soviet humor to be classified informa-

---

[21] Cf. Smirnov, "Sotsrealizm," p. 19, as well as Borenstein, "The Plural Self," p. 668.

Fig. 10. Cartoon reprinted from the Czech newspaper *Rude Pravo*. *Literaturnaia gazeta*, February 23, 1952. First frame: "Hitler's attempt..." Second frame: "...and what came out of it." Third frame: "The dreams of Truman and Co..."

tion.[22] By signing treacherous pacts and spreading lies about the Soviet Union, virtually every Western office-holder committed numerous sins against the demands of normal human decency and mutual respect.[23]

"The goal of artistic typization is in making all details of an image expressive of the internal essence,"[24] the 1956 Great Soviet Encyclopedia entry on typization explains. This double nature of the typical—*external* markers pointing to a more general category are considered to be expressive of the subject's *internal* essence— is at the core of Stalinist ideological practices in general, which, according to Igal Halfin, are based on the assumption that "every interior had been externalized."[25] The very same principle is also at the heart of caricature. Usually, these revealing markers are external to the bodies of the people depicted. Such, for example, are

---

[22] Boris Efimov's cartoon accompanied by Samuil Marshak's satirical poem appeared in *Literaturnaia gazeta*, September 9, 1952.
[23] See, e.g., Zhitomirskii's satirical photo montages to this effect, such as the one from March 21, 1953, satirizing the West German government having signed military agreements with other Western allies, and from November 30, 1949, where we see Lyndon Johnson speaking into a microphone, while a ghost of Goebbels is feeding him lies about the Soviet Union.
[24] "Tipicheskoe."   [25] Halfin, *Stalinist Confessions*, p. 4.

the accompanying accessories in nearly all the images of characters depicted as types—top hats, dollar bills, purses, cigars, striped trousers, masks, skeletons of dead predecessors. Quite often, however, these markers are external to the very species: insects' legs, pigs' snouts, dogs' muzzles. Either way, in the cases examined here, there is hardly any difference between animalizing the humans, turning their physical characteristics into markers of their social belonging, or making use of accessories that are purely external (with respect to the body). These accessories signal one's affiliation with a certain (social) class, just as being drawn with an ape's face or a pig's muzzle marks one as a member of an alien species. The social class and the biological one are no longer distinguishable. Capitalists have fat cheeks and bellies just as spiders have many feet; imperialists have wicked grins just as pigs have snouts.

By equating the significance of one's physical appearance with the symbolic markers of the person's position in the world, caricatures reverse the otherwise accepted semantic mechanism according to which one's "'name,' 'titles,' 'insignia' are semiotically reliable, [while] appearance [is] semiotically void."[26] In political satirical drawings, one's appearance becomes symbolic, just as accessories become inseparable from one's appearance in every single situation. One's very body becomes an insignia and one's insignia becomes part of the body, never changing, forever fixed. Thus, de Gaulle is tall (Fig. 1) because he is being "tortured by the question of how to come into power"; Churchill is fat and never without a cigar because he is the prototype of a capitalist; Truman has a certain hairstyle because he is a copy of Hitler; and so forth.

The more one is unlike oneself, and the more markers there are to establish one's belonging to a general category, the easier it is to classify a character within the general order of things, phenomena, and people. Supposedly, thus, the caricatures end up being even more reflective of the true nature of things than photographs, since "photography creates a fragmentary glimpse of truth, [while] the artist [including the caricaturist] selects, composes, and gives a synthesis of truth, therefore a higher and truer picture than the camera."[27]

Reflecting the Real Reality

Unlike traditional character caricature, political caricature in general, and the examples of it that were generated by a system most concerned with positioning itself with respect to its enemies, were designed to serve as guidance on whatever was happening in the world rather than as a study of human nature. With what might seem to be the least realistic and least serious genre of Soviet daily

---

[26] Petrey, "Pears," p. 52.   [27] Topolski, "Contemporary Comment," p. 166.

propaganda appearing alongside reports and analytical pieces that claimed to be reflective of a higher order reality, it made perfect sense for caricatures to replace actual portraits of foreign leaders in the Soviet press, so that "any official announcements quite often evoked associations with caricatures."[28] Keeping this in mind, Boris Efimov's claims that "Soviet caricatures of that period reflect, as if in a mirror, the butting muzzles [*bodlivye fizionomii*] of imperialists," or that "a caricature artist gets to the "core of the fact" at once, removing the covers whose function was to conceal this core,"[29] no longer sound intentionally absurd—we are dealing here with the "hyperreality of the typical," when that which was postulated as characteristic, and fixed, was more real than what actually existed.[30]

The Marshall-plan-crazy imperialists are like Colorado beetles because they do exactly what Colorado beetles do: they damage and destroy, so that the newspaper report accompanying the image becomes a metaphorical description of the real pest from which Europe is suffering. A pig with Wehrmacht insignia breaking out from behind the European Treaty may not be there in reality, but this is what the European Treaty *really* hides; John Foster Dulles looks like a pig because he engages in a pig-like behavior; one gets to see the characters involved in painting the White House brown (Fig. 11) because the drawing shows what these people are *really* engaged in. By this logic, it does not matter whether the Western leaders had actually been caught conspiring with Nazis to gain control over the world; if they had not, they could have been, because in fact, this is what they do—whereby "in fact" refers not to what really did or did not happen, but to the essence of things, beyond the layer of appearances and of what is known to have actually happened. Even if Lyndon Johnson may not be literally speaking in the voice of Goebbels's ghost, he would, if this were possible, and hence one would be justified in saying that he does. Even if these people do not really paint the White House in brown and do not literally cook the next war in a big "aggression" pot, even if they are not really as ridiculously tall, as fat, as evil-looking, these depictions are still truthful—in essence.

In 1931, Lunacharskii appealed to Soviet artists to "not only describe what is, but... to go further, to show those forces which are not yet developed, in other words, from the interpretation of reality it is necessary to proceed to the disclosure of the inner essence of life."[31] Some twenty years later, the Great Soviet Encyclopedia taught readers who decided to look up the entry on "the typical"

---

[28] Golubev, "Interwar Europe," p. 131. The author of these words analyzes primarily caricatures from the 1920s–1940s, but the sheer number of caricatures that continued to appear in the central newspapers after the war justifies the assumption that this was also the case for at least some time after the war.

[29] Efimov, *Rabota*, p. 23; Efimov, *Osnovy*, p. 45.

[30] The connection between Baudrillard's notion of the hyperreal which is "more real than the real itself" and the concept of the typical in the Soviet context was made by Dobrenko, *Political Economy*, p. 21.

[31] Bonnell, *Iconography*, p. 38.

Fig. 11. Caricature by Boris Efimov. *Literaturnaia gazeta*, November 4, 1950. Adenauer is depicted painting the White House (apparently) brown from a jar marked: "The Brown Paint of Nuremberg."

that "an unfolding, an expansion to their limit of the potentialities that an artist has detected in the real people he knows" is of primary importance in creating a truly "typical" image.[32] Both Lunacharskii's instructions for artists and the article in the encyclopedia allude to detection of a potentiality, to that which has not yet made its appearance. This is not surprising, since most references to "the typical" concerned the depiction of positive heroes—and one of the paradoxes of the era frequently commented upon was that "realistic" depictions of its heroes had little to do with their own physical, human selves. "The Soviet person in reality [was] better than he appear[ed] to be in his everyday life"[33] because the only temporal dimension in which this person existed was that of potentiality, of the future. This future may not be there yet; hence the mistake of a photographer creating a "superficial depiction of life," which "comes not from him *photographing* a ready, true material of life, but from his starting off by *seeing* the world as ready, ordered once and for all. But the world is 'not ready' yet."[34] The world may not be ready yet, but it is already visible to those who have the right capacity to see through the appearances, while the reality of antiheroes is, by definition, that of the past. The clash is not just between the young and the old, but between different

---

[32] "Tipicheskoe."
[33] Spasskii, "O poeticheskom geroe," quoted in Bogdanov, *Vox Populi*, p. 101.
[34] Atarov, "18 x 24," p. 151.

"temporal styles" of the regime, its "temporal pluralities."[35] The comic plays out at the point where these temporal pluralities meet, wherein those that are nearly gone are always at a disadvantage with respect to those who are "not yet" what they should be—but who are moving in the right direction.

The coexistence of these temporal pluralities defined the vocabulary of the Soviet political caricatures throughout the years of the Cold War, regardless of whether a particular drawing featured a juxtaposition between heroes and anti-heroes or not. Examining the topic with reference to the conflicting temporalities also helps us explain the otherwise perplexing fact that most Soviet caricatures, "their 'message' apart, could have come from any Western country,"[36] with most stock images (such as "a fat cigar-smoking capitalist with a piglike face surrounded by money bags") having originated in Western European sources in the late nineteenth and early twentieth centuries.[37] To a contemporary Western viewer, the incongruity between the fashion accessories, clothes and objects of everyday life that surrounded capitalists in the Soviet caricatures and the items that were actually available, fashionable, or recognizable in Western countries at the time was striking: "... too often in Soviet cartoons capitalists still have the fat white waistcoats and wear the out-of-date top hats of sixty years ago, although obviously the reality has changed. His dollars likewise, are symbolized still in coins and in bags, not in notes in bundles."[38] In the vocabulary of the Soviet caricature, faces and physical features played as significant a role as did accessories *from another time*. De Gaulle's height, Churchill's corpulence, Marshall's spider-like hands, Attlee's mustache, once repeated in dozens and hundreds of images in nearly every newspaper, would have soon become recognizable as associated with creatures who are stuck in another time just as much as those wearing top hats and dispensing coins from bags.

With caricatured representations far outnumbering realistic ones and whatever likeness there was being based on other caricatures rather than on other portraits, let alone the actual appearance of a person, in the Soviet context it was probably even truer than in any other that "a caricature is best contrasted not with a face but with already existing modes of representing that face."[39] Western leaders and general stock characters were depicted along similar lines by different artists: Efimov's bloodthirsty American general posing as a lover of peace for a photographer in a poster from 1958 entitled "A Peace-Lover from Overseas" may differ in technique, but not in narrative and message from Kukryniksy's numerous similar images; the image of the proletarian fist crashing those conspiring for world domination is pretty similar, whether it is drawn by L. Samoilov in his often

---

[35] Sabrow, "Vremia."   [36] Low, "Review," p. 169.
[37] Bonnell, *Iconography*, pp. 200–1. Cf. also Stephen Norris as a general reference for how Western examples influenced Soviet caricature (Norris, "The Sharp Weapon").
[38] Low, "Review," pp. 168–9.   [39] Ross, "Caricature," p. 290.

reproduced poster *Po rukam!* (1952)[40] or Kukryniksy in several of their works; the threatening shadow of fascism is a common element in many drawings regardless of their creators or the characters depicted. De Gaulle's scrawny figure and Churchill's chubby cheeks had already been copied and recopied so often that they probably turned into a sign of things already seen and long past just as top hats and dollar coins. Here one can speak quite literally of stereotypes in the primary meaning of the word, as "image[s] produced from a plate whose characters are fixed and which [are] preserved for subsequent prints."[41]

Such stereotypes were, unquestionably, quite useful as mnemonic exercises for training the right reactions to certain names, events, and images. Boris Efimov justifies the rather limited set of easily recognizable figures and images in more down-to-earth terms:

> It is unlikely that someone would hit upon the idea of chastising, for example, chess players for using the same "boring" chess pieces, say, the queen or the rook. After all, these "habitual" pieces serve to create an unlimited variety of new, interesting, and unexpected combinations and variations that bring true artistic enjoyment to those who love chess. In the same way, the British lion, Uncle Sam, and dozens of other similar allegories are the chess pieces of caricature artists, which serve us to create satirical situations that are always new, depending on the particular political events and facts of the day.[42]

In general terms, this description would hold for any self-contained semiotic system: fixed primary units of meaning obeying a special grammar of what is considered to be "typical," which defines the interrelationships between elements—and, ultimately, meaning itself. Thus, the outdated sartorial habits of the characters are not just clichéd representations of yesterday's fashion appearing ridiculous. They are defining features of the characters' status, which regulates their positioning in the network of relationships. They fix the characters' type on the temporal scale. As fashion items from a few decades ago, reproduced in many an image in various countries and contexts, the accessories of these figures are *still* recognizable, but as elements of satire of the past decades, they are *already* recognizably ridiculous.

This emphasis on recognizability, when images are supposed to be perceived as funny only in so far as they are *recognized* as having been established as funny, seems to run counter to the basic convention of caricaturistic humor, which usually calls for a combination of familiarity and of "the shock moment of an image."[43] It might well be, however, that in the Soviet political caricature the

---

[40] The title can be translated either as "Done deal!" or as "Caught red-handed." Both readings are possible, as the strong hand of a vigilant Soviet citizen lands on the miniature figures of capitalists conspiring to start a new war.

[41] Amossy and Herschberg-Pierrot, *Stéréotypes*, p. 25.   [42] Efimov, *Osnovy*, p. 58.

[43] Behrmann, "Bild," p. 93.

tension between the recognition and the "shock moment" that should create the humorous effect is simply of a different nature. Efimov is right when he says that the caricatured characters are just the means that "serve [artists] to create satirical situations that are always new, depending on the particular political events and facts of the day": it is not the images themselves, but rather the behavior of the habitually distorted figures in ever-changing situations that should be funny. There may be nothing new in how ridiculous de Gaulle, Marshall, Churchill, Attlee, Bevin, Johnson, and Adenauer look, but the incongruity between the world going forward, with new situations being created every day, and the predictability of the characters' set traits and habits should be humorous. Konrad Adenauer is ever an awkward, scrawny clerk desperate to please his new masters, but unable to give up on the Nazi models (Fig. 1); Harry Truman is always trying to think of new ways to shape American foreign policy so as to endanger the very existence of the Soviet Union, from attempting to physically bring down the invincible Soviet fortress to actually painting the White House brown, but he is as doomed to failure as all the aggressors that had preceded him, all those in whose shadow and with whose help he is trying to pursue his dark goals (Fig. 11); de Gaulle is pitiful in his attempts to make it "up there," which is inextricably linked with the need to sell himself to the highest bidder.[44] Their only connection to the future is predictability, as their behavior is based on past patterns inherited either from fascists or fat capitalists of the previous age, or else on the most primitive animalistic impulses; their only function in the present is to embody the past.

Hieroglyphics and Their Readers

The range of these emblems and allegories is just broad enough to make each character different from the others, but limited enough to make these characters recognizable as types defined by allegorical props. In a caricature nothing can be wasted, nothing is "just so" and everything has to be loaded with as much significance as possible, in full conformity with the etymological origin of both "karikatura" and "sharzh" (both *caricare* and *charger* meaning "to load"). Such is the nature of any example of political caricature in general, it being nothing else than "a calligraphic shorthand character, a convenient hieroglyphic sign"[45]—but this is especially in line with the Soviet indexical thinking of the time when everything stood for something, when every single action, fact, or phenomenon was to be perceived as charged with a significance beyond its appearance, its immediate function and the intention of its creator. In a Kukryniksy cartoon (Fig. 12) the gnawed dollar-shaped bone, the broken bowl, the lion's ridiculously

---

[44] See, e.g., Kukryniksy's "Passing a Viva to Qualify for the Rank of a Führer" in *Literaturnaia gazeta*, January 17, 1948; Efimov's "A Dollar-Patterned Horse," *Literaturnaia gazeta*, 7 September 27, 1947; Efimov's "The 'Judgment of Paris' Today", *Literaturnaia gazeta*, December 13, 1947.
[45] Topolski, "Contemporary Comment," p. 166.

narrow jacket that looks more like a baby apron, Uncle Sam's ungainly outfit that is apparently worn out and badly in need of repair—all point at the state of affairs in the capitalist world. In Fig. 5, the nails/claws holding the fake constitution, the blood dripping from the fingers, the dirty stains on the cover of the foundational law, the fat cigar, the grin on the ugly face with the eyes concealed behind dark glasses, the trousers whose belt barely closes on an extremely fat belly, covering extremely thin legs, the gun in the pocket and the dollar coin clutched in the other hand are all details that convey to the audience the clear message about the true nature of imperialism. In Zhitomirskii's depiction of Truman as a mad warmonger (Fig. 13), the message is not just in the ridiculous posture of the hysterical drummer and the agitated drumming, but in the suggestion that the body language, the hairstyle, the gestures, and the drumming itself are in fact a bad copy of Hitler's posture, Hitler's image, and Hitler encouraging his followers to march to a drumbeat.

But hieroglyphic signs are only of use if they can be understood as the minimal elements of a language—or at least of a narrative based on repetitive patterns. The Soviet political caricatures of the time published by central newspapers, with their fixed characters and a predictable set of references, can most certainly be seen as "sequences of discrete, juxtaposed pictures that comprise a narrative, either in their own right or when combined with text"[46]—in other words, comic strips. The reader to whom these cartoons are addressed would be someone who would be "enjoying it [the story] because of the recurrence of a narrative that remains constant...respond[ing] to the infantile need of hearing again always the same story, of being consoled by the 'return of the Identical,' superficially disguised."[47] Such, according to Umberto Eco, is the nature of a serialized narrative. This was by no means the only Stalinist genre that had features reminiscent of comic strips. Political cartoons, for obvious reasons, come closest to "real" comic strips, the only difference between the two genres being that the caricatures were mostly spread over many issues of newspapers rather than (at least originally) contained between the covers of a book, and the characters' adventures were not the fruit of an author's imagination, but (at least in theory) actual events in different parts of the globe. Like the characters in a comic strip, the actors on the international scene had to be always "in character," in accordance with the requirements of the type to which they belonged, just as they always wore the same clothes, smoked the same cigarettes, and had the same grin on their faces. Only if the heroes were recognizable could their adventures be truly entertaining—and only then could the news reports follow the strictly fixed plotline of a world populated by characters with fixed roles, in which contingency had no place.

---

[46] Hayman and Pratt, "What Are Comics?", p. 423.   [47] Eco, "Innovation," p. 168.

Fig. 12. Caricature by the Kukryniksy, *Pravda*, October 1, 1947. The bag restraining a human figure is inscribed: "Greece." Title: "Under solid protection." Caption: "Anglo-American gentlemen: —We will not let anyone interfere with the independence of Greece!"

Umberto Eco suggests that the particularity of any serialized narrative is in that it always "presupposes and constructs" a double "Model Reader (let us say, a naïve and a 'smart' one)."[48] A "naïve" reader would be one who sees each installment of a story as a separate event, rather than as part of a pattern, while a "smart" one

[48] Ibid., p. 174.

172 STATE LAUGHTER

Fig. 13. Montage cartoon by A. Zhitomirskii. © Vladimir Zhitomirskii. *Literaturnaia gazeta*, March 24, 1948. Caption: "Harry Truman—a hysterical drummer of war."

would take pleasure in recognizing the pattern and constructing a meaningful message out of the interplay of repetitions of the same and deviations from the same. The implied viewers of the Soviet caricatures, just as the implied addressees of all of the Soviet propaganda of the darker decades, were supposed to be both at the same time. On the one hand, they were supposed to be the addressees of lengthy articles on the political situation in the world, with satirical drawings supplied for ease of understanding. They were also supposed to be in need of a multi-level explanation of the constellation of characters and events (Efimov's cartoon published in *Izvestiia* on December 4, 1951 shows how a digested, one-sentence summary of news reports works as an introduction to, and an explanation of, the news of the day). But on the other hand, those same readers were expected to be able to decipher the clues that every single caricature presented them with, identifying the types, the specific persons, and the relationships between them. In the case of a completely "naïve" reading, the interpretative focus would be on the textual reports; in that of a "smart" one, it would be on the images. This constellation works contrary to the usual premise that an ability to interpret texts should be perceived as superior to a tendency to privilege images in the reception, and interpretation, of information, and highlights the particular relationship between text and image in Soviet propaganda. The correctly trained Soviet readers are those who could "read the caricatures" correctly. One had to recognize the various Western leaders depicted in the often elaborate combinations of characters; one had to be familiar with the content of Marshall's speech in Chicago (Fig. 7) and to know what the connection between Winston Churchill, Hector McNeil, and Ernest Bevin was (Fig. 9)—otherwise the caricatures simply would not work. Since the semantics of the Soviet regime, and of the Cold War in general, was largely dependent on a stable association of the actors with the roles assigned to them, the readers had to prove that they were "smart" by being able to recognize the images as part of a larger pattern, without the assistance of a text or with the most minimal assistance. In this case, the pleasurable moment when a character is identified as humorous would come not so much from the appreciation of a skillful, meaningful distortion of the familiar, as from the satisfaction of seeing these characters act predictably ridiculous regardless of what the day brings, as they are embodiments of personalized distortion-turned-norm (in behavior as well as appearance).

At the same time, an insufficient knowledge of the actual configuration of forces on the international arena at the particular moment would not be a handicap. In fact, the readers who are able to read the images "etymologically"—that is, who can draw on past associations connected with the unit of meaning (in this case, an image)—are "smart" not despite, but exactly because they may not have sufficient knowledge of the events of the day: they know that what really matters is recurrent patterns rather than minor changes brought about by the particular moment. It is, after all, a special feature of caricature that it "always clearly and unambiguously resolved this or that political moment even for those who were not at all engaged in the political affairs of the day."[49] On this reading, the caricatures would appear funny because of an instant recognition of the *individuals as types*. The predictably clumsy, stupid, fat, ugly, and servile characters look predictably ridiculous in situations of which a short description would be sufficient to give one an idea of what the "adventures of the day" were. If one already knows that Dulles is always out to buy cheap favors, that Spain's infantile leader with the inflated self-esteem is unable to function without external support, or that General MacArthur is a bloodthirsty butcher, then one is likely to "get the joke" when the characters appear in new situations that make them look just as ridiculous and pitiful as ever. The Europeans are servile as ever, only too eager to oblige; Franco unfailingly behaves like a boy with an inferiority complex trying to make himself accepted by grown-ups; MacArthur is forever busy trying to fool the world by appearing to be a dove of peace, even

---

[49] Varshavskii, *Nasha politicheskaia karikatura*, p. 9, quoted in Golubev, "Nash otvet Chemberlenu," p. 123.

though his nature never changes; the US Secretary of State Dean Acheson, and Americans in general, are rats—no surprise there, either.

Those readers who may not necessarily have been able to immediately recognize the (proto)types of the satirical drawings, and who were, hence, "naïve" in that they needed a detailed explanation of the background for the episodes to which the particular caricature referred, were also smart in their own way—or were at least informed. They would have read the analytical articles and the news reports preceding and surrounding a caricature in order to be able to truly appreciate why it is, indeed, ridiculous when General MacArthur is praised for his achievements, why Franco joining the Marshall Plan is a joke, and why French politicians really do act like prostitutes in their interactions with the USA. In this case, the comic effect would be based on a reaction to the behavior of *specific individuals in a specific situation* (the depiction of Dulles visiting Paris in order to decide which of the French politicians to support in their fight for power is funny because it discloses the true nature of Franco-American relations; Franco holding on to an American official's walking stick is ridiculous as an illustration of the American intention to extend the Marshall Plan zone to Spain; General MacArthur showing his true face in the context of Acheson's words makes one laugh; the Acheson/rat cartoon figure is a biting satire of the American actions in Korea).

A good example of how and why image-text relations matter in the context is Efimov's illustration to an article on the use of biological weapons in Korea (*Izvestiia*, March 25, 1952). The caricature is that of Acheson as a particularly revolting-looking rat with a banner. The stars and stripes on the banner are rat's paw prints and barbed wire; the subject of the short text is the "terrifying American atrocities" in Korea, where American aggressors have made use of bacteriological weapons. On a "smart" reading, the caricatured image can be seen as yet another example of a more or less skillful animalization of the American politician, and as an allusion to the nature of American foreign policy in general; it might thus prepare the viewer for a reading of the text to the left about the evil deeds of the American warmongers—or else it might simply be understood as yet another instalment in the series about Acheson the rat and the Americans using biological weapons. On a "naïve" reading, the drawing can be understood in conjunction with the text only, with the image being an illustration of one of Truman's "plague-stricken allies" to which the text refers. This definition has its counterpart in the caricature in so far as both are more than just an insult based on a metaphor: they are puns in the definition of Arthur Koestler, that is, an invitation to consider something "from the perspective of two self-consistent but normally incompatible sets of reference."[50] And puns have their most adequate visual equivalent in caricature, which brings such two sets of reference together by

---

[50] Cefalu, "What's So Funny," pp. 44–58, quoting Arthur Koestler from Martin, *The Psychology*, p. 63.

visual means, with its customary combination of the human and the animal and downgrading of the symbolic to the literal. The American politicians are both people and rats, the rats are both vermin and American allies, "plague-stricken" can refer to all of them to an equal extent, and it is both an insult, a metaphor, and a truthful description of the situation; a reference to a type and a comment on the current state of affairs. It is on the level of "both...and," rather than "either...or," that the satirical impact is created, with the figures and events to which reference is made never being quite what they appear to be.

In the Stalinist and early Cold War propagandistic context, commentaries (or, broadly defined, any form of textual production that was secondary to a certain set of core texts) were of primary importance (pun intended). The fabric of Soviet reality was largely defined by multiple levels of texts, images, and pronouncements that existed in parallel to each other, all of them referring to a limited number of primary sources. The obligatory obsessive quoting of whatever had been said, written by, or attributed to the leaders of the state has been discussed in scholarship; but the words and actions of enemies were also frequently quoted, albeit in a different way. The only crucial difference between the two kinds of quoting the primary pronouncements and commenting on them was that while the "sacred" texts were supposed to be preserved and multiplied in repetitions by many speakers and writers and in many genres, the commentaries on whatever was deemed to be coming from the other camp had the opposite function: they were to take the primary texts apart.

Scaling Down and the Logic of Wit

And this is what they did, retelling the same stories, the same news items, the same episodes from the political biographies of high public officials again and again in a shorter, and lighter, form: as satirical verses or as epigrams, as more or less witty cartoon captions or digested versions of news reports ("from the papers"), as caricatures and as satirical texts accompanying these caricatures.

It is not easy to say whether satirical verses that frequently accompanied caricatures illustrated the images or the other way round; nor is it relevant. Nor is it about the summary of the news, whose intentionally imprecise attribution ("from the press") made it impossible to verify their veracity, being a supplement to the cartoons, or being illustrated by them (Fig. 4 is but one of many examples). All of these are secondary with respect to the actual event—or rather, with respect to the reporting of the event in the media as an item of news. What is important is the very multiplication, the density of retellings and re-presentations of the events and people in a variety of short and conventionally satirical genres. The same persons, the same events are depicted in one caricature after another; they are made fun of in an accompanying satirical piece; they become the subjects of an epigram and feature in a satirical poem, again and again, and again. In a commentary on recent developments in West Germany (*Izvestiia*, December 4, 1951), the same piece of news is rewritten three times in three different (but very short) forms: as a news flash, supposedly serious, but with the use of the ubiquitous quotation marks signaling irony, then as a caricature (by Efimov), then as a satirical verse (by Samuil Marshak). On February 20, 1951, the newspaper featured a long article with a rather self-explanatory title ("Prime-Minister Attlee Needs Lies About the Soviet Union"), followed by a lengthy subtitle ("Why the British Parliament Won't Pass the Law for the Defense of Peace as Recommended by the Warsaw Congress"). The text of the article framed a caricature that is preceded by a succinct explanation of how by "persecuting advocates of peace and casting aspersions on the Soviet Union, British Prime Minister Attlee showed to the whole world the real price of his fake love of peace." The caption to the caricature clarifies that the character depicted is the god of war Mars, who complains that "unfortunately, this mask of a peace-loving democrat is no longer suitable."

The sheer accumulation of retellings and re-presentations of the same information in forms and genres that are far removed from the "serious" reporting of the event in the same newspaper becomes significant in more than one way. First of all, the principle of tautology replacing truth value in Stalinism worked just as well for negative propaganda as it did for propagating the words of the leaders: things repeated again and again began to be perceived as the truth (or as a mocking rendition of a lie) without necessarily being the truth (or without the original quotation necessarily being a lie). But for the repetitions themselves to be convincing as a means of promoting a particular view on every piece of the news, every phenomenon, and every person, they must not be identical to the primary pronouncement, since otherwise they would not be perceived as separate messages, as a new view on the same issue. An illusion of multiple perspectives had to be created—not an easy task in the Soviet Union of the late 1940s and early 1950s.

When neither the message nor the source can be varied, the only thing that can change is the form of (re-)presentation—that is, the genres. Here, the practice of accumulating genres of a certain kind to introduce a variety into repetition is a consequence of ideologically defined discursive limits, or even of the limits dictated by the size of a newspaper page. The more commentaries there were on a certain character or event (and, as suggested above, it was important that there be a few), the shorter they had to be. The events and the characters thus were, quite literally, scaled down: from the reports on international affairs to the one-sentence digested versions of the same, to a caption, to a cartoon; from the regular publication of updates on the new intrigues of the wicked capitalists to a comic strip-like "weekly review" (see, for example, Fig. 3); from lengthy articles on the acts of specific characters in the international arena to the densely populated group cartoons with explanatory notes on the side. When Efimov proudly declares that "only political satire and journalistic poetry are capable of keeping up with the events these days,"[51] he is certainly right in that these two genres are more appropriate than others for dealing with the task at hand—if only because artists working in these genres are supposed to be capable of producing short works.

Scaling down in conjunction with repetition is an inherently comic gesture. The very act of retelling an event in a shorter form suggests that in the act of retelling, only the essential information must be conveyed, the very core of the occurrence or the character, the bare truth. But when the retelling is framed as a satirical, or—in broader terms—comic, statement, it is the *gesture*, rather than the essence, that is preserved; or rather, the gesture *is* the essence. An evil politician is squashed by the heavy weight of facts, a judge is observed treading on the law, reactionary Western politicians are caught trying to stop the train of peace and progress in Fig. 5, and in Fig. 6, the spiderweb of the Marshall plan covering Europe is a real spiderweb. These are, indeed, "weekly reviews," with all the events of a certain period reduced to visual, shortened versions of gestures chosen as characteristic, because they bring together the literal and the metaphoric, the ridiculous and the somewhat terrifying—in short, they are caricatures.

As obvious as it might appear, this is still crucial: cartoons dispense with words, or make do with an absolute minimum of them. This is the ultimate economy governing the use of caricature as a genre of propaganda: what is cut off in the cartoon-event relationship is the very process, and the very idea, of analysis. The access to information that they provide should be immediate and direct in the most literal sense of the word, with reaction to recognizable visual stimuli replacing almost any kind of linguistic mediation, when a re-presentation of events "makes events and situations concrete, translates facts from the language of logical concepts into the language of visual images." This is why, Efimov claims, "caricature as a form of artistic expression is more understandable and easier to respond to than any literary presentation."[52] Even a sympathetic Western colleague agrees that the ability to convey complex messages in a simple manner is a major achievement of the Soviet artists: "Their points are easily understood. With a few exceptions the *Krokodil* cartoonists keep to simple compositions to convey simple meanings."[53] Simple meanings—and those that could be understood quickly, with no precious time wasted and no possibility of conflicting interpretations: "From the point of view of ease of understanding and the economy of time a drawing, with its internal compositional elements, can be understood in a split second. The viewer may choose to explore it in detail—or not; in any case, its meaning becomes clear faster than the meaning of an article, a satirical piece, a short report."[54] It is in the guaranteed speed of perception that contemporary

---

[51] Efimov, *Rabota*, p. 18.   [52] Efimov, *Osnovy*, p. 45.   [53] Low, "Review," p. 167.
[54] Golubev, "Praktiki," p. 352.

authors detect a similarity between political caricature and other related genres of visual propaganda: "Whether the images appear in flyers, on posters, in the form of popular woodcuts, or in printed newspapers...the masses become familiar with the political moment before reading the editorial, before they turn to an article on a particular topic."[55]

Thus, even if allowing for the possibility of a reading that we defined, somewhat counterintuitively, as "naïve" in that whoever practices it would first need to read the texts in order to understand the drawings, it is still imperative that a political caricature worthy of its name make it possible for a reader to grasp at least the general essence of the matter without reading—and quickly. Seen from this perspective, truly successful political caricatures should guarantee that transmission and reception of the message are *immediate* both in the sense of them being completely direct, straightforward presentations of events and people such as they are, there being no analytical or descriptive mediation, and in the sense of timing. If these images can be seen as primary to texts, then it might be not in terms of their importance, but in the sense of them functioning at a level that exceeds language and possibly even dispenses with it altogether. As the British caricaturist David Low put it: "How do these Soviet cartoonists do their jobs? Do they agitate well? Do they evoke, do they stir? If, judging deceit excusable in a 'sound' cause, they deceive, is their deceit adroit? Yes. They do. It is. The sparkling wit survives even the handicap of translated captions."[56]

Wit in caricatures, then, is closely linked to an appeal to emotions: agitating, evoking, stirring. We might conclude these reflections the way we started, with a reference to Carl Schmitt: "communication through images [*Bild-Kommunikation*]...is superior to verbal communication in that it appeals to [emotional] affects in a more immediate way, because information is not transmitted in a sequential form but appears instead as instantly decodable, and thus open to perception [*wahrnehmbar*]."[57]

An Enemy in Words

Sardonic Realism: The Art of Verbal Caricature

Textual caricature works with tools similar to those of visual caricature, but it does so in a special way. First of all, it makes extensive use of a virtually limitless range of expressive language tools to create acoustic and visual images. One of the greatest masters of this type of satire was Samuil Marshak, an astonishingly

---

[55] Varshavskii, *Nasha politicheskaia karikatura*, p. 9. [56] Low, "Review," p. 167.
[57] Balke, "Regierbarkeit," p. 120.

inventive author of astonishingly inventive poems replete with a variety of tropes that caricaturized the objects of his mockery. In *Poultry Farm*, the said farm stands for France, and each bird has its special voice. The main character, de Gaulle, is a rooster who used to be a "migrant bird" (a hint at de Gaulle's emigration during the Nazi occupation of France), but who is now "thumping his chest." As befits a rooster in popular folklore, he is a pretentious impostor: "De Gaulle is all puffed-up, / Like a king! / So what does he want, / The rooster?" As it turns out, he wants to sell France to the Americans and engage it in warfare: "'Cock-a-doodle-do! / On to Moscow!'— / The rooster drawls. / His neighbor, the turkey, / Mumbles 'Blum-Blum!' / Full of self-importance." The onomatopoeic effects intensify until at a certain point the soundtrack turns into the main feature of the poem: "'What is this noise / My friends?' /—Goose Shu-uman asks. / 'It's Ha-ha-ha-harry Truman come / To give us corn!'"

In another case the surnames of politicians targeted for ridicule imitate funeral bells. The poem *A Bell* opens with an epigraph: "Eisenhower, Clay and other warmongers have declared a 'Crusade for Freedom.' From Berlin they delivered the USA a 'Freedom Bell' cast from bronze on special order (from the press)." The "warmongers" do not just ring the bell ("Doing merry rounds / Dulles, Clay, McCloy"), but actually *produce* the "toll," which is the effect the politicians' names have in Marshak's poem:

> This gloomy toll
> Is whining with an echo,
> As if repeating
> Several names:
> "Eisen-hower.
> Ade-nauer.
> Clay, McCloy,
> Clay, McCloy."
> These are the ones
> Who want the world
> To have a reason
> To mourn its new dead!...

These satirical verses clearly expose the comic devices that make them work, and in doing so, they are clearly "formalist." Why is it that the formalism that had been banned from all genres, that was condemned in comedy (lyrical comedies were often criticized for being too "genre-reliant," that is, for following the conventional vaudeville devices of Scribe and Labiche), was welcomed in Cold War satire? The reason becomes clear once we remember what the nature of caricature is. In the 1920s, one of the leading theoreticians of theatre Vladimir Vol'kenshtein (who was later accused of being a formalist himself) explained it thus: "Since pure comedy is characterized by a struggle that is totally awkward and ignoble, its characters are not types but caricatures, and the more colorful a comedy is, the more caricature-like its characters are."[58]

Soviet aesthetics saw caricature as a satirically exaggerated representation of types, and any juxtaposition of caricature and type was regarded as a manifestation of formalism. By this logic, the more of a caricature a certain character type is, the more long-lasting its comic effect. The characters of Russian classical literature—Gogol's *Inspector General* (*Revizor*) or Saltykov-Shchedrin's *History of a Town* (*Istoriia odnogo goroda*)—are showrooms of comic types. In the Soviet satire of the Cold War, things worked the opposite way: Soviet writers modeled their characters on real politicians, whom they turned into types and thus deprived of their status and personality. But while the prototypes may have been different, the Soviet satirists created *the same type*, again and again. The dramatic personas of Soviet satire are alike because their prototypes, while representing completely different political views and biographies, were a priori appointed to be enemies. *This* is the common denominator for creating one "type" out of the French Minister of Defense and socialist Jules Moch and the Pope; the French Prime Minister and socialist Léon Blum and the conservative Catholic Portuguese dictator António Salazar; the Belgian Prime Minister, one of the main ideologists of a united Europe, and a top NATO official and socialist Paul Henri Spaak and a fierce French nationalist, a sworn anti-NATO man and conservative, Charles de Gaulle. This is exactly what happens in "A Ballad of One Circumstance" by Vladimir Mass and Mikhail Chervinskii. Populated by "spaaks, de gaulles, julesmochs," the poem recounts an event following which "Black dinner jackets / — Blum, Salazar and other spaaks — / Became agitated, / And everybody, from Jules Moch / To the Pope / Raised / Their shaking paws."

Usually, what was common to these texts is a total absence of self-reflection, which makes the following example all the more interesting. Samuil Marshak chose to introduce his poem "Classified Humor" with an epigraph "from the press": "Dr Raymond Bauer from Harvard announced at the 16th annual congress of the American Psychological Association that from now on scientific research on Soviet humor is to be regarded as secret." Marshak's poem talks about how the rulers of America have decreed that "it's not just missiles and bombs / That are top secret now, / But even humor itself / Is under lock and key / In Mark Twain's motherland." Since "the learned men / Are working on a top secret report" on "what, why and how often / The Soviet people find amusing," Marshak decides to disclose the secret: "Humor is a dangerous weapon! / It cannot be studied under a magnifying glass.... / Soviet people laugh / At everything that is mediocre and stupid."

Had it been true, the post-war Soviet Union would have been the merriest country in the world.

---

[58] Vol′kenshtein, *Dramaturgiia*, pp. 146–7.

Adventures of Tropes: Political Trolling of the Pre-Internet Age

Let us now turn to a concrete example that shows how the modes and devices of verbal caricature promoted discursive strategies that much later, at the time of social networks and hybrid wars, came to be called *political trolling*. The term is to be understood as an intentional offense against the ethics of communication that expresses itself in aggressive, mocking, or insulting behavior. Below we will focus on *aesthetic* tropes in special types of political trolling. As we will see, the toolbox of this particular kind of Cold War discourses included a whole range of comic devices.

David Zaslavskii, one of the most influential journalists of the era and a member of Stalin's inner circle, was a skilled master of the genre. His satirical features that were later reprinted in the collection *Cavemen in America* (*Peshchernaia Amerika*, 1951) can be studied as a manual on political trolling, a real catalog of literary figures and tropes used for mockery and ridicule. The basic structural principle of all these texts is the same: an anecdote, an untested news item, a curious event or a figment of someone's imagination is taken out of context, blown out of all proportion, and exaggerated beyond reason and is then served as a significant and highly symbolic fact, supposedly disclosing the very essence of contemporary America.

Thus, for example, the satirical piece "Mammoths of the American Congress" describes the "brouhaha" in the USA around the question of whether the capital of the country should be moved from Washington to a different, safer place. At the center of this text is a ***metaphor***. A member of the Congress from the state of Iowa suggested that the Congress be transferred to his native Des Moines, which is surrounded by cornfields with plants high enough for the leaders of the United States to hide in an hour of need. His opponent is a representative of Texas, whose suggestion is to "hide the congressmen deep inside the continent, somewhere to the west of Mississippi." All of this is but warmongering hysteria. These appeals are devoid of any sense since American democracy is but a smokescreen, and in fact, "the USA is ruled not by a parliament, but by the government of an 'invisible empire' operating behind the scenes: bankers, moguls of coal, steel, oil, and electrical power." This brings Zaslavskii to the "wildest" proposal made by a member of the Republican party, who

> invited the Congress, together with the government and with all the ministers, to move to his state—Kentucky. There they would find a comfortable shelter in the famous Mammoth Cave, the biggest cave in the world. Once it was home to cavemen, and it is quite possible that mammoths lived there, too. Having the mindset of a caveman, the congressman can be excused for thinking that

the most appropriate place for the American Congress in its present state would be a cave. (6)

The transformation of a toponym into an extended political metaphor culminates in a reassessment of the whole situation. A senseless discussion concerning the transfer of the American capital because of a non-existent Soviet threat acquires meaning. Recalling the Russian saying "for telling so many lies, a fool ends up telling the truth," Zaslavskii turns "empty lies" into "the truth": "Nothing at all will change in the policy of the United States if the reactionary congressmen are transferred to Mammoth Cave. After all, the nations of the world already see many American politicians as cavemen." The metaphor starts living its own independent life, as more and more sarcastic remarks emerge from it: "Once upon a time the Roman emperor Caligula led his horse into the Senate. The American congressman Morgan could lead a mammoth into the American House of Representatives, as a contemporary of its deputies" (p. 6). The text concludes with the device laid bare, when Zaslavskii directs "merciless, accusatory mockery against the clownish plans of the mammoths of the American Congress," just as "progressive humanity thwarts the intrigues of the hysterical warmongers."

The kind of ridicule that seeks to expose the truth needs the object of its mockery to be permanently estranged. This is where *allegory* comes in especially handy, where the real meets the symbolic. In another satirical piece Zaslavskii speaks of a "lynch" when referring to the trial of Harold Medina (Fig. 14)—the main character in the drama of the famous "Trial of Eleven Communists," where not only the leaders of American communists but also their lawyers ended up sentenced for contempt of court. The satirist draws an absurd image of a new kind of court session, where "any distinction between defendants and lawyers has been abolished," and both parties "have their place in the shared prisoners' dock." Witnesses, too, may end up in prison, which is why "from now on every American citizen who enters a court-house as a witness should be prepared to leave it as a prisoner" (p. 8).

The device of a comic exaggeration is exposed. It is not just the witnesses, but the audience, as well: "The spectators' benches are also to be viewed as defendants' benches. If members of the audience do what they did at the trial of the eleven communists, that is, if they laugh at the spies and instigators from the prosecution, they will be jailed." The jury is likely to follow, too. The text concludes with a sarcastic remark:

In the modern American court-house there are but two positions that can be safely occupied: that of the prosecutor and the judge. All the others are potentially prisoners. This is what they call "democracy" in America, and all nations of the world would do well to copy these new ways of American jurisprudence so as not to end up in the defendants' dock.

Soviet readers would not be familiar with the system of American jurisprudence, and Zaslavskii explains it by using wild tribes from Africa and Australia as examples. These tribes, he says, are not seeking to import American "democracy" because "in the past they themselves had exactly this kind of justice: no lawyers; the defendant was simply barbecued and then eaten." The American system, Zaslavskii continues, is just as (literally) wild. In the American court-house "there are no complicated distinctions. There are simply those who lynch, and those who are lynched. That's it." The reader is invited to come to the required conclusion: "Cracking down on lawyers, which would be unthinkable in any other country, is evidence of the American justice system turning fascist. Judge Medina is a fascist and a Ku Klux Klan man." This statement, full of pathos, is followed by a comment full of Zaslavskii's usual sarcasm: "This wild scene in the jungles of New-York clearly shows the true worth of all the drivel in the American press about 'democracy'!"

Note the stylistic vibrations: sarcasm is followed by pathos, which is then followed by a Socialist Realist image of the Soviet penitentiary idyll, which is then followed by a passage in the spirit of farce:

> The pitiful figure of judge Medina was thrashing about with wrath, in a powerless fury, while the lawyers were exposing the prosecution's lies and forgeries. A person with a limited horizon and a limitless baggage of a numb hatred against all things progressive, he could not juxtapose anything to the intelligence, talent, honesty, and ideals of the communists and their lawyers. He tried to threaten them so they would shut up. It didn't work. And then he paid them back for his humiliation by making the lawyers go to prison without any legal process, just by the power of his own executive order. (9)

The whole piece was most assuredly written for the only logically possible coda, when the Medina incident is raised to the level of an allegory:

> The USA does not have enough prisons to sentence everybody who finds judge Medina ridiculous. His name has already acquired a sinister notoriety, and satirical pamphlets around the world are already reprinting his pitiful image with the expression of an enraged and frightened ferret. Now he is the face of American "justice." More than that: now all those approaching New York from the ocean see that the famous Statue of Liberty holds a torch with Medina in it. This is what the much praised American "democracy" looks like. (10)

This grotesque symbol provides an allegorical conclusion to the story of the horror trial:

At the basis of many comic texts is *personification* as a main trope of fables. Thus, the satirical piece "How Mr Acheson Flogged Himself" opens with a saying:

"They say that if a hare is flogged for long enough, it will learn to light matches. An American diplomat, unlike a hare, can be flogged for a very long time, but he will still not learn anything" (p. 16). The reference is to the publication of the "White Paper on China" by the US State Department—a collection of documents concerning American policy in relation to China, testifying to a failure of the American attempts to save Kuomintang. More than a thousand pages of documents were accompanied by Acheson's foreword that Zaslavskii summarized thus: "We have committed one stupid action after another, and we will continue doing so."

Acheson accuses Kuomintang members of corruption, moral decay, hunger for power, and an unjustified certainty that the Americans will guarantee their power in the country. For Zaslavskii this is not only a sign of the US being powerless, but also an indication of the fact that they are in no way different from their Chinese allies: "Acheson is ruthlessly flogging Chiang Kai-shek: he is a good-for-nothing! he is a failure! he has capitulated! But with each of these blows he ends up hitting himself: The most incompetent American policy in China! Failure after failure! One stupid action after another! So what makes Chiang Kai-shek in any way

Fig. 14. Boris Efimov. Illustration to the satirical piece by D. Zaslavskii "The Trial of Lynch-Medina" in the collection *Cavemen in America* (Moscow, 1951).

worse than his American associate?" Acheson sees the reasons for the defeat of Kuomintang and American policy in China in the Soviet intent to spread its influence through the Far East. In Zaslavskii's opinion, that is a lie: "the American politicians have not learned a thing, and even a hare that has been flogged would be able to learn more from such a shameful defeat." Here we have a reverse personification: Acheson is like a flogged hare, just like a hare is like Acheson who has flogged himself. The title of Zaslavskii's text carries a reference to the NCO's widow from Gogol's *Inspector General* who supposedly flogged herself as a model of an endless self-punishment for having repeatedly committed the same foolish deed. Boris Efimov illustrated it beautifully in the image accompanying Zaslavskii's piece (Fig. 15).

Mixing similes is considered a sign of bad taste until it becomes a discursive strategy. A clash of similes can be the result of piling up objects of ridicule and at the same time—a consequence of searching for a successful *periphrasis* to debase these objects. In the piece "A Postwar Cat House," the "house" in question is the newly formed European Council. The cosmopolitan idea of a world government, the striving for a "united Europe" when half of Europe is Soviet, retired European politicians (Spaak, Churchill), and much else becomes a target for a stream of mocking comments. Everything starts from the basics: the local cuisine. "Strasbourg," we are told, "once famous for its pies, is now looking to become famous for its 'European Council' (p. 20). But the Strasbourg council will never be able to compete for popularity with Strasbourg pies. This latter product was made from goose livers of the highest quality, while the council of Strasbourg is stuffed with the ministerial and parliamentary tripe of the most doubtful provenance." As he scoffs at European "political corpses" and local idiots (such as Garry Davis), Zaslavskii finally comes up with an appropriate anecdote: "According to the French press agency..., the Funeral Society of Luxembourg demands that 'the future statute of Europe feature an article that would give every European citizen the right to dispose of their corpse'" (p. 21). This, according to the author, is what should occupy "the European clowns," who are not just "political corpses" themselves, but also

> political undertakers, longing for Europe to be turned into one big political cemetery. Death permeates everything that the European agents of American imperialism undertake. Death is at the heart of their political plans, death is the starting point of their philosophy and culture. A direct goal of the reactionary half-European council is the death of European democracy, the death of the national sovereignty of West European countries. (21)

Zaslavskii turns the Council of Europe into a brothel, whose inhabitants, though dead, are now also fulfilling additional functions. Here,

Fig. 15. Boris Efimov. Illustration to the satirical piece by D. Zaslavskii "How Mr. Acheson Flogged Himself" in the collection *Cavemen in America* (Moscow, 1951).

half-dignified delegates are spending time discussing with great care and dedication the issue of the rights of political half-corpses.... At the same time in the back rooms, those who have been put at the disposal of the Council of Ministers, Mr. Harriman can console himself with eight half-European ministers at once. He brings them together, he threatens them, he caresses them; and Mr. Spaak is there, entertaining the party in the uniform of a renowned matchmaker, with a skittish apron on his voluminous bust. (22)

This periphrasis creates the effect of caricature.

Among the most efficient devices of the comic are **hyperbole** and **litotes**. In both of them the proportions of whatever it is they refer to are distorted. In the case of litotes, the low status of the object of mockery finds a literal expression. Thus, in the essay "Acheson Overthrows... Karl Marx" the American Secretary of State is represented as a greenhorn ignoramus who dares to argue with Marx without even having read his works. A digested version is all he could master:

As is well known, in the USA classical works are published in simplified versions. For example, all of *Anna Karenina* takes up 24 pages. There is probably such a version of *Das Kapital*, on 12 pages—an American pill as an antidote to Marxism. Acheson has swallowed it—and that's it! Now he can defeat Marxism easily! (32)

As if this debasement were not enough, Zaslavskii claims that the hero of his sketch would be mentally incapable of comprehending Marx even if he were to read his oeuvre in its entirety. Acheson has the brains of Saltykov-Shchedrin's provincial town mayor:

Respectable gentlemen, honorable inhabitants of the Wall-Street jungle could never read Marx's texts in a non-abridged version. Saltykov-Shchedrin's *History of a Town* features a senior official in the town council, Nikodim Osipovich Ivanov, who was so short that he couldn't contain complicated laws within himself. He died from overexertion, trying to fathom a particularly complicated piece of legislature. (32)

The only reason the US Secretary of State Secretary "runs no risk of dying from overexertion is because he learns 'complicated' laws of historical science from the simplified editions provided by the American bourgeois lifestyle." To make the relative proportions completely clear, Efimov drew Acheson as a tiny figure banging his head against the unassailable fortress of Marx's volumes (Fig. 16).

The comical device of **hyperbole**, on the other hand, is used not so much to magnify the physical proportions of the object of ridicule as to emphasize the scale of its inferiority. Thus, the satirical piece "Petty Politics of a Large Power," whose very title hints at incompatible proportions, talks about the ban against selling pacifiers to "the countries of people's democracy." The author indulges in mocking comparisons between pacifiers and tanks, aircraft and torpedo motor boats, using the contrast to show that "having no practical, real effect, bans imposed by the American government are like petty jibes, a kind of political grimacing." The implication is that the significance of the pacifiers is exaggerated to reflect political interests. At the same time, if one were to understand "political grimacing" as referring to trolling (which it is, in actual fact), this definition could be applied to Zaslavskii's own satirical pieces.

Displacements of meaning are at the basis of **alogism**, one of the most common comic devices that Zaslavskii uses with a literary slant in a number of his pieces. Thus, his text "Headless Detectives" features FBI detective Coombs, who discovered that a Stanford University student had with him the prohibited "Fučík Paper." The incident immediately attracted the attention of the Committee on Un-American Activities, which demanded that the author be "fished out," thus exposing their ignorance of facts. Searching for Fučík predictably led to nothing,

Fig. 16. Boris Efimov. Illustration to the satirical piece by D. Zaslavskii "Acheson overthrows... Karl Marx" in the collection *Cavemen in America* (Moscow, 1951).

but it provided Zaslavskii with ample material for drawing a surrealistic image of contemporary America:

> There is no doubt that mental deficiency is a feature of American reactionaries and of American sleuths alike. We have an amazing image: people who set out to fight communism have never heard of Fučík, they do not know that the chairperson of the Second World Peace Congress in Warsaw concluded the sessions with a quotation from Fučík, and that Fučík has been awarded the Honorary Peace Prize. (47)

As the author of these words provides a rationale for the behavior of the enemies, he magnifies its absurdity (even though, in doing so, he simultaneously exposes the futility of Soviet efforts to convince the world of the USSR's peaceful intentions). The same effect is achieved by employing the opposite device—a concluding metaphor:

Detective Coombs disgraced himself. American tribesmen from the investigation committee exposed their ignorance. They are now conscious of their impotence. They have no power over ideas. Let them look for Fučík all over America. They will find him in every university, in every school, in every town, in every workers' neighborhood and—what is most important—in thousands and thousands of minds and hearts that are not accessible even to somebody like agent Coombs, a headless detective. (48)

Using the same "fact" in its literal as well as metaphoric sense (a headless detective trying to look into people's heads), Zaslavskii demonstrates an ability to work extremely economically, making do with just a handful of facts, with everything else having to be fabricated. Here, the main trope is *metonymy*. Thus, Eisenhower's short stay in Rome and the speech in which the American military commander made a reference to the coming of the "apostle of peace" to Rome some 2,000 years previously becomes the target of elaborate mockery in the satirical piece "General Dwight's Epistle to the Romans." From this text the reader learns that Eisenhower supposedly "tries to pass for a new apostle and indulges in reminiscences of Ancient Rome, parodying characters from ancient history and mythology to the music of Leoncavallo's *Pagliacci*." Juggling quotes from the Bible, Zaslavskii performs a secondary metonymic displacement, comparing the American general not to an apostle but to a barbarian. He suggests that the general might consider going at least 1,500 years back in time:

> It was then that another unwelcome foreigner visited Rome—Alaric. He brought hordes of Visigoths with him, or, as we would say today, West Germans. Alaric did not compose any epistles to the Romans, he did not arrange for any press conferences to take place. Instead, he proceeded straight to the destruction of Rome. General Eisenhower is in no way inferior to Alaric when it comes to being decisive. In brutality he would probably surpass Attila, who also paid a visit to Italy and was near Rome. But modern-day Romans are quite different from their ancestors, even though De Gasperi and Scelba probably do have a lot in common with the noble Romans of the period of decline and disintegration of the Roman Empire. Eisenhower had a good opportunity to see for himself that present-day Romans are not slaves, that they, like all Italians, can stand up for their country's independence and thwart any aggressive schemes of boorish invaders. (61–62)

These references to ancient history and metonymic substitutions/transformations, in which Eisenhower turns into Apostle Paul or Alaric, Americans become barbarians, and Italian politicians are a reincarnation of the senators of Ancient Rome, are supposed to ensure that a relatively insignificant event—a general's press conference—is amplified to the scale of the second invasion of barbarians into Europe.

A most illustrative example of such metonymic displacement is found in the satirical piece "Three American Sisters," which is based on the trope of *synecdoche*. The three sisters are Helen, Peggy, and Gussi (the first two being actual sisters, while the third one is their cousin). Helen and Peggy have a brother, John Sherman Zinsser, who is a real "Wall Street shark." He has managed not only to become the director of the Morgan Bank but also to arrange for the most advantageous marriages for his sisters: Helen is now married to the Chief Commander of the US in West Germany, General John MacCloy, Peggy's husband is the American ambassador to Great Britain, Lewis Douglas, while Gussi is the wife of West Germany's Chancellor, Konrad Adenauer, who is also the director of the largest German bank, Deutsche Bank. The three sisters thus represent America's key interests in Europe in the spheres of politics, intelligence, warfare, economy, and finance. As he paints comical imaginary scenes where family matters and political considerations mix, the author leads the reader to believe that through these people, "the masters of Wall Street" solve all the key problems that Germany faces: "All of Bonn's parliament is but the 'servants' quarters' in the side wing of the castle where Helen and Gussi discuss their concerns related to family life and diplomacy."

The piece concludes by *laying bare* a *device*: "They have not yet been able to find an appropriate name for West Germany. Bizoneland, Trizoneland, Federal Germany, Westdeutschland—nothing sounds right. Its true name is Zinsserland, the promised land of the Zinsser family." These two words ("promised land"), thrown in as an aside at the very end, have a clear referent: the new international conspiracy is modeled on a Jewish conspiracy wherein Jewish wives are "distributed" in exactly this way among the masters of the world. In the stream of sarcastic remarks, the reader accepts this idea with no difficulty whatsoever.

From a "Negative Realism" to the "Realistic Grotesque"

In its appeals to "the Leninist theory of reflection" Soviet aesthetics assumed the primacy of a "reality" that art was supposed to "reflect." It was reality rather than art that contained all forms of aesthetic reactions, including the comic: "Laughter is a subjective reaction to the objectively comic in life."[59] It was postulated that

> the comic, the funny, whatever causes laughter,—these are traits that are objectively characteristic of certain phenomena in reality. They are targeted by a writer's wit and humor. The significance of a particular comical trait from the point of view of its role in social life can vary. The character of humor will vary,

[59] Dzeverin, *Problema*, p. 168.

too, if the essence of a given comical trait in a certain phenomenon is assessed correctly.[60]

Thus, the comic exists "objectively," while wit and humor are subjective and evaluative reactions to it. This fixation on the allegedly objective nature of the comic programmed the Soviet aesthetic theory to expose the link between the comic on the one hand and realism on the other. Since the grotesque appealed to an imaginary rather than real world, it was associated with decay and mysticism, and, as such, it was juxtaposed to realism, which was a mark of the "progressive worldview." Hence, as realism acquired a canonical status by the mid-1930s, the grotesque was gradually pushed out of literature and the arts. Its rehabilitation only started after 1952, following the call for "Soviet Gogols and Shchedrins." At first it was handled with caution, as "a means of exaggeration, a sharpening of an image in order to more fully bring out its typical traits."[61] It was only much later, in the late 1960s, following the publication of Bakhtin's book on Rabelais, that it came to be seen as a legitimate aesthetic mode.

The grotesque was understood rather broadly in readings of Russian classic literature (Gogol, Saltykov-Shchedrin, Sukhovo-Kobylin) and foreign authors (Rabelais, Swift, Hoffmann). However, it was measured carefully when applied to Soviet satire and recognized as valid only in texts that featured enemies (political caricature) or life in the West (Cold War satire). As a result, the Soviet theory of the comic developed a concept of the *realistic grotesque* in which realism was in no need of verisimilitude and the grotesque was in no way irrational. Now it was claimed that "the grotesque, hyperbole, and other forms of artistic convention can be realistic or non-realistic depending on how truthful they were in exposing the objective laws of life, the essence of the things they reflected.... Verisimilitude is not an obligatory feature of realism."[62]

Having lost the skill of creating new works in the genre after decades of not being allowed to experiment with the form, Soviet satirists were now engaging in numerous experiments in the grotesque mode, recycling the same tropes again and again, to compensate for the low quality of humor. One of the most common metaphors was that of a lunatic asylum, which became a recurrent motif of anti-American verses.

We will start with a poem by two of the most popular and productive satirists of Stalin's era, Vladimir Dykhovichnyi and Moris Slobodskoi. Their numerous sketches, plays, and features (including those on international topics) were probably the most widely performed satirical pieces in the Soviet Union from the 1940s through the 1960s. The protagonist of their poem "A Mad Day" is a certain Mr. Smith. Hospitalized in a lunatic asylum after the war, he is finally discharged,

---

[60] El'sberg, "Satira," p. 8.   [61] Nedoshivin, *Ocherki*, p. 215.
[62] Nikolaev, *Satira Shchedrina*, p. 27.

and is trying to adjust to "normal life" in present-day America. He is shown a headline in a newspaper: "It is our duty to defend / Korean borders against China!" He thinks he must have forgotten his geography. He then asks for the radio to be turned on: "Through the sounds of tango mixed with a funeral feast / A fierce voice (like the 'Führer's' own) / Screams: 'We must use the bomb to entrench / The American lifestyle everywhere!'" Smith asks for his pulse to be measured, concluding that his "brain is not yet strong enough" and he is "still under the spell of hallucinations, / Apparently not quite cured." The poem ends with Smith being "accompanied by paramedics": he is back in the lunatic asylum. "It's over. In his new straitjacket / He declared solemnly to the doctor / 'I am back, I want / To return to a normal life again.'"

Of course, depicting America as a land of madmen symbolized by Soviet propaganda's favorite comic character—the first United States Secretary of Defense, James Forrestal, who jumped out of a window in an emotionally volatile state—was supposed to intensify the mass psychosis and mobilize the people, seeing as the madmen had control over weapons of mass destruction. But there was a special aesthetic aspect to these propagandistic exercises, too. Realism demands that there be a cause-and-effect sequence, and a lunatic asylum was an ideal framing for "the realist grotesque": madness implies alogical thinking and the most fantastical understanding of the world.

"A Lunar Eclipse," another poem by Dykhovichnyi and Slobodskoi, talks about how "Among other kinds of madness, / Among many forms of psychosis, / In America dealers and mountebanks / Have already opened travel tours to the moon." The business, the authors write, is booming, and 120,000 "lunar tickets" have already been sold. Such is the number of students who have despaired of finding a job, or simply people who do not think they would be able to save themselves in the case of a nuclear invasion. A teacher from Massachusetts, for example, has "but one hope—to sit it out. Having emphasized the name of the main character by quotation marks, the authors make it obvious that all these people are mad: "Those dreaming of open space / Are not brave explorers, nor romantic youths/Charmed by voyages into the unknown. / It's 'Mr. Smith,' scared out of his mind."

As the 1946 Party resolutions on the arts were published and artists had to avoid depictions of any conflicts when describing Soviet reality, satire on foreign policy topics was becoming more and more attractive, and the grotesque was back in fashion.

The action of Nikolai Pogodin's play *Missouri Waltz* (*Missuriiskii val's*, 1949) takes place after the war in the largest city of the state of Missouri, Kansas City. The choice of the location is not random. It was here that Harry Truman at the dawn of his political career became involved with the corrupt local leader of the Democratic Party, Tom Pendergast. This involvement proved to be an enduring stain on Truman's reputation, and using this fact to discredit the President was one of the main goals of the Soviet campaign. The characters of Pogodin's play meet in the hotel Cosmopolitan, which Chicago gangsters call "the most comfortable brothel in America." All the characters are profoundly cynical, this being not just their shared character trait but an important device that relieves the author of the need to explain anything to the audience. A man by the name of Johnny Gennari, for example, who calls himself "the king of swindlers and bandits," is not at all embarrassed when the journalist Kerry asks him how it is possible that he is a friend of "Mr. Brown," the same "Mr. Brown [who] is the leader of the local branch of the Democratic Party? How can it be, if you are the king of swindlers and bandits?" Gennari's response is simple: "This, Kerry, is practically the same thing." Such jibes could well be captions to Boris Efimov's caricatures, or else have those same caricatures as illustrations.

This play, and others of the same type, were examples of "negative realism," wherein existing reality was sharply criticized and juxtaposed to an ideal.[63] "Negative realism" results in caricature because it is based on an extreme form of exaggeration, when political views are divorced from those who are supposed to have them. Thus, when Pogodin makes Gennari a cosmopolitan, this is not so much in order to flesh out the character, but rather to explain what a cosmopolitan is, as the play was published at the height of the anti-cosmopolitan campaign in 1949. Gennari explains:

> It is just that I am a cosmopolitan. Your great president is as precious to me as the last Turkish sultan. I am an Italian who grew up in Spain. In my youth I was a vagabond in Portugal and France, but matured in England, from where I escaped to Canada, then from Canada I made it to America where, as you can see, I found myself. Which one of these blessed countries would you call my motherland?

One can conclude that "negative realism" is different from "critical realism" in that the characters' actions lack motivation. While the power of traditional realism is in the representation of characters' motives, "negative realism" works by introducing coarse generalizations, quick effects, and pure rhetoric. To emphasize even more the already rather exaggerated traits of the leading gangster figures in the play, Pogodin introduces positive, reasonable, level-headed heroes (a progressive party activist, a trade-union leader), who provide helpful generalizations for the audience:

> I am not sure how it happens in other states, or in other towns, but here, in Kansas City, the place is ruled by political gangsters who know they are

---

[63] Timofeev, *Teoriia*, pp. 80-7. In using the term "negative realism," Timofeev was echoing Lunacharskii who spoke of "negative realism" ("otritsatel'nyi realizm").

invulnerable... Elections are approaching... They will be ready to burn down Kansas, if that's what it takes to have their senator in Washington.

The audience learns how exactly "Johnny Gennari, a millionaire, a nobleman and a convict on the run" "rakes in millions" for Brown:

> All the syndicates of swindlers and conmen with their gambling houses dutifully pay him a percentage of their profits. The top gangsters of America come to him to hatch their shady deals and crimes.

Such exposure of other people's faults is followed by passages where characters expose their own moral imperfections. The absurdity of the technique must emphasize the absurdity of the American political system itself, thus serving the actual purpose for which these dramatic works were created in the first place: discrediting the American election system and, in particular, President Truman himself by describing monstrous machinations that make it possible to score a victory in American elections. Brown's far-reaching influence is due to his being

> similar to a giant, monstrous squid... The city is split into districts where so-called district captains are endlessly busy. These are the tentacles of the political machine.

The farcical character of these operations is drawn with thick and heavy strokes. This is how Brown's second-in-command explains the workings of the Democrats' party machine:

> GENNARI: Look, Fren: soon they will be putting together ballot lists. We must make sure all the strips of no-man's-land, all the gasoline stations, and all the abandoned slums and empty warehouses are populated. Your lists should feature these places as residential blocs whose residents are all dying to vote for our candidates. We call them ghosts.
> MACDONALD: It's pretty clear.
> GENNARI: Then there are also "sleepers" and "horsemen." The "horsemen" are our boys who drive around the city in automobiles and vote some thirty times wherever they want. And then...

But "negative realism" was quite risky in that it contradicted the Socialist Realist demand for a "positive ideal" and "historic optimism." In this context it is interesting to look at some interventions by Pogodin's colleagues during a discussion of the play at a board session of the Soviet Writers' Union, where typical and quite predictable reproaches were addressed to the author (at that time *Missouri Waltz* was already being performed in Moscow theaters):

COMRADE N: Tikhonov thinks that people are not given a voice in the play; it is as if this were a play from the life of gangsters.
COMRADE A: Surov believes the play romanticizes gangster life.
COMRADE A: Perventsev also believes the play shows the criminal world and there is no sign at all of the American people.
COMRADE K: Simonov talked about how he is uncomfortable with the play veering towards gangsterism...[64]

Thus, satire based on "negative realism" turns out to be insufficiently realistic. But in this case the introduction of positive characters or themes could not solve "the problem of the typical" (as it was expected to do in satirical works on domestic topics, where it was necessary to balance off the positive and negatives sides of Soviet reality). America was not supposed to have redeeming qualities or positive features. To be realistic, the Soviet anti-American satire had to become demonstratively non-realistic. This is how "negative realism" turned into "realistic grotesque."

Anatolii Surov prefaced his play *The President's Countryman (A Mad Haberdashery Seller)* (*Zemliak prezidenta*, 1950) with the following remarks:

> All of this might appear incredible, but it is true. As the Americans say, sometimes truth is stranger than fabrication. This saying could be a good epigraph to the play. And if anyone finds the events depicted here exaggerated, the paint laid too thickly, it is not the author who should be blamed.[65]

He then shared some important considerations concerning the genre of the play:

> We called this play a satirical comedy. It could also be called a pamphlet. The author is not at all interested in blindly reproducing details of everyday American life. But let the actors and the director be truthful in what matters most: in depicting the characters, the thoughts, the motifs and the actions of the plays' heroes, let them not be afraid to accentuate the characters' traits in a satirical manner. In this case the satirical and the realistic coincide.

In other words, the grotesque made it possible to depict gangsters without romanticizing them and without making them attractive. The plot of Surov's play follows the pattern of the *Missouri Waltz*, except that here the action takes place in a provincial town in Missouri rather than in Kansas City. Once again, one

---

[64] A personal report of the Propaganda Department of the CPSU Central Committee to M. A. Suslov on the debates concerning N. F. Pogodin's play *Missouri Waltz* at the Union of Soviet Writers on August 11, 1949 (*Stalin i kosmopolitizm*, pp. 473–4).

[65] Surov, *Zemliak*.

of the leading characters is "a local boss of the Democratic Party," whose name is Robert Hard. He is known to be "the kind of man who does everything. He sells jobs and publishes newspapers. He buys human souls and makes senators." He is surrounded by swindlers and bandits of the same kind, and this is the spirit in which he is preparing for elections to the Congress. There is, however, one character in Surov's play that was not in *Missouri Waltz*—an American trickster.

Charlie Mitchell is a shallow dreamer and loser who keeps drifting from job to job. The audience meets him when he works at a haberdashery selling ties. The trade is far from booming in the provincial town, and the shop goes bankrupt; Pauly, the owner of the store, terminates the lease, and Charlie finds himself yet again unemployed. But he does not want to work. When his father-in-law suggests he seek employment in the post office, Charlie responds that such work is beneath him. He thinks in global terms:

CHARLIE: I have already achieved a thing or two in my life. I cannot allow myself to fall that low. One should know one's own worth! An American's way is forward and upwards! We are Americans, father! The world trembles before us. And you say—*the post-office?* ... Fill out receipts and lick stamps? At a time like this!

He focuses on a talent he has just discovered in himself—a talent for transformation that, he hopes, will help him find his place among the local party bosses:

CHARLIE: Because in this world there is Robert Hard. Our Bob—our boss! He will not let a guy like me go down like that. (*Holds a mustache to his upper lip, removes his glasses, parts his hair, lets a lock of hair fall down on his forehead. Looks at himself in the mirror.*) Now that was a man we did not appreciate. (Snaps up his arm into a salute.) Heil! ... (*Rotates his eyes wildly.*) Drang nach Osten! Russisch! Hände hoch! Drang nach Pauly! Pauly kaputt! (*Tears off the mustache, puts it in his side pocket.*) But what can I do? There are no joys for me at home. Let's go to "The Lion of Missouri," raise a glass worth a tie or two.

In "The Lion of Missouri" Charlie spends whatever little money he has in hopes that the local men of influence will accept him as one of their own. He finally succeeds, after discovering that there is someone else to whom he looks quite similar:

(*Sits back in his chair, looking at the president's portrait as if he were looking in the mirror. Adjusts his hair, his bow-tie—and suddenly he does look like the president.*) This is somebody who will never abandon me in an hour of need! Bet you didn't realize we are relatives, did you?

Passing himself off as Truman's relative, Charlie finds a position with one of Hard's newspapers, whose editor has been tasked by the boss with looking for anti-communist sensations. He has a brilliant idea: Charlie is actually Hitler, who managed to flee Germany and has now surfaced in Missouri. Tsissi Schlesinger becomes the new Eva Braun. A cleaner from the Reichskanzlei is fetched from somewhere so he can "identify" the newcomer as Hitler. The rest of the action in the play unfolds like a farce, when "the new Hitler" has trouble "recognizing" his wife, who explains the confusion by the fact that "he suffers from lapses of memory" because "he has had a hard life." Fortunately, her "Adolfchen" remembers the most important German words: "Deutschland! Vaterland! Drang nach Osten! Russisch, Hände hoch!...Sprechen Sie Deutsch?"

Hard organizes for a senator to come to Missouri and orders that "a book by the Führer be prepared overnight for the senator's visit." This would be "a sequel to *Mein Kampf*—a new volume in his magnificent oeuvre." Each of Hard's journalists is assigned a chapter, each chapter to be dedicated to a special "thesis":

> The last days of great Germany: This chapter will deal with the tragic war against the Reds.... Me and Churchill.... The Führer's warning to the Americans: do not underestimate Russia.... My experience of fighting against German communists.... Why it is necessary to defeat the Cominform.... America needs me—and I need America!... There will be no peace, war is inevitable.

These theses were omnipresent in the Stalinist propaganda of the time—in the media, poems, novels, and "serious" plays and films. But here, built into the fantastical plot of the play, they seem to be deprived of any real ideological significance. They are presented in a form in which they could be most easily taken in by the mass audience. They turn into chest-thumping, which finds its best expression in sardonic laughter and nourishes the feeling of resentment. The more grotesque the action of the play, the more farcical the characters, the more organic "Hard's theses" fit the general image of "mad America." In this particular play, the former cleaner from the Reichskanzlei is invited to share "juicy details" from Hitler's private life, including his memories of how he "accompanied a *Frau* more than once on her way out from the Führer's bedroom" and how the Führer "mostly loved watching...eeeh.. pornographic films with Miss Eva Braun."

This parade of circus attractions concludes with a strike in Hard's household, with most of his staff declaring that they "refuse to serve this resurrected toad."

Modes of "Popular Democracy": Between Resentment and Bravado

The extreme attention that the country's government dedicated to satirizing the actions of other states cannot be explained away only by reference to the "totalitarian" nature of the Soviet regime, which endeavored to control all and everything. It is also important to remember that the first decade of the Cold War, starting with Churchill's "Sinews of Peace" speech (1946) and up to the emergence of the "Geneva spirit" (1955), marked a collapse of diplomacy. The Soviet Union and its East-European satellites found themselves isolated in international organizations (such as the UN) and in their relations with Western democracies.

In the absence of an efficient diplomacy, almost the only remaining tool of international political communication is a set of signs that are transmitted by means of public gestures ("loudspeaker diplomacy"). This type of communication took a range of forms, from speeches by the leader of the state, official statements and activities of various "public organizations for peace" (such as the Soviet Committee for the Defense of Peace, the World Peace Council etc.), which functioned as expressions of Soviet "soft power," to texts and images featured in the press. These latter included the heavy-handed *Pravda* headlines, Il'ia Erenburg's pathos-charged lectures, Leonid Leonov's angry diatribes, Kukryniksy's and Boris Efimov's scathing caricatures, the sarcastic fables of Sergei Mikhalkov and Samuil Marshak, David Zaslavskii's satirical feature articles, as well as Vladimir Dykhovichnyi and Moris Slobodskoi's grotesque sketches, biting satirical plays, verses, and pamphlets.

The production of such "satire from above" directed at international matters was first of all addressed at the internal audience, supplying not so much information or an interpretation of certain events as affirming a sense of the Soviet community's own value and might. Ridiculing an enemy has always been an instrument of its demonization. Those who laugh are a priori in a position of power, and laughter is a mighty weapon of empowering the national ego, a key element in the culture of resentment that dominated the Soviet political discourse in the late Stalinist period. Since these texts were highly toxic (as we have seen, their humor was mostly contemptuous, humiliating, cynical) and since they made use of strong comic tools (sharp satire, sarcasm, grotesque), the sense of might grew into a sense of national arrogance, which became a central element in the Soviet nation building.

This is how "satire from above" began to simulate "satire from below," which in the repertory of the Cold War played the role of a special kind of "popular diplomacy." Even though it was always based on a narrative supposedly on behalf of the Soviet subject (who was shaped by this very narrative), its stylistic range was quite broad: from the usual sarcastic trolling to a double stylization—a simulation of *skaz*, which was itself a stylization of colloquial speech.

A good example of the first type of satirical exercises is Konstantin Simonov's poem "A Speech by My Friend Samed Vurgun at a Dinner in London" (*Rech' moego druga Sameda Vurguna na obede v Londone*, 1948) written like a report on a speech by the most celebrated Azerbaijani poet in the British Parliament. Simonov makes ample use of sarcasm in his description of the event. Stalin's poet and deputy of the Supreme Soviet had to

>Listen for no pay
>To a hundred and five speeches
>On how in the year one thousand ... may God not let me
>Err, something ...
>They cut off a king's head here.
>And how three hundred years later
>They passed all those bills of freedom
>And that's how they became so free
>As we can see today,
>So free, everyone cries tears of joy,
>Both they themselves, and the population.
>We listened to all this for a month,
>Ate three meals a day in the breaks
>And patiently—what else can you do?—
>Listened again, from morning till night.

Finally, when the poets had had enough of "smiling and listening to polite lies" and realized they were running out of their "resilience and patience," Samed Vurgun, urged on by other Soviet delegates to "tell them a few words" and to "spoil their devil's dinner!", decided he should speak:

>And then the son of Baku rose
>Over the crystal and the dinner jackets,
>Over those marks of hereditary
>Gout they displayed on their blue cheeks,
>Over the lords, so proud
>Celebrated by Kipling,
>Dressed in starched collars
>Old muzzles,
>Old bottles,
>Red necks,
>White heads
>Of colonels from India.

This parade of freaks does not just provide a background to the intervention by the poet and the people's deputy; it magnifies its sarcasm. Vurgun talks about his native Azerbaijan as a "free country" that is part of the "Soviet state"—"a union of true friends." But most of his speech is not so much talking about his motherland as exposing his hosts' imperialism:

> And even though my country has
> All the riches of oil,
> It is the only one in the world
> Where you have no mandate,
> Which is not at your feet,
> Not made a pawn in your City,
> Not robbed on ships from Dover,
> Not forced to accept petty freedoms
> Like India, as if in mockery,
> My country is really mine,
> Completely useless to you,
> For which I offer you
> My full sympathy.

His listeners' reaction, as rendered by Simonov, is supposed to make the reader feel superior to the occupants of the British Parliament, as it betrays the enemies' impotence (and they are described as enemies). Their faces betray

> First fear,
> A voiceless cry: "Police!"
> Then they went red,
> Their veins swollen,
> As if that speech
> Was a mustard plaster on their skin.
> They don't want to be sitting there, listening to that speech,
> They want a gun in their hands, their finger on the trigger!
> They want a whip
> To flog this nobody from Baku!
> They want to dance on his back,
> To crack his bones,
> Instead of sitting here, like equals,
> With me and with him, their guests,
> To sit and listen to his speech
> Idiotically helpless,
> To sit and to know: these ones cannot be burnt,
> Cannot be eaten alive,

> Cannot be shot, like those twenty six
> In the dunes near the town of Krasnovodsk.

The last words are a reference to the twenty-six Baku commissars executed some thirty years previously for their belief in the revolution and the victory of communism. One would be hard pressed to find a better description of the collapse of diplomacy: if both sides have such a strong, literally deadly, hatred of each other, why do they organize meetings, and why do they exchange parliamentary delegations and speeches? It is unlikely that the Soviet delegation would go to London to spend a whole month there eating "three meals a day in the breaks" for the sole purpose of poisoning their generous hosts' appetite.

One might ask how the authors of these works (and that culture as a whole) saw the Stalinist subject (reader): Who needed *this kind* of satire to nourish self-esteem? What is the moral and intellectual profile of the subject who can only affirm his or her own worth by demonstratively humiliating and insulting the other, even while enjoying the benefits of the other's generous hospitality? This question, however, became irrelevant once satire was accorded supreme legitimacy. In order to help the reader understand how right the Azerbaijani poet was in choosing to behave in this manner, Simonov concludes by introducing the Father of the People:

> My friend is standing over this wolf pack,
> Protected by the union of brotherly hands,
> He doesn't hear how Stalin, silently,
> Took a stand behind him while he is talking.
> Stalin is standing there, smiling—
> Apparently he likes the speech.

As this satire moved farther into the territory of colloquialisms, transmogrifying into the "direct speech" of the author speaking on behalf of the subject who was also the reader, and becoming more and more "popular," it was also becoming less and less witty. The loss of wit was compensated by an increase in what was perceived as authenticity. Particularly interesting are cases when the quality of humor falls below zero. They reveal a great deal about the kind of subject that was constructed in these texts, as well as about the mental profile of the authors, who themselves were exemplary Stalinist subjects. In the Ukrainian satirist Stepan Oleinik's poem "A Diplomat" (*Diplomat*, 1952) the situation is reversed. There, it is an ordinary kolkhoz member who finds himself in the role of "diplomat," and the encounter has a distinctly mundane feel to it. Gnat, a kolkhoz team leader, has a visitor: a diplomat from Washington. The hosts do not waste too much time getting ready for the visit:

"Hey, wife! Did you hear? Now that's a true wonder!
Look, they say here, in this note,—We're about to receive a guest from
   America,
Apparently he is visiting people around here!..."
The wife has a custom:
When a new guest arrives, he is always welcome,
But a guest of this kind, that's a first,
Especially seeing as he is a diplomat.
She dons a new garment:
A new apron, fitting tightly.
She fastens
The Order of the Golden Star
And other medals
Onto her husband's jacket.

The conversation between Gnat and the diplomat is described in the same buffoonish tone, to stress the gap between the diplomat's exaggerated politeness, his true intentions, and the Soviet reality. Gnat is happy that "sir.../ Is not opposed to learning from the kolkhoz" and offers "to entertain... slightly" the distinguished guest, even though "sir is almost breathless with a deep-rooted fury." The American is confused: Whom should he trust? On the one hand, there is the American radio, monotonously reciting news of how "hail and locusts... are bringing / Devastation to the Soviet harvest...," how "there, in all of Ukraine, / There are no fish in the rivers," and how "there is no electricity there, / Huts are blackened by oil lamps." On the other hand, there is what he sees with his own eyes, when "the lady of the house is bringing freshly baked bread," "carp is served for dinner," and "the chandelier is so bright that the diplomat is blinded."

Following the logic of ridicule, the kolkhoz member turns out to be a mirror-reversed diplomat. His diplomacy is not the art of lies but that of telling the truth; not the art of dialogue but that of burning bridges and causing scandals; not the art of concealment but that of exposure; not the art of peace but that of (cold) war—the art of trolling.

This diplomacy in the eyes of readers is the diplomacy of winners. Even though the diplomatic efforts of the poet and the kolkhoz team leader result in failure in both cases, from the viewpoint of militant satire they culminate in a Soviet victory and a humiliation, even symbolic annihilation, of the enemy. This is the familiar "laughter of victors," the function of which is to promote Soviet superiority. This may be a purely rhetorical exercise, but the rhetorical aspect is not to be discarded. When diplomacy no longer works, these imaginary rhetorical escapades simulate victories. Laughing at furious and helpless British MPs, or at a hapless American diplomat, the Soviet reader simultaneously learns the voice of power ("satire from above") and internalizes it through the "satire from below"—which nonetheless was also generated from above. In the Cold War "satire from above," language played a key role. It was the main tool that helped it perform its main function: a domestication of the country's foreign policy so that the mass consciousness of the nation's subjects internalized it.

As we can see, trolling Western enemies did not require any special motivation, and could be employed without connection to any concrete events. But when such events did take place, the propagandistic wave they caused could go on for years. This is exactly what happened after a successful testing of the Soviet nuclear weapon. Since at first, on August 29, 1949, it was only a nuclear "device" that was tested, and the bomb itself was to be assembled by December 1, the project was kept secret to prevent the US from taking retaliatory steps. It was only after Truman's public speech that mentioned the Soviet nuclear tests, when there was no point in keeping things secret any more, that a statement by TASS appeared on September 25, 1949 "in connection with President Truman's mention of nuclear tests in the USSR." This was the official Soviet response to the West, but in practice its addressee was the home audience (in the West, the news was no longer new). Except that the heavy-handed language of state media, which was the only form of communication possible for TASS, was not suited to mobilizing the masses. Hence, two weeks later, on October 8, 1949, a poem by Sergei Mikhalkov was published, translating the statement by TASS into the "language of the people":

> Blowing, blowing their whistle,
> Every day and every hour,
> Threatening everyone,
> Seeding panic.
> And then
> One day there came this message:
> TASS was informing the world
> Calmly, modestly, without any pretence,
> That, you see, we, too,
> Now have atomic weapons,
> Not just you.
> Yes-s-s!

Here, the comic effect is created primarily by the author's distinct style. He speaks of the hapless enemies in third person, never directly addressing them except for the very last line ("Not just you!"), and only once using personal pronouns in the "Not just you"—"we, too" juxtaposition. He thus makes it clear that the text has no function except for pure trolling—a spiteful teasing and picking on the enemy. Mikhalkov speaks in the voice of the Stalinist subjects, for whom this was the only way to express their attitude to the fact of the Soviet Union now having a nuclear bomb.

The official discourse (the communication by TASS) offers a serious take on the events, while the "satire from above" exposes its true content. The technological breakthrough that made the creation of the bomb possible is presented as something perfectly natural and ordinary, something that can be described in an exaggeratedly calm tone ("Calmly, modestly, without any pretence"), since there can be no doubt as to the victory of Soviet science and technology anyway. This restrained and matter-of-fact tone is contrasted with the reaction of the West, which is presented as panicky. At the same time the actual fact of the successful nuclear test is clouded in secrecy.

Another poem by Sergei Mikhalkov, "On the Soviet Atom" (*Pro sovetskii atom*, 1950; the poem was put to music by Vano Muradeli and performed by an army choir as a "soldier song"[66]), was an almost literal translation into a more accessible set of emotional and meaningful references of the many sophisms from Stalin's interview given to a *Pravda* correspondent following the testing of the bomb.[67] Here Stalin's exaggeratedly serious maxims, addressed to the foreign audience, are transformed into folk couplets—*chastushki* with the characteristic tone of spiteful glee. First the reader learns the happy news, which is both top secret and somehow mundane:

> Not long ago we made a test
> To see whose power is the best;
> We're quite pleased, You'll understand
> Our accomplishments are grand!
> It all splendidly succeeded—
> It exploded right where needed!
> The outcome's made us very happy:
> The Soviet atom's not too shabby!

In the next lines the leaders of the panic-stricken West are mocked for having been fooled. Here, too, "Soviet pride" is affirmed exclusively through sarcasm and bravura:

> The foreign press, with ears alert
> To headlines did the news convert
> The whole world heard it shout:
> "Now our precious secret's out!
> And now the Russians have for sure,
> What was only ours before!
> But why were the Russians all so daring

---

[66] Mikhalkov, *Oni*, p. 79.   [67] Stalin, "Otvet," pp. 151–2.

When Attlee and Truman both were staring?!"
Did they really,
Look so silly,
Actually?
Ha, ha, mind!
The Achesons
And Morrisons
Will get you in a bind!

The rest of the poem contains thinly disguised threats to the enemies that were somewhat out of sync with the allegedly peaceful nature of the Soviet political discourse. The true meaning of the Soviet "politically correct" messages was thus disclosed in the satirical verses ridiculing the West.

By changing the stylistic and generic modes—translating Stalin's text into rhymed sentences in the style of popular entertainment, or into a soldier song—Mikhalkov not only brings the message closer to the reader but also constructs the actual meaning of the message. His poem is a Stalin text adapted for the mass audience, painting the rivalry between the two camps the way it was supposed to be (and was most often) perceived by the common Soviet reader. The leader and the poet alike simultaneously responded to the readers' demands and shaped these demands, creating a level of discursive familiarity and approachability, a unified community of sympathetic readers and listeners, who, after all, formed the solid basis of the "moral and political unity of the Soviet people" with their ruler. The role of satire in this process can hardly be overestimated: the discourse that cemented this link could only be "popular."

On the other hand, this satire/humor divide becomes a distinguishing device that marks figures associated with specific camps as possessing certain features: the Stalinist subject is laughing, while the enemy can only frown. Consequently, the opposition "smile"/"sour face" is a meaningful, distinctive opposition. In the satirical piece "With a Sour Face" V. Medvedev reflects on how happy he is to see the happy smiles of friends around the world and the enemies' sour grimaces. The USSR is a country of smiles where "with each passing day there are fewer and fewer sour faces, and it cannot be any other way." This is the discourse of Soviet "kind humor," obsequiously self-congratulatory. The satirical tone is completely different: at a certain point the author confides to his readers that he "wanted to visit America just to look at the sour grimaces of the gentlemen from a certain well-known street in New York." This is the voice of bravura—threat drowned in laughter—and it is the defining characteristic of Cold War satire. Except that in this case there is no attempt to conceal the threat. The opposite is true: the threat is exposed. It creates a vivid emotional background to what is, in fact, a most obvious weakness: dependence on the enemy, at a moment when this enemy is in the process of being constructed by the very agents threatening him.

The Art of Double Entendre: Transference as a Satirical Device

The enemy's function is to provide a screen for the projection of a negative identity, and laughter plays a very important role in the process. Two fables that were both written in 1947 and that complement each other in quite a remarkable way provide a sort of manual on the technique of satirical transference at work.

Samuil Marshak's fable "The Dollar and the Pound" (*Dollar i funt*, 1947–51) tells the story of an encounter between the two currencies. One day "in an old bank on the banks of the Thames / The English Pound met the snobbish American Dollar." The dollar tries to convince the pound "to go into depreciation," which would make the British currency "healthier and younger," while the dollar would become "even more expensive." The dollar's behavior toward the "old friend" may seem unprecedented, but that would be a wrong impression. There is a precedent; it can be found in Sergei Mikhalkov's fable "The Ruble and the Dollar" (*Rubl' i dollar*, 1952). In it the arrogant, "puffed-up American dollar" encounters the Soviet ruble and starts "putting on airs" and boasting: "All of humankind trembles before me! / All doors are open to me, all borders." But the ruble, unlike the British pound, is not going to bow down before the dollar. He calmly affirms his superiority, since the ruble stands for Good, while the dollar symbolizes Evil: "I am the people's own Ruble, I am owned by the people / Who are building peace and are calling the world to follow the path of peace. / And I am getting stronger year by year. / Hey, you, step back: let the Soviet Ruble pass!"

As is evident, from among the three characters of these two fables it is the ruble rather than the dollar that is by far the most arrogant. Marshak had enough good taste to use the pound to expose the dollar's empty vanity, but Mikhalkov failed to understand that, by juxtaposing the dollar and the ruble, he essentially makes them swap places. His conceited dollar is, in fact, the Soviet ruble, who is even more full of himself than the dollar. The latter's behavior becomes a case of simple transference and projection of the Soviet national haughtiness. Mikhalkov failed to see the ruble's rhetoric of superiority as a mirror reflection of the dollar's behavior, thus demonstrating not so much malice as lack of insight.

While transference is a real semantic minefield for satire, satire is still the most appropriate form for its realization, based as it is on a clash of two levels: the visible (expression) and the hidden (content). The hidden level works by rejecting the visible. Soviet dissident satire thematized this logical mismatch, demanding to be deciphered and making use of "Aesopian language." Obviously, in Stalinism this satire was outside the public field, and now it is well researched. What is of special interest to us here are cases when the level of expression generated—intentionally or not—an ambiguous content.

Dykhovichnyi and Slobodskoi, as their work of the post-Stalinist period showed, sympathized with dissidents and nourished no illusions concerning the nature of the Soviet regime—unlike Mikhalkov and most other official Soviet satirists. At the same time, they were skillful masters of creating subversive and ambiguous (*supposedly* satirical) texts about America. Presented as unquestionably typical Soviet examples of anti-Western trolling, these texts can just as easily be read in an anti-Soviet vein, since the kind of West they described could not but make Soviet readers think of the realities of Soviet life. The same holds for the authors themselves: they did not know America at all, but the everyday reality of existence in the Soviet Union was all too familiar to them and easily reproducible in their texts. "A Little American Song" (which is how they defined the genre of their poem "Completely Free" [*Sovershenno svobodno*, 1953]) painted the instantly recognizable story of the horrors of American life:

> Who said there is slavery in America?
> Who said there are people who are not free?
> No, guys, we know that it is
> A land of free brothers.
> Our noble regime has been helping us
> To follow a destiny of free men:
> From our youth we have been free
> From doing any work at all.
> We were vagabonds, we walked for miles and miles,
> We needed rest—which is why
> We were sentenced in full freedom
> And put here—in prison.
> Be merry! Life itself
> Has provided for shelter and meals,—
> We are now free to drink waste water
> Under the guise of a brew.
> Who else is there, unemployed, hungry,
> Unhappy? There is room for him here—
> The way will be free for him
> To go into prison instead of us, once we are corpses.

This typical anti-American text talks of America in the early 1950s. It goes without saying that this picture was hardly reflective of reality at that particular point in time, since these were the years of unprecedented economic growth. Ironically, in the year this "little song" appeared, unemployment in the US sank to an all-time low, 2.5%. The prison life to which the American citizens are supposedly condemned brings us back to a completely different statistic: in 1951 (a double irony!) the population of Gulag camps reached a record number: more than 2.5 million people. The words about how US citizens have the right to "be completely free to kick the bucket in a completely free country" obviously correspond to the Soviet experience, not to the American one.

One could object that the real conditions of life in both countries (the US and the USSR) were not known to the citizens of the Soviet Union, but their main features were, of course, no secret to the authors of these verses. This is transference at work, but not in the Freudian sense of the word. Instead, the authors make use of transference as a subversive practice so as to demonstrate their total political loyalty, while at the same time leaving a loophole for uncontrollable interpretations that could only be made explicit beyond the limits of the legally permissible frame of interpretation. The very act of creating such a semantic field demanded a professional mastery of the art of *double entendre* (which was colloquially known among the intelligentsia as "showing a finger in the pocket").

The readers of another poem by the same authors, "A Spy from Buffalo" (*Shpion iz Buffalo*, 1951) would probably recognize local echoes of the supposedly "American" reality rather quickly. The poem opens with an epigraph: "All schools in Buffalo (in the state of New York) received an FBI directive encouraging children to spy on their parents." The source is indicated, too: "From the press," with the implication that this was *Soviet* press, as was usually the case with such epigraphs to caricatures and satirical poems. The poem talks about how the FBI teaches children "to pick up the pen": "They stick their nose into everything anyway, / So let them put their youthful eagerness to good use: let them report on others." The main character of the poem is nine-year-old Tommy, who, having taken the instructions of the agency to heart and being eager "to set a patriotic example," is now busy writing reports on all the members of his family. His top target is Aunt Mag,

> a nit-picker and a dangerous person.
> Once she was out for a walk with brother Harry,
> And then she said: "Our Harry is a fool!"
> But let us get this straight.
> I will tell you everything about this beast.
> Brother Harry is no fool! And I will find out
> Whom Aunt Mag had in mind,
> When she said out loud: "Our Harry is a fool!"
> My conclusion is: the aunt must be made to spill it all! ...
> Please pay me urgently for the report.

Here the authors are laying bare the device: since the aunt meant not "brother Harry," but Harry Truman, her words should be read subversively, at the level of a subtext—but this can be interpreted as an invitation to the poets' own audience to read their own text in a similar manner. Considering that the conclusion of the poem actually declares America to be a direct heir to Nazi Germany ("This is how it used to happen in Berlin, / But it would never have happened in Buffalo / If the White House had not become brown"), the subversive meaning of the scenes depicted here becomes as obvious as it is unexpressible. In a country where writing reports on others had been an officially encouraged national pastime since the 1920s, and where these reports had been used as an instrument of mass terror, where the paragon of childhood heroism was Pavlik Morozov, hardly anybody could misunderstand "whom aunt Meg had in mind."

In 1949, Dykhovichnyi and Slobodskoi created a cycle of one-act comedies about modern America. Their shared motifs are the lies about "American values," a disintegration of social ties, a general fear of losing one's job and status, becoming victim to politically motivated repressive measures, total corruption, the cynicism of the political system, the hypocrisy of the bourgeois family, and the like. Each of the plays featured the level-headed philosophizer Robert Cooper—a scriptwriter, communist, and fighter for peace.[68] The masterfully plotted plays were excellent examples of situation comedy.

Did the authors realize that their "America" was a replica of Stalin's Russia? It was their own country that was so governed by fear that it became a key motif of national literature, from the poems by Osip Mandelstam and Anna Akhmatova up to the cinematic works of the post-Soviet era, such as Aleksei German's *Khrustaliov, My Car!* (*Khrustaliov, mashinu!*, 1998), which is set in the time described by Dykhovichnyi and Slobodskoi in their poems and sketches. The satirists did not criticize the USSR, not even in the voice of its enemies. In their scathing criticism of America and only America they were guided by a simple logic: rendering the similarity explicitly *would have been possible* only in a position that would have been *fundamentally impossible* in Stalinism. Even thinking of such a comparison would have been a life-threatening act of political dissent.

Evil, once personified, becomes ridiculous because human nature is weak. As Nikolai Chernyshevskii remarked,

> evil is so horrible that it is not funny, however ugly it may be. But it often happens that a person harbors only a desire to be evil, even though his weakness and the insignificance of his character do not let him be evil for real; and such a helpless evil person, not terrifying or harmful to anyone, is a comic figure; his

---

[68] See Dykhovichnyi and Slobodskoi, "Tri oproverzheniia."

very death can be funny if he perishes through his own weakness and stupidity; and this can happen frequently, because all evil, every type of immoral behavior is stupid, reckless, and senseless at its core.... The realm of everything that is harmless / ludicrous is the realm of the comic; the main source of the ludicrous is stupidity, idiocy. Which is why stupidity is the main target of our mocking remarks, the main source of the comic.[69]

For all their rational tone, the reverse of these statements is also correct: that which is declared comic, that is, caricature or satire, is ludicrous, idiotic, stupid (it is not by chance that after making these remarks, Chernyshevskii goes on to discuss farce). In other words, caricature does not so much *portray* the ridiculous as it *produces* it. Since Socialist Realism was an art of producing reality, and since production of the enemy was one of its political and aesthetic functions, it provides fertile ground for satire. Everything that it marks as negative and deficient, everything that is to be rejected, it turns into caricature. Caricature, then, can be understood as a process of disarming the enemy.

[69] Chernyshevskii, "Vozvyshennoe," pp. 188–9.

5
The Gogols and the Shchedrins
Lessons in "Positive Satire"

>—Well, let me see what you have there... Is it a long report you've written?
>—The text itself is, as you know, about 45 minutes long. Plus the reaction of the audience: laughter, applause...
>—Is there humor?
>—(*darkly*) There is. There is! I was reading it in front of a mirror, I myself was laughing.
>
> Sergei Mikhalkov, *Lobsters*

The Satire of the Impossible

That April day in 1952 was a turning point in the history of Soviet satire. *Pravda* ran an editorial titled "Overcome the Lag in Playwriting" (*Preodolet' otstavanie dramaturgii*) that declared "conflictless" plays to be "harmful," claimed that "the strength of Soviet dramaturgy is in its truth to life," and asserted that

> the main reason for the feebleness of dramaturgy and the weakness of many plays is that the playwrights do not build their work around the serious conflicts of life, but evade them. If one were to judge by plays of this sort, everything is fine, everything is ideal, there are no conflicts. Some playwrights feel they are almost forbidden to criticize the bad and negative in our life....
>
> We should not be afraid to show shortcomings and difficulties. Shortcomings should be cured. We need Gogols and Shchedrins. There are no shortcomings where there is no movement, no development. But we are developing and advancing, which means that we have both difficulties and shortcomings.[1]

The "Gogols and Shchedrins" passage came from something that Stalin had said the day before, during a discussion of Stalin Prize candidates. As noted by Konstantin Simonov, who had been at that meeting, Stalin's actual words were:

---

[1] *Pravda*, April 7, 1952.

State Laughter: Stalinism, Populism, and Origins of Soviet Culture. Evgeny Dobrenko and Natalia Jonsson-Skradol, Oxford University Press. © Evgeny Dobrenko and Natalia Jonsson-Skradol 2022.
DOI: 10.1093/oso/9780198840411.003.0006

"We need Gogols. We need Shchedrins. There's still quite a lot of evil here. Quite a lot of shortcomings."[2]

Political circumstances prompted the campaign to revive satire, since just before and following the Nineteenth Party Congress in October 1952, Stalin was ramping up to another "great purge" in the higher echelons of power. Valerii Kirpotin, formerly a prominent Party functionary and after his ouster a scholar of the history of Russian satire, recorded his impressions of a recently appointed General Secretary of the Soviet Writers Union Aleksandr Fadeev speech in these terms:

> Contradictions never held Fadeev up. One day, before a large audience, he developed the idea that one should write without the exaggeration of Gogol and Shchedrin and that Chekhov would make a good role model. But a few years later, with identical enthusiasm, he started arguing that one should exaggerate, one should write like Gogol and Shchedrin. Both times, the directive had been authored by Stalin. Before the war, no satirical, critical attacks were allowed in literature. After the war, when Stalin was getting ready to settle scores with his closest associates, when the Politburo had been replaced with the broader Presidium, he gave Fadeev a directive to begin amassing society's critical potential. Conflict was now permitted in plays and there was now a need for the satire of Gogol and Shchedrin, who should be the mirror in which, without scaring the citizenry overmuch with grotesque forms, Soviet reality should be reflected.[3]

"After the war" refers to 1952, and as for concerns about the citizenry, the best response to that was provided by the magazine *Krokodil*, which published the following epigram by Iurii Blagov in its twelfth issue for 1953:

> We're for laughter! But we'd like
> Shchedrins of a kinder stripe
> And Gogols of the sort that don't
> Needle us, as was his wont.

But the satire that was being "revived" by a decision from above could fulfil only the functions assigned to it:

> In working out a theory of satire, we must begin by concentrating our attention on the cardinal problems that define its essence, especially the issue of the direction to be taken by Soviet satire, of its character, of which manifestations

---

[2] Quoted from Simonov, *Glazami cheloveka*, p. 233.   [3] Kirpotin, *Rovesnik*, p. 637.

of vice it is especially important at the given time to cauterize away with the fire of satire.[4]

Since the point at issue was the development of a *Soviet* satire, its direction had been decided long before: satire was to be a tool used in reinforcing the Soviet order and, as such, should be directed against a defined range of defects:

> The speeches of Lenin and Stalin and the documents issued by the Nineteenth Congress contain many specific pointers towards the vices that should be the object of unflagging attention and ruthless assault with the means available to art. The slackening of vigilance, complacency and woolgathering, various kinds of anti-state activity, a formal and bureaucratic attitude towards one's duties, a reluctance to listen to criticism from below, the suppression of that criticism, conceit, lying to the Party, smoke and mirrors, a heartless attitude towards people, hiring practices rife with nepotism and cronyism, immoral conduct in everyday life, and so on—all this should be made the target of merciless satire.[5]

Soviet satire hit its peak in 1953, a year that brought dozens of satirical plays, the best known of which were Nikolai Virta's *The Last Day of Pompeev* (*Gibel' Pompeeva*), Leonid Lench's *A Lot of Fuss* (*Bol'shie khlopoty*), Semen Narin'iani's *The Anonymous Letter* (*Anonim*), Sergei Mikhalkov's *Lobsters* (*Raki*), Nikolai Pogodin's *When Swords Are Crossed* (*Kogda lomaiutsia kop'ia*) and *Knights of the Soap Bubbles* (*Rytsari myl'nykh puzyrei*), Andrei Makaenok's *So Sorry* (*Izvinite, pozhaluista*) (also known as *Liver Stones* [*Kamni v pecheni*]), Vasilii Minko's *Mentioning No Names* (*Ne nazyvaia familii*), and Vladimir Dykhovichnyi and Moris Slobodskoi's *Sunday on Monday* (*Voskresen'e v ponedel'nik*). Toward the end of 1954 that surge of satire had ebbed to nothing.

The political underpinnings of the campaign fell away after Stalin died. *Kommunist* (the Central Committee's principal theoretical journal) told its readers in 1957: "Some people are incorrectly interpreting the Party's call to raise the chastising power of our satire to the level of Gogol's and Shchedrin's. And it is being forgotten that Gogol's satire, and especially Saltykov-Shchedrin's, aimed to shake the foundations of the then-existing order." Not so, though, in the Land of the Soviets: "The goal of our satire is the ruthless mockery of all that hinders the people's movement towards communism—that is, the affirmation of the Soviet order through a criticism of shortcomings."[6]

In 1958 the journal *Oktiabr'* published yet another discussion of satire, and this one spoke volumes. This time Nikolai Akimov, one of the most lively figures in Soviet theatrical comedy, declared in no uncertain terms:

---

[4] Onufriev, "Povysit' teoreticheskii uroven'," p. 9.   [5] Ibid., p. 10.
[6] *Kommunist* 3 (1957): p. 21.

I would have been completely calm and collected if it had been authoritatively explained to us that for the next fifty years we would have no need for comedy. There was plenty else to do. But if we are told that comedy is needed, and needed without fail, then it is our duty, the duty of professionals, to stand up and ask: Under what circumstances may it physically exist and occupy a worthy place in Soviet dramaturgy?!⁷

He was echoed by Rostislav Iurenev, a leading Soviet film critic and theoretician of comedy:

It is long past time for someone to come right out and say: "We don't need satire. We don't need Gogols and Shchedrins!" I am sick of the amicable unanimity at every conference. The same people keep getting together—people who really love comedy, who work in comedy, who are convinced that the satirical genre is essential—and speaking words of truth to each other. But a person who comes right out and says, "We don't need satire, comrades"—now there's a person we never see. Yet there are such people! Except that they don't say anything, they don't make speeches; all they do is sometimes write articles under pseudonyms, not expressing their basic position on the acknowledgment of satire but carefully and oh-so-ponderously annihilating the genre.⁸

The staging of Mayakovsky's *The Bathhouse* by Valentin Pluchek's Moscow Satire Theater, which had its premiere on December 5, 1953, was quite the event, since no Mayakovsky comedy had been publicly performed in the Soviet Union for a quarter-century. The third act of *The Bathhouse*—the "play within a play" in which the Pobedonosikov prototype takes on the censor's role and starts explaining how satire is to be written—presented a unique kind of parody on Stalinist satire, itself now a target of satire (suffice it to recall Comrade Ogurtsov in the movie *A Carnival Night* (*Karnaval'naia noch'*, 1956; dir. El'dar Riazanov). Rather than "condensing," satire should "poeticize," not dig at the bosses, not generalize, not typecast, and show no initiative, but instead mock only the things that have been pointed out by higher-ups. Its images should be symbolic, unlike their prototypes, and ideally should not make anyone laugh. Thus spake Pobedonosikov the censor, in lines that Mayakovsky had not really invented, but could perfectly well have drawn from speeches trashing satire (including the satire of Mayakovsky himself) dating back to the 1920s.

After Stalin's death, a view of the history of Soviet satire emerged according to which satire had blossomed in the 1920s and been revived during the Thaw, but could not by definition have existed in Stalin's time:

---

[7] Akimov, "Sovetskaia komediia," p. 149. [8] Iurenev, "Kakaia nuzhna," p. 164.

Satire was unable to develop under the cult of personality, when important satirical genres such as the fable, the epigram, the fel'eton, the parody, and so forth, were entirely consigned to oblivion. It could not have been otherwise, since the cult of personality betokened the abnegation of any kind of criticism, including the unique kind of criticism that satire represents.[9]

This is not how it was. Satire did indeed develop in all genres during the era of Stalinism but it differed significantly from what was and is traditionally understood as satire.

Iurii Tynianov's *Dostoevsky and Gogol: Towards a Theory of Parody* (*Dostoevskii i Gogol [K teorii parodii]*, 1921) closed with the following aphorism: "While the parody of a tragedy will be a comedy, the parody of a comedy may be a tragedy."[10] If this is so, there could indeed be no comedy under Stalin, since Socialist Realism had no truck with tragedy. But the picture is far more complex than that. Stalinist culture was one of heroics and sermonizing, and this, when turned inside out, becomes satire. Paradoxically, the form of comedy that was the most organic fit for Stalinism, which eschewed humor and irony, was satire, which corresponded to the spirit of Stalinism by virtue of its inherent and profound conservatism, since the satirist is less a revolutionary than a sermonizer. A satirist, as Robert C. Elliott has aptly observed,

> claims, with much justification, to be a true conservative. Usually (but not always—there are significant exceptions), he operates within the established framework of society, accepting its norms, appealing to reason (or to what his society accepts as rational) as the standard against which to judge the folly he sees. He is the preserver of tradition, the true tradition from which there has been a grievous falling away.[11]

A patch covering a tear in the fabric of wholesale heroism, satire always points toward the heroic, reproducing the heroic situation in reverse: "In fact, satire derives from the heroic personality and holds it to be a present spiritual requirement of society, but actualizes it in the 'hero-less' present situation."[12] The self-debunking character of satire should, however, be viewed in that heroic light: "Just as the fictional being of the heroic character concentrates and culminates in the noble deed [*podvig*], the fictional being of the satirical character becomes whole in a cartoonish quasi-*podvig* of involuntary yet cleansing self-negation, of self-immolation in the flame of laughter."[13]

---

[9] Makarian, *O satire*, pp. 3–4.
[10] Tynianov, "Dostoevskii i Gogol'," p. 226. Vladimir Vol'kenshtein repeats the first half of this paradox in his book from the 1920s: "Comedy is a parody of tragedy: Aristophanes parodied Euripides" (Vol'kenshtein, *Dramaturgiia*, p. 149).
[11] Elliott, *The Power*.   [12] Tiupa, *Khudozhestvennost'*, p. 117.   [13] Ibid., p. 120.

Satire began to suffer its "developmental problems" at the point when the power structure formulated an official requisition for it, imposing on it a "positive program" of regulation, prohibition, and censorship. From the viewpoint of traditional satire, "Soviet Gogols and Shchedrins" is an oxymoron, as is "Soviet satire" per se. Blium and other critics of satire in the 1920s had opined that if it wanted to continue being Soviet, satire could not be satire, and if it wanted to be satire, it would have to stop being Soviet. But Stalinist satire was aesthetically unique in having been fashioned by the power structure, which established prohibition and censorship as conditions under which the genre would have to develop. Stalinist satire was *the satire of the impossible*, and that is what makes it interesting.

It simply could never have occurred to Blium and his fellow-critics of the 1920s that the power structure itself would ever issue a requisition for Gogols and Shchedrins. They did not know how aesthetically radical the regime they were defending against satire actually was. As soon as the power structure transitioned from word to deed and started to throttle satire in the late 1920s, a lively discussion began of the main factors that characterized the originality of strictly Stalinist, Socialist Realist satire. Even into the early 1930s, critics were talking about the unprecedented novelty of Soviet comedy. So, for instance, at the First All-Union Congress of Soviet Writers, Boris Romashov spoke of the emergence of a transitional form in Soviet dramaturgy achieved by dint of combining genres: "[T]he canonical framework of comedy, drama, and tragedy," he noted, "is too narrow for the new content."[14] Due to the "narrowness" of the genre and the breadth of the "new content," tragedy, as we know, simply disappeared. Yet the consequences of abandoning the "canonical framework" for comedy were no less dismal.

The focus on a neutral genre form that possessed no distinctive features was ubiquitous in the 1930s. How that turned out for comedy is evident from an article that Emilii Mindlin titled "A Conversation About Comedy" (*Razgovor o komedii*, 1940). Mindlin shored up his argument that comedy could not possibly be "a unified genre" with references to the Russian classics: "The line of demarcation between realistic comedy and realistic drama can sometimes be highly approximate (in Ostrovskii, for example)." Mindlin spoke against "vacuous tomfoolery" and in favor of "injecting the serious" (*oser'eznivanie*) into the comedy genre by reference to specific problems. In the process, he again referred to the classics:

> Realistic Russian comedy—the comedy of social thinking—plays down the role of the purely comic, "ludicrous" element. In Russian playwrighting, that "purely comical" element retreats into the genre of vaudeville, of entertainment pure and

---

[14] *Pervyi Vsesoiuznyi s'ezd*, p. 428.

simple. To Russian comedy writers, the mockery addressed to an audience of given negative traits in society, of certain mores and aspects of life, was by no means the same thing as "amusing, diverting, or entertaining" that audience. At any rate, "funny" as a goal in itself is entirely alien to the nature of Russian comedy. In his comedies, Ostrcvskii is known to have almost never resorted to "funny," purely comic elements.[15]

As a result, satirical comedy was moving closer to drama, but inasmuch as drama could only be set in the "production" environment of an industrial enterprise or collective farm (in what also could be called a drama of *nomenklatura*, since it featured mainly a roster of Party-endorsed officials—district committee secretaries, executive committee chairmen, plant and factory directors, collective farm chairmen, etc.), satire too was turning into a kind of "a drama of *nomenklatura* (lite)." Soviet satire became essentially an amalgam of "production play" and vaudeville.

Vaudevillian Satire: No Gogols or Shchedrins Here

By the late 1930s, the production of "conflictless" plays was in high gear. Soviet vaudevilles, romantic comedies with singing and dancing shamefacedly dubbed "lyrical comedies"—with their hard-working heroes and heroines, high passions at home and at work, feelings put to the test, on the lines of Viktor Gusev's plays *Friendship* (*Druzhba*, 1938) and *Fame* (*Slava*, 1935)—packed the Soviet stage and screen. An idea of that popular genre may be garnered from Ivan Pyr'ev's film *The Swineherd and the Shepherd*, which was based on a Gusev play. The critics were pleased by the "verisimilitude" of those plays and films, one stating, for instance, that *The Tractor Drivers* (*Traktoristy*, 1939) (another Pyr'ev film) "presented real relations in the life of the collective-farm village, which have taken shape on the basis of socialist relations to labor and property."[16]

Soviet reality was still being satirically portrayed in the 1920s. But to visualize what the "positive satire" that took the place of satire proper was like, we should turn to one of the most popular comedies of the early post-war years—Dykhovichnyi and Slobodskoi's 1945 play *King for a Day* (*Fakir na chas*).

A hotel is expecting the arrival of a stage hypnotist who has had a room reserved for him (the hotel is otherwise booked up; new arrivals have to sleep in the foyer). The writer Karavanov is mistaken for a hypnotist and promptly shown to "his" room. The hotel staff start coming to him, asking to be hypnotized and

---

[15] Mindlin, "Razgovor," p. 118.   [16] Vaisfel'd, *Epicheskie zhanry*, p. 125.

cured of various ailments (a fear of upper management, a craving for alcohol, apathy, a penchant for bureaucratism, a stutter, and other disorders).

When Mironov, the town's housing and utilities director, appears in the supposed hypnotist's room, the play starts to look a lot like Gogol's *The Inspector General*. Karavanov thinks he is about to be unmasked, but instead he is moved to a better room; Mironov has actually come to see the "doctor" so he can learn how to read the minds of the higher-ups.

Making the most of his position, Karavanov forces the bosses to be more attentive to the residents, and the hotel is transformed. Clean curtains, linens, and flowers appear, the electricity is turned on, the water and radio start to work, the bathhouse is repaired, the guest registration form is shortened... And the main problem—the lack of rooms (which higher-ups have been occupying)—is also solved.

The vaudevillian storyline on which the "satirical" construction turns then brings Tania, Karavanov's lady-love, to the stage. It is her uncle, the bureaucrat Mironov, who is to blame for the hotel having been made into a huge hostel for the relatives and acquaintances of the local bosses. Tania threatens her uncle that if he does not put in for retirement, the "hypnotist" will make him think he is a dog:

[H]e will hypnotize you, set you on all fours, and send you off to your bosses looking like that. You'll go into the front office, lick the personnel director's hand, bark at the trade union people, and take a piece out of the city soviet chairman's thigh!... Your choice—either go there yourself on two legs, or you will be driven there on all fours.

But Mironov himself is a victim of the system: if he is afraid of the higher-ups, they are to blame for that:

I'm not deciding because I'm not in the habit.... And why is that?... Again, probably because for all these years my bosses have been impressing on me, and I've been impressing on myself, to remember that I have a head on my shoulders. "Why was it given to you?" they ask. "For you to figure out what'll happen to you if you start using that head on your own account." So I got used to assuming that my head's not there to think with, it's there to be kept safe!... And all of a sudden, there's a call for initiative: "Come on now, use your head for its intended purpose," they say. "All by yourself!"... But here I am, out of practice. I've forgotten.

Then the real hypnotist turns up, the deceit is discovered, and Mironov comes to his senses. In a panic, he demands that everything be restored to how it was before the "hypnosis."

As the story ends, Mironov's bosses express their gratitude and a conflict arises between Karavanov and Tania. She is falling in love with him but thinks this is due to the "hypnosis." Karavanov explains to her that, although he had been trying to free people from hypnosis rather than hypnotizing them, she is indeed under hypnosis,

> the most persistent, the most dangerous kind—the hypnosis of the past! The most damaging, the most hateful hypnosis for me is the hypnosis of distrust in other people.... That is a terrible hypnosis, Tat′iana Alekseevna! Under its influence, one goes blind and stops seeing the good in people!

In other words, the soulless bureaucrat, the rude boss, the perpetually drunk custodian (in short, all the play's characters) are nice people. And if you see the good in them, everything will fix itself.

As the curtain comes down, Karavanov reveals his real name and a relieved Mironov sighs: "Well, what do you know—he writes *fel′etony*. He could just as well have raked us over the coals in the press, which stings worse than any hypnosis! But he, so to speak, restricted himself to a reprimand. Very noble of him!"

The same may be said of Dykhovichnyi and Slobodskoi, for having elected not to write a *fel′eton* and producing instead a "noble satire" in which there were no satirical types (the bureaucrat recovers from his bureaucratism as efficiently as the stutterer from his stuttering) and no "negative manifestations"—just good people and discrete, easily corrected shortcomings. This 1945-vintage satire tells us that everything bad surrounding the Soviet person results from "the hypnosis of the past," which is distrust in people. Gogol, who saw his characters as nothing but "pigs' snouts," never discerned the good in them. Not so Soviet satire, whose "nobility" lies in its rejection of satire: good-for-nothing workers should not be "ousted and bounced"—no, one should instead see the good in them. All the characters in *The Inspector General* are propelled by fear, whereas the Soviet "hypnotist inspector," by contrast, "cures" everyone of fear.

Menacing Laughter: Stalin the Satirist

When Stalin turned to satire in 1952, it was not for the first time. The explosion of the satirical genres during the war had been guided from beginning to end. Military satire had melted fear down into laughter by portraying the enemy, and nothing but the enemy, as a satirical caricature. On this side of the front lines, meanwhile, only satire inspired by the Leader himself was permitted. Aleksandr Korneichuk's *The Front* (*Front*, 1942) was very much of that ilk.

The usual reason given for the publication of this play is that Stalin needed to offload the early wartime fiascos onto someone:

> It is a known fact that German tank columns had penetrated deep into Russia in a matter of months. Stalin should have been made to answer for the unheard-of

defeat that brought the Soviet Union to the brink of catastrophe. But he invariably ducked the answer, instead shifting the guilt onto "specific perpetrators." So, for instance, when 8 million peasants were exiled during collectivization, he explained in the article "Dizzy with Success" [*Golovokruzhenie ot uspekhov*, 1930] that the fault lay with local officials who had been "overdoing it." And in the summer of 1942, after Hitler's troops had broken through the line protecting the Volga and the Caucasus, new scapegoats were in urgent demand. So it was that Korneichuk's play *The Front* ran in *Pravda* from August 24 through 27—a first for *Pravda*, which rarely, if ever, published stage plays rather than novels. The wholly banal meaning behind Korneichuk's piece was that the perpetrators were at fault, and its prime scapegoat was front commander Gorlov, who does not want to learn anything new and is proud that he "never went to any universities" and is, in general, "not a theoretician but an old warhorse."... So, Korneichuk's message to readers was that these Gorlovs and Khripuns, jotted down so hurriedly (or, rather, in panicky haste) here and united by their obsolescence and blindness, are the ones to blame for the tragedy visited upon the people, for the retreat in which millions were killed and taken prisoner. This hot-button excuse for a play was naturally awarded a Stalin Prize First Class.[17]

Yet it is unlikely that Stalin had Korneichuk in his office in the Kremlin twice in less than a month during the most desperate days of the war (on July 24 and August 20, 1942) and personally edited the script just so that someone else could take the fall for his mistakes. He evidently had a different goal, which was first to lay the blame squarely on the Gorlovs, Khripuns, Tikhiis, Krikuns, and Udivitel'nyis, and then to announce a new army staffing policy that replaced incompetent commanders with new ones, with educated modern strategists—with Ognevs.

An order appointing General Zhukov First Deputy People's Commissar (to take Marshal Budennyi's place) was promulgated the day after the play appeared in *Pravda*. By the autumn of 1942, the iconic heroes of the Civil War had been forced into positions of secondary importance, while the key posts in the combat army were now filled by new commanders who had proved their superior professionalism later, during the Battle of Stalingrad and in further engagements.

Korneichuk's play centers on the conflict between Gorlov and Ognev, "a military leader of the new generation." Gorlov cannot take criticism and demands unthinking obedience; he is ambitious, rude to his subordinates, an easy mark for flattery, and surrounded by sycophants. He not only is unfamiliar with the science of war but flaunts his unfamiliarity, investing all his hopes in "General Frost" and "the courage of those heroic warriors, our stalwarts." Gorlov responds to doubts regarding the lack of sophistication in his projected operation, which is based on

---

[17] Svirskii, *Na lobnom meste*, pp. 484–5. See also Pechenkin, "Iskusstvo PR."

ignorance of the enemy's plans and potential, with "And what if there's an earthquake?...(*Laughs*) The main thing is to rush them, to dumbfound and destroy them!" The main thing, then, is valor and audacity. But, as Ognev maintains,

> there's no audacity in that order. Not even a whiff of it. Because there's no thought in it. This is all about cheering and hallooing and sheer dumb luck, as if the enemy before us is a fool and fast asleep. Is that really how positions are encircled? All you've done is drawn a sweeping circle and told us "Gallop on, lads, close 'em in on both sides!"

In the upshot, as Ognev foresaw, the enemy escapes the encirclement and surrounds Ognev's army, which, at great risk to itself, performs a truly audacious and successful maneuver, not only breaking out its own encirclement but also beating the enemy back from the contested village, and thus, to all intents and purposes, achieves what the operation had been intended to achieve. Meanwhile, Gorlov just goes on issuing his disastrous orders.

While the qualities of a modern, educated commander who enjoys the support of Headquarters and thinks in the categories of modern warfare are underscored in Ognev, his opponents, by contrast, are resistant to the new and think in terms of old concepts based on unintelligible class sentiments:

GORLOV: They've never had any blisters, so how can they be properly schooled?
UDIVITEL'NYI: Never was a truer word spoken! Take me, for one. Though I didn't work in a factory very long, only three years and two weeks, I can't for the life of me understand how I got enough proletarian guts in me to last a lifetime. Somebody else, y'know, might be all cultured and have graduated from university, but then you go and take a good look at him, and he's just not right. Not right at all.
GORLOV: Clear as day. There's culture on top but nothing earthy in the guts. That's why he doesn't come out right.

This recurrent motif in the play is also underscored in the additions Stalin made to it. So, for instance, we have some lines of dialogue inserted in his own hand for one of the sermonizing heroes:

> We still have a lot of uncultivated commanders who don't understand modern war, and that's our misfortune. War cannot be won by valor alone. What you need to win a war, besides valor, is the ability to fight in the modern way. You need to learn to fight in the modern way. For that, the experience gained in the Civil War is insufficient.

At one point, a deus ex machina makes an appearance, in the form of a representative from Headquarters on the staff of the Gaidar Front, who comes from Moscow bringing an order that sends Gorlov into retirement and appoints Ognev in his place. And in that order Stalin's style is recognizable:

> You are a brave man, and devoted to our great cause. That is very good, and for that you are respected. But that is not enough to be victorious over the enemy. To be victorious, the ability to fight in the modern way, the ability to learn from the experience of modern warfare, the ability to cultivate new young cadres rather than pushing them away is also needed. But you do not have that ability, unfortunately. Of course, knowing what you're doing and having the ability to fight is something that can be acquired. If today a person doesn't know how to fight, if today he doesn't have enough military know-how, tomorrow he will—the ability both to fight and to know what he's doing, if, of course, there is a strong desire to learn, to learn from the experience of war, to work on oneself, and to develop. But you do not have that desire. Can old commanders develop and become experts in the techniques of modern warfare? Of course they can, and not less so but perhaps even more so than the young ones, provided only that they want to learn from the experience of war, that they don't think it's a shameful thing to learn and develop further. As the wise folk proverb says, and with good reason, "You learn something new every day." But the whole trouble is that you, meaning certain old military leaders, don't want to learn. You are sick with conceit and think you're already schooled enough. And therein lies your principal shortcoming, Comrade Gorlov.

Here we have all of Stalin's writing techniques: rhetorically paired questions and answers, pleonasms, proverbs, and redundant syntactical constructions. Stalin either inserted those passages himself or spoke them, leaving Korneichuk to write them in for him. And that sacred text was never edited thereafter.

The play predictably infuriated the officer corps. Whereas previously, individual junior commanders had been criticized, now Korneichuk's devastating criticism was being leveled at a front commander and his entourage. Never before had the army command been presented in such a cartoonish light in the Soviet press. The *Pravda* editors and the Party Central Committee received outraged letters, telephone calls, and telegrams from highly placed readers who were unaware that there was on Stalin's desk a typescript of the play with "Text contains my corrections, St." written in his own hand on the title page.

Literally the day after the play's publication, a telegram came for Stalin from Marshal Timoshenko, commander of the North-Western Front, telling him that "the play will harm us for a long time to come, and must be withdrawn. The author must be held to account, and all those culpable therein should be investigated." Stalin replied the same day:

I have received your telegram about Korneichuk's play. Your assessment of the play is incorrect. The play will be of great educational significance to the Red Army and its commanding staff. The play correctly notes the Red Army's shortcomings, and it would be incorrect to close one's eyes to those shortcomings. One must have the courage to admit to shortcomings and must take steps to eliminate them. This is the only path to improving and perfecting the Red Army.

Stalin was, in essence, not only the client for and editor of this play but also its author; hence the significance of the conflict portrayed in it. Korneichuk (and his supreme editor and co-author) had taken great care with the portrayal of Gorlov, applying to it a precise delineation of light and shadow. He is presented as a patriot, devoted to the Party's cause, who for all that has lost touch with advanced military science and is falling apart because of his entourage. Thus, a conflict flourished between the good and the better, in which "the good" is a euphemism to denote what yesterday was good but today is "out of touch" and needs to "give way to the new."

It became clear that in the Stalinist world, a *nomenklatura* hero would get no chance to remake himself: once he became a target of satire, the verdict was in. He would, to quote *Pravda*, be "implacably cast aside by life." And that is why postwar satirical plays patterned on the *Front* would admit the "remaking" of "simple people" but never of high-ranking characters from the *nomenklatura*.

The war gave shape to a unique elite. The exemplar for the Soviet manager became the military director—a person of unchallenged authority whose focus was on completing the assignment whatever the cost. This was a special archetype of a societal character, a whimsical and psychologically complex combination of bureaucrat, factotum, and adventurist. This hero was the true "reflection of life," a representative of a Stalinist *nomenklatura* that stood in need of constant "purging" and intimidation. Whereas the basic work was being done invisibly by the departments of Party committee administrative bodies and personnel departments at every level, satire was one of the few *publicly accessible* ways of publicizing a particular political decision in the arena where management of the *nomenklatura* cadres took place. This engendered a new type of satirical play that was *politically topical in its form* and *nomenklatural in its content*.

Menacing Laughter: The *Nomenklatura* Tragicomedy

After the war, and especially after the 1946 Central Committee Resolution on the theaters' repertoire, what is known as the "production play" began to dominate the Soviet stage. But, since those plays invariably centered on the image of "the strong leader," and their basic plot conflict usually amounted to the discrediting of that leader, it would be more accurate to call them *nomenklatura* plays. Those plays were "realistic" to the extent that they faithfully reflected the structure of the bureaucratic Party regime. But the continuous calls to portray "simple people" went unanswered in them, because "production relations" (and that was what they were supposed to portray) boiled down to nothing but the "relations" between the people in whose hands the power lay.

"The endless clashes with the directors, managers, heads, and chairmen of the Soviets and Party secretaries, and all the changes played thereon, have yet another important aspect, this being that Soviet playwrights are paying too little attention to the image of the simple Soviet worker," wrote Anatolii Surov, who himself composed plays of that kind.

> By concentrating their attention on sketching images of directors and bosses and losing sight of the life of the simple folk who are building the communist society, our playwrights sometimes end up distorting reality, whose hero and creator is less the individual comrades in a position of responsibility than the triumphant Soviet people. Plays such as, for example, Virta's *The Last Day of Pompeev*... in general contain no images of simple Soviet people. There are instead the collisions and conflicts of various "nomenklatura" characters, as Mikhalkov described them in his comedy, who are detached from the people and know neither how the latter live nor what they need.[18]

Although the title of that Virta play parodies the title of what is probably Russia's most famous painting, Briulov's *Last Day of Pompeii*, Virta was not writing a parody on the production play. He was, rather, only caricaturing certain characters (revealing the full gamut of positive and negative heroes) and plot clichés that typified the genre.

Daniil Romanovich Pompeev, a forty-eight-year-old regional executive committee chairman at the height of his career in the *nomenklatura*, is a sort of postwar Gorlov. He has hatched a scheme to construct a huge, 60,000-seat stadium and now wants "to put on a humdinger of a song festival for the First of May." His wife cannot understand what her husband's critics want from him:

> But you already know Daniil's a go-getter. They sent him a three-year animal husbandry plan, and Daniil resolved to complete it in two years. And all sorts of eager beavers and blockheads started yelling, "Bunkum! Smoke and mirrors!" But like it or not, half the plan has already been completed in a year, if you can imagine that! What more do they want? No, I don't understand them at all, and I don't want to.

---

[18] Surov, "Nashi zadachi," pp. 311–12.

But the Pompeevs have reason to worry, because something has changed there since the arrival of the new Party regional committee secretary. And, although that character never appears on stage, his presence is felt in everything.

The play runs along the well-worn furrow of the *nomenklatura*-production play, until the author has the protagonist himself resort to "the sharp weapon of satire." Pompeev, who is to give a report to a meeting of the regional soviet, asks his daughter to help him: "Iul'ka, go and pick out five quotations or so from the classics for me. About bureaucrats, you know, and toadies.... As cutting, as biting as they can be.... That's how it's done now to bad-mouth the bosses, girlie." But the quotations she collects prove to be an exercise in self-debunking that make a laughing stock out of the speaker, as we learn from the public prosecutor after the meeting: "He certainly knows his stuff, that one! Those quotations about Sobakievich and the bear in the province—did he put them in there to tell us about himself?" Pompeev sends his minion to find out what is being said about his report behind the scenes: "Go and listen to what they're saying. And remember who said what. Then report back to me. I love criticism, I promote people for being bold in their criticism. And you need to be speaking out too, get it? The more criticism, the better." But when Supreme Soviet Deputy Glybov turns up and starts criticizing him, we realize that Pompeev really cannot stand to be criticized and that there are dark clouds on his horizon:

GLYBOV (BANGING HIS FIST ON THE DESK): We will not permit you to go on deceiving the people with your blowhard plans. We will teach you to see real people and real causes. And if even that teaching doesn't help, there's precious little chance the people will do you the honor of seating you as a deputy a second time.

What comes next is only to be expected: "the people" withdraw their trust from Pompeev and close the play by saying, through the proxy of a group of workers just back from Moscow, "Yesterday we went to the Satire Theater and saw a play. One actor was playing Pompeev to the life—so like him, so very like him that I thought 'You might as well be portraying his nibs.'" "They *will* portray his nibs," Lomov, Pompeev's deputy, tells them.

Virta's play is in the genre of satirical comedy, but there is, strictly speaking, nothing comic in it. This is a typical *nomenklatura* play about a high-handed boss. The project of "injecting the serious" into satire had borne fruit, in that this play has nothing funny about it, other than a cartoonishly vulgar wife and an insolent secretary. The satire on this *nomenklatura* braggart is based on demonstrating the untenability of his claims on the power of the regime. Pompeev's "Last Day" comes when the system cleanses itself.

Only the Soviet order as a whole possesses the power to which this overweening bureaucrat lays claim. After hearing Pompeev has lost his job, his wife panics: "But what will he do? He can only be a manager. All his life he's been managing something." Putting an official like that in his place means showing him the door. The loss of a job is a tragedy for him (but a comedy for the audience). So, in so far as the Soviet satirical comedy parodies tragedy, it parodies the *nomenklatura* tragedy of Pompeevs large and small. But whatever the scale of the boss being ridiculed, his tragedy is so demonstrably petty that there is really no sense in parodying it at all.

What, then, was this satire's function? Typification (*tipizatsiia*) was a key to the Soviet theory of realism. In the Soviet interpretation, there could be no satire without "types." Thus, Gogol's and Shchedrin's satirical characters were all "types." But, whereas prior to the Revolution satirical types were "the most widespread" phenomenon, in Soviet satire (which bore no resemblance to its pre-revolutionary counterpart, since, among other things, the former undermined the regime and the latter strengthened it), "types" reflected "the essence of the phenomenon." The *nomenklatura* characters of Soviet satire, however, manifestly had no bearing whatsoever on "the essence of the phenomenon" precisely because they were "typical." In fact, the greater a Soviet satirical character's "typicality," the greater, paradoxically enough, his *specificity*. Pompeev is a typical bureaucrat, braggart, despot, what you will, but not a typical representative of the Party *nomenklatura*.

The more varied and motley the *nomenklatura* freak show became (and Stalinist satirical dramaturgy created a whole gallery of *nomenklatura* "monstrosities"), the more the political content of the *nomenklatura* system that had given birth to them all was concealed. The point of contention was always the characteristics of a *particular* repository of the bureaucratic evil, the protagonist's own delinquencies, rather than how *system-specific* those characters were. The operative principle here was "the worse the better": the more negative traits a satirical character had, the more opportunities there were to censure those traits, which were offered and accepted as a deviation.

But how can the protagonist's behavior be explained, other than by class and political status? The art of Stalinist satire is an escape from satire, whereas "the technique of the comic" is an escape from generalization, a kind of *detypification* through what is ostensibly typification. Mikhalkov's comedy *Lobsters* (1953) is a veritable handbook on the practice of safe (satirical) writing.

This is a comedy attacking woolgathering[19] that is written "à la Gogol." Mikhalkov furnished his play with an epigraph designed to clear him of any suspicion that he was "threatening the founding principles":

---

[19] In the political context of Stalinism, "woolgathering" (*rotozeistvo*) was more than just a foible or character trait that might be slightly amusing, because (in a person of responsibility) it implied criminal negligence or even treason.

MR. P.: Well, then, judge for yourself. What do you make of it? It's all vices and more vices. What example is that for an audience?
MR. B.: But are those vices being praised? No, They're being made to look ridiculous.
MR. P.: Well, say what you will, old chap, but then there's respect. This is how people lose respect for officials and the jobs they do.
MR. B.: There's no respect lost for officials or the jobs they do but for those who make a mess of their jobs.

—Gogol, "Leaving the Theater After the Performance of a New Comedy" [*Teatral'nyi raz"ezd posle predstavleniia novoi komedii*]

Having thus smoothed the feathers of both officials and readers, Mikhalkov went on to portray a cabinet of *nomenklatura* curiosities in a provincial town:

STEPAN FEOFANOVICYH LOPUKHOV: A member of the *nomenklatura*, some fifty years of age. A self-enamored bureaucrat, heavyset, undereducated, and out of touch with life. His "management" style may be guessed from how he conducts himself at home. He cannot stomach objections from his subordinates. He has such a high opinion of himself that he permits himself to judge everything categorically and abstrusely.
AGLAIA IVANOVNA: His wife. Her only interests are tasteless outfits, tasty meals, gossip, and tittle-tattle. She dotes on her daughter and, weak-willed as she is, always lets her have her way. She considers her husband one of the town's most deserving white-collar workers. Despite her age, she loves light blue and pink.
SERAFIMA: Their daughter. A spoiled brat, thoughtless and frivolous. She lords it over her mother and is a little scared of her father. She has no principles at all.
LEONID ARKAD'EVICH LENSKII: An unknown quantity with the face of a positive hero, some thirty-five years old, a swindler by trade. He considers honest labor the lot of plebeians. Not a stupid man, and not untalented when it comes to role-playing and improvisation. Likes to find common ground with everyone he talks to. Distinguished by his habit of not immediately answering questions that are put to him.

And so forth.

To see a Gogol comedy as a play about "woolgatherers" is tantamount to seeing *Crime and Punishment* as a standard-issue detective story. The source of laughter for Mikhalkov is not an emotional appeal to the audience's societal awareness but the situational lampooning of certain secondary manifestations of bureaucratism. One of the recurrent "ploys" of this kind of "satire" is that the bureaucrats' aides write their reports for them, upon which hilarity ensues. For his reports, Lopukhov relies entirely on Ukleikin, his assistant, with whom he is, even so, perennially displeased. "He'll stretch it out to the bitter end, and then you have to take the fall. The last report he fobbed off on me would have tied the devil's own tongue in knots. The words he crammed in there! And not one of them to the point." Lopukhov's wife also bewails her husband's excessive gullibility:

> Oh yes.... My Stepan Feofanovich has a heavy load to haul!... But you can't put your trust in everybody. No indeed, not everybody! This one or that one will write goodness knows what for you, and you'll take it in the simplicity of your soul and deliver it from some podium. It's all well and good if parts of it escape them, but if they don't and then the nit-picking starts, there'll be no end of unpleasantness.

A speaker reading someone else's text verbatim is supposed to be good for a laugh. But Lopukhov's incompetence combined with his actor's ability to "enter into the role" is supposed to be even funnier. So, Ukleikin tells him that in the report he has written, "you level criticism at our woodworking complex." Lopukhov then enters organically into the role of author, while Ukleikin steps out of it with equal ease:

LOPUKHOV (*RAISING HIS SPECTACLES*): So I'm criticizing it?
UKLEIKIN: Of course you are! Here! (*Shows the passage.*)
LOPUKHOV (*AFTER READING THE PASSAGE*): Aren't I being too hard on it?
UKLEIKIN (*WITH CONVICTION*): No, you're not, Stepan Feofanovich. Not a bit! I would even say you're going easy on them. Highly placed organizations have taken the factory's flawed practices sharply to task.
LOPUKHOV: Seems like I missed that.
UKLEIKIN: There's going to be a special piece in the paper. Don't you worry, now, I won't steer you wrong. That would hurt me worse than it hurts you.
LOPUKHOV (*THOUGHTFULLY*): Then perhaps I'd do good to give it to 'em good? Right? Criticism's a wholesome thing: no one's died of it yet. (*Laughs.*)
UKLEIKIN: You're a cutup, Stepan Feofanovich. You take criticism well, like water off a duck's back.
LOPUKHOV: And you, Uleikin—do you take criticism?
UKLEIKIN: That I do, Stepan Feofanovich. I take it when it's prescribed to me. A tablespoonful three times a day. Because more than that isn't advisable. (*Laughs.*)
LOPUKHOV (*GOING BACK TO THE REPORT*): Then add two or three more tablespoons here. And spike it with something!... So criticism seems to be OK now. But what about the self-criticism? Won't they say it's coming up a bit short?

UKLEIKIN: Now, now, Stepan Feofanovich: they won't say anything of the sort! I gave it my all. I took past reprimands into account, that I did!... Did you skip those pages? Page twenty-two, page twenty-three, and there's another half-page here. (*Points.*) I came down hard, with all integrity, with all, so to speak, asperity. On you personally, on Comrade Kareglazov.... In a word, you'll be pleased.
LOPUKHOV: Then thank you for that, old chap.
UKLEIKIN: Well, it's all for the cause, Stepan Feofanovich.

This *metasatirical* scene reveals one of Mikhalkov's techniques. Here, he has assumed the role of Uleikin, so that his play resembles a report complete with "criticism and self-criticism." Its epigraph could well have been the slogan that we see in Lenskii's office, which is "Be Bolder in Criticizing Isolated Shortcomings!" The main thing here is to "isolate" shortcomings from system-wide problems, and use the former to obscure the latter. So, for instance, Lopukhov's status remains undefined throughout the play: he criticizes various enterprises for doing bad work and behaves toward the town's officials as if he owns the place, yet we learn from the text that he does not represent the authority of either the Party or the local soviets.

UKLEIKIN: If he wants to complain, let him address himself to the soviet authorities. It sits in the executive committee. You're not soviet authority!
LOPUKHOV: You're right about that. What kind of soviet authority am I? We have nothing in common!

Then what does he represent? The one certain thing is that he has allowed himself to be fooled by a petty crook. But while the self-deception of the officials in *The Inspector General* is explained by fear, the gullibility of the characters in *Lobsters* is inexplicable. And that inexplicability is what makes it intriguing, and so much so that the label of "woolgatherer" seems to supply all the answer we need.

To discredit every character in Lopukhov's orbit, Mikhalkov portrays them in the light of one "principal" shortcoming—that of "woolgathering." Not only are the Lopukhovs tarred with this brush but also the chief of police, who issues Lenskii a new passport on the strength of "forged documents," and the chief accountant, who hands public funds over to a con man, and the head of the personnel department, who did not check his documents and so on. They all suffer from the malady of woolgathering. This is the "Soviet Gogol."

Just as Soviet satire portrayed negative phenomena in ways that concealed the crux of it all, so that it could be neither ridiculed nor even simply articulated, so too the critics came nowhere near to censuring the thing that prevented the satire in those texts from being satire at all. For instance, Nikolai Pogodin, who gave his article on *Lobsters* the title of "Satire in Watercolor" (*Satira akvarel'iu*), criticized

Mikhalkov for focusing on Lopukhov in order to blacken his character and for adding Lenskii to the dramatis personae while doing nothing to show us who he is. In like style, Iakov El'sberg demanded something "above and beyond" from Mikhalkov, on the grounds that at that time, in 1954, satire was needed to help with the incipient "cadre renewal" and it would not have been out of place at all to tackle the political dimension of "woolgathering."

> The woolgathering type in S. Mikhalkov's *Lobsters* cannot truly satisfy audiences here. In drawing the woolgatherer, a writer should take aim at woolgathering as a serious flaw engendered by political immaturity, the slackening of vigilance, complacency, conceitedness, carelessness, and the inability to discern the enemy and tear the mask from his face. The negative type of the woolgatherer should encompass and expose the most dangerous forms of woolgathering, which is often enough masked by sham vigilance and fine words and is apt to inspire confidence in itself. A satirist's duty is to castigate and ridicule woolgathering to the extent needed to run to ground even tricky and slippery woolgatherers with pretensions to authority and intellect.[20]

But the qualifications ascribed here to the woolgatherer contradict the very essence of the phenomenon: no mask will do a nitwit any good—if he is not a woolgatherer, he must be a slippery spy. Harking back to Mayakovsky's challenge to the satirist ("hook the big fish, the kulaks and the bureaucrats, the fools and the toadies" [from the 1929 fragment "Something Gloomy about Humorists" (*Mrachnoe o iumoristakh*)]), El'sberg demanded that the shortcomings of "the big fish"—who in this instance were the woolgatherers—be "boldly uncovered," wherever they were hiding, but also said that as things currently stood, it was impossible to "ramp up the satirical generalization," since the "uncovering" was contingent upon analysis of the reasons why the Lopukhovs had flourished in the Stalinist *nomenklatura* system. The political offense under which El'sberg, master of the genre of political denunciation, had subsumed Mikhalkov's characters was less effective in "uncovering the social roots of woolgathering" than it was in concealing them behind an inappropriate explanation.

Criminal Laughter: Gogols and Shchedrins in the Age of Ostap Benders

Then who managed to give the *nomenklatura* woolgatherers the slip? The above-referenced plays are devoid of politically colored conflicts of any kind, leaving the

---

[20] El'sberg, *Nasledie*, p. 23.

discussion to center on a miscellany of "crooks and thieves." The presence of such characters in very nearly every satirical play was supposed, on the one hand, to indicate the unstable boundary between a ridiculed phenomenon (bureaucratism, careerism, vulgarity) and a criminally punishable offense and, on the other, not simply to morally discredit but also to delegitimize the ridiculed bureaucrat. Satire was being transcended, not because criminally punishable offenses could not be an object of ridicule but because, as we shall see, the invocation of the Criminal Code as an instrument of moral criticism was a sure sign that the genre was in crisis.

Il'f and Petrov made Soviet literature's principal satirical protagonist Ostap Bender "honor" (read: circumvent) the Criminal Code because this served as an inexhaustible source of comical situations. Furthermore, they, unlike the "Soviet Gogols and Shchedrins," understood that the satirical exposure of criminal culpability transforms satire into sermonizing and the satirist into a policeman on the beat. And indeed, in many Stalinist satirical comedies, policemen and prosecutors actually do assume the role of ultimate authority. The aesthetic threshold separating satire from tautology and distinguishing it from propaganda and caricature, which had been felt strongly in the 1920s, was overstepped in Socialist Realism.

Corroboration of the extent of the changes in Soviet reality and "realism" when compared to the 1920s is found in the fact that the only place for the con man was now in a *nomenklatura* storyline, because in order to remove the crook from the *nomenklatura* structure, he would have to be ejected from the action itself. The foothold that *Lobsters* has in *The Inspector General*, needless to say, predetermined a situation in which strictly official relationships cause the action to develop. Although Gogol's Khlestakov did not belong to the bureaucracy, he was supposed to be perceived as part of it. But the cipher Khlestakov became a swindler by happenstance, whereas Lenskii is an imposter and a scoundrel on purpose.

The Soviet Khlestakov contrived to fool everyone and abscond with public funds. But even if Mikhalkov had not given his character such a scintillating "career path," that would only have changed the scale of the deception. And the critics sensed this accurately. Pogodin reproached Mikhalkov for making Lenskii this comedy's protagonist:

> It is not the plot of *Lobsters* that is open to objection (the plot is true to life and valid), but Lenskii as a type, because, first and foremost, a professional crook cannot personify the idea of an artistic image in a modern work. What is there of interest, of social significance for an artist to reveal in the image of a crook who has chosen fraud and swindling as his trade? Nothing, if you ask me.[21]

---

[21] Pogodin, "Satira," p. 75.

Pogodin, moreover, saw Lenskii as a character from a *fel'eton*, and not typical in any way: "He is manifestly and even somewhat emphatically copied from modern *fel'etony*," because the Soviet exposé-style *fel'eton*

> deals with facts. There is no need to belabor the idea that, whatever fact of life it uses as its springboard, a Soviet denunciation play should deal with a social phenomenon. The tale of Lenskii's shenanigans at the Lopukhov home is legitimate as a fact, but as a social phenomenon, it is not. And not due to the actual incidence of types similar to that con man but only because the character itself restricts the play to the random and concrete nature of a given fact, providing no material for far-reaching societal generalizations.[22]

Pogodin's argument is interesting as evidence of the impasse in which Soviet satire found itself. On the one hand, a crook cannot be at the center of attention due to the negative aura that surrounds him. But on the other hand, that aura is insufficiently negative to "gel" ideologically and transform the crook into a full-fledged foe. El'sberg demanded that Mikhalkov provide full clarity regarding Lenskii:

> Mikhalkov informs us that the scoundrel he is portraying perpetrates swindles. He is probably capable of any kind of criminal behavior. But criminals such as this are characteristically hostile to the Soviet order and often enough in a position to commit the most grievous crimes against the motherland. But how did such a man come to be, and what crime is he still capable of, unless he is rendered harmless? The answers to these questions are to be found nowhere in the play.[23]

The critics were constantly urging satire to "cast light on" its fraudster characters, being justifiably concerned that, when seen against a background of tedious bureaucrats, they could well engage the audience's sympathies with their directness and their disinclination for sermonizing. Such was Lenskii, and for this reason, the critics rejected him.

A far warmer critical reception awaited Kleshchov, deputy to Director Bokov at the Fact Sheet publishing house and the con man in Leonid Lench's play *A Lot of Fuss* (*Bol'shie khlopoty*, 1954). A reference book titled *In and Around Zarechnyi* and published under Bokov's leadership is such a sloppy job that it omits an entire town from a map. Meanwhile, though, Kleshchov has been merrily booking bonuses for himself and others. A scandal erupts, and Usachev, Bokov's daughter's

---

[22] Pogodin,"O komediiakh," p. 33.   [23] El'sberg, *Nasledie*, p. 113.

fiancé, decides to show Kleshchov up. Having gotten wind of this, Kleshchov first doctors the editorial board meeting minutes and then accuses Usachev of producing incorrect maps. Usachev in turn accuses Kleshchov of breaking the law: "[D]ocuments don't appear of their own accord," he says. "People compile them. And people vary. From counterfeit people come counterfeit documents. This document is counterfeit!"

The district Party committee bureau fires Bokov and Kleshchov, hands the Kleshchov case off to the prosecutor's office, orders the unfortunate reference book be withdrawn from sale, and rules that Kleshchov be sued for the recovery of all losses.

Lench's play (another *fel'eton* written for the stage) points to the basic contradiction within Stalinist "realistic satire," since on the one hand, it is structured on moral denunciation and on the other, it invokes the Criminal Code. The distinction between moral and criminal condemnation boils down to the factor of violence, and by introducing violence into the satirical equation and thereby imparting to it an aesthetic quality, Soviet satire showed its true colors.

The invocation of the Criminal Code resulted from a unique kind of compromise. Since the bureaucrat, as a product of the *nomenklatura* system, could not be made over into a full-fledged foe (which would have taken him beyond the bounds of satire), his entourage, a congeries of crooks, con men, and toadies, is criminalized instead. But sometimes the bureaucrat himself is not simply a "woolgatherer" but is also, if not actually a culprit, then at least an accomplice in criminally punishable acts.

Andrei Makaenok's *So Sorry (Liver Stones)* describes just such a situation. As the curtain rises, a voice from the loudspeaker informs us that "The Party Regional Committee has pointed out to Comrade Kaliberov his flawed working style, in which practical and specific leadership is replaced by one pointless meeting after another. In the preparations for the harvest, it is essential to..." From Kaliberov's conversation with his wife, we learn that he landed in the district center after being banished from a high position in a big city: "It offends me even to remember the post I held in Minsk, the apartment we lived in! And I had a real car for my own use, far and away better than that crummy runabout." But his wife hints that he is still part and parcel of the *nomenklatura*, so all is not lost.

> Well, so what if they didn't appreciate you in Minsk? At least they didn't give up on you. They sent you here instead, a little lower on the scale, so you could show your worth. Show it, then! Stand out! Otherwise we've as good a chance of seeing Minsk again as of seeing our own ears. And if you don't find a way to show your worth, they'll hustle you out of here too. Then what d'you think will happen? You're not really qualified for anything. Your education... (*flaps her hand*). What will you go in for then? Herding sheep? Because there too you have to know how to handle a whip.

Moshkin, a staffer in the procurement office, puts Kaliberov on to a way of distinguishing himself:

> There are two distilleries in the district here. They can issue standard receipts to the collective farms but for the time being, they take their IOUs instead of the grain. And later, we start leaning on them to come up with the grain, so they can get their IOUs back.

That way, the collective farms go on record as top performers but do not have to deliver the grain until later and Kaliberov and Moshkin get a good deal of the credit.

Moshkin applies threats and blackmail to embroil the chairmen of underachieving collective farms, the director of one of the distilleries, and a whole host of smoke-and-mirror operators in his plan. Needless to say, though, the "simple people" stand in his way. Moshkin tries to intimidate them too, but never does find a way to "shut the people's mouth."

The district prosecutor Kurbatov then makes his entrance. After receiving a letter from a distillery worker, he has started looking into Moshkin's scam. Gradually, everything is made clear: the culprits try to duck the blame, and Kaliberov takes refuge in political accusations ("You understand his intentions, don't you? This is neither more nor less than sabotage or political adventurism"), but his platitudes no longer scare anyone. Since a reporter is present when the secret comes out, the next day the newspaper publishes a *fel'eton* that will certainly not be the end of the matter.

Although "senior district official" Kaliberov had been motivated solely by a desire to further his career, he is criticized for his "bureaucratic working style." He is best at holding vacuous meetings, which lead to fiascos that lead in turn to reprimands and firings. What keeps him going is his fear of the next fiasco. And the upshot, via a few logical shortcuts, is that *bureaucratism leads to crime*—or, in other words, that bureaucratism *is* a crime. The task of this kind of satire is therefore to disclose the criminal in the bureaucrat, but to disclose him in such a way that bureaucratism is perceived as deriving from careerism rather than from the *nomenklatura* system itself.

Stalinist satire simultaneously generalizes, typifies, and individualizes. The author and the consumer are basically required to understand the point at which a politically beneficial process morphs into its opposite. Another requirement is that the narrative accommodate a fundamental lack of consistency, in that an idea that has been brought to a given point then has to be interrupted and rerouted in order to avoid politically inappropriate inferences. This kind of "realistic satire" totally dislocates the course of natural inferences and associations with reality (in that phantasms are passed off as reality and reality as a "distortion") and thus becomes alogical and akin to the theater of the absurd and to farce.

Nomenklatura Slapstick: The Soviet Kafkas

As a political instrument, Soviet satire was expected not only to "amass society's critical potential" as a prelude to purges but also to mold a publicly acceptable discourse of societal criticism. That being so, all generalization and typification became, as Malenkov aptly put it, "a political problem" ("The problem of the typical is always *a political problem*"). That criticism was fully controlled in "realistic satire," but the transition to another dimension (farce, slapstick, the absurd) rendered satire unable to avoid some less manageable "generalizations." Retention of control became a crucial task for the satire industry.

We are dealing here with two representational extremes, at which the evil being ridiculed is either absolutely recognizable or absolutely unrecognizable. The functional mechanism in the former instance is that of personalization, so that we see *not bureaucracy but bureaucrats* (Lopukhov, Pompeev, and Gorlov), not a system but discrete individuals. In the latter instance, the operational mechanism is that of complete depersonalization, which generates caricatures. Those caricatures do, of course, resemble certain abstract vehicles of societal defects, but they are so thoroughly stripped of their individuality that they are perceived either as bearing no relationship to reality or exclusively as images whose principal purpose is to communicate distortion. But the societal realia are not easy to invoke in a deliberately distorted reality.

The problem of the bureaucracy and its portrayal was an exceptionally serious matter. Trotsky, in fact, saw Stalin's strength in what was being called in the Trotskyite political jargon of that time "the degeneration (*pererozhdenie*) of the apparatus." Trotsky also labeled Stalin's encouragement and exploitation of that bureaucratic degeneration "a betrayal of the Revolution." The bureaucracy was both the foundation of the regime and a living reminder of the collapse of revolutionary ideals, and for that reason its image had to be made simultaneously attractive (in the positive characters—the Party organizers and captains of industry) and somewhat repulsive, since it was a convenient arena for documenting the manifestations of mass dissatisfaction. Its positive traits were therefore associated with "simple people," while the bosses were quite often portrayed as "bureaucrats" isolated from the masses. A bureaucrat could be surrounded by fawning subordinates or even accomplices, but usually he was alone, and was never seen as a representative of bureaucracy as a system. Only "the people" were a "system"; the bureaucrat was a "distortion." That is why Comrade Byvalov in *Volga-Volga* stands against *the entire population of the movie*. Byvalov is Stalin's response to Trotsky. The real bureaucracy (Stalin as the bureaucrat in chief and the *nomenklatura* system he created) was portrayed in an exclusively positive light (with all levels of the Party leadership getting good press) while the source of the masses' dissatisfaction was rendered alien and concentrated in a satirical image. The *bureaucrat is always the Other in authority.* And the creation of the image of that Other became authority's pivotal function.

Soviet satire did less to *remove itself* from the thorny topics, as it is commonly held to have done, than to *remove the consumer* from them. The "satirical generalizations" touched on three facets of the Soviet bureaucracy: its genesis ("the degeneration of the apparatus"), its evaluation ("prudishness," "complacency," "cynicism"), and its excesses ("formalism," "smoke and mirrors," "soullessness"). We shall now examine three plays written in the 1953–7 period (when there was a shift from the satire being commissioned in 1952 as preparation for a new wave of terror to satire that was produced to "overcome the cult of personality" and "restore the Leninist norms") that bring these three facets to light.

Mikhalkov's 1957 comedy *A Monument to Myself* (*Pamiatnik sebe*) centers on Kirill Spiridonovich Pochesukhin, a bureaucratic "degenerate" who manages a town's public services. This *nomenklatura* farce begins with a chance occurrence: Pochesukhin's wife discovers a strange pre-revolutionary monument at the cemetery—a marble armchair on a granite plinth. The deceased had been a merchant of the First Guild, and his wife had had that monument put up to commemorate the fact that he had traded in furniture. But the merchant and Pochesukhin have exactly the same surname and initials. Pochesukhin's wife is horrified. Pochesukhin summons the cemetery director to his office and explains the situation to him:

POCHESUKHIN: It won't do for a man of that social estate to have my last name and my initials! Especially since I occupy a certain official capacity and am descended from merchants. So I called you here in connection with that monument. You'd think it was a trifling matter, but it can be blown out of proportion. Any matter can be blown out of proportion, this I know from personal experience. But afterwards, just try proving that you're not a merchant of the First Guild!

Vecherinkin, the enterprising cemetery director, makes Pochesukhin the following offer: he will not only remove from the monument any reference to anyone having been a merchant but even write the grave off as abandoned and register both grave and monument to the present-day Pochesukhin, which means that only the name will remain on the monument. Pochesukhin feels so at home with the armchair-monument that one day, while leaning back in it, he dozes off and dreams that he is drinking "in a pre-revolutionary chophouse, in the company of Kondratii Savvich Pochesukhin, merchant of the First Guild." After Pochesukhin and the merchant plant kisses on each other's cheeks in the dream, the astonished Pochesukhin muses: "I've been unceremoniously exchanging kisses with the private mercantile sector, and what of it? I feel no class self-awareness at all."

And, once thoroughly "propagandized" by his namesake, he is thrilled by the prospects that now open up to him:

> Your worship! Kondratii Savvich! You dear, precious man! You have understood my soul! And no one understands, but you puzzled it out. What a clever one you are! And that's why I love and respect you! Drink! Drink, I'm paying. This really is the life—wine and women and for you, not a lick of responsibility!

Pochesukhin visits "his" grave very nearly every day. But the merchant's eighty-year-old daughter unexpectedly appears, and the deception is discovered.

It is also revealed that Vecherinkin has been involved in machinations of which the "woolgatherer" Pochesukhin was wholly unaware. Now the cemetery director is blackmailing him, demanding a good character reference to present to a court. And Pochesukhin agrees to provide one for him.

Toward the end, Pochesukhin is visited by a crowning catastrophe, when the new bathhouse burns down. It had no water supply, and its drunken superintendent had to be dragged feet-first through a window. Pochesukhin is frantic:

> The new bathhouse? What will the people say now? They will say, "Pochesukhin bungled this one!" Again Pochesukhin's in the paper! The stuff of fables! Grist for the cartoons! They'll make a monkey out of me! (*Clutches his head.*) And in the anteroom! In the bathhouse anteroom?... What did just one of those chandeliers cost? (*Turning around.*) Why are you all staring at me? It's not the bathhouse that's burning, it's me! And there's no one to put out the flames!

In the epilogue, we see our hero at night in the snowbound cemetery, tipsy and carrying his perpetual briefcase. He walks around the monument.

POCHESUKHIN (*READS*): "Merchant of the First Guild!" (*Ruefully*) They've put it back.... Because how could a Soviet person ever occupy that place?... Where's the logic?... It's not clear.... In all candor, I admit: it's not clear. (*Brushes the snow from the armchair seat with his briefcase and, puffing, clambers onto it; sits down; puts the briefcase on his knees; speaks contemplatively, as if remembering something.*) Kirill Spiridonovich... Pochesukhin... I haven't changed, and I don't intend to... Year of birth: one thousand nine hundred and ten. Place of birth: The Back of Beyond... He never hesitated... was never investigated... never captivated... never extricated... Education: incomplete... Foreign languages: not a one... Inventions: no... Reprimands: yes. (*Plaintively*) Dear comrades! My healthy body bears the accursed birthmark of capitalism! But! Even with it, I have given myself entirely, free and clear, to the cause of building a new society! (*Suspiciously*) I've been publicly accused of obtusitism [*glupizm*] and dull-witterism [*tupizm*]! Where's the sense in that?... They said there's no way of getting into communism with people like me around! But where else can I go?... They told me off for being a merchant! But, permit me to ask, in what way? (*Defiantly*) If I'm a merchant, then I'm one of yours, a Soviet merchant, my dear comrades!

The "birthmark" explanation for "bureaucratic degeneration" was already being ridiculed in the 1920s, so here, Mikhalkov was stating the obvious, that "the greater Soviet life" is passing Pochesukhin by and that his place is in the cemetery, on "the trash heap of history." He and his wife are seen as old fogies, even though he is only forty-seven years old. Age is of secondary importance here, since the mores and the value-related and behavioral frames of reference of the characters in these plays, while labeled "birthmarks of the past," were acquired *under the Soviets*. And, since the *nomenklatura* was generated by the reversion to a prerevolutionary hierarchical societal model, "the degeneration of the apparatus" was nothing more than the restoration of a societal praxis of "Russia the Eternal." But that secret of the system's genesis Mikhalkov simultaneously flaunted for all to see and hid from view.

The "degenerate" official is without doubt a "generalization"—but a deliberately inaccurate one. The cartoonish bureaucrat is being compared here to a merchant who, like him, "sprang from the petty bourgeoisie," but the merchant is strikingly unlike the faceless, pitiful Soviet official. While the merchant represents capitalism, the *nomenklatura* as personified by Pochesukhin is more closely associated with feudalism, the nobility, the aristocracy; the character's "birthmarks" manifestly belong to *another* past. And to call that past by its name would be to reveal the system's true genesis, which has nothing to do with either the mercantile estate or with capitalism. But that societal genetics was the least of Soviet satire's concerns, because there was nothing at its core except the establishment of demonstrably false diagnoses and the indication of false directions. And the most reliable way it knew to conceal that core was to rely on stereotypes.

Soviet satire may be said to have done *less to typify than to stereotypify* reality. Its principal stereotypes included "formalism" and "bureaucratic literalism," which were repeatedly made the target of satire. And in Dykhovichnyi and Slobodskoi's 1954 play *Sunday on Monday* (*Voskresen'e v ponedel'nik*), they were carried to the absurd.

Dykhovichnyi and Slobodskoi's humor was characterized by its ubiquitous use of snappy wordplay, beginning with the name of the institution in which the action is set. The director of the KUKU directorate that reports to the city-level GorKUKUREKU directorate (both entities sporting ridiculous names that yield acronyms reminiscent, respectively, of "cuckoo" [in the sense of "off one's rocker"] and "cock-a-doodle-doo"), is named, appropriately, Petukhov (based on *petukh*, "rooster"). He is so profoundly afflicted by "bureaucratic formalism" that, for the sole reason that a certificate presented to him contains a misprint (the female surname "Matveeva" has been turned into the male surname "Matveev" by the mere omission of the terminal "a"), he refuses to sign an order that will grant this pregnant woman statutory leave and refer her to a specialized rest facility for women in the latter stages of pregnancy. Petukhov rejects all the arguments put forth by Fikusov, his deputy, to the effect that one look at the person's shape will prove she's a woman:

> When this citizen leaves, that shape will leave too, but the certificate will stay in the file. And while your Matveev is sitting in the house of rest, calmly waiting to become a mother, [satirical magazine] *Krokodil* may well be publishing a piece based on that certificate telling its readers that you and I have sent a man off to give birth! I think I hardly need describe the consequences to you!

Later, though, Petukhov himself becomes a victim of "formalism" when all his documents are stolen at the railroad station and the thief is run over and killed by a truck. Fikusov, brought to the police station to identify the body, refuses to view the victim but still signs a document confirming the identification. Petukhov is officially declared dead.

After coming in to work the day after his own funeral, Petukhov encounters his deputy, who is in no hurry to give up his new office. He cannot retract the order terminating Petukhov's employment. But Petukhov is not upset by this, only puzzled: "You know, Fikusov, I've been fired for every possible reason—for failure to meet requirements, and for having sticky fingers, and for messing up, and for falling behind. But for being dead and gone? This is a first!" In the end, Petukhov despairs of securing official acknowledgment of his existence and readies himself to submit to the bureaucratic "reality": he lies in a grave and demands to be buried. A scandal ensues. A policeman shows up and everything falls back into place.

To prevent the reader from developing too gloomy a picture of the Kafkaesque bureaucratic world, Dykhovichnyi and Slobodskoi "bookend" the action with police monologues. It begins and ends with a policeman addressing the audience. He says that his "standby profession" is *fel'eton* writer and continues:

> Remember: we have no positive types here. So where are they? you ask. I'll tell you where (points to the auditorium)—right there! In the auditorium. And there are far more of you. And if you are going to laugh at them (points to the stage), then it must be because you're stronger. And that's how it is. So you can laugh. We aren't fining people for that these days.

The interest of this play lies in its organic combination of absolutely "well-intended" and politically appropriate satire and intellectual irony, and the policeman who confides in the audience is a remarkable part of this. This unique kind of *police-force satire* transforms the bureaucrat into an outcast, by alienating him from the image of authority. Author, audience, and policeman are on one side of the barricades, and the bureaucrat is on the other. The "generalizations" are thus in no way associated with bureaucracy as a system. Furthermore, the actions of petty bureaucrats are shown to be both absurd and utterly unrelated to the author-policeman-audience's "wider world." Petty bureaucrats can cause only petty inconveniences. The absurdity of the bureaucratic system is reduced to the absurdity of individual features within it.

The two gloomy protagonists in Pogodin's 1953 comedy *Knights of the Soap Bubbles* (*Rytsari myl'nykh puzyrei*)—superintendent of savings banks Utiugov (his name based on *utiug*, "iron") and grain procurement consultant Mel'kaev—terrorize an entire town with their prudish demands for "moral purity." Utiugov is portrayed as a veritably maniacal gossipmonger. Even Mel'kaev calls him "a disagreeable sort" and says he is "weary of the leaden pressure he exerts." He is convinced that Utiugov is

> the only one of his kind. I don't think he's ever sniffed a rose. He hasn't ever loved a woman. He hasn't ever known the poetry of a first kiss. He might be married and have a beauty of a daughter, but I'm sure that beauty of a daughter isn't his. A phoenix can't hatch from a boa constrictor's egg.

In hopes of "putting up a fight with putrid appeasement and its putrid ways," the "knights" go to the editorial office of the lace factory newspaper. Editor Romashkina declares that she sees nothing wrong in the trysts taking place in the town park that have Utiugov so bent out of shape. This results in a denunciation being sent up the chain, to inform "the higher agencies" that:

> under the convenient cover of a communal garden lies concealed a seedy hangout for mass romantic rendezvous that are protected by the town police and tolerated by the Party and social organizations in the factory, which is itself a den of iniquity. But to uproot evil, it is necessary first and foremost to grub up the roots of that specific evil. So, on the very next day, we immersed ourselves in a study of the issue in general. And what came to light?... That here, in full view of the Party and social organizations, at the factory's main gates, meetings and rendezvous, again on a mass scale, are taking place between young female workers and people of the opposite sex. In the past week, we presented ourselves on a daily basis at the factory gates in time for the evening and night shifts to let out and recorded eleven hundred assignations, not counting various random, puny efforts to strike up an acquaintance.

The denunciation produces no results, but Utiugov will not let it go, the end result being that a visiting commission sends him "out to pasture, into retirement."

This comedy exposes the double-think of a "Party prude" and provides a "caricature" on the Soviet versions of Chekhov's "man in a case" (*chelovek v futliare*). But the satirical characters are such nonentities that it is impossible to understand how these "knights" have gained so much power over the town and how everyone in the town lives in fear of people who can produce nothing but "soap bubbles." Since these "Tartuffes of the Party" are by no means profligates themselves, it is unclear what forms the gist of their prudishness, which is characterized by prohibitions of an exclusively sexual nature. This gender shift and the conventions of farce provide a convenient camouflage, so that the real outlines of the object of ridicule are lost to view behind the caricature. In presenting "Party prudishness" in so demonstrably inappropriate a manner, Pogodin covered up the topic without ever having touched on it.

The Comedies of Fear: 1939–1949–1953

Not only did Stalinism disallow the public expression of dissatisfaction: it also *simulated public disclosure* in the guise of "criticism and self-criticism," one of whose forms was satire. While denunciation was the covert way to express dissatisfaction, the official public way was satire, which did less to express real dissatisfaction than to model the targets and discourse of dissatisfaction that the power structure found acceptable (or beneficial). *Soviet satire was dissatisfaction as the authorities wished to see it.* Hence both the political instrumentalization of satire and the interest in fine-tuning it. Stalinist satire, as a "reflection" of the denunciation, came complete with the "genre memory" of denunciation. The storylines of most of these plays were therefore structured on the revealing and concealing of secrets, fear of exposure, and devastating failure for whoever was behind the cover-up.

The most suitable arena for the demonstration of failures of this kind is science, it being a place where a person's status is confirmed through institutionally public procedures, through proof and verification. It is, therefore, no coincidence that many satirical comedies are set in scientific establishments, where pseudoscientists, plagiarizers, and scientific paper-pushers are unmasked. The scientific sphere also offers the ideal décor for sermonizing—a rostrum from which to deliver the emotionally charged unmaskings.

Professor Borodin, the protagonist of *Fear* (*Strakh*, 1931), Aleksandr Afinogenov's nothing-like-a-comedy, declares that his study of societal groups has disclosed that the principal behavioral stimulus for Soviet people is fear.

> Eighty percent of those studied live in never-ending fear of being scolded or losing their foothold in society. The milkmaid fears the confiscation of her cow; the peasant, forced collectivization; the white-collar Soviet worker, ceaseless purges; the Party worker, accusations of deviations; the scientist, accusations of idealism; the technical worker, accusations of sabotage. We live in an age of towering fear. Fear forces talented intellectuals to disown their mothers, to fake

their societal origins, to worm their way into high positions. The person becomes mistrustful, withdrawn, unscrupulous, slovenly, and unprincipled. Fear engenders absenteeism, makes trains run late, disrupts production, and causes general poverty and hunger. A rabbit that has seen a boa constrictor is unable to budge from the spot. Its muscles have seized, and it waits submissively for the boa's coils to tighten and crush it. We are all rabbits. The remaining 20 percent of those studied are workers under someone's wing, who have nothing to fear: they own the country. They enter our institutions and our science with proud faces and clattering boots. Annihilate fear, and you'll see the country richly alive and thriving!

In 1939, as the Great Terror, which had confirmed the conclusions drawn by Professor Borodin, was coming to an end, Kondrat Krapiva wrote a comedy on that topic, *He Who Laughs Last* (*Kto smeetsia poslednim*), whose principal characters are Gorlokhvatskii, director of a geological institute, a certain Professor Chernous, and Tuliaga, a research scientist.

A passer-by mistakes Tuliaga, who is afraid of his own shadow, for a colonel in Denikin's army. The unnerved Tuliaga makes easy prey for Gorlokhvatskii, whose directorship of the institute is only through the good offices of influential friends. Gorlokhvatskii's ambition is to put Chernous, the institute's leading scientist, out of a job. He forges documents, thwarts the publication of Chernous's book, spreads gossip about his political unreliability and moral turpitude, and calls the institute where Chernous's daughter is enrolled to report that her father "is implicated in sabotage" and that he has "reliable data" to that effect. But Chernous is not so easily frightened.

Gorlokhvatskii then blackmails Tuliaga into writing a scientific paper for him. Tuliaga agrees but reveals the secret to Party Organizer Levanovich, who ultimately "tears the mask" from Gorlokhvatskii.

Since Krapiva's play was an ideal match for the concept of "Soviet satire," it was immediately "added to the gold reserve of Soviet multinational dramaturgy." It was politically timely, simultaneously urged humaneness with respect to "honest cadres" and reprisals against enemies, and fostered vigilance. But had Gorlokhvatskii not been presented as an enemy within, who had maneuvered his way into the *nomenklatura* with assistance from his "pals" (themselves presumably enemies comfortably ensconced even farther up the hierarchy), had his exposure not resulted from a counterplot devised by a vigilant Party organizer, and, most importantly, had Krapiva's play not been a response to the 1939 campaign censuring the excesses of the Great Terror and uncovering its pretended culprits, it not only would not have survived the Stalinist epoch but would never even have been staged. Because that was exactly what happened with Anatolii Sofronov's *Beketov's Career* (*Kar'era Beketova*, 1949).

Sofronov's *nomenklatura* comedy centers on a clash between three friends—Plant Director Privalov, Chief Engineer Beketov, and Kutasin, a "responsible official" on the Regional Party Committee. Beketov, who longs to be plant director and knows all about the defects in the combines produced at the plant, goes for a two-month stay at a health resort to "cure an ulcer," and, through his housemaid back at home, sends anonymous letters to the ministry accusing the director of suppressing criticism. Privalov is removed, and Beketov is made acting director. However, Beketov is brought to justice by his son, who happens upon the drafts of the anonymous letters in a volume of their encyclopedia.

When asked why he did it, Beketov replies: "I was sick of being second. I wanted to be first." But as "first," his leadership amounts only to berating his subordinates, debating the placement of walnut furniture in the director's office, and arguing the right paint color for the plant's facade. In 1949, Sofronov could not make his protagonist an "enemy within"; instead, Beketov is a typical Soviet bureaucrat. But he had to make his play a whodunit, in order to skirt a discussion of the nature of *nomenklatura* careerism.

Careerism is unacceptable because it is an attempt to forcibly co-opt the system. This aspiration to manage one's own career is tantamount to attempting an escape from authority, to disengaging from the chain of command by ensuring one's own invulnerability, to receiving the "net yield" of *authority without fear*. This essentially betokens an undermining of the foundations of the Stalinist regime. But lest the reader or audience be visited by thoughts such as these, the Regional Party Committee functionary Kutasin explains to Beketov:

> You aren't a Soviet person. You wanted to make a career for yourself! But you've got the wrong system, the wrong conditions for that. The people don't put up with careerists here. Honest folks are thought highly of. You've got the wrong soil! Because everything rose up against you, your son went against you, don't you understand? Your son! That's how strong we are. Our Soviet world is good, and it will not be defiled by your kind—never, Beketov! And the closer we come to communism, the more evident your kind becomes, wherever it may be, even somewhere as respected as the intelligentsia. Don't you understand that thousands make it into the first tier honorably, with one accord, shoulder to shoulder, without ever trying to pull the carpet out from under each other? Singletons sometimes break through—the likes of you, I mean—and they come to grief. People like that soon take a tumble here on our soil, go flying out of the saddle. No, Beketov, we won't be hauling that filth with us into communism. That filth will be left at the doorstep. Do you understand, Beketov? At the doorstep!

Not having the rich "storyline" of 1939 at his disposal, Sofronov could not employ the stratagem of plot and counterplot, and therefore resorted instead to the detective genre. But in trying to retreat from the real issues and transforming Beketov's comeuppance into mere serendipity, he was hoisted with his own petard. His play, which won first prize in a competition for the best Soviet comedy organized by the Committee for the Arts and the Union of Writers,[24] was slammed by *Pravda*, and a leading article in the journal *Teatr* chided Sofronov for the "happenstance" both of what Beketov did and of the way he was brought to account:

> Sofronov has provided an improper, distorted portrayal of our reality and our people. Instead of showing how a healthy Soviet collective exposes any manifestations of careerism, lack of integrity, and double-dealing, the author wants to assure the audience that his protagonist, the engineer Beketov, who uses the most despicable methods to step into the shoes of the plant director, would never have been exposed had his son not accidentally come across a copy of an anonymous letter he had written.[25]

The author of another article questioned how Beketov and Privalov, chief engineer and director of the same plant, as well as Kutasin, deputy secretary of the Party regional committee for machine building, could have been such close friends for twenty years:

> How could it be, other than by dint of criminal myopia and lack of foresight unworthy of genuine Party members, that Kutasin and Privalov went for twenty years without figuring out what a small-minded and morally degenerate nonentity Beketov was? Yet the author, contrary to life's logic, recommends Kutasin and Privalov to the reader as the communist vanguard, as genuinely positive heroes of our time.

Even the play's conflict is questioned: "The Soviet collective combats the careerist, the status seeker, the person deficient in morals, and does not allow him to advance into responsible supervisory posts."[26]

Instead of real issues, the play offers a predictable selection of motifs: Beketov is a careerist and a status seeker. No longer a societal phenomenon, careerism is now transforming into a moral flaw, but, since Sofronov's play is satirical, the concentration of negative traits in one character renders any analysis superfluous. Beketov's cartoonish careerism was expected to simulate "the correct response."

---

[24] Characteristically, the prize jury's decision was criticized for having categorized Sofronov's play as a comedy to begin with: "The erroneous decision of the jury for the competition for best comedy is especially surprising in that the genre of Sofronov's play is not comedic at all. It contains neither comic characters nor comic situations" ("Sezon zakonchen," p. 16).

[25] Ibid., p. 5. Aleksandr Fadeev also said: "The exposure of the careerist Beketov is random in nature and does not stem naturally from what is special about our social order. The play does not show the social life in our enterprises. And, first and foremost, it fails to present the plant's Party organization, which, as we know, is the soul of its social life." (Fadeev, "O literature," p. 62).

[26] See "O neudachnykh p'esakh," p. 10.

But Sofronov "neutralized" the problem by declaring Beketov "small-minded" and a "nonentity."

Beketov, like Pompeev, ends badly. After learning that he is being summoned to speak with the chairman of the Party Commission, he panics and implores Privalov to help him:

> You can save me. I'm scared. I'm being brought up before Kuzin. (In a singsong voice) Ku-u-zin, do you understand?... Beketov was and Beketov is no more! I ask one thing of you: tell him that I shouldn't be kicked out, ask him not to have me kicked out. Because you realize what'll happen if I'm kicked out!

The manifestations (which are sometimes hysterical fits) of *nomenklatura* fear at the end of many satirical plays make it clear that *fear, and only fear* underpins the power of the *nomenklatura*. These characters are ready to stop at nothing, but not for the commendations and decorations, not for the "honor" of it and a personal dacha at the Khimki reservoir. At the end of the day, the desire to fight free of dependency on a system whose principle begins and ends with the formula "Beketov was and Beketov is no more!" is elicited by *fear of the tenuousness of one's position in that system*. But the reason posited in these plays is the "moral dissolution" of one or more of the characters, caused by everything from petty vanity to inordinate ambition. The principal mechanism of Socialist Realist mimesis (the replacement of the real problem with the simulation of superficial "decisions") is especially clear here: the plays were written not to pose questions but to head them off and cover them up.

The Anonymous Author (*Anonim*), a play by Semen Narin'iani, a famous writer of *fel'etony* for *Pravda*, appeared in 1952 as a response to the call for "Gogols and Shchedrins." Narin'iani had taken "the lessons of Beketov" to heart—his satirical protagonist not only did not belong to the *nomenklatura* but was also "the most ordinary" worker, "just like all the rest." The action is set in an architectural workshop, where the married couple Aleksei Dmitriievich and Anna Grigor'evna Kravchenko work. The husband has offloaded all the household chores on his wife: "Every man has his weaknesses. Some write poetry, others run after women, and I, Annushka, play cards. But don't go and hang me for that harmless hobby." Anna Grigor'evna is disgruntled: "People call you a boor out loud, and they make no bones about it." But no one is more disgusted with him than Galina Voronova, editor of the workshop's wall newspaper, who is demanding that he be fired for unprofessionalism. All conceivable jurisdictions are then swamped with anonymous letters in which Voronova is subjected to a slew of indiscriminate accusations, but numerous commissions find no basis for any of them.

Although the situation becomes entirely absurd, what we have here is not a run-of-the-mill bureaucratic farce, since the target of the satire is *not the bureaucracy but the anonymous author*. The play presents the bureaucracy per se in a quite decorous light, showing that it cannot disregard even anonymous letters because it operates on a presumption of integrity.

Eventually, at the latest in a string of commission meetings, the representative from the prosecutor's office determines that this is a case of libel and establishes the author's identity. The audience is then treated to the following conversation:

PETROV: Just don't confuse what's permitted in this country and what isn't. Writing complaints... by all means, write away. But libeling honest people? Excuse me, but no, that we won't allow.
LELIA: Then why are we going back and forth with him? Send him to trial and then to prison!
ALEKSEI DMITRIIEVICH: Well, isn't she fast on her feet—to prison, indeed! What, pray tell, is the legal precedent for prison?
PETROV: Such a smart mouth! See that, Comrade Prosecutor?
ALEKSEI DMITRIIEVICH: Look here, Comrade Prosecutor will tell you what's what! There's no article in the Criminal Code that would lock me up.
LELIA: Well, there might not be, but we'll ask the government to make one. Because it's our government, the Soviet government.
PETROV: Quite right. The court shouldn't just fine libelers, but imprison them, too.
GLAZOV: Very well, comrades, all in favor, raise your hands!
LELIA: See there? It's unanimous.

And that last aside to the audience brings to an end a play whose principal premise was *the criminalization of "libel."*

Narin'iani's play was sharply criticized in the press, but not as keenly as *Beketov's Career* had been. Since the power structure was "upping the ante" in 1953, the criticism in *The Anonymous Author* was deemed insufficient: it had been said that in the type portrayed by Beketov, Sofronov had "gilded the lily" for no good reason, yet the direct opposite was asserted relative to *The Anonymous Author*:

> The further this comedy develops, the more and more evident it becomes that its principal point is not the incriminating revelation of the character of a dangerous and artful enemy (who actually remains *anonymous* to us until he comes to grief) but the exposition of an incident involving anonymous letters that disturb the peace of a small architectural workshop. But the exposition of an event that *is not conducive* to comprehension of a societal type (which is always the artist's principal desideratum in his work) attests in and of itself to the weakness of this piece of writing and the creative unfitness or incompetence of its author.[27]

---

[27] Surkov, "Ne po tomu puti," p. 105.

This was a demand for the broaching of the *political* content of a societal phenomenon. Displeased as the critics were with the way the political component in the actions of the character being ridiculed was being "blurred," that political component had to be created after the fact.

> Unfortunately, Narin'iani has not revealed *the true motives behind the provocative activities [provokatsionnaia aktivnost']* of his Aleksei Dmitriievich. His comedy also contains no attempt to associate the fight against libellers with the fight *against the last vehicles of the bourgeois ideological contagion, against the remnants of groups hostile to Soviet power that the Party has not quite finished working over.* ... No efforts are made to scrutinize from the Party's point of view the *harmful "activity"* of the anonymous letter writer and also to note the numerous representatives of various central organizations that wasted no time, as Narin'iani assures us, to set up entire fact-finding commissions to study the denunciations they had received.... And it does not so much as occur to even one of those inspectors who swan around squandering their travel allowances how unseemly it is for Soviet people to take their cue from a ruffian, how necessary it is for an enquiry to be launched, not into declaring him to be what he is, but into his personality. In other words, *the anonymous letter writer's chicanery must be politically decoded and the collective mobilized to expose him.*[28]

A slice-of-life storyline is thus transformed into one involving politics and criminality, thus imparting a special meaning to a sentence that Surkov dropped into his analysis of Narin'iani's play: "Laughter," he wrote, "really does have an enormous capacity to strike terror into evil."[29]

It is precisely because the protagonist was not a member of the *nomenklatura* that the critics were demanding "generalizations," for which it normally failed to see a need. "True satire always belabors evil at its very foundation, strikes a vice at its very root. Behind the individual character in a satirical comedy, the soil from which he sprang must without fail be palpable. It was therefore a mistake to seize on the theme of libel and libellers while restricting the explanation of the conflict arising to the individual and the everyday," Surkov lectured the author of *The Anonymous Author*.[30] Such demands could not have been made of the author of *Beketov's Career* (*Kar'era Beketova*, 1949), since uncovering the "roots" of what the critics had taken to calling "Beketovshchina" would have recalibrated the conversation to political categories, and in the year of the play's publication, that was unthinkable.

The situation in 1952 and 1953 was different. As El'sberg wrote, by underscoring only the philistine inclinations of his protagonist and by portraying him as a vulgar man, Narin'iani was essentially disavowing satire:

---

[28] Ibid., pp. 106–7, 109 (emphasis added).   [29] Ibid., p. 104.   [30] Ibid., p. 107.

One of the characters describes [Kravchenko] at the end of the play as "a person who is not what he seems." But if Kravchenko really is a phony, he would reveal that essence of his in various ways, not just by libelling a work colleague. The play, though, has nothing to say about that. And again the bewildering questions arise: How did such a low character come to be? What is his true essence? *Where is Kravchenko going?*[31]

The critics, the author, the play's other characters, and even the audience would have liked to see Kravchenko imprisoned, and on a political charge at that; the blame for that not having happened was laid squarely on the author.

Terror by Laughter

All of these plays are characterized by the recognizability and triteness of their storylines and character types, which attests to the fact that they were reproducing a series of traumatic experiences that had been enshrined in a specific political ritual (since these plays were undoubtedly the product of political campaigns). The range of characters, the relations among them, and their personal outcomes left no doubt that what was being portrayed there was *the political ritual of the purges*. And that is why this genre assumed its definitive shape immediately after the war, because during the Great Terror there was no need to show on stage what was actually happening in real life.

These plays essentially tapped into something in which "the rank-and-file theatergoer" of the 1930s had been well-trained: "criticism and self-criticism." The campaign that Stalin began in 1928 was aimed at focusing criticism on the "middle-tier" *nomenklatura*. "Self-criticism is a controlled burn that leaves the upper echelons of power untouched and casts no doubt on the chosen policy,"[32] but at the same time it provided an outlet for mass dissatisfaction with the power structure. In everyday life, though, "self-criticism" assumed the form of the familiar and ubiquitous denunciation, and that is exactly what these plays are—denunciations furnished with a plotline. Therefore, in order to understand the societal impetus concealed within them, one has to understand the nature of denunciation in Stalinist Russia. As François-Xavier Nérard, who has studied the practice of denunciation in Stalinism, observes, it was "a means of vicarious violence" exercised by the weak who had been "slighted when they strove to attain the acme of power."[33] And for that reason,

denunciation is basically a pursuit of the intermediate strata of Soviet society—blue-collar workers, collective farm workers, white-collar workers, or low-level

[31] El'sberg, *Nasledie*, p. 114.   [32] Nérard, *Piat' protsentov*, p. 97.   [33] Ibid., p. 267.

managers. Sometimes they are Party members possessing a modicum of symbolic power and are thus far from the most defenseless members of Stalinist society. But the general disarray and everyday violence renders these people vulnerable too. By engaging the state as their proxy in the infliction of violence, they are seeking confirmation of their societal status. Virtually all of Soviet society is defenseless with respect to the state.[34]

Not coincidentally, almost all these plays feature journalists or the writers of anonymous letters and/or involve a skirmish over publishing something (over making certain facts public, that is). And the more important the place occupied in a play by the figure of the bureaucrat, with his career aspirations and his sights set on power, the stronger the political coloration of its plot. This was exactly where denunciation came in: it was the sole legitimate form of protest. And the non-public nature of the populace's interaction with the power structure in this spoke to the fact that, by channeling the masses' dissatisfaction into sending up written "flares," the power structure was actually trying to keep a lid on all the possible ways in which people might seek to take information public. That is why there was such significance attached to the publication of a letter or a *fel'eton* in a newspaper, because, after transitioning to the public dimension, denunciation visibly entered the feedback loop. It was substantiated merely by virtue of having been published in a newspaper and, once there, it was not subject to verification but nonetheless was to serve as a guide to action. Shortcomings were now to be swept away, along with their "specific perpetrators." Such was the plotline of Stalinist satire.

A "bombardment of the headquarters" that is orchestrated from the top is a time-tested tool of regimes such as Stalin's. But terror cannot be permanently maintained, and, for that reason, society should always be on the lookout for the dormant volcano to reawaken (when ordered from above). Keeping society on a "combat footing" is a vital political task. What happened countrywide during the Great Terror was not a one-time-only exercise; the assumption was that it would be replicated indirectly, in venues such as the theater, which provided an arena in which the purge scenario could be acted out. What was being portrayed on stage was supposed less to "sugar-coat" Soviet reality, as is commonly thought, than to reflect and elucidate the real political structure of Soviet society. There was a threat implicit in that constant reminder of lived experience; time and time again, by re-enacting the purge ritual on theater stages everywhere, Soviet laughter—a transmuted form of fear—performed its basic function, which was *to terrorize*.

---

[34] Ibid., p. 272.

6
The Soviet Bestiary
Genealogy of the Stalinist Fable

> ...like children we prefer the familiar stories, the fables we have been told before.
>
> Alan Bennett, *Kafka's Dick*

If Angus Fletcher is right in claiming that it is impossible to understand political language without understanding the allegories it uses,[1] it makes sense that we should dedicate a chapter to the most allegorical kind of texts that existed in the Soviet Union: satirical fables. Fables were an extremely popular genre of the official satire of the first socialist state. Apparently their very structure, which allowed for a combination of moralizing with entertainment in short rhyming pieces, made it particularly attractive to the Soviet ideologues. The direct association of the genre with the classical Russian fable writer Ivan Krylov was also useful to the propaganda machinery of the regime, even if this association was not always explicit or even intentional. Krylov's fables, familiar to every speaker of Russian from childhood, linked high and low culture, the world of children with that of adults, fairy-tale imagery with everyday reality. This was the kind of synthesis the masters of the new culture sought to create. The claim of an encyclopedia article from 1925 that "after Krylov the fable disappeared as a distinct genre of literature, and its remnants only exist in the form of jokes or parody"[2] is mistaken. Much more reflective of the true state of things is an observation made by the author of an article published in 1961 in *Voprosy literatury*: "The fascination with fables has acquired the size of a literary epidemic, and it does not look like it is going to subside any time soon: on the contrary, the fable flood is gaining strength, the numbers of fable-writers multiply."[3]

This "epidemic" began immediately after the Revolution or even in the years preceding it with the fables by Dem'ian Bednyi, and reached its culmination after the war, with Sergei Mikhalkov's texts. These two poets will be in the focus of our analysis here, whereby we are particularly interested in the question of how

---

[1] Fletcher, "Allegory," p. 78.   [2] Eiges, "Basnia."   [3] Lipelis, "Sovremennost'," p. 36.

State Laughter: Stalinism, Populism, and Origins of Soviet Culture. Evgeny Dobrenko and Natalia Jonsson-Skradol, Oxford University Press. © Evgeny Dobrenko and Natalia Jonsson-Skradol 2022.
DOI: 10.1093/oso/9780198840411.003.0007

transformations in the relationship between the implied reader/implied subject of the Soviet state and the state power were reflected in the allegorical satirical images and in the changing stylistics of the new type of fables, and what conclusions one can draw from this concerning the differences between the ideal consumer of the Soviet satire in the early years of the period of terror and toward its end. We will also dedicate some attention to Ivan Batrak, a much less known figure, to help us better outline some key elements of the discussion and the transition from Bednyi to Mikhalkov. There were, of course, other authors writing in the genre—or rather, other producers of this type of texts. There were dozens, probably hundreds of them. The reasons we chose to focus on just these particular ones are twofold. First of all, these were the names with whom the very concept of the Soviet fable was associated for decades (this may be less true in the case of Batrak, to whom we dedicate but a small section of the chapter). Second, a proliferation of texts did not result in a greater degree of variation or distinct character. Whatever else these texts were, most of them did not read as original works. They were repetitive and endlessly repeated exercises in what was to be laughed at, without the exercises themselves necessarily being funny. Though a comic genre, the Soviet fables were mostly about training the audience in developing the correct attitude to various manifestations of whatever was unwelcome in the new (for Bednyi) or the perfectly regulated (for Mikhalkov) world. The authors we focus on are representative of the development of the genre through the three decades of Stalinism when it comes to state-sanctioned allegory.

Actually, the very concept of *official* Soviet allegorical texts is somewhat of an oxymoron. More often than not, scholars speak of two main kinds of Soviet literature which are supposed to stand in a complementary relationship to each other: either there were official texts which speak in the all too direct language of official ideology, sticking to the safe, tested images of the optimistic present and the bright future,—or else there was "authentic," honest literature, those other writings that said one thing but meant another, appealing to their trained readers' ability to read between the lines, to understand and respond to the Aesopian language of hints, implications and indirect allusions. It would seem that allegorical writing belongs, unquestionably, to the latter group, never to the former.

Or do they? In fact, Soviet satirical fables are an example of a multi-layered discursive structure that undermines this simple division. They speak in Aesopian language, as befits fables—but the truth behind this language, the implied meaning which is revealed to those who are party to the conventions of reading is the truth of the politically correct message, fully compatible with the line of the ruling ideology. They may appear to defy official conventions and strict limits of state propaganda—but only in order to establish them more firmly by constructing a type of reader that is best suited for the new regime. Below we will look at how this is done, and why.

Dem'ian Bednyi

New Soviet Animals

In the early 1960s, a Soviet critic quoted Mayakovsky's pronouncement on Bednyi as an example of the highest praise a poet can receive: "Dem'ian Bednyi's poetry is today's political order correctly understood, a determined, target-oriented position."[4] Regardless of whether the critic's own understanding of Mayakovsky's words was correct, it is certainly true that the new regime welcomed Bednyi's poetry. His poems were printed in numbers that clearly show he was more than "a modest mouthpiece for Lenin's ideas," as the author of a 1923 review put it.[5] And in the words of another critic writing a few years later, "fables are most certainly the best that Dem'ian produced."[6] As the genre conventions demand it, most of the allegories in Bednyi's fables come from the animal world. One of his contemporaries notes with satisfaction: "Dem'ian's animal world is picturesque, and he knows it. His hens, mongrels, jades, bugs, pikes, ruffs, loaches, panthers, marmots, hamsters etc. are used in total correspondence with their nature, personifying exactly the right things, acting in accordance with their main features."[7] Maybe they do, indeed, "personify the right thing," even though a picky reader may have questions, for example, as to the legitimacy of describing the young Soviet state in one of the texts as something that is "sharp-clawed..., not only horned." Still, such descriptions are not beyond the genre conventions—and it is here that we can find one of the first points of approximation between traditional fables and early Soviet imagery, where animals, or at least non-people, also occupied a special place. According to Muireann Maguire, in the 1920s the Soviet literary and general discursive space was populated with composite creatures, half-animals/-half-machines/half-humans, whom the scholar defined as the "Soviet gothic bodies" and with whose help the newly created society tried to work out the characteristics of its heroes, both present and future.[8] A kind of bestiary was being created by collective efforts—a collection of allegorical images, with a set of certain characteristics assigned to each of them, more or less randomly.

However, from the point of view of an analysis of the place of fables in early Soviet discourse and its role in the education of a model Soviet citizen it appears much more interesting to examine not the presentation of human subjects, individual or collective, as animals, but a consistent "animalization" of human images. This "animalization" of humans is traceable primarily in the language of

---

[4] Monastyrskii, "Rytsar'," pp. 41–2.
[5] Sosnovskii, "Pervyi proletarskii poet." Igor' Kondakov writes that "the popularity of Bednyi in the 1920s can be measured by the print run of his books. In the first post-revolution decade over two million copies of his books were published, in addition to numerous booklets and flyers which saw light in the years of the Civil War without any publishing identification."
[6] Voronskii, *Iskusstvo*, p. 284.   [7] Ibid., p. 318.   [8] Maguire, p. 34.

the characters, since, as befits a fable-writer, Bednyi offered his characters the right to express themselves in the first person. The animalistic humans that abound in Bednyi's texts and that usually, though not always, personify negative characters, are not quite capable of speaking human language, this human language being obviously the language of the new power. The wife of Gordeich, a stupid and greedy merchant from a cycle of fables that went on for quite a few years, is literally unable to put together two words after she heard from her husband that the workers are starting to get interested in "ideas":[9]

> Uhh... thieves... uh-h... scoundrels!
> Look here... smarty pants!..
> What...
> Sort...
> Of ideas?

Gordeich himself has it even harder with normal human speech after he went through a severe shock—the sight of a worker reading a newspaper. Unable to pronounce the words just learnt, he must break them into awkward syllables: "ca-pi-tu-la-ti-on... Le... Le-nin" (acknowledging that he "has never seen a word like that" and trying to reproduce it "by the sound" rather than relying on the meaning. As he is beaten up by his own employee to whom he failed to pay the wages, the merchant learns a new concept: "Ad-van-ce pay-ment!"; as he gets to hear a political speech given by his own shop assistant, Gordeich is trying to repeat a slogan he has never heard before: "Get u-ni-ted!" When rendered by Gordeich, the speech of revolutionary workers does not particularly resemble human language, either. They "roar like beasts," concludes he, because "the devil himself couldn't figure out / What is what and who is flaying whom." At home, trying to show his wife how "the little Jew" in his shop "howled," the merchant himself "bellows." Not wanting, or else being unable, to actually describe the verbal battles between workers and their employers, he calls an incident at the shop a "brawl," where nothing but "shouts, curses, howling" is heard. Gordeich does, however, acquire the powers of speech at least once, when he describes a menshevik—but only in order to explain to his wife why he did not understand a word said by this suspicious type, whose manner also appears to be not a little similar to that of an animal:

> This one—one sees at once—is no bolshevik,
> A petty breed! Walks around all shaking,
> Hitting himself in the chest.

---

[9] All quotations are according to: Bednyi, *Sobranie*.

> That was no talk, but a dance.
> You think I understood a word?
> I am, my darling, no foreigner.

In other fables, mensheviks are not depicted in a particularly flattering way, either. They are sheep-like not only in their cowardice but also in the way they speak:

> Isn't it a good example of sheep's convictions,
> So pleasing to the wolves
> (To all the Denikins and other Kolchakovs),
> Meee... meee... methods of political planning
> Of the meee... meee... mensheviks?)

Neither are animals particularly eloquent, especially those personifying negative characters. Fish call each other "a blockhead" and "a headless coward," they talk "gibberish," "cry wo-wo" and "jabber." The speech of all these creatures is on the border between the human and the animalistic, the meaningful and the onomatopoeic. They speak not in order to express anything, but in order to show that they are incapable of speaking, thus turning into "typical representatives," coded personifications of those who cannot belong to the new society, the implication being that the ability to speak (the right kind of language) is a prerequisite of belonging to (the new) human political community. Those who do not speak, and do not belong, are ridiculous—at least this is the way it seems to be. We will come back to this point below.

Bringing together the human and the animal has always been a popular comic device.[10] It appears, however, that in the context of the early Soviet imagery this device was valuable also because it allowed a nearly zoological classification of individual people and social groups based on easily identifiable criteria. In Bednyi's straightforward texts, not overloaded with considerations of style or artistic value, political types are represented as natural species by means of their speech or its absence, when their very nature is expressed through their inability to use human language on the one hand, and to keep silent—on the other. Indeed, allegorical characters in fables are not entitled to silence, they have no choice but to speak. According to Louis Marin, who offered an intriguing political and philosophical analysis of the Western fable tradition, inability to speak is a traditional way to signal the similarity of any character with an animal, thus marking this person's place in the hierarchy of signs and meanings.[11] In this

---

[10] See, e.g., the following observation in an article on ancient Greek plays: "Existing on a plane between the gods and animals, human beings frequently become in comedy creatures whose concerns illustrate their ties to the animal world" (Saxonhouse, "Comedy," here p. 888).

[11] Marin, *Food*, p. 45. Cf. also Avital Ronell on stupidity: "The French term denoting stupidity is of course *bête*, tying dumbness to the animality of animals" (Ronell, *Stupidity*, p. 320 [endnote 9]).

connection we can remember traditional verbal formulas, Russian and not only, where animal images are used to point to a place of non-belonging; the popular curses where one is called a dog, or an ass, are remnants of these.[12] The language of the negative characters in Bednyi's satirical fables stops being a means of communication and turns into yet another, external, characteristic of the nature and behavior of those who express their attitude to the new regime not so much by means of words but rather by making inarticulate noises or else by making a certain expression show on their "mug" (*rozha*). These creatures can best react to the political and economic situation in the country at the level of pure physiology, either "losing fat" or "growing fat."

Here, however, we encounter a problem, since Bednyi's rather limited poetic talent and his extremely rude style do not allow us to conclude with any degree of reliability where the characters' inability to speak is a deliberate device, and where it is just a consequence of the author's own limitations. Whoever practices too deep a textual analysis of Bednyi's fables runs the risk of "reading into them" motives and meanings. There is no doubt that in the texts of the period, human speech which stops being human turns into a special sign marking enemies of the system. But it is also true that few of Bednyi's ideal readers, that is, those who sided with the Revolution or at least did not belong to the wealthy and the educated classes, could read and write, and even fewer understood the meaning of political slogans. It stands to reason, thus, that they would have not been much different from Gordeich in finding all those sophisticated words in *Pravda* articles and in the agitators' speech confusing and unpronounceable:

> A "diplomatic... orchestra,"
> A "communist... sequestration,"
> And "devaluation,"
> And "restoration,"
> And... the devil himself would break his neck.

In so far as Gordeich is obviously a personification of the dying class of merchants and exploiters, it would seem logical that the readers laugh *at* him; but in so far as most instances of verbal communication are ridiculed in general in the fable, it appears that the readers are invited to laugh *with* him, and with all the other characters who would otherwise appear negative. Even though Gordeich and the likes of him certainly personify enemies of the Revolution, the mocking attitude to a certain kind of language that these characters display turns them

---

[12] "A thief caught and put in jail could be, according to an expression used by the newspaper *Russkaia pravda*, killed 'in place of a dog' [*vo psa mesta*], that is, with impunity, like a dog" (Afanas'ev, "Iuridicheskie obychai," p. 330). Cf. also Kafka's "like a dog" at the end of *The Trial*.

into generalized allegorical representations of failed attempts at meaningful communication as such.

This is exactly why Bednyi is so interesting for an analysis of early Soviet allegorical imagery. Keeping in mind Walter Benjamin's understanding of allegory as a mode of expression which replaces verbal language in describing the organization of the world, one can say that Bednyi's verses are an example of absolute, pure allegory—exactly because the first Soviet fable writer could not write. In the kind of communication he depicts language as such recedes, giving place to other forms of contact. Predictably, the negative characters find the language of the new regime unintelligible and hence ridiculous, but in so far as the readers are offered access to this language almost exclusively from the perspective of these negative characters, the status of linguistic communication as ridiculous, meaningless is reaffirmed by the texts. A space of empty meaning is created, whose only function is to signal the simple fact of the characters literally making themselves heard, but not necessarily saying anything coherent.

The above statement might sound like a paradox: why would the regime encourage the writing, and reading, of texts that appear to satirize, however implicitly, the keywords and slogans that form the core of its propaganda? We would like to argue that the propagandistic allure of Bednyi's texts lay exactly in that they used the conventions of allegorical narrative to translate verbal language into a mode of communication that we would call *funny violence*.

But first—a few examples.

Funny Violence

Animals in Bednyi's texts suffer a lot. A discussion between a pike and a carp ends with the latter being led away by the guards with "damages to his spine and tail" and it is only at the very end of the fable that "The carp, all chewed up.../ Smelling awful, / Was puked up by the pike"; a bull manages to save himself from a lion at the very last moment; a sheep is reminded that "a wolf is a wolf, and you are a sheep," and as to the poor gudgeon, one is not sure whether he was "swallowed up by the pike, / Or else a crawfish's claw broke him." Like in most traditional fables and fairy-tales (and quite in accordance with the eating/speaking semiotic paradigm developed by Louis Marin),[13] many animal characters in these poems either devour somebody themselves, or else are devoured by somebody.

But the human characters, too, mainly communicate with each other by means of punches and curses. In the poetic foreword to a newly published edition of some of his pre-revolution fables the author rejoices that now the people have

---

[13] "The animal figuring in fables is properly animal in that it is presented as a body that both eats and is eaten." Marin, *Food*, p. 44.

finally "extracted all fangs" from the "broad jaws" of the enemies of the revolution. The brave writer himself becomes a victim of some wicked devils in his own dream: "And some devil dragged me into a hole: / Will you please... into the pot... m'sieur fable-writer!" The relations between Gordeich the merchant and his workers are not particularly subtle, either: the merchant punches "the little Jew... in the haberdashery" in his "snout, bang," and is immediately made to pay for it by receiving a "punch between the eyes" from a politically conscious worker. Gordeich himself, offended by the new power, feels a burning desire "to smash his noddle against the wall" and "to conk / One of the toothy guys." He feels sorry one is no longer allowed to "smack one on the snout." In one of the last fables of the series Gordeich, already in a flat he must share with a few other families, daydreams about how his former workers, "dogs" and "ragged fellows," will beg to be taken back, how they will "respond to the owner's curses and shouts / With a tender, loving, shy neighing," and he will have his revenge when he smacks "each of them on the mug, ha-ha, with his own hands, / Like a fly... into boiling water!".

Gordeich should be forgiven for some zoological inconsistencies in this emotional speech; as we said, he is unable to find himself and his language in the new world. What is important is that all this punching in the "snout," hitting "in the mug" and "between the eyes," putting somebody in boiling water and extracting all the "fangs," as well as devouring and "puking up" reflects the essence of communication between the characters of the fables. Violence becomes a non-verbal expression of social relations, actually turning into a general signifier that brings together political theory (in this case—revolutionary ideology) and the actions of its supporters and adversaries; it defines social and personal roles, it is used to explain and to convince; it comes from that grey zone where the human and the animal, primary instincts and modern political realities merge into one—and fables offer a perfect generic framing for such merging. Eric Naiman suggested that in an analysis of Stalinist realities we should consider not only direct manifestations of terror and violence, "but also the discourse—or representational system—that facilitated that violence by *not* speaking about it."[14] We would add to this that we would also do well to consider the function of those discursive models that made real violence possible by offering an alternative way of speaking about it—such as presenting it as something funny.

"Funny violence" is reminiscent of slapstick comedy, where even the most terrifying outbursts of violence end completely innocently. In Bednyi's texts those swallowed are "puked up," those hit on the head completely recover by the beginning of the next "chapter" in the fable series, and damages to "spine and tail" do not prevent the little fish from leading a successful life as a British minister. The fables appear to be an early version of cartoons, where the beaten up, maimed,

---

[14] Naiman, "Discourse," p. 297.

devoured and killed animals and people come back to life, again and again; more than that—all these acts of violence, inflicting bodily injury, physical annihilation are a most mundane part of the characters' life, in fables as in cartoons. It stands to reason that rendering political transformations in a language of "funny violence," "as-if violence," which made it possible to express the straightforward, unhindered power of natural impulses, but did not entail heavy consequences, was helpful in relieving the tension and fear in connection with the real, total, annihilating violence that the new order brought with it.

Mark Lipovetsky wrote about the co-existence of mythological and fairy-tale motifs in the language which the Soviet power used to communicate with the people.[15] Fables can be seen as the most "fairy-talish" of all adult genres, whose value lies in the fact that, as Lipovetsky points out, "fairy-tales actually offer probably the most democratic cultural code, which hardly requires any preparation in order to be understood."[16] Hence their importance in appealing to an adult audience with openly moralizing messages. In the first post-revolutionary years there was hardly a major event which was not rewritten in the language of "funny violence," be it political disputes, the civil war, NEP, diplomatic statements, managing residential policy, dispossession of the kulaks... In the fables grotesquely simplified, conventional images and language patterns, reminiscent of characters and speech in childhood stories, were united with politically relevant messages for the adults. This combination was crucially important for the political propaganda after the revolution.

Much has been written on the function of infantilizing audiences in the early Soviet discourse.[17] We would like to suggest that Bednyi's political fables are examples of a particular kind of infantilized language that catered to the kind of audience that was especially characteristic of post-revolutionary Russia. This was a language, or rather—a way of expression, that relieved political theory and the troubling events of everyday post-revolutionary reality of their aura of fatal incomprehensibility, translating them into concrete, physical expressions of emotions and feelings. William Reddy, one of the pioneers of "emotional turn" in historical science, encouraged scholars analyzing the propaganda of revolutionary ideas to consider "how real people could have lived... an abstraction."[18] Bednyi's texts solve this problem by translating abstractions into a kind of prelinguistic form of communication in which political and socio-economic concepts become concrete, turning into raw material for the amusement of the masses.

---

[15] Lipovetsky, "Skazkovlast'." See also Goscilo, "Introduction." [16] Lipovetsky, "Skazkovlast'."
[17] See, e.g., the chapter on "infantilizatsiia" in Heler's *Mashina*; Dobrenko, *Metafora*; Clark, *The Soviet Novel*.
[18] Reddy, "Sentimentalism," p. 144.

The Language of Truth

It is possible that such translation of abstract ideas into the most concrete and down-to-earth images was helped by the lack of any stylistic sophistication whatsoever in Dem'ian Bednyi's poetic language. In a recent article on Bednyi's fables, Igor' Kondakov particularly emphasizes the importance of "simplicity" in the poet's judgment of his own works. The critic concludes his remarks with a quote from Bednyi: "My songs are simple and rude, / But poor people like them."[19] The author of a 1923 article about Bednyi, having solemnly declared: "And so, they have come together: the poet and the masses," explains thus the importance of this union:

> ...simplicity and accessibility is not the lowest, but the highest level of poetry. Not everyone can make it that high. In addition to the talent, one needs to be prepared to invest a tremendous amount of dedicated labor and the greatest courage to tear off the misty-mystical veils covering the nature of poetry and to display it not as a muse and not as a "dreamy princess," but as a common, full-fleshed, coarse woman—the Truth.[20]

Characterizations such as "simple" and "rude" were unquestionably compliments in the harsh post-revolutionary years. Another critic writing in the same year concluded that Dem'ian Bednyi "reflected in poetry for the first time ever... the proletarian face of the Russian Revolution, but with its peasant features." The critic described this face, or rather—the Russian Revolution itself, in the following words:

> It has an open, stubborn, firm forehead and blue eyes, the color of fields, the color of forests. Its cheekbones are strong and its nose is a bit "potato"-shaped; its hands are those of a working person, covered in oil, with a firm grasp and strong muscles. It walks with a sway, in that measured way that peasants have. It smells of a mix of machine oil, wormwood and hay.[21]

It is no wonder that RAPP proclaimed a "Dem'ianization of Poetry" as one of its objectives.[22] Apparently true supporters of the Revolution were expected to find the language of educated liberals as ridiculous and awkward as Gordeich did. No wonder that the foolish carp who tried to hold a speech in the spirit of enlightened liberalism in "the legally defined form, / So as not to diverge from the norm" citing "historical examples," was cut short by another fish speaking in a much more

---

[19] Kondakov, "'Basn'ia'." [20] Sosnovskii, "Pervyi proletarskii poet."
[21] Voronskii, *Iskusstvo*, pp. 303–4. [22] Egorova, *Istoriia*, p. 207.

straightforward language. "Not even your scales are convincing" is all the arriviste carp gets to hear in response to his harangue.

The positive characters in Bednyi's texts call each other "gobs," "first-rate son of a bitch" and "dunce"—the list can go on for pages. Thus, the concretization of political relationships happens not only at the physical level (punching somebody, devouring them, spitting them out etc.) but also at the level of vocabulary. As Konstantin Bogdanov noted, "in writing strong emotions demand means that are beyond the purely lexical [*vneleksicheskie*]."[23] Curses and insults, the whole strata of language that had been traditionally considered "the inversion of official, measured speech,"[24] now became an acceptable means of expressing interpersonal and social relations in writing. This appears to be a standard carnivalesque situation. But let us dwell a bit on the importance of these two words: *in writing*.

Roland Barthes, comparing the essence of oral and written speech, came to the following conclusion: "What makes writing the opposite of speech is that the former always *appears* symbolical, introverted, ostensibly turned toward an occult side of language, whereas the second is nothing but a flow of empty signs, the movement of which alone is significant."[25] The semantic density of symbolic and allegorical allusions in fables (their "introverted" nature) can be regarded as an expression of the very essence of writing. Curses, swearing, on the other hand, are expressive of the essence of oral speech, figuring as "empty signs"—not because they are devoid of meaning, but because the simple fact of their use matters more than their semantic properties. In Bednyi's fables, speech replaces written language as the final link in a long chain of stylistic dislocations, as words and expressions which clearly belong to the realm of official writing appear ridiculous and give place to a disrupted, unstructured, often nearly nonsensical oral speech. This act of replacing written language by oral speech completes the chain of stylistic shifts when words and expressions that belong to the semantic category of written, literary, language are made to seem more ridiculous than verbal communication of a much lower level, whose primary function is to convey an emotion rather than a piece of information.

In the beginning of *Writing Degree Zero*, Barthes refers to this very expressive function of curses and swear words in politicized speech:

> Hébert, the revolutionary, never began a number of his news-sheet *Le Père Duchêne* without introducing a sprinkling of obscenities. These improprieties had no real meaning, but they had significance. In what way? In that they expressed a whole revolutionary situation. Now here is an example of a mode

---

[23] Bogdanov, Konstantin, "Otkrytye serdtsa," pp. 136–54.
[24] Halfin, "The Bolsheviks' Gallows Laughter," p. 262. Cf. also from Bakhtin: "This 'loud' talking image of the crowd is, as we have seen, built exclusively on oaths, in other words, outside the norms of official speech" (Bakhtin, *Rabelais*, p. 191).
[25] Barthes, *Writing*, p. 19.

of writing whose function is no longer only communication or expression, but the imposition of something beyond language, which is both History and the stand we take in it.[26]

By addressing this lowest level of the sense of humor, by setting up an alternative to language as an organized system of communication ("written" language), just as the examples of rude, impulsive violence quoted above are an alternative to abstruse slogans and political theories, Bednyi's fables celebrate this "something beyond language," this characteristic allegorical impetus that the revolutionary situation in Russia with its orientation at orality brought with it.[27] The appeal of Bednyi's work in the 1920s was so great that a contemporary critic claimed:

> By the way, it is practically impossible to write poetry *à la* Dem'ian. Dem'ian does not really have a style of his own at all. His style is the style of the Soviet power itself, the style of bolshevism as such,—militant, rude, disturbingly monosemantic, thoroughly ideological. Not simple, but supremely simplistic.[28]

If we reread this conclusion with reference to Barthes's pronouncement on literary style being a kind of abnormality, a deviation from a canon,[29] then Bednyi's style is defiantly bold in so far as it is oriented toward orality and a rejection of ordered, "correct" discourse, in so far as it presupposes rude cartoonish violence, foul language instead of argumentation and curses instead of names. And at the same time, style is completely absent from his works in so far as it is dissolved in the general spirit of the discourse of the time. The radically abnormal style turns into its opposite—an absence of style and correspondence to (new) norms. As a researcher of Italian fascism writes (rephrasing the words of Pier Paolo Pasolini), "is it possible to transgress when transgression itself becomes institutionalized?"[30] The introduction of an extreme form of orality into a traditionally highly conventional, "written" genre signals the presence of a new modality of expression in principle—that very modality which we can call, together with Igor' Kondakov, "supremely simplistic" (*prosteishii*).

Elsewhere in the book we refer to some of these sources discussing the ideology of "simplicity" in the presentation of ideologically reliable and transparent thoughts in totalitarian contexts in general, and in the Soviet Union in particular. However, in poetry, especially in highly conventional genres such as fables, this

---

[26] Ibid., p. 1 (Introduction).
[27] Murašov, "Pis'mo," p. 599. See also Iampol'skii, "Lenin," where the author talks about the privileged status of the voice in post-revolutionary rhetoric.
[28] Kondakov, "'Basn'ia'."
[29] "Style is then seen as the exception (though coded) to a rule; it is the (individual, yet institutional) aberration of a current usage" (Barthes, *The Rustle*, p. 91).
[30] Ravetto, *The Unmaking*, p. 101.

category acquired a special significance. The characterization "supremely simplistic" is applicable to Bednyi's texts not only as a description of the vulgarity of language, the primitivity of jokes; rather, it can be taken to define the very essence of the images inhabiting his texts. The human-animals, the allegorical images (defined as such by the strict conventions of the genre) communicating with each other by means of punches and disjointed insulting phrases, are indeed "supremely simplistic"—they are as simple as the simplest forms of life, protozoa-like.

These protozoa (with the pun on "the simplest form of life" working better in Russian) with their communication style which is "beyond language" have an important discursive and political function. In his reflections on the nature of the German baroque drama, in a passage where he discusses the striving of the baroque world view to differentiate between oral speech and writing, Walter Benjamin notes: "The spoken word, it might be said, is the ecstasy of the creature."[31] *Kreatur* (understood as "divine creation") is a concept which is loaded with multiple layers of philosophical, religious and socio-political meaning in Benjamin's text, and one would hardly think of discussing it alongside the creatures in Bednyi's fables. They do, however, share *creatureliness*, understood as belonging to the lowest, the most basic level of existence in the world. My use of the term is inspired by the writings of Eric Santner, especially his monograph on Rilke, Kafka, and Sebald. Without in any way suggesting the possibility of comparing Bednyi to the three great European writers, we would, however, like to quote a few words from Santner's book which may be helpful for understanding the function of early Soviet *creatureliness*:

> ...creaturely life—the peculiar proximity of the human to the animal at the very point of their radical difference.... The "essential disruption" that renders man "creaturely" for these writers has, that is, a distinctly political—or better, *biopolitical*—aspect; it names the threshold where life becomes a matter of politics and politics comes to inform the very matter and materiality of life.

In Santner's interpretation, *creatureliness* is an ultimately paradoxical zone, that place where the human and the animal overlap, which in the end defines man as subject and object of politics. In the context of our analysis here it seems possible to claim that a schematic, genre-determined bringing together of people and animals in this raw, crude manner politicizes the most elementary, "animalistic" facets of human existence. On this basis it can, indeed, be claimed that the introduction of offensive expressions as the dominant mode of communication between characters in satirical political fables literally introduces animalistic essence into an allegorical representation of political discourse. The concept of

---

[31] Benjamin, *The Origin*, p. 201.

creatureliness, with its emphasis on the essential physical nature of being, helps see how one could detect a "healthy strong realism" in Bednyi's writings, which was welcomed as something that "always protects the reader against all kinds of boffinry [*zaum'*]."[32] This *creatureliness* is a dominant humoristic element in Bednyi's texts exactly because of its expressive character: bodies talk, quite literally, without being in any way restricted by conventions and rules of behavior. Desires and impulses are translated into action without the mediation of language. The result is funny or ridiculous, depending on the reader's perception—but it is also useful as a means of propagating a new kind of interpersonal relations.

In Bednyi's fables it is exactly this bringing together of the human and the animalistic, reducing the resolution of conflicts and the general view of the world to the most primitive forms of grotesque physical violence, that emphasizes the allegorical nature of his satirical images, allegory being, according to Walter Benjamin, a composite construction by its very nature. These first Soviet satirical allegories are on the borderline between the threatening and the comic, the terrifying and the grotesque. It is exactly as a mixture of opposites that they are useful as a device of didactic writing.

Some two decades after the texts examined here saw light, the composite images combining mutually exclusive features found their further development in the Soviet rhetoric of the 1930s, when alleged enemies of the people were called upon to "tear off the masks" and "show their real faces."[33] Not that there was necessarily a direct intertextual connection between the images of Bednyi's fables and the vocabulary of denunciators and investigators, when defining the inhuman essence of the accused became an integral part of court verdicts[34] and when the State Prosecutor Andrei Vyshinskii execrated the "rabid dogs," "Szlachta-like spiders," "a cursed vixen-pig cross," "evil bipedal rats," "anthropomorphic beasts."[35] But one can argue that the roots of the presence of political mutants in judicial contexts are in this exceedingly primitive language which politicizes combinations of the human with the animal, of the archaic with the modern in the name of political ideals.[36] After all, according to Pierre Bourdieu, pronouncements of the lower levels of language, such as curses, aspire to the same degree of performativity as the language of law.[37]

---

[32] Voronskii, *Iskusstvo*, p. 317.   [33] Fitzpatrick, *Tear Off the Masks!*
[34] Cf. on this: Orlova, "Rozhdenie"; Brossat, "Le bestiaire," pp. 309–46.
[35] Vyshinskii, *Sudebnye rechi*.
[36] Cf. also Mircea Eliade's reflections on the overlapping of the totalitarian and the mythological discourses quoted by Mikhail Golovin'skii: 'All the epithets repeated at the communist trials...: Trotskyite, an accomplice of Tito, murderer an agent of imperialism.... It is as if there were no 'individuals' at the Soviet trials, but only types, archetypes, roles. Just like in archaic societies living outside of history" (Golovin'skii, "'Ne puskat'," p. 152.
[37] "Legal discourse is a creative speech which brings into existence that which it utters. It is the limit aimed at by all performative utterances—blessings, curses, orders, wishes or insults" (Bourdieu, *Language*, p. 42).

Years later, in 1956, the two canonical Soviet fable-writers—the already dead Dem'ian Bednyi and Sergei Mikhalkov—were praised for their fables in which "the fairy-talish flavor is disappearing, allegories can no longer be interpreted broadly. The language is more politically concrete, since fables are related to specific social phenomena."[38] True—Bednyi's texts can hardly be "interpreted broadly." Thus, the readers know exactly who hides behind the image of a particular fish: "The carp, all chewed up / Was a minister just the other day / Calling himself MacDonald Ramsay." They are told that "This gudgeon from Shchedrin's tales...has made it to our days, / And his name is Webb Sidney." Here, however, we confront yet another paradox stemming from the extreme simplicity of Bednyi's style. So as to ensure that his images will be understood directly, as concrete representations of specific people and phenomena, his texts include a great number of intertextual "explicatory" layers—epigraphs, citations from classics of Russian satire, quotes from newspapers, references to encyclopedias on animal behavior. The author explains clearly what his sources are: "I am writing like Shchedrin, / Putting in something from myself here and there, / And snapping a couple of quotations from Brehm." He even allows himself to make indirect references to Biblical imagery, such as when the carp, "swallowed by the pike for supper.../ Is then puked out by it." The texts themselves often include guidance on what the allegories mean:

> I gave here a precise translation of an Arab fable,
> And one shouldn't look for some hidden meaning in it.
> But were I to make a connection with the present day,
> I would use it to mock Lloyd George's manner.

We are dealing here with a somewhat paradoxical assumption when a multilayered allegory, awkwardly bringing together the animalistic and the human, newspaper headlines and conventional imagery is apparently more helpful in explaining to the reader the true state of things in the world than a direct interpretation of politicians' actions. The function of allegories in Bednyi's fables is to make the reality which the newspapers talk about understandable to the broad masses. In the spirit of traditional cheap woodcut accompanied by unpretentious and memorable rhymes, quite often the "paratextual" framing of the fables (titles, epigraphs, explanations, introductions) carried at least as much information as the poems themselves. This, for example, is one such title, which was followed by an epigraph from George Bernard Shaw: "About a Carp the Idealist and a Gudgeon the Socialist, Or In Other Words, About MacDonald Ramsay and Webb Sidney (Which One is Worth What, the Reader Knows

---

[38] Zheltova, "S. Mikhalkov," p. 427.

Better)" (*O Karase-Idealiste i Peskare-Sotsialiste, Sirech' o Makdonalde Ramzae i Uebbe Sidnee* [*Kto chego stoit, chitateliu vidnee*]). The cumbersome intertextual constructions are supposed to expose the readers to the nature of politicians behind words and actions, the true meaning of events behind newspaper reports, and the reliable criteria for a division into friends and enemies behind confusing diplomatic protocols.

The multiple intertextual and stylistic layers narrow down the number of possible interpretations of the texts, thus justifying the existence of satirical fables as a genre that propagates nothing but the truth. Intertextuality becomes a code which fixates and popularizes a certain set of images as sacred, allowing for one interpretation only; one is reminded of Roland Barthes's remarks on an extreme degree of codification that is characteristic of Marxist writing.[39] Intertextuality, or para-textuality, becomes a code which, on the one hand, points at a direct connection of the fable plots to real events, and on the other hand—exposes the parodic nature of the verses, revealing the essential truth without the shackles of a realistic narrative. The function of this code, thus, is simultaneously to simplify and to limit the understanding of images to a single possible interpretation. Just as primitive violence simplifies communication by transferring it to a pre-verbal level, so the multiplication of sources, by creating interpretational frames, is meaningful not by virtue of having a certain content, but through its sheer quantity. The intertextual codes are also an important element in the satirical effect these texts were supposed to produce, with the formal newspaper language and political realities directly translated into the blatantly inappropriate images. As with any other instance of humorous practices in totalitarian regimes, the audience is invited to laugh at the right things so as to prove that they can interpret the codes in accordance with the demands of the new order.

When speaking of the function of intertextual parodic allegory as a way to train the readers to discern the essence of a certain personality, one must pay special attention to the use of personal names of real people in combination with traditional expressions of mockery and curses. Here is a typical example from a passage ridiculing the leader of socialist revolutionaries:

> "Who? Me?.. —groaned Kornei.—I'd rather drop dead!"
> And that very night
> Robbed clean old Egor's house!
> Who awaits repentance from Viktor Chernov?
> Oh no, he is incorrigible, the Kornei of socialist revolutionaries!
> He is still that old white guard officer at core.
> So as not to let the white guard wolf hunt for meat,

---

[39] Barthes, *Writing*, pp. 23–4.

> Don't leave him with teeth—leave him no roots, either!
> That should do it!

We can detect here, too, a motif that found its full development somewhat later, in the epoch of great terror, with predication becoming "replaced with direct identification."[40] Long before the Soviet great terror, and before Dem'ian Bednyi, the nineteenth-century researcher of folklore Aleksandr Potebnia in his analysis of the fable genre spoke of the predicative function employed in fables. According to him, a fable should aim "to be the constant predicate of changing subjects."[41]

The mechanism of instrumentalizing names and personal qualities is essentially the same in fables as in terror. While there may be different specific individuals whose personal qualities undergo changes, the predicate (another person's name applied as a nickname, or else the whole image construction of the kind we encounter in fables) remains the same. In a revolutionary, and later totalitarian, regime the personal and the changeable is meaningful only as a manifestation of the typical because only a fixed, general predicate is believed to expose the true essence of an individual; only as a representative of a group does one become understandable. Coming back to the image brought to the fore by Sheila Fitzpatrick, we can say that the "tearing off of masks" is only possible by making people assuming other masks, more appropriate for the demands of the day.

This change of masks, this transition from the particular to the general, when a nickname turns into the name, plays a key role in the humorous appeal of Bednyi's allegories. Replacing names with nicknames, trading the particular for the general, and the introduction of masks into daily communication are among the characteristic features of post-revolutionary Soviet carnivalesque reality. Probably no other genre captured the very moment of transition better than Bednyi's fables, with their combination of the incombinable in political allegories (as with the thief Kornei turning into the socialist revolutionary Viktor Chernov turning into a wolf hungry for meat) and the reduction of multiple semantic layers to one simpler level.

If history is a place of names, then fables, by assigning to individuals strange (though supposedly more appropriate for them) names under the guise of allegory are most suitable to educating readers in accordance with the demands of a new historical era and making sure that the people are trained to actually "recognize" certain individuals as belonging to a certain type. A "true" reading of a text like Dem'ian Bednyi's is comical in the same way as a moment of the recognition of something that tried to remain unrecognized might be comical (assuming there is no danger involved). Sigmund Freud calls the moment of recognition in the production of pleasure from jokes and humor in general as *lustvoll* (pleasurable).

---

[40] Halfin, *Stalinist Confessions*, p. 125.   [41] Potebnia, *Iz lektsii*, p. 17.

Naturally, not everybody could enjoy this moment of recognition, and not everybody would find it funny. Those who could not fathom the scale of the transformations, those who had remained captives to the old world order, would naturally be surprised or frightened by the changes. Such is, for example, the case of an old woman who sees an orthodox priest trying to pass for a red army soldier:

>Darling, my precious!
>Why did you have your hair cut, father?
>Or have they abused you, poor soul?

As to those who have a correct understanding of things—they will laugh, detecting here yet another confirmation of how ridiculous some fake heroes of the new life can be, with their failed transformations. Of course, at first they need somebody to direct them, to show them what is funny and what is not, what is correct and what is not. They are in need of an instructor, somebody who, in literary texts, usually assumes the role of an enlightened witness and narrator of events. When present at a particular event, or observing the behavior of a person, or studying a phenomenon, this enlightened witness would be the one able to see everything from the right perspective, which often implies finding what they see ridiculous. An enlightened witness would also be able to interpret correctly what it is that he or she has just seen, who could translate the hieroglyphics of the new life into a simpler—"supremely simplistic"—language. A good example is the narrator of one of Bednyi's fables finding himself at the meeting of a political society, where he is the only one among many "petty intellectuals" who is able to see through a fake "political activist":

>As I found myself at a meeting the other day,
>I was quite surprised
>To see there Psoi [a doggy-man]. Dishevelled and angry,
>He was shouting: "Out! Out!"
>Cursing the bolsheviks and threatening them,
>To the great joy of social democrats.
>The petty intellectuals were beyond themselves with love for Psoi:
>Hear, hear, they cry, the wisdom of the people speaks!
>But what the cheapskates are trying to hide
>Is that the blood-sucker has come to them for support!

The moralizing voice here is what allows us to call these texts fables even when they probably could not be defined as such on the basis of strict genre criteria.

Paradoxical as it may sound, the allegorical fables of the not particularly talented poet Dem'ian Bednyi were a perfect propagandistic tool for the Soviet regime of the first decades. Though only for the first decades, or even the first years. Some time around 1930, Bednyi's intuition as to what would be most appealing to the masters of Soviet ideology started to fail him. He was accused at the highest level of ridiculing Russian national heritage and folk literature. A few years later, in 1936, a satirical opera for which he wrote the libretto was banned from being ever staged again after just one or two performances.[42] Apparently Bednyi did not recognize a change in the treatment by the state ideology of all things traditional, which were no longer to be ridiculed but treasured. However, the actual pretext for excluding Bednyi from the ranks of preferred poets seems to be what Igor′ Kondakov so aptly calls "Dem′ian's 'excessive' simplicity, which started to look like a conscious mockery of the primitive ideas he propagated." The children of the revolution had grown up, and speaking to them in the language of their childhood was no longer appropriate; worse, it was becoming suspicious. The vulgar, simplistic, completely transparent style was starting to be suggestive of a mask that the poet was wearing.

Ivan Batrak

But at least Bednyi lived. Another fable writer who was writing at about the same time, Ivan Batrak was arrested and executed in 1938. Batrak's real name was Ivan Kozlovskii. He shared with Bednyi and many other self-professed poets of his generation the love for pen-names marking his class affiliation, and "batrak" (a landless peasant) seemed like a good choice. His tragic fate, unfortunately, does not make him special, and nor do his poems. In the late 1920s and early 1930s he was the author, and the subject, of some polemical articles on the function of poetry (including fables) in the new era—and that's about it.[43] Despite the fact that in his lifetime he published quite a few collections and had some of his poems, including fables, reprinted posthumously,[44] he was deservedly forgotten—much like Dem′ian Bednyi by whom he was influenced, despite his eagerness to make old genres serve the new times. Also similarly to Bednyi, it is exactly his ordinariness that made Batrak appealing to those who labored on defining the language of the revolutionary era, and that makes him of interest to us here. He differed from his more popular contemporary not only in that he was less prone to using offensive language in his writings, but also in that he neither saw nor depicted the revolution as a simple matter of a (re-)distribution of power and of (physical)

---

[42] The story of Bednyi's fall from grace was no secret even in the Soviet post-Stalin time. See, e.g., Monastyrskii, "Rytsar′," pp. 45–6, and Kondakov, "'Basnia'."
[43] Batrak, "V chem my raskhodimsia"; Batrak, "Krest′ianskaia literatura"; "Ocherednye zadachi"; Bekker, "Nuzhna li nam basnia?"; Polonskii, "Tovarishch Batrak"; Kotomka, "Basni"; Rudov, "Basnopisets."
[44] Here we used two editions: Batrak, *Basni* (1933) and Batrak, *Stikhi i basni* (1956).

force. To him, the new life was not only about the new, liberated classes, personified by energetic and cunning animals being always ready to declaw, devour and destroy those who spoke, lived or thought differently. He was much more sensitive than Bednyi to changes in the administration and management of the state. His fables featured not only the traditional foxes and bears, wolves and cats, sharks and carps, spiders and flies, but also wheels and nails, numerous items of agricultural equipment, technologically advanced machinery, village correspondents, kolkhoz managers, and community council officials. He is, thus, somewhat of a connecting link between the militant drive of Dem'ian Bednyi and the pedantic, strictly conformist (non-)satire of Sergei Mikhalkov which we will analyze below.

Batrak's topics are split relatively equally between the classical fable themes (general human virtues and vices personified by animals, with the hard-working and the conscientious always ending better off than the lazy and the careless, with the selfish ones losing to those who are willing to cooperate etc.) and those inspired by events of the day. Among the texts belonging to the latter categories there is one thematizing an announced sale of agricultural equipment at a kolkhoz rental station ("Machines' Complaints" [*Zhaloby mashin*]), a response to the establishment of the League of Nations ("The League of Beasts" [*Liga zverei*] in Batrak's rendering), a poem about pieces of equipment, from harvesters and tractors to harrows and triers, that have gathered in the village square to celebrate an anniversary of the revolution ("Two Plouws" [*Dva pluga*])... The laughable figures—depicted whether as humans or in some other form—are not only lazy and stupid class enemies, as it would mostly be the case in Bednyi's texts. There is also a speaker with an inflated sense of self-importance, who holds forth on "Schelling, Fichte, Schlegel / The dialectical Process / That Hegel introduced us to"—except that he then turns out to be just an empty "professorial cap" addressing "comrades sheepskins and peasants' overcoats" and "hareskin coats" ("The Speaker" [*Orator*]). There is a wolf trying (unsuccessfully) to cull favor with a politically conscious village correspondent in order to gain access to sheep in the kolkhoz ("A Village Correspondent and a Wolf" [*Sel'kor i volk*]). There are "freeloaders" eager to serve as "managers of general affairs" or "archival managers" when their immediate supervisor has been promoted to a better place, even though they are incompetent ("Freeloaders" [*Nakhlebniki*]). There is also an inconsiderate political agitator who ends up being thrown down by the platform he was speaking from as he forgot to acknowledge its support, the moral lesson being the following:

> Comrade! You should never
> Forget about the masses
> And about your working class;
> Always keep an eye
> On what is happening among the rank-and-file,

Otherwise you will meet the same fate
Or, maybe, even a worse one ("A Speaker and a Stand").

In "A Cart with a Wooden Run" (*Telega na dereviannom khodu*) a hapless peasant stuck in the past is reproached by the wheel of his own old-fashioned cart (with a wooden run) for not having "acquired / A cart with an iron run." Understandably, quite a few fables thematize the attitude to enemies and their evil doings. Having compared the cunning strategies of saboteurs to the doomed attempts of some animals set on making a gain at the expense of others, the narrator of "A Behemoth and a Catfish" (*Begemot i som*) sums it up:

> This, more or less,
> Is the way of all saboteurs.
> We have already made sure
> That petty scoundrels
> Do not interfere with our united labor effort.
> But one day we will
> Also get to the hippopotamus himself.

In another instance ("Spiders and Flies" [*Pauki i mukhi*]) the author is yet more direct:

> But we won't be negligent,
> When the enemies are baking
> Not cakes for us,
> But gas, and canons, and shells.

In the original Russian, Batrak's texts are hardly more readable and more stylistically pleasing than they are in the verbatim English translation. A legitimate question to ask seems to be why he chose the fable form at all, if the content would probably have had just about the same effect on the readers if presented as a short opinion piece in a peasant newspaper or a flyer? All he is doing is pointing out a phenomenon, an event, or a form of behavior and saying: this is ridiculous; we should not tolerate this; this is similar to another event, phenomenon, or type of behavior that we would also find laughable. One line of conclusion would have sufficed: it is important to work hard, it is not good not to work; it is better to use modern machines rather than to rely on old-fashioned agricultural technologies; it is better to be on the side of the revolution than to be a counter-revolutionary. It could be, of course, that Batrak quite simply fancied himself a poet and a fable-writer. This is a possible explanation, but hardly sufficient if we are talking about the reason these verses resonated with the readers at the time, even if the readership was limited just to publishers and related authorities. Rather, it is likely that in the new reality, especially in non-urban areas, signs of the new life (better-quality equipment, a new type of management, new administrative hierarchies, previously unheard of professional functions) carried with them a sense of novelty that implied a significance transcending their immediate function. Just like wolves, foxes, spiders and ravens had for centuries populated the collective consciousness of the people, personifying powers of good and evil, so village correspondents, kolkhoz chairmen, tractors, and motorized carts were to become part of the new era's narrative about the new order of things. The short episodes rooted in mythological tales, however unsophisticated and badly written, reflected the need for the creation of a new folklore, which would be a response to the overwhelming novelty of the transformations and the need to normalize this very novelty.

It is as if the narrator, together with other creators of similar creative responses to what they saw happening around them, driven simultaneously by the spirit of the Revolution and that of the tradition, was eager to create a traditional frame narrative for the momentous changes before this traditional narrative had had time to evolve naturally. At around the same time the much loved children's author Kornei Chukovskii, seeing no other options left after a campaign against him had been unleashed, signed a letter declaring his willingness to write a series of children's poems and songs that would be an ultimate expression of the popular mood, "the new folklore": "Undoubtedly this folklore will be created in a natural way [stikhiinym putem] over the coming decades. But it is necessary to anticipate this process and, if possible, to create a whole range of such folk [narodnye] children's songs that would be propagating the new life in the village and affirming the new everyday [novyii byt]."[45] The oxymoronic imperative—to create folk songs—is discernible behind most other attempts at a forging of new cultural arche- and prototypes in popularly accessible genres.

Except that just a decade, or a decade and a half, after the Revolution the new life had not yet quite had time to become the new life in a full sense of the word. That very "new everyday" that Chukovskii refers to and that, as Lunacharskii claimed, was the true goal of the revolution and a measure of its success,[46] would not yet have become routine by the 1930s. At that time it would still be in that intermediate state between the uniqueness of the exception brought about by the revolutionary moment and the normalized functioning of a communal life, regulated by unspoken conventions and clearly defined rules. Bednyi's radical, crude, animalistic, impulsive, all-or-nothing humor expresses the nature of the revolutionary moment, but less so that of the transition to a society regulated by habits and customs. The humor encoded in Batrak's texts is of a different kind. It is more declarative, when the simple gesture of pointing at something in writing

---

[45] Kornei Chukovskii's letter of December 10, 1929 quoted in Lukianova, *Kornei Chukovskii*, p. 129.
[46] Lunacharskii, *O byte*.

and declaring it inappropriate, ridiculous, inadequate to the new reality counts as a humorous pronouncement. This is the humor of the time when the revolution, as an event, is already over, but before the new grammar of humor has been developed, when the general structure of the new reality is still as unstable and unpredictable as that of Batrak's sentences.

It was with Sergei Mikhalkov that the syntax and semantics of the Soviet moralizing humor came into their own.

Sergei Mikhalkov

Katerina Clark juxtaposes the complex, disparate imagery of the post-revolutionary years and "the more abstract, more unified and more economical" range of fixed images of the later period, which the researcher likens to an alphabet.[47] Even though Clark writes about Socialist Realism, her conclusions are significant in many respects also for an analysis of the transformations that occurred between the early 1920s and the late 1940s in the special genre of fable satire.

A critic wrote about Bednyi in 1924: "Dem'ian writes in the old way...all according to the old grammar."[48] He had in mind the style, of course, but also archaic images—those which, combined with political events of the day, were supposed to create a humorous effect. The author of the preface to the 1933 edition of Batrak's collection notes that some critics believe that fables, as a genre, belong to the past, because, in their opinion, "in the period of a gigantic socialist construction taking place under the conditions of an intense class struggle open satire should replace the periphrastic genre, the allegorical fable."[49] According to the preface, Batrak proved them wrong and managed to confirm the contemporary value of the old genre. Some twenty years later, when Mikhalkov was at his most prolific, the question of whether fables could be relevant was no longer asked.

The most productive fable-writer of the first post-war years wrote in a very different way: his grammar and imagery were completely Soviet. While Bednyi's images were constructed around clashes of incompatible elements (regardless of how realistic or fictional they were) and Batrak eulogized the new order by combining it with old narrative patterns, Mikhalkov's satirical imagery was grounded in the language of a well-established, perfectly functioning system. While in Bednyi's texts it is physical violence that is made to look funny and that turns into an allegory of the general principles organizing the new world, and in Batrak's writings the new everyday is awkwardly making its way into the

---

[47] Clark, "Polozhitel'nyi geroi," p. 571. [48] Voronskii, *Iskusstvo*, p. 317.
[49] Korenev, "Basni," p. 6.

archaic form, in Mikhalkov's poems physical violence is completely absent, and the socialist everyday is the only reality known and described. There is no physical contact between his characters at all. Bednyi has his human-animals, who are incapable of coherent human speech, fight each other, curse and swear, go through multiple grotesque and archaic transformations. Batrak experiments with anthropomorphic tools and pieces of equipment that are called upon to clearly introduce themselves, define their qualities and state where they stand politically. In Mikhalkov's fables, by contrast, the most that happens is conversations of conventionally animal figures in mundane, predictable situations. Now it is about the greatest possible economy in the use of narrative and images.

If we were to discuss the allegorical nature of Mikhalkov's works in the context of Benjamin's reading of allegory as an alternative to regular speech, we could conclude that Mikhalkov's images and the situations in which his characters find themselves are almost the opposite of the allegorical. They are an embodiment of an ordered, correct speech, the only kind of speech that is acceptable in the society of which they are part. Here there are no forms that would even allow for a possibility of an alternative mode of expression. The images that Mikhalkov uses are something like the primary units of the state discourse of his day. This core feature defines both the subject and the content of his satire. Mikhalkov targets not enemies as an ontological category, but the lowest level of incompatibility with the system: faults within its functioning and minor deficiencies of some of its representatives. While Bednyi laughs at those who cannot speak, Mikhalkov ridicules those who make mistakes in the new grammar; while Bednyi and Batrak's characters mock those who are strangers to the newly established order, in Mikhalkov's world there are no strangers. In the years that had passed since the voices of Bednyi and his followers counted everybody had become literate and enlightened enough to know what the rules are. This difference, as we will see below, is crucial.

Zoomessing

The more fixed the elements of the Soviet "alphabet" of images were becoming, the more ambiguous the Soviet critics were starting to be toward elements of writing that did not fit completely into the Socialist Realist canon—even if only because such elements implied an allegorical, that is, indirect, interpretation. In the 1950s, literary critic Zheltova praised the Soviet allegory which was grounded in a realist tradition. As an example of solid realism she mentions the elephant in Sergei Mikhalkov's fables, whose role "corresponds to his true image: elephants are nice, kind animals."[50] However, a few years later another critic expressed his

---

[50] Zheltova, "S. Mikhalkov," p. 429.

dissatisfaction with the growing trend to use allegories. According to him, "a purely allegorical image does not seem to be... appropriate for modern poetry, especially for fables, because it is extremely 'general' in its content, offering nothing for our aesthetic feeling 'to hold on to'."[51] He recommends to Soviet fable writers to concentrate on the character of the Soviet man and woman, "because it is in character that the artistic and satirical thinking of a fable writer resides." Some twenty years later Sergei Mikhalkov was, indeed, complimented by the author of an introduction to a collection of his fables for "having left behind the traditional dressing up of fable characters as all kinds of animals" and for being brave enough to approach a topic directly, "without all kinds of 'zoomessing' [*zverookolichnosti*], without playing zoo games."[52] It is true that by that time more and more fables featured simply "a friend" who got married "in order to get registered [i.e., as a resident in a city with a strict residence quota]," tourists who were "out on a wild holiday" and who "borrowed" freely potatoes from a kolkhoz field, construction workers "doing hackwork"... However, at the time which is of interest to us here, that is, in the last years of Stalinism, most of Mikhalkov's characters were still animals.

Back in the nineteenth century, the scholar of folklore Aleksandr Potebnia shared his thoughts on the function of animals in fables:

> How this came about that a fox stands for a cunning person, a wolf symbolizes somebody who is greedy, while an ass means that this person is stubborn and somewhat stupid,—I am not going to talk about it now. This is too broad a question. I will only say that the practical advantage of this convention for fable-writing can be compared to what happens in some games, for example, in chess, where each piece has a certain way of performing its function: a knight moves a certain way, the king and the queen move another way. Anybody who starts playing knows this, and it is very important that everybody know this, because otherwise people would need to agree on the rules each time, and they would never make it as far as the game itself.[53]

In the case of Mikhalkov, however, the situation is somewhat different: by the time he had joined the game, it had already been going on for some time. The roles had already been divided. In most of his fables these are not people behind the animal masks, but *person(a)s* in the initial meaning of this word, that is, masks referring to a function: "a poet-accountant" (*bukhgalter-poet*) and his "boss" (*nachal'stvo*), the "second-in-command" (*zam*) and the "head-of" (*zav*), poor speakers at meetings and hopeless poets, judges and defendants, high officials and sycophants, jealous colleagues and way too eager subordinates, poets and editors, drunkards

---

[51] Lipelis, "Sovremennost'," p. 36. [52] Isaev, "Vstupitel'naia stat'ia," p. 3.
[53] Potebnia, *Iz lektsii*, pp. 26–7.

and teetotallers, bribetakers and honest officials, representatives of public interests and traitors... These *person(a)s* deliver to each other rare delicacies by way of bribes ("A Goat, a Bear and a Deaf Ass" [*Koza, medved' i glukhoi osel*]), they pay respects to a stupid donkey simply because he is in charge of the fodder at a communal farm ("A Much-Needed Ass" [*Nuzhnyi osel*]), they drag the proceedings on a legal case on and on and on for fear of taking responsibility for a decision ("A Rabid Dog" [*Beshenyi pes*])... The animal images turn out to be masks placed on top of masks. They are conventional in a double sense: as figures in a fable, and also because they refer to socially defined roles.

In her monograph on the nature of comedy Alenka Zupančič argues against the common belief according to which laughter is triggered when the bearer of a social role exposes his or her "lower," physical, human nature. In Zupančič's opinion the opposite is true, namely, people laugh when the emphasis is on somebody being "not only human," not only a physical and biological entity. In her understanding, the ridiculous reminds us that a significant part of being human is about being "more than human"—it is about one's social role, one's status in society etc.[54] It would appear that the essence of the characters in Mikhalkov's fables is defined exclusively by these "more than human" elements, by the rules of the social game which had come to determine all interactions in the society. Hence the direct connection to specific socially significant and familiar situation: a city council, an exhibition, an editorial board, a house, a human resources department. This is the natural environment of Mikhalkov's animal characters—no longer seas, rivers, forests, fields; no creaturely presence as an expression of the post-revolutionary openness to the instinctive, the spontaneous, the animalistic. In this sense, Mikhalkov was writing in the tradition of Batrak much more than in that of Bednyi, except in a more adroit style and having transferred his characters to the urban environment of Soviet officialdom.

But then, if animal characters are completely deprived of their animal nature, why does one need them at all? One possible reason for their appearance in fables which are so directly related to contemporary everyday situations is that they were necessary in order to signal the very fact of this being a conventional use of a conventional satirical genre. The tautology is intentional: these fables were supposed to be *conventionally funny*, even if in reality many of them read simply as rhymed descriptions of routine daily encounters. To continue with Potebnia's analogy, we can say that Mikhalkov's verses not only set up pieces for a game which was already in progress. They actually created, and maintained, the genre of *pretending to play a game*, and they did so with great insistence, almost obsessively, their author increasing more and more the number of short rhyming narratives that were supposed to address nearly every situation in the reality of

---

[54] Zupančič, *The Odd One In*, p. 49.

victorious socialism. Batrak had already made a step toward erasing the line between "traditional" and "new" plots, writing fables in response to a variety of everyday interactions. But while for him things were still in the making and the novelty of the new thrashers and tractors made them almost as exotic as talking pigs and spiders, there were few surprises in Mikhalkov's satire.

It is obvious why it was necessary to play the game: this was the only way the illusion of satire as a free critical voice could be preserved, without saying anything that might be adverse to the regime. But in order to exclude the possibility of misunderstanding the rules that defined this "as-if game," nearly each fable-like episode is concluded with an explicit and often unduly lengthy "laying bare" of the device: the readers are told who should "learn a lesson" from the story and how it should be understood, so that "the meaning of this fable [become] clear," lest somebody forget that "Our fable has a goal: / To fight against evil." The narrator explains patiently why, for example, he decided to make one of his characters a brick (as it turns out, "the brick reminded [him] of certain people"), why he chose the allegorical form of satire in the first place ("I made chalk the subject here intentionally, / In order not to touch upon more serious matters") and what a particular image symbolizes ("What we call here 'pantry' / Is actually one's head"). At least one of the texts ("A Five-Minute Meeting" [*Piatiminutka*]) even features an explanatory subtitle: "A Joke" (*Shutka*). It was safer to repeat an explanation one time too many than to allow for the possibility of an ambiguous interpretation.

Tautology As a Device

For Mikhalkov, just like for all other skilled speakers of the official Soviet idiom, repetitions were important—though it would probably be more appropriate to speak of logorrhea or of graphorrhea rather than just repetitions. The readers would be excused for thinking that after the end of the war Mikhalkov produced a fable in response to every single event, every single occasion that he heard of, experienced directly or indirectly. The narrator informs the reader that "It was in the waiting room of the city council / That [he] got an idea to write on this topic," or: "Recently [he] read a critical review, / And, as [he] disagreed with it, / [he] added a new fable to [his] book of fables"; or: "The other day [he] was reading a foreign newspaper." The cause-and-effect chain is almost automatic: trigger—response; event—fable. Repetitions as such, of course, kill humor. But then, humor was not high on the list of the effects the author was trying to achieve. Rather, it was about marking a certain situation as humorous, as something that should be laughed at. Any deficiency, any malfunction in the otherwise smoothly working machinery of the social relations would need to be marked this way, just like a teacher marks any grammar mistake made by a pupil in a composition in order to correct it, and also as a warning for the future. By the early 1950s, mistakes in the Soviet grammar were much less obvious, because often less radical, than at the time of Bednyi and Batrak; all the more important was it to be able to detect a general tendency in a specific case, and intervene before it evolved into a chronic problem.

Slavoj Žižek points out that the Soviet discourse left no space for the "empty speech" which, according to Lacan, is the basis of human communication as such. In an ideal society, which is what the Soviet Union aspired to be, everything that is said and written should have a meaning.[55] This rejection of "empty speech" and the insistence on having everything fixed in writing could be an explanation of the obsessive urge to generate more and more writing, which was a characteristic feature of the Soviet discourse throughout the years of the regime's existence and across genres, even if the imperatives behind the writings thus produced differed from author to author and from period to period.[56] While Bednyi was about breaking the conventions of written language, and Batrak was among the first to introduce the new Soviet reality as routine rather than as a moment of revolutionary violence extended in time, Mikhalkov was driven by the need to eradicate anything not conforming to the norm. A socially conscious typesetter, appearing to a hapless writer in a dream, speaks to him in the language of a *Pravda* editorial:

> I read your work. Its message is not clear to me.
> I cannot agree
> With the actions of the people you describe!
> The heroes of your lines are fake and shallow!
> Where did you find them in your surroundings,
> Where did you see them? Or rather,
> Why did you humiliate the living heroes of our days
> With your slander?

The moral lesson of the fable "Just Some Information" (*Prostaia spravka*), where the author unsuccessfully tries to find out from the workers of a local zoo how long lions live, sounds like an entry in a registry of complaints:

> Nowadays some people try to stay so "vigilant"
> In order not to be responsible for anything,
> While at the same time leaving
> Their round seal in an open safebox!

---

[55] Žižek, *In Defense*, pp. 219–21.
[56] Fitzpatrick, *Tear Off the Masks!*, p. 167. See also Galkovskii ("Poeziia"), who defined the essence of Socialist Realist poetry as "parodically graphomanian" (referred to in Kozlova, "Sotsrealism," p. 150).

"The Sparrow Who Does Not Drink" (*Nep'iushchii vorobei*) ends like a letter of reference from the party committee at someone's place of work:

> There are some who once made a mistake
> (And then feel sorry for it!).
> Then they mend their ways,
> Do not stumble again,
> And become wiser and much more modest.

Mikhalkov's writing is the complete opposite of art. It is an embodiment of the very spirit of bureaucracy in a supposedly creative genre, a triumph of the rigid style that is as vital to the maintenance of the system as its legal machinery. It is the kind of style which, not constrained by the limits of formal judicial proceedings and state officialdom, provides a discursive framework of the regime—and graphorrhea is necessary here, as the enjoyment of the very process of producing writing which repeats and reaffirms discursive patterns is an integral trait of state bureaucratic discourse.[57] It seems justified to say that the excessive bureaucratization of life in Stalinism defines to a great extent a totalized vision of the world in general, when all deficiencies acquire a social significance and should be corrected immediately. As Andrei Platonov wrote in his diary in the mid-1930s, "Everything ordered, all the 'happiness,' etc. of the world is the hyperbolic imagination and practical philosophy of an office clerk."[58]

Mikhalkov's fables are an embodiment of Platonov's phantasy, in so far as humor in them presupposes total normality, against the background of which the most insignificant deficiencies in familiar, mundane situations are supposed to trigger laughter: red-tape, a lack of professionalism on the part of officials, the exaggerated self-confidence of minor bosses. Mikhalkov's animals do not even pretend to be anything but transparent stand-in figures for everyday imperfections personified ("Here we are, writing about animals, birds and insects, / But we end up hitting people we know all the time..."). These are no longer the forces of good and evil with a political flavor from Bednyi's poems, though Mikhalkov's pieces are sometimes reminiscent of Batrak's badly rhymed declarative responses to not particularly extreme instances of everyday incongruities. The reader is invited to laugh at relatively inane faults—half-heartedness, lack of initiative, narcissism, sluggishness, greed, irresponsible attitude to communal property...

The one thing all three of the authors discussed here have in common is that they, each in his own special way, express the essence of the Soviet power itself, in

---

[57] See, e.g., Richard Heinemann in his analysis of the bureaucratic style in Kafka: "In Josef Olszewski's 1904 study, a penchant for 'Schreiberei' ('writing') is included among the four characteristics most commonly associated with the bureaucrat" (Heinemann, "Kafka's Oath," p. 259).

[58] Platonov, *Zapisnye knizhki*, p. 172.

so far as they renounce authorship in favor of speaking in the voice of the community. Walter Benjamin opens his notes on Kafka with an anecdote on a courtier at the Russian tsar's court, who played a joke on a minor official for bothering him for a signature at a wrong moment by signing all the documents in the official's own name.[59] This episode is an allegory of authorship turned into a parody of itself. Mikhalkov's essentially tautological writings are akin to the mockingly reproduced signature of the Russian petty clerk. The multiple repetitions of the same, erasing the author's voice, become an affirmation of the ubiquitous presence of the superior power. And with the (non-)author being an ideal Soviet joker, always conscious of the need to conform to the norm even in his jokes, that is, in deviations from the norm, it stands to reason that the implied readers of these texts would need to be ideal Soviet readers always willing *to laugh tautologically*, that is, in response to conventional images that have been previously tested on multiple occasions. Mikhalkov's ideal implied reader is *an ideal consumer of normative bureaucratic language as the language of humor*. When the characters and narratives aimed at triggering laughter are so highly predictive, laughter itself is supposed to become a predictable reflexive reaction.

Boredom, Laughter, and the Norm

At the risk of committing blasphemy by mentioning Kafka and Mikhalkov in one sentence we can say that Mikhalkov as an anti-Kafka. His satirically-didactic pieces powered by awkward clichés of bureaucratese are a reversed mirror image of Kafka's texts, where a near indefinite multiplication of bureaucratic fantasies creates alternative dimensions of meaning. Compared with Kafka's writings the main feature of Mikhalkov's verses becomes especially noticeable: they are boring.

This is not just to say that a potential reader is likely to be bored, lose interest, become distracted. Rather, being "boring" is an essential core characteristic of these texts. Their images, style, message are always extremely predictable. There is no secret in them, they do not promise a surprise, there is no discrepancy between what one sees and hears in the course of going about one's daily life and what one reads in these short pieces. In Bednyi's fables the revelation of the true nature of some of the characters was supposed to come as a moment of shock, which was supposed to amuse the readers and make them more interested in the new social dynamics. In Batrak's poems about the new village life the very novelty of what he was describing would have been enough to trigger at least some interest. In

---

[59] Benjamin, "Franz Kafka," p. 409.

Mikhalkov's rhyming sketches, however, the possibility of anything unexpected happening is excluded, and where there are no surprises, boredom rules.

This is a paradoxical situation, seeing as it is a supposedly satirical genre we are talking about here, something that should ridicule and amuse. Reduced to its essentials and taken to the extreme, the formula seems to be that boring equals funny equals normative. This leads to the logical (though equally paradoxical) conclusion that, as the ideal readers read the endlessly multiplied examples of bureaucratese (with lazy bosses promising "not now, but later... we'll check this... it'll be sorted out"; with those enjoying even the most minimal influence making sure that "one hand washes the other one / And both hands grab, where possible"), they must be ready to laugh at the bureaucratic structure itself, but at the same time they should also accept this very structure as a given. Even more: it should be perceived as a kind of ideal language, a model of perfect communication, it being the only form of communication that was used by the Soviet power itself to communicate with its citizens.

In the Soviet universe, neither constituent of this triangle (the familiar and the predictable—the ridiculous—the normative) should be incompatible with the other two. On the contrary, the three elements should complement each other, creating an ideal product for the ideal consumer of official satire. In the context of Soviet didactic humor those who are laughed at and those who laugh, the object of a joke and the joker merge together. We already mentioned a similar paradox which is noticeable in Dem'ian Bednyi's writings, where the language of the new power is represented as ridiculous and obscure when seen through the eyes of enemies of the revolution, even though this was probably an impression shared by most of Bednyi's readers who identified themselves with the revolutionary cause. Mikhalkov's fables continue this tradition of bringing together the object of laughter and the one who laughs. Ideal consumers of Soviet satire should be able to laugh at a reflection of themselves as either those who are confused about the language of the new power (as with Bednyi), or as those who make mistakes in its grammar (as with Mikhalkov). Ideal Soviet citizens understand that they should not trust their own subjective perception of the Soviet tongue as something incomprehensible, or cliché-ridden, or simply boring, because this is how language is perceived (in Bednyi's texts) or used (in Mikhalkov's fables) only the heroes of didactic satirical pieces (we are leaving Batrak out because his style is too nondescript, and the language of his characters too basic, to provide any meaningful material for analysis). The bottom line is that the ideal consumers of satirical texts of the kind analyzed here should be prepared *to laugh at the fact that they find something to laugh at in the language of power*. Such is the ultimate tautology of the discursive strategy of Soviet ideology.

This merging together of an ideal and a subject of ridicule, a friend and an enemy reflects a fundamental belief of Soviet ideology in language being a dangerous substance so that even repetitions and citations might potentially undermine the foundations of the society. Gordeich, trying unsuccessfully to repeat the words he does not understand, is ridiculous—but what makes him ridiculous is, ultimately, the language of the new power. Officials neglecting their professional duties in Mikhalkov's fables are funny because they use the language of central newspapers' editorials to cover up their actions which are far from the Soviet ideal—but by doing so they, too, simply reproduce the "politically correct" language. Repetitions are necessary, learning by rote is a must—but repetitions can become a parody just as much as they are an expression of one's loyalty to the system. This "mirroring" quality of the Soviet language reached its climax in the years of the Great Terror when, as Igal Halfin points out, both the investigators and the accused spoke the same language.[60]

If so, how could any attempt at subversive thinking under the guise of obedience be prevented?

Moralizing was one possible way.

The Moral of the Story

The "moral" here is to be understood as referring to both the final part of a fable, and that politically and ideologically loaded quality which was supposed to determine the behavior and beliefs of every Soviet citizen. The author of a relatively recent article on the genre of fables writes that in each narrative the characters are "introduced to moral principles for the first time, that is, they undergo a moral experience [scbytie morali]."[61] In other words, the characters (or rather—readers) in a fable find themselves in the position of children discovering the world, and by explaining the meaning of whatever happens to them, the creator of this world (the author of the fable) prepares them for adult life.

The structure of Mikhalkov's fables is much stricter and much more clearly expressed than that of Bednyi's and Batrak's. In the revolutionary poets' writings, the moralizing conclusion is frequently not even singled out as such, with the reader just invited to observe the exchanges between the characters and draw supposedly obvious conclusions. Mikhalkov, however, is careful always to provide a clearly and unambiguously formulated explanation of the meaning of whatever it is he described and mocked in the particular piece. Here is one example out of dozens, coming at the end of a short fable:

> I wrote this fable as a lesson for those people
> Who are always dancing around their bosses,
> Ready to take even a simple sneeze

[60] Halfin, *Stalinist Confessions*, p. 3.   [61] Nesterenko, "Proizvedenie," p. 102.

Of their superior
For an instruction.

Playing the satire game required that any representation of a malfunction in the ideally harmonious picture of the world be immediately compensated by an unconditional explanation, and any such explanation had to be absolutely transparent so as not to leave room to a dangerous ambiguity which otherwise accompanies humor. In the spirit of the *fort-da* game in Freud's famous interpretation, any ironic deviation from the official discourse had to be followed by a reintroduction of order and an annihilation of even the most minimal humorous charge.

This expedient narrowing of the space of interpretation, this urge for an immediate resolution of any conflict with the system is yet another manifestation of the infantilization which is characteristic of totalitarian discourse in general. Appropriately, the most celebrated Soviet fable-writer himself admitted that "of course, [he] owed his fables to children's literature. This literature is unimaginable without a sense of humor, because children have a better sense than grown-ups for everything funny."[62] But when dealing with children, even when playing and making jokes with them, it is important to never forget to explain what is what, what is right and what is wrong, and how things are. This is why a small episode involving dubious characters must be followed by setting things right; this is why there is no room for physical or verbal violence in the literature for (future) ideal citizens of the state, not even as a joke; this is also why it is important to keep the texts short and written to one pattern—this way children can understand them better. It is, then, no wonder that Mikhalkov's fables are like short illustrations of the laws of the genre for beginning writers and readers.

Mikhail Iampol'skii writes about the living voice as an ideal in Lenin's post-revolutionary Russia; Valerii Podoroga notes the canonized status of the written law under Stalin.[63] If we take fables to be an expression of the spirit of the age, then it makes sense that Bednyi's writings were mostly about a shockingly informal language, with the moralizing lesson being to a great extent related to the simple fact that such language could now be used in writing. Batrak's voice was insipid to the extent that it bore no distinctive features of either class, stylistic register or markers of the medium in which it was best rendered. Decades of Stalinism, with its canonization of writing, produced Mikhalkov's didactic tales for grown-ups with their heavy-handed moralizing. Bednyi marked the beginning of the narrative of the Soviet fable, Batrak introduced the new topics of the socialist everyday, and Mikhalkov concluded it—not necessarily in terms of actual chronology, but in affirming and maintaining socialist normativity. This normativity required that

---

[62] Mikhalkov, "Iasno videt'," p. 155. [63] Podoroga, "Golos," p. 109.

the moralizing lesson transcend a particular case and point at a recognizable model of behavior, as the conventions of the genre require. This is why the main lesson of Mikhalkov's fables is the very fact that there is a moralizing lesson, that there is a completion of the narrative, guaranteeing that all cases of inappropriate behavior will be made public, however insignificant they might be. It turns out that satire itself can be but a convention, framed by explanations and reservations that repeat and affirm the solidity of the rules at the foundation of the Soviet society. Hence the accent on vague and generalized pointers at the conclusion of most fables: "and if, by chance"; "I am referring here to many"; "a magazine known to us"; "we know there are still some families around"; "we know of courthouses of this kind"; "one can meet such ignoramuses"; "some show such 'vigilance'"; "excessive praise is bad for some." These "some" and "certain" refer, of course, to those who are known to everyone, who are everywhere, those at whom the fables are addressed. The short verses in their exaggeratedly schematic, "Mikhalkovean" version are one of characteristically Soviet genres, especially appropriate for the education of an ideal and obedient subject. Whoever happens to be wrong or mistaken, or in the grip of some false beliefs, is corrected or punished quickly and adequately, their case becoming a lesson both for the guilty party themselves, and for the others. Having reached the end of a fable, its readers should be able to detect in the most minimal transgression a manifestation of a ridiculous (and thus offensive, and thus potentially dangerous) *pattern*.

A *pattern*, however, should be distinguished from the *law* in a broad sense of the word, the law that evolved from the blind post-revolutionary violence through the initial stages of an awkward bureaucratization of daily life and up to the victory of a total normativity, the kind of law that Mikhalkov's fables affirm. This last stage in the development of Soviet legality, less bloody, but no less total than the preceding ones, is incorporated in Mikhalkov's satirical pieces as an ideal, almost fairytale-like order of things, where crimes are reducible to minor deficiencies, and where a verdict is replaced by a wise moralizing statement at the end of a fable.[64] Satirical educational tales for grownups with unpretentious rhymes can be regarded as an incarnation of the primary unity of poetry and law, oversimplified to the point of parody.[65] The two realms of language turn out to be similar not in that they share an elevated style, but in that they are governed by principles of normativity. The main moralizing lesson of Mikhalkov's fables is an affirmation of normative satire and a delineation of the rules, and limits, of what can be presented as ridiculous and inappropriate once socialism has established itself.

---

[64] The parallels between allegorical poetry and judicial practices of the regime are inspired by the reflections in Lipovetsky, "Skazkovlast'."

[65] Afanas'ev, "Iuridicheskie obychai," p. 329 (with reference to an article by Jakob Grimm).

Bakhtin spoke of "a great migration of seriousness" which happens at turning points in history.[66] This "migration of seriousness," relieving genres and forms of their old content, inevitably implied also a shift in the functions of traditional forms, with "non-serious" genres coming to fulfill quite important educational and propagandistic functions. As the Soviet reader was growing up, evolving from a witness of the revolution, barely familiar with the new language, to the hero of the new world order, speaking its language as a native tongue, the forms of communication with the audience were also changing, as were the principles of education and political training. This is especially noticeable on the examples of genres such as fables, which are on the borderline between the archaic and the politically relevant, combining childishly simple, conventional plots with a propaganda of political ideas. As a "borderline" genre, fables illustrate the transformations of stylistic and textual codes which modelled the ideal reader, the ideal consumer of Soviet satire—the ideal citizen.

---

[66] Bakhtin, "K voprosam," p. 51.

7
The Merry Adventures of Stalin's Peasants
Kolkhoz *Commedia dell'arte*

> Laughter requires not only the laughable persons that we are; it demands the inconsequential crowd of those who laugh.
>
> Georges Batailles,
> *Inner Experience*

"The Colonel Will Find It Funny": Constructing Soviet Humor

Comedy can be traced back to a time in human history when art was inseparable from ritual. The word comes from Greek: *Kōmos*—"revel" and *aoidos*—"singer." Over time the reveling masked crowds and improvised choirs celebrating Dionysus were replaced with types, characters, dialogue, and action.[1] Comedy has retained its proximity to its folk roots, popular entertainment, celebrations on fixed days of the year, and wedding feasts. This link manifests itself in obscenities, vulgar jokes, rude comic masks, and carnival transformations. The low origins of the comic were readily exploited by Soviet aesthetics, which never tired of emphasizing the "popular" roots of humor: "People are rich in humor, and this humor nourishes comedy. In humor lies the power of popular optimism; humor is how people express their contempt, their joy, their sadness."[2] This grounding of the comic in low popular culture points at a defining characteristic of the genre that has long been acknowledged by scholars, namely, its greater national/ethnic specificity as compared to other aesthetic categories. The social and national roots of Soviet state laughter are the same as the roots of Stalinist political culture as a whole: in the psychology of semi-urbanized peasants that provided the social basis of Stalinism.[3]

"Sense of humor" is a relatively new concept. From the seventeenth century, wit has been associated in the Western tradition with arrogance and mockery, as a marker of sarcastic intellectualism and aggressive resentment. Humor, on the contrary, evoked images of goodwill and sympathy. It became a sign of a

---

[1] Ozmitel', *O satire*, p. 35.   [2] Frolov, *O sovetskoi komedii*, p. 14.
[3] See Lewin, *The Making* (part I).

democratic spirit and emotional health. This distinction was followed by Freud, who differentiated between good-natured, psychologically healthy humor and aggressive wit.

However, in the eighteenth and early nineteenth centuries, English philosophers had already developed a conceptual vocabulary for a range of aesthetic and moral sentiments. Such sentiments came to be seen as a sign of "sensitivity," that is, an ability to show a deep understanding and appreciation of various qualities. One spoke of the sense of beauty, of honor, of decency, moral sense, common sense and the sense of the comic, which toward the middle of the nineteenth century came to be called the "sense of humor." At that time, the notion of a "sense of humor" already had an aesthetic connotation. An ability to perceive, generate, and evaluate humor was likened to the "sense of beauty" in art or "perfect pitch" in music. In other words, from the very beginning it was an evaluative category denoting one's intellectual development, level of general culture, and degree of sophistication in responses to the outside world.

There are completely objective ways of evaluating the quality of humor. There is, for instance, Rod Martin's "Coping Humor Scale," in which humor is classified on the basis of its complexity, from pre-set notions to those created by imagination and fantasy. The closer one's humor is to the upper limit (ascending from sexual to nonsexual; from simple to complex; from personal and situation-specific to impersonal and abstract), the more developed it is.[4]

However, the democratization that the twentieth century brought with it (especially in Russia, where it took the most radical forms) led not so much to a development of "sentiments," but to an averaging of taste (*obshchepit*—"community catering"); fashion (*shirpotreb*—articles for popular consumption); and, finally, of the sense of humor itself, the ultimate expression of which became "Grandpa Shchukar'" from Mikhail Sholokhov's *Virgin Soil Upturned*. He was probably the first humorous character to be included in the Soviet literary canon and became familiar to every Soviet citizen, since the novel was part of the school curriculum.

If one compares the era of Stalinism with the 1920s, it becomes apparent that the level of Soviet humor had been declining for some time. Even though characters somewhat similar to Grandpa Shchukar' can be found in the literature of village correspondents from the 1920s, they did not dominate the Soviet culture of laughter, which remained predominantly urban. As more and more peasants were moving into cities, the mental profile of the consumers of culture was acquiring more and more semi-peasant features. The sense of the comic was becoming increasingly blunt, the imagery was becoming more and more simplistic, until finally archaic popular culture characters found themselves on stage—

[4] See Martin, *The Psychology*.

first as extras, and then as leading characters. Humor understood as "empty laughter" is as alien to this semi-peasant culture as the idea of "art for art's sake" is alien to Socialist Realism. It is not humor that utilitarian cultures recognize but satire, which performs important social and political functions of a primarily sanitary nature. While the authorities' need for manipulative satire is politically justified and understandable, their interest in humor appears inexplicable. Or rather, in order to elicit laughter, it requires a level of consciousness that is either in the margins of culture or else completely outside its limits.

The comic is often dependent upon the recipient and, as such, it is a trait of the object as much as of the subject. State laughter was always oriented toward the subject: the jokes, character types, and anecdotes it favored clearly appealed to the audience of yesterday's peasants. As Il'ia Kalinin noted, "Soviet laughter is not so much about an *effect* produced through mechanisms of the comic as about an *affect* generated by the collective spirit."[5]

In the mid-1950s, for the first time in Soviet aesthetics, Iurii Borev introduced a list of fundamental conditions that needed to be satisfied for something to be considered witty. First, there were certain moral ideals without which humor could become cynical, bawdy, vulgar, or obscene. The second condition concerned a dialectic flexibility in registering and accentuating contradictions. One also had to have a high level of critical thinking so as to apply common sense to the accentuated contradictions, lest humor be degraded to skepticism and nihilism. A developed aesthetic sensibility and a sense of moderation were also needed, as was the ability to think associatively, to produce and respond to a broad range of varied, unexpected comparisons, whereby phenomena are taken out of their primary contexts.[6] It is obvious that *all* these parameters imply that being witty and having the ability to respond to wit cannot become a mass phenomenon. In fact, the opposite is true: they define the perception of the Soviet consumer of culture, who had at this point been introduced to just the basics of culture and whose consciousness was utilitarian, undeveloped, limited and poor in associations, whose thinking was slow, and who was as yet unable to exercise a critical attitude to the surrounding reality. Hence the inability of the Soviet consumer of culture to respond to wit. The comic as generated by state laughter in accordance with the demands of this consciousness was not only lacking in any degree of sophistication; it inevitably appealed to the concrete imagery specific to infantile thinking, the vulgar jargon of a semi-urban milieu, a primitive thematic range (rude mockery, crude jokes, exploitation of gender, national, or racist stereotypes) and an undeveloped taste.

When humor is defined by parameters that are fundamentally antagonistic to wit, it inevitably results in a degradation of laughter. However, this was exactly the

---

[5] Kalinin, "Nam smekh," p. 128.   [6] Borev, *O komicheskom*, pp. 88–9.

type of humor that was promoted by Soviet "masters of the comic." One of them, Leonid Lench, drew the attention of his colleagues directly to this "horizon of expectations" in a speech he gave in February 1944:

> The humorous and satirical literature of our time must be oriented towards the masses and organically popular, if it wants to develop and to grow. A comic writer whose works make one and a half snobs laugh, wherein the "half" is represented by the humorist's own aunt, is of no use to anyone, and he might as well go sleep. The audience of a Soviet comic writer is millions of readers.[7]

There is no doubt that Lench, himself one of the leading Soviet comic writers who had joined the Writers' Union upon Mikhail Zoshchenko's recommendation, well understood the nature of "mass" laughter and the guidelines he was following. After a histrionic appeal to the writers to write for the masses, he explained to his colleagues the special nature of one such acceptable form of comedy, which was being called "army humor." He shared a story about how once he and a number of other satirists and comedy writers

> were summoned to a high office and invited to think about the creation of a military satirical magazine. We considered the situation—a military magazine, the commander's position of authority, the hierarchy, and so on—and then asked, "Who does one laugh at in a military magazine?" They told us we can laugh at people not above the rank of major. Then someone asked, "But will it be funny?" And I think it was Ryklin [the editor-in-chief of *Krokodil*] who answered from his seat: "A colonel will find it funny."[8]

The transcript recorded the reaction of those present: "Everyone burst out laughing." Soviet "masters of the comic" knew very well *what kind* of humor they were required to produce, and they produced it in industrial quantities.

Laughter "not above the rank of major" is, of course, an extreme case of laughter that creates hierarchy, despite the fact that it supposedly is called upon to undermine it. Here, however, it is not just about hierarchy, but also about a division into social strata. A soldier's humor is defined by an extremely primitive range of devices ("flat" and/or "dirty" jokes, obscenities) and topics (sexual, naturalistic/bodily, and household-related). Striving to be accessible, Soviet culture gravitated toward this type of "totalitarian humor"[9] since it was the kind most preferred by the masses.[10]

---

[7] RGASPI F. 17 (Agitprop TsK 1938–48). Op. 125. Ed. khr. 282. L. 58. (Union of the Soviet Writers Plenum, February 5–8, 1944. Transcript).
[8] Ibid., L. 63.   [9] Stolovich, *Filosofiia*, p. 270.
[10] See Melekhov, "Umoritel'naia gil'otina."

By the early 1930s, the nature of the comic underwent a transformation, as biting satire gave way to a gentle, harmless, good-natured humor, light-hearted jocularity with a generally happy intonation. This was in line with the political mandate of the 1930s to strengthen life-affirming motifs, to compose works in an optimistic tone, to depict everyday Soviet life in consistently cheerful colors so as to make the new type of hero—the rank-and-file builder of socialism—appear "warmer" and "more human." The previously dominant spirit of austerity and self-restraint was no longer on the agenda. Rather, now it was all about joy, merriment, and abundance, and action was to be set during celebrations, on holidays, with characters singing, dancing, and participating in sports activities. The new comedy was a stream of gags, puns, and almost variety-show episodes, hastily put together around the axis of an unsophisticated plot. The life in these plays was filled with "the poetry of Soviet reality" to such an extent that their characters lost the ability to express in prose the feelings that overwhelmed them and started talking in poetry. Now their songs opened and concluded nearly every Soviet comedy play and film.

To avoid the accusation of "vilification" of Soviet reality the authors of these plays and films chose to set the action of their works in spa retreats or out in nature, thus isolating their characters from social and historical conflicts. For lack of any form of social antagonism, the characters' social relations could display their dramatic potential only in extraordinary circumstances. Thus, exceptional events were always required in order to drive the dramatic plot. There were ships stuck in ice, natural catastrophes, and outbreaks of lethal diseases.

Satire, by its very nature, was unsuitable for "reflecting" Soviet reality, so a special kind of comedy emerged, one that "started to acquire a somewhat different shape from classic comedy."[11] This makes sense, since if, according to Aristotle, comedy depicts the worst of human nature, and tragedy the best, then comedy must "die out as perfection of human nature is achieved." However, far from declining, the number of comedies was steadily growing, and their heroes were "not the worst, but the best people." Since satire with its annihilating laughter is reserved for "the worst" people, a depiction of "good people" in comedy demands "kind laughter":

> We are not going to eliminate "our people"; we look at them with a friendly smile, we expose their weaknesses, but they remain the best. However, if laughter serves not just the best or the worst people, but in that area specifically where these people are even worse, then the logical conclusion is that laughter is connected with personal deficiencies and that as these deficiencies are gotten rid of, laughter also begins to disappear.[12]

---

[11] Iuzovskii, "Osvobozhdennyi Promete.," p. 125.   [12] Ibid.

In fact, laughter started dying off a long time before these lines were written. The year before that, Richard Pikel presented the following statement as a foregone conclusion: "Comedy found itself in the backyard of theater repertoire, like Cinderella after secretly making her way onto the stage."[13] These words were written in the early 1930s. By the late 1950s, there was no longer any need to explain to the Soviet audience that "a comedic playwright's desire to make people laugh is no more wanton than a cook's desire to feed them, a doctor's to cure them, and a builder's desire to build"; nonetheless, it had to be acknowledged that humor on stage and on screen had died, and "for some time now humor in comedy had been akin to smuggled goods."[14]

In reality, however, this state of affairs was a sign of comedy winning, except that in this comedy Socialist Realism was gaining an upper hand over Aristotle, and the depiction of heroic characters was no longer exclusively the prerogative of tragedy or drama. Now, these characters were just as at home in comedy, in "that kind of comedy whose characters are truly the best people, heroes whose status as heroes is affirmed in this way—through comedy, because comedy is the genre that shows them as what they are, that is, the best people."[15]

Here the critic turned to classical comedy, which was born out of the tradition of performing songs at phallic harvest rituals celebrating fertility and Dionysus. These folk celebrations took place in an atmosphere of merriment, jokes, erotic songs, drinking, nocturnal circle dancing, and torch processions of dressed-up characters moving to drumbeat. Since those celebrations "were a result of the processes of labor and its achievements, possibly originating directly from the era of primitive communism," comedic playwrights would do well to turn to dramatic folklore—after all, Gorky himself had encouraged poets to look to poetic folklore in his speech at the Writers' Congress.[16]

In this chapter we discuss the consequences of this folklorization, which rapidly brought state laughter closer to the mass consumer, completely shifted the threshold of the comic, and radically transformed the very nature of Soviet laughter. First, however, we should understand how the fact that Soviet aesthetics perceived comedy as a tool for shaping a politically correct optics led to a lowering of this threshold in the selection of devices in order to increase the tool's efficiency.

In the 1930s, the attention of readers and viewers, authors and critics alike shifted from satire (which was a constant focal point for discussions in the 1920s) to humor. The true meaning of the Soviet transformations of comedy was not a secret to anyone. As the Czech historian of Soviet literature Miroslav Mikulášek remarked in 1960, "now it became especially evident that lyrical comedy... was to a certain extent a cowardly modification of satirical comedy, a consequence of the false assumption that in Soviet literature humor and satire had to take a back seat,

---

[13] Pikel', "K probleme," p. 49.   [14] "Sovetskaia komediia v nashi dni," pp. 152, 153.
[15] Iuzovskii, "Osvobozhdennyi Prometei," p. 125.   [16] Ibid., p. 126.

a fruit of the community spirit where the life of the country appeared in the form of 'a smiling prosperity'."[17]

Iurii Borev explained that laughing at "mainly expressions of the positive" meant laughing at weaknesses that were, however incredibly, a continuation of "our" positive qualities:

> When negative aspects of the positive and of the beautiful are comic, comedy is not a manifestation of the general inadequacy and corrupt nature of a phenomenon, but of a conflict between a beautiful phenomenon and those aspects of it that impede its further development and its reaching a greater degree of perfection.[18]

This "conflict between the good and the excellent" resulted in a truly dialectic formulation of the distinction between satire and humor: "A special emotional *negative* critique and a critique that *confirms* its object in its essence—such is the core of the distinction between satire and humor."[19]

This was a kind of humor that had been previously unheard of, in all respects. It was "realistic"; never before had humor been classified in such terms. According to this logic, if there is romantic irony and "realistic satire," why should there not be "realistic humor"? Now it was claimed that "wit is only valuable when it is grounded in real life experience, when it helps reveal the characteristic traits of heroes, when it shows these heroes' feelings."[20] And it was not just that humor had to be realistic. It had to be Socialist Realist, that is, had to be inspired by ideas and popular spirit: "As popular wisdom shows, people are in favor of laughter, but are against aimless buffoonery. The laughter of the people is profound and intelligent, despite the fact that it sometimes appears in a playful and jocular packaging."[21]

It should be no surprise that this new humor demanded a new kind of comedy: "A distinctive feature of our comedy is that its characters are positive heroes, and the plot is structured not on conflict, but on mutual competition and solidarity."[22] And since humor came to be associated with "certain weaknesses of generally positive phenomena and characters," the genre that was most adequate for its expression was vaudeville.

Vaudeville is a product of *urban* culture, as is evident from the etymology of the word: the genre that emerged in Paris in the sixteenth century was called *voix de ville* (the voice of the city). A century and a half later, popular urban satirical songs turned into small dramatic performances, which then came to be known as "vaudevilles." They reached the climax of their popularity as an urban genre in the nineteenth century. However, their Soviet audience was not truly urban, which

---

[17] Mikulášek, *Puti*, p. 200.   [18] Borev, *O komicheskom*, p. 55.   [19] Ibid., p. 152.
[20] Frolov, *O sovetskoi komedii*, p. 325.   [21] Ershov, *Sovetskaia satiricheskaia proza*, p. 19.
[22] Shchupak, "Zametki," p. 101.

led to the emergence of two Soviet versions of the genre: "lyrical" and "kolkhoz" comedy. "Kolkhoz vaudeville" is a degraded form of urban comedy, brought down to the level of peasant humor. This is how the genre adapted to the social composition of the Soviet cities that were populated with erstwhile peasants.

In addition to the social factors that led to this transformation of the genre, there were also political and aesthetic ones. From the 1920s onward, Soviet theoreticians of satire saw vaudeville as an absolute evil. Boris Alpers claimed that it was "impossible to use the traditional vaudeville form in a modern play."[23] He believed that "restoring a genre that had been rejected by life itself" was "a useless enterprise, doomed to failure."[24] Other critics of the 1920s were less ingenuous in their formulations, claiming that "the task of a modern vaudeville writer is to revise the masks of the eighteenth century Italian comedy and to adjust them to our daily life."[25] This was the beginning of the Soviet "lyrical comedy," or the "comedy of positive characters," even though vaudeville as such was still not welcome. However, the development of the theory of "positive satire" in the 1930s brought with it a rebirth of vaudeville—even though the use of the term itself was tabooed as being directly evocative of the petty-bourgeois lifestyle, referring to a genre whose presence "made perfect sense in contemporary bourgeois theater," but that "could not contain events and phenomena of Soviet reality."[26] Regardless of the definitions preferred by the critics, the "comedy of positive characters" was nothing other than vaudeville.

During the war, these concerns about ideological purity were temporarily put aside, and "light comedy" returned to the stage and on screen. The effort at the front and in the interior of the country demanded distraction, pure entertainment, and light-hearted humor. Among the new creative teams put together in 1942 by the All-Union Association of Touring Concerts there was a troupe called "Old and Soviet Vaudeville." The vaudevilles *Taxi to Heaven* (*Vozdushnyi izvozchik*, 1943; dir. Gerbert Rappaport), *A Noisy Household* (*Bespokoinoe khoziaistvo*, 1946; dir. Mikhail Zharov), and *A Girl with Character* (*Devushka s kharakterom*, 1939; dir. Konstantin Iudin) broke records of popularity in the cinemas, and theaters around the country were staging vaudevilles by Valentin Kataev, Tsezar' Solodar', Vladimir Dykhovichnyi and Moris Slobodskoi, Aleksandr Galich, Konstantin Isaev, Vladlen Bakhnov, and Iakov Kostiukovskii.

Light comedy received a hard blow when the resolution of the Party Central Committee *On the Repertoire of Drama Theaters and Its Improvement* was passed on August 14, 1946; in it, nearly all the plays mentioned as unworthy of the Soviet theater were comedies. The second blow came with the decree *On the Journals "Zvezda" and "Leningrad,"* passed on the same day, where the attack against

---

[23] Alpers, a review of Boris Shkvarkin's *Vrednyi element*, p. 27.   [24] B. M. "Vodevil'," p. 8.
[25] Gutman, "K vodeviliu," p. 4.   [26] Frolov, "O putiakh," p. 46.

Zoshchenko was also perceived as targeting the comic genre. Critics were quick to add their voices to the chorus:

> The historic decree brings home most clearly the main, final conclusion concerning *true realistic comedy being based only on solid ideological premises and the significance of life phenomena depicted.* This conclusion rejects the standard formalistic devices of bourgeois "entertaining" comedy that result in spurious jocularity and a perverse depiction of the Soviet people.[27]

But only in 1952 would a *Pravda* editorial of April 7 open the audience's eyes to the problematic state of affairs in the genre:

> Why are there no satirical plays being written? Denunciatory comedies have all but disappeared. And what about vaudevilles? There are simply no comedies about everyday life. The genre of comedy has been gradually withering and falling into disregard.... Satire has come to be seen as a highly inflammable genre, almost harmful, as something to be annihilated.[28]

Suddenly critics remembered that vaudeville, too, was a democratic genre, "loved by people, close to them,"[29] one of the distinctive characteristics of which is its "realistic, true depiction of the life of the people."[30] This was especially true of the Soviet vaudeville, which was defined as "a truthful, cheerful performance with dancing and couplets, saturated with the merriment of the people's life and with humor, representing in a witty and entertaining form the rich world of the Soviet people."[31]

The Kolkhoz Vaudeville: Strategies of Contamination

Kolkhoz comedy made fun of the patriarchal order. However, its ridiculing of the patriarchal structure of the society was the best reflection of this very structure, which was a key feature of the Soviet society itself. In the Stalinist era, it was the kind of humor that was equally accessible to the characters and the audience alike. The key to that accessibility was in the origin of this comedy, which went back to the popular farce and the general paradigm of the traditional Italian commedia dell'arte.

Commedia dell'arte provides the most natural matrix for analyzing Soviet kolkhoz comedies, and not only because of its popular spirit but also because it is the one popular genre that best reflects the state of social transitioning.

---

[27] Frolov, *O sovetskoi komedii*, p. 194.   [28] Ibid., p. 228.   [29] Ibid., p. 48.
[30] Ibid., pp. 47, 252.   [31] Ibid., pp. 47–8.

Commedia dell'arte was born on the threshold between the palace and the street. Half of its characters are city dwellers (from an ingénue modestly averting her eyes to greedy old rogues), while the other half is identified as "the Zanni"—servants who moved to the city from the countryside (yesterday's village lummoxes and silly girls, sassy maidens and funny-men). Kolkhoz comedy emerged and developed in a similar situation of social transition, but because it reflected the mental profile of erstwhile peasants who found themselves not just in a new environment but in a new era, folk theater often turned into a real theater of the absurd on the Soviet stage.

On the one hand, the traditionally more popular and less sophisticated situational comedy was attacked by Soviet critics for "shallow jocularity" and "lack of ideological content." On the other hand, the comedy of characters (morals) was seen as more static, since its characters were strictly defined and required no intrigue, no plot, and no clearly outlined conflict. Elements of both varieties merged in the Soviet kolkhoz comedy, where a synthesis of the comedy of characters and the comedy of situations became a bureaucratic comedy of *nomenklatura* roles.

The Soviet kolkhoz comedy is populated with chairmen and -women of kolkhozes and the party organizers with whom they work closely; agricultural and zootechny experts; secretaries of regional party committees and warehouse managers; team leaders, tractor drivers and farm machinery operators; calf- and pig-barn attendants, pig-women and milkmaids; procurement officers and kolkhoz watchmen, and yet others. All of these professional/bureaucratic roles are inscribed into fixed behavioral models, resulting in an apparent mix of a typical kolkhoz job directory and a list of the roles in a commedia dell'arte performance. Out of this hybrid new characters emerge: kolkhoz versions of soubrettes and ingénues; the almost indispensable proud, power-hungry, witty and sarcastic grande-coquette; male romantic heroes of two kinds—either arrogant and jealous, or gentle and amiable; eccentric grandpa jesters; and, finally, the special breed of kolkhoz Zanni—Brighellas, Columbinas, and Harlequins.

The kolkhoz comedy was governed by the principle of *tipi fissi*, in which the same character types (masks) were involved in different plots and story lines, while retaining their own functional, social, and psychological characteristics. This transposition of the characters of medieval open-air theater into the context of Stalinist officialdom constituted the very core of kolkhoz comedy. The greedy old Pantalone found a new life as a kolkhoz chairman who is preoccupied only with revenues for his own collective farm. The heavy-handed reasoner turned into a party organizer or a local party committee secretary who can understand and explain everything, and who can easily switch between the role of a manager, an agricultural specialist, or a matchmaker. The hapless warrior Scaramouche who likes to brag, but is not known for his courage, is now an energetic and self-aggrandizing young team leader whose team members fall behind on the fulfilment of a plan or are negligent in their attitude to work (weeds in kolkhoz fields, high levels of harvest waste) and who in the end suffers a failure in his career as well as his private life. In almost every comedy, talkative jesters of both sexes were a must: these were old men who remembered the old times, older females who were illicit dealers or fortune-tellers; or they might be con men who specialized in procuring goods in high demand, such as spare parts for tractors and electrical milking machines, thus demonstrating "certain weaknesses" of the planned Soviet economy; sometimes there were even theatrical evildoers weaving webs of intrigues.

But we should point out one major difference between commedia dell'arte and the kolkhoz comedy. In contrast to commedia dell'arte, kolkhoz comedy was thoroughly eclectic, put together as it was from fragments of vaudeville, fixed comic roles (of which the Italian templates were a subset), topics of industrial production, and elements of farce. But though it operated with a fixed range of templates and comic roles, at the same time it adapted these templates and roles to the reality of the nomenklatura roles and functions. For example, the stingy head of a kolkhoz who makes an appearance in nearly every play of this kind, the person who fails to understand "the cultural needs of his kolkhoz members" and who tries to retain the best team leader for his collective farm, a young woman who ends up marrying a young team leader from a progressive neighboring kolkhoz—this man is a new version of Pantalone, the avaricious guardian from commedia dell'arte. Except that in the Soviet context this hero was not so much a satirical figure as a comical one, presented lovingly. There was no doubt of his being a positive character, a kind of Pantalone in reverse. Sometimes a curious contamination of the genre occurred, in which features of Pantalone (a rich miser) were mixed with those of Pulcinella, who was simultaneously a household tyrant and a henpecked cuckold husband. Obviously, there were no adulterous wives in the kolkhoz comedies, but there were plenty of independent and willful women who were more intelligent and stronger personalities than their husbands and admirers, with more distinct individual traits.

Besides the secondary characters that were almost direct replicas of those in commedia dell'arte, there were also others with similarly fixed roles, even minor ones. For example, one can easily recognize versions of Petimetre—a dandy, a society man, a vacuous and ignorant nobleman who slavishly imitated anything and everything foreign. In Pyr'ev's kolkhoz comedies these are young people obsessed with how they look, intent on following the latest city fashion, inevitably unsuccessful in romantic endeavors. Such were Kuz'ma in *The Swineherd and the Shepherd* and Vasia Tuzov in *The Kuban Cossacks*.

Sometimes such contaminations brought quite unexpected results. Thus, in Aleksandr Korneichuk's comedy *In the Steppes of Ukraine* (*V stepiakh Ukrainy*, 1940) the principal boy turned out to be none other than the secretary of the local party committee: everyone mistook him for a chauffeur because he was modestly dressed, while the bespectacled chauffeur was taken for the boss. The party secretary, like a king in a common man's clothing, used this misunderstanding to his advantage in order to learn about the true state of affairs in the kolkhoz.

Female roles underwent similar transformations. Antolii Sofronov's kolkhoz comedies (*The Cook* (*Striapukha*, 1959), *The Cook Gets Married* (*Striapukha zamuzhem*, 1961), *Pavlina* (1964), *The Cook Becomes Grandma* (*Striapukha-babushka*, 1978), and others) center on the image of a Soviet grande-coquette. This character was energetic, willful, sharp-tongued, a "boisterous female." Another almost indispensable character in these comedies is a Soviet "grande-dame." These figures usually appeared as middle-aged "honorable women"—mothers or grandmothers, keepers of the families' "Bolshevik heritage." At times these older women, who were an embodiment of the Soviet moral code, performed the functions of a chaperone, sometimes bringing lovers together, sometimes hindering their union.

Just like the commedia dell'arte, the kolkhoz comedy always featured two parties—for example, there would always be two couples in love and funny older characters (Soviet versions of Pantalone, il Dottore). It also followed the pattern of a three-part division of action: a romantic intrigue at the basis of the plot, attempts by the "old people" to prevent the young couples in love from coming together, and sharp-witted "Zanni" (the lovers' friends) thwarting the older people's determination to stand in the way of lovers' happiness. Even though some of these "old people" were not at all old and were quite good at resolving their own matrimonial problems, they were in conflict with the younger couples. The romantic plots that were developing in parallel always included a Soviet version of Servetta—the brave, sharp-witted, resourceful chambermaid. No longer a servant helping her masters find happiness in love, she could now be a junior team leader and the fiancée of a record-breaking team leader from a neighboring kolkhoz who competed with him—and almost always won the competition. The other couple inevitably included the ingénue-type character of a progressive milkmaid or swineherd—sincere and naïve, charming and deeply feeling, but also a bit mischievous and coquettish. Male characters were quite predictably schematic, too: there was a hero-protagonist and a hero-lover, a hero-dandy and a hero-neurotic, a hero with distinct individual character traits and a simple-minded hero, as well as a raisonneur-hero.

These comedies were full of chaos, meaningless commotion and fuss, noise and hubbub. Their action usually developed in the presence of a large number of people (in a village square or a kolkhoz club, during community gatherings, engagement parties, or weddings). Characters in them were busy trying to shout each other down, so that everything felt like a community masked celebration. The usual vaudevillian encounters and slapstick moments took place against the background of these public events: unintentional and intentional eavesdropping and spying on others; falling from staircases and jumping out of windows;

changing clothes and misrecognitions; mixing up names and surnames, mistaking people for animals and the other way round (like, for example, when a piglet is mistaken for a crying baby); hiding behind furniture or being locked up in a garden shed, and so on. According to the golden rules of vaudeville, characters in all these plays had to go through a tripartite conflict, a series of mistaken identities, mutual misrecognitions, and repeated situations.

Since the connection of kolkhoz comedies to vaudeville and commedia dell'arte was as obvious as it was ideologically unacceptable, it demanded to be either covered up or else publicly refuted. In the introduction to Sabid Rakhmanov's comedy *Welcome* (*Dobro pozhalovat'*, 1949) Aleksei Faiko reminded the actors that

> the characters are all people of a modern Azerbaijani village. This is why it would be wrong to interpret, for example, Mirab Dzhavad as a traditional vaudevillian confused old man. Nor should one see Zakir as a schematic operetta-type simpleton, always getting himself into a mess. The play itself does not give any reason for this interpretation, but some directors and performers can become too excited by fake theatricality, which would inevitably lead to a diminution of the social significance of the comedy. The more successful a theater is in revealing the main theme of a play, the merrier, brighter and wittier this modern, energetic and life-affirming comedy will become.[32]

"The main theme" of comedy was understood to be some "serious" deep meaning of a plot that, as a whole, was not serious at all. And the "trifling" nature of these plays was perceived as some annoying circumstance that had to be allowed for.

Kolkhoz comedy emerged after collectivization as one of the genres that were designed to normalize and domesticate the new reality of the kolkhoz. However, after the end of the Stalinist era it quickly lost its political relevance and came to be seen as something atavistic, as evidenced by numerous parodies from the mid-1950s. It is worth mentioning that all of these parodies targeted the most overused plot devices. Such, for example, was the most famous parody of Stalinist literature—the chapter "A Literary Conversation" from Aleksandr Tvardovskii's poem *Distance After Distance* (*Za dal'iu—dal'*, 1960), where the recognizable characteristics of a typical Socialist Realist plot template were associated with a masked performance:

> See—it's a novel, and all is as it should be:
> A new method of brick laying is described,
> There's a conservative second-in-command, a progressive head,

---

[32] Rakhman, *Dobro pozhalovat'*, p. 4.

>And a grandpa moving towards communism.
>Both he and she are record-breakers,
>There's an engine started for the first time,
>A party organizer, a snowstorm, a breakthrough, an "all hands ahoy,"
>A minister at the factory and everybody dancing.

What is remarkable in Tvardovskii's parody is that it is about an industrial novel that bears no connection to a vaudeville. Nonetheless, the same words can be applied to kolkhoz comedy, which emerged from a synthesis of industrial comedy and vaudeville.

Pre-war kolkhoz comedy was nothing but vaudeville in a kolkhoz setting. Such was the first kolkhoz comedy, Nikolai Pogodin's *La Gioconda* (*Dzhokonda*, 1938), which later became the basis for the playwright's own screenplay of the best-known work in the genre, *The Kuban Cossacks*. The action here took place in a kolkhoz holiday house where every detail was nothing short of amazing: the living conditions, the spa treatments, the daily routine, the menu. The guests, however, did not see this as anything extraordinary, as they were quite well-off and often talked about their high standard of living. "Haven't I earned this pleasure? It's not like I have hungry children at home," one character says, and another one agrees: "Me, I have a young daughter... I don't deny her anything." The dramatic intrigue corresponds to the general sense of well-being: the protagonist wants to run away from the holiday house, because he is, of all things, bored there ("The menu is, as always, stewed apricots in cream sauce"). Throughout the first part of the play, other characters try to convince him to go to the holiday house, and throughout its second part they try to convince him not to run away from there. Since there is no production-related conflict, and since the only discomfort the characters experience is that "even though every day is a holiday, they wouldn't let us get drunk," everything revolves around drinking, getting hold of alcohol without being noticed, and getting drunk without being exposed.

But it was a different play that became the first truly successful kolkhoz comedy: Korneichuk's *In the Steppes of Ukraine*. Written in 1940, it became immensely popular and was performed for decades in theaters around the country, from the capitals to provincial towns. Having read it, Stalin wrote the following letter to its author:

Dearest Aleksandr Evdokimovich!

I've read your *In the Steppes of Ukraine*. A brilliant thing it is – artistically whole, super-merry. My only worry is that it might be too merry and there is a danger that this riot of merriment in the comedy might distract the reader/spectator from its content. By the way, I've added a few words on page 68. It's for greater clarity.

Greetings!

J. Stalin
28.12.1940[33]

It is important to understand what Stalin saw as the play's "content," what function he attributed to the laughter that was to be generated by it, what exactly he liked about the "merriment in the comedy," and why he singled out this particular play by Korneichuk, deciding to send the author a letter of encouragement. And this was not all: a year later Korneichuk was awarded a Stalin Prize First Class.

Stalin intuitively understood why Soviet art had to include this kind of entertainment and why a comical (but not satirical!) element in depictions of Soviet reality was necessary. Similar to Aleksandrov in *Volga-Volga*, Korneichuk gave readers and viewers humor masked as satire. From Stalin's point of view, a simulation of satire was not only acceptable but also useful in peaceful times. Several years later, with the war raging, he needed satire that would justify a purging of high military leadership, and commissioned Korneichuk to write another play: *The Front* (*Front*, 1942).

Korneichuk's humor was of the lowest possible level. In her study of the play in the context of pre-war Ukrainian mass culture, Tat'iana Sverbilova showed that the extraordinary kitsch that permeates every scene of the play, next to which even Pyr'ev's films are examples of good taste, is evidence of Korneichuk having succeeded in creating a kitschy kitsch—that is, a sample of the most primitive forms of laughter.[34] Stalin was particularly sensitive to this type of humor. This was exactly the style of his jokes when he was looking to entertain the audience during his speeches.

In Korneichuk's play, a Ukraine who was just recovering from the great famine was shown as wallowing in plenitude, merrily dancing and singing. But the less recognizable the reality that was presented here, the more recognizable (more "popular") the humor was. Stalin was the first to recognize this. And since there was no need for "Soviet Gogols and Shchedrins" after the Great Terror, Korneichuk's play was declared the herald of a new genre—kolkhoz comedy. However, not everyone agreed with this judgment, and the publication of the play unleashed vivid debates. Some critics accused the playwright of creating a work that "contradicted common sense," with characters borrowed from an old Ukrainian vaudeville.[35] These articles touched upon the main nerve of the new genre: its connection with folk comedy. On the one hand, this connection was seen as something positive, a democratic core of the genre. On the other hand, it could also be regarded as something that denigrated its level. One of the critics summarized this twofold nature of the genre and of Korneichuk's play: "In his

[33] Stalin, "Zapiska," p. 209.
[34] See Sverbilova, "Podvodnaia lodka."
[35] Borshchagovskii, "Vopreki."

merry, entertaining, and very modern comedy Korneichuk borrowed from old Ukrainian vaudevilles not only the most characteristic masks, but also, and mainly, a characteristic rivalry of ambitions that constitutes the very basis of a play like this."[36]

Indeed, Korneichuk skillfully combined popular farce with a party meeting. The kolkhoz comedies that were a result of this combination were in the most literal sense "works of profound truth in their depiction of life," since they truthfully reflected the mental profile of the audiences that loved these works. Korneichuk borrowed freely from the nineteenth-century Ukrainian popular comic opera (a local version of vaudeville)[37] and played with the conventions of the "play within a play" for double effect. His two young protagonists rehearse *Romeo and Juliet*, and the play concludes with an equine sport performance with Marshal Semyon Budyonny, one of the top army commanders closest to Stalin, as one of the participants. Even in the most farcical episodes of the play, Korneichuk's comic devices are derivative, relying mostly on Gogol, whose "folk" laughter the Soviet playwright tried to imitate—and on Stalin, who both shared and appreciated this aspiration.

Having succeeded in this first combination of vaudeville and a production (kolkhoz) comedy, Korneichuk returned to the genre after the war. In his first post-war play, *Come to Zvonkovoe* (*Priezzhaite v Zvonkovoe*, 1946), a vaudevillian plot carried a new, ideologically relevant political message: a general mobilization against "the spirit of complacency." The play is interesting as an example of a vaudeville in which the central conflict is not comic but instead related to the process of (agricultural) production. The main character is the moralizing head of a local kolkhoz party committee. He organizes people, engages those with little faith, and his determination is contagious: "We will flood all of the Soviet Union with crops, and we will beat the French themselves when it comes to grapes. A PhD holder said that all of Europe lacks the richness that is to be found in Ukraine."

At the same time, the play features four vaudevillian couples in love (the party organizer and the chairman of the kolkhoz; the agricultural technologist and the architect's daughter; the stableman and the head of the village council; and the tractor driver and the doctor), all of whom enjoy a predictably happy ending. There are also exaggeratedly comical characters: an architect with his head in the clouds, a naïve artist, a local drunkard, and a coquette who has come back from the war full of "city style." Korneichuk faced a difficult task in translating the challenges of post-war reconstruction into vaudevillian character types, and he went a bit over the top in stressing the importance of pursuing "a dream." The picture he painted was unrealistic not only because of how the reconstruction of

---

[36] Borovoi, "Uvlekatel'naia komediia."   [37] Sverbilova, "Podvodnaia lodka," p. 248.

villages was depicted (with new cottages for kolkhoz members) but also because of the "life situations" shown. Even the characters themselves struggled to imagine the head of a local council married to a stableman, or a tractor driver wed to a doctor.

Combining vaudeville with the genre of the production play was a difficult balancing act for the writers of kolkhoz comedies. Often the comic elements in a play were so scarce and so rudimentary that a particular play could be classified as a comedy only based on some schematic plot devices. Otherwise, a production-related conflict was in the foreground. Thus, the plot of Dmitrii Deviatov's *In Lebiazh'e* (*V Lebiazh'em*, 1950) revolved around the problem of expanding the territory and management area of kolkhozes, with two party organizers calling for a merging of their two kolkhozes to facilitate joint construction efforts and improve the efficiency of a hydraulic station. The head of the more successful kolkhoz is "out of sync with the times" and is reluctant to join efforts with the "less successful" kolkhoz. Not one, but three romantic plots develop in parallel, wherein local kolkhoz members fall in love with either someone from the other kolkhoz or professionals from Moscow. In the end, the less politically advanced head of the kolkhoz understands he is wrong, all three couples resolve all misunderstandings, and all production-related conflicts come to a happy resolution.

Playwrights working in the genre of kolkhoz comedy developed a variety of tools to help them keep the balance between "serious content" and "comic form." First of all, production-related and matrimonial conflicts and their resolution received equal attention. Production-related conflicts and romantic ones were resolved simultaneously, and the resolution of the former led to a resolution of the latter almost automatically. In both Elizaveta Bondareva's *Towards the Dawn* (*Zare navstrechu*, 1949) and Abdulla Kakhkhar's *Silk Suzani* (*Shelkovoe siuzane*, 1950), recognizing one's mistaken beliefs with relation to the way collective labor should be organized is inseparable from finding happiness in love.

The second (related) device involves a complete correspondence between socialist competition and romantic conflict. A common motif is for the bride or the bridegroom from different kolkhozes at first being in competition with each other, and then joining their beloved in his or her own kolkhoz. Thus, the production-related conflict acquires a more intimate touch, with the competition between two kolkhozes being also a competition between lovers. Vladimir Churkin's *Against All Odds* (*Naperekor*, 1953) and Kondrat Krapiva's *Larks Singing* (*Poiut zhavoronki*, 1950) (the latter play a 1951 Stalin Prize winner) are characteristic examples: in both these works a union of young lovers brings with it a welcome merging of previously competing kolkhozes.

"Life Has Become Better, Life Has Become Merrier": A Comedy of "Serious Content"

It was Stalin, the chief playwright of the Soviet Union, who linked vaudeville with a production play when he declared on November 17, 1935 at the First All-Union Conference of Stakhanovites that "life has become better, comrades, life has become merrier. And when life is merry, work becomes more effective."[38] Historians usually notice the optimistic tone of this statement that did not bode well on the eve of the Great Terror. But the other, more direct significance of these words is no less important: people work "effectively" when they are merry. The goal of art is to make life merrier so as to make the process of labor more joyful—and thus more productive.

Thus, it is not by chance that an obligatory link came to be established between the comic and the "serious," as if the "content" of comedy existed inseparably from comic devices. Comedy had to become serious since "merry, true-to-life [sic!] vaudeville"[39] was expected "not to hide in the bushes, behind various transparent shields of 'merry playwriting' while there is an ongoing struggle to establish the ideals of a new, communist world."[40] However, later Soviet critics had to acknowledge their profound disappointment with the ability of kolkhoz comedy to be both comic and realistic. One of them complained bitterly that "there is hardly a 'kolkhoz' comedy without a rivalry between two (inevitably neighboring) kolkhozes." The only consolation he found in the present state of affairs was that "a 'happy' ending to the comic plots is true to life, reflecting the laws of the development of our reality."[41]

While traditional dramatic and comic conflicts could emerge as a result of certain social, political, economic, and psychological circumstances and problems, now they were a result of a too-rapid improvement in the standard of living. In Georgii Mdivani's comedy *New Times* (*Novye vremena*, 1952), the head of a kolkhoz realizes that the speed with which the wellbeing of his people grows is such that he can barely catch up:

> I used to know our land, I managed the harvest, knew how much milk each cow yielded. In short, I knew everything any clever man must know.... But then we decided we want to live even better, be wealthier, as it were, come closer to communism. And why not, with all the help from the party.... So we've become wealthy... proud.... And there is no limit to our desires. You understand—no limit at all! We decided we want to live the way they live in the city, in mother Moscow herself. And that's how we live now! There's a club, a library, a movie theater, schools.... And look at our young people!... They study in universities

---

[38] Stalin, I. "Rech' 17 noiabria," p. 89.   [39] Romashov, "O komedii," p. 265.
[40] Ibid., p. 274.   [41] Frolov, *O sovetskoi komedii*, p. 288.

and colleges, and on holidays they dress up as if they were in the Bolshoi Theater rather than just strolling down a kolkhoz street.

Clearly this diatribe is not at all about the kolkhoz chairman's difficulty of keeping up with the growth of the prosperity, but about the prosperity itself, which bore no similarity whatsoever with the reality of Soviet villages after the war. It is just that annihilating the difference between the city and the village was one of the main markers of communism, and Soviet art was finding it everywhere. The normalization of the institution of kolkhozes in these texts ended with a complete derealization of life. The kolkhoz inhabitants in the play talk about themselves and their high standard of living as if they were merchants from one of Nikolai Ostrovskii's plays, rather than what they really were: people with no rights to either a pension or a passport, not allowed to move to a new location, and forced to tolerate poverty and famine. In these texts, they are "well-to-do," but also "frugal," as good peasants should be. One of the characters of *New Times* states this explicitly:

> It's not a secret to anyone that I am a wealthy person. Once my son has got married, I will build another house!... My daughter will find a husband, so I'll build another one.... And she'll get the best car as her dowry! That's the kind of man I am! I'm not sorry to give away what I have...

In this world of fully resolved material problems people pursue exclusively symbolic values: they worry about "the glory of their kolkhoz," "honor awarded for hard labor," "the authority and reputation of a team leader," or "a team's honor."

In Aleksei Kozin's *In the Native Land* (*V kraiu rodnom*, 1953) the plot revolves around a kolkhoz chairman's inability to understand how the kolkhozniks can best be motivated to work. He opts to give them too much bread flour for their labor-day credits (*trudodni*) whereupon they, the beneficiaries of his generosity with kolkhoz resources, just sack him. As one socially conscious member of the community tells him, she has "more than enough bread, even left over from last year, to last another year." She is frustrated by the inability of the chairman to understand the spirit of the times: "Pfui! What's the point of talking to you? I'm in a hurry to get to communism, and you're trying to force-feed me bread." One of the reviewers was appalled by the playwright making the kolkhoz member speak of bread with disdain: "How can one give a kolkhoznik such words, how could she be made to express contempt for the bread she received, almost spitting at the granaries filled by the kolkhoz?!"[42] This is what the critic found unrealistic. The existence of "the granaries filled by the kolkhoz" was not doubted.

---

[42] Mar'iamov, "Konflikt."

A Soviet Vanity Fair: Matrimonial Problems of Socialism in the USSR

As is customary in commedia dell'arte, matrimonial issues had to be central to the plot of any such play—even in its Soviet version, where romantic sub-plots developed in parallel with production-related conflicts. What both these conflicts have in common is the topic of a dowry, which is addressed in nearly every kolkhoz comedy. Naturally, under Soviet conditions material considerations did not play any role, since the standard of living in kolkhozes was such that young people had no reason to worry about, or be interested in, these aspects of life. They needed a dowry because they did not need anything. In Aleksei Simukov's *Wedding* (*Svad'ba*, 1936), the romantic situation is typical for the genre: a young man and a young woman from different kolkhozes are to be married. The chairman of the bride's kolkhoz tries to convince the groom to move to his collective farm rather than have the young woman follow her husband. The groom is very clear on his position in the matter.

Holding a certificate with a record of his labor-day credits, he explains that it doesn't matter to him at all where he is going to live, since the material aspect of marriage is of no importance to him. The chairman has no trump card that could attract the husband-to-be, but he gives it a try:

> Come join us, and we'll give you anything you want. If your cottage is small, we'll give you a separate one with a huge garden, with cherry trees and bees. You step out of your front door with your young wife, and nightingales are singing.... Any wish you have, we'll make sure it is fulfilled.

But Petro, the groom, is unmoved:

> I can have all this. (*Takes out a piece of paper*). See, here's the certificate. This is all I need to get nightingales, and cherries, and a good suit—anything I want. This one certificate is worth 400 poods... (*Throws it up in the air*). And all this wealth would be happy to welcome a young wife, but it looks like the young wife has enough wealth of her own. It's hard to decide to leave the place where you've grown roots.

But if neither a dowry nor a ransom attracts enough interest, what can become the basis of an intrigue? This is where socialist competition comes in handy. In one of the most popular Stalin-era kolkhoz comedies, Nikolai D'iakonov's *Wedding with a Dowry* (*Svad'ba s pridanym*, 1948), the chairman of the bride's kolkhoz reacts with extreme annoyance to the suspicion expressed by the groom's party that his kolkhoz may not have enough bread flour. He insists his kolkhoz would have no problem offering a dowry for the bride, a dowry of a new kind, of the Soviet, kolkhoz kind.... We were just talking about socialist competition between our two kolkhozes.... [The bride] has committed her team to harvest 135 poods of barley per hectare.... Now she is moving to your kolkhoz; you are winning, we are losing. And here's what I suggest: even though she's leaving, her team will still guarantee the same amount, plus we'll add about five more poods, in the bride's honor.... How's that for a dowry?... Except that the groom, too, would need to respond in the Soviet way, like a real kolkhoz member.... So how about that? What will you do for our beauty, your fiancée? What will your gift to her be?

The socialist competition leads to a true romantic rivalry that makes everybody nervous, except for the local party organizer, who declares: "I like it, honestly; I really do. What matters is not the amount, but the fact that socialist competition has now become as necessary as air to us." Indeed, so necessary that when the groom says to his future wife at the engagement party, "Ol'ia, let's not talk about barley now," the Soviet audiences do not laugh: when, indeed, is one supposed to talk about barley if not at this moment?

But before they can come together in a happy union, the young couple must overcome various adversities. The protagonist's fields are overgrown with weeds. The two team leaders love each other, but neither can concede leadership to the other. At a certain point the young woman seeks comfort from the party secretary—a scene that her fiancé witnesses and that makes him suffer attacks of jealousy until the end of the play, when he learns that the party organizer in fact loves Ol'ga's sister Galia, not Ol'ga. There is no attempt to pass this misunderstanding off as a conflict. The schematic adherence to genre conventions and a total lack of interest in the characters' psychology make it obvious that there is no claim to a truthful depiction of reality. The social (socialist competition) and the private (jealousy) neutralize rather than complement each other. The young couple's falling-out is not supposed to be psychologically justified in any way. When the heroine turns to the party organizer for understanding and support, she complains not about her beloved's explosive nature, but about his professional incompetence.

The socialist competition between kolkhozes is a constant reference in these plots, which creates the necessary suspense and supports the action. The production play was linked with vaudeville on the plot level in these performances through a connection between socialist competition and matrimonial rituals. This worked without fail in all kolkhoz comedies where it was the only basis for plot action. Thus, in Simukov's *Wedding* everything revolves around an engagement party where the chairmen of two kolkhozes spend all the time of the play arguing over whether the bride will move to the groom's kolkhoz or the other way round.

The wedding preparations turn into a competition of tempting proposals, with each of the two chairmen doing their best to attract the young couple to his kolkhoz. Since material stimuli are of no interest to shock workers who have accumulated more than enough labor-day credits, the chairman of the groom's kolkhoz decides to secretly infiltrate the bride's kolkhoz as a spy. Pretending to be somebody else, he learns that the young woman dreams of attending professional training courses. The chairman in disguise concludes that

> apparently [the chairman of the competing kolkhoz] refuses to let her go, worried about her beating him on the path to worldwide fame. That's OK, Katia. Don't you worry, we'll take care of you! You will decide for yourself which kolkhoz is best. The regional party committee will support us. It is important to promote local cadres. We will have our own student... And you, Il'ia [the chairman of the competing kolkhoz], will be made to pay for being stingy!

But the rival chairman follows the same strategy of attracting the young couple to his kolkhoz, since the groom, too, is keen to study. The preparations are kept secret by both chairmen until the last minute, which creates numerous misunderstandings and confusions: the young people receive vouchers for the same professional courses and must urgently leave their villages to go to the city to study.

The competition between the two chairmen does not stop until the very last scene, when the former village drunkard, now the official "kolkhoz artist," prepares a secret gift for the young couple: a chest of drawers on which the two young people are depicted standing on a globe and holding hands. The gift is praised by those in attendance, including the two chairmen, as a new type of "icon" to "bless" the newly wed couple. The scene clearly signals not only the impossibility of resolving the question of which kolkhoz is better than the other but also the inevitability of competition. Competition is painted in exaggeratedly comic tones, as both inevitable and senseless. As an inevitable element of life, it is promoted at every opportunity as healthy socialist rivalry; as an activity devoid of all sense, it is refuted as the empty ambitions of the chairmen. Only true socialist competition has a harmonizing potential; any other form of rivalry is an embodiment of discord. The harmony of true socialist competition culminates in orgiastic scenes of collective merriment. Usually the vaudevillian plot in these final scenes becomes reduced to a simple pretext for celebration that marks the end of a conflict centered around issues of production.

"Maximum Indiscretion": Reluctant Lovers

Commedia dell'arte brought together two realms—an elevated, lyrical interpretation of the topic of love, and a buffoonish, flat take on the same topic. In kolkhoz comedy, for all the similarities between the two genres, the latter was replaced with a production-related conflict. While the plot of commedia dell'arte revolved around winning the battle for love, in kolkhoz comedy the action was propelled by the production-related conflict. This led to a lowering of the lyrical tone of the romantic intrigue. As a result, both of the couples in love move between role functions within the same character, as they are motivated solely by the need to increase the efficiency of a production process.

Since the squabbling between kolkhoz managers does not have much comic potential, there is a surplus of comic potential in the interactions between young couples, and this is where the main action usually takes place: comic passions, misunderstandings, jealousy, bouts of anger, minor conflicts, reconciliations, stormy arguments. Because it is young lovers who assume the role of comic characters, kolkhoz comedies are charged with boundless vaudevillian dynamics.

In Vladimir Vasil'ev and Petr Romanovich's comedy *The Lyrical Suburban* (*Liricheskaia podmoskovnaia*, 1953), the action revolves around a workers' team from an industrial facility who have come to a kolkhoz in the Moscow region to help with harvesting potatoes. Almost immediately it is revealed that young men from the city have either fallen in love with young women from the kolkhoz, or else they are already in love with female colleagues from their own factory. There is jealousy, there are misunderstandings, unfair accusations, and suspicions—but everything ends well, and only one of the characters, frivolous Edik, is left dancing Western-style dances with pretty Tamara without worrying about unnecessary matrimonial obligations.

The absence of kolkhoz chairmen from this play almost turned it into a pure vaudeville, which is why the authors needed a plot move to supply it with "serious content." It turns out that the parents of one of the young men are opposed to their son marrying a kolkhoz girl and leaving the factory. They travel from Moscow to the kolkhoz to set things straight, but are put to shame, as their attempts to talk reason into their son are interrupted by the fiancée rushing in, throwing herself onto her beloved to tell him that they finally "can be happy." The reason for this excessive joy is "a resolution adopted by the Central Party Committee... All support to the kolkhozes... The party calls on specialists to relocate to motor-transport stations. Now nobody can accuse you of being disloyal to your factory, of deserting!" The young man's father surrenders without a fight, acknowledging that he and his wife are "behind the times" and that he himself is "just an old conservative fool." Another colleague from the factory also makes the decision to move to the kolkhoz and marry his newly found love.

The superimposition of comic character types from commedia dell'arte upon the professional functions of characters from the kolkhoz play led to a total jumble. The new models of theatrical action that were born out of this jumble were completely alien to classical comedy. Traditional comic character types had been rooted primarily in the particular social and dramatic functions of a character that were to be associated with a certain psychological type and temperament. With the social functions changing, character types could now be defined only by psychological particularities. For example, the difference between an ingénue and a chambermaid had always been marked not just by their character traits, but also by their social status: a chambermaid is a servant, an ingénue is a mistress. Clearly in the "classless" Soviet society this last circumstance could play no role. As a result, dramatic character types lost their fixed nature.

In *Gardens in Bloom* (*Sady tsvetut*, 1939) by Vladimir Mass and Nikolai Kulichenko, a young wife overhears a conversation between her husband and his father. The older man explains that he understands the young man's frustration with having chosen the wrong woman, one about whom there is "nothing special" and who "obviously, is not a match" for his son. Confronting her husband with this, the young wife adamantly declares that they can get divorced any time, "even today"; at least she "won't feel responsible for having destroyed somebody's life." Her husband is appalled by this ridiculous statement, and accuses her of "talking like a petty-bourgeois woman." The senseless exchange culminates in a predictable falling-out, with him calling her "a silly girl" and her calling him "a fool." The young woman's dramatic function is that of a typical ingénue; her character type is that of a chamber woman. The dramatic function and the psychological type of the heroine are disjointed; as a result, her behavior becomes unpredictable, hysterical, and unconvincing.

The more of the kolkhoz there was in a comedy, the less realistic it became. And it worked the other way around, too: the more farcical the behavior of a character was, the more recognizable it became, since it could be immediately cast as a familiar commedia dell'arte type. This is especially true in the case of satirical characters, of which there was no shortage among couples in love. There always had to be those who had to part ways with each other so that, ultimately, they could find true love, which meant that the "wrong" partner in a couple by definition needed to be somehow faulty. The most common types were those that were traditionally satirized in Soviet comic genres: the idler, the coquette, "the plunderer of socialist property," and other similar characters.

In the same comedy by Mass and Kulichenko, the function of a "fake bride" is given to an intern who works for the groom's father. Vera is a good-for-nothing young woman from the city who has no interest in doing gardening work and is never short of excuses, explaining that the day before she had "neuralgia," and now "it's because of circumstances" that she cannot work, and that she has recently "developed apathy" and feels "dreadful" because she is being "ignored and disregarded," even by the people whom she had "idealized," which "disorients" her. In the end Vladimir, the young husband-to-be, rushes off to prevent his beloved, Tania, from leaving. Through a muddled conversation, the father mistakenly thinks his son has lost his heart to the lazy Vera, and he blesses their union. Shocked, Vladimir of course rejects Vera, whereupon she breaks into one of her characteristic monologues. She threatens that she is "not going to leave it like that," that Vladimir has "created some kind of chaos," and that she does not even know "how to classify" his "maximal indiscretion" and "this kind of absurdity" from a "well-behaved man."

The word "absurd" may sound like a parody when coming from someone like Vera, with her grandiloquent style of speech, but in fact what she says is not far from the truth. The behavior of these people is, indeed, absurd, because the old comic dramatic roles could not be mechanically applied to the new social roles. As a result, the characters of kolkhoz comedy seem to be put together, as it were, from different heroes of commedia dell'arte, when Columbina's head is attached to the body of Isabella and Brigella's feet are shod in Pantalone's shoes.

There is, however, one character type in kolkhoz comedy that especially stands out.

When "The Skirt Wouldn't Let the Trousers Have Their Way": The Soviet Amazons

Kolkhoz comedy was born in Stalinism and it died with it. However, even though the Soviet theater lost interest in the genre after the Stalinist era, there is one notable exception: Anatolii Sofronov's *The Cook* (1959) was a return to vaudeville in a kolkhoz environment with no "serious content" whatsoever. It was still a thoroughly Soviet comedy, but it was more "popular," adapted to a less primitive kind of propaganda. No longer living and breathing socialist competition, striving for the Red Banner or a labor award, couples in love now turned their attention almost completely to courtship and to the arrangement of their private lives. The masks of kolkhoz comedy had by now lost their ideological functions, and the characters' professional occupations were no longer central to the plot. Only pure character types were left. But once the vaudevillian axis of kolkhoz comedy was exposed, its difference from commedia dell'arte became clear: it was *women's* comedy.

This is especially striking when one considers that the original sets of masks (each including four characters) in commedia dell'arte include only male masks in both the northern (Venetian) and the southern (Neapolitan) traditions. Of course, a female presence was necessary for the action to develop, which is why there was also Isabella (inamorata) and a female servant (Columbina). In kolkhoz comedy, by contrast, women played a more important role than in any other Soviet dramatic genre. Everywhere else, be it plays on historical and revolutionary topics or on matters related to industry or agriculture, men ruled. Historical personalities, party leaders, factory directors, kolkhoz chairmen, engineers, pensioners, dreamers, and simpletons—all of them were men. There are at least three reasons that explain why the gender balance shifted in kolkhoz comedy.

First of all, kolkhoz comedy reached the peak of its popularity in the post-war period, when demographic balance was simply not a realistic idea. Even before the war, women had constituted the core workforce in kolkhozes. As Sheila Fitzpatrick writes, "according to the 1937 census, women outnumbered men by a factor of almost two-to-one in the working (*samodeiatel'noe*) population of agricultural collective farms in the Soviet Union."[43] After the war this imbalance became even more pronounced. Now they were not simply the main workforce; during the war many of them had become managers.

Second, at the center of a kolkhoz comedy is a romantic intrigue, which implied the active participation of women in the plot. Here it is appropriate to point to the link between laughter and sexuality that Freud saw as the origin of wit, claiming that

> where a joke is not an aim in itself—that is, where it is not an innocent one—there are only two purposes that it may serve, and these two can themselves be subsumed under a single heading. It is either a *hostile* joke (serving the purpose of aggressiveness, satire, or defense) or an *obscene* joke (serving the purpose of exposure). It must be repeated in advance that the technical species of the joke—whether it is a verbal or a conceptual joke—bears no relation to these two purposes.[44]

In the former case it would be satirical comedy; in the latter—vaudeville. Since kolkhoz comedy is not just a sub-genre of vaudeville, but also an attempt to construct "popular" comedy, the motifs of sexuality in it are not implicit but rather open (that is, its references fit precisely into the category of obscenities). The reference of kolkhoz comedy to folk theater, marketplace farce, and folklore make one conscious of the kind of sexual imagery that is often defined as "salacious." This kind of laughter is associated not just with the body, but specifically with its lower part, and in any national folklore, including the Russian tradition of erotic jokes,[45] this humor evokes images of copulation, excrement, crude physiology. Naturally, like any other form of Soviet culture, kolkhoz comedy was careful to avoid direct references to sexual imagery, hiding behind the façade of prudish literariness. But, as Paul Hollander noted, as eager as these people were to expurgate officially accepted texts, even "negative characters are often presented as sexually alluring," since "sexual self-denial need not go so far as to interfere with procreation."[46] And since the humor of the patriarchal society was rooted in nuptial games, the topic of procreation could not be eliminated from a comic plot that was built around romantic relationships. This, too, meant that women had to play a key role in these texts.

---

[43] Fitzpatrick, *Stalin's Peasants*, p. 218.   [44] Freud, *Jokes*, pp. 96–7.
[45] See Zazykin, *O prirode*.   [46] Hollander, "Models," p. 358.

Last, but not least, the Soviet woman was visible proof of the progressive nature of the Soviet regime and the success of the Soviet experiment, living evidence of achievements in the elimination of gender inequality. Placed at the center of dramatic action, these women almost always were more significant, more active, more intelligent, and more successful than their male counterparts. There was no shortage of backward-looking managers, con men, braggarts, and other satirical characters, but almost all of them were men; very rarely were they women.

Commedia dell'arte had just two distinct female types, with all the female roles being variations on these two. One type was that of a willful, proud, mocking, sarcastic female character, eager to subjugate her lover to her needs; the other was gentle, soft, obedient, lyrical, whose lover can twist her around his little finger. This second type was rather rare in kolkhoz comedy.

In the traditional setup of kolkhoz comedy, the main lovers couple was formed by two progressive leaders of high-performing workers. The woman was quite noisy, strident, described in different plays as "quite militant," "sharp-tongued," or a rebel who can "raise the masses" and is always ready to "criticize the management." The man mostly sought to impress and almost always lost out to the woman. In the secondary couple, everything was the other way round. He was the main groom's best friend, courageous and even reckless. She was either the bride's sister or her best friend. There were, of course, no servants, and the traditional pairing of a chambermaid and an ingénue was brought together as a result of comic entanglements and confusions, various misunderstandings that passed for a conflict, with the obligatory socialist competition thrown in. Without all these "complications," it was not quite clear how the lovers would be able to find their way to each other. They were either too embarrassed to declare their feelings for each other, or else there were work-related obstacles preventing them from getting together. Who would win the banner of honor? Who was going to outperform whom in setting a crop harvesting record? Who was certain to surpass the plan to 300%? Who was looking to be awarded the Star of the Hero of Socialist Labor? The certain victory of women (almost always energetic and strong-willed) in these labor battles was made to look all the more natural by the fact that the mockery in kolkhoz comedy was directed against pre-kolkhoz life, the old-fashioned forms of the individualistic household, the traditional family, religious prejudice, and old family structures. All of these structures and forms of behavior were defined around their attitude toward women, and, as a consequence, the women's victory meant a victory of the new forms of life over the patriarchal world order, over old customs and family relations. Because social conflicts had no place on stage, they were replaced with gender-related issues—a topic that the writer could develop safely in the Soviet context and that provided some driving energy to the dramatic action.

The figure that made the most frequent appearance in these comedies was an "energetic," "boisterous," "sharp-tongued" woman. A typical example is provided by the characters of Palashka and Paraska, which Korneichuk borrowed from nineteenth-century Ukrainian farce for his play *In the Steppes of Ukraine*; other national authors followed their respective national traditions in producing similar characters. These mature women often argued with each other, but they argued with men even more, always leaving the men to feel conquered. As to the younger female characters, they turned from Isabellas to Columbinas and now quite frequently manifested their belief in feminist ideals. For example, in Krapiva's comedy *Larks Singing*, the bride-to-be not only refuses to move to her future husband's kolkhoz but also accuses the matchmakers of male chauvinism. When the matchmaker's response to her surprised "Why is it that I am supposed to move to his kolkhoz, and not the other way around?" is simply that "that's how it has always been," her reaction is quick: "Lots of things were a certain way for a long time, and then changed. There used to be no socialism, and now we've built it.... Women used to be slaves in their household, and now I am a free Soviet woman." She has the last word in the argument when she declares that she suspects the matchmakers of "holding outdated beliefs in everything." A character in Simukov's *Wedding* explodes at the engagement party, protesting against others talking of her "being given away" ("What a stupid term: giving away") or "taken for a wife" ("How is that—you are 'taking me'? I am not for the taking! I myself decide whom I want to take, and I'd be the first to decide!"). However broad the range of roles involved in these clashes over gender issues (and it was rather broad, from the lovers to kolkhoz chairmen), the general structure was always the same: men ended up manifesting their comic weakness, while women came out of these encounters even more energetic and affirmed in their progressive views.

In these plays, the idea of "masculinity" was mostly associated with boastfulness and chest-thumping. Personified by young and older characters alike, these qualities were always the object of ridicule. Self-obsessed Salim from *Welcome* considers himself to be an irresistible bachelor, and he deserves a put-down from the young woman whom he wants to tell him "who the most impressive guy in the village" is, with "the best horse" and "the tallest house," managing "the biggest kolkhoz." Her reply is curt: "One's heart cannot be ordered to love a grey horse and a two-story house."

Some men start off determined to fight the "injustice" in gender relations, but still end up defeated. In *Come to Zvonkovoe* the male protagonist, undergoing an ideological re-education, spends most of the play suffering from not being needed and not being as good as the others. His frustration makes him consider gender inequality over and over again: his wife is head of the village council, which leaves him feeling depressed and resentful. He does not believe that "there is anything useful to be done with these females here" and is permanently angered by how things are:

Who is the head of our kolkhoz? A female. Our team leaders, junior heads—who are they? Again, females. And who are we? I am a staff sergeant. I have, if I may say so, four medals and five injuries. And now I am back home—and there are females ordering me around! It's time we changed this state of things.

Declaring "war on females" is a favorite topic of all the "Grandpa Shchukar'" characters that were to be found in every kolkhoz comedy.

Naturally, in reality there were plenty of people who were unhappy about the "domination," real or imagined, of not just women, but also of particular social or ethnic groups in certain domains. The positions of power recently gained by the party *nomenklatura*, Jews, or Russians in national republics irritated many. These topics, however, were taboo and could not be voiced publicly. The topic of gender inequality was a substitute for all these controversial subjects, and those who were complaining about how these days "the skirt wouldn't let the trousers have their way" were to be ridiculed, as they are in *Come to Zvonkovoe*.

One of the most famous playwrights to put the post-war gender conflict at the center of his works was Anatolii Sofronov, whose *The Cook* became fantastically popular: in 1960 alone there were 4,637 performances in 175 theaters.[47] Sofronov was able to capitalize on this success, and the play was followed by *The Cook Gets Married* (wherein Pavlina, the central character, becomes the manager of a village restaurant), then by *Pavlina* (where she is the head of a kolkhoz) and, finally, by *The Cook Becomes Grandma*.

Sofronov was very sensitive to the masses' demand for kolkhoz comedy, and his success was due to his ability to retain the vaudeville axis of dramatic action while removing the bulky ideological superstructure. But without this superstructure, the mind-bogglingly schematic, predictable plot of these plays became all too apparent, as did their tasteless, kitschy character, reminiscent of Pyr'ev's productions. In Stalinist kolkhoz comedy, these features of the genre had been camouflaged by political conscientiousness and the depiction of an imaginary reality; with the demise of Stalinism, things became different. Sofronov sensed intuitively that the mass audience he was trying to please hungered for the crude humor of comedies that revolved around the adventures of village bachelors, sharp-tongued female cooks, and the obscene jokes of village simpletons. Pavlina's "quick wit," just like the "fighting spirit" of other kolkhoz Amazons that populated every such comedy, created an illusion of freedom. Dubious jokes, popular dialect, emotional intensity, and unselfconsciousness all imitated a world that was free of conventions, fixed social roles, and political conscientiousness, a world where one could just as easily be insolent to one's "beau" as to the kolkhoz chairman. By doing this,

---

[47] Rybakov, "Sofronov," p. 156.

Sofronov's comedies promoted orderliness and imprinted traditional values on the popular imagination.

"Time to Merge": A Card-Carrying Pantalone

The genre of kolkhoz comedy was built around two foci: the focus on industrial (agricultural) progress and on making use of the traditional tools of the genre of comedy. These are built into the vaudevillian plot, a standard set of masks borrowed from commedia dell'arte and fixed dramatic roles. The resolution of a production-related conflict (that is, exactly the reason these were *kolkhoz* comedies) was almost exclusively the prerogative of the (usually two) chairmen. Along with the pairs of lovers competing with each other in the realization of their romantic goals and in overfulfilling the production plan, the kolkhoz chairs performed a key role in kolkhoz comedy: their presence normalized the existence of kolkhozes in a manner that was both entertaining and accessible. This was the "content" from which an excess of "merriment" could distract the audience, as Stalin warned the author of *In the Steppes of Ukraine*. It is not by chance that *In the Steppes...* was awarded the Stalin Prize First Class. It created a prototype of the new genre by focusing on two old friends and irreconcilable rivals, heads of two competing kolkhozes: Salivon Chesnok of the "Death to Capitalism" kolkhoz and Kondrat Galushka, whose kolkhoz is called "A Quiet Life." Galushka symbolizes the petty-bourgeois attitude to life, while Chesnok "toes the line."

This was a true comic farce, with characters arguing, fighting, and even at one point attempting to kill each other on stage. All of this was so obviously fake that it seemed more like a parody of Gogol. The two wives of the kolkhoz chairmen, Palashka and Paraska, are especially like talking puppet masks from a market fair—two cantankerous middle-aged women from the early nineteenth-century Ukrainian "booth comedy." With their love of imaginative swearing, they were a caricature of the caricature that both their husbands represented.

The end of Galushka's career as head of the kolkhoz comes when it becomes obvious that he does not think enough about the needs of the state, being too preoccupied with the requirements of the private household. Romaniuk from Korneichuk's other play, *Viburnum Grove* (*Kalinovaia Roshcha*, 1950), is yet another kolkhoz chairman whose career was doomed to end in much the same way. Unable to understand that a true communist can only be someone "who in their soul is no longer a peasant," Romaniuk is offended by this suggestion: "What am I—some kind of aristocrat?"

In this context a peasant is a kulak, a money-grubber. This is exactly what Romaniuk is like, thinking only about "the kolkhoz members' private households." It is not enough simply to not be "some kind of aristocrat." It is also important to manifest a communist attitude to property that is alien to a peasant.

On the other hand, the chairman's "managerial thrift" passes for his care of the kolkhoz members. This is why a kulak chairman is simultaneously an object of satire (with his mentality of a private property owner) and someone to be celebrated (as a strong manager). This latter quality became important as the helplessness of the kolkhoz economic model was increasingly exposed in the face of normal economic laws (material stimuli, just reward of labor, profit-and-loss accountancy). However, even when accepting the legitimacy of such economic laws, it was still necessary to subscribe to the rhetorical framing of kolkhoz life.

While Galushka's pre-war petty-bourgeois spirit was somewhat buffoonish, kolkhoz comedy after the war presented such figures as an increasingly serious obstacle on the way to developing "the communist foundations of life." Thus, the tight-fisted kolkhoz chairman Korolev from Deviatov's *In Lebiazh'e* manifests features associated not just with a "solid peasant type," but with a true kulak. As he agrees to help out a neighboring poorer kolkhoz with some equipment, he thinks as a capitalist would—only about his own kolkhoz's profit: "We'll get seven per cent of the harvest for our kolkhoz. After all, it's not for free that we are helping!" Unlike feeble Pantalone, Korolev is still firm on his feet, but he is just as stingy and just as determined to interfere with the young lovers' happiness. This happiness is, of course, to be realized in love, the way to which lies through socialist competition. And this is where we learn that the young people follow completely different principles from those that guide the likes of Korolev. The bride refuses to move to the more successful kolkhoz of her husband-to-be, explaining that "since my kolkhoz is going through a hard time, I will not leave it. The time when kolkhozes were crashing each other with their spikes is long gone. Now the path has been opened for all of them."

Pantalone is old. The young lovers are young. But their conflict is not a generational one, since the young people have the party on their side, as personified by the local party secretary—once again, a woman. She explains to grandpa Prokopych why the young people are right, why kolkhozes should be expanded, quoting "with pride and joy" from Stalin's "Response to Comrades from the Kolkhozes":

> Until recently the attention of kolkhoz workers has focused on the organization of large kolkhoz units, "giants," whereby these "giants" quite often grew into unwieldy paper-pushing command points with no structural connections to the villages and agricultural settlements... Now the attention of the workers should be attuned to the organizational and managerial work of kolkhozes in these villages and settlements. Once these efforts have borne fruit, the "giants" will appear naturally.

The old man wants to make sure he understands the significance of the guidelines correctly: "That means it's time to merge, right?"

What, then, is the status of the Soviet Pantalone who stands in the way of the happiness and the advancement of the ever-victorious new life? In commedia dell'arte the class target of the satire was obvious: it was directed against Venetian merchants (Pantalone) or Bolognese jurists (il Dottore). Traditional popular comedy affirmed the victory of the democratic spirit. Kolkhoz comedy, it would appear, does the same. In one of the episodes, when Korolev is annoyed after being reprimanded for calling the members of the other kolkhoz "good-for-nothings," he explains: "After all, I understand that the people are the same everywhere, that everything depends on management." The party secretary is quick to correct him: "This is true, but not quite. The managers are in our power, right? Which means that they should not be let off the hook, they should not be allowed to imagine themselves supreme leaders. Everything depends on us!"

This "us" clearly does not include Korolev. It does not include executives at all. But it does include party secretaries, with Stalin at their apex. Zanni now assist party leaders in controlling local executives, for which they are rewarded by being allowed to believe that they share the power with party secretaries. This is where the main catch of the genre is revealed. In it, managerial functions are split (as in Tvardovskii's formula) into two: "a conservative second-in-command, a progressive head." In reality this was not the case: managers were subordinate to party functionaries. In this sense, and in no other, this power was "ours." Just as the head of the party was also the head of the government, in the same way the secretary of a regional party committee was the senior manager not only of the local party secretaries but also of all the kolkhoz chairmen and chairwomen. In order to make the concept and practice of kolkhozes appear more natural, despite the fact that it was a complete catastrophe both in the 1930s and after the war, it was necessary to create a kind of lightning rod. This is where the figure of a "chairman lagging behind" came in handy: the function of this character was to be discarded. In this respect, kolkhoz comedy was on the opposite pole to that of the democratic tradition in commedia dell'arte. The latter proclaimed victory over the existing social hierarchy, while the former celebrated this very hierarchy.

The fate of the Soviet Pantalone was a lamentable one. Subjectively, these were honest Soviet people, dedicated to the idea of collective farms and serving it with their heart and soul. Their transformation into ridiculous, feeble old men, whose downfall constituted the plot of many a kolkhoz comedy, is the price they had to pay for their inability "to keep up with life": they had to bear the responsibility for the anti-democratic nature of the kolkhoz system. The audience learned that in their kolkhoz there was no cultural center, hospital, maternity ward, library, and so forth, not because such was the nature of the Soviet regime and the kolkhoz economy, but because this particular head of this particular kolkhoz was thinking according to old patterns. Except that even an acknowledgment of this "truth" had its price: in exchange the kolkhozniks had to agree that they lived in prosperity and abundance.

Kondrat Krapiva's play *Larks Singing*, awarded the Stalin Prize in 1950, follows a familiar pattern. We are introduced to two kolkhoz chairmen, one from a successful kolkhoz, the other from a less prosperous one. The key conflict is also recognizable from many other such plays: two young people fall in love and it must be decided who moves to whose kolkhoz. The chairman of the successful kolkhoz "thinks in an old-fashioned way." For him, what matters most is how much someone gets in exchange for a labor-day credit: "four kilograms plus another eight rubles—that has some weight." As a man of the capitalist yesterday rather than the communist tomorrow (or rather—today), he does not understand either the "cultural needs" of his kolkhozniks or the importance of dreams as materialized in production plans. In the Stalinist economy daydreaming was a key factor, since in reality, the average labor-day credit on a kolkhoz was worth not four kilograms of wheat plus eight rubles, but some 600–800 grams of bread flour. Thus, this particular manager proves his inadequacy as a chairman, and his own kolkhozniks refuse to follow him. The bride, a progressive team leader, would not move to his kolkhoz because "people need wings in order to fly higher and higher, and people like [the chairman] clip these wings with their views, their regulations." She "cannot be happy" in a place where there is "no space for [her] dreams," where someone who "strives towards the light is told, 'just eat the bacon'," and for whom "the agricultural production plan is just a piece of paper." The chairman refuses to see that the kolkhozniks have had all the bacon they can eat and now demand "cultural life." He does not recognize the achievements of the kolkhoz economy. In an argument with the other, more progressive, kolkhoz chairman he summarizes his vision of things thus:

> We will never come to an understanding, you and I. You will keep saying collective farms, and I will be talking about labor-day units. You will be talking about your palace of culture, but I will be prouder of a kolkhoznik who has earned a hundred poods of bread flour. I think people should first have enough food and enough clothes; only then can you start thinking about a palace of culture.

The audience was offered a typical false choice. Preoccupied with the question of whether having enough flour was better than a palace of culture or the other way around, the people were supposed to forget that they had neither one or the other. The derealization of the reality of the kolkhoz was such an important function of kolkhoz comedy that for its sake the authors had no trouble sacrificing the demands of the genre, turning comedy into an ordinary play about kolkhoz life. Krapiva's comedy ends with a regional party committee meeting where the hapless Pantalone-type character nearly loses his party card, and where he (or rather—the audience) must listen to the following summary of the deliberations on the complaints against him: "Comrade Pytlevanyi does not take good care of maintaining the communal property and the daily functioning of the kolkhoz; he misunderstands the individual needs of the kolkhozniks.... He has not yet rid himself of the mentality of a private property owner." People were supposed to forget about the value of their labor-day units, what with all the flour and bacon that they had. It was time to think about "the communal property and the daily functioning of the kolkhoz" that symbolized the germinating seeds of communism. And just as the intrigues of a feeble, wealthy old miser could not prevent the lovers from uniting, the intractability of the "conservative second-in-command" was broken by members of the local party committee as the "conflict" was resolved and the "will of the broad kolkhoz masses" was affirmed. In this way the regime purified itself, affirming its popular spirit.

One should not think, however, that comedy could undermine the authority of characters who occupied official positions in this way—they were hardly ever the objects of satire. Thus, throughout *Viburnum Grove* the (female) head of the village council argued with the kolkhoz chairman, Romaniuk, whom she saw as a manager with a limited horizon, a conservative person, and a petty-bourgeois. At the same time, as critics noted, "in Romaniuk's character, elements of satire are intertwined with a rich and warm type of humor, since at his core Romaniuk is a good person and a healthy Soviet character."[48] The same can be said of nearly all the other "negative" figures in kolkhoz comedies: they were "healthy characters" who were portrayed not so much in a satirical light but rather with warm humor, by a sympathetic playwright.

The exceptional generosity with which kolkhoz comedy forgave the sins of the arrogant and self-centered team leaders who rested on their laurels and did not see themselves as part of the collective is explained by the fact that the vaudevillian core of this non-satirical comedy outweighed the conventions of a production play. Probably the best proof of this was the role played by the "kolkhoz lazzi."

"A Grandpa Walking Towards Communism": The Kolkhoz Lazzi

We would like to open our discussion of the least serious character in Soviet comedy—a buffoonish kolkhoz grandpa—somewhat unexpectedly, with reference to the most serious character of the Soviet pantheon: Stalin himself. With respect to his mental profile and personal qualities, Stalin was the complete opposite of his predecessor, although he made sure that the image of Lenin created and popularized under his rule was a reflection of his own manner and way of talking. Lenin was quite sincere and spontaneous in the expression of his attitude toward his

---

[48] Parkhomenko, *Aleksandr Korneichuk*, p. 182.

audience and his interlocutors, and there was no distinction between his private and public humor: the latter was a continuation of the former. Not so Stalin. His laughter was completely situational, performative, and instrumental. Its purpose was to intimidate the addressee.

This, however, was the private version of Stalin. The Stalin who sought to amuse a public audience with his jokes was very different. His humor was strikingly awkward and disingenuous. It was a flat, primitive type of humor, the kind that was associated with figures like Grandpa Shchukar'. Why did Stalin—a suspicious, malicious, and vindictive person with an intense stare, the paralyzing effect of which was noted by almost all those who had personal interactions with him, a gloomy misanthrope who preferred dark humor—turn to "sneering," "buffoonery" and "flat jocularity," using the words of a fellow writer against the creator of Grandpa Shchukar'?[49] Stalin played the fool in front of his audience not because he was a buffoon, but because he believed that such was to be the public image of "comrade Stalin"—the people's leader and orator. What Stalin found most attractive about this image was its "popular spirit."

The jester is one of the perennial figures in world literature; but there is also a different, though related, comic figure, that of the village idiot. The village idiot is quite different from the mean, bitter, and witty jester in that he is an ignorant simpleton well-known to locals. The buffoons of village farce performances are a characteristically Russian phenomenon.[50] The combination of canniness and naivety, wit and stupidity turns the marketplace buffoon into a character who is both eternal and contemporary. The "kolkhoz grandpas" confirm Vsevolod Meyerhold's remark: "Popular farce comedy is eternal. Its heroes do not die. They only change their masks and assume new shapes."[51] Indeed, the ancestors of the marketplace "buffoon grandpa" were Harlequin and Pierrot, performance announcers of traditional French comedy. Most of the village buffoon's jokes are about a mean wife. His mockery of the wife's peevishness and his own mishaps, his witticisms mainly followed the pattern set by Old Russian literature. According to Dmitrii Likhachev, "some elements of the world of laughter of Old Russia survived into the nineteenth century. One of such remnants was the buffoonery of marketplace grandpa-type jesters. This buffoonery was an attempt to reproduce the seventeenth-century world of laughter, but it lacked the sharp wit of that century's democratic literature when it came to addressing socially relevant issues."[52] In other words, by the nineteenth century numerous taboos and allegories were in place to neutralize references to police stations or flogging, mass poverty, and misery.

The Socialist Realist grandpa "moving towards communism" was no longer in need of allegories. Far from wishing to ridicule the authorities, the opposite was

---

[49] *Vtoroi Vsesoiuznyi s"ezd*, p. 401.
[50] See Kelly, "Territories."
[51] Meierkhol'd, "O teatre," p. 222.
[52] Likhachev et al., *Smekh*, p. 57.

true: his buffoonery strengthened the existing power structures and Socialist Realist conventions that were simultaneously profoundly populist and thoroughly antidemocratic. By the nineteenth century this buffoonery had become a politically conscious jesting, with the "buffoonish grandpa" himself seen as a symbol of departure from democratic satire, whose antics are "laughter for the sake of laughter, buffoonery devoid of any satirical character whatsoever."[53]

In Socialist Realism this trend was consolidated. Without having an active role to play in the plot, the kolkhoz lazzi were an important instrument for normalizing and domesticating the kolkhoz as an institution. Providing a defamiliarized perspective on the innovations of kolkhoz life, they were a living embodiment of the ideology affirmed through buffoonery—the very core strategy of state laughter. But before turning into kolkhoz buffoons, Soviet jesters had gone through a lot of transformations. The comic characters of the 1920s were "marginal characters," and as such, they could freely cross clearly outlined borderlines and discuss forbidden topics that by the end of the 1920s no one else could address. They could talk about the people's attitude toward the Revolution and the communists, toward private property and Soviet power, toward the idea of labor enthusiasm without reward, the probability of a future war, voluntary and non-voluntary membership in kolkhozes, and even the "only true" ideology.[54]

Nothing of the kind could be possible in a Stalinist play, where political topics were raised only so that the characters' gratitude to the Soviet power and their love for the leader could be expressed. Everything forbidden was simply absent from these texts. For example, the question of what the people think of the Revolution and the communists could not exist in these works, the people being one with the revolution and the communists. Private property belonged to such a distant past that one could only talk about it as a joke or else when ridiculing "the bourgeois world." Unrewarded enthusiasm was no longer an issue, since everyone was enthusiastic and no one was looking for a reward, except for negative characters who could only be satirized, but who could never appear in comedy. Nor could questions concerning the war or the "only true" ideology by any means be the subject of comedy. As to a discussion of voluntary or involuntary kolkhoz membership—it would not even occur to anyone to bring it up.

The similarity between the Stalinist comedy and the early Soviet comedy was of about the same degree as the similarity between Tatlin's tower and the Palace of the Soviets: both projects were conceived as high-rise buildings, but that is about all they have in common. The genesis of the Stalinist comedy was linked to Soviet laughter becoming progressively more archaic, as a new image of the people was created, and a new type of the comic filled the space. This is how Grandpa Shchukar' appeared.

[53] Ibid., p. 59.   [54] Ibid., p. 249.

Grandpa Shchukar' is a hero of the era of collectivization, of which Sholokhov's *Virgin Soil Upturned* is a monument. The novel made an old buffoon from a village farce into one of the main literary heroes of Socialist Realism. Soviet critics tried hard to conceal the link between the old kolkhoz man moving toward communism and the old buffoon from a comic farce. They never tired of celebrating him as a literary character of universal scale: "In the breadth of the topic he covers and in his very distinct character traits Grandpa Shchukar' continues the tradition of other heroes from a variety of national literatures: Cervantes's Sancho Panza, De Coster's Till Eulenspiegel, Rolland's Colas Breugnon, Hašek's good soldier Švejk."[55] But even in the ranks of such distinguished personalities this "most beautiful humoristic creation"[56] occupied, as it were, a special place: he was "the first of the folk heroes of world literature—jesters and wise men, cunning jokers—who stepped over the border separating the old from the new and joined a society building socialism."[57] Soviet critics claimed that Grandpa Shchukar' is "an heir to the tradition of folk jesters, story-tellers, raconteurs, who never lost their belief in the people, not even in the periods of utmost difficulty for the nation, and whose sense of humor helped the people overcome all adversities."[58] Sholokhov, the critics claimed, "tried to look at the past with the eyes of a philosopher, the eyes of a historian. One of the channels of his broad, truly popular, wise, and mischievous glance was Grandpa Shchukar'."[59]

In Sholokhov's novel every single statement by Grandpa Shchukar' is supposed to elicit the reader's laughter. Taken together, his pronouncements create a faithful image of the implied reader of the text. This one character that has barely any connection with the plot of the novel became one of its most popular figures. As a book known to everybody in the vast country, since it was on the school curriculum, it should be recognized for what it was—a mirror image of Soviet "popular humor," the humor of peasants from days past (and the present day)—crude, revolving primarily around topics of peasant life and the body. These readers found a story about Grandpa Shchukar' being tricked into buying an apparently well-fed horse, which turned out to have been blown up like a balloon, incredibly funny. They also laughed at his story about concocting a dish with a frog that he was hoping to pass off as an oyster, and his account of his confrontations with a goat called Trofim that nearly resulted in "a deadly murder." Since most of the novel's readers for several decades were schoolchildren, it is not surprising that these anecdotes proved popular.

Grandpa Shchukar''s function was not only to amuse the readers but also to distract them. This is why Sholokhov places him in the foreground at the most dramatic moments of the narrative that deal with the collectivization. Such, for example, is the episode when he is attacked by a dog when fleeing from the estate

---

[55] Moldavskii, "Ot zhizni," p. 2.   [56] Ozmitel', *O satire*, p. 22.
[57] Moldavskii, *Tovarishch*, p. 286.   [58] Ibid., p. 264.   [59] Ibid., p. 285.

of a wealthy peasant whose property is about to be confiscated. Zooming in on this insignificant experience lowers the level of intensity of the main event. The same occurs at a different point in the novel when the villagers decide to slaughter their livestock to keep it from being repossessed by the kolkhoz. Shchukar' is determined to keep up with the others, and after eating too much cooked bacon over lunch, he finds himself needing "the shelter of the tall sunflowers behind the shed, despite the great cold, for days on end."

This "kolkhoz humor" found multiple reincarnations in Soviet literature. Only the appearance of the "village prose" in 1960s brought with it a change in how kolkhoz reality was seen, with the loss of its automatic association with the comic. After the publication of the second volume of *Virgin Soil Upturned* in 1959, in which Shchukar''s presence was even more pronounced, even the critics and writers closest to Sholokhov started talking about how "it might be a good idea to somewhat 'cut down' on Grandpa Shchukar''s talkativeness and his antics,"[60] because sometimes "his witty talk loses the comic seriousness that used to be its defining characteristic and falls out of sync with the main thread of the narrative."[61]

Even though Shchukar' was supposed to evoke sympathy in the readers, their only response to his appearances in the book was laughter. This was understandable, since Sholokhov's own humor, as is obvious from his public speeches, was full of cheap jokes and sneering, and had nothing to do with the true ideals of Russian populism; instead, it was ruthless and deeply antidemocratic. His Grandpa Shchukar' turned out to be a good-for-nothing chatterbox. No matter how hard the critics tried to explain that "those years of endless adversities—the things that people call 'bad luck'" were what had made Shchukar' "a lousy worker"[62] (rather than the other way round!), the reader felt no sympathy for him.

All the more remarkable is the fact that this character, whose behavior and manner signal a deeply antidemocratic position, was appropriated by Soviet aesthetics. Iurii Borev in his book *On the Tragic* (sic!) dedicated several passionate pages to Shchukar'. The logic of his interpretation of the character is summarized in the following conclusion: "Is there a misfortune that can be more devastating to a horseless peasant household than the loss of a long hoped-for horse, for which they had been saving precious pennies for months?!" And still, Sholokhov laughs at Shchukar' and his bad luck. "Why is it that the artist, who is so sensitive to the most subtle aspects of the spiritual life of his heroes, is at the same time so 'indifferent' and 'heartless' when it comes to what Shchukar' has to bear," this "little man, whose plight has always solicited sympathy from the world's artists and who would have never been the object of such loud, gleeful, and merciless ridicule? Why is it?" Borev asks. As it turns out, it is because

---

[60] Alekseev, "Khudozhnik." [61] Iakimenko, *O "Podniatoi tseline"*, pp. 128–9.
[62] Moldavskii, "Ot zhizni," p. 2.

Sholokhov's laughter at Shchukar' is the laughter celebrating departure from a past that has become obsolete.... The little man now belongs to the past in literature and life alike. You see, Shchukar''s misfortunes are no longer a historical inevitability; they have been overcome [by the October Revolution]. This being the case, there is no reason one should not be able to laugh at the personal (and no longer universal, historically predetermined), small misfortunes of this little man, misfortunes that would not result in either death or particularly heavy consequences for the little man himself, and most definitely not for the whole nation.[63]

This unexpected turn made Shchukar' into "a kind of 'the last of the Mohicans' when it comes to the depiction of little men in Russian literature." And tragedy became, however unexpectedly, comedy:

For [Gogol's] Akakii Akakievich to lose a coat was almost tragedy, but for Shchukar' to lose a horse is just comedy. This is a testimony to an increase of the historical and social value of individuals compared to the material values that surround them.... Grandpa Shchukar' is, in a way, a comic conclusion to the tragic theme of the little man. It is quite possible that the author even unconsciously parodied this image in Russian literature.[64]

As if he foresaw such a reading of his character, Sholokhov made him speak the following words: "There isn't a thing alive that hasn't offended me at some time in my life! Geese, and guys, and dogs—I've had dealings with them all, and so much else has happened to me. Somebody even left an orphan at my doorstep once." When even complaints make the reader laugh, it is clear that this is exactly the kind of reaction the author sought to elicit. With the same ease with which Soviet aesthetics turned tragedy into comedy, it turned an old marketplace jester into "the little man," and anti-democratic convictions and behavior into the popular spirit of Socialist Realism. In so doing, Soviet critics followed the logic of the genre: kolkhoz comedy was a brightly painted screen for the tragedy of collectivization.

* * *

In its derealization of life, Socialist Realism consistently fabricated images of reality to correspond to the political goals of the regime. As the destruction of the Russian village was progressing, intense efforts were being made to create a new "kolkhoz culture" that would replace peasant culture. Its audience, semi-urbanized peasants, had already lost their connection to their original village culture, but had yet to become part of the urban cultural community. The new

---

[63] Borev, *O tragicheskom*, p. 365.   [64] Ibid., p. 366.

(shared) national culture that was equally familiar, supposedly, to kolkhozniks and to engineers, to factory workers and to party officials, to army officers and to teachers, was grounded in an understanding of reality and cultural stereotypes that the residents of the workers' suburbs of yesterday brought with them. This mass culture of semi-industrialized cheap urban neighborhoods was behind the emergence of what has been called "raree show communism." This definition was first used by Grigorii Kozintsev in his diary in the early 1950s, when he was reflecting on Ivan Pyr'ev's films. He wrote that just as Dühring spoke of "barracks communism," the author of the famous kolkhoz comedies "Van'ka Pyr'ev" had created "raree show communism." But as we can see, Pyr'ev was part of a far-reaching literary and dramatic tradition, whose radical take on vaudeville and cheap comic farce as cultural sources helps us understand the central role of state laughter in the political and aesthetic project of Stalinism.

8
"A Total Racket"
Vaudeville for the New People

> There have been periods, of course, when no distinction was made between public and private, and others when such concepts didn't even exist.
>
> Roberto Calasso, K.

The Soviet project is often cited as an example of a political regime that sought to take possession of people's emotions. This, however, was a two-way street. Just as it was crucial that people accept the collective enterprise as a personal matter close to their hearts, the truly personal matters (love, friendship, desire for intimacy, for home and family) could not be discarded, either. The first decade of the new regime, characterized by a resistance to a "petty-bourgeois conspiracy against new forms of daily life," was followed by a time when "personal relations [came to be] at the heart of the Soviet project,"[1] even if only because there was always the danger that people's private lives might be just slightly too private and allow them to avoid the omnipresent eye of the state.[2]

In his lectures on the body politic and the physical body in modernity, political philosopher Eric Santner reads Shakespeare's drama *The Merchant of Venice* as a key text of the modern era; he says it reflects a new pattern of relations between the public marketplace and the private household, the alien and the familiar, the communal and the private.[3] In the Stalinist cultural empire, a similar function was performed by urban romantic comedy. In its structure and main themes, the genre followed that of traditional vaudeville. "Vaudeville" is what we will be calling it in this chapter, putting aside the question of whether particular authors or critics of the time would have found this definition acceptable. We will argue that, counter-intuitively, it is exactly where the genre would be reasonably expected to depart from the core principles of the Soviet ideology and its worldview that it reflected

---

[1] Pikel', "Ironiia," p. 5. See also: Fürst, *Stalin's Last Generation*, p. 250; Dunham, *In Stalin's Time*.
[2] Fürst, *Stalin's Last Generation*, p. 252. Cf. also Rebecca Balmas Neary: "In a state where one's first obligation was to the collective, the fear of oppositional familism-unresponsiveness or resistance to appeals on behalf of the motherland resulting from strengthening family ties—ran high. The party could claim to have had some experience in this arena: tolerance of the private sphere during NEP was believed to have resulted in a weakened sense of social responsibility and loyalty to party and state" (Balmas Neary, "Mothering Socialist Society," pp. 406–7).
[3] Santner, *The Weight*, p. 66.

State Laughter: Stalinism, Populism, and Origins of Soviet Culture. Evgeny Dobrenko and Natalia Jonsson-Skradol, Oxford University Press. © Evgeny Dobrenko and Natalia Jonsson-Skradol 2022.
DOI: 10.1093/oso/9780198840411.003.0009

and promoted those very core values from a slightly different perspective. No genre was more suitable to training people to form the "correct" kind of desires in the intimate sphere and to go about satisfying these desires and resolving whatever confusions might arise in a socially acceptable way, and no genre was more popular—with the possible exception of the romantic comedies set in the kolkhoz. The play with the unlikely title *Another Man's Child* (*Chuzhoi rebenok*, 1933) by Vasilii Shkvarkin, which a critic called "truly... the first mature Soviet comedy-vaudeville,"[4] was performed around 500 times in the year it was created. Thirty years later, in the 1960s, there were about 300 performances each year.[5] The success of another play, Aleksandr Galich and Konstantin Isaev's *Taimyr Calling* (*Vas vyzyvaet Taimyr*, 1947), was described as "staggering... in no way equal to its modest merits."[6] Vladimir Kirshon's *The Miraculous Alloy* (*Volshebnyi splav*) was awarded the second prize for the best play of the year in 1933 (the first prize was not awarded) by a committee especially created to examine "theater plays of a high artistic quality that could promote enlightenment of the masses in the spirit of socialism."[7]

Like kolkhoz comedies, the Soviet urban romantic comedies of Stalin's time were addressed to an audience familiar primarily with peasant life, either through immediate experience or from recent family history. Unlike the kolkhoz romantic comedy, vaudeville was an urban genre not only, and not so much, because it was set in a city (as we will see below) but primarily because its recurrent themes were associated with progress and development, the promise of a better life in the near future, and the demands of coming to terms with unfamiliar and less than perfect conditions in new places. Socially and professionally, its heroes were mainly young professionals, people in the process of changing social roles—or learning to combine multiple such roles, occupying new spaces, and learning to adjust to measuring the new time in new ways.

The acceptance of vaudeville as a legitimate addition to the Soviet comic genres was not unequivocal, even with enough voices admitting that "the development of Soviet comedy to a great extent depends on a recognition of a need for every comic genre—from high comedy to vaudeville,"[8] and that "in the big household stock of Soviet comedy there is, of course, a need for a Soviet vaudeville as well,"[9] with the stipulation that "a vaudeville should possess the defining features of a vaudeville, a lyrical comedy those of a lyrical comedy, and satire those of a satire."[10] One always had to remain mindful of the primacy of ideological constraints, never forgetting that "all genres are good [only] if they contribute to the communist education of

---

[4] Shtok, "Vasilii Shkvarkin," p. 76.
[5] "Shkvarkin, Vasilii Vasil'evich." *Wikipedia*. Wikipedia.org, n.p. https://bit.ly/2wqWCsm. Accessed on April 1, 2020.
[6] Pliatt, "Diskussiia," p. 4.
[7] "Ob organizatsii sredi pisatelei."
[8] Akimov, "O komedii," p. 3.
[9] Simonov, "Diskussia," p. 28.
[10] Osnos, "Geroi," p. 228.

the people,"[11] that "entertaining does not mean frivolous, and an engaging plot cannot and should not replace ideological content,"[12] and that Soviet authors of vaudeville had to "avoid self-serving intrigues [in their plots] so as to preserve the social direction and ideological depth."[13] Nobody could ever argue against the proposition that the function of "true comedy [is to exercise] an educational influence on people's social consciousness,"[14] and it was important to be completely certain that "our spectators, so demanding and strict in their evaluations, decisively rejecting platitudes and shallow intrigue in theater, would unconditionally accept a merry comedy built according to the conventions of vaudeville only if this comedy affirmed something great and serious in what is fun and humorous."[15]

As we will show, the Soviet vaudeville did in fact affirm "something great and serious." Vaudeville as a comedy of situations in a society driven by striving for a higher cause; vaudeville as a genre of unpredictable collisions in a planned society; vaudeville as a light-hearted take on romance in a society governed by the primacy of labor; vaudeville as a comedy of the private space in a society fixated on communal values; vaudeville as a compressed sequence of comic mis(-understandings, -takes) and trans(-formations, mutations) in a society obsessed with knowing exactly who was who and what was what; vaudeville as an urban comedy in a society largely composed of recent peasants—all these features of the vaudeville promoted exactly the features of the Soviet order to which they might at first seem to run counter. It was a textbook of the right kind of behavior in matters that mattered most. This might sound paradoxical, which warrants asking questions in the spirit of Adam Phillips, the psychoanalyst especially interested in paradoxes related to formations of subjectivity and upbringing: What is the problem to which vaudeville was the solution? What was it supposed to provide education in?

The most logical answer is that vaudeville trained its audience in the difficult art of being "correctly" confused.

"You are Mistaking Me for Someone Else": Confusions

As in other—classical—vaudevilles (and probably in much of classical comedy ever since the Greeks, where "recognition by one character of another, or by both characters," would be "routinely delay[ed]"), characters in the Soviet examples of the genre need to go through a series of confusions and misunderstandings before everything falls into place. Unlike in tragedy, though, where a letter arriving too late or ending up in the wrong hands, or a person mistaken for someone else can

---

[11] Uralov, "O sovetskom vodevile," p. 192.
[12] Prokof'ev, "Nedostoinoe uvlechenie," pp. 137–8. [13] Mikulášek, *Puti*, p. 192.
[14] Mindlin, "Razgovor," p. 117.   [15] Dikii, "Zabytyi zhanr," p. 87.

result in a catastrophic outcome, misunderstandings in these texts are always humorous, because we can be certain that the course of events is only temporarily disturbed, and that the pleasure of recognition, of order emerging out of chaos, will be all the greater for that. The audience, knowing the laws of the genre, should not feel guilty for laughing, and the satisfaction of a perfect closure will be shared alike by the characters and the audience. Just as in the grand Soviet narrative that encompasses the future as well as the present, a moment will arrive where there are no conflicts between good people, where the bad ones are punished, perfect harmony and happiness rule the day, and laughter—a sign of emotional health—will be heard everywhere.

But until this moment comes, there must be confusions. In the Soviet take on the traditional genre, two main types of confusion are allowed. The first one concerns the interrelationship between people and functions (the same people performing different functions, or else different people performing the same functions, or else, in more general terms, a conflation of person and function). The second type relates to a conflation of realms (usually the private and the professional realms) to which an activity, a state of affairs or a pronouncement is attributed.

Examples of both of these confusions abound. Sometimes they are (or rather appear to be, as we will show below) of a more classical, straightforward vaudevillian nature. In Valentin Kataev's wartime vaudeville, *Blue Handkerchief* (*Sinii platochek*, 1942), officers on a short leave from the front try to track down the authors of letters and the senders of parcels to soldiers. Not addressed to anyone in particular and often not signed, the parcels and letters nonetheless contained objects and words that left no doubt as to the identity of those who put them together: pretty young women. Except that, of course, this was not always the case. A blue silk handkerchief turns out to have been skillfully embroidered by a boy—who, however, prefers to think of himself as a Young Pioneer rather than as a boy: "*Valia*: I am not a boy. *Babushka*: I know, I know! You are a Young Pioneer." The following exchange takes place as the officer Fedia is considering how he will marry his beautiful Valia ("Valechka"), the sender of the parcel containing the said handkerchief: "*Fedia*: That's what I think. My Valechka has golden hands. *Vasia*: Who is this Valechka of yours? *Fedia*: The one who embroidered this handkerchief for me.... *Vasia*: And how do you know she is Valechka? *Fedia*: There's a letter. It's signed 'Valia'." The plot revolves around these comic confusions, with one officer looking for a woman who turns out to be a boy and another one convinced he has finally managed to find his fiancée–only to find out that the said lady is a grandmother and to experience the awkward moment of realizing he has been calling a wrong woman a wrong name.

In Boris Romashov's *A Noble Surname* (*Blagorodnaia familiia*, 1944) various characters are confused as to others' intentions for several reasons. The mother of two sons is upset because she believes her older son is courting the fiancée of the younger one ("Andriusha's a fine one, too! He's after his own brother's girlfriend. And she just laughs, without saying a word about it."), while in fact the suspect brother's only intention is to make the younger one understand how much he truly loves his girlfriend and induce him to return to her after their precipitous break-up. Elena, a fearless circus tamer whose fiancé had gone missing at the front the previous year, also tries to help the younger brother; to find a way to speak to him, she pretends to be in a similar occupation, but then offers his bewildered girlfriend a classic vaudevillian (and obviously inadequate) explanation: "You are mistaking me for someone else."

As befits a vaudeville and romantic comedy in general, where "the pleasure lies in being different or in passing for another" and where, ever since the classical Greek comedies, audiences particularly enjoy "faked and mistaken identities [conveying] the excitement, the advantages and perils of pretending to be someone else," the Soviet examples of the genre feature characters who frequently assume the identities of others.[16] In a society obsessed with both the implications and the consequences of people pretending to be someone they are not, as well as the importance of knowing who is who (as the characters in Sergo Amaglobeli's *A Good Life* [*Khoroshaia zhizn'*, 1934] put it in an exchange that is just short of being threateningly serious: "Doubting is safer than trusting.... A person—that has a suspicious sound"), vaudeville provided a channel for translating these anxieties and obsessions into the mode of a harmless, happy game, the final goal of which was to make everybody even happier. We may never know whether the audience laughed at the interlude in Amaglobeli's play or mostly shuddered with recognition, but the play ends with everybody singing a song rather than being arrested.

In *A Noble Surname*, we learn that the adopted teenage son of an army officer has been writing letters he pretends were dictated by a soldier who had been killed some time ago, simply in order to spare the unbearable grief to the soldier's widow. It is only through a vaudevillian scene, when the widow comes looking for the young man's father (who has, we learn, fallen in love with her) that she discovers the deceit—and immediately forgives the boy. It is one of many examples of a meeting point between the real tragedy of World War II and the conventional comedy of misrecognitions and confusions: people disappeared; other people took on their identity; still others believed and were confused. In Aleksei Simukov's *A Discharged Captain* (*Kapitan v otstavke*, 1952) the male protagonist, back home after the end of the war, is trying to find out whether the woman he likes (and in whose provincial town he found himself by pure chance) is the author of a beautiful poem that somehow reached him at the front, and is disappointed when it turns out the romantic lines had been composed for

---

[16] Roger Caillois quoted in Ehrmann et al., "*Homo Ludens*," p. 37; Welsh, "State-of-the-Art," p. 1061.

the girl by an older male worker when she came to the town as an evacuee. The true author of the poem, however, sees no reason for the young man to feel deceived, since for him it is a most natural thing for someone to pass on to someone else something that had made him or her happy: "*Sergei*: Wait a minute... So, you mean she had nothing to do with it? *Zakhar Denisych*: Who? *Sergei*: Zhenia. *Zakhar Denisych*: What do you mean? It was her, after all, who sent the poem to the front! Somebody helped her, and she wanted to cheer up somebody." Realizing, however, that the brave captain is keen on finding a partner and settling down, and hoping to make him stay in the town where they urgently need good professionals, Zakhar Denisych takes a chance by persuading a young neighbor to pass as his (only) daughter—just as his wife walks into the same room with yet another young neighbor whom she *also* introduces as their (only) daughter. Given the personnel shortages, apparently any young woman would do, as long as the young man stayed. In *A Noble Surname* again, even in the tragic situation of possibly losing his son at the front, a father finds consolation in meeting a man who looks very much like his son who has gone missing. In *A Girl with Character* a young woman who ends up on a train without a ticket through a lucky coincidence comes into possession of a ticket issued to another woman with whom—through an even luckier coincidence—she shares a name and surname. The film follows the "impostor" not only assuming the identity of the lawful ticket owner but also fulfilling her mission (convincing young women in Moscow to move to the Far East). After a successful campaign in the capital, the confusion is resolved to everyone's satisfaction, the two women depart for the Far East in the company of numerous new friends, and the main character finds love. In all of these instances we are invited to recognize the misrecognitions as an element of the (comic) genre, but underlying it is the promise that for true Soviet people a discovery of what they really are and what motivates their actions is never traumatic. The spectator laughs happily with them, rather than sneering at them.

In other instances, the confusions are, according to a critic, "beautiful scenes that subtly manifest the qualities of the new relationships gradually emerging among Soviet people."[17] This came from a reviewer of Vladimir Kirshon's *The Miraculous Alloy*, a play about a team of young researchers developing a particularly robust alloy. The cleaner Nastia, who is about to leave for a spa holiday, mistakes the new researcher Natasha for a cleaner who has been sent to replace her and instructs her on the right way to handle mops, cloths, and cleaning materials. "This is no longer that old type, a frightened person meekly doing whatever is asked of her," the critic continues, "but rather a proud keeper of the house, passing on not just equipment, but also her care for the people working at the institute and the responsibility for making sure that everything there is in

---

[17] Mikulášek, *Puti*, p. 187.

order."[18] One of the young (male) researchers, Gosha, is then mistaken by Natasha for a fireman on duty, while his colleague Dvali becomes infatuated with another cleaner, Tonia, whom he mistakes for the new colleague. Dvali engages in a series of intense and passionate monologues about the importance of a serious and responsible attitude to work to ensure that the whole team works as one unit, but Tonia misunderstands him as talking to her about the importance of cleaning the facility and making sure the men turn off the lights and leave for lunch on time. Later in the play, Dvali offers to help the pretty cleaner prepare for entrance exams at the workers' faculty. The comically awkward native speaker of Estonian uses a quiet moment to declare his love for her, while she misunderstands him—yet again—as speaking about her professional future rather than a romantic union:

DVALI: Can you feel it, Tonia?
TONIA: Very much.
DVALI: And do you want to, Tonia?
TONIA: Who wouldn't want to!
DVALI: Do you agree to this change in your life, to this new fate?
TONIA: Well, of course! Now I'm a cleaner, but I will be an engineer.
DVALI: Of course... Come, come here, I will press you in my embrace! (Takes her hand.)
TONIA: What did you say? We were talking about the workers' faculty, and suddenly it's you embracing me. Shame on you! (Runs away).
DVALI: Some kind of misunderstanding, again. I was explaining everything so clearly, and she just got it all wrong. Why is this?

A similar moment occurs in Vodop'ianov and Laptev's *Emergency Landing* (*Vynuzhdennaia posadka*, 1943), where mechanic Antonych is reflecting on the time it takes for a man to find true love, while the woman he is talking to assumes he is complaining of how long it takes to locate the cause of a technical malfunction.

These moments, of course, are supposed to be funny. But for them to be funny, at least according to the intention of the playwrights, such misunderstandings have to be possible—that is, the two realms of existence must be so close to each other that they can be easily confused: the thoughts of becoming an engineer are as natural to a young woman's mind as the thoughts of love are to a young man's; one feels almost as passionate about one's friendship with work colleagues as one does about romantic relationships with one's lover. When in *A Discharged Captain* Sergei, who at this point still sees himself as just a temporary visitor in a strange town, tries to get in touch with a woman staying in a hotel and hears in

---

[18] Ibid.

response that she "has just left... she was crying," one might think that it's because there is something romantic going on, but in fact, the young woman is devastated because the equipment she was charged with commissioning for a primary school has not been delivered, and Sergei is determined to make sure it is all sorted out. Likewise, in Vasilii Shkvarkin's *Just a Girl* (*Prostaia devushka*, 1936), young women who are becoming close friends no longer exchange intimate stories about their boyfriends as they would have a generation ago. Instead, the excited question one is eager to ask the other is "do you know how to calculate the volume of a pyramid?" This is even before she learns that her new friend is preparing to become a student at an elite Moscow university. In *A Good Life*, a young wife is having trouble making her husband jealous because he fails to understand her hint that the child she is carrying is not his. He misinterprets her "this child is not ours" as referring to the fact that he is, "of course, not ours. He is a son of the international family of the proletariat," driving his wife almost to despair and making her cry out: "No... it's not your child!"

These misunderstandings can be perceived as humorous by two mutually exclusive readings. The first one would see the very possibility of a misunderstanding in these circumstances (a young father reacting to the announcement "it's not your child!" the way the character does in the play; two young women getting excited over the volume of a pyramid; a woman crying her eyes out over a failed product delivery rather than a personal misfortune) as something one may be forgiven for at least smiling at. This, needless to say, would not have been an ideologically acceptable option at the time. The other take on the characters' reactions would have probably been more in line with the intentions of both creators and critics. By this reading, the humorous effect arises from an encounter between traditional expectations concerning appropriate pronouncements and reactions in certain situations and the new reality that overturns these expectations. For this humor to work, one must assume that both the old and the new would be equally close, equally recognizable to the audience, that one could easily switch between the alternative interpretations.

In some of the scenes, the confusion is multi-layered. Clearly the man and the woman are talking at cross purposes, but a much greater and more ideologically significant point is made by a confusion of the second order—that between one's identity at the present moment (a cleaner) and the same person's potential identity (an engineer). One is misrecognized by being taken for what one is, because in the new reality, one is as much what one can be as what one is (or appears to be) at present. In *Just a Girl* the main character, Olia, comes to Moscow to prepare for university exams and while doing so, works as a household helper in a private house. Through a misunderstanding, a rumor is spread that she is a "not household help but a writer, a journalist" collecting material on the socially reprehensible behavior of people residing in the apartment block where she works. Her employers, a middle-aged couple who are still very much of the old world, mistake her notes on algebra ("An analysis of infinitesimally small numbers") for a journalistic report on the deficiency of their own moral principles. Olia's uncle, the manager of a large factory, resolves a stream of comic confusions at the play's end by suggesting that the greatness of the new society is that one's status is never fixed; calling somebody "just a girl" is wrong not because this does not correspond to the factual truth at a given moment, but because "'just a girl,' not 'just a girl,' then again 'just a girl,' then no longer that... And what does it mean—'just a girl'? Today she is 'just a girl,' and three years later she is an engineer, a teacher, a lawyer."

Keeping up with these transformations is no easy task, since they concern both the development of individuals and profound changes in the society, as is illustrated by an episode in Valentin Kataev's play *A Million Torments* (*Million terzanii*, 1931). In it a middle-aged man who spends his days longing for the good old days to come back mixes up his daughters' future husbands. He simply cannot believe that an erudite and well-mannered young man whom he takes for a "consultant on matters of art" is a simple worker, while the other one, a rude and annoying presence, actually specializes in high art. When a woman (as in *A Good Life*) writes in a letter to a famous doctor, apparently asking him for help with an abortion-related matter, "I cannot bear it any more, I have already missed the deadline," this is not an indication of her having been unfaithful to her partner, as in the old days—and as her partner believes at first. Instead, she is a socially conscious staff member inviting the doctor to deliver a talk of general interest at the research institute, which was approved at the last "meeting of the local committee"; the "deadline" in question refers not to the term of a woman's pregnancy, but to the eager audience's expectations and the finalization of the agreement with the lecturer ("still no agreement with him, and that's me getting reprimanded for it"). Once the misunderstanding is resolved, a scene of general hilarity follows, with one of the characters "dying" laughing.

With the old signs of how to decipher behavior no longer valid and the new ones in flux, it is especially older people and those who have not fully incorporated the spirit of the new age that have trouble reading others correctly. In Tsezar' Solodar''s *In the Lilac Garden* (*V sirenevom sadu*, 1954), a morally irreproachable young man and a very principled young woman who meet in a "house of rest" (one of the Soviet spa-like vacation establishments) are mistaken for secret lovers, when in fact the only reason they seek quiet moments is to compose a letter to a newspaper alerting the authorities to the financial shenanigans of the management. In *A Discharged Captain* an older husband and wife keep getting the younger people's actions comically wrong. The wife, Efrosin'ia Mikhailovna, assumes that the brave army captain Sergei is keen to go out in the evening because "the man misses female company": "just arrived—and then runs off on a date," but in fact Sergei is eager to get to the Kolkhoz Members' Cultural Center to help out with an amateur dramatic studio performance. At the same time, when Efrosin'ia Mikhailovna hopes Sergei might settle down ("I wish he'd just stayed for good"), she thinks of him as a valuable addition to the workforce in their small provincial town. On the other hand, the husband, Zakhar Denisych, just cannot understand that a young woman might want to attract a man for a reason other than promoting an industrial project—which in this case happens to be his own project for a drying apparatus:

ZAKHAR DENISYCH: If only he stayed.... Like you were saying: tactics and strategy ... He must be made to take an interest, do you understand?
ZHENIA: But I don't like him one bit.
ZAKHAR DENISYCH: Doesn't matter.
ZHENIA: Why wouldn't it?
ZAKHAR DENISYCH: Just so. It's all the same. Who knows this business better than you?
ZHENIA: What business? What are you talking about?...
ZAKHAR DENISYCH: Well, the dryer, the dryer!
ZHENIA: So, you're talking about the dryer?
ZAKHAR DENISYCH: What else would I be talking about? That's what I've been telling you all along: you must make Sergei Ivanych take an interest in the dryer.

Like an unwitting parody of Kafka's Odradek, the industrial dryer turns up throughout the play as a ubiquitous and awkward presence. When Sergei misses the last chance to say goodbye to his love interest, who has just left for the Far East, his hopes rise for a moment when he discovers what he at first takes to be a love letter—only to realize it is a note about that very dryer, with a "supplement": an *Izvestiia* article by one Professor Salomatin entitled "Clearing the Way for New Technology," which also includes "a plan for redesigning a drying chamber based on high frequency currents." It is not that the old people are necessarily behind the times; nor are they doomed to being conservative or longing for what was but is no more. Far from it; in many of the Soviet vaudevilles, as in the examples examined here, they are only too eager to embrace the new way of life. Their role is to elicit laughter by being unable to switch between different registers quickly enough, or to recognize that two registers can actually coexist, so that any interaction at any given moment can be defined to an equal extent by the social and the private, the professional and the personal, the rational and the emotional. Confident in their knowledge and understanding, they misunderstand again and again—but only in a way that testifies to their eagerness to know and to understand.

In the general cultural and political context of the time, these plot devices in the various plays and films can be seen, to quote Hannah Arendt's essay on Kafka, "not [as a] report of a confusing event, but the model of confusion itself."[19] This comes close to a core question of Soviet reality, that of "how...identities [were] to be determined,"[20] whether of people, events or facts. While it was acceptable to be confused, there were only certain types of confusion that were acceptable, that could become the target of friendly, kind laughter. While a happy resolution was always guaranteed, conditions applied, and these conditions could not be ignored, as we will show below.

"Am I a Soviet Person?": The "Both...And..." Principle

Somewhat counterintuitively, the whole point of instructing the audience in the right perception of the new way of life and the right attitude to the situations presented was often based on a recognition that there could be no clear resolution. An obvious, unambiguous revelation is only possible where there is an unquestionably correct state of affairs that must be restored, for example, when people alter their appearance or are mistaken for the other gender, or when one's criminal or immoral nature must be exposed (as is the case with the corrupt managers of the "house of rest" in *In the Lilac Garden*, or with the superficial, flirty, and self-obsessed women in the same play and in *Just a Girl*). In most other cases, what is special about the Soviet vaudevilles is that the moment in which the true identity and function of a person or a phenomenon is established and the mistaken one is discarded does not necessarily come. Rather, what is affirmed is the inherent duality of every character in Soviet vaudevilles—and in Soviet society. The secret of the new personality is that any individual is more than one person at any moment of his or her life. One is *both* a boy and a Pioneer; a dedicated worker and a person in love, used to conversations where matters of the heart and those of work are discussed with equal passion; a cleaner and a (future) engineer or journalist; a simple worker and an intellectual (which is how one of the characters in *A Discharged Captain* introduces himself: "a foreman of an assembly workshop, a trained carpenter...a lover of literature").

Likewise, just as a person is not reducible to any one function, just as he or she can be and do many things, the performance of any function is never reduced to just one person. No moment of realization comes, for either the audience or the characters, that a particular mission or job has been carried out by the wrong person, no matter how frequently it happens that it is performed by someone not originally designated for it. The humor often stems from this very duality, from a lack of juxtaposition between the primary/authentic self and the social (secondary, inauthentic) function. Any woman can be (mis)taken for a cleaner—or for a new

---

[19] Arendt, "Franz Kafka," here p. 78.   [20] Halfin, *Stalinist Confessions*, p. 16 (Introduction).

researcher; the author of a beautiful poem can be a young romantic woman or a middle-aged, down-to-earth man; a letter to the front can be written by anyone and received by anyone; one person is just as good at conducting a recruitment campaign for the developing Far East as any other. Romantic unions are the only realm of human life where the principle of "one is as good as the other" does not seem to hold in these texts. There and only there, "the one" can be just one, and no transgressions are tolerated. One brother may not court the fiancé of another except in a make-believe sort of way and when driven by noble motivations; more than one woman may be presented to an desirable bachelor to make him stay, but he will only choose one; any woman may write loving letters to any man at the front, but there can only be one meeting between the two particular people that will seal their future.

Unlike traditional vaudevilles, neither element of the dual structure here is more "authentic," more primary than the other one. As Sheila Fitzpatrick notes, "many lives are double rather than binary"[21]—and the vaudevilles clearly show how the two sides complete rather than contradict each other. It is true that it might well be that in a particular conversation one interlocutor talks about love (or work), while the other misunderstands it as being about work (or love); it is true that there is a specific person, for example, Katia Ivanova, for whom a particular train ticket was issued in *A Girl with Character*, or who first thought of the lines of the beautiful poem in *A Discharged Captain*. But these revelations do not restore the order of things to what it should be, as would be the case in a traditional vaudeville. Rather, their function is precisely to show that "both... and..." and "one is as good as the other" are the guiding principles upon which the organization of Soviet society is based. Many other comic moments in these texts grow out of the implication that realms of human existence that used to be uncombinable are now brought together into a bigger unified whole. When Efrosin'ia Mikhailovna in *A Discharged Captain* thinks that Sergei is off on a date, when in fact he is going to an amateur dramatics club, or when she wishes he had decided to stay as an employee, and then he does decide to stay, but as the partner of a woman, it is not that he reveals himself to be a man in love—nor a newly recruited employee; he is both. When a man in *A Girl with Character* invites the girl to go with him so he can introduce her at her future place of work, the fur trading center, or when several men on the train compete for her attention, each interested in her as a diligent employee ("we'll just see whose employee she is," one of them says angrily to the other), this is not meant to be a comic sublimation of the erotic drive; the desire may well be there, on the part of the audience or the characters, but recruiting her as a worker is at least as important as winning her heart. When men in nearly all the other plays and films compete with each other

---

[21] Fitzpatrick, *Tear Off the Masks!*, p. 152, referred to in Lipovetsky, *Charms*, p. 42.

professionally when in love with the same woman, or when they declare their love in terms more appropriate for descriptions of a professional competition, in neither of these cases do the characters commit the fallacy of falling into the wrong genre at the wrong moment; rather, both affairs of the heart and work targets are equally important. Members of a team in *The Miraculous Alloy* have "a difficult situation: the team leader has fallen in love"; learning this, they try to convince the love-stricken colleague to tell the new chemist Natasha about his feelings immediately, otherwise they will fall behind their rivals in reaching research targets. In one of the opening scenes of *The Goalkeeper* (*Vratar'*, 1936; dir. Semen Timoshenko), robust women are shown rowing a heavy boat—and singing about love. When in *A Discharged Captain* a man and woman who love each other but are too embarrassed to acknowledge their mutual interest start speaking in passionate poetry about increasing the production rates at the local industrial facility, or when in *A Noble Surname* a love-stricken young train conductor feeds his beloved stories about locomotives, finally arriving with his technically advanced machine just in time to win her heart forever and to guarantee a timely delivery of crucial goods to the front, in neither case have the priorities been wrong at any one moment, deciding either for the beloved or for work, because both are equally essential. When in Viktor Gusev's *Springtime in Moscow* (*Vesna v Moskve*, 1941) an aspiring young researcher turned individualist declares her decision to leave the institute for historical research in a scene more reminiscent of a woman leaving her lover ("I beg you: do not protest, / Do not make my grief worse, / And I will somehow manage / To find interest in myself and love / In a different institute"), it is not that she is more of a disillusioned researcher than a woman who feels unloved; she is equally both of these things. When in *Emergency Landing* the kolkhoz chairman does not know where to find enough workers to fulfil the plan, and the managers announce a (fake) wedding so that people come and help them work the fields, and the fake wedding then turns into a real engagement celebration, the real event is no more authentic than tricking the people into fulfilling the plan. Nadia in *In the Lilac Garden* is not just a doctor diagnosing the state of a man who (his fiancée is concerned) might die from sorrow thinking she does not love him ("he won't die"), nor just a woman giving advice to another woman ("he won't fall out of love [with you]"), but is both. The jet pilot Lena in *Fame* (*Slava*, 1935) is both a pilot and an attractive young woman in love whose very appearance in the sick room of her injured beloved might make him agitated (his surgeon cautions "It's dangerous to let women visit a patient"); she is simultaneously a dedicated professional and a much treasured daughter (as her father, worried about her being sent on dangerous missions, explains to her boss: "Look, she is a fiancée.... But Lena for you is mostly a jet pilot, / While for me she is mostly a daughter"). In the same way, this short exchange between two members of a kolkhoz in Aleksandr Korneichuk's *Come to Zvonkovoe* is about both work and a man's recognition of his feelings for a woman: "*Marina*: I came to ask you: who did you survey the hills over the river last night with? Are you intending to do something without me again? *Prokop*: When did I ever do anything without you?"

Here it is helpful to come back to Mladen Dolar's notes on the nature of the comic and on doubling in the production of a comic effect:

> ... one is not funny, two is funny, but provided that two is the replication of one, its imitation, its likeness, its mimetic double, its similar twin.... What happens between one and two to produce the comical effect? Not between one and two, but between two ones that don't quite add up to two; they are just clones of each other, same and different at the same time. Where there should be difference there is replication, a crack in the midst of the same.[22]

Pascal (to whom Dolar refers in this passage) speaks of faces; Dolar speaks of individuals; my claim is that the same can be extended to include expressions of duality as such, in different semantic categories and phenomena. In the Soviet vaudevilles as in Soviet society, functions, people, and actions are duplicated and multiplied, with the comic effect coming not from the fact that the false one takes over, and then the true one wins, but from the fact that both happen at once, but at any given moment one part takes over, without the other one fully disappearing: misunderstandings, confusions, and simply comical moments occur not because a truth is disguised, but because it is "two ones," such that one speaks both as a record worker, a kolkhoz chairman, a jet pilot, a journalist, an engineer, a cleaner—and a man or woman in love, a future engineer, a future journalist, an aspiring scientist. When in *Fame* a young woman's mother scolds her daughter's admirer, her exclamation "Pestering a girl—and you a postman!" and plea "Lord, please keep postmen / From stealing daughters in broad daylight!" do sound comical, but they also point to that very blurring of boundaries between function and private life that was celebrated on and off stage. There should be nothing surprising in the fact that a "foreman of an assembly workshop, a trained carpenter [and] a lover of literature" is actually a self-taught inventor of a new commercial dryer, though he acknowledges that he has "no formal connection to drying matters" (*A Discharged Captain*). Nor should it strike anybody as extraordinary that in *The Goalkeeper* two groups of industrial designers are also top-notch soccer players, introduced at one point to their fans at a stadium as "design engineers and soccer players from two factories." It is enough for a famous surgeon to change his clothes to be transformed from a professor of medicine into a quasi-magician who can bring awkward lovers together after an unfortunate misunderstanding, as it happens in *Fame*. After some feeble remonstrations in

---

[22] Dolar, "The Comic Mimesis," p. 582.

response to his young patient's request to bring back his beloved ("Well, that's really too much, young man!/Soon you'll send me to fetch water, / You'll make me sweep the floor. But I am a surgeon, and here / There are no reasons for a surgical intervention. / Here you could maybe do with a sorcerer: / Somebody to sprinkle holy water on your chest"), he reluctantly agrees ("Well, stop moaning. I'll try to bring her back. [*Starting to change.*] I'll bring the fiancée back into this house. / I'll open the gates of paradise, as it were"). It appears to be completely natural that in *Just a Girl* a militiaman and a newspaper photographer are more than willing to spend as much time as might be needed to help a young sailor locate in Moscow a young woman he met on the train and fell in love with. In fact, representatives of the forces of order seem to be particularly amenable to reaching out to people above and beyond the call of duty. In *Fame*, two young lovers have a moment of embarrassed panic when they think they might be told off by a militiaman for kissing in a public park, but all the kind officer does is politely apologize for disturbing them before disappearing discretely. In *Springtime in Moscow*, the militiaman who finds the distressed Nadia on a bridge appeals to her friends for help, hoping they can alert her to the beauty of the world around her and chase away whatever unwelcome thoughts may be making her sad: "Tell her, you know, something / About the spring, the river..." Worried that Nadia might be too emotional to be outside at night on her own, he contributes his own opinion: "I am personally of the opinion / That sadness is best dealt with / In a sheltered space... / Worries should be overcome indoors." Nadia is lucky to live among people, friends and strangers alike, who are never indifferent to each other, so that when the man who loves her writes to a famous captain, "a hero and a [people's] deputy," in the hope that "An external intervention / Such a radical one, will help her," the hero captain does not need to be asked twice. This makes the immoral characters appear all the more ridiculous for being unable to grasp this notion of unified existence, as in *In the Lilac Garden*, when the crafty manager of a "house of rest" is shocked that "even though I serve in the area of leisure, I am criticized in the area of work!"

"Omnicompetence" is the word Hannah Arendt uses in connection with Kafka's texts, defining it as "the motor of the machinery in which Kafka's heroes get caught."[23] For the characters in Soviet vaudevilles, omnicompetence is a defining characteristic. People assume the professional (and personal) responsibilities of other people with the ease of actors getting dressed for a masked ball. In *Taimyr Calling*, the whole plot is structured around an endless chain of assumed professional identities, when a hotel guest ends up sharing his professional responsibilities with the residents of the rooms next to his, and in return, he is asked to step in for each of them, assuming a different role each time, from testing

---

[23] Arendt, "Franz Kafka," p. 76.

the vocal abilities of aspiring opera singers to resolving a romantic complication with a woman. In an episode from *Just a Girl* the motif of people being both themselves and more them themselves, both private individuals and professionals, both amateurs and omnicompetent experts, reaches its comic pinnacle when a neighbor comes looking for help from Ol'ga, whom everybody believes to be a journalist:

WOMAN: Ol'ga Vasil'evna, admittedly, I'm from the house next door, but please do attend to what I have to ask... My husband drinks...
OL'GA: But what can I do?
WOMAN: Advise...
PAVEL IVANOVICH: Ma'am, we do not cure alcoholics here.
WOMAN: So where should I inquire?
PAVEL IVANOVICH: Go ask them in the theaters, the Writers' Union, they should know there.

Though an obvious ironic reference to the self-image of the writing and acting professions of the time, this last example is nonetheless indicative of the special role of "omnicompetence" in the Soviet society. It may have provided fertile ground for comedy, but the reason it could be counted upon to elicit laughter was because it was a recognizable feature of the new life—and by no means something to be ashamed of.

This is what distinguishes the people in these plays and films from the modern subject in the era of capitalism who suffers from what Eric Santner calls "the crisis of investiture," when the symbolic function cannot be properly "metabolized" (in Santner's vocabulary) by one's organic being.[24] There is no such crisis for the ideal members of the Soviet society that populate the vaudevilles of the time. For them, being in "office" or bearing an "investiture" encompasses their very being. If anything, they are so eager to encompass everything in themselves and to share themselves with everybody that it leads to inevitable comic consequences.

Of particular interest in this sense is a scene that takes place in the beginning of *A Discharged Captain*. The young male protagonist, Sergei, finds himself by pure chance in the small town and in the office of a local manager, forced to answer phone calls concerning the supply of materials to socially important construction sites. At first, he attempts to claim ignorance of the matters at hand, explaining that he is "just a stranger." However, after the person at the other end of the phone responds by reminding him that "in this matter there can be no strangers" and asking Sergei whether he is a "Soviet person," he realizes that the only appropriate

---

[24] Cf. Kevis Goodman's introduction to Santner, *The Weight*, p. 3, with reference to Santner's discussion in his earlier monograph on the mental illness of Daniel Paul Schreber (*My Own Private Germany*).

reaction is to take the matter in his own hands: to start responding, clarifying, passing on messages, getting personally involved, giving instructions, inquiring, making calls, exercising pressure. In the next scene, when mistaken by a resident of the town for someone else, he tries to explain that he is "just a regular Soviet person"—to which the answer is: "What do you mean, a regular person? There are no regular people anymore."

Such is the world of the Soviet vaudeville—and of Soviet reality, where an individual action is only valuable in so far as it is replicable by others, and only those functions that are not dependent on a specific individual are recognized as valid. The multiplication of the same, which is a common comic technique, works on the same premise. The fact that "thirty per cent of the young women are called 'Valia'" in the provincial town where one of the heroes of *A Blue Handkerchief* spends a few days off from the front extends the young soldier's romantic quest by a few hours, and clearly communicates to the audience that he will find the right one not despite but *because* all these women are so similar: everybody is helpful, friendly, nice. In *A Girl with Character* the female protagonist, having finally made it to the citizens' advice bureau in Moscow, delivers her pre-prepared complaint about the wrongdoings of a corrupt kolkhoz manager to the wrong person, a visitor like herself. The awkwardness of the moment is quickly forgotten as it is obvious that the only reason she could mistake a fellow complainer for an official is because everybody is equally approachable and eager to assist. In *Springtime in Moscow*, the aspiring historian who succumbed to the sin of individualism emerges from her despair after she answers a phone call from someone who had misdialed and tells this stranger about her problems. In the same way, the fact that there are so many women drivers in *A Discharged Captain* makes it easier, rather than more difficult, for the initially annoyed but then love-smitten male protagonist to find the right one: people have no secrets from each other, everybody knows everybody else, so it is no problem when the young man, "alone in an unfamiliar town, with no address, no luggage... decided to knock on every door, street after street, asking for a woman driver." In *In the Lilac Garden* the janitor on (apparently permanent) duty, Agafonova, sees nothing wrong with leaving a visitor alone with the office phone, instructing him before she leaves: "Make sure you write down those telephone messages carefully!" In some instances, being mistaken for someone else enables people to become better versions of themselves, apparently because everyone has the potential to be equally good. Such is the case in Mariam Baratashvili's *Dragonfly* (*Strekoza*, 1953),[25] where a good-natured but lazy young woman from a Georgian village comes to Tbilisi to stay with a professor uncle, whose family mistakes her for a celebrated Hero of

---

[25] *Strekoza*. Dir. Semen Dolidze and Levan Khotivari. Based on Mariam Baratashvili's play *Marine* (1953). Gruzia-Film, 1954.

Socialist Labor. The comic confusion leads to a happy end: "Marine returns to her native kolkhoz a new person, no longer in the shackles of the mindlessness, carelessness, light-heartedness, and thoughtlessness that were such an obstacle to the development of her character and to her work."[26] In *Just a Girl*, when an orphan baby is left at someone's door, the man who has to pretend he likes caring for the baby ends up becoming genuinely attached to her and adopts her.

Even when women are mistaken for men, as is the case with aircraft technician Shura in *Emergency Landing* (later in the same play we learn that another young woman, Niushka, is a blacksmith—the plays and films are full of women doing traditionally male jobs), or in *A Discharged Captain* (where Zhenia, a lorry driver, is at first mistaken by her future fiancé for a man), it is more than just a simple vaudevillian classic genre confusion, but a recognition of a world where everybody is equal, women can easily do men's work, and children dream of becoming heroic adults (as they do in *Fame*, where the boy and the girl at the site of the disaster speak like miniature versions of the two adult heroes). A family embraces strangers not because they know no better but because everybody is equally loveable (as in *A Discharged Captain*, where the former bureaucrat Klavdii, who had spent all his life with his parents and is now about to set off to conquer virgin lands with his young wife, is happy to introduce a newcomer and his bride to his mother thus: "Here you have, mother, a second son and a second daughter to replace us").

These are examples of traditionally comic devices whose function in the Soviet context is almost the opposite of what it would have been in the past. If there is anything comic about them in the new reality, it is only because they are recognizable as what had been deviations from the norm—and as evidence of the fact that this norm has now changed. Everybody is equal or, in a more sinister version of the same principle, "nobody is irreplaceable." Vaudeville bypasses the more realistic and less cheerful scenario of being misidentified in the Soviet society of the time and the paramount preoccupation with knowing who is who. The inherently vaudevillian pattern reflects perfectly the imaginary foundations of the Soviet world order. What Viktor Orlov writes angrily about a failed vaudeville in 1960 where "conflicts are replaced with misunderstandings, and clownish *quid pro quo* takes the place of real-life confrontations"[27] is, in fact, a model of the ideal Soviet society.

In many instances even slapstick performs the same function of emphasizing the equality between different people and different functions. There are, of course, still plenty of instances of classical slapstick performance that do not go beyond physical comedy, such instances being a homage to the traditional vaudeville as a comedy of situations, in contradistinction to satire, which is a comedy of

---

[26] Osnos, "Geroi," p. 227.   [27] Orlov, "Vodevil'," p. 70.

characters. Soviet positive heroes were legitimate objects of a kind, hearty laughter, devoid of any *Schadenfreude* that would be appropriate when laughing at an enemy. But even the most unsophisticated physical comedy in most of these works is only admissible because it is laughter shared by equals, whether as subjects or as objects. In *A Girl with Character* the impostor Katia Ivanova unsuccessfully tries to escape from the young women eager to meet the other, real Katia Ivanova at the train station in Moscow—but subsequent events reveal that there was no point in hiding anyway, because the "impostor" is just as passionate and dedicated about doing the job as the "original." In *The Miraculous Alloy* one of the longest scenes takes place in the research lab with the team leader, Grisha, who has taken off his torn trousers and is hiding this fact behind a desk. He is thus unable to come forward either to shake the hand of the manager, who is there to congratulate him on impressive research results (which makes him appear "horribly shy"), or to embrace his girlfriend (whose endearing "Well come on, come here!" he rejects with a dry "No, I can't!"). In *Late for a Date* (*Devushka speshit na svidanie*, 1936; dir. Mikhail Verner and Sergei Sidelev) the hapless vacationer Gurov takes on a variety of roles: as a patient due for a shower treatment, stepping in for those eager to spend their time doing more exciting things at the spa; as a self-proclaimed shoemaker; and even as an acrobat in a circus. Everything ends well, of course; slipping in and out of these various "selves" was only a slightly more extreme realization of what was the order of the day anyway.

In cultural historical research, these quick transitions from one role to another in the Soviet context of the time have been associated with trickster-like figures. Scholars argue that "the very process of 'reforging' social identities, which laid the foundation for the 'Soviet project,' required trickster-like qualities from ordinary people," that tricksters reflected something fundamental about the essence of the Soviet society, and that "in the political environment of the early Stalin years, which was characterized by theatricality, hyperbole, and reckless arrogance and lacked all caution and restraint, [a] daring con artist with [an] inflated identity was in the most fundamental sense a Soviet man."[28] Analysis of the vaudevilles, however, seems to suggest that these ideal subjects, the residents of the Soviet fairyland, were not so much *changing* identities as *combining* them, being many things at once, containing multitudes, never fully coinciding with themselves because they were more than themselves at any given moment, but also less than themselves. A lover who cannot lose him- or herself in a romantic moment because (s)he is thinking about labor records is probably an imperfect partner; a militiaman who leaves his post to console a distressed woman or to help two excitable young people reunite may not exactly be doing his duty because he is

---

[28] Lipovetsky, *Charms*, p. 42, with reference to Fitzpatrick's *Tear Off the Masks!*, p. 152 (this is also the main thesis of Lipovetsky's own book); Alexopoulos, "Portrait," p. 776.

going above and beyond it; a cleaner who is also (potentially) an engineer or a journalist may not be completely, fully inhibiting her cleaner "identity." In *In the Lilac Garden* a happy resolution of multiple confusions is sealed with a kiss between a loving husband and wife, but first they must clarify whether they are allowed to kiss within the confines of their social roles at the moment: "*Shorina*: Kiss me, Serezha. *Rybtsev*: How can you! I am here on business. *Shorina*: But I am here on holiday. And I am allowed to kiss you." There is a certain "provisionality" to the existence of all these individuals in any one capacity; their every function is bracketed by another one. The audience is never allowed to forget that the characters in the plays are almost impostors, regardless of how sincere they are in what they are and what they do, and this is simply because they are (or could be) at the very same moment something (or someone) completely different. Their every state of being is predicated by what else, or where else, they could be, and it is in the space between the different functions, states, identities that the humor is generated.

This space—literally—is that of vaudeville.

"You Share the Flat Anyway": Space, Public and Private

Vaudeville creates a zone that is both governed by special laws that have very little to do with mundane everyday existence, and immediately recognizable from one's own daily experience. It is a space of intense social activity and at the same time of absolute privacy and intimacy. As Jennifer Terni writes, vaudeville has been traditionally "drawn to settings that privileged impromptu social interactions, like those fostered in restaurants, waiting rooms, drawing rooms, and offices."[29] The challenge for the Soviet master-creators of vaudeville was to show how the Soviet concept of private and borderline public spaces, and the relationships that develop in them, transgress the limits of traditional ones.

Those traditional spaces were, according to a Soviet historian of classical Russian vaudeville, quite predictable:

> a hotel room, a bakery, a badly furnished living room, a classroom, a writer's study, offstage in a provincial theater. Knightly armor was replaced with bonnets and scarves, military uniforms and merchants' three-piece suits; "gothic" parlors gave way to a glazed tile stoves, a chest of drawers, a piano, an embroidery frame, bookshelves, curtains, baskets—all the multifaceted and varied everyday reality of a real, regular life.[30]

---

[29] Terni, "A Genre," p. 237.   [30] Dikii, "Zabytyi zhanr," p. 90.

The author of these words meant to argue, predictably, that the Soviet vaudeville had left all those objects and settings behind, but the truth is that their more modern incarnations were thoroughly Soviet in their essence. Everyday objects of easily identifiable labor and shared leisure, settings that mark an existence not so private as to be completely hidden from the eyes of strangers, but not so public as to be fully exposed to the outside world, either: these were the markers of the new world and the new vaudeville.

In these spaces the boundaries between the inside and the outside, the private and the public, the domestic and the communal are as blurred as they are in the constructions of personal identity. While Ol'ga Matich's claim that the early Soviet "utopian organization of daily life, meant to overturn the concepts of the private and the communal... in practice led to a total erasure of the boundaries between the social and the private life of an individual"[31] may not be completely true, this erasure of boundaries was definitely a proclaimed ideal, an extreme and condensed version of which was presented in the vaudevilles we examine here. The special zones of vaudeville, just like the new social reality, are a bit outside the social conventions that would be familiar to the previous generations and established by cultural traditions. In these zones the comic effect arises from a combination of, on the one hand, a supposedly non-formalized setting, and, on the other, exceptional, exaggerated situations, where everything is made just the slightest bit more extreme. As it would be, for example, in that quintessentially Soviet space, communal apartments.

"If there had been such a thing as a Soviet cultural unconscious, it would have been structured like a communal apartment—with flimsy partitions between public and private,"[32] writes Svetlana Boym. There is no shortage of literature about and historical testimonies to the crowded living conditions in the Soviet Union at the time these vaudevilles were created, and the impact it had on the daily life of the people.[33] There were "tens of thousands of work communes sprouted across the vastness of the Russian land—in the form of phalansteries, apartments carved into open space, tents and barracks planted beside great steel works and power stations,"[34] where "the Stalinist regime persistently cultivated just such an army spirit, while at the same time never allowing the society to fully close in upon itself and become one gigantic barrack."[35]

Army barracks, or anything remotely similar to them, might seem an unlikely location for a vaudeville, but in fact they were perfect. Brushing shoulders with strangers with whom one was forced to share the most intimate aspects of one's

---

[31] Matich, "Sueta," p. 80.   [32] Boym, *Common Places*, p. 123.
[33] Zubkova, *Poslevoennoe sovetskoe obshchestvo*, p. 29. Fitzpatrick, *Everyday Stalinism*, pp. 140–1; see also Attwood, *Gender*.
[34] Stites, *Revolutionary Dreams*, p. 219.
[35] Zubkova, *Poslevoennoe sovetskoe obshchestvo*, p. 29. Fitzpatrick, *Everyday Stalinism*, pp. 140–1; see also Attwood, *Gender*.

life provided fertile ground for comic scenarios. The postman in *Fame* who is courting a beautiful student actress would not have to think of various tricks to find a private moment with his beloved, were she not sharing a room with her mother. None of the comic mix-ups in *Taimyr Calling* would have happened, were it not for the shortage of rooms in a typical Soviet hotel, with strangers sharing rooms. In *A Discharged Captain* there would have been no chance for two happy couples to come together at the end of the play, had not the two young women, Zhenia and Liusia, shared a room; the same holds for *At 6 P.M. After the War* (*V 6 chasov vechera posle voiny*, 1944; dir. Ivan Pyr'ev). On screen (and, if the directorial notes are anything to go by, on stage) these rooms did not fall short of the comfort provided by the traditional bourgeois interiors occupied by the heroes of the vaudevilles of previous generations and in more advanced countries. The rooms we are shown in *At 6 P.M. After the War* are neat and cozy; in *A Noble Surname* we are introduced to a family room where "everything bears the stamp of tidiness, coziness, and order"; in *A Discharged Captain*, we are invited to a "spacious, brightly lit room.... To our right, to our left and in the back wall there are doors. In the center of the room there is a table covered with a blindingly white tablecloth." These may be shared living spaces, but they promise security and the assurance that even if something were ever to go wrong there, it would never be so bad as to get out of hand.

And even if shared, these rooms and apartments offer all the comforts one can wish for, with the additional benefit of a completely relaxed behavior being the norm. As a character in *Fame* puts it, "Nowadays a Soviet play / Always ends with a mighty meal." They do indeed. In the final scene of *Springtime in Moscow* a secondary male character, exhausted by his long struggle to help the female protagonist maintain her moral integrity and by the search for the object of his own romantic interest, walks into a room where the reconciled lovers are kissing and declares: "Of all human sensations / I can feel only appetite. / My nerves have become wires, / The world is but a dead sketch to me. / Tell me, what do you use to open cans? / Stop kissing and give me a knife. (*Eats canned food*)." In *A Good Life* one of the last statements made is: "Here is a hot pie!" Nobody expresses any dissatisfaction with the crowded conditions in the hotel nor the exhausting series of misidentifications in *Taimyr Calling*. Instead, in the morning following a long night a newly formed couple welcomes the newly found friends, and everybody celebrates together.

In *At 6 P.M. After the War* the officers on leave who have come looking for a beautiful nursery school teacher are invited to what is supposedly a regular event in the block of flats: an evening of dancing and merriment, with delicious food served by anonymous older women, always ready to serve more, always helpful, but never intrusive.

Of course, offstage and off-screen, living in a block of shared flats was a different experience. A historian made an approximate calculation of what it would have been like for the residents of the house in *At 6 P.M. After the War*: with approximately 140 flats, there would be some 530 rooms, which, as we learn from a merry song sung by the house management around minute 17 of the film, roughly translated here into 2,000 "inhabitant souls." The room in *A Noble Surname* that exhibits "a stamp of tidiness, coziness, and order" also features a piece of furniture that, without intending it to be a too heavy-handed pun, one can characterize as revealing: a room screen, behind which there is a bed. Just as Svetlana Boym says, under Soviet conditions "the minimum of privacy is not even a room but a corner in a room, a hidden space behind the partition."[36] However neat and tidy the dining car on the train in *A Girl with Character* may be, however well-dressed its occupants, the two protagonists, travelers of opposite genders who have just met on the train, are expected to share a compartment. The many doors from the sunny room in *A Discharged Captain* lead to what is either multiple rooms in a big communal apartment, or else corridors leading to other flats with other rooms, with walls so thin that one need only call someone's name for that person to appear.

In de Sade's *Philosophy in the Boudoir* the libertine Domancé reads a manifesto calling for the creation of a state "in which every citizen has a right to summon any other person to freely use his or her body." Giorgio Agamben concludes his analysis of the passage by saying: "Intimacy becomes here what is at stake in politics; the *boudoir* is totally substituted for the *cité*."[37] The life philosophy of a scandalous French anti-moralist and that of a socialist state coincide at a point where the most intimate spaces are politicized simply through the enforced sharing of private spaces and an equal distribution of the right to full access to each other's intimate sphere. In de Sade the vision of an oppressive total equality remained a fantasy. In the Soviet Union it progressed beyond the stage of an imaginary construct, though it did not immediately result in the coming of a golden age. "Persons who live in adjoining rooms and must share the same hallway, kitchen, and clothes washing facilities are not always the best of neighbors,"[38] two Sovietologists in the early 1950s drily concluded.

Obviously, for the authors and intended audience of the Soviet vaudevilles this was an enemy voice speaking. Only those who remained strangers to the new world order found the new living conditions to be incongruous; only they behaved incongruously. For example, a ridiculous petty-bourgeois character from *A Million Torments* "keeps guard at the bathroom, making sure the residents turn off the light" and defines this activity as "social activism"; or the licentious storehouse manager in *Just a Girl*, whose idea of home does not go beyond "a young maiden's room, soft lighting ... Some vodka on the table, sliced ham." In days long gone, or

---

[36] Boym, *Common Places*, p. 150.   [37] Agamben, *The Use*, p. 92.
[38] Geiger and Inkeles, "The Family," p. 399.

in other countries, the inhabitants of old-fashioned apartments with their heavy locks and thick walls suffered from "the difficulty of knowing what goes on behind the walls and doors across the street, and by extension what goes on in someone else's mind."[39] No such dangers in the happier Soviet world, the citizens of which knew to appreciate the shared intimacy of communal existence. Thin those walls may have been, but they nourished proximity between the father and the daughter in *Fame*, with the father realizing just how worried, and how much in love his heroic pilot daughter actually is:

> MEDVEDEV: She is calm? I wish!
> We have thin walls; it's a new house.
> I can hear: she gets up, then lies down, and again,
> She picks up a book, or a jug of water,
> And sometimes she cries out as she hears the clock chime.
> Then suddenly—in a thunderstorm!—she opens the window.
> On the outside, she's strict—a commander,
> But inside she is just a girl, a little child.

Having one's voice heard by next-door neighbors, no matter how quietly one speaks, guarantees instant help in a moment of need and nourishes the feeling of true community. Instead of discomfort, with "the Soviet 'family romance'... adulterated by the fluttering sound of a curious neighbor's slippers in the communal apartment, or by an inquisitive representative of the local Housing Committee," the "romance with the collective"[40] brings with it the safety of a loving, supportive extended family, and the comical moments that inevitably accompany this co-existence only emphasize this. In *Just a Girl*, even the typical vaudevillian motif of an infant left on a stranger's doorstep turns into a happy event. The initial confusion as to which one of the two men sharing the apartment is supposed to be the adoptive father is resolved by an intervention from a young female neighbor: "What are you arguing about? You are the dad, you are the granddad, and you share the apartment anyway." The uninterrupted coming and going of strangers turned into neighbors by no will of their own in an overcrowded hotel in *Taimyr Calling* becomes a testimony to all the good qualities that Soviet people share, so that the question of whether "it is possible to represent in a comic mode the positive qualities of Soviet people [and whether] it is possible to look at a positive image of a Soviet man through the prism of comedy"[41] is a

---

[39] Welsh, "State-of-the-Art Impersonations," p. 1063.
[41] Nezhin, "Veselyi spektakl'."

[40] Boym, *Common Places*, p. 123.

rhetorical one: the answer is obviously yes. There may be no end to misunderstandings in the course of the play, but in the end,

> the plot of the comedy is driven by the characters' noble motives. Comedy reveals the best features of the Soviet person: his constant readiness to help a compatriot, his personal interest in any affair of the state, his highly developed sense of civic duty, and, finally, his empathy, compassion, and transparency and simplicity in his relationships with people who are just like him.

It did not much matter how restricted the living conditions were at the present moment, because these people lived in the full knowledge that "an endless summer vacation (communism) was always considered to be just around the corner."[42] Nor did it matter that bathrooms and kitchens had to be shared with many others, because everyone knew that the whole country was their true home. The young officer in *A Discharged Captain* feels it intensely when he declares his decision to settle down in a small provincial town and build his house there with the woman he loves: "And here's what's strange: this house seems so big that it has room enough in it for all the people of my Motherland. Our Motherland is our sunny home!" As befits a strong Soviet man, he is uncomfortable talking about his feelings and a bit shy when it comes to confessing his only concern: "I am not sure if a particular person will want to be there with me." Of course this other person agrees, and the happy ending is guaranteed. Whatever small mishaps, incongruities, misunderstandings, or confusions happen in these settings, it is always nothing more than "the humor one knows 'from one's own home,' extended to the scale of a big human collective."[43]

These last words could be a good response to *Pravda*'s editorial of April 7, 1952, which deplored the absence of "household comedies" (*bytovye komedii*). Far from a dearth of household comedies, one could argue that regardless of where a particular play or film was set, it was always about relationships within a household, a family. Urban comedies these might be, but the traditional orientation toward family could be expected to appeal to yesterday's peasants. At the same time, given that the uncomfortable and noisy communal apartments are just a stand-in for a boundless new world, it is not surprising that the most mundane settings acquire the aura of an almost magical state where conflicts are resolved easily and harmony reigns. In *In the Lilac Garden* the cunning and deceitful manager of a vegetable storehouse, trying to get into the good graces of a man he believes might be useful to him in his financial operations, is determined to act through this man's wife and is surprised when he is told she will not tolerate any advances. His verdict is: "There are no good wives in practice," to which

---

[42] Hanson, *Time*, p. viii (Preface).   [43] Iuzovskii, *Voprosy*, p. 178.

the wise and all-knowing janitor, who has seen enough guests to realize that the fundamental nature of people has changed, responds: "Maybe that's the way it is at your storehouse, but in real life..." This "in real life" is key to understanding how things now worked—or at least how they should work. "In real life" means experiencing the discomforts of daily life as if they were simply props in a game. The nosy neighbors on the other side of the wall, or unwelcome guests at the wrong moment, or the ubiquitous presence of grown-up lovers' parents—these are but opportunities to laugh together, to indulge in a collective game. For example, the game of hide-and-seek, which is by far the most popular one in vaudeville in general, is particularly prominent in the Soviet examples of the genre.

No matter how confined the premises might be, there never seems to be a shortage of opportunities for playing hide-and-seek. In *Springtime in Moscow*, despite the fact that in reality it was highly unlikely that free rooms would be available in a Moscow hotel for the use of unexpected visitors at any moment, the people's deputy has no difficulty ensuring that his guests who are not supposed to see each other just yet are each taken to a different room. In almost every scene in *In the Lilac Garden* there is at least one character who is not supposed to be seen by others and who therefore is hiding behind whatever piece of furniture, curtain, or partition there is. In *A Noble Surname* the teenage son of one of the protagonists arranges for a date between his father and the woman he loves, and organizes for a quick hiding place for the father's mother (in the bushes, under a martial cloak). In *The Goalkeeper* a young man from a Ukrainian village announces his unexpected appearance in a construction bureau in Moscow after he is unable to keep to himself, hiding behind a curtain, the gifts he has brought: a piglet, a hat, and a watermelon. In the same film, various characters hide intermittently either behind that very curtain or else inside a robot that one of the engineers had constructed. In *A Girl with Character* the boss in Moscow seems to be unaware of the fact that a cheeky young employee is engaged in, right behind his back, persuading other female colleagues to leave Moscow and join her on her journey back to the Far East. Even the numerous doors leading to adjacent rooms and corridors in *A Discharged Captain* turn out to be useful in playing such games. When the two young protagonists are finally alone, slightly embarrassed because they are unable to confess their mutual feelings, their positions with respect to the door make it possible for a neighbor to grimace and make signs to the young woman to remind her to mention his project of an industrial dryer to her interlocutor:

> *Zakhar Denisych, peeping from behind the door, is making signs—puffing his cheeks, blowing air. Finally, unable to restrain himself anymore, he whispers, "The dryer, the dryer." Sergei turns around. Zakhar Denisych barely manages to hide behind the door.... He spells in the air with his fingers the word that he wants Zhenia to write down for Sergei after he asks, playfully, for a sample of her handwriting: "Dryer."*

As Roger Caillois writes, "Play is a luxury and implies leisure. The hungry man does not play."[44] Nor, we can add, does the man who lives in uncomfortable conditions; nor somebody who is distressed, or worried, or unhappy. The Soviet vaudevilles make it clear that the spaces occupied by the citizens of the new society are in no way inferior to the plush and velvety interiors of the bourgeois mansions in which the traditional vaudevilles had been set. If anything, the Soviet way of life is superior to that of the capitalist neighbors, offering as it does all the potential for play plus the luxury of having friends and strangers alike as members of one's extended family. In this context, people hiding behind things, emerging unexpectedly, or interrupting other people is not just an old vaudevillian device. It is a legitimization tool for turning the cramped living conditions into something normal, acceptable, something that is a source of joy and happiness rather than discomfort and suffering. If humor differs from satire in that it invites identification with the character, it would make sense that a happy character would make the viewers believe that they, too, should be happy. The audience's laughter at what they see on stage and screen would imply a recognition that they, too, should enjoy the potential for the play and comical interactions their daily life offers.

However, even in the happy reality where every room, object, and surface is potentially a playground, some spaces are still, even if only symbolically, more appropriate for playing games than others, in keeping with a key principle of game theory according to which "play must be accomplished 'in an expressly circumscribed time and place'."[45] Such are, for example, trains (*A Girl with Character*), hotels (*Taimyr Calling*), and dormitories (*Springtime in Moscow*). In all such transitory places, halfway between home and not-home, stationary and mobile, permanent and temporary, one can be forgiven, and even expected, to be confused and to cause confusion, to be surprised and to surprise. But the best examples of such special places were the "houses of rest," where *In the Lilac Garden* and *Late for a Date* are set. Representative of the ideal Soviet space both of never-ending active holiday and of total control, the houses of rest combine the uncombinable: on the one hand, as much freedom as one could imagine, in all senses, which led at least one observer to condemn these establishments as "places of slothful indulgence,"[46] and, on the other, the most stringent regimen and round-the-clock supervision, where visitors were caught, to use Svetlana Boym's words, "between control and intoxication."[47] The guests are welcome, but they cannot do much without presenting their ID, and the need to comply with this

---

[44] Roger Caillois's *Encyclopédie des jeux* quoted in Ehrmann et al., "Homo Ludens," p. 45.
[45] Ehrmann et al., "Homo Ludens," p. 42.
[46] Gorsuch, "'There's No Place'," p. 765, with reference to a source from the late 1940s.
[47] Boym, *Common Places*, p. 123.

requirement causes much merry confusion in both *In the Lilac Garden* and *Late for a Date*. They are on holiday and should be free to spend their time as they wish, except that, of course, "the door is locked for quiet time," which makes two honest people in *In the Lilac Garden* look like deceitful lovers, and the guest in *Late for a Date* is expected to follow religiously the instructions in the "Vacationer's Memorandum" he is given at check-in. Guests must fill out questionnaires and write applications. They must also remember that at all key points there will be an inevitable observer who, though disguised as an insignificant servant appointed to satisfy their needs, will have supreme control over their comings and goings, possibly of their very life. In *In the Lilac Garden* it is the middle-aged female janitor, who lets no one enter or leave without depositing an ID with her; in *Taimyr Calling* it is the "on-duty administrator assigned to the 13th floor" who has the power to decide on who gets what room in the hotel and, indirectly, causes a whole series of substitutions and confusions; in *At 6 P.M. After the War* there is someone known as "Aunt Dasha" who occupies an indeterminate position between being the caretaker of the big housing block, the janitor, and the head of staff, and who presides over all the encounters and leisure activities in her territory, making sure that the officers who come looking for the pretty "Aunt Varia" are not allowed to come in without first identifying themselves. These liminal figures are akin to fools in Shakespeare, or court assistants in Kafka; they know something that others do not, they guard something that others want, but the rules they follow are not explicit, so that the comic episodes involving them are never quite free of a somewhat sinister tinge. They are simple people, an embodiment of the democratic principle of the new society—but they are also an incorporation of the random, arbitrary force to which others' lives are hostage. They mark the key paradox of Soviet reality: a celebration of freedom, movement, and change, combined with the requirement for total control and identification of a person with external markers: provenance, address, occupation, affiliation.

The anxiety of authorities when faced with the reality of "people on the loose" was not unique to the Soviet regime. A historian of European modernity identifies the same concerns in early twentieth-century France, where "location was paramount, for it allowed one to be known, to have identity in a community,"[48] and the same is true of other societies. But it is probably safe to say that it was primarily in the Soviet context that the reality of anxious surveillance on the one hand, and the ideologically driven fantasy of free movement and permanent reinvention of the self on the other were in such permanent tension, thematized as playful and endearingly comical in the vaudevilles of the time.

---

[48] Matsuda, "Doctor," p. 76.

"Walk Around the World with a Light Step": Moving in Space And Time

Another comparison with de Sade's novels is called for at this point: there, as Roland Barthes notes, "we travel a great deal,"[49] though only to discover that nothing much changes. According to Barthes, the transition from one location to another signals a transition to a world of fantasy, of private pleasure where questions pertaining to the essence of one's subjectivity and relations to others are posed and explored.

The same can be said of vaudeville as a genre, and especially of the Soviet vaudevilles. *Another Man's Child* was praised for following a foundational principle of vaudevillian comedy originally mentioned by Chekhov: "ceaseless movement."[50] Another text of the time reminded readers of the "necessity to saturate Soviet playwrighting with constant action" because of the need for "activization of the repertoire,"[51] though without offering a clear explanation of what this meant. Yet another critic was less pretentious in his explanation of the (literally) moving principles behind the genre, stating simply that the humor of the Soviet vaudeville is one "that needs space, air, changes of location, unexpected landscapes, surprising encounters, different people."[52]

The classical vaudevillian motif of being on holiday, enjoying leisure time, is by no means the only context in which the characters of the Soviet vaudevilles move. They move simply because their audiences predominantly consisted of the working class that is, according to a critic writing in 1934,

> a laboring class, active, fighting, constantly transforming nature, social relations, and the forms of communal coexistence.... The culture of the classless society that we are creating is dynamic and rich in events.... The concept of freedom includes the notion of movement, change, and action that follows a goal-specific plan.... These people are not "statuary."[53]

The author of these words was probably unaware that Samuel Harper, an American professor who had visited the Soviet Union in the late 1920s had concluded that the Soviets placed a great emphasis on "*aktivnost'* or *activeness*, a word that, Harper argued, denoted not merely concrete activity but a state of mind."[54]

---

[49] Barthes, *Sade*, p. 15.
[50] Mikulášek, *Puti*, p. 226, with reference to Chekhov, Anton. *Polnoe sobranie sochinenii*, vol. 8 (Moscow, 1948), p. 391.
[51] Kirpotin, "Sovetskaia dramaturgiia," p. 12.   [52] Iuzovskii, *Voprosy*, p. 178.
[53] Kirpotin, "Sovetskaia dramaturgiia," pp. 10–11.
[54] Alexopoulos, "Soviet Citizenship," p. 522, with reference to Harper, *Civic Training*, pp. xv, 1–2.

This is most certainly true for most of the protagonists of the Soviet vaudevilles. The war years provided a setting for numerous arrivals and departures, occasional meetings and rapid good-byes, chance encounters and predictable disappearances. *A Blue Handkerchief, A Noble Surname, At 6 P.M. After the War* are only a few of the numerous vaudevilles where the plot revolves around the "front:home front" axis, with the central characters or token objects moving between the two locations, two forms of existence, without knowing where they will be the next day— or whether they will be anywhere at all. But even in peacetime, active movement was an integral part of these people's existence. In *Fame* the young female pilot is constantly given just an hour to prepare for her next heroic flight, so that her exhausted father, an old actor, can only sigh: "Me, I'm an actor, I've been a vagabond all my life, / But you, you've outdone me." In the same play, the mother of the male protagonist who has just saved a whole village from a catastrophe is busy preparing for a family reunion, for which she expects, in addition to the hero son who is now at the site of a disaster, the arrival of "my son Nikolai from Kazan', / My son Ivan from Vladivostok." In *A Discharged Captain* a secondary character, a young man who used to be a bureaucrat and a lazybones living with his parents, has an epiphany and announces his departure to an exotic region of the country to build a new life with his newly found love, while the female protagonist, a young transport driver, decides to accept the invitation to join a work brigade in the Far East. *A Blue Handkerchief* ends with the young couple going to Ural to work at a factory. In *Springtime in Moscow* the people's deputy captain Krylov must depart for the Far North the next morning. Another character in the same film finally manages to find the factory where the woman he has fallen in love with works, only to exclaim in desperation:

> My soul was full of hope,
> I flew to the factory like a bird.
> But what did they tell me there?
> She, Katia, has left the factory...gone to study!
> And some old man, having learned of my love,
> Of my new defeat,
> Told me: "Look for her, quick!
> Because everyone is in motion these days,
> Time itself is rushing forward now,
> Days are flying by.
> While you're looking for her, she'll finish her studies,
> She'll have gone far away, and all will be lost!"

In real life, the chances of a young woman wanting to leave Moscow for a provincial town were apparently rather slim, as historical evidence from the time shows—all the more reason for the magical world of the vaudevilles to counterbalance this unfortunate state of things. In them, cities retain the attraction as centers of learning for those seeking professional training, and, in this particular Soviet sense, these vaudevilles were truly *urban* comedies. In *The Goalkeeper* a simple woman from a Ukrainian village manages to convince some engineers from Moscow to take her "to the city, to study," and on several later occasions she repeats "I am working in a lab" with the same sense of profound bliss with which women of previous generations declared that they were about to marry desirable young men. Young village girls all over the country would be able to identify with the emotion, regardless of whether the longing was for education or for a good husband. In *Dragonfly* the female protagonist leaves a Georgian kolkhoz for the capital, Tbilisi, in order to study at a university. In *Just a Girl* the heroine of the title conceals from the family that employs her as household help the fact that she has actually moved to Moscow from a provincial town to study for her university entrance exams. At the same time, socially conscious young professionals are looking to leave the capital. In *A Discharged Captain* Zhenia, the transport driver who previously "worked as a secretary for the plant manager," one fine day "left and got twenty girls from the administration follow her to the driving school—imagine that," only to then lead a group of fellow drivers to explore a faraway terrain. In *A Girl with Character* it does not take much effort for the guest from the Far East, when she sings in her melodious voice "I can on my own / Walk around the world with a light step," to convince the most intelligent, prettiest, most courageous, and boldest young women to leave their boring office jobs and surrender to the magical pull of the unknown in the beautiful and wild country. On screen only the lazy and the incapable stay behind, like the spoiled and self-centered "Madlene" from *In the Lilac Garden*, who, even though she "studied in a technical college," did not move anywhere because "I then learned that working in the country would be bad for my nervous system, and... got married," or like the clerk Klavdii, from *A Discharged Captain*, who in the first half of the play, before his transformation, is dreaming aloud: "If only you knew... Sometimes I would be working through paperwork... And there is an invoice from somewhere far away, say, from Turkmenistan... And I would lay it out in front of me like a map, as if I were not a finance clerk but a conqueror of the desert, and sitting not on a chair, but riding a camel." As is evident from the complaint of a critic, this, too, was a real plot device, a "motif related to the characters' unwillingness to live anywhere except in the capital" in many vaudevilles of the time,[55] intended to make some characters appear ridiculous.

However, there are plenty of examples in these works of lazy and incapable people spending much of their life moving, too, at least as much as the ideologically loyal citizens do. What differentiates the good ones from the bad is that they

---

[55] Osnos, "Geroi," p. 234.

do so in different ways. Like particles obeying their special laws, they follow other trajectories and exist in states that are mutually incompatible. Their movements are, as Alenka Zupančič calls them, "mismovements."[56] In Valentin Kataev's *Path of Flowers* (*Doroga tsvetov*, 1934) one of the most repulsive characters is Zavialov, who sees himself as a "person of the future" and professes a freedom of love and of movement. In *Just a Girl* the shabby forty-something storehouse manager Egor Gavrilovich, one of the whole class of those who, "in accordance with his theory of 'free movement,' keeps changing the objects of his love and his places of residence,"[57] appears to be courting a superficial and desperately pretentious young woman. However, he deflects her declaration that she is prepared to marry him, explaining:

> I'm not rejecting you. But marriage—no, that's not something I'd be interested in. I've been married. And more than once or twice. I've tasted that brew. *Ira*: So what were you hoping for? Why did you keep coming? *Egor Gavrilovich*: I was looking for something poetic. You know, somewhere to crash after work... I want romanticism! But all of that "Where have you been?", "Why are you late?", "How much money did you bring?"—No, that's bad taste, that doesn't interest me.

The corrupt managers of the "house of rest" in *In the Lilac Garden* keep drifting from job to job and from location to location—a lifestyle that appears out of sync with the new norms. Even the young son of one of them complains: "As a Young Pioneer, I'm ashamed to keep changing schools. Why are you and Semen Semenovich always moving, like some migrant birds?" Offended by somebody's suggestion that they had "left" a previous position, he explains the subtle difference: "Managerial cadres do not leave; they are transferred. You get the difference?"

The difference between the two forms of movement is indeed substantial. The vocabulary these people use is telling: they speak of being "transferred" or "moved up," or "passing through" somewhere (*In the Lilac Garden*). They frankly declare that their ideal form of existence is being "here, there, everywhere. The main thing is to hit it right, then make a move," and they think it acceptable to answer a question about their marital status ("are you single, Willie?") with an evasive "on the one hand, I am; on the other, not quite" (*A Noble Surname*).

"On the one hand, I am; on the other, not quite" is very different from the "both ... and ..." principle that guides the actions of the successful, respectful, inspired and inspiring heroes of the same plays. Mark Lipovetsky characterizes the figure of the Soviet trickster as a "gentleman of the road,"[58] and it would

---

[56] Zupančič, *The Odd One In*, p. 130. For a critical response, see Vandaele, "Narrative Humor," p. 78.
[57] These words are spoken by Zav'ialov in Kataev's *Doroga*. [58] Lipovetsky, *Charms*, p. 30.

appear that these characters fit the description: always on the move, but never arriving; always in transition, but never becoming anything, always moving away, but never quite aiming for much beyond their own immediate gain. These self-professed quintessential Mercurian figures display "certain qualities demanded by the epoch of modernity, qualities traditionally associated with internal strangers, service nomads, professional "others" (such as merchants, craftsmen, middle men, entrepreneurs, and actors, for example)."[59] The occupations of the ridiculous individuals in the Soviet vaudevilles are more mundane: storehouse managers and corrupt circus janitors, railway administrators and managerial assistants in holiday facilities, or even those who, like the dormitory caretaker in *Springtime in Moscow*, spend their days feeling desperate about how "It's becoming harder to live in the world. / It's harder to understand the cause of events," moving from one function to another in the eager anticipation of how someday they will be able to just figure out everything and achieve what they long for: "And me, I'm striving for the system with my whole being, / I'm striving for a long-term management job."

However, it is important to note that the activity of these "gentlemen of the road" is in no way subversive, unlike that of the classical trickster figures; nor do they always pretend to be someone they are not. If anything, they take at face value the injunctions of the new order, above all the principles of self-reinvention and of free movement, and apply them literally. These are grotesque characters, objects of satire in a genre otherwise driven by positive heroes; the latter can be objects of humor, but never of satire. While it may be true, as a contemporary critic contemptuously wrote, that many characters of the wildly successful vaudeville *Another Man's Child* are shallow, lacking a "biography..., a past and a future,"[60] one could never accuse them of the sin of passivity in a workers' state. Far from passive, these parasites are always busy, never standing still. What distinguishes them from the good citizens of the new society—and what is supposed to make them ridiculous—is that they are not active, but restless. Their lot is "busy-ness," which Eric Santner defines as engaging in "work that [keeps] one busy beyond reason."[61] And they are exactly that: busy beyond reason, because in the community of shared big goals and limitless expanses, there is simply no reason for them to get involved in the transportation of illegally acquired strawberries in train carriages dispatched off the record (*In the Lilac Garden*), procure coffee and chocolate through dubious channels (*A Noble Surname*), find—and keep— husbands that are beyond redemption (*Just a Girl*), seek favors, exchange empty promises, work hard to establish connections, only to realize that they have missed the boat once again. This inherently tautological state of being—being busy with busy-ness—is potentially ridiculous in the same way as any inherently tautological

---

[59] Ibid., p. 12.   [60] Mikulášek, *Puti*, p. 221, quoting Shokhin, *O tragicheskom geroe*.
[61] Santner, *The Weight*, p. 23.

or self-contained activity would be, any activity that is out of sync with the mechanisms that drive the world in which these people exist. In this new world, there are right and wrong ways to be on the move. They move too much, and too fast. They are comical figures because they exaggerate and accelerate.

All the transformations they undergo, all their movements, whether the space is literal or metaphorical (between different states of being, different social roles), are associated with new people in the new society. Rather than introducing a subversive element into the plot of life, these people seek a fulfilment of the new society's promises to its citizens: happiness, wellbeing, abundance of material comforts in exchange for work. Once the immediate post-revolutionary years were over, it became apparent that "even the ruffian has become... different. He no longer tries to stand out from the general community...; on the contrary, he tries to blend in."[62] What distinguishes the actions of these "ruffians" from the ideologically sanctioned version of being on the move, changing and being changed, and what makes them appear ridiculous in these texts and performances, is the simple fact that in their case things are sped up. The path between a notion of how a collectively shared desire may be satisfied and its eventual satisfaction is short-circuited, and ideas in which the guiding principles of the society are grounded are given an immediate realization. Is this a community of individuals eager to help each other? By all means; "you get me ceylon lingerie, I get you a train carriage," in the neat formula of petty criminals arranging for illegal transport of stolen fruit in *In the Lilac Garden*. Loyalty to one's team, to the point of seeing no difference between one's collective and one's family? The same play features characters who are truly dedicated to this idea, prepared to satisfy every need of a potentially important guest of the holiday home they manage:

DUSHECHKIN: Today Rybtsev is second-in-command of the municipal health board, but tomorrow he'll be head of the local council! Head of the regional council! A member of the High Board! Deputy minister! And no matter where he's transferred, no matter how high he climbs, I'll always be following him!
...
SHOK: And I'll be following Semen Semenovich! You mustn't destroy a family!

A unity of person and social role? But of course; in *A Noble Surname* a petty and crafty circus administrator inquires of his interlocutor almost immediately upon being introduced: "Excuse me, Stepan Petrovich, what is your occupation?", and reacts with an excited "I adore this. Classic" to the other's curt reply: "Inspector." The same comic device is used, far too heavily, when a selfish hysterical woman in *In the Lilac Garden* refers to her supposedly numerous admirers not by names or

---

[62] Pavlovskii, "Skuchnyi smekh," p. 219, quoting I. Sel'vinskii.

any other personalized forms of identification, but by occupations: she misses "oilfield workers in the spa town of Kislovodsk" who had provided her with a "more sophisticated society," and wonders why her husband "is so fiercely intrigued by the railroads official," because "he had not even been so jealous of scientific researchers." Heroism? For lack of opportunities to commit a truly heroic deed right there and right now, the male characters in *Another Man's Child* compete with each other in their willingness to sacrifice themselves by marrying a woman who supposedly carries another man's child, and one of them is bitterly disappointed when it turns out that there is no child: "Because I spent nights admiring myself, feeling so sentimental, crying...I started to respect myself. I even talked to myself respectfully! Then suddenly—oops! No baby. No heroic deed for me. Deceived, dishonored! Give me back the other man's child!" Equality? In the mini-world ruled by these shadowy characters, the people who really know how things are done are those on the lowest step of the social ladder, and in order to make arrangements, a visitor is advised not to "chat... with anyone else but Klava, the girl who serves at the counter." Professional education that would open up new vistas in life? Good-natured but lazy Marine from *Dragonfly* dreams at the beginning of the play about how wonderful it would be if "scientists invented some kind of pill so you could take one and immediately become an agronomist, a teacher, or a doctor."

A significant speeding up of action is not uncommon in comedy; Alenka Zupančič writes of "comic acceleration"[63] as a special narrative trope in the genre. According to a Soviet encyclopedia of literary terms, "rapid action"[64] is a key feature of any vaudeville plot. Critics of the time speak of "a fast, even lightning-fast development of dramatic action, a rapid succession of impressions" and "a quick change of contradictory emotions"[65] as markers of the vaudeville, Soviet or not. Some found this particularity of the genre quite irritating, finding it to be a "putrid influence of bourgeois boulevard playwriting" on Soviet art and claiming that Soviet audiences could feel nothing but disdain when forced to witness how "it is a total racket. People fall out and come back together, fight and kiss several times, all in just three acts."[66]

It is understandable how the excessive speed with which romantic unions were established and broken would be suspect in a society that was moving more and more toward traditional family values, promoting the importance of an impeccable and formally verifiable personal record. It was only during the war that the hastily concluded arrangements for a "happily ever after" life together were welcomed, just as letters written by women to unfamiliar men at the front were a sign of high moral principles, not of loose morals. *A Blue Handkerchief, At 6 P.*

---

[63] Zupančič, *The Odd One In*, pp. 58–9. [64] "Vodevil'."
[65] Mikulášek, *Puti*, p. 225; Dikii, "Zabytyi zhanr," p. 94.
[66] Uralov, "O sovetskom vodevile," p. 192.

M. After the War, and *Emergency Landing* are characteristic examples (though in this last one the authors must have felt that the announced marriage was a bit too prompt even against the background of the war, and settled for a more appropriate engagement). But what is truly special about the Soviet context is that in the depiction of negative characters this exaggerated fast-forwarding not only is applied to emotions and events but also is used to present a certain way of life that is to be perceived as hopelessly ridiculous. These are the people who lack the telescopic vision that guides their better compatriots on the way to a better world. Their conflation of prosperity with immediate gain, personality with functionality, is evidence of a failure to maintain the state of productive confusion that is celebrated in these works. What these unworthy people want, they want now—objects, privileges, favors, status—and they legitimize their demands in the vocabulary they borrow from the language meant to describe a more enlightened (and more confused) world.

We started with confusion as a defining feature of vaudeville. It is likely that at least part of the reason why works of the genre appealed to the audience of the time, and why they were a good tool to promote the new values, was precisely because they thematized living with (unresolved) confusion and dealing with the confusing discomforts of the daily life, all against the background of one big question formulated by an enthusiastic young person in *A Good Life*: "Yes,... a new world is in the making. But where is the new man? When will he come?... Or is it just a dream, a myth?" And, we might add: how will we recognize this new man or woman when they appear on stage? How will we know what defines these new people? How will the audience know, the playwrights, the actors? Vaudeville, Jennifer Terni tells us, is a "dramatization of a kind of performance anxiety—the anxiety felt when one is asked to perform a new social script or try on a new persona in unfamiliar social settings."[67] When unfamiliar and ever-changing social settings were the social norm, when transformations, identity games, substitutions and extreme acceleration were the order of the day, vaudeville provided a frame for dealing with these experiences that otherwise might have proved disturbing and potentially destructive.

[67] Terni, "A Genre," p. 246.

9
Metalaughter
Populism and the Stalinist Musical Comedy

> There is no better starting point for thought than laughter.
> Walter Benjamin,
> *The Author as Producer*

"Popular spirit" (*narodnost'*, sometimes translated as "populism") was one of the key categories of Socialist Realist aesthetics, one that radically distinguished Stalinist culture from the revolutionary culture preceding it. Nowhere else does popular spirit appear in such a pure form as in the comic genres, which occupied a low position in the Socialist Realist genre hierarchy and were addressed to the widest audiences. This is because "popular spirit" is itself an image of the masses as the regime would like to see them. The very raison d'être of state laughter was essentially the production of "popular culture" that would create cheerful, laughing and singing masses. The Soviet cinema of the Stalinist era was the medium in which this was most noticeable.

We shall examine the dynamics of comic forms in two dimensions: theater and music, which came together in musical film comedies. Here we can see, in fixed patterns, the discrepancy and conflict between the classical and the mass-oriented, between the "high-cultural" and the "entertaining," discrepancies that were characteristic of the Soviet cultural situation from the very beginning of the period of revolutionary change. The transformations of Socialist Realist popular spirit reflect not only the dynamics of the image of the masses in the eyes of the regime but also the attempt made to balance the dichotomy. As we will see, these discrepancies and conflict became a system-forming factor of internal readjustments inside Socialist Realism, a regulator in the mechanisms of change in the strategy regarding the masses that the state followed.

"The Rest, As They Say, Just Endured It"

The new audience for art in the early Soviet era was born of the cultural collapse that occurred when the "old culture" grew to include a new recipient. The new spectators formed their perceptions through the very process of being given "access to culture." This was a difficult and painful process. It was accompanied by a crisis of all the traditional forms of receptive activities and, consequently, by an overwhelmingly negative attitude of the masses toward culture in general—both the "old culture" and the new revolutionary counterpart that arose from the paroxysms of that "old culture." The rejection of the consumption of art, and the concomitant desire of the masses to create their own art instead, both began as a result of this process. This situation regenerated the audience by making them, at first, participants in the "creative process" and, subsequently, authors.

The social class that was newly awakened to cultural life was required to make its own art practically from nothing; it had to satisfy its artistic hunger with prehistoric means. This is what we learn from the book *Workers on Literature, Theater and Music*:

> At the same time, the treasures of art and culture in our theaters, museums, academies, and the like, are rotting because they have no consumers among the workers and peasants. The satiated, anemic, fatigued brains of the petty-bourgeois intelligentsia, who still find themselves, willingly or not, in the role of the main consumer of the arts, are unable to digest all these riches and make them accessible to a society ruled by the proletariat that is following the path to communism.... The more art comes into direct contact with the proletariat and with peasants, the more it will be transformed and reconstructed, the more communist it will become.[1]

But until that moment came, the new spectators had to acknowledge that the "old culture" did not belong to them. "I don't know who this performance is for," writes a workers' correspondent after visiting a performance in Vakhtangov's studio,

> but since I received the tickets through a workers' organization, I expected to see factory and plant representatives there. It came as a total surprise to me when I saw only three or four workers scattered among the general masses. The rest of the spectators seemed to be "gentlemen," ladies all dressed up and younger ones made up and powdered, with rings and bracelets. I felt totally out of place. Remember, this the first time ever that the performance was free. But if none of the spectators at a free performance were workers, what is it going to be like later when you have to pay for performances? (34–5)

---

[1] Krylova, *Rabochie*, pp. 32–3. Hereafter the worker correspondents' responses to their visits to theater and concerts are cited from this edition, with page numbers noted.

As it turned out, however, it was not just the metropolitan and academic theaters that failed to attract workers—the same held for local ones. "Why are there so few people in the theater?" a workers' correspondent asks, bewildered. "More than half the theater (and it's not like the theater is big) is empty. Awfully annoying that a theater in the middle of a workers' neighborhood has no audience of workers. Who is to blame?" (p. 35).

It was obvious, however, that workers were in no rush to consume the "old art" made available to them by the new state. Nor did art itself "regenerate, rebuild itself, become Communist" (p. 43). The result was dissatisfaction: "If we look at the performances from the workers' point of view, then none of them presents anything except the same rotten old stuff. All there is to be seen at performances are lovers, dancing, legs flying around and flimsy skirts puffing out"; "They performed Chekhov's plays, things that meant nothing to the workers, that didn't touch the mind or the heart either" (ibid.); "We watched *Uncle's Dream*, based on Dostoevsky... You feel compelled to ask what the point is of presenting on stage a degenerating courtly figure, a noble type that we've learned to detest and who is out of his mind. A worker has no need for such topics"; "In the daytime I watched a premiere about life in Roman times (*Anthony and Cleopatra* by Shakespeare) and I thought: why does a worker, busy all day long with hard physical work, need this rotten historical trash?"[2]

Approaching the "old trash" as the "new owner," the worker-spectator denied entire genres and forms of theatrical art the right to exist. This was particularly true for musical theater. Opera and ballet were rejected outright. The reaction of the new mass audience to these forms of musical art was notable for its particularly aggressive rejection of "aestheticism."

Workers' correspondents' reviews of opera and ballet give us a sense of the cultural dead end in which the attempts of mass culture to "take possession of the cultural heritage" culminated.[3] A real cultural abyss can be seen here, where any form of "reshaping the old culture" is out of the question: "Why do they show us workers things that have become obsolete and that don't teach us anything?" one workers' correspondent objected after seeing Tchaikovsky's *Eugene Onegin*. "All these ladies and gentlemen [Onegin, Lenskii, Tatiana] lived at the expense of the serfs, not doing anything, and, out of sheer idleness, not knowing what to do with themselves!"; "We think the content of [Tchaikovsky's opera] *Queen of Spades* is now completely a thing of the past and it should no longer be performed. I would like to point out especially that at the end of the third act Catherine the Great makes an appearance, and the choir glorifies her in song.... One can hardly think

---

[2] The responses are cited from Alatyrtsev, *Pochva*, p. 12.
[3] On the consequences of the transformation of opera and ballet as a response to the mass demand, see Fairclough, *Classics*; Raku, *Muzykal'naia klassika*; Iakovleva, *Mariinskii teatr*.

of anything more offensive than singing an anthem to a Russian empress from the stage of state academic theaters"; *Swan Lake* is rejected as "the story of a prince's love for a princess, followed by the dance of the dying swan as a result of his infidelity. This most boring of boring stories, of no use to anyone...takes place over the course of four acts." The state of mind of the worker spectators during the performance is predictably uninspired: "Out of seven of us, three were constantly going to sleep, and we had to badger them: 'Hey, guys, just don't snore.' The rest, as they say, just endured it" (pp. 73–6).

However, there were significant difficulties with understanding not only the "historical trash" but also the avant-garde theatrical performances of Meyerhold and Vakhtangov: "Despite the fact that I followed the scenes intently, I couldn't make any connection between them," declares one bemused spectator. "I didn't understand a thing." "The thing seemed very difficult and muddled to me," states another. "In my opinion the thing wasn't written for workers. It is really difficult to understand and wears the spectator out." "The first part is followed by muddle, the second part is followed by muddle, and the third part is followed by muddle." "In the new performances there are a lot of incongruities. No general impression at all" (45–7).

> There are works of photomontage that might be called "A jump into the unknown" or "A bloody nose," or "A hanged Moor," or anything else. They might also have a bottle of home-made vodka, and a gun, and people in various outfits and poses, and cars, and steam trains, and torn-off arms, legs, heads...It's all good, except...who knows what it's all about? You can look at it from top to bottom, or else from the bottom up, but still, the devil only knows what it all means! It's the same with this show. It has a little of everything. There is the Pope, and books, and libertines, God and angels, carousing, dancers, the foxtrot, bombs, meetings, and they've even got a worker in there for some reason. All of this is presented in such a sequence that you can't even tell where it starts and where it ends. A worker who ends up watching a play like this leaves completely baffled and bewildered. (pp. 45–7)

Factory theater, which arose "unaided," piqued by far the greatest interest from the mass audience; here the spectator was involved in the "production of art" through his or her own authorship and a "familiar plot." This is what the workers' correspondents wrote:

> The state theaters only serve the town center, for example, the bourgeoisie and Soviet intelligentsia. The working masses do not go to these "real" theaters. They only watch performances put on by drama circles in their workingmen's clubs. These are the clubs that carry the whole burden of providing theater for the working masses..."That's it: that's ours!" the workers say.

The club is described as putting on performances "written by the guys themselves under the direction of the club director" and, as a result, "the performances captivate the workers."[4]

It is obvious that the "mass spectator" was unprepared not only to understand traditional artistic forms but even to be a recipient of art as such. Nearly every report by workers' correspondents contains statements like the following: "we collectively wrote some plays"; "we have developed our own adaptation of the original text for the theaters"; "we have an initiative group that is working on plays and textual adaptations for our amateur drama group"; "we work in close contact with the amateur literature group and with workers' correspondents who supply us with material." The masses were eager to be creators in their own right, and this eagerness nourished first the rhetoric of Proletkult and later of RAPP, whereby the gulf between the mass recipient and the cultural repertoire of the era became all the more obvious. Overcoming this gulf became a primary aim of Socialist Realism, which set out to "bring together" the masses and high culture.

If there was anything in the "classical heritage" that attracted the mass spectator and listener, it was "operas from the life of the people." Bizet's *Carmen*, Tchaikovsky's *Mazeppa*, and Moniuszko's *Halka* all met with quite a warm reception in the masses' auditoriums. Judging by the spectators' responses, they were mostly attracted by "a familiar plot" and "memorable, beautiful music." "Plotless" symphony music, by contrast, was completely rejected. "I want the Proletarian Musicians' Association to answer this for me," demands a "new listener":

> Do we need these endless concerts with particular programs in the... conservatory halls? One hardly ever runs into a proletarian there, or people like us, from the Young Communist League. At such concerts they usually end up yawning or doze off completely. Seeing this, some people conclude that workers "get bored" at such concerts because they are "not mature enough," "not used to music," or "not accustomed to it." Well, that's nonsense! Why do workers like choirs? Why do they like contemporary songs, or folk melodies?   (p. 80)

The new listener demanded songs. This genre was particularly attractive owing to its "familiarity," "comprehensibility," and "jolliness." The last characteristic is particularly important. Music or theater that was "not ours" (whether old or new and revolutionary) was, above all, boring. "The guys just endured it," "dozed off," or were "bored," as the workers' correspondents inform us. In the club, on the other hand, everyone is cheerful, everybody is familiar, and everything is familiar: "We pay a lot of attention to the song-march, the song-game and song-staging,"

---

[4] Krylova, *Rabochie*, p. 56.

recounts a factory club leader, "and work in this direction is proceeding happily, joyfully, and enthusiastically" (ibid., p. 80). Is it by chance, then, we might ask, that the "musical theme" was later sanctioned in the Stalinist cinema, precisely in the jovially enthusiastic comic genre?

The goal is "conquering culture," to which end it was necessary "to bring the guys further into music by creating new amateur groups"; "not to play waltzes and mazurkas that hint at the petty-bourgeois lifestyle and parties, but rather folk melodies and revolutionary songs, and also, if possible, the works of the great composers"; "to organize singing at demonstrations, in clubs, and for workers, rather than preparing oneself to be an 'artiste'." These are all excerpts from statements made by "club members." Revolutionary culture, with its strategy of "conquering" cultural heritage, could not quite work out this agenda.

The most radical advocates of the new "proletarian" culture in the 1920s, who were later accused of having taken "a tail-end position," suggested that it was possible to bring art and the masses together:

> The working class needs professional theater, and in the future, it will be able to satisfy the demands of the masses. But for this to happen it first needs to be transformed, to become proletarian, to shed its rotten decadent roots, to become healthy. For this to happen, it will need to master the many achievements and many distinctive features of the factory theater, first among which is a connection with the masses and with the party... The factory theater creates new dramatic forms and new content... Its achievements must be used, consolidated, developed, and explored by the professional theater, whose future staff must come almost entirely from today's factory theater.[5]

As they accused the modern theater of being victim to "decadence and neurasthenia" and urged it to become "proletarian," the proponents of a radical mass-oriented transformation of culture suggested that "the proletarian audience should be infused into directorial councils and repertory committees," that "new playwrights and actors [should] be created," that actors and directors must "listen to the workers criticisms and adjust their work accordingly," that they should "orient themselves in the organizational and management sense to the proletarian audience."[6] It was clear, however, that the kind of proletarian audience for whom the whole theatrical repertoire was either "old trash" or "avant-garde nonsense" had nothing to contribute to directorial councils and repertory committees. It was clear that for the same reason it was not a good idea for actors and directors to "adjust their work" in accordance with the workers criticisms, and that the

---

[5] Krylova, *Rabochie*, pp. 60–1.   [6] Ibid., p. 65.

"creation" of "new playwrights and actors" was but a theatrical version of the motto previously proclaimed in literature, that of creating "red Leo Tolstoys." The task of systematically creating a new culture could be achieved only by Stalinism—not by proponents of the revolutionary cultural ideals.

However, to accomplish this task, it was necessary to forgo artistic radicalism, something that revolutionary culture was organically incapable of doing. Socialist Realism took this "historical mission" upon itself. Having dispensed with the avant-garde project, Soviet culture, more consistently than its revolutionary predecessors, went to "meet the masses." It had removed the traditional inferiority complex of the masses in the face of "highbrow art." At the same time, attempts to make art more "worker-friendly" had already become a thing of the past. The idea of replacing "directors and actors with jaded, perverted intellectual taste" (who were alien to Soviet culture) with "the best members of amateur drama clubs, factory workers who were to be given the opportunity to master all aspects of the theatrical arts,"[7] was no longer on the agenda. At the same time, "jadedness and perversion," just like "decadence and neurasthenia," became for many years characteristics attributed to Western art in the demonology of Soviet aesthetics. What happened was, in accordance with the traditional Stalinist scheme, an averaging out of the extremes: members of the amateur drama clubs, remaining at their workstations, became the "Soviet spectators" they were supposed to be; "decadence" was transferred to the West, avant-garde theater died, and in its place came the art of Socialist Realism, which "belonged to the People." No longer following the revolutionary strategy of substitution, Socialist Realism adopted the policy of absorption /synthesis, a complete "reshaping of culture." This reshaping was a process of constant balancing and rearrangement, even as the mass "consumers of art" of the 1920s and early 1930s, those "jolly fellows," were becoming a thing of the past.

Genuine Music for the "Broad Masses Of Workers" (Jazz)

Three popular songs came out of the first Soviet musical comedy, Grigorii Aleksandrov's *Jolly Fellows* (*Veselye rebiata*, 1934). One is about a song, the other two are about love. Both songs about love are sad; the song about a song is an expression of bravura. The songs about love are closely linked to the plot of the film. The song about a song has a more general character and, in contrast to the love songs, is not personal; it speaks about "all of us," is directed to "everyone," and its protagonist is "we":

---

[7] Krylova, *Rabochie*, p. 66.

A cheerful song lightens the heart;
It always chases off boredom.
The countryside and villages love a song,
The towns and big cities love it too.
Songs help us to live and to love,
Like a friend, they call and lead.
And those who go about life with a song,
Will be at home anywhere.
We will sing and laugh, like children,
Amid the constant battle and work.
This is what we were born for, you see:
Never to surrender anywhere.

This song only conveys the mood, without becoming the pivot of the plot (as will be the case later in the film *Volga-Volga*). The shepherd Kostia Potekhin not only sings well, he also takes violin lessons and "studies Beethoven." His first appearance "before an audience in a frock coat" is an embarrassment, and not only because Kostia's herd breaks into the house and the place turns into an "animal carnival." The vacationers from the "Black Swan" resort, mistaking the shepherd for the Paraguayan conductor Kosta Frankini, are at first enraptured by his pipe playing, but when they realize he is a shepherd, they throw him out of the house: "A shepherd has nothing to say to my daughter," says the mother of "the singer Elena." Elena and her circle are incapable of appreciating Kostia's art. The only person able to do so is the maid Dunia. Kostia loves Elena; Dunia loves Kostia. At first, the shepherd cannot recognize Elena's "philistinism," but by the end of the film he will have seen how wrong he was. The lovers' plot and the musical plot motivate rather than just accompany one another: Elena is untalented, Dunia is talented. Aleksandrov's musical comedy consciously makes use of conventions of the operetta. For example, everyone mistakes Kostia for a "foreign conductor" although he speaks Russian with a strong Odessa accent (whereas the real conductor, as becomes clear later, does not speak Russian at all); "the singer Elena," who dreams of making it to the Bolshoi Theater stage, has no musicality at all and can only croak; the plot hinges on a succession of "chance meetings" between the characters; and so forth. The film opens with a juxtaposition of two types of space, the "Crystal Springs" farm and the "Black Swan" resort for "Unorganized Vacationers." The almost fairytale counterpoint of the clear spring to the demonic black swan is evocative of *Swan Lake*. The juxtaposition occurs again at the end of the film, when the ballerinas in their white tutus encircle Utesov's jazz orchestra as extras on the stage of the Bolshoi Theater.

The Bolshoi Theater is the goal of both the jazz musicians and "the singer Elena." Aleksandrov depicts the path of the jazz musicians to the theater as one of merry adventures. But the Bolshoi Theater itself does not appear in the film as a sacred space. On the contrary, the sacredness of the "serious" (including the classics) is constantly profaned in the film. The herd of farm animals wreaks havoc in the resort house, smashing everything to smithereens, from the expensive crockery to a copy of the Venus de Milo. During a music hall concert, the conducting of the ersatz "maestro" Kostia, who has found himself in the place of the touring artiste, is depicted through a succession of rhythmic substitutions. There is much running about on stage, falling down stairs, knocking over of bottles, and other similar slapstick action. A rehearsal of the orchestra turns into a fight in which the "creative workers" use musical instruments as weapons. A funeral march during a somber procession turns into a jazz improvisation. Finally, the jazz players, dirty and dressed in rags, along with drunks, a maid, and a cab driver all appear on the stage of the Bolshoi Theater itself.

This clearly met the requirements of "the masses' demands." Pandemonium on the "grand stage" and the audience's laughter turning into the sound of applause are supposed to symbolize the victory over the classics. The "Friendship" (Druzhba) musical collective, which finally "takes the stage" of the Bolshoi Theater, is an idiosyncratic model of how the classics can be "mastered." This model, however, was already becoming outdated when the film was made. The "nihilistic, couldn't-care-less attitude towards the classical heritage" that the film celebrates was no longer acceptable in Stalinist culture. In Aleksandrov's film, there is hardly any difference between classical music and jazz; there is no conflict—simply because classical music is dead. It is as if jazz fills an empty space: nothing opposes it except for lovers of classical music, who are "philistines."

Nonetheless, the "philistines" are not the heirs of high culture. They only "chase after" whatever happens to be fashionable and only need classical works of art as a spurious sign of refinement, like the copy of the Venus de Milo in the lounge or the busts of composers on the grand piano. The classical heritage has no successors and is therefore not an "aesthetic problem"—or rather, this "problem" has been resolved by time itself. The true creators are the "innovators" (the jazz musicians), Aleksandrov's comedy seems to suggest, as it concludes with a familiar vignette: On the stage is the ragged amateur workingmen's ensemble and the cheerful song about a song that "helps us to live and love," but the whole episode is framed by the image of the chariot that tops the portal of the Bolshoi Theater.

Like Gogol's famous troika from the finale of Part I of *Dead Souls*, the chariot rushes on and... does not give an answer.

"Overcoming the Noise, Screeching and Grinding of the Orchestra"

The answer came two years later, in 1936. The ground rules were laid in a series of newspaper and magazine articles, the channel the authorities chose to express their new aesthetic demands. On January 28, *Pravda* published its editorial

"Muddle Instead of Music," establishing the new criteria for Soviet opera; on February 6, the editorial "Falsehood in Ballet" spoke to those in charge of the new ballet; on February 20, "Cacophony in Architecture" set the new standards for architects; and on March 1, "On Sloppy Artists" addressed the painters. Needless to say, the new trend was immediately taken up by the "party press" and the "Soviet public." On February 14, *Komsomol'skaia pravda* printed the editorial "Against Formalism and 'Leftist Deformity' in Art," followed by "A Staircase Leading Nowhere: Architecture Upside Down" on February 18 and "Far From Life," on March 4. Vladimir Kemenov wrote a long text "Against Formalism and Naturalism in the Arts," published in *Pravda* on March 6 and 26, and another one—"On Formalists and the 'Undeveloped' Audience" in *Literaturnaia gazeta* on February 24. The sixth issue of the periodical *Under the Banner of Marxism* featured P. Lebedev's "Against Formalism in Soviet Art." The list could be continued.

In January through March of 1936 there was a true Socialist Realist revolution in Soviet art. "Popular spirit" became a hallmark of the new Socialist Realist art. This, however, was not about "destruction of formalism"; as a direction of revolutionary culture, "formalism" had been practically eliminated from the "artistic front" by the end of the 1920s. Rather it was about a synthesis of the "classical heritage" with the taste of an average representative of the masses. This synthesis gave birth to a new set of stylistics, combining the accessible and "the beautiful." Synthesizing became the main aesthetic strategy of state power, waging a war simultaneously on two fronts: one against "formalism," the other against "naturalism." Formalism came to be exemplified by the works of Shostakovich, supposedly an example of a "dissonant, confused current of sounds...rolling, grinding, and screeching" in which "singing is replaced by shouting," melody is substituted by "a maze of cacophony," expressiveness became "furious rhythm," and passion was nothing but "noise." This was music that had been deliberately turned "upside down." All these features were decried as signs of "petty-bourgeois formalist efforts and claims of creating originality by means of cheap affectation."

On the other hand, the music of Shostakovich used jazz, which was defined as nothing more than "nervous, spasmodic, epileptic music," naturalistic and vulgar, vibrating "crudely and primitively"; it "grunts, bangs, puffs, and pants." It was made clear that such music is "confused and absolutely apolitical," that it had been intentionally encoded with all its sounds confused so that it would reach "only those aesthetes who have lost all healthy taste," and that Shostakovich's opera *Lady Macbeth of Mtsensk* could only "tickle the perverted tastes of bourgeois listeners with its throbbing, loud, neurasthenic music."

Shostakovich's ballet, on the other hand, is (according to *Pravda*) "sugar-sweet" and exhibits a "doll-like, fake attitude to life." Since ballet in general is "one of our most conservative genres of art" and since it is "particularly challenging to break conventions in this genre," its creator has failed to depict faithfully the daily life of a Kuban kolkhoz. Instead, there are "kitschy *paysans*, as if copied from a prerevolutionary chocolate box, who are supposed to express 'joy' in dances that have nothing in common with folk dancing in Kuban or anywhere else. On the Bolshoi Theater stage, dolls painted 'à la Kolkhoz folk' are broken," while Shostakovich's music "just tinkles and expresses nothing."

These are not just insulting remarks. If we are to see this as a "warning call" from above and as "party interference in the arts," then it is only these in so far as the 1936 campaign against "formalism and naturalism" had an important positive message: it formulated, by a "reversal of logic," a new aesthetic program. Because the "rolling, grinding, and screeching" of Shostakovich's music was "difficult to follow," it was "impossible to remember." There should be singing in opera, not screeching. Instead of cacophony, "a simple and comprehensible melody" should be heard. Instead of "a furious rhythm" there should be "expressiveness." Music made "topsy-turvy" had to be "turned the right way around again," toward "symphonic sounds and simple, popular musical discourse." Shostakovich's music was "built upon the principle of a negation of opera," but the affirmation of opera was "simplicity, realism, comprehensibility of image, the natural sound of words." To this "leftist mumbling" *Pravda* juxtaposed "a natural, human music" and its ability to "captivate the masses." This was what "the Soviet audience expects and hopes to get from music."

However, the campaign against "formalism and naturalism" that erupted in 1936 contained an important, positive idea: a new aesthetic program was formulated "from its opposite." How could this be achieved? "If the creators of a ballet, for example, want to show a kolkhoz on stage, they should study a kolkhoz, its people, its daily life. If their goal is to show specifically a Kuban kolkhoz, they should familiarize themselves with the distinct features of the kolkhozes in this region... Then the creators of the ballet and the composer would discover limitless sources of creative energy in folk songs, dances, and games." Otherwise one could never "put together a folk, kolkhoz ballet" but only "make one's artistic creation into a ridicule of the audience and the listeners, making a life full of the joy of artistic labor appear as kitsch." Obviously, the creators of this particular work of art had failed to follow the advice of those who knew better, because on the Bolshoi Theater stage "some people in clothes that have nothing in common with the actual costumes of Kuban Cossacks jump about, rave... An unnatural mix of supposed folk dances with classical ballet moves performed by ballerinas wearing 'tutus' passes for a ballet based on kolkhoz life."

The basic aesthetic strategy, which was expressed in angry party invectives, was that of synthesis built upon the appeal of a ready-made set of stylistic devices. Works of art had to be accessible, predictable, "expressive," and "natural." All of these elements were present to an equal extent in both classic and folk art that was not "trashy," to use the favorite definition of Stalin, the country's greatest judge of aesthetic matters. Only their proposed synthesis could offer art that would appeal to the "Soviet audience." Such art would welcome superimposition, doubling, and repetition—all devices exemplified in the tautological title of the film *Volga-Volga*.

A True New Music (Song-Song)

Compared to his 1934 film *Jolly Fellows*, Grigorii Aleksandrov's *Volga-Volga* (1938) represented a more advanced stage in the development of Soviet genres, and not only chronologically. *Volga-Volga* is, of course, a film about the Volga, more specifically about how an unknown female postal worker writes about the Volga in a wonderful song that everyone admires. Except that only the refrain of this song is really about the Volga: "Folk beauty, like the full-flowing sea, / Like the free Motherland—wide, deep, strong." The song itself is not about the river, properly speaking:

> Many songs about the Volga have been sung,
> But they still haven't made one
> Warmed by the Soviet sun,
> And that would ring out across the Volga.
> That by bursting into song resoundingly and bravely,
> Our strength would live in it,
> It would fly to the sun itself
> It would penetrate the heart itself.
> Many songs have rung out across the Volga
> But the songs did not have the right refrain:
> They used to sing of our yearning,
> But now they sing of our joy.

This is, in fact, a song about a song. The film could have been called "Song-Song," except that the authors chose to emphasize the location rather than the genre. Central to the film is the concept of song and singing, that "most popular" musical genre "beloved by all." From the very beginning of the film, viewers realize that the most important person in the town of Melkovodsk is Comrade Byvalov. Everyone knows him—from the janitor to the ferryman, from the woodcutter to the water-carrier—though Comrade Byvalov has only recently arrived in town and does not have a very important job: he is not the head of the town's administration, nor a party leader, but simply the director of a small, "local industry." We learn that his "enterprise" produces, of all things, balalaikas. So, where has such fame come from?

Since everyone in the town spends time indulging their amateur interest in music (without, as far as the viewer can tell, doing much else), Byvalov assumes the role of an official manager of this popular amateur work. He makes no claims to this role: his only aim is to make a career and to move to Moscow. However, finding himself at the head of a "true mass movement," Byvalov also lands in a situation of conflict with the "popular element." Once again, we should remember that his "enterprise" produces "the folk instrument," and, as he himself says at the end, "makes no pianos."

This symbolic opposition of the balalaika and the piano is reproduced in a different (but also musical) conflict in the film. Also at the center of Aleksandrov's comedy is a couple in love, one half of which (the mail carrier, Strelka) directs the "popular talents," while the other (Trubyshkin, an accounts clerk) conducts a classical brass orchestra. Both collectives are amateur, and at the very beginning Strelka says to her beloved accounts clerk, "Your rehearsal is my rehearsal." However, it soon turns out that Strelka finds his music boring. She thinks Wagner is "a total bore," and the *Death of Isolde* irritates her: "What a long time she takes to die!" Her clerk responds that this is how it is done "classically." These key definitions ("classically" and "a total bore") would be familiar to Aleksandrov's audience since the times of the Proletkult clubs. Trubyshkin suggests that Strelka "simply does not understand classical music." This is, however, not the point. What one should remember is that Strelka (typifying the masses) is a creator rather than simply a performer. Here is their dialogue:

STRELKA: Aleshka, did you never want to create something yourself?
TRUBYSHKIN: Never.
STRELKA: If I knew music like you, I would be creating something all the time.
TRUBYSHKIN: You would never be successful.
STRELKA: And why is that?
TRUBYSHKIN: Because you are a mail carrier.

Comrade Byvalov says roughly the same thing to Strelka a bit later in the film: "You'd need to study twenty years to be able to sing like that." For Strelka, however, whatever one makes or does oneself is by definition better than what is ready-made: "But our Uncle Kuzia plays better on the trumpet he made himself than you do on the one you bought," she says. A bought trumpet, like a bought balalaika, is bad *a priori* (the balalaika produced by Byvalov's enterprise, for example, "sounds like a log"). Classical music is something ready-made and, therefore, in the eyes of Strelka, impaired. For the accounts clerk, on the other hand, all these "Uncle Kuzias and Aunt Mashas" are "low farce." This opposition is, however, not absolute: both points of view, seemingly opposed to each other, are no longer fixed, and the plot of the film traces the trajectory of the initial conflict, resulting in a final synthesis. The dialectics of conflict in *Volga-Volga* are, in fact, the dialectics of "reshaping the classical heritage" and its conversion into "the property of the broad masses of workers."

On the other hand, "popular talents" like Strelka prove themselves in part through the performance of classics as well. We are introduced to the courier

Simka, who performs Tatiana's aria from Tchaikovsky's opera wonderfully well; there is Mishka the engraver, who can recite the whole of Lermontov's *Demon* by heart, and even the local street sweeper is no stranger to opera. When the "popular talents" perform folk songs, it is because such songs in Soviet culture were elevated to the ranks of a respectable genre. Trubyshkin's "symphony orchestra" goes on a tour and "takes Beethoven, Mozart, Schubert, and Wagner to Moscow," all the officially approved classics that are seen as in no way alien to the "popular masses."

An intersection of these two repertoires creates an official anthology of what is to be considered "classic" and made available to the masses. "Popular talents" like Strelka do not perform anything "bawdy," nor does the accounts clerk's "Neapolitan orchestra" produce any of the formalist "muddle" or "transrational" music, but only melodic, memorable tunes (like Schubert's *Moments musicaux* or the march from *Aida*). The extremes are severed. The spectator ends up in a holistic, organic musical space in which the apparent opposition dissolves, and the conflict becomes playfully comedic.[8]

This apparent opposition develops at the beginning of the film: the ferry with the "populists" moves to the sound of folk music, while the steamship with the "classicists" is accompanied by opera. But even Byvalov likes the folk music coming from the ferry ("They sing well!"), and the operatic music, the well-known march from *Aida*, turns out to be no less popular than the folk song. The musical space thus preserves its heterogeneity, with tradition and innovation both being dialectically organic. Finally, even the parties in conflict—the accounts clerk and the mail carrier—come to understand each other. Ending up by mistake on different boats (Strelka with the "classicists," Trubyshkin with the "populists"), they stop their musical "arguments" and finally create The Song.

The song was incomplete. Its first performance by Strelka at the very beginning of the film is still amateur, monophonic, and too personal. But once the song is "set to notes" (a synthesis of the classicists and populists) toward the end of the film, it "matures" very rapidly. Finally, the entire musical "ado" retreats (the "classics" versus the "folk songs"), and only the "Song of the Volga" remains, the "Song About a Song," a song about itself. This egocentrism of the created work deserves to be studied more carefully.

The song becomes a metasong and a synthesis of previously opposed elements. At the beginning of the film, the "populists" play the song on the ferry using whatever they can get their hands on (a saw, bottles, anything at all); they play it

---

[8] Reviewers responded thus: "The director had to overcome serious faults of the script. The main vice of the original script was a harmful juxtaposition of modern art and classical musical heritage.... The author of the film succeeded in avoiding a nihilist, contemptuous attitude to musical classics" (Korchagin, "Volga, Volga"). This was just four years after *Jolly Fellows*.

"the wrong way" (as someone says, the result is "low farce"). Then the song is performed on violins, flutes, and trumpets by the "classicists," who had earlier played "the wrong thing" (the "colossal bore," "boring enough to kill a fly"). The "populists" understand that a song is what is needed, and the "classicists," having perfected their performance techniques by learning from "Beethoven, Mozart, Schubert, and Wagner," finally realize what they need to play. The synthesis of the symphony orchestra (which Strelka now conducts) and the folk choir (with Trubyshkin as their new conductor) gives birth to a work that truly becomes fantastically popular: the vacationers and the river divers, the woodcutters, and even the pilots of river planes discover the song. It is performed by literally everyone: from Young Pioneers to military brass bands. Eventually the song is converted into a symphonic production thanks to a talented Young Pioneer ("Your theme—my orchestration," he tells Strelka). The final rendition of this "theme" in the symphonic "orchestration" raises the song to the status of high culture, converting it into a super-genre.

The song acquires a triumphal-majestic ring, which marks it as a hallowed text. Here, there is a merger of popular and classical culture, music, theater, cinema, and literature (Strelka is not only a composer but also a poet). The finale of "the musical comedy" is a stage backdrop with the emblem of the USSR and flags of the national republics. This closing image reveals to the spectator the "conversion" of art, the final stage of its reshaping in Stalinist culture. This is achieved without the classics being debased to cater to mass taste, without a clear preference for either the classics or popular music (something for which reviewers nonetheless faulted the director). Instead, what we have is the beginning of a synthesis of arts and styles, of that elevated image of the "complete work of art" into which the life of the Soviet people was being molded. Here the song is simultaneously a film about the Volga, a film about the flourishing of talents in the Soviet Union, and a film about music and theater: a *Gesamtkunstwerk*.

Volga-Volga represents a condensed history of the consolidation of Socialist Realist aesthetics: from the battle with classical genres and works, through the notion of "taking possession of the classical heritage," and right up to the creation of one's own classical heritage, based on a symbolic synthesis of the symphony orchestra with the folk choir. It could be said that Aleksandrov's "musical comedy" is the very manifestation of Socialist Realism and, in this sense, a pure spectacle of the image of state power in 1938. This is, however, not yet the end of the Soviet "musical story."

The Real New Music: The Classics (Opera as Operetta)

Two years after *Volga-Volga* the Soviet audience was presented with another work of the genre: *A Musical Story* (1940; dir. Aleksandr Ivanovskii and

Gerbert Rappaport). Here, we move one level up in the hierarchy of musical styles, to opera.

The genre of this film was somehow new, different from the familiar standard of "musical comedies." There were no predictable, traditional, and hastily refashioned situations and characters. It did not follow the conventions supposedly "assigned" to this genre. There were no "musical episodes" included artificially with justifications of variable validity. Instead, there was true musical content.[9]

Opera was a symbol of whatever was considered "classic," a symbol of that which was fixed, something to which Stalinist culture aspired. In Ivanovskii's and Rappaport's film, operatic music is a constant presence. Opera also represents three pivotal points of the plot: there is *Carmen* (the exposition), *Eugene Onegin* (the climax), and *May Night* (the denouement). The selection of operatic texts is telling: a foreign opera, a Russian opera "from the old life" and a Russian opera "from folk life." The screenplay by Evgenii Petrov and Georgii Munblit originally featured a performance of *Eugene Onegin* at the end, but the director chose Rimsky-Korsakov's *May Night*. There is a certain logic in this choice, for *May Night* is simultaneously a classical piece of music, an opera, and a folk narrative. The pure operatic cliché is ridiculed in the very first scenes of the film when a fat Carmen and Jose appear on the set, singing out-of-tune and laughing in a schooled, unnatural manner. But *Eugene Onegin* is a beloved opera known to everyone in the film. Every member of the car mechanics' club, from the driver to the senior watchman, knows the words of the libretto, cheering on Petia Govorkov by singing the beginning of Lensky's aria in chorus. By 1940, works of the musical classics had become part of the "folk" heritage, that is, "loved by the people," and the honor of "The People's Artist" was awarded under Stalin, almost exclusively to those performing classical works. After an embarrassing failure in *Eugene Onegin*, Petia delivers a triumphant performance in *May Night*, where his character, Levko, dances and sings in orchestrated folk songs. It is significant that when Petia (while still a chauffeur) sings folk songs at home, the communal kitchen comes to a standstill. Everyone listens to his singing. But later, when he (as a student at the conservatory) practices scales at home, it provokes extreme indignation among the residents of the communal flat.

Yet the conservatory is now presented as an essential part of the "training of masters in the trade": being one of the "talents" is no longer enough. In *Jolly Fellows*, the jazz musicians had appeared directly after the funeral procession in a completely inappropriate state on the stage of the Bolshoi Theater, and in *Volga-Volga* the "popular talents" stepped directly onto the Moscow stage from the town square. But here the stage is not that of the Bolshoi; this time the setting is much more appropriate—an amateur theater, which, significantly, is housed in the

---

[9] Dobin, "Muzykal'naia istoriia," p. 34.

premises of the River Terminal. In *A Musical Story* there is no place at all for the anarchy of *Jolly Fellows*: the only way one can make it to the Theater from the car mechanics' club is through the conservatory. There is no longer an opposition between the amateur club and the professional theater, as was the case in *Jolly Fellows*. Instead, there is a sequence of steps: the amateur club, then the conservatory, then the theater. For all that, the main vector of movement is preserved: real art comes from below, from the amateur workers' club. The main thing is to detect natural talent.

One could say that Ivanovskii's and Rappaport's comedy was more realistic than the Hollywoodesque buffoonery of Aleksandrov's musicals both in terms of style and in a conceptual sense. Although *A Musical Story* preserves the myth about the outstanding talent of the masses, in the end, talent only manifests itself as an individual phenomenon. This was different in *Jolly Fellows* and in *Volga-Volga*, in which talent made its appearance mostly in the plural: talents as a collective rather than "talent" as an attribute of individuals. To quote the head of the local trade union committee, who supports Petia Govorkov's application to the conservatory and speaks "in the name of all employees of the car workshop"; "We have, comrades, a talent among us." The "realism" of *A Musical Story* is not limited to the depiction of details of everyday life: in this film there are no "coincidences" (like those in Aleksandrov's or Pyr'ev's films). One might say that it presents a version of the world that is governed by an objective consistent pattern.

Recognition of talent and experience in the conservatory are two new prerequisites (or rather, traditional ones, now newly recognized) that one must go through in order to make it in the world of high art, "from rags to riches." This colloquial idiom is quite appropriate when describing the "radiant path" of the shepherd to the Bolshoi Theater in *Jolly Fellows*, or of the mail carrier from a godforsaken provincial town to the (amateur) stage in Moscow in *Volga-Volga*, or of a chauffeur to the stage of the "Kirov State Order of Lenin Academic Opera and Ballet Theater." However, with each successive film this path becomes more and more complicated. Petia Govorkov's teacher Makendonskii repeats again and again that "a lot of serious work is needed," and that "opera is hard work." Such maxims would not be taken seriously by the characters of *Jolly Fellows* or in *Volga-Volga*, where the path to the stage is a cheerful journey with singing, dancing, and amusing adventures. In *Jolly Fellows*, it is the lovable and funny teacher Karl Ivanovich, speaking with a heavy German accent, who holds forth on such subjects, and in *Volga-Volga* these sentiments are voiced by the bureaucrat Byvalov. Importantly, both *Jolly Fellows* and *A Musical History* depict the progress toward a metropolitan stage of not just actors, but of stars particularly beloved by the public—Leonid Utesov and Sergei Lemeshev.

In *Jolly Fellows* the path toward "popular art" culminates in playing jazz on a central stage (with opera being at the opposite pole). *A Musical Story* traces the path to an operatic stage that has already become "popular." A mere seven years separates the making of the two films, but, on a wider cultural plane, it is a significant fragment of Soviet history, when classical works were integrated into high Soviet culture. There remained no trace of the former opposition between the genres.

The critic who wrote about the film's "clear and light atmosphere," its "bright and celebratory flavor," the "atmosphere of a young and happy meeting between Soviet youth and the arts, the sense of having just fallen in love with the music that has entered their lives," quite justly noted that the scenes in which the amateur opera group meets the "jazz folks" are "full of lively comedy."[10] Indeed, pure comedy is all that is left from the previously acute conflict. The organizer of the amateur jazz band says, "It is better to play bad jazz that will be enjoyed by the broad masses of workers than bad opera that nobody will want to see." To which Makedonskii, the head of the amateur opera group, responds reasonably, "Jazz is healthy, entertaining music, but it must not stand in the path of sacred art." In the context of the film, both are right: "sacred art" has earned its right to exist, and has come to be loved and cherished by "the broad masses of workers." As the director of the club says, "we are trying hard, mastering the classical heritage."

In *Jolly Fellows*, opera is associated with the satirically depicted "bourgeois characters." The petty-bourgeois Alfred Tarakanov in *A Musical Story* is completely indifferent to music, whereas a love of classical music is inherent to the positive heroes of the film, all of whom have come entirely from "the broad masses of workers." Significantly, music accompanies the films' characters everywhere. In *Volga-Volga*, the radio broadcasts popular songs much loved by the people; in *A Musical Story*, listeners enjoy opera broadcast by the same radio stations; in *A Tale of the Siberian Land* (*Skazan'ie o zemle sibirskoi*, 1948; dir. Ivan Pyr'ev) it is symphonies that the "broad masses of workers" listen to on the radio. This coming together of opposing poles is important: while the classical works are made more approachable (by simplifying their complexity or "Tchaikovskyization"), folk music is made more "academic."

A year after *A Musical Story* Ivanovskii made another film on the same subject: *Anton Ivanovich Gets Angry* (*Anton Ivanovich serditsia*, 1941; dir. Aleksandr Ivanovskii). Its protagonist is a conservatory professor and a passionate lover of classical music who worships Handel, and for whom even opera is a suspicious genre because it is possibly "too light," who sees Puccini as an embodiment of "muddle instead of music," and who fervently protects his daughter from contagion by frivolous genres such as jazz. Toward the end of the film, however, he has an epiphany and gives his blessing to his daughter, Simochka, acknowledging her

---

[10] Ibid., p. 32.

love for the composer Mukhin, a writer of music "for the people," and argues that the people need music of all genres: opera, operetta, variety songs, jazz. As if to counterbalance the prejudices of the father, the talented Simochka takes on the main role in Mukhin's musical comedy. Almost all of the characters in *Anton Ivanovich Gets Angry* are sympathetic: Anton Ivanovich, Simochka, and Mukhin.

There is only one unlikeable character: Kerosinov. Played in the film by Sergei Martinson, this satirically depicted, untalented but pompous "composer" is a symbol of "the image of a formalist." The viewer is introduced to him at a point when he has been busy for two years composing some sort of "physiological symphony" that no one has heard. Only noises that can best be described as "musical muddle" reach others from his room. The idea of a "physiological symphony" is an oxymoron, akin to "material spirit," and it is supposed to reveal the image of a formalist who does not want to be part of modernity: to understand and accept "the demands of life," to be inspired. Instead he creates something cold, something superfluous. Formalism is cold, but creativity is warm. A symphony with such a provisional title by a composer with such a name cannot possibly bring warmth to other humans (except by using kerosene). Indeed, all genuine creators in Soviet musical comedy films are able to create mainly because they are "warmed by the heat of love." There can be different kinds of love. It can be a person that one loves (*Jolly Fellows*), or else a person and a river (*Volga-Volga*), a person and an opera (*A Musical Story*), two people loving each other and music (*Anton Ivanovich Gets Angry*), or a person and Siberia (*A Tale of the Siberian Land*).

One's attitude toward music is a sign of "culturedness" (*kul'turnost'*). The masses are supposed to perceive music as their own, but at the same time the very content of "their music" in Stalinist culture constantly changes. Jazz, operetta, opera, or symphonies—all these genres in turn were at the center of the Stalinist idea of the "right" music for the masses. But whatever genre it might be, once it has been declared "popular," all of them average out, and "genre memory" again rewrites itself. If we acknowledge that popular spirit is the image of the masses as the state would like to perceive them, then it follows that the process of erasing "genre memory" is the result of erasing a previously celebrated image of the masses.

Just as the bureaucrat represents the former image of state power, the philistine represents the former image of the masses. Therefore, the opposition of philistine and creator is a stable element in musical cinematic comedies. In *Jolly Fellows* the philistines are grotesque characters, revealing traits of the profiteers from the New Economic Policy period of the 1920s. Their "bad taste," their passion for "plush curtains" and "foreign things" (the symbolic features of the 1920s—potted ficus, canaries, and porcelain elephants—may not be present on screen, but their presence is always implied), become a trigger for comic situations (for example, in the scene where Elena talks about the "artificiality" of a live sheep, assuming that it is not real and claiming that "they make them better abroad"). Their wealth is ostentatious, they wear "foreign bathrobes," and they love everything "chic." The bourgeois version of "culturedness" is supposed to emphasize the discrepancy between the "philistine" and the role of the "cultured person" that the philistine is attempting to play. The discrepancy between one's being and one's social role is a key feature of the satirical image. In the case of "the singer Elena" this discrepancy is particularly important, as she lays claim to the role of "an artistic worker," "a person organized in a refined way," yet at the same time she does not possess the required refinement (as in the scene where she attends the concert of the "foreign conductor" and takes handfuls of sweets and munches them during the performance), nor does she possess the required "interest in art" (during the concert she does not even look at the stage, preferring to scrutinize those sitting in the boxes). All this is designed to reflect her artificiality (this is apparently why Aleksandrov makes her laugh in a rather unnatural way: her laughter is vulgar, yet at the same time lays claim to being a "trilling coloratura"). Genuine creators are, in contrast, natural and unrefined (Kostia and Dunia). In *Volga-Volga* the image of the satirical bureaucrat Byvalov follows the same pattern of incongruity with one's social role, except that Byvalov aspires to be the best at "management" rather than the arts, which is why he is juxtaposed as an example of a "bad manager" to creative types from outside his circle.

If Elena is "the face of yesterday" of the masses as perceived in 1934 (when the memory of NEP was still vivid), then Tarakanov from *A Musical Story* is "the face of yesterday" of the masses from the second half of the 1930s (with the inevitable move from a "luxurious" flat to a communal apartment). The modern face of the masses is presented in minute detail in *A Musical Story*: they are an artistic, talented, and cultured "mass," one and all in love with classical music. The opposition between Govorkov and Tarakanov is sustained throughout the film. At the start of the story Govorkov, a taxi driver, spends an evening in the theater, and at the end Tarakanov, also a taxi driver, sits in his car waiting for passengers to come out of the theater after a performance, in exactly the same spot where the opening episode of the film took place. The opera theater is a place where everyone (even the neighbors from the communal apartment) ends up at a certain point in the film—except for Tarakanov. Tarakanov does not participate in the shared "artistic process," although even the head of the local trade union committee takes part in it, though unable to sing, overweight, and constantly wiping sweat from his forehead. The head of the committee is a comical character, unlike the grotesquely satirical Tarakanov. Still, Tarakanov constantly talks of "culture" and "culturedness." One might say that he is "in his element," verbally, when he says "mass consumption." This, for example, is how he speaks of his gift for the woman he loves: "Cologne is not a luxury, but an item of mass consumption and of a cultured life." Tarakanov's views on "cultivation" form an entire encyclopedia of "philistinism" as perceived in the late 1930s: they are materialistic, in contrast to the romantic ideas of real artists; they are pretentiously-profound ("fate is a life stimulus in the dimension of scholarly disputes") and "bureaucratic" (Tarakanov suggests to Klava that they "get registered," that is, get married, without saying to her even once that he loves her, as Govorkov does). Tarakanov's speech register is that of the cliché, evidence of his lack of sensitivity to words. The speech of a philistine, so thoroughly explored in Zoshchenko's texts, has the effect it has because of the superimposition of different discursive layers that by definition cannot overlap. As a result, the words are always "misplaced": "I, Klavdiia Vasil'evna, in the sense of family life, am a person who is reliable and categorical." Satirical characters are (literally) sheer nonsense because everything in them is in conflict: the personal and the socially defined, their social function and their appearance (suffice it to remember the roles played by Erast Garin and Sergei Martinson, highly eccentric character actors, both leading figures of the Meyerhold theater company), their social function and their speech, even their social function and their surnames (a man in love is called "Tarakanov," recalling the word for "cockroach," *tarakan*; a composer is called "Kerosinov"). This discrepancy is the result of the hero's groundless claims to a social role that is "not his." In Tarakanov's case these claims become part of the character's very being. Tarakanov is grotesquely pretentious, as, for example, in the episode during the "Polar Ball", in which he tells "Klavdiia Vasil'evna" how much he loves "all things beautiful and demands from love beauty above all," how he changed "the trivial name Fedor," that his "backward parents" had given him, and took "the beautiful and mysterious name Alfred," how every day between four and six in the afternoon he "works on himself, and then enjoys a free and cultured leisure time." It is noteworthy that the philistine is called "a fool" both in the film (by Klava, when she is being ironic) and in critical reviews ("this hopeless and complete fool, wrapping himself in a robe of importance and significance"[11]). Clearly this word is imprecise here: in fact, any satirical character is a "fool" by definition (if he were clever, he would not be an object of satire).

The social and aesthetic function of a satirical character is much more important. It is no accident in Soviet comedy that there is a clear demarcation between satirical and humorous characters. In *Jolly Fellows*, Elena and her "bourgeois circle" are satirical characters, while Karl Ivanovich and the touring Paraguayan artist are humorous characters. Byvalov is a satirical character in *Volga-Volga*, while the pilot is a humorous one. In *A Musical Story*, Tarakanov is a satirically painted figure, while the sweat-wiping chairman of the local trade union committee and the amateur Onegin are humorous characters; in *A Tale of the Siberian Land* the pianist Olenich is satirized, while his gluttonous colleague, a violinist, is, undoubtedly, a humorous character.

---

[11] Ibid., p. 33.

Such clear delineation is linked to the diverse functionality of humor and satire in Soviet comedy. Soviet satire was always an image of what the state declares today to be "yesterday's." Hence the persistent categorization of "negative aspects of our reality" as "vestiges of the past": they are, as it were, still present today, but already defined as "the past," and thus implicitly eliminated. The entire potency of the statement is directed at the future in the present (as stated in the official definition of Socialist Realism, "life in its revolutionary development"). Soviet satirical comedy is a continual process of de-realization, of a change in how reality is to be perceived. Here we have focused on the changing image of the masses in the eyes of state authorities, as illustrated in the way that the musical heritage is portrayed in Soviet musical comedies of the 1930s. Party spirit (*partiinost'*) now defined the authorities' strategy with respect to the masses, while the masses themselves were now perceived by the authorities through the prism of popular spirit (*narodnost'*). The dynamics depicted above manifest the aesthetic phenomenon of socialist mimesis.

Zhdanov and the Muses

We started with a monologue of the masses (workers' correspondents on music and theater), then discussed a monologue of the authorities (newspaper editorials), and now we will turn to a dialogue of a special kind: between the authorities and composers. We will start with a socialist realist text of a different genre: "A Stenographic Report of the Conference of Soviet Musicians at the Central Committee of the All-Union Communist Party (Bolsheviks)."[12] The session convened in mid-January 1948 and lasted for nearly three days.

This is a somewhat special dialogue. One side in it was represented by the Secretary for Ideology of the Central Committee, Andrei Zhdanov, and the other side was represented by thirty participants in "the debate," as one of them defined the interaction. The word "debate," however, does not quite reflect the nature of what happened there, since at this "conference" there was no "keynote presentation." There was only the opening speech by Zhdanov. However, this opening speech was delivered by Zhdanov not quite on his own behalf, as it were. Rather, he spoke as an interpreter of the Central Committee's decree "On Vano Muradeli's opera *The Great Friendship*," which had been passed on the eve of the session. Zhdanov's aesthetic program quite closely follows the pattern set twenty years previously:

---

[12] *Soveshchanie deiatelei*. Subsequent references are to this edition with page numbers in brackets.

there is not a single memorable tune in the opera. The music does not reach the audience... The replacement of musical harmony with improvisations that are both discordant and very noisy results in the opera being mostly a muddled mixture of strident sound components... stormy, discordant, and often cacophonic interventions, getting on the nerves of listeners and violently perturbing their mood... a depressing effect of lack of harmony... the music is confusing, boring, much poorer in content and much less beautiful than ordinary folk music... The vocal part of the opera is weak and does not stand up to critical comparison with the richness of tunes and range of the singers' voices that we've learned to expect from classical opera... The music has a shocking effect on the audience. Some verses and episodes have an elegiac or half-harmonious character; some are potentially melodious, but they are suddenly interrupted by *fortissimo* noise and shouting, so that one cannot help but being reminded of a construction site with excavators, stone crushers, and cement mixers operating. These noises, alien to the normal human ear, disorganize the listener. (5–6)

Constant appeals to "the normal human ear" and naturalism in the descriptions of one's own perception of "degraded music" suggest that Zhdanov feels personally offended by his inability to comprehend the "cacophony," that he himself suffers from the "muddle," and wants to bring music back to the "lost paradise"—to "ordinary folk music, beautiful and rich in content," to "the wealth of melodies and the vocal range of classical opera." Here Zhdanov speaks, indeed, on behalf of "the broad masses of workers," who were nowhere close to understanding classical music, let alone this "musical muddle." It is also worth noting that the Secretary of the Central Committee is ready and strangely able to talk about music, using musical terminology with ease (he uses terms such as atonality, dissonance, consonance). Zhdanov is prepared to speak with confidence in front of leading Soviet composers, conductors, professors of the conservatories of Moscow and Leningrad, and the Bolshoi Theater's leading performers and soloists. Not only that; he accuses others of "ignorance and unprofessionalism in matters of music" (p. 133). Zhdanov's status is the least likely explanation for this "courage." Even as Central Committee secretary he would understand that by "giving music lessons" to Shostakovich, he might find himself in quite an unenviable (or downright ridiculous) position. Stalin himself, who several years later decided to try his hand at linguistics, opened his famous *Marxism and the Problems of Linguistics* by acknowledging that he lacked a professional background in the specific field of linguistics. But the fervor of Zhdanov's speeches was grounded, it would appear, in his complete conviction that he was right. This stance can be explained (however paradoxically) not by the fact of his position in the Central Committee, but—on the contrary—by this being the position of "a regular listener" who has the right not only to convey his opinion to musicians but also to demand that they respect his taste as being representative of that of the masses. One might say that Zhdanov assumes here the role of a "quintessential workers' correspondent," one of those "club members" quoted above, except a generation later, when they have already matured enough to be able to listen, finally, to Tchaikovsky. Hence the full range of invectives (fully in the spirit of the old Proletkult style) was directed at composers who "serve the solely individualistic concerns of a small group of select aesthetes" (p. 136), as was the demand for an art that would be "natural, beautiful, and human" instead of these "ugly, false, vulgar, often simply pathological" works that are "alien to the popular masses and designed for... 'the elite'" (p. 137). Zhdanov voices the opinion of the Central Committee—or rather "the people's opinion"—when formulating the laws of an art that would be expressive of "popular spirit": "Ignoring the demands of the people, its spirit, and its creativity means that the formalist trend in music has a distinctly expressed anti-popular character" (p. 137); "the people do not need music that they do not understand. Composers need to point the finger not at the people, but at themselves" (p. 144); "music that intentionally ignores normal human emotions, that traumatizes one's psyche and nervous system, cannot be popular, it cannot serve society" (p. 145). And finally, "Not everything that is accessible is a work of genius, but every work of genius is accessible, and the more accessible it is to the broad masses, the more it is a sign of genius" (p. 143).

This is evidence of "violence against art," but is a result of an earlier "violence of art against life." In Zhdanov's understanding it is not just an aesthetic problem, a "deviation of natural, healthy forms of music" (p. 142); nor is it just an ideological problem when dealing with an "unserious and wild eagerness to swap the heritage of Soviet musical culture for the pitiful rags of modern bourgeois art" (p. 147). Rather it is an almost physiological matter, since "a deviation from the norms of musical art is an offense against the foundations of not only a normal functioning of musical tones, but the very foundations of the physiology of normal human auditory capacities... Weak, disharmonious music undoubtedly disturbs the correct psychological and physiological functioning of a human being" (p. 146).

In this, the authorities manifested a certain "realism" as they verbalized the intentions of the masses. The "realist trend in music" that Zhdanov was calling for was in this sense realistic not only stylistically but also conceptually. This extreme (pragmatic) realism might be called an aesthetic strategy of power. Hence the appeal to "the populist spirit," which also includes a mass culture of laughter.

The physiology of a beautiful person with an "all-round education" demands that the world around them be "beautiful" (including the world of sounds). Hence the demand by "the Central Committee of the Bolsheviks" that music "be beautiful and graceful... We stand for beautiful, graceful music" (p. 143). Hence the designation of "innovation" as a "drilling engine or a musical gas chamber" (p. 143), as "Herostratus's attempt to destroy the temple of art" (p. 146). It had taken years for the mass consciousness as formulated in the writings of the workers' correspondents to come to recognize that "beautiful and graceful" are adjectives that can be applied to classical music. Now Zhdanov, pointing to the "growth of the artistic taste and demands of the Soviet people," had the right to demand that they have "their own, Soviet 'Mighty Group'," with reference to the famous nineteenth-century group of distinguished composers (pp. 147–8).

Since opera was, according to Zhdanov, "the highest synthetic form of art, which combines within itself the achievements of all the main types of musical and vocal art" (p. 7), it found itself "in the firing-line of the musical front." The synthetic nature of opera fitted comfortably into the synthetic project of the authorities as they set out to turn life into a *Gesamtkunstwerk*: it was exactly in this way that Wagner had imagined a realization of his idea. The stage of an "academic opera theater" became an ideal replacement for "mass amateur creativity" (*Jolly Fellows, Volga-Volga*) "in the city square." At the same time, classical works, having proved their victory over time, were perceived by the authorities as an ideal (although as yet unachievable) exemplar for associating themselves with the eternal as they were busy exercising their main function: self-representation.

A True Soviet Classic (A Symphonic Oratorio)

From the merry jazz of Kostia Potekhin who "made it to the Bolshoi Theater" to the imperial sounds of the "Song of the Volga," from a synthesis between a symphony orchestra and a folk choir to a mass fascination with the classics, from a talented performance of classical compositions to the creation of one's own classical compositions (a symphonic oratorio): this is the path of the "development of popular spirit in the Soviet arts." This path is traceable in the history of Soviet musical comedy, and its foundations were set in the early days of the formation of the Socialist Realist project.[13]

March 25, 1936 was the opening night of Ivan Dzerzhinskii's opera *Quiet Flows the Don* (*Tikhii Don*) in the Bolshoi Theater. On the same evening, the creators of the opera met in the governmental suite of the theater with government representatives who had watched the performance. It was on this occasion that Stalin's laconic challenge to Soviet art was voiced for probably the first time: "It is time we had our own Soviet classics." Now, the idea of "learning from the classics" that had previously been propagated by the now extinct RAPP had a definite goal. In the culture of late Stalinism, the problem of the "Soviet classics" became a central aesthetic problem. In 1951, the editor in chief of *Literaturnaia gazeta* Boris Riurikov proclaimed: "The writers of our country are facing the task of creating Soviet classics, Socialist Realist classics." A year later, the same idea was repeated by the chief director of the Bolshoi Theater, Nikolai Golovanov, in the article "For a Classical Soviet Opera": "We are looking forward to the birth of the

---

[13] For a discussion of some trends in Soviet musical criticism of the time, see Ryzhkin and Safarova, "Sovetskaia muzykal′naia estetika."

'Mussorgskys' of our time." The same kind of appeals (to create "classic Soviet artworks") were coming from the Academy of the Arts, which had been reorganized just a few years previously, in 1947. The periodical *Architecture of the USSR* called for the creation of "eternal, classical examples of Soviet architecture."

"Soviet classics" is a formulation of the relationship between Socialist Realist culture and eternity, a belated answer given by Socialist Realism to the challenge of the avant-garde. But most importantly, it was an attempt to bring together highbrow and lowbrow culture.

Ivan Pyr'ev's *A Tale of the Siberian Land* is probably his most complex film in terms of genre. At its core is a synthesis of melodrama and comedy that can be explained by his attempt to convey an internal thematic dichotomy between the "folk" and the "classical."

The film is built on a seemingly irreconcilable juxtaposition of two dimensions: a conservatory and a tearoom. However, by 1947, such a juxtaposition already belonged to the past, to an era before popular spirit won the day. Were this juxtaposition of the two elements absolute in Pyr'ev's feature film, it would not make much sense to turn to it after a discussion of Aleksandrov's and Ivanovskii's musical comedies. But the *Tale* offers an essentially new level of "resolving the problem of popular spirit." In it the two dimensions are not so much opposed as conjoined. The time of "learning from the classics" is over, and it would not be right to claim that "the tearoom was supposed to teach the Conservatory art, in all seriousness."[14] It is no longer about "teaching," but about unification.

The opening scene of the film is set during a short lull in the battle of Breslau. The accompanying soundtrack is that of a folk song that is evolving into a classical, symphonic score. In the ruins of a destroyed house where the soldiers are singing the folk song, senior lieutenant Andrei Balashov starts performing a classical piece on a piano, over which the soundtrack brings in a symphony orchestra. The pensive fighters who were singing "our song, the Siberian one," are immediately visibly transformed by the classical music. Their faces become sterner, more animated—and they launch an attack. There is no opposition between the two types of music. On the contrary, there is an organic transition from a folk song to symphonic music. The two elements merging into one sublime element is illustrated in the film by unambiguous images: as the sound of classical music becomes more and more overwhelming, the warriors' facial features are incrementally more monumental, until they freeze completely, just like Vuchetich's sculpture of the soldier-liberator in Berlin's Treptower Park.

Not an opposition between the tearoom and the conservatory, then, but their unification. The era of a "nihilistic attitude to the cultural heritage" (*Jolly Fellows*) was now over. In fact, there is not even a transition between the two spaces. Both

---

[14] Turovskaia, "I. A. Pyr'ev," p. 140.

are united by the central characters of the film, who feel completely at home in the conservatory and the tearoom alike. As we remember, in *Jolly Fellows* the plot was driven by the motif of the "creators" from among the people being pushed away from the "high" cultural space, whose "sanctity" they consistently profaned. According to the new high Socialist Realist canon, the tearoom and the conservatory are in no way inferior or superior to each other. Tellingly, it is the ideologically "alien" character of Olenich who calls everything that happens in the tearoom "buffoonery" (which is exactly the word Trubyshkin uses at the beginning of *Volga-Volga* before he undergoes "reforging"). Olenich contrasts Natasha Malinina, whose voice holds a promise of "fame, America, Europe" to Andrei Balashov, the "tavern accordionist."

It turns out that there is hardly any difference between the two spaces, that of the conservatory and that of the tearoom. True, the conservatory is the territory of ladies in white opera-length gloves, velvet evening gowns and furs, and of gentlemen in dinner jackets who speak Russian like actors of the Maly Theater ("doubtlessly, dear col-league"), while the tearoom is frequented by a different crowd. Despite this, both locations are merely manifestations of the same—Soviet—cultural space. It is not by chance that the motif of space is a key one in the film. The characters are constantly moving within the borders of the country. Balashov leaves the frontline and goes to Moscow; then he leaves Moscow to go to a construction site in Siberia, from whence he goes to the Far North, which he then leaves to go back to Moscow, where he triumphs as a performer, only to return to Siberia. Natasha Malinina follows in his steps (like some kind of "Decembrist wife," Olenich sneers). "Foreign countries," "America, Europe"—this is Olenich's space. The year 1947 falls within the period of fighting against "kowtowing to the West," and there is evidence of that in the film, but the stronger the opposition between "the Soviet" and "the non-Soviet," the stronger the integrative fervor in the description of what is Soviet. It is as if the symphonic oratorio "brings all of Russia together." This hymn to Siberia is composed above the Polar Circle and performed in Moscow, before it returns to its "native land," the Siberian city of Krasnoiarsk. A meeting between the Conservatory and the Tearoom is an illustration of this new unity, when the artists of the Conservatory "gift their art" to the masses:

>I travelled far and wide across my mother land,
>But now I am in love with this corner of it.
>Our greetings, and honors, and respect
>Go to you, victorious builders.
>"The masses" express their deep gratitude as they whirl around in a waltz:
>Thank you for your art,
>We are always happy to see you here.

Pass on our feelings to people in Moscow,
Come and visit us more often.

In both the historical sense (the integration of the classics and folk art) and the spatial sense (the unified Soviet territory), the *Tale* is a demonstration of the great potential for integration that Socialist Realism carries within itself.

The tearoom's suitability for "high art" is one of the key motifs in the film. The audience does not yet know anything about the future of the central character when the "real" folk music is "purged" of its "bawdiness." There is a scene where Andrei Balashov receives the gift of an accordion from a "merry fellow" who has just been reproached by a "rube" for bawling something that was "not pretty": "The accordion can tell more about beauty than a person can, but you..." This episode of presenting an accordion to a better player marks a point at which "real folk music" is sacralized: everybody joins in a song about "our Siberia." Just as everyone in the tearoom is impressed by Balashov's art, "everyone" (that is, two characters—Burmak and Nasten'ka) is in awe of his symphonic oratorio.

The tearoom is the foundation of the Soviet space. "Here," Andrey tells Natasha, "you see just a tearoom, while I see the people, our simple Russian people.... They helped me believe that I am still capable of something, that I am a musician.... They come here as if it were a celebration, and demand my music, my songs." The tearoom enriches the conservatory, but the conservatory is not a "passive object"; it is an elevated image of these "simple Russian people." Balashov's symphonic oratorio is a beautiful, inspiring, "true" image of the masses in the eyes of the authorities. In other words, it is an embodiment of popular spirit. At the same time, Olenich's "performative mastery" is condemned as just showing off: "You just keep hitting the keys. You are living only for yourself, admiring your own playing and loving only yourself," Natasha tells him. "So that means I am a selfish philistine?" Olenich quite reasonably inquires. "Yes," his beloved answers. Needless to say, Olenich is not as much a "philistine" as Tarakanov or Kerosinov is, but is quite similar to "the singer Elena" from *Jolly Fellows* (she is talentless, he "follows technique"). He is nothing but a very skilled performer. As Balashov's teacher says, he "brilliantly imitates preset patterns," but he is by no means a "creator." It is not by chance that the pianist Balashov becomes a composer, that is, a "creator," while Olenich remains "just a pianist." A technique "without the soul" is identical to a total lack of talent (which is the case of "the singer Elena"). Who needs "skill" if it does not "elevate" the masses, if it does not express anything, in other words, if it does not come "from the people"?

Just as *Volga-Volga* was a film about a song, the *Tale* is a film about a symphonic oratorio. The genre is the film's protagonist, and as such, it sets claim to its rights. At the same time, we should not exaggerate the distance between a song and a symphonic oratorio. The *Tale* was already foreshadowed in the magisterial sounds of the Song in *Volga-Volga* when the melody was rearranged by a "talented Young Pioneer." In itself, the genre of a symphonic oratorio is based on an antinomy, with an inherent tension between instruments and voice. However, as pointed out above, the contraposition of genre is also the foundation of Pyr'ev's film: the film about music has the word "tale" in its title. The oxymoron is resolved by a significant broadening of the realm of the Word. There is, of course, an expansion of the Word in music: Balashov's "artistic development" is depicted in the film as a progression from words to the music that will accompany these words. But there is more: as the film progresses, the characters' own speech turns into a "tale." Whenever verbal exchanges exceed three sentences, the dialogues turn into a declamation, which in one instance then progresses to a poem, and in another, to a song. The "symphonic oratorio" itself is a declamation set to music, celebrating the endless expanses of Siberia. In its essence, Balashov's work is an extreme instance of verbalized music. The progression from word to song to opera and, finally, to a programmatic piece of topical symphonic music culminates in a complete victory of the recital of the sacred Word accompanied by a symphony orchestra. The *Tale* has nothing of the buffoonery of Aleksandrov's early comedies. Instead it produces the sublime image of the people.

A synthesis of high and low in which the "low" is raised to the level of the "classical" explains the reduction of the comic elements in the *Tale*. The comic requires that such extremes be at least present, but such synthesis is self-sufficient. Only declamation can emerge from it, as the word is transformed into a "tale," into an epic. This is potentially not a comic situation but rather a heroic one, which does not find a genre framing in the *Tale*, which itself is built on an intersection of comedy and melodrama. It is this generic incompatibility that makes the film "unbearably schematic":[15] this is a case of genre aphasia. But this aphasia is not the result of a wrongly chosen optics by the maker of the film. In the Soviet epic, comedy is reduced to a limited range of forms not because of an external "pressure from above," but because it cannot find adequate channels (forms) of expression.

Thus, at first (1934) it was made clear that the people love the kind of music that is produced by Kostia Potekhin's shepherd pipe in *Jolly Fellows*, and no one needed classical music. Bach was only good for breaking eggs on his nose when practicing singing, and ballerinas were at their best as extras in a scene when bedraggled jazz-players filled up the stage of the Bolshoi Theater.

Then a shift occurred in what was supposed to be the right attitude toward music. Now, it was the people who created the right kind of music, regardless of whether it was a work for a symphony orchestra or for a folk choir. Only a synthesis of the different genres would give birth to the true Song (*Volga-Volga*, 1938).

Then this thesis was reformulated more precisely. In order to create the true Song, people learned, one had to study. Perhaps an academic course lasting twenty years, as comrade Byvalov postulated, was not always necessary, but at least a year

---

[15] Ibid.

in the conservatory was a must—and there had to be some talent, too. The Song was no longer the same, either. Now, the Song most loved by "the broad masses of workers" was classical music (*A Musical Story*, 1940).

Balance was everything. Not only jazz but opera, too, had to be defended against orthodox conservatory professors. Granted, these professors turned out to be capable of "changing their pattern of thinking," they responded to the demands of "the broad masses of workers" and were able to manifest an enviable tolerance in matters aesthetic, from Handel to operetta. Their own hearts may have been dedicated to Handel, but the hearts of their happy children accepted "anything that is talented" (*Anton Ivanovich Gets Angry*).

And finally, as Stalin announced, "our Soviet classics" were born, a synthesis of folk song, symphonic music, and patriotic declamation. Traditional distinctions between genres were removed, and there was no longer an opposition between what the masses liked and high-brow culture. The dialectical synthesis that replaced them culminated in a symphonic oratorio where there was no jazz, no popular song, no opera, no operetta. It is a new phenomenon that cannot be reduced to its constitutive elements—a true *Gesamtkunstwerk*.

The strategy of a dialectical removal of oppositions is, of course, a strategy of transformed comedy across the full range of manifestations: from a discrepancy between the persona and the role to carnival shifts in the relationship between high and low. Transformations of this kind became inscribed in Soviet musical comedy like growth rings in a tree trunk. One can trace them to reconstruct the memory of the new Soviet comic genres and, more broadly, the emergence of the Socialist Realist popular spirit. This pattern is displayed here so clearly because it is superimposed upon a grid of previously valid (in this case, musical) genre forms.

The erasing device of Socialist Realism had a clear "constructive potential," but it could only work when there was complete concordance between art and life. If the latter refuses to comply with the demands of a total political and aesthetic doctrine, the unified process of life-building is disturbed and there is "muddle instead of music." The erasing device stops working, and the original memory of the genres, the original grid, resurfaces. The layers of the palimpsest start peeling off, and the face of a singing and laughing authority is exposed.

"You'd Need to Study Twenty Years to be Able to Sing Like That": Twenty Years Later

But Socialist Realism, simultaneously an encoding device of both the masses' desires and the voice of authority, transformed the consciousness of the masses in a very special way. These transformations included, of course, the culture of laughter and the comic. We will conclude this outline of the problems of populism and laughter in Soviet musical comedy with a comparison of two films: *Volga-Volga* (1938) and *A Carnival Night* (1956) in order to point out some essential characteristics of state-appropriated laughter.

There is an almost twenty-year slice of history between these films. They reflect two distinct moments of Soviet history and culture. *Volga-Volga* is an exemplar of the Socialist Realist aesthetics of the 1930s, and of the classic canon of Socialist Realism. *A Carnival Night* brings with it the spirit of Khrushchev's Thaw and reflects a new version of the canon. However, the two films prove to be so similar that the second must be considered as a sequel to the first one. Both films portray the same motif of the popular masses and the collective creative spirit in opposition to the bureaucratic "scornful attitude towards people" and "a lack of belief in the creativity of the people." Both films portray a victory of the joyous, laughing collective over a swaggering, boring bureaucracy.

How do the festive masses in *Volga-Volga* occupy themselves? Exclusively with amateur performances: singing, dancing, and other amusements. Nothing else. The characters in *Volga-Volga* are identified by professions (a letter carrier, a water carrier, a yardman, a militiaman, a cook, a waiter, an accounts clerk, and so on), but none of them actually works. The letter carrier refuses to send telegrams; the water carrier is drunk all the time; the yardman sleeps; the militiaman does not protect anyone, nor does he preserve order; the cooks and waiters in the restaurant, instead of serving patrons, sing about their "winning the many sweet victories on the food-front"; the accounts clerk spends his time with an amateur symphony orchestra. All of the action supposedly takes place in the busiest hours of the workday, but all the characters joyously and habitually occupy themselves with non-work activities during work time, as appears to be the norm here. It would seem that all these singing cooks and instrument-playing accountants are supposed to abolish the basic rule of "amateur artistic performance," which is normally understood as leisure time creative activity.

In *A Carnival Night*, the situation is radicalized. We see characters for whom amateur performance is work; it is their actual profession. They organize the carnival the way people organize a theatrical production, a carnival in which there is no main carnivalesque happening, no participatory event, but instead there are actor-performers and spectators of the show presented on stage and in the auditorium. Let us return, however, to *Volga-Volga*, twenty years earlier. The characters here are marked as "simple people," and in this they differ from the bureaucrat, Byvalov. One could suppose that amateur performance is, in fact, the work of the town's residents. The bureaucrat does not hinder them in this; he only prevents them from going to Moscow to a big amateur artists' festival.

The festival in Moscow goes on without regard to time. One could even say that it goes on *all the time*. The time of the trip to Moscow is deliberate, and each day of the six days' journey—a working week—is noted by special captions during the film. At the same time, the temporal boundaries of the Moscow festival are not at all clear; the characters are summoned to the festival, and nothing is said about how long it will last. When the Melkovodsk delegation arrives, the festival is already going on. While they search for the author of the song about the Volga, the festival shows no sign of ending. The presidium and spectators remain seated, although absolutely nothing is happening on the stage. What we are seeing is a permanent holiday: the spectators and members of the presidium enter and leave, but the plot action takes place elsewhere: behind the scenes, on a boat, even under the presidium's table. The character of the performance—which here is called an amateur artistic festival—strongly resembles everything that takes place in Melkovodsk. This is, as it were, a microcosm of Soviet reality, completely submerged in a world of amateur performance, of joyous creative activity and *dolce far niente*. The temporal aspect of events is weakened at the expense of the actualization of the spatial aspect: time turns into space, which is measured by the degree of proximity to the capital. Space is thus future-oriented. One could assume that all this "joyous holiday of free creative activity," when no one works, is in fact the future—Communism.

Through the whole film we see movement in a utopian space: the space of perfected utopia, such as Moscow appears to be. The contrast of movement and immobility is central throughout the film. The steamer *Sevriuga*, the ferry, and the rafts upon which the heroes are transported are demonstratively in decline. They constantly break down: a wire flies off, pipes fall down, decks collapse. Every aspect of the movement toward Moscow is uncomfortable, but with the transfer to the motor ship *Iosif Stalin*, dispatched from Moscow, a striking change takes place to the interior: the yardmen, letter carriers, and water carriers, now also outwardly transformed, spend their time in cabins furnished with luxurious furniture, draperies, and fittings.

The summit of the harmonious space, its center, is the "competition headquarters," which is encamped on a stage and pompously decorated with Soviet slogans and the medallion-like USSR state coat of arms, with members of the presidium sitting dressed in national costumes of the Soviet republics. What we see is a poster. Space in the film is, as it were, completed on the stage area, directed toward the proscenium. All the action of the film has been taking place on a riverbank or on a ship's deck, constantly bearing toward Moscow and finally coming to a climax on the stage.

So, is what we are seeing a carnival, or theater? Socialist Realism engenders performance of a unique kind. This performance can be briefly characterized thus: carnival takes place on the court stage. Or, we are seeing court theater in the form of a carnival, or a carnival in the form of court theater. This book is about how this transformation became possible. As Bakhtin pointed out, the popular carnival culture resists the official one. But the phenomenon of Socialist Realist laughter forces one to ponder the source of the "radical populism of the carnival." And from this begins the symbiosis that engenders the unique phenomenon of a laughing ideology, a laughing state, and laughing power. The laughter of the authorities is so radical that it is practically impossible to separate it from that of the laughing masses. Moreover, the plot of both *Volga-Volga* and *A Carnival Night* is based on the premise that authority defends the laughing masses from the unsmiling bureaucrat. The intentions of the carnival directly coincide with the intentions of authority. The bureaucrat Byvalov in *Volga-Volga* is condemned for not wanting to see the talent of the laughing masses; the bureaucrat Ogurtsov in *A Carnival Night* is condemned for being boring, for his unwillingness to laugh with everyone else.

The figure of the bureaucrat reflects that which the authorities do not want at present, and it exposes the former face of authority. Earlier, in the time before Byvalov, they did not believe in the creative potential of the people, but now, with Byvalov as a comic character, they have changed their faces, traded their masks and voices. Thus, the boring past is abolished. Now, as Stalin said, "life has become better, life has become merrier." Something similar occurs in *A Carnival Night*. Before the bureaucrat Ogurtsov appeared, people misunderstood the notion of the typical, and many typical characters were boring and joyless. Now things are different. The boring past is being abolished again, and the joyous future is coming. Rephrasing Marx's famous idea that mankind merrily and laughingly parts with its past, one might say that in Soviet comedy, authority laughingly parts with its past. More precisely, authority changes its mask, changes its old image, laughing all the while. That is, using the mechanism of the carnival, parting with its past, it dies and is reborn into a new shape. Soviet comedy is the mechanism of legitimization of the process of re-creation and resurrection of authority. Thus, laughter acquires the function of a cleansing device. Stalinist literature, film, and painting are the eyes and ears of the authorities, their voice and optical instruments, but they are all these things also for the masses, for whom the whole spectacle is designed. In the action one sees on the screen, power is the only actor, and the only "happening" is the very existence of power. But the spectators are not outsiders here.

The spectators of the film are simultaneously the spectators of this carnival-theater. At the very beginning we find ourselves on the proscenium and see a theatrical prologue, with a direct address to the spectator, with all the attributes of a theatrical performance, where not only are the actors introduced, but the characters are also described ("here you see Byvalov.... He is a gigantic bureaucrat, he is played...by the actor Il'inskii"). It is exactly the same in the finale: in *Volga-Volga* the actors, located squarely on the stage, turn to the spectators with words of thanks and explain the moral of the performance they have just seen. *A Carnival Night* ends with "Comrade Ogurtsov" addressing the viewers. This theatrical projection is there throughout the course of the action: in *Volga-Volga*, for example, the actors mostly speak directly to the camera (that is, to the spectator in the audience), rather than to each other. Nonetheless, it would be hard to find two things more fundamentally opposed to each other than carnival and theater.

The level of Socialist Realist laughter was continuously adjusted to reflect the level of mass culture from the lower reaches, such level at the time being fundamentally different from that of the times of Rabelais, as described by Bakhtin. In Socialist Realism this is no longer a different culture. The process of the "degradation of laughter" that Bakhtin discussed has been completed: the previously opposing cultures have emerged together in a new synthesis. This is the source of the modern spectator's sense of a theatrical "playing at carnival" and of the miscalculated effort to draw the Stalin-era spectator into the events of the motion picture. We can hardly say, however, that the spectators for whom all of this is being played on the screen find themselves outside the performance. The nature of the characters' relations on-screen had to be quite accessible to the mass spectator: Strelka and Trubyshkin relate to each other like children, calling each other fools and each trying to shout down the other, rather like the childish taunts of "it takes one to know one, it takes one to know one!" Viewers are presented with demonstrations of the indomitable energy and strength of the collective, popular art; they recognize a bureaucrat; they are introduced to a couple in love. Soviet comedy allows us to reconstruct not only the portrait of the authorities but also that of the mass audience, as it was perceived by the authorities.

It is significant that in *Volga-Volga*, with so many characters, there are no signs at all of anyone having a family. There are no wives, no husbands. There are only the two main characters in love with each other, which provides fertile ground for comic situations. All the same, the feeling of family life is palpable in everything that happens in the film. Essentially, the collective replaces the family. It is the same in *A Carnival Night*. The presence of such a big "family" of characters compensates for the absence of any conventional family. It is true that Ogurtsov in *A Carnival Night* reveals that he is married, but the context of this statement (to "This is a dance about beauty, youth, and love," he responds "I know. I'm married myself'") reveals this declaration as having "zero inflection," a significant absence of a trait.

The main distinctive feature of the amateur world of the collective is the fact that it is not mediated by someone else. A bureaucrat, on the contrary, apprehends the world through mediation. Byvalov, for example, naturally tends to use indirect forms of communication: He talks on the telephone with "the garage," when the chauffer is just outside his window; he sends a "top secret" telegram. We can observe similar features in *A Carnival Night*.

Ogurtsov is the 1956 version of Comrade Byvalov, and the role is played by the same actor, Igor′ Ilinskii. Ogurtsov wants to organize the upcoming New Year's carnival according to the traditional canon, with a speech and lectures, and without "jokes" ("I don't like making jokes myself, and I won't allow other people to, either"). But in *A Carnival Night* we find ourselves already in a space of perfected utopia. Strictly speaking, the very situation of this film is oxymoronic: the carnival is organized in a Palace of Culture, on stage. In *Volga-Volga* the carnival aspired to reach the stage, and reaching it was the culmination of the plot, which began on a city square. In *A Carnival Night* the stage is equivalent to the square. The transformation of the carnival into theater is complete. In *A Carnival Night*, the stage itself, and the whole Palace of Culture, are the only setting for all of the onscreen action. The characters are transformed, they change clothes, but all this takes place exclusively on the stage, in the wings, or else under the stage. One could say that, in general, "the making of a spectacle" is the favorite plot of Soviet film comedies, and its preferred location is "behind the scenes." This is true of *Jolly Fellows*, *Volga-Volga*, *The Circus* (*Tsirk*, 1936; dir. Grigorii Aleksandrov), *A Musical Story* (*Muzykal'naia istoriia*, 1940; dir. Aleksandr Ivanovskii and Gerbert Rappaport), *Anton Ivanovich Gets Angry*, *A Tale of the Siberian Land*, *A Carnival Night*, and others. Thus, the carnival takes place on stage, and has footlights and wings.

It can be said that *A Carnival Night* begins where *Volga-Volga* ended twenty years earlier. The object of ridicule in both films is identical—the bureaucrat played by Igor' Il'inskii. But the bureaucrat is an authority figure, and the films make it possible for the authorities to distance themselves from their own outdated mask. Whereas in the usual carnival practice social roles are "abolished," in the theatricalized carnival of Socialist Realism they are accentuated. Hence the distinct recognizability of the masks, most of all that of the bureaucrat; it is through him that authority changes its appearance. This singling out and clearly marking the bureaucrat are signs of an abrupt change in the focus of the ideological "chronotope." Just yesterday the authorities had spoken with Byvalov's voice, but now they have turned "popular," and thus they speak with Strelka's voice. Just yesterday the authorities had spoken with Ogurtsov's voice (in his very words, "music should lead," "the musical collective should be inspired by the masses and serious," everything should be "typical [and] in the forms of life itself," and finally a direct quotation from Malenkov's address at the 19th Party Congress: "We need Gogols and Shchedrins"), but today he must appear ridiculous. The "bureaucrat" is always yesterday's face of authority. He is a sign of the change in the image of authority.

A reference to a "completed past" is imprinted in the very surname of the main satirical character in *Volga-Volga*—Byvalov. The idea of "something-that-used-to-happen-sometimes" (*byvalo*) grounds the film in a certain mode. It is not that something "was" (as a state of things), but rather, it "used to happen sometimes" (a reference to something indefinite that took place in the past). This also explains the fact that all satirical characters are obviously and tellingly lonely—something that is not true of positive ones. Positive characters are, by definition, members of a mass: they are "typical." A bureaucrat or a philistine cannot be typical, as per the well-known maxim regarding the depiction of negative phenomena in Soviet art: "The most important rule is to never generalize." A satirical character is there to "personalize" the negative, to individualize it. A bureaucrat and a philistine are the two images for an officially acceptable channeling of "negative discourse" in Soviet aesthetics: the bureaucrat embodies a negative image of authority, while the philistine embodies the negative image of the masses. Both are clearly defined. Characteristically, the most memorable images of the bureaucrat in Soviet film comedy are associated with Igor' Il'inskii, an actor beloved by audiences; it is his words from *Volga-Volga* and *A Carnival Night* that became popular sayings. This bureaucrat is not scary, and may be yesterday's face of authority, but he is still part and parcel of state power (despite his association with the past). He is not supposed to insult the authorities or evoke disgust in the audience (a disgusting character cannot be funny). The same can be said of the philistine characters. They are not there to insult the masses. Their function is to make the masses laugh at the image of what they themselves were yesterday.

The strategy of laughter in Socialist Realism finds its own forms of likeness, "a representation of life in the forms of life itself." This is laughter that is both entertaining and explanatory. For example, in *Volga-Volga*, almost all of the basic comic effects are built on a preliminary announcement of an event, with its subsequent literal realization. The pilot says that the steamer will not run aground, and then it immediately runs aground; Strelka is swimming in the river and says, "I'm going to faint—water!" There and then, the boundless watery expanse of the river is shown full-screen; Strelka is told that her collective will "fall through" (that is, fail) at the competition in Moscow—and she immediately falls through the deck of the steamer. The space of entertaining laughter swallows up whatever does not fit into the space of satire. After twenty years of Soviet power in Melkovodsk there is no water supply, but there is a water carrier; the only telephone in the town doesn't work; the streets are not paved; the "express" telegram is taken on an old ferry; and there is only one old steamship, which America had gifted to Russia before Soviet times. None of these should be understood as objects of satire in *Volga-Volga*, but as something secondary, simply amusing. In *A Carnival Night* there are no such moments at all.

Satire is the flip side of heroism. In heroic mode, what is personal and what is assigned by one's social role coincide, but not in satire. Satire starts out from the heroic as a potential spiritual necessity of society, but artistically realizes this necessity in an unheroic situation. At the core of satire is the inadequacy of personal existence in relation to one's social role. This is why the "ego" of what Hegel calls the hero is present in real life only as an "empty swelling of subjectivity." The hero in satire follows a path of unrestrained self-affirmation in his subjective pretension (this is especially noticeable in *Volga-Volga* in Byvalov's continual self-affirmation: "my water carrier," "my system," "thanks to my responsive leadership," and, with complete absurdity, "How can there be misfortune, if I am here?"). But on the way to self-affirmation, the hero arrives at a point of complete self-repudiation. The main hero of a satirical work is the satirical hero—the bureaucrats Byvalov and Ogurtsov in *Volga-Volga* and *A Carnival Night*, respectively. All the other characters are located in a different space—a space of heroism that is required to support the satire. This is the space in which the new image that authority wishes to adopt becomes fixed. In fact, one might say that Soviet satirical comedy fixes only this moment when authority changes its "costume"; its main content is the striptease of authority. But from this comes also the second key feature of state-appropriated laughter: it is threatening. In the merriness of Soviet comedy there is a constant aggression that is aimed at the audience. Spectators must laugh, since a refusal to laugh is understood as a sign of dangerous dissent, a refusal to participate in a performance of authority, as an attempt to escape. A heroic note, whether in emotion or in style, always implies a threat.

Only humor is truly alien to the heroic-satirical world. This is why we see a process of constant degradation and reduction: from humor to amusement, from amusement to satire, and from satire to fervor and heroic emotion. This mechanism quite literally reveals itself in *A Carnival Night*, in stages, when at the insistence of Ogurtsov, the clowns' scene becomes at first unamusing, is afterwards reduced to an emotive gesture, and finally becomes a statement of heroic dedication.

Byvalov, who does not believe that there are native talents in his town, even when the letter carrier sings an operatic aria, declares: "You'd need to study twenty years to be able to sing like that." In fact, the letter carrier is the composer of the song about the Volga, about how in the songs from old days "we used to sing of our yearning, / But now it is of joy we sing." This time period—twenty years—was, as it turned out, prophetic. Exactly twenty years passed after the October Revolution before *Volga-Volga* appeared, and then another twenty before *A Carnival Night*. Over these years the Soviet song of joy matured, and Soviet art learned how to perform it—dancing, making merry, and laughing—in the carnival theater on the state-sanctioned grand stage.

The stunning success of *A Carnival Night*, one of the very few Soviet films that have remained enduringly popular, is a testimony to the triumph of the revitalized urban culture over primitive populism. It also demonstrates how a society that seemed to have forgotten how to laugh can emerge from the state of anabiosis in which it had spent years, made numb by the deadening *state laughter*—the product and instrument of a repressive political culture and totalitarian kitsch.

Bibliography

Abramskii, Isaak. *Smekh sil'nykh: O khudozhnikakh zhurnala* Krokodil (Moscow, 1977).
Afanas'ev, Aleksandr. "Iuridicheskie obychai. Po povodu vyzova Etnograficheskogo otdela Imperatorskogo Russkogo geograficheskogo obshchestva." In *Proiskhozhdenie mifa: Stat'i po fol'kloru, etnografii i mifologii* (Moscow, 1996).
Agamben, Giorgio. "Friendship." *Contretemps* 5 (December 2004).
Agamben, Giorgio. *The Highest Poverty: Monastic Rules and Form-of-Life*, translated by Adam Kotsko (Stanford: Stanford University Press, 2013).
Agamben, Giorgio. *Potentialities: Collected Essays in Philosophy*, edited, translated and introduction by Daniel Heller-Roazen (Stanford, California: Stanford University Press, 1999).
Agamben, Giorgio. *Profanations*, translated by Jeff Fort (New York: Zone Books, 2007).
Agamben, Giorgio. *State of Exception. Homo Sacer II.1*, translated by Kevin Attell (Chicago and London: University of Chicago Press, 2005).
Agamben, Giorgio. "Das unheilige Leben" (Interview mit Cornelia Vismann und Hanna Leitgeb). *Literaturen* 1 (2001).
Agamben, Giorgio. *The Use of Bodies. Homo Sacer IV.2*, translated by Kevin Attell (Stanford, California: Stanford University Press, 2016).
Akimov, Nikolai. "O komedii i teatre komedii." *Izvestiia*, April 10, 1940.
Akimov, Nikolai. "Trudnosti i perspektivy zhanra." *Oktiabr'* no. 6 (1958).
Alatyrtsev, M. "Pochva pod nogami.'" *Literaturnyi ezhenedel'nik* no. 8 (1923).
Alekseev, M. "Khudozhnik ispolnil svoi dolg." *Literaturnaia gazeta*, February 12, 1960.
Alexopoulos, Golfo. "Portrait of a Con Artist as a Soviet Man." *Slavic Review* 57, no. 4 (Winter 1998).
Alexopoulos, Golfo. "Soviet Citizenship, More or Less: Rights, Emotions, and States of Civic Belonging." *Kritika: Explorations in Russian and Eurasian History*. New Series 7, no. 3 (Summer 2006).
Alpers, Boris. [Boris Shkvarkin's *Vrednyi element*. Review]. *Repertuarnyi biulleten'* no. 2 (1927).
Alpers, Boris. "Zhanr sovetskoi komedii." *Sovetskoe iskusstvo*, August 15, 1932.
Amossy, Ruth and Anne Herschberg-Pierrot. *Stéréotypes et clichés: Langue, Discours, Société* (Paris: Éditions Nathan, 1997).
Andreev, German. "O satire." In *Odna ili dve russkikh literatury?* International symposium organized by the Faculty of Literary Studies at the Geneva University and the Swiss Academy of Sciences (Lausanne: L'Age D'Homme, 1981).
Arendt, Hannah. "Franz Kafka: A Revaluation. On the Occasion of the Twentieth Anniversary of His Death." In *Essays in Understanding (1930–1954)*, edited by Jerome Kohn (New York: Harcourt Brace & Company, 1994).
Arendt, Hannah. *The Origins of Totalitarianism* (New York: Penguin, 2017).
Atarov, Nikolai. "18x24." *Nashi dostizheniia* no. 7 (July 1935).
Attwood, Lynne. *Gender and Housing in Soviet Russia: Private Life in a Public Space*. (Manchester: Manchester University Press, 2010).

Averintsev, Sergei. "Bakhtin, smekh, khristianskaia kul'tura." In *M. M. Bakhtin kak filosof*, edited by Sergei Averintsev et al. (Moscow, 1992).
B. M. "Vodevil' v 'Satire'." *Rabochii i teatr* no. 13 (1928).
Bakhnov, Vladlen. "Otvety na voprosy ankety 'Pochemu ia stal satirikom'." *Voprosy literatury* no. 12 (1967).
Bakhtin, Mikhail. *Estetika slovesnogo tvorchestva* (Moscow, 1979).
Bakhtin, Mikhail. "Formy vremeni i khronotopa v romane. Ocherki po istoricheskoi poetike." *Voprosy literatury i estetiki. Issledovaniia raznykh let* (Moscow, 1975).
Bakhtin, Mikhail. "K voprosam teorii romana. K voprosam teorii smekha. (O Maiakovskom)," vol. 5, *Sobranie sochinenii v semi tomakh* (Moscow, 1996).
Bakhtin, Mikhail. *Problems of Dostoevsky's Poetics*, edited and translated by Caryl Emerson, introduction by Wayne Booth (Minneapolis: University of Minnesota Press, 1984).
Bakhtin, Mikhail. *Rabelais and His World*, translated by Hélène Iswolsky (Bloomington: Indiana University Press, 1984).
Bakhtin, Mikhail. *Speech Genres and Other Late Essays*, edited by Caryl Emerson and Michael Holquist, translated by Vern W. McGee (Austin, TX: University of Texas Press, 1986).
Balke, Friedrich. "Regierbarkeit der Herzen. Über den Zusammenhang von Politik und Affektivität bei Carl Schhmitt und Spinoza." In *Politische Theologie: Formen und Funktionen im 20.Jahrhundert*, edited by Jürgen Brokoff and Jürgen Fohrmann (München: Ferdinand Schöningh, 2003).
Balmas Neary, Rebecca. "Mothering Socialist Society: The Wife-Activists' Movement and the Soviet Culture of Daily Life, 1934–41." *Russian Review* 58, no. 3 (July 1999).
Barmin, Aleksandr. *Sokoly Trotskogo* (Moscow, 1997).
Barthes, Roland. *Sade, Fourier, Loyola*, translated by Richard Miller (Berkeley and Los Angeles: University of California Press, 1989).
Barthes, Roland. *The Neutral: Lecture Course at the Collège de France (1977–1978)*, translated by Rosalind Krauss and Denis Hollier (New York: Columbia University Press, 2005).
Barthes, Roland. *The Rustle of Language*, translated by Richard Howard (Berkeley and Los Angeles: University of California Press, 1989).
Barthes, Roland. *Writing Degree Zero*, translated by Annette Lavers and Colin Smith, preface by Susan Sontag (New York: Hill and Wang, 1968).
Batrak, Ivan. *Basni*, edited by Gennadii Korenev (Moscow, 1933).
Batrak, Ivan. "Krest'ianskaia literatura k XVI s″ezdu VKP(b)." *Literaturnaia gazeta*, June 26, 1930.
Batrak, Ivan. *Stikhi i basni* (Moscow, 1956).
Batrak, Ivan. "V chem my raskhodimsia s Polonskim." *Literaturnaia gazeta*, January 20, 1930 and January 27, 1930.
Beard, Mary. *Laughter in Ancient Rome: On Joking, Tickling, and Cracking Up* (Los-Angeles: University of California Press, 2014).
Bednyi, Dem'ian. *Sobranie sochinenii v vos'mi tomakh* (Moscow, 1965).
Begak, B. "Kto smeetsia poslednim." *Znamia* no. 11 (1945).
Behrmann, Carolin. "Bild–Actus–Ausnahme: Zur Ikonologie des Ausnahmezustandes." In *Ästhetik der Ausschließung: Ausnahmezustände in Geschichte, Theorie, Medien und literarischer Fiktion*, edited by Oliver Ruf (Würzburg: Königshausen & Neumann, 2009).
Bekker, Mikhail. "Nuzhna li nam basnia?" *Na literaturnom postu* nos. 13–14 (July 1928).
Belova, L. "Nam Gogoli i Shchedriny nuzhny!" *Iskusstvo kino* no. 10 (1952).

Benjamin, Walter. "Fate and Character." In *Selected Writings*, edited by Marcus Bullock and Michael W. Jennings, vol. 1 (Cambridge, MA: Harvard University Press, 2004).

Benjamin, Walter. "Franz Kafka: on the Tenth Anniversary of His Death." In *Illuminations*, translated by Harry Zohn, edited and introduction by Hannah Arendt (New York: Schocken, 2007).

Benjamin, Walter. *The Origin of German Tragic Drama*, translated by John Osborne (London: NLB, 1977).

Bergler, Edmund. *Laughter and the Sense of Humor* (New York: Intercontinental Medical Book Corp., 1956).

Bergson, Henri. *Laughter: An Essay on the Meaning of the Comic*, translated by Cloudesley Brereton and Fred Rothwell (London: Macmillan, 1911).

Billington, Sandra. *The Social History of the Fool* (Glastow: Harvester, 1984).

Blium, V. "K voprosu o sovetskoi satire." *Zhizn' iskusstva* no. 30 (1925).

Blium, V. "Po linii naimen'shego soprotivleniia (O 'sovetskoi satire')." *Sovetskoe iskusstvo* nos. 3–4 (1925).

Blium, V. "'Prochev' otvety..." *Zhizn' iskusstva* no. 37 (1925).

Bogdanov, Aleksandr. "Taina smekha." *Molodaia gvardiia* no. 2 (1923) (2).

Bogdanov, Konstantin. "Otkrytye serdtsa, zakrytye granitsy (O ritorike vostorga i bespredel'nosti vzaimoponimaniia)." *Novoe literaturnoe obozrenie* no. 100 (2009) (6).

Bogdanov, Konstantin. *Vox populi: Fol'klornye zhanry sovetskoi epokhi* (Moscow–Saint-Petersburg, 2009).

Boguslavskii, Aleksandr. "Bor'ba za stilevoe mnogoobrazie sovetskoi komedii v 20-e gody." *Filologicheskie nauki* no. 2 (1962).

Boichevskii, V. "Puti sovetskoi satiry." *Zemlia sovetskaia* 1 (1931).

Bonnell, Victoria. *Iconography of Power: Soviet Political Posters under Lenin and Stalin* (Berkeley, Los Angeles, London: University of California Press, 1997).

Borenstein, Eliot. "The Plural Self: Zamiatin's We and the Logic of Synecdoche." *The Slavic and East European Journal* 49, no. 4 (Winter 1996).

Borev, Iurii. *Komicheskoe* (Moscow, 1970).

Borev, Iurii. *O komicheskom* (Moscow, 1957).

Borev, Iurii. *O tragicheskom* (Moscow, 1961).

Borovoi, L. "Uvlekatel'naia komediia" *Literaturnaia gazeta*, March 11, 1941.

Borshchagovskii, Aleksandr. "Vopreki zdravomu smyslu." *Teatr* no. 12 (1940).

Bourdieu, Pierre. *Language and Symbolic Power*, edited and introduction by John B. Thompson, translated by Gino Raymond and Matthew Adamson (Cambridge, MA: Polity, 1991).

Boym, Svetlana. *Common Places: Mythologies of Everyday Life in Russia* (Cambridge, MA: Harvard University Press, 1995).

Boym, Svetlana. "Paradoxes of Unified Culture: From Stalin's Fairy Tale to Molotov's Lacquer Box." *The South Atlantic Quarterly*. Special issue: Socialist Realism Without Shores, edited by Thomas Lahusen and Evgeny Dobrenko, 94, no. 3 (Summer 1995).

Bremmer, Jan and Herman Roodenburg. "Introduction: Humour and History." In *Cultural History of Humour: From Antiquity to the Present Day*, edited by Jan Bremmer and Herman Roodenburg (Cambridge: Polity, 1997).

Brooks, Peter. *Reading for the Plot: Design and Intention in Narrative* (New York: Vintage, 1984).

Brossat, Alain. "Le bestiaire du délirium." In *Moscou 1918–1941: De "l'homme nouveau" au bonheur totalitaire*, edited by Catherine Goussef (Paris: Editions Autrement, 1993).

Burke, Kenneth. "Auscultation, Creation, and Revision." In *Extensions of a Burkeian System*, edited by James Chesebro (Tuscaloosa and London: University of Alabama Press, 1993).
Burke, Kenneth. "Four Master Tropes." In *A Grammar of Motives and A Rhetoric of Motives* (Cleveland and New York: Meridian Books, 1962).
Burke, Peter. "Overture: The New History, Its Past and Future." In *New Perspectives of Historical Writing*, edited by Peter Burke (Cambridge: Polity, 1992).
Burov, A. "Smekh—oruzhie v bor'be novogo so starym." *Iskusstvo kino* no. 11 (1952).
Burton, Frank and Pat Carlen. *Official Discourse: On Discourse Analysis, Government Publications, Ideology and the State* (London, Boston and Henley: Routledge & Kegan Paul, 1979).
Butler, Judith. *Excitable Speech: A Politics of the Performative* (New York & London: Routledge, 1997).
Cefalu, Paul. "What's So Funny about Obsessive-Compulsive Disorder?" *PMLA* 124, no. 1 (2009).
Chegodaeva, Maria. "Massovaia kul'tura i sotsialisticheskii realizm." *Voprosy iskusstvoznaniia* 10, no. 1 (1997).
Chernus, Ira. "War and the Enemy in the Thought of Mircea Eliade." *History of European Ideas* 13, no. 4 (1991).
Chernyshevskii, Nikolai. "Vozvyshennoe i komicheskoe." In *Stat'i po filosofii i estetike*, vol. 4, *Sobranie sochinenii v 5-ti tomakh* (Moscow, 1974).
Chickering, Roger. *Imperial Germany and the Great War, 1914–1918*, 2nd ed. (Cambridge: Cambridge University Press, 2004).
Clark, Katerina. "M. M. Bakhtin and 'World Literature'." *Journal of Narrative Theory*. Special issue: Benjamin and Bakhtin: New Approaches—New Contexts, edited by John Docker and Subhash Jaireth, 32, no. 3 (2002).
Clark, Katerina. "Polozhitel'nyi geroi kak verbal'naia ikona." *Sotsrealisticheskii kanon*.
Clark, Katerina. *The Soviet Novel: History as Ritual* (Chicago and London: University of Chicago Press, 1981).
Clover, Joshua. "Genres of the Dialectic." *Critical Inquiry* 43, no. 2 (Winter 2017).
Corbeill, Anthony. *Controlling Laughter: Political Humor in the Late Roman Republic* (Princeton, NJ: Princeton University Press, 1996).
Custine, Astolphe de. *Empire of the Czar: A Journey through Eternal Russia* (New York: Doubleday, 1989).
Davis, Natalie Zemon. *Fiction in the Archives: Pardon Tales and Their Tellers in Sixteenth-Century France* (Stanford, California: Stanford University Press, 1987).
Deleuze, Gilles. *Desert Islands and Other Texts, 1953–1974* (New York: Semiotext(e), 2004).
Dikii, Aleksei. "Geroika i satira." *Literaturnaia gazeta*, September 9, 1954.
Dikii, Aleksei. "Zabytyi zhanr: Zametki o vodevile." *Teatr* no. 11 (1953).
Dmitriev, Anatolii. *Sotsiologiia iumora: Ocherki* (Moscow, 1996).
Dobin, E. "Muzykal'naia istoriia." *Iskusstvo i zhizn'* no. 10 (1940).
Dobrenko, Evgeny. "Grustnaia istoriia sovetskogo smekha. A review of Gérin, A. *Devastation and Laughter: Satire, Power, and Culture in the Early Soviet State (1920s–1930s)*. Toronto, 2018; Waterlow, J. *It's Only a Joke, Comrade! Humour, Trust and Everyday Life under Stalin*. Oxford, 2019; Etty, J. *Graphic Satire in the Soviet Union: Krokodil's Political Cartoons*. Jackson, 2019." *Russian Literature* 116 (2020).
Dobrenko, Evgeny. *Metafora vlasti: Literatura stalinskoi epokhi v istoricheskom osveshchenii* (Munich: Verlag Otto Sagner, 1993).

Dobrenko, Evgeny. "Mezhdu istoriei i proshlym: Pisatel' Stalin i literaturnye istoki sovetskogo istoricheskogo diskursa." In *Sotsrealisticheskii kanon*.
Dobrenko, Evgeny. *Political Economy of Socialist Realism*, translated by Jesse M. Savage (New Haven & London: Yale University Press, 2007).
Dobrenko, Evgeny. "Raeshnyi kommunizm: poetika utopicheskogo naturalizma i stalinskaia kolkhoznaia poema." *Novoe literaturnoe obozrenie* 98, no. 4 (2009).
Dobrenko, Evgeny. "Russkaia literatura mezhdu chitatelem i pisatelem: Ot sotsrealizma do sotsarta." In *Reading in Russia: Practices of Reading and Literary Communication, 1760–1930*, edited by Damiano Rebecchini and Raffaella Vassena (Milan: Ledizioni, 2014).
Dolar, Mladen. "The Comic Mimesis." *Critical Inquiry* 43, no. 2 (Winter 2017).
Dostoevsky, Fyodor. *Podrostok*, vol. 13, *Polnoe sobranie sochinenii v 30-ti tomakh*, (Leningrad, 1975).
Drubek-Meyer, Natascha. "Mass-Message / Massazh mass: Sovetskie (mass-)media v 30-e gody." *Sovetskoe bogatstvo: Stat'i o kul'ture, literature i kino*, edited by Marina Balina, Evgeny Dobrenko and Jurij Murašov (Saint-Petersburg, 2002).
Dunham, Vera S. *In Stalin's Time: Middleclass Values in Soviet Fiction* (Durham: Duke University Press, 1990).
Dykhovichnyi, Vladimir and Mor.s Slobodskoi. "Tri oproverzheniia." In *Za mir, za demokratiiu: reperturarnyi sbornik* (Moscow, 1949).
Dzeverin, Igor'. *Problema satiry v revoliutsionno-demokraticheskoi estetike* (Kiev, 1962).
Eco, Umberto. "The Frames of Comic 'Freedom'." In *Carnival!*, edited by Umberto Eco et al. *Approaches to Semiotics* 64 (Berlin, New York, Amsterdam: Mouton Publishers, 1984).
Eco, Umberto. "Innovation and Repetition: Between Modern and Post-Modern Aesthetics." *Daedalus*. Special issue: The Moving Image 114, no. 4 (Fall 1985).
Edele, Mark. "Paper Soldiers: The World of the Soldier Hero according to Soviet Wartime Posters." *Jahrbücher für Geschichte Osteuropas*. Special issue: Magnaten und ländliches Gewerbe. Neue Folge, 47, no. 1 (1999).
Efimov, Boris. *Desiat' desiatiletii. O tom, chto videl, perezhil, zapomnil* (Moscow, 2000).
Efimov, Boris. *Osnovy ponimaniia karikatury* (Moscow, 1961).
Efimov, Boris. *Rabota, vospominaniia, vstrechi* (Moscow, 1963).
Efimov, Boris. *Rovesnik veka: Vospominaniia* (Moscow, 1987).
Egorova, Liudmila (ed.). *Istoriia russkoi literatury XX veka (Pervaia polovina). Kniga 1.* Textbook. 2nd ed., revised (Moscow, 2014).
Ehrmann, Jacques, Cathy Lewis and Phil Lewis. "Homo Ludens Revisited." *Yale French Studies*. Special issue: Game, Play, Literature 41 (1968).
Eiges, Iosif. "Basnia." *Slovar' literaturnykh terminov*, vol. 1 (Moscow, 1925).
Eikhenbaum, Boris. "Kak sdelana 'Shinel'" Gogolia." In *O proze* (Leningrad, 1969).
El'sberg, Iakov. "Klassiki russkoi satiry i sovetskaia literatura." *Bol'shevik* 22 (1952).
El'sberg, Iakov. "Nasledie Gogolia i Shchedrina i sovetskaia dramaturgiia." *Teatr* no. 2 (1953).
El'sberg, Iakov. *Nasledie Gogolia i Shchedrina i sovetskaia satira* (Moscow, 1954).
El'sberg, Iakov. "Otritsatel'noe i polozhitel'noe v satire." *Iskusstvo kino* no. 7 (1953).
El'sberg, Iakov. "Satira, komicheskoe, iumor." *Literatura v shkole* no. 6 (1954).
El'sberg, Iakov. "Velikie traditsii Gogolia i Shchedrina." *Literaturnaia gazeta*, July 24, 1952.
El'sberg, Iakov. *Voprosy teorii satiry* (Moscow, 1957).
El'sberg, Iakov. "Za boevuiu sovetskuiu satiru." *Voprosy filosofii* no. 2 (1953).

Eliade, Mircea. *Myth and Reality*, translated by Willard R. Trask (New York: Harper Torchbooks, 1968).
Elina, Elena. *Literaturnaia kritika i obshchestvennoe soznanie v Sovetskoi Rossii 1920-kh godov* (Saratov, 1994).
Elliott, Robert C. *The Power of Satire: Magic, Ritual, Art* (Princeton, NJ: Princeton University Press, 1966).
Erenburg, Il'ia. *Na tsokole istorii...: Pis'ma 1931–1967*, edition prepared by Boris Frezinskii (Moscow, 2004).
Erenburg, Il'ia. *Voina* (22 June 1941–10 May 1945), vol. 5, *Il'ia Erenburg: Dela i dni (v dokumentakh, pis'makh, vyskazyvaniiakh i soobshcheniiakh pressy, svidetel'stvakh sovremennikov)*, edited by Viacheslav Popov and Boris Frezinskii (Saint-Petersburg, 2001).
Ermilov, Vladimir. *Nekotorye voprosy teorii sovetskoi dramaturgii: O gogolevskoi traditsii* (Moscow, 1953).
Ermilov, Vladimir. "Russkii voin Vasilii Terkin." *Literatura i iskusstvo*, no. 44 (October 31, 1942).
Erren, Lorenz. *Selbstkritik und Schuldbekenntnis: Kommunikation und Herrschaft unter Stalin, 1917–1953* (Munich: Oldenburg Wissenschaftsverlag, 2008).
Ershov, Leonid. "Nekotorye voprosy teorii satiry." *Uchenye zapiski AN Latviiskoi SSR* no. 12 (1955).
Ershov, Leonid. *Sovetskaia satiricheskaia literatura* (Leningrad, 1955).
Ershov, Leonid. *Sovetskaia satiricheskaia proza* (Moscow & Leningrad, 1966).
Etkind, Aleksandr. "'Odno vremia ia kolebalsia, ne antikhrist li ia': Sub"ektivnost', avtobiografiia i goriachaia pamiat' revoliutsii." *Novoe literaturnoe obozrenie* 73, no. 3 (2005).
Eventov, Isaak. "M. Gor'kii i sovetskaia satira." *Zvezda* no. 9 (September 1960).
Fadeev, Aleksandr. "O literature i literaturnoi kritike." In *Ideinost' i masterstvo*.
Fairclough, Pauline. *Classics for the Masses: Shaping Soviet Musical Identity under Lenin and Stalin* (London: Yale University Press, 2016).
Fateev, Andrei. *Obraz vraga v sovetskoi propagande 1945–1954 gg.* (Moscow, 1999).
Faulkner, Joseph (ed.). *Sociology Through Humor* (St. Paul, MN: West Publishing Co., 1987).
Fedoseev, G. "*Vystrel* Bezymenskogo." *Zemlia sovetskaia* no. 5 (1930).
Fitzpatrick, Sheila. *Everyday Stalinism: Ordinary Life in Extraordinary Times* (New York: Oxford University Press, 2000).
Fitzpatrick, Sheila. *Stalin's Peasants: Resistance and Survival in the Russian Village After Collectivization* (New York: Oxford University Press, 1994).
Fitzpatrick, Sheila. *Tear off the Masks! Identity and Imposture in Twentieth-Century Russia.* (Princeton, NJ: Princeton University Press, 2005).
Fletcher, Angus. "Allegory Without Ideas." *Boundary 2* 33, no. 1 (2006).
Foucault, Michel. *The Abnormal: Lectures at the Collège de France 1974–1975*, edited by Valerio Marchetti and Antonella Salomon, translated by Graham Burchell (London: Verso, 2003).
Foucault, Michel. "Two Lectures." In *Power/Knowledge: Selected Interviews and Other Writings 1972–1977*, edited and translated by Colin Gordon (New York: Pantheon, 1980).
Freud, Sigmund. *Jokes and Their Relation to the Unconscious (1905)*, translated and edited by James Strachey (New York: W. W. Norton & Co., 1960).
Frezinskii, Boris. *Ob Il'e Erenburge: Knigi, liudi, strany* (Moscow, 2013).
Frolov, Vladimir. "O putiakh razvitiia sovetskoi komedii." *Teatr* no. 4 (1949).
Frolov, Vladimir. *O sovetskoi komedii* (Moscow, 1954).

Frolov, Vladimir. "Ob osobennostiakh komediinogo zhanra." *Iskusstvo kino* no. 10 (1952).
Frolov, Vladimir. *Sovetskaia komediia* (Moscow, 1954).
Frolov, Vladimir. *Zhanry sovetskoi dramaturgii*. (Moscow, 1957).
Fürst, Juliane. *Stalin's Last Generation: Soviet Post-War Youth and the Emergence of Mature Socialism* (Oxford: Oxford University Press, 2010).
Galkovskii, Dmitrii. "Poeziia sovetskaia." *Novyi mir* no. 5 (1992).
Gantar, Jure. *The Pleasure of Fools: Essays in the Ethics of Laughter* (Montreal: McGill-Queen's University Press, 2005).
Gasparov, Boris. *Literaturnye leitmotivy: Ocherki russkoi literatury XX v.* (Moscow, 1994).
Gatrell, Vic. *City of Laughter: Sex and Satire in Eighteenth-Century London* (London: Atlantic Books, 2006).
Geiger, Homer Kent and Alex Inkeles. "The Family in the U. S. S. R." *Marriage and Family Living*. Special international issue: Family 16, no. 4 (November 1954).
Gentile, Maria Teresa. *Educazione linguistica e crisi di libertà* (Rome: Armando, 1966).
Glovin'skii, Mikhal. "'Ne puskat' proshlogo na samotek': Kratkii Kurs VKP(b) kak mificheskoe skazanie" (translated by Konstantin Dushenko). *Novoe literaturnoe obozrenie* no. 22 (1996).
Golino, Enzo. *Parola di Duce: Il linguaggio totalitario del fascismo* (Milan: Rizzoli, 1994).
Golubev, Aleksandr. "Interwar Europe through the Eyes of Soviet Caricature." *Evropa* 3, no. 8 (2003).
Golubev, Aleksandr. "Nash otvet Chemberlenu: Sovetskaia politicheskaia karikatura 1920–1930-kh godov." *Istorik i khudozhnik* no. 2 (2004).
Golubev, Aleksandr. "Praktiki vizualizatsii sovetskoi povsednevnosti: Plakat i kinematograf." In *Povsednevnyi mir sovetskogo cheloveka 1920–1940kh gg.*, edited by Evgenii Krinko, Irina Tazhidinova and Tat'iana Khlynina (Rostov-na-Donu, 2009).
Golubev, Aleksandr. "'Zverinyi stil'' v sovetskoi politicheskoi karikature mezhvoennogo perioda." In *Ot velikogo do smeshnogo...: Instrumentalizatsiia smekha v rossiiskoi istorii XX veka*, edited by Igor' Narskii (Cheliabinsk, 2013).
Gomel, Elana. "Aliens Among Us: Fascism and Narrativity." *Journal of Narrative Theory* 30, no. 1 (Winter 2000).
Goodrich, Peter. "Of Law and Forgetting." In *Law in the Courts of Love: Literature and Other Minor Jurisprudences* (London: Routledge, 1996).
Gorbatov, Boris. "O sovetskoi satire i iumore." *Novyi mir* no. 10 (1949).
Gorky, Maksim. "Kakim dolzhen byt' 'Za rubezhom'." In *Sobranie sochinenii v 30-ti tomakh*, vol. 26 (Moscow, 1953).
Gorky, Maksim. "O zhenshchine." In *Sobranie sochinenii v 30-ti tomakh*, vol. 27 (Moscow, 1953).
Gorsuch, Anne E. "'There's No Place like Home': Soviet Tourism in Late Stalinism." *Slavic Review*. Special issue: Tourism and Travel in Russia and the Soviet Union 62, no. 4 (Winter 2003).
Goscilo, Helena. "Introduction." In *Politicizing Magic: An Anthology of Russian and Soviet Fairy Tales*, edited by Marina Balina, Helena Goscilo and Mark Lipovetsky (Evanston, Illinois: Northwestern University Press, 2005).
Griesse, Malte. "Soviet Subjectivities: Discourse, Self-Criticism, Imposture." *Kritika: Explorations in Russian and Eurasian History* 9, no. 3 (Summer 2008).
Groys, Boris. "Grausamer Karneval. Mihail Bachtins 'Aesthetische Rechtfertigung' des Stalinismus." *Frankfurter Allgemeine Zeitung*, June 21, 1989.
Groys, Boris. "Mezhdu Stalinym i Dionisom." *Sintaksis* (Paris) 25 (1989).
Groys, Boris. "Totalitarizm karnavala." *Bakhtinskii sbornik* no. 3 (1997).

Groys, Boris. *Utopiia i obmen* (Moscow, 1993).
Günther, Hans and Evgeny Dobrenko (eds.). *Sotsrealisticheskii kanon* (Saint-Petersburg, 2000).
Gural'nik, Uran. "Russkaia revoliutsionno-demokraticheskaia kritika i voprosy satiry." *Vestnik Akademii nauk SSSR. Seriia literatury i iazyka* 12, no. 3 (1953).
Gus, Mikhail. "Sovremennye kollizii." *Teatr* no. 12 (1940).
Gusev, S. "Predely kritiki (O paskviliakh, poklepakh, klevete i kontrerevoliutsii)." *Izvestiia TsIK SSSR i BtsIK*, no. 100, May 5, 1927.
Gusev, Viktor. "Mysli o geroe." *Literaturnaia gazeta*, June 30, 1940.
Gusev, Viktor. *Slava* (Moscow, 1935).
Gusev, Viktor. *Vesna v Moskve* (Moscow and Leningrad, 1946).
Gus'kov, Nikolai. *Ot karnavala k kanonu: Russkaia sovetskaia komediia 1920-kh godov* (Saint-Petersburg, 2003).
Gutman, D. "K vodeviliu." *Zhizn' iskusstva* no. 11 (1927).
Halfin, Igal. "The Bolsheviks' Gallows Laughter." *Journal of Political Ideologies* 11, no. 3 (October 2006).
Halfin, Igal. *Intimate Enemies: Demonizing the Bolshevik Opposition, 1918-1928* (Pittsburgh: University of Pittsburgh Press, 2007).
Halfin, Igal. *Stalinist Confessions: Messianism and Terror at the Leningrad Communist University* (Pittsburgh: University of Pittsburgh Press, 2009).
Halliwell, Stephen. *Greek Laughter: A Study of Cultural Psychology from Homer to Early Christianity* (Cambridge: Cambridge University Press, 2008).
Hanson, Stephen E. *Time and Revolution: Marxism and the Design of Soviet Institutions* (Chapel Hill & London: University of North Carolina Press, 1997).
Harper, Samuel Northrup. *Civic Training in Soviet Russia* (Chicago: University of Chicago Press, 1929).
Hayman, Greg and Henry J. Pratt. "What Are Comics?" In *Aesthetics: A Reader in Philosophy of the Arts*, edited by David Goldblatt and Lee B. Brown, 2nd ed. (Upper Saddle River, NJ: Pearson-Prentice Hall, 2005).
Heinemann, Richard. "Kafka's Oath of Service: 'Der Bau' and the Dialectic of Bureaucratic Mind." *PMLA* 111, no. 2 (March 1996).
Hellbeck, Jochen. "'The Diaries of Fritzes and the Letters of Gretchen': Personal Writings from the German-Soviet War and Their Readers." *Kritika: Explorations in Russian and Eurasian History*. New Series 10, no. 3 (Summer 2009).
Heller, Mikhail. "Kloun i komissar." In *Odna ili dve russkikh literatury?* International symposium organized by the Faculty of Literary Studies at the Geneva University and the Swiss Academy of Sciences (Lausanne: L'Age D'Homme, 1981).
Heller, Mikhail. *Mashina i vintiki: Istoriia formirovaniia sovetskogo cheloveka* (London, 1985).
Herzen, Aleksandr. <O pis'me, kritikuiushchem "Kolokol">. In *Sobranie sochinenii v 30-ti tomakh*, vol. 13 (Moscow, 1954-66).
History of the Communist Party of the Soviet Union (Bolsheviks). Short Course (New York: International Publishers, 1939).
Holland, Norman. *Laughing: A Psychology of Humor* (Ithaca: Cornell University Press, 1982).
Hollander, Paul. "Models of Behavior in Stalinist Literature: A Case Study of Totalitarian Values and Controls." *American Sociological Review* 31, no. 3 (June 1966).
Holman, Valerie and Debra Kelly. "Introduction. War in the Twentieth Century: The Functioning of Humor in Cultural Representation." *Journal of European Studies* 31 (2001).

Iakimenko, Lev. *O "Podniatoi tseline" M. Sholokhova* (Moscow, 1960).
Iakovleva, Iuliia. *Mariinskii teatr. Balet. XX vek* (Moscow, 2005).
Iampol'skii, Mikhail. *Demon i labirint: Diagrammy, deformatsii, mimesis* (Moscow, 1996).
Iampol'skii, Mikhail. "Lenin provozglashaet Sovetskuiu vlast': Zametki o diskurse osnovaniia." *Novoe literaturnoe obozrenie* 26 (1997).
Isaev, Egor. "Vstupitel'naia stat'ia." In Mikhalkov, Sergei. *Basni* (Moscow, 1984).
Istoriia Vsesoiuznoi Kommunisticheskoi Partii (Bol'shevikov). Kratkii Kurs (Moscow, 1945).
Iurenev, Rostislav. "Kakaia nuzhna komediia?" *Oktiabr'* no. 6 (1958).
Iuzovskii, Iu. "Osvobozhdennyi Prometei. Stat'ia pervaia." *Literaturnyi kritik* no. 10 (1934).
Iuzovskii, Iu. *Voprosy sotsialisticheskoi dramaturgii* (Moscow, 1934).
Jakobson, Roman. *Iazyk i bessoznatel'noe* (Moscow, 1996).
Kalacheva, S. "Chto zhe takoe iumor?" *Sovetskaia kul'tura*, June 14, 1956.
Kalinin, Ilya. "Nam smekh i stroit' i zhit' pomogaet (politekonimiia smekha i sovetskaia muzykal'naia komediia, 1930-e gody)." *Russian Literature* 74, nos. 1–2 (2013).
Karasev, Leonid. *Filosofiia smekha* (Moscow, 1996).
Karen, V. "Vyzhigat' po-shchedrinski." *Sovetskoe iskusstvo*, December 10, 1952.
Kataev, Valentin. *Doroga tsvetov* (Moscow, 1934).
Kataev, Valentin. "Million terzanii." In *Komedii* (Moscow, 1934).
Kelly, Catriona. "Territories of the Eye: The Russian Peep Show *(Raek)* and Pre-Revolutionary Visual Culture." *Journal of Popular Culture* 31, no. 4 (Spring 1998).
Khalizev, Valentin. *Tsennostnye orientatsii russkoi klassiki* (Moscow, 2005).
Khimich, Vera. "Karnavalizatsiia kak stilevaia tendentsiia v literature 20-kh gg." In *XX vek: Literatura. Stil'. Stilevye zakonomernosti russkoi literatury XX v. (1900–1930)*, edited by Viola Eidinova and Leonid Bykov (Ekaterinburg, 1994).
Kirpotin, Valerii. *Rovesnik zheleznogo veka: Memuarnaia kniga* (Moscow, 2006).
Kirpotin, Valerii. "Satira Shchedrina i sovremennost'." *Oktiabr'* no. 1 (1953).
Kirpotin, Valerii. "Sovetskaia dramaturgiia." In *Pervyi Vsesoiuznyi s"ezd sovetskikh pisatelei*.
Kirshon, Vladimir. *Volshebnyi splav* (Moscow, 1934).
Kiselev, Nikolai. *Problemy sovetskoi komedii* (Tomsk, 1973).
Kogan, L. "V chem sila iumora?" *Sovetskaia kul'tura*, July 12, 1956.
Kol'tsov, Mikhail. "Rech' na Pervom s"ezde sovetskikh pisatelei." In *Pervyi Vsesoiuznyi s"ezd sovetskikh pisatelei*.
Kondakov, Igor. "'Basnia, tak skazat', Ili 'Smert' avtora' v literature stalinskoi epokhi." *Voprosy literatury* no. 1 (2006).
Korchagin, A. "Volga, Volga." *Moskovskii ekran*, no. 6 (1938).
Korenev, Gennadii. "Basni Ivana Batraka." Introduction to Batrak, Ivan. *Basni*.
Korneichuk, Aleksandr. *Priezzhaite v Zvonkovoe* (Moscow, 1947).
Kotomka, L. "Basni Ivana Batraka." *Zemlia sovetskaia* 8 (1932).
Kozintsev, Aleksandr. *Chelovek i smekh* (Saint-Petersburg, 2007).
Kozintsev, Aleksandr. "Smekh i antipovedenie v Rossii: Natsional'naia spetsifika i obshchechelovecheskie zakonomernosti." In *Smekh: Istoki i funktsii*, edited by Aleksandr Kozintsev (Saint-Petersburg, 2002).
Kozlova, Natal'ia. "Sotsrealism: Proizvoditeli i potrebiteli." *Obshchestvennye nauki i sovremennost'* no. 4 (1995).
Kozlova, Natal'ia. "Uproshchenie—znak epokhi!" *Sotsiologicheskie issledovaniia* 7 (1990).
Krylova, S., L. Lebedinskii, L. Ra-be (A. Bek), L. Toom. *Rabochie o literature, teatre i muzyke* (Leningrad, 1926).
Krynetskii, N. "O krasnom smekhe." *Krasnaia pechat'* no. 20 (1923).
Kuzmin, Mikhail. "Skorokhody istorii." *Zhizn' iskusstva*, June 26–7, 1920.

Lenin, Vladimir. "Kriticheskie zametki po natsional'nomu voprosu." In *Polnoe sobranie sochinenii*, 5th ed., vol. 24 (Moscow, 1970).
Lenin, Vladimir. "Politicheskii otchet Tsentral'nogo Komiteta RKP(b) XI s"ezdu RKP(b), 27 marta 1922 goda." In *Polnoe sobranie sochinenii*, 5th ed., vol. 45 (Moscow, 1970).
Lewin, Moshe. *The Making of the Soviet System: Essays in the Social History of Interwar Russia* (New York: New Press, 1985).
Likhachev, Dmitrii. *Poetika drevnerusskoi literatury* (Leningrad, 1967).
Likhachev, Dmitrii. *Razvitie drevnerusskoi literatury. Epokhi i stili* (Leningrad, 1973).
Likhachev, Dmitrii, Aleksandr Panchenko and Natalia Ponyrko. *Smekh v Drevnei Rusi* (Leningrad, 1984).
Likhachev, Dmitrii and Aleksandr Panchenko. *Smekhovoi mir drevnei Rusi* (Leningrad, 1976).
Lipelis, A. "Sovremennost' starogo zhanra." *Voprosy literatury* no. 7 (1961).
Lipovetsky, Mark. *Charms of the Cynical Reason: The Trickster's Transformations in Soviet and Post-Soviet Culture* (Brighton, Mass.: Academic Studies Press, 2011).
Lipovetsky, Mark. "Skazkovlast': 'Tarakanishche' Stalina." *Novoe literaturnoe obozrenie* 45, no. 5 (2000).
Litovskii, O. "Segodnia sovetskoi estrady." *Sovetskii teatr* nos. 11–12 (1930).
Lotman, Iurii. "Gogol' i sootnesenie 'smekhovoi kul'tury' s komicheskim i ser'eznym v russkoi natsional'noi traditsii." In *Istoriia i tipologiia russkoi kul'tury* (Saint-Petersburg, 2002).
Lotman, Iurii and Boris Uspenskii (eds.). "Novye aspekty izucheniia kul'tury Drevnei Rusi." *Voprosy literatury* no. 3 (1977).
Low, David. "Review: Krokodil Cartoonists." *Soviet Studies* 2, no. 2 (October 1950).
Luk, Aleksandr. *Iumor, ostroumie, tvorchestvo* (Moscow, 1977).
Lukianova, Irina. *Kornei Chukovskii* (Moscow, 2019).
Lunacharskii, Anatolii. "Budem smeiat'sia." In *Sobranie sochinenii v 8-mi tomakh*, vol. 3 (Moscow, 1964).
Lunacharskii, Anatolii. *O byte* (Leningrad, 1927). http://lunacharsky.newgod.su/lib/o-byte/. Accessed on October 25, 2020.
Maguire, Muireann. *Soviet Gothic-Fantastic: A Study of Gothic and Supernatural Themes in Early Soviet Literature*. PhD dissertation, Jesus College, University of Cambridge, October 2008. https://www.repository.cam.ac.uk/handle/1810/224215. Accessed on October 24, 2020.
Makarian, Anushivan. *O satire* (Moscow, 1967).
Makarov, Aleksandr. *Vospitanie chuvstv: Literaturno-kriticheskie stat'i i ocherki* (Moscow, 1957).
Malenkov, Georgii. *Otchetnyi doklad XIX s"ezdu partii o rabote TsK VKP(b)* (Moscow, 1952).
Malovichko, A. "Pogovorim o komedii." *Sovetskii Kazakhstan* 7 (1955).
Mandelstam, Osip. *Slovo i kul'tura* (Moscow, 1987).
Mar'iamov, A. "Konflikt ili proisshestvie." *Literaturnaia gazeta*, February 27, 1954.
Marin, Louis. *Food for Thought*, translated by Mette Hjort (Baltimore and London: The Johns Hopkins University Press, 1989).
Martin, Rod. *The Psychology of Humor: An Integrative Approach* (New York: Academic, 2006).
Marx, Karl. "Contribution to the Critique of Hegel's Philosophy of Law." In *The Collected Works of Karl Marx and Frederick Engels*, vol. 3 (Moscow: Progress Publishers, 1975).
Mass, Vladimir. "O sovetskoi satire." *Novyi zritel'* 33 (1925).
Mass, Vladimir. "Smekh na teatre." *Zrelishcha* no. 14 (1922).

"Materialy fevral'sko-martovskogo Plenuma TsK VKP(b) 1937 goda." *Voprosy istorii* nos. 2-3; 4-5; 6-7; 8-9; 10 (1992).
Matich, Olga. "Sueta vokrug krovati: Utopicheskaia organizatsiia byta i russkii avangard" (translated by Irina Prokhorova). *Literaturnoe obozrenie* no. 11 (1991).
Matskin, Aleksandr. "Kniga nachal i prodolzhenii." *Literatura i iskusstvo* no. 13 (March 25, 1944).
Matskin, Aleksandr. "Pisatel' v stroiu." *Znamia* no. 11 (1942).
Matsuda, Matt K. "Doctor, Judge, Vagabond: Identity, Identification, and Other Memories of the State." *History and Memory* 6, no. 1 (Spring-Summer 1994).
Maugham, Somerset W. *The Partial View* (London: William Heinemann Ltd., 1954).
McKenna, Kevin J. *All the Views Fit to Print: Changing Images of the U.S. in Pravda Political Cartoons 1917-1991* (New York and Washington: Peter Lang, 2001).
Meierkhol'd, Vsevolod. "O teatre." In *Stat'i. Pis'ma. Rechi. Besedy*, vol. 2 (Moscow, 1968).
Melekhov, Aleksandr. "Umoritel'naia gil'otina. Totalitarnyi iumor." *Zvezda* no. 2 (1996).
Mel'nichenko, Mikhail. "Fenomen frontovogo anekdota: Narodnoe tvorchestvo ili instrument agitatsii." *Rossiiskaia istoriia* 6 (November-December 2009).
Merleau-Ponty, Maurice. *Humanism and Terror: An Essay on the Communist Problem*, translated and with notes by John O'Neill (Boston: Beacon Press, 1969).
Mikhalkov, Sergei. "Iasno videt' tsel'." *Voprosy literatury* no. 3 (1969).
Mikhalkov, Sergei. *Oni bez maski* (Moscow, 1952).
Mikulášek, Miroslav. *Puti razvitiia sovetskoi komedii 1925-1934 godov* (Prague, 1962).
Mindlin, Emilii. "Razgovor o komedii." *Teatr* no. 3 (1940).
Moeller-Sally, Stephen. *Gogol's Afterlife: The Evolution of a Classic in Imperial and Soviet Russia* (Evanston, Il.: Northwestern University Press, 2002).
Moeller-Sally, Stephen. "'Klassicheskoe nasledie' v epokhu sotsrealizma, ili Pokhozhdeniia Gogolia v strane bol'shevikov." *Sotsrealisticheskii kanon*.
Moldavskii, Dmitrii. "Ot zhizni i skazki–Ded Shchukar'." *Literatura i zhizn'*, March 9, 1960.
Moldavskii, Dmitrii. *Tovarishch smekh* (Leningrad, 1981).
Monastyrskii, A. "Rytsar' revoliutsionno-pisatel'skogo dolga." *Voprosy literatury* no. 4 (April 1963).
Morokhin, Nikolai. "Dokument v antifashistskoi satire I. Erenburga." In *Problemy zhanra i stilia khudozhestvennogo proizvedeniia: Mezhvuzovskii sbornik* (Vladivostok, 1988).
Morokhin, Nikolai. *Satira v russkoi sovetskoi khudozhestvennoi publitsistike voennykh let (1941-1945 gody)* (Sarov, 2001).
Mosse, George. *Fallen Soldiers: Reshaping the Memory of the World Wars* (New York and Oxford: Oxford Univesity Press, 1990).
Mulkay, Michael. *On Humor: Its Nature and Its Place in Modern Society* (Cambridge: Polity Press, 1988).
Murašov, Jurij. "Pis'mo i ustnaia rech' v diskursakh o iazyke 1930-kh godov: N. Marr." *Sotsrealisticheskii kanon*.
Murašov, Jurij. "Schrift unter Verdacht. Zur inszenierten Mündlichkeit der sowjetischen Schauprozesse in den dreißiger Jahren." In *Politische Inszenierung im 20.Jahrhundert: Zur Sinnlichkeit der Macht*, edited by Sabine Arnold et al. (Wien, Köln and Weimer: Bohlau, 1998).
Mushchenko, Ekaterina, Vladislav Skobelev, and Lev Kroichik. *Poetika skaza* (Voronezh, 1978).
Nadtochii, Eduard. "Drug, tovarishch i Bart: Neskol'ko predvaritel'nykh zamechanii k voproshaniiu o meste sotsialisticheskogo realizma v iskusstve XX veka." *Daugava* 8 (1989).

Nadzhafov, Dzhangir (ed.); compiled by Dzhangir Nadzhafov and Zinaida Belousova. *Stalin i kosmopolitizm: 1945-1953. Dokumenty Agitpropa TsK* (Moscow, 2005).
Naiman, Eric. "Discourse Made Flesh: Healing and Terror in the Construction of Soviet Subjectivity." In *Language and Revolution: Making Modern Political Identities*, edited by Igal Halfin (London and Portland, OR: Frank Cass, 2002).
"Na puti k satiricheskoi komedii." *Literaturnaia gazeta*, April 11, 1953.
Narskii, Igor' et al. (eds.). *Ot velikogo do smeshnogo...: Instrumentalizatsiia smekha v rossiiskoi istorii XX veka* (Cheliabinsk, 2013).
Nedoshivin, German. *Ocherki istorii iskusstva* (Moscow, 1953).
Nelson, William. *Out of the Crocodile's Mouth: Russian Cartoons about the USA* (Washington: Public Affairs Press, 1949).
Nérard, François-Xavier [Fransua Nerar]. *Piat' protsentov pravdy: Razoblachenie i donositel'stvo v stalinskom SSSR (1928-1941)*, translated by Elena Balakhovskaia (Moscow, 2011).
Nesterenko, Vitalii. "Proizvedenie morali: Analiz basni." *Voprosy literatury* no. 2 (1998).
Nezhin, B. "Veselyi spektakl': Retsenziia na 'Vas vyzyvaet Taimur'." *Ogonek* no. 22 (1948).
Nietzsche, Friedrich. *Human, All-Too-Human: A Book for Free Spirits*, translated by Paul V. Cohn (New York: Russell & Russell, 1964).
Nikolaev, Dmitrii. *Satira Gogolia* (Moscow, 1984).
Nikolaev, Dmitrii. *Satira Shchedrina i realisticheskii grotesk* (Moscow, 1977).
Norris, Stephen. "The Sharp Weapon of Soviet Laughter: Boris Efimov and Visual Humor." *Russian Literature* 74, nos. 1/2 (2013).
Novichenko, L. "Zametki o satire." *Izvestiia*, April 17, 1953.
Nusinov, I. "Voprosy zhanra v proletarskoi literature." *Literatura i iskusstvo* nos. 2-3 (1931).
"Nuzhna li nam sovetskaia satira?" *Literaturnaia gazeta*, January 13, 1930.
"O neudachnykh p'esakh i netrebovatel'noi kritike." *Teatr* 7 (1949).
"O putiakh sovetskoi satiry." *Literaturnaia gazeta*, July 15, 1929.
"Ob organizatsii sredi pisatelei SSSR konkursa na luchshie p'esy. Postanovlenie SNK SSSR ot 17.02.33." *Sovetskoe iskusstvo*, February 20, 1933.
"Ocherednye zadachi VOKP (Rezoliutsiia, priniataia na noiabr'skom plenume TsS VOKP)." *Zemlia sovetskaia* 1 (1930).
Onufriev, N. "Povysit' teoreticheskii uroven' i vospitatel'nuiu rol' prepodavaniia literatury." *Literatura v shkole* no. 1 (1953).
Orlov, V. "Vodevil' s rydaniem." *Iskusstvo kino*, no. 3 (March) (1960).
Orlova, Galina. "Rozhdenie vreditelia: Otritsatel'naia politicheskaia sakralizatsiia v strane Sovetov (20-e gody)." *Wiener Slawistischer Almanach* 49 (2002).
Ortenberg, David. "Iiun'—dekabr' sorok pervogo" (Moscow, 1986).
Osnos, Iurii. "Geroi i zhanr: Nekotorye problemy sovetskoi komedii i satiry." *Druzhba narodov* 3 (1954).
Oushakine, Serguei and Dennis Ioffe (eds.). *Totalitarian Laughter: Images-Sounds-Performers*. Special issue of *Russian Literature* 74, nos. 1-2 (2013).
Ozmitel', Evgenii. *O satire i iumore* (Leningrad, 1973).
Ozmitel', Evgenii. *Sovetskaia satira. Seminarii* (Moscow & Leningrad, 1964).
Palmer, Jerry. *Taking Humor Seriously* (London: Routledge, 1994).
Parkhomenko, Mikhail. *Aleksandr Korneichuk* (Moscow, 1952).
Parvulescu, Anca. "Kafka's Laughter: On Joy and the Kafkaesque." *PMLA* 130, no. 5 (2015).
Parvulescu, Anca. *Laughter: Notes on a Passion* (Cambridge, MA and London, England: MIT Press, 2010).

Passet, Eveline. "Im Zerrspiegel der Geschichte: Deutsche Bilder von Ilja Erenburg." *Osteuropa: Zeitschrift für Gegenwartsfragen des Ostens* 57, no. 12 (December 2007).
Pavlovskii, A. "Satira i obshchestvennyi konflikt." *Sibirskie ogni* no. 4 (1954).
Pavlovskii, A. "Skuchnyi smekh." *Zvezda* no. 8 (1957).
Pechenkin, Aleksandr. "Iskusstvo PR v ispolnenii Stalina: Svoiu vinu za porazheniia v 1941 i 1942 gg. Khoziain khotel svalit' na starykh kavaleristov." *Nezavisimoe voennoe obozrenie*, September 27, 2002. https://nvo.ng.ru/spforces/2002-09-27/7_stalin.html. Accessed on October 20, 2020.
Pervyi Vsesoiuznyi s"ezd sovetskikh pisatelei: Stenograficheskii otchet (Moscow, 1934).
Petrey, Sandy. "Pears in History." *Representations*. Special issue: Monumental Histories 35 (Summer 1991).
Pfaller, Robert. "Comedy and Materialism." In *Schluss mit der Komödie! Stop That Comedy!: Zur schleichenden Vorherrschaft des Tragischen in unserer Kultur / On the Subtle Hegemony of the Tragic in Our Culture*, edited by Mladen Dolar et al. (Sonderzahl Verlag, 2005).
Pikel', Richard. "Ironiia i lirika." (A review of K. Finn's *Vzdor* in the theaters of MOSPS and VTsSPS). *Literaturnaia gazeta*, January 24, 1934.
Pikel', Richard. "K probleme sovetskoi komedii." *Teatr i dramaturgiia* no. 6 (1933).
Pimenov, Vladimir (ed.) *Ideinost' i masterstvo. Sbornik statei sovetskikh pisatelei o dramaturgii (1945–1953)*. Moscow, 1953.
Platonov, Andrei. *Zapisnye knizhki: Materialy k biografii*, 2nd ed. (Moscow, 2006).
Pliatt, Rostislav. "Diskussiia o komedii." Contribution to the special section "Za komediiu!" *Teatr* 5 (1952).
Podoroga, Valerii. "'Golos vlasti' i 'pis'mo vlasti'." In *Totalitarizm kak istoricheskii fenomen*, edited by Aleksei Kara-Murza et al. (Moscow, 1989).
Poeticheskii slovar'. http://www.endic.ru/poet/Skaz-400.html. Accessed on February 24, 2018.
Pogodin, Nikolai. "O komediiakh." In *Iskat', myslit', otkryvat'* (Moscow, 1966).
Pogodin, Nikolai. "Satira akvarel'iu." *Teatr* 3 (1953).
Pokhlebkin, Vil'iam. *Velikii psevdonim* (Moscow, 1996).
Polonskii, Viacheslav. "Tovarishch Batrak i ego uchitel' Beskin." *Literaturnaia gazeta*, January 6, 1930.
Popov, Aleksei. Contribution to the special section "Za komediiu!" *Teatr* 5 (1952).
Potebnia, Aleksandr. *Iz lektsii po teorii slovesnosti. Basnia. Poslovitsa. Pogovorka* (The Hague and Paris, 1970).
Powell, Chris and George E. C. Paton (eds.). *Humor in Society: Resistance and Control* (London: Macmillan Press, 1988).
Prokof'ev, Vl. "Nedostoinoe uvlechenie." In *Sovetskii teatr i sovremennost'. Sbornik materialov i statei*, edited by Mikhail Miringof (Moscow, 1947).
Propp, Vladimir. *Problemy komizma i smekha* (Moscow, 1976).
Protsess Antisovetskogo Trotskistskogo Tsentra. 23–30 ianvaria 1937 (Moscow, 1937).
Pumpianskii, Lev. "Gogol'." In *Klassicheskaia traditsiia. Sobranie trudov po istorii russkoi literatury* (Moscow, 2000).
Purseigle, Pierre. "Mirroring Societies at War: Political Humor and the British and French Popular Press During the First World War." *Journal for European Studies* 31 (2001).
Rakhman, Sabit. *Dobro pozhalovat'* (Moscow, 1950).
Raku, Marina. *Muzykal'naia klassika v mifotvorchestve sovetskoi epokhi* (Moscow 2014).
Raskin, Victor. *Semantic Mechanisms of Humor* (Dordrecht, Boston and Lancaster: D. Reidel Publishing Company, 1985).

Ravetto-Biagioli, Kriss. *The Unmaking of Fascist Aesthetics* (Minneapolis and London: University of Minnesota Press, 2001).
Reddy, William M. "Sentimentalism and Its Erasure: The Role of Emotions in the Era of the French Revolution." *The Journal of Modern History* 72 (March 2000).
Riumina, Marina. *Estetika smekha: Smekh kak virtual'naia real'nost'* (Moscow, 2003).
Robin, Regine. *Socialist Realism: An Impossible Aesthetic* (Stanford, California: Stanford University Press, 1992).
Rogi, M. "Puti sovetskoi satiry (Ob oshibkakh tov. Bliuma)." *Literaturnaia gazeta*, June 22, 1929.
Romashov, Boris. "O komedii." *Ideinost' i masterstvo: Sbornik statei sovetskikh pisatelei o dramaturgii (1945–1953)* (Moscow, 1954).
Ronell, Avital. *Stupidity* (Urbana and Chicago: Univesity of Illinois Press, 2003).
Ross, Stephanie. "Caricature." *The Monist* 58, no. 2 (April 1, 1974).
Rubashkin, Aleksandr. "Erenburg na voine." *Voprosy literatury* no. 2 (February) (1985).
Rudov, Mikhail. "Basnopisets Ivan Batrak." *Uchenye zapiski filologicheskogo fakul'teta Kirgizskogo gosudarstvennogo universiteta* no. 12 (1964).
Rüger, Jan. "Laughter and War in Berlin." *History Workshop Journal* 67 (Spring 2009).
Rybakov, Iurii. "Sofronov." In *Mir i voina: Ocherki iz istorii russkoi sovetskoi dramaturgii 1946–1980 godov*, edited by Inna Vishnevskaia (Moscow, 2009).
Ryklin, Mikhail. *Prostranstva likovaniia: Totalitarizm i razlichie* (Moscow, 2002).
Ryklin, Mikhail. *Terrorologiki* (Tartu and Moscow, 1992).
Ryzhkin, I. A. and Z. Safarova. "Sovetskaia muzykal'naia estetika v 30-e gody." In: *Iz istorii sovetskogo iskusstvovedeniia i esteticheskoi mysli 1930-kh godov* (Moscow, 1977).
Sabrow, Martin [Sabrov, Martin]. "Vremia i legitimnost' v nemetskikh diktaturakh XX veka (sravnitel'nyi analiz)" (translated by Il'ia Afanas'ev). *Novoe literaturnoe obozrenie* 100 (2009).
Samoilenko, Grigorii. *Stikhotvornaia satira i iumor perioda Velikoi Otechestvennoi voiny* (Kiev, 1977).
Santner, Eric. *My Own Private Germany: Daniel Paul Schreber's Secret History of Modernity* (Princeton, NJ: Princeton University Press, 1996).
Santner, Eric. *The Weight of All Flesh: On the Subject-Matter of Political Economy*, with commentaries by Bonnie Honig, Peter E. Gordon and Hent de Vries; edited and with an introduction by Kevis Goodman (New York: Oxford University Press, 2016).
Sarasin, Philipp. "Die Visualisierung des Feindes. Über metaphorische Technologien der frühen Bakteriologie." *Geschichte und Gesellschaft*. Neue Wege der Wissenschaftsgeschichte 30, no. 2 (April-June) (2004).
Sarnov, Benedikt. "Shest'desiat let 20-go veka." *Voprosy literatury* no. 5 (2005).
"Satira i iumor v dni Velikoi Otechestvennoi voiny." *Voprosy literatury* no. 5 (1985).
Saxonhouse, Arlene W. "Comedy in Callipolis: Animal Imagery in *The Republic*." *The American Political Science Review* 72, no. 3 (September 1978).
Schmid, Ulrich [Shmid, Ul'rikh]. "Konstitutsiia kak priem (Ritoricheskie i zhanrovye osobennosti osnovnykh zakonov SSSR i Rossii)." *Novoe literaturnoe obozrenie* 100, no. 6 (2009).
Schmitt, Carl. *Political Theology: Four Lectures on the Concept of Sovereignty* (1922), translated by George Schwab (Cambridge, Mass.: MIT Press, 1985).
Senin, Sergei. "Za proletarskuiu satiru." *Rost* no. 23 (1931).
"Sezon zakonchen." *Teatr* 7 (1949).
Shafir, Iakov. "Pochemu my ne umeem smeiat'sia?" *Krasnaia pechat'* vol. 17 (1923).
Shapiro, Kam. *Sovereign Nations, Carnal States* (Ithaca and London: Cornell University Press, 2003).

Shchukin, Vasilii. "Dukh karnavala i dukh prosveshcheniia (Bakhtin i Lotman)." *Voprosy filosofii* no. 11 (2008).
Shchupak, Samuil. "Zametki o tvorcheskikh zadachakh dramaturgii." *Literaturnyi kritik* nos. 7–8 (1934).
Shkvarkin, Vasilii. *Prostaia devushka* (Moskva, 1938).
Shokhin, Kirill. *O tragicheskom geroe i komicheskom personazhe* (Moscow, 1961).
Shtok, Isidor. "Vasilii Shkvarkin." *Rasskazy o dramaturgakh* (Moscow: Iskusstvo, 1967).
Simonov, Konstantin. "Diskussiia o komedii." Contribution to the special section "Za komediiu!" *Teatr* 5 (1952).
Simonov, Konstantin. *Glazami cheloveka moego pokoleniia* (Moscow, 1988).
Simons, Anton. *Carnival and Terror: The Ethical Meaning of Bakhtin's* Rable (Utrecht: University of Utrecht, 1996).
Simukov, Aleksei. *Solnechnyi dom, ili Kapitan v otstavke. Vorob'evy gory* (Moscow, 1977).
Skradol, Natalia. "Laughing with Comrade Stalin: An Analysis of Laughter in a Soviet Newspaper Report." *The Russian Review* 68, no. 1 (January 2009).
Smirnov, Igor'. "Sotsrealizm: Antropologicheskoe izmerenie." In *Sotsrealisticheskii kanon*.
Smith, Adam. *An Inquiry into the Nature and Causes of the Wealth of Nations* (1776), edited by Roy Harold Campbell, Andrew S. Skinner and William B. Todd (Indianapolis: Liberty Classics (authorized by Oxford) and Oxford University Press, 1979).
Snow, Charles Percy. "Introduction." In *Tyorkin and the Stovemakers. Poetry and Prose by Aleksandr Tvardovskii*, translated by Anthony Rudolf (Cheadle: Carcanet Press, 1974).
Solodar', Tsezar'. *V sirenevom sadu* (Moscow, 1954).
Solomon, Peter H., Jr. *Soviet Criminal Justice under Stalin* (Cambridge University Press, 1996).
Sosnovskii, Lev. "Pervyi proletarskii poet Dem'ian Bednyi." *Na postu* no. 1 (1923).
Soveshchanie deiatelei sovetskoi muzyki v TsK VKP(b) (Moscow, 1948).
"Sovetskaia komediia v nashi dni." *Oktiabr'* 6 (1958).
Soviet Humor: The Best of Krokodil (Kansas City: Andrews and McMeel, 1989).
"Sowjetische Kritiken an Ehrenburg." *Osteuropa: Zeitschrift für Gegenwartsfragen des Ostens* 13, no. 4 (April 1963).
Spasskii, Iu. "O poeticheskom geroe nashikh dnei." *Teatr* 2 (1940).
Stalin, Iosif. "O proekte Konstitutsii Soiuza SSR: Doklad na Chrezvychainom VIII Vsesoiuznom S"ezde Sovetov 25 noiabria 1936 goda." In *Sochineniia*, vol. 14 (Moscow, 1951).
Stalin, Iosif. "O sotsial-demokraticheskom uklone v nashei partii: Doklad na XV Vsesoiuznoi Konferentsii VKP(b) 1 noiabria 1926 goda." In *Sochineniia*, vol. 8 (Moscow, 1948).
Stalin, Iosif. "Ob oppozitsionnom bloke v VKP(b): Tezisy k XV Vsesoiuznoi Konferentsii VKP(b). 26 oktiabria—3 noiabria 1926 g." In *Sochineniia*, vol. 8 (Moscow, 1948).
Stalin, Iosif. "Otvet korrespondentu *Pravdy*." In *Sochineniia*, vol. 16 (Moscow, 1997).
Stalin, Iosif. "Pis'mo A. M. Gor'komu." In *Sochineniia*, vol. 12 (Moscow, 1949).
Stalin, Iosif. "Rech' 17 noiabria 1935 g. na Pervom vsesoiuznom soveshchanii rabochikh i rabotnits—stakhanovtsev." In *Sochineniia*, vol. 14 (Moscow, 1951).
Stalin, Iosif. "Rech' na predvybornom sobranii izbiratelei Stalinskogo izbiratel'nogo okruga goroda Moskvy 11 dekabria 1937 goda." In *Sochineniia*, vol. 14 (Moscow, 1997).
Stalin, Iosif. "Zakliuchitel'noe slovo po dokladu 'O sotsial-demokraticheskom uklone v nashei partii' na XV Vsesoiuznoi Konferentsii VKP(b). 3 noiabria 1926 g." In *Sochineniia*, vol. 8 (Moscow, 1948).
Stalin, Iosif. "Zapiska A. E. Korneichuku." In *Sochineniia*, vol. 18 (Tver', 2006).
Stalin, Joseph. "Letter to A. M. Gorky." In *Works*, vol. 12 (April 1929–June 1930) (Moscow: Foreign Languages Publishing House, 1954).

Stalin, Joseph. "On the Draft Constitution of the USSR: Report Delivered at the Extraordinary Eighth Congress of Soviets of the USSR, 25 November 1936." In *Works*, vol. 14 (July 1934–March 1939) (London: Red Star Press, 1978).
Stalin, Joseph. "The Opposition Bloc in the CPSU(b): Theses for the Fifteenth All-Union Conference of the CPSU(b)." In *Works*, vol. 8 (January 1926–November 1926) (Moscow: Foreign Languages Publishing House, 1954).
Stalin, Joseph. "Reply to the Discussion on the Report on 'The Social-Democratic Deviation in our Party. 3 November 1926." In *Works*, vol. 8 (January 1926–November 1926) (Moscow: Foreign Languages Publishing House, 1954).
Stalin, Joseph. "The Social-Democratic Deviation in our Party. Report Delivered at the Fifteenth All-Union Conference of the C.P.S.U.(B.). 1 November 1926." In *Works*, vol. 8 (January 1926–November 1926) (Moscow: Foreign Languages Publishing House, 1954).
Stalin, Joseph. "Speech at the First All-Union Conference of Stakhanovites. 17 November 1935." In *Works*, vol. 14 (July 1934–March 1939) (London: Red Star Press, 1978).
Stalin, Joseph. "Speech Delivered by Comrade J. Stalin at a Meeting of Voters of the Stalin Electoral Area, Moscow. December 11, 1937." In *Works*, vol. 14 (July 1934–March 1939) (London: Red Star Press, 1978).
Stallybrass, Peter and Allon White. *The Politics and Poetics of Transgression* (London: Methuen, 1986).
Starinkevich, E. "Nasushchnye problemy sovetskoi komedii." *Sovetskaia Ukraina* 9 (1954).
Steinberg, Mark. *Proletarian Imagination: Self, Modernity, and the Sacred in Russia, 1910–1925* (Ithaca and London: Cornell University Press, 2002).
Stites, Richard. *Revolutionary Dreams: Utopian Vision and Experimental Life in the Russian Revolution*. (New York and Oxford: Oxford University Press, 1989).
Stolovich, Leonid. *Filosofiia. Estetika. Smekh* (Saint-Petersburg–Tartu, 1999).
Surkov, Evgenii. "Ne po tomu puti." *Teatr* 4 (1953).
Surov, Anatolii. "Nashi zadachi." In *Ideinost' i masterstvo: Sbornik statei sovetskikh pisatelei o dramaturgii (1945–1953)* (Moscow, 1953).
Surov, Anatolii. *Zemliak prezidenta (Besnovatyi galantereishchik)* (Moscow, 1950).
Sverbilova, Tat'iana. "Podvodnaia lodka 'V stepiakh Ukrainy': Kolkhoznyi vodevil' A. Korneichuka 'V stepiakh Ukrainy' v matritsakh kitcha i problema kul'turnoi identichnosti mnogonatsional'nogo fenomena sotsrealizma." In *Trudy "Russkoi antropologicheskoi shkoly,"* vol. 7 (Moscow, 2010).
Svirskii, Grigorii. *Na lobnom meste* (Moscow, 1998).
Tarasenkov, Anatolii. *Sila utverzhdeniia: Sbornik statei o sovetskoi literature* (Moscow, 1955).
Terni, Jennifer. "A Genre for Early Mass Culture: French Vaudeville and the City, 1830–1848." *Theater Journal* 58, no. 2 (May, 2006).
Terts, Avram. "Chto takoe sotsialisticheskii realizm?" In *Fantasticheskii mir Abrama Tertsa* (New York, 1967).
Tihanov, Galin. *The Master and the Slave: Lukács, Bakhtin, and the Ideas of Their Time*. (Oxford: Clarendon Press, 2000).
Timofeev, Leonid. *Teoriia literatury* (Moscow, 1948).
"Tipicheskoe." In *Bol'shaia sovetskaia entsiklopediia*, 2nd ed. (Moscow, 1949–58).
Tiupa, Valerii. *Khudozhestvennost' literaturnogo proizvedeniia* (Krasnoiarsk, 1987).
Topolski, Feliks. "Contemporary Comment and Caricature." *The Burlington Magazine for Connoisseurs* 83, no. 484 (July 1943).
Trotsky, Lev. *Novyi kurs* (Moscow, 1924).

Tsipursky, Gleb. *Socialist Fun: Youth, Consumption, and State-Sponsored Popular Culture in the Soviet Union, 1945–1970* (Pittsburgh: University of Pittsburgh Press, 2016).
Tsurikova, Galina and Igor' Kuz'michev. *Utverzhdenie lichnosti* (Leningrad, 1975).
Turovskaia, Maia. "I. A. Pyr'ev i ego muzykalnye komedii. K probleme zhanra." *Kinovedcheskie zapiski* no. 1 (1988).
Turovskaia, Maia. *Zuby drakona: Moi 30-e gody* (Moscow, 2015).
Tvardovskii, Aleksandr. *"Ia v svoiu khodil ataku…": Dnevniki. Pis'ma. 1941–1945* (Moscow, 2005).
Tvardovsky, Aleksandr. "Kak byl napisan 'Vasilii Terkin'." *O pisatel'skom trude: Sbornik statei i vystuplenii sovetskikh pisatelei* (Moscow, 1953).
Tvardovskii, Aleksandr. "Otvet chitateliam 'Vasiliia Terkina'." *Novyi mir* no. 11 (1951).
Tvardovskii, Aleksandr. *Vasilii Terkin: kniga pro boitsa* (Moscow, 1969).
Tvardovskii, Aleksandr. *Vasily Tyorkin: A Book about a Soldier*, translated by Jill Higgs (Spalding: Hub Editions, 2003).
Tynianov, Iurii. "Dostoevskii i Gogol' (k teorii parodii)." *Poetika. istoriia literatury. Kino* (Moscow, 1977).
Tynianov, Iurii. *Poetika. Istoriia literatury. Kino* (Moscow, 1977).
Uralov, Roman. "O sovetskom vodevile." *Novyi mir* no. 4 (1947).
Vaisfel'd, I. *Epicheskie zhanry v kino* (Moscow, 1949).
Vaiskopf, Mikhail. *Pisatel' Stalin* (Moscow, 2001).
Vandaele, Jeroen. "Narrative Humor (II): Exit Perspective." *Poetics Today* 33, no. 1 (Spring 2012).
Varshavskii, Lev. *Nasha politicheskaia karikatura* (Moscow, 1930).
Vershina, Viktoriia and Aleksandr Mikhailiuk. "Smekh v kontekste nesmeshnogo." *Doksa* (Odessa). Special issue: Logos i praksis smekha no. 5 (2004).
Veshnev, Vladimir. *Kniga kharakteristik* (Moscow and Leningrad, 1928).
Vishnevskaia, Inna. *Komediia na orbite* (Moscow, 1979).
"Vodevil'." In *Kratkaia literaturnaia entsiklopediia* (Moscow, 1962).
Vodop'ianov, Mikhail and Iurii Laptev. *Vynuzhdennaia posadka* (Moscow and Leningrad, 1943).
Vol'kenshtein, Vladimir. *Dramaturgiia*, 2nd ed. (Moscow, 1929).
Voronskii, Aleksandr. *Iskusstvo videt' mir: Stat'i. Portrety* (Moscow, 1987).
Vtoroi Vsesoiuznyi s"ezd sovetskikh pisatelei. Stenograficheskii otchet (Moscow, 1956).
Vykhodtsev, Piotr. "Osobennosti tipizatsii v poemakh Aleksandra Tvardovskogo." *Zvezda* no. 1 (1954).
Vykhodtsev, Piotr and Leonid Ershov. "Smelee razrabatyvat' teoriiu sovetskoi satiry." *Zvezda* no. 2 (1953).
Vyshinskii, Andrei. *Sudebnye rechi* (Moscow, 1955).
Weber, Samuel. "Between Part and Whole: Benjamin and the Single Trait." *Paragraph* 32, no. 3 (2009).
Weiner, Amir. *Making Sense of War: The Second World War and the Fate of the Bolshevik Revolution* (Princeton and Oxford: Princeton University Press, 2001).
Weis, Daniel. "Parazity, padal', musor: Obraz vraga v sovetskoi propagande." *Politicheskaia lingvistika* 1, no. 24 (2008).
Welsh, Alexander. "State-of-the-Art Impersonations for Comedy and Everyday." *Social Research*. Special issue: Fraud 75, no. 4 (Winter 2008).
Wepler, Ryan. "Nabokov's Nomadic Humor: Lolita." *College Literature* 38, no. 4 (Fall 2011).

White, Hayden. *Figural Realism: Studies in the Mimesis Effect* (Baltimore and London: The Johns Hopkins University Press, 1999).
White, Hayden. "The Value of Narrativity in the Representation of Reality." In *On Narrative*, edited by William J. T. Mitchell (Chicago: University of Chicago Press, 1981).
Zazykin, V. I. *O prirode smekha: Po materialam russkogo eroticheskogo fol'klora* (Moscow, 2007).
Zheltova, Ninel'. "S. Mikhalkov i russkaia basnia." In *Voprosy sovetskoi literatury*, edited by Valentin Kovalev and Vera Timofeeva, vol. 3 (Moscow and Leningrad, 1956).
Zhurbina, Evgeniia. "O mere sarkazma." *Nashi dostizheniia* no. 8 (1936).
Zhurbina, Evgeniia. "Zametki o satire." *Oktiabr'* no. 9 (1936).
Žižek, Slavoj. *Absolute Recoil: Towards a New Foundation of Dialectical Materialism* (London and New York: Verso, 2014).
Žižek, Slavoj. *In Defense of Lost Causes* (London and New York: Verso, 2008).
Žižek, Slavoj. *The Sublime Object of Ideology* (London and New York: Verso, 1989).
Žižek, Slavoj. "When the Party Commits Suicide." *New Left Review* 238, no. 1 (1999).
Zorkaia, Neia. "Ot *Maksima* do *Komissara*: Sovetskoe kino kak agiografiia." *Kul'turologicheskie zapiski* no. 11 (2009).
Zubkova, Elena. *Poslevoennoe sovetskoe obshchestvo: Politika i povsednevnost', 1945-1953* (Moscow, 2000).
Zupančič, Alenka. *The Odd One In: On Comedy* (Cambridge, MA and London, England: The MIT Press, 2008).

Index

For the benefit of digital users, indexed terms that span two pages (e.g., 52–53) may, on occasion, appear on only one of those pages.

acceleration, as a comic device 359–60
"Aesopian language" 19, 206, 251; *see also* fables
Afinogenov, Aleksandr: *Fear* 241–2
Against All Odds (Churkin, Vladimir) 301
Agamben, Giorgio 24, 90–1, 102, 141, 347; *see also* state of exception
Aleksandrov, Grigorii 24–6, 43, 123–4
  The Circus 394–5
  Jolly Fellows 367–9, 376–80, 388–95
  The Shining Path 8
  Volga-Volga 23–4, 43, 235–6, 368, 372–5
allegory 28–9, 168, 182, 250, 273–6; *see also* fables
alogism 187–90
Amaglobeli, Sergio: *A Good Life* 329, 331–3, 346, 360
Another Man's Child (Shkvarkin, Viktor) 325–6, 353, 357–9
anti-semitism 37–8, 42–3, 192–3
Anton Ivanovich Gets Angry (Ivanovskii, Aleksandr) 378–9, 390, 394–5
Arendt, Hannah 157–8, 334–5, 339–40
At 6 P.M. After the War (Pyr'ev, Ivan) 345–6
Averintsev, Sergei 30–2

Bakhnov, Vladlen 57, 292
Bakhtin, Mikhail 18*n*, 43, 142, 284
  on carnival 20–5, 29, 31, 85, 92–3
  vs carnival, Stalinist 20, 24–5, 27–9, 31–2
Baratashvili, Mariam: *Dragonfly* 341–2, 354–5, 359
Barthes, Roland 74–5, 86–7, 260, 265
Batrak, Ivan 28–9, 250–1, 268–72, 281–4
Baudrillard, Jean 165*n*
Bednyi, Dem'ian 24, 27–9, 252–84
Beketov's Career (Sofronov, Anatolii) 242–6
Benjamin, Walter 94–5, 146–7*n*, 256, 262–3, 273, 278–9
Bergson, Henri 57, 138, 148
Bezymenskii, Aleksandr: *Shot* 56, 66–7
Blue Handkerchief (Kataev, Valentin) 328, 341–2, 354, 359–60

body, and physicality 122–3, 137–9, 143–5
  carnivalesque 147
Bogdanov, Aleksandr 44–5
Bondareva, Elizaveta: *Towards the Dawn* 301
Bonnell, Victoria 152–3*n*
Borev, Iurii 18*n*, 57, 287, 291, 322–3
Bourdieu, Pierre 82–3*n*, 263
bourgeois, as a pejorative concept applied to art 47, 58–9, 90, 107–8, 293, 359, 362, 366, 370, 384
  as a pejorative concept applied to negative characters 25–6, 40, 42–3, 55, 107, 238, 292, 308, 314–15, 318, 320, 325, 345–6, 379–81
Boym, Svetlana 105–6, 345–7
Bukharin, Nikolai 89–99, 107–8
Bulgakov, Mikhail 19, 22, 41–2, 56
bureaucrats, as negative characters 28, 40, 42–3, 84, 229–41, 245–6, 379–81; *see also* enemies, internal; Mikhalkov, Sergei; nomenklatura comedy
Burke, Kenneth 131–2, 139–40
Burton, Frank and Pat Carlen 76, 87

campaigns 40–1, 292–3, 369–72, 382–5
caricature 27–8
carnival, Stalinist 20, 24–5, 27–9, 31–2; *see also* Bakhtin, Mikhail
Carnival Night, A (Riazanov, El'dar) 214, 390–7
chastushki 204
Chernyshevskii, Nikolai 30–1, 35, 57, 209–10
Chervinskii, Mikhail 180
Churkin, Vladimir: *Against All Odds* 301
Circus, The (Aleksandrov, Grigorii) 394–5
Clark, Katerina 85, 258, 272
classics 36, 52–4, 59, 84–5, 191, 216–17, 321–3;
  place of, in the new society 363–90; *see also* Gogol, Nikolai; Saltykov-Shchedrin, Mikhail
Cold War, the 28; *see also* enemy, external
Come to Zvonkovoe (Korneichuk, Aleksandr) 300–1, 312–13
comedy *see* laughter and the comic
commedia dell'arte 29, 285
communal apartments 345–50, 380–1

Conference of Soviet Musicians at the Central Committee of the All-Union Communist Party (Bolsheviks) (1948) 382–5
conflictlessness 28, 58–63, 211–17, 327–35, 341–2; *see also* laughter, harmonizing
constitution (Stalinist) 79, 85–6, 88

Deviatov, Dmitrii: *In Lebiazh'e* 301, 315
Diakonov, Nikolai: *Wedding With a Dowry* 304–5
Discharged Captain, A (Simukov, Aleksei) 329–42, 345–7, 349–50, 354–5
Dolar, Mladen 145–6, 150, 338–9
Dostoevsky, Fedor 34, 36
Dragonfly (Baratashvili, Mariam) 341–2, 354–5, 359
drama *see* theater
Dunaevskii, Isaak 23–6
Dykhovichnyi, Vladimir 19, 29, 37, 191–2, 198, 207–9, 292
   King for a Day 217–19
Dzerzhinskii, Ivan: *Quiet Flows the Don* (opera) 385–6

Eco, Umberto 170
Efimov, Boris 19, 153–60, 166, 184–6; *see also* Cold War
El'sberg, Iakov 35n, 40–1, 60, 66, 230, 247–8
Emergency Landing (Vodop'ianov, Mikhail and Laptev, Iurii) 331, 336–8, 342, 359–60
emotions, instrumentalization of 258–61; *see also* vaudeville
enemies, external 116, 129–33; *see also* Cold War
   internal 42–3; *see also* Stalin, speeches; Stalin, writings; types, in Stalinist comedy, negative
Erdman, Nikolai 19, 22, 41–2, 56
Ermilov, Vladimir 18n, 23, 38–9, 53, 59–60, 65–6, 120–1
Erenburg, Il'ia 27, 116, 129–33
Etkind, Aleksandr 102–3n

fables 24, 28–9, 84–5, 206; *see also* fairytales
Fadeev, Aleksandr 115, 212, 244n
fairytales 27, 29, 258
Fame (Gusev, Viktor) 217, 336–9, 342, 345–8, 354
Fear (Afinogenov, Aleksandr) 241–2
fel'eton 19, 47, 130, 215, 232, 245; *see also* Erenburg, Il'ia; newspapers, as the voice of the people
First All-Union Congress of Soviet Writers 44, 216

Fitzpatrick, Sheila 263, 266, 277, 310, 336–8, 343–5n
folk culture *see* popular culture
fools 28, 136, 351–2, 380–1; *see also* Ivan the Terrible; jesters; laughter and the comic, general theories of, general
formalism 28, 62, 179–80, 236, 238, 369–71, 379; bureaucratic 238–9
Foucault, Michel 68–9, 89n, 101
Freud, Sigmund 126–8, 138–9n, 145, 285–6, 310; *see also* laughter and the comic, general theories of
Frolov, Vladimir 18n, 23, 39, 54, 62–4, 285, 292, 302
Front, The (Korneichuk, Aleksandr) 219–23, 299–300

Galich, Aleksandr 292; *Taimyr Calling* 325–6, 339–40, 345–6, 348–9, 351–2; *see also* vaudeville
Gardens in Bloom (Kulichenko, Nikolai and Mass, Vladimir) 308–9
gender relations 304–6, 309–14; *see also* vaudeville
Gioconda, la (Pogodin, Nikolai) 298
Girl With Character, A (Iudin, Konstantin) 329–30, 336–8, 341–3, 346–7, 350, 354–5
Goalkeeper, The (Timoshenko, Semen) 336–9, 350, 354–5
Gogol, Nikolai 40–1, 52, 64–5, 80
   as Stalin's favorite writer 86
   The Inspector General 65, 180, 218–19, 229, 231
"Gogols and Shchedrins" (campaign) 40–1, 53–6, 59–60, 63–5, 211–12, 214, 216, 231, 299–300, 314; *see also* campaigns
Good Life, A (Amaglobeli, Sergio) 329, 331–3, 346, 360
Gorky, Maxim 28, 46, 50–1, 56, 130, 290
Grandfather [Grandpa] Shchukar' 20, 286–323
Great Friendship, The (Muradeli, Vano) 382–3
Groys, Boris 23–5, 27, 92–3n
Gusev, Viktor 29, 59, 217
   Fame 217, 336–9, 342, 345–8, 354
   Friendship 217
   Springtime in Moscow 336–9, 341–2, 346, 350–2, 354, 356–7

Halfin, Igal 68, 74–5n, 83, 92, 97, 114, 148–9, 195, 280–1
Harmful Element, A (Shkvarkin, Vasilii) 56
He Who Laughs Last (Krapiva, Kondrat) 242
Hellbeck, Jochen 129–30, 138, 145–6
Heller, Michael 41–2

heroic, the, and the comic 18, 27, 44, 111–12, 126–7, 134, 396–7
History of the CPSU (Short Course), The 101–2, 104–14
household comedies 349–50
human vs non-human 135, 146–51, 159–64, 173–5, 252–7, 262–5, 272–5; *see also* fables
humor *see* laughter and the comic
hyperbole 187, 191, 343–4

Iampolskii, Mikhail 261*n*, 282–3
Il'f, Il'ia 19, 59, 231
In Lebiazh'e (Deviatov, Dmitrii) 301, 315
In the Lilac Garden (Solodar', Tsezar') 333–9, 341–4, 349–52, 354–9
In the Steppes of Ukraine (Korneichuk, Aleksandr) 295–6, 298–300, 311–12, 314
infantilization 77–8, 84–5, 250, 258, 281–2, 287
insults 19, 43–7
   as a general comic device 147, 260; *see also* Bednyi, Dem'ian
Isaev, Konstantin 292; *Taimyr Calling* 325–6, 339–40, 345–6, 348–9, 351–2
Iudin, Konstantin 25–6, 29, 292 *A Girl With Character* 329–30, 336–8, 341–3, 346–7, 350, 354–5; *see also* vaudeville
Iuzovskii, Iu 57–8*n*, 290, 340–1
Ivan the Terrible 31–2, 71
Ivanovskii, Aleksandr: *Anton Ivanovich Gets Angry* 378–9, 390, 394–5
A Musical Story 375–81, 389–90

jesters 30, 134; Stalin as a j. 319; *see also* fools; Grandpa Shchukar'; Ivan the Terrible
Jolly Fellows (Aleksandrov, Grigorii) 367–9, 376–80, 388–95
Just a Girl (Shkvarkin, Vasilii) 331–3, 335, 338–42, 347–9, 354–6

Kafka, Franz 26, 93–5, 98, 279, 334, 339–40, 351–2
Kakhkhara, Abdulla: *Silk Suzani* 301
Kamenev, Lev 74, 76–7, 102–3, 106–8
Karasev, Leonid 32
Kataev, Valentin 19, 22, 56
   Blue Handkerchief 328, 341–2, 354, 359–60
   A Million Torments 333, 351–2, 355–6; *see also* vaudeville
King for a Day (Dykhovichnyi, Vladimir and Slobodskoi, Moris) 217–19
Kirshon, Vladimir 56–8
   The Miraculous Alloy 325–6, 330–1, 336–8, 342–3

Knights of the Soap Bubbles (Pogodin, Nikolai) 240–1
kolkhoz comedy 20, 27, 29; *see also* peasant culture and comedy; Pyr'ev, Ivan; vaudeville
Kol'tsov, Mikhail 44, 51*n*, 55–6
Korneichuk, Aleksandr: *Come to Zvonkovoe* 300–1, 312–13
   The Front 219–23, 299–300
   In the Steppes of Ukraine 295–6, 298–300, 311–12, 314
   Viburnum Grove 314–16, 336–8
Kozin, Aleksei: *In the Native Land* 303
Kozintsev, Aleksandr 23, 30
Kozlova, Natalia 70*n*, 83*n*
Krapiva, Kondrat: *He Who Laughs Last* 242
   Larks Singing 301, 311–12, 317
Krokodil (periodical) 18–19, 24, 27, 153
Kuban Cossacks, The (Pyr'ev, Ivan) 24, 295, 298
Kukryniksy, the 19, 154–5, 159–62, 168–9*n*, 171; *see also* Cold War
Kulichenko, Nikolai: *Gardens in Bloom* 308–9

Lacan, Jacques 71–2, 97, 277
language, colloquial 79–89, 99–104 *see also* orality, vs writing; Vasilii Terkin
Laptev, Iurii: *Emergency Landing* 331, 336–8, 342, 359–60
Larks Singing (Krapiva, Kondrat) 301, 311–12, 317
Last Day of Pompeev, The (Virta, Nikolai) 224–6
Late for a Date (Sidelev, Sergei and Verner, Mikhail) 342–3, 351–2
laughter and the comic: general theories of 18–20, 22, 25, 32, 57, 119, 123, 133, 180, 266–7, 285–6
   (Soviet), traditional approaches to 18–20, 22–30, 41–2, 207–9
   Russian 24, 35–6, 39, 285–6
   Soviet debates on 39–41, 43–67, 83, 143–4, 150, 190–1, 286–8; *see also* Sovietology; state laughter
law in Stalinism 68–112
Lench, Leonid 19, 37, 213, 232–3, 287–8
Leonov, Leonid 56, 198
Likhachev, Dmitrii 27, 32–3, 46, 71*n*
Lipovetsky, Mark 258, 356–7
litote 186–7
Lotman, Iurii 32–3
lubok 27, 35
Lunacharskii, Anatolii 45–6, 165–6, 193, 302
lyrical comedy 29, 39, 56, 58, 62–3, 179–80, 217, 290–2, 326–7
Lyrical Suburban, The (Romanovich, Petr and Vasil'ev, Vladimir) 307

Makaenok, Andrei 27, 213, 233–4
Malenkov, Grigorii 40, 117–18, 162–3, 235, 395
Marshak, Samuil 27, 115, 154–5, 163–4n, 178–80, 206
Marshall Plan 155–7n, 162–3, 173–4, 177
mass culture *see* popular culture
Mass, Vladimir 47, 49–50, 180
   Gardens in Bloom 308–9
Mayakovsky, Vladimir 19, 22, 28, 51n, 53n, 56, 214, 230, 252
Mdivani, Georgii: *New Times* 302–3
meta-laughter 28–9
metaphors, as a comical device 71, 159–62, 174–5, 177, 181–2
   concrete understanding of 98, 104, 119
metonymy 189–90
Mikhalkov, Sergei 20, 24, 203–5, 206, 213, 224, 272–3
   Lobsters 222–31
   A Monument to Myself 236–8
Mikulášek, Miroslav 50, 290–1, 326–7, 330–1
Million Torments, A (Kataev, Valentin) 333, 351–2, 355–6
Minko, Vasilii 213
Miraculous Alloy, The (Kirshon, Vladimir) 325–6, 330–1, 336–8, 342–3
Missouri Waltz (Pogodin, Nikolai) 192–5
mobility (country-city) 233, 293–4, 304–6, 312, 317, 325–6, 330–1, 334, 341–2, 387, 392
Mubblit, Georgii: *A Musical Story* 376
Muradeli, Vano: *The Great Friendship* 382–3
Murašov, Jurij 88n, 94, 261n
Musical Story, A (Ivanovskii, Aleksandr and Rappaport, Gerbert) 375–81, 389–90

Naiman, Eric 257
names, personal 95–6, 102–3, 265–6; *see also* insults; nicknames
Narin'iani, Semen 19, 213, 245
narodnost' (popular spirit) 21, 361, 382; *see also* popular culture
nationalism and nation-building 21–2, 198
"negative realism" 46–7, 195
New Times (Mdivani, Georgii) 302–3
newspapers, as the voice of the people 234, 237, 249, 333–4
nicknames 28–9, 37, 71, 107–10, 266; *see also* insults
Nietzsche, Friedirch 32
nomenklatura comedy 216–17, 223, 230–41
Norris, Stephen 153, 166–7n

Oleinik, Stepan 201–3
Olesha, Iurii 22, 41–2

On the Journals "Zvezda" and "Leningrad" (decree, 1946) 292–3
On the Repertoire of Drama Theaters and Its Improvement (resolution, 1946) 292–3
orality, vs writing 82–3, 88, 91, 94, 113–14, 119, 260–2
Orlova, Galina 83n, 101n, 105–6, 263n
outsiders and liminal characters 22, 351–2; *see also* Grandpa Shchukar'; jesters

Panchenko, Aleksandr 33
Parvulescu, Anca 26
patriarchy 22–5, 30–1, 293
peasant culture and comedy 22, 24, 28–9, 321; *see also* kolkhoz comedy; patriarchy
periphrasis 185
personification 184–5; *see also* allegory; fables; metaphors, as a comical device
Petrov, Evgenii 19, 59, 231
   A Musical Story 376
Platonov, Andrei 22, 41–2
Podoroga, Valerii 82–3, 282–3
Pogodin, Nikolai 229–32
   The Kuban Cossacks 298
   La Gioconda 298
   Knights of the Soap Bubbles 240–1
   Missouri Waltz 192–5
   When Swords Are Crossed 213
popular culture 20–1, 23–33, 204
   as integrated into the mainstream culture 21–38, 198, 202–3, 286; *see also* kolkhoz comedy; *Vasilii Terkin*
populism 18–29, 361
Potebnia, Aleksandr 266, 274
prizes and awards 25–6, 211–12, 220, 243–4, 299, 301, 314, 317, 325–6
Propp, Vladimir 18, 29n, 39
proverbs 79–81, 83–5, 222
Pumpianskii, Lev 19–20, 38
purges 40; *see also* show trials; terror
Pyr'ev, Ivan 19
   At 6 P.M. After the War 345–6
   The Kuban Cossacks 24, 295, 298
   The Rich Bride 24, 27
   The Swineherd and the Shepherd 20, 23, 217
   A Tale of the Siberian Land 378, 386, 388–9; *see also* popular culture; kolkhoz comedy; Pogodin, Nikolai

Quiet Flows the Don (opera; Dzerzhinskii, Ivan) 385–6
quoting, as ridicule 71–2, 100–1, 107–10

Raikin, Arkadii 37
Rakhmanov, Savid: *Welcome* 297
RAPP 52–3, 55, 259–60, 365
Rappaport, Gerbert: *A Musical Story* 375–81, 389–90
  Taxi to Heaven 292
Raskin, Viktor 83–4n, 133
'realistic grotesque' 190–210
repetitions, as a comic device 90–1, 100–1, 104–6, 138, 150–1, 166–7, 169–70, 175–6, 191, 336–9; *see also* types
Riazanov, El'dar: *A Carnival Night* 216, 390–7
Rich Bride, The (Pyr'ev, Ivan) 24, 27
Romanovich, Petr: *The Lyrical Suburban* 307
Ryklin, Grigorii 19, 51n, 288
Ryklin, Mikhail 21n, 23, 80–1, 88, 98

Saltykov-Shchedrin, Mikhail 19, 37, 52–3n, 84, 180, 191, 213
Samoilov, Lev 167
Santner, Eric 143, 262–3, 325–6, 340, 357–8
satire 34, 38–44, 213, 234–6, 396–7
  as non-satire 226, 229–30, 289
  debates on 43–67, 211–16, 229–32, 293
  documentary 130–2, 142, 145–6
  positive 44–67, 215–19, 292, 318, 357–8
  realistic 233–5, 291
  vs humor 39, 282, 286–7, 299, 318, 351–2, 396–7; *see also* laughter and the comic
Schmitt, Carl 94–5, 152–3, 178
self-criticism 27–8, 45–6, 50, 54, 229, 241–8
serialized comic narratives 169–75, 177
Shining Path, The (Aleksandrov, Grigorii) 24
Shkvarkin, Vasilii: *Another Man's Child* 325–6, 353, 357–9
  A Harmful Element 56
  Just a Girl 331–3, 335, 338–42, 347–9, 354–6
  Swindler 56; *see also* vaudeville
Sholokhov, Mikhail: *Virgin Soil Upturned* 20, 25–6; *see also* Grandfather [Grandpa] Shchukar'
Shostakovich, Dmitrii 27, 370–1, 383–4
show trials 68, 99–104, 111–12
Sidelev, Sergei: *Late for a Date* 342–3, 351–2
Silk Suzani (Kakhkhara, Abdulla) 301
Simonov, Konstantin 25–6, 199–201, 211–12
simplicity vs complexity 70, 76–7, 259, 291
  as a feature of enemies 146, 261–2, 264–8, 367; *see also* Dem'ian Bednyi
Simukov, Aleksei: *A Discharged Captain* 329–42, 345–7, 349–50, 354–5
  Wedding 304–6, 311–12
Sinyavsky, Andrei 37–8, 41–2
skaz 126–8, 142, 198–9; *see also* colloquial speech
slapstick 27, 35, 235, 257–8, 342–3, 368–9

Slobodskoi, Moris 19, 27, 29, 37, 191–2, 198, 207–9, 292
  King for a Day 217–19
Socialist Realism
  and carnival 23, 395
  and comedy in 33–5, 37–8, 42, 215, 231
  and general principles of 46, 53, 57, 65–6, 128, 194–5, 290–1, 297, 382, 396
  and populism 21–2, 25–9, 286–7, 319–21, 323, 361, 367, 370, 375, 385–94
  and a traditional analysis of 24–5, 27
Sofronov, Anatolii 19
  Beketov's Career 242–6
  as author of kolkhoz comedies with female characters 309–14; *see also* kolkhoz comedy; nomenklatura comedy
Solodar', Tsezar' 29, 292
  In the Lilac Garden 333–9, 341–4, 349–52, 354–9
Sovietology (as a traditional approach to the study of Soviet culture) 18–20, 24–5, 41–2
Springtime in Moscow (Gusev, Viktor) 336–9, 341–2, 346, 350–2, 354, 356–7
Stalin, as a participant in collective rituals of mockery 89–99
  involvement in the arts 219–23, 299
  sense of humor of 37, 318–19
  speeches 27, 69–89, 116
  writings 27, 101–2, 383–4
state laughter, key features 18–67, 127
  and criminal punishment 74
  and fear 22, 24–5, 27, 32, 219–23, 241–8
  as educational 49, 53, 115, 230–1, 235, 241, 267, 280, 283
  as 'laughter of victors' 202–3
  as legitimising the regime 20, 23, 33–4
  as a stranger to irony 37–42
  transformations of 40–1, 55, 92, 114, 216, 249, 272, 286–91, 322
  audience participation in 69–79, 89–99, 101–2, 110, 112–13, 265
  harmonizing 57–67; *see also* satire, positive
  no place for humor in 33–7, 39, 44–6, 67, 276–7, 287–8
  satire vs humor in 205, 215, 290–1, 397
state of exception 24, 93–7, 104
subject (Stalinist) 21–2, 24, 27, 42, 280, 284; *see also* state laughter, as educational
Sunday on Monday (Dykhovichnyi, Vladimir and Slobodskoi, Moris) 213
Surov, Anatolii 195–7
Swindler (Shkvarkin, Vasilii) 56
Swineherd and the Shepherd, The (Pyr'ev, Ivan) 20, 23, 217
synecdoche 190

Taimyr Calling (Galich, Aleksandr and Isaev, Konstantin) 325–6, 339–40, 345–6, 348–9, 351–2
Tale of the Siberian Land, A (Pyr'ev, Ivan) 378, 386, 388–9
tautology 86, 176, 231, 276–9; *see also* quoting; repetition, as a comic device
Taxi to Heaven (Rappaport, Gerbert) 292
terror 23–4, 27, 32, 40, 50, 68–9, 88–104, 114, 235, 241–9, 299–300, 302; *see also* campaigns; carnival, Stalinist; fear; show trials
theater 28, 60–7, 211, 292–3
Timoshenko, Semen: *The Goalkeeper* 336–9, 350, 354–5
Towards the Dawn (Bondareva, Elizaveta) 301
transference, as a feature of state laughter 206–10
trickster 195–7, 230–5, 343–4, 356–8
Trotsky, Leo 69–79, 235–6; *Trotskyite* 37, 71, 107, 110; *see also* nicknames
Turovskaya, Maya 27
Tvardovskii, Aleksandr 27, 115–50, 297–8
Tynianov, Iurii 18*n*, 127–8*n*, 215
types, as a comic device 49, 158–64, 180, 293–5
and new social roles 211, 307–14
in Stalinist comedy, negative 28, 40–3, 48, 50, 60, 76, 83–4, 180, 226, 234, 238–40, 247, 249
positive 54–7, 61; *see also* commedia dell'arte; non-human; satire, positive; typical, the (as a category)
typical, the (as a category) 54–5, 61–2, 65–6, 117–18, 153–67, 225, 395–6

unmasking 39, 52, 55, 57–9, 263, 343–4
Uspenskii, Boris 33

Vaiskopf, Mikhail 84–5*n*, 112

Vasil'ev, Vladimir: *The Lyrical Suburban* 307
Vasilii Terkin (Tvardovskii, Aleksandr) 27–8, 116–29, 148–50
vaudeville 16–17, 216–18, 291–2; *as traditional genre* 353; debates on 291–3; 326–7
Verner, Mikhail: *Late for a Date* 342–3, 351–2
Viburnum Grove (Korneichuk, Aleksandr) 314–16, 336–8
Virgin Soil Upturned (Sholokhov, Mikhail) 20, 25–6; *see also* Grandfather [Grandpa] Shchukar'
Virta, Nikolai 27, 60–1, 213
The Last Day of Pompeev 224–6
Vodop'ianov, Mikhail: *Emergency Landing* 331, 336–8, 342, 359–60
Volga-Volga (Aleksandrov, Grigorii) 23–4, 43, 235–6, 368, 372–5
Vyshinskii, Andrei 99–104

war humor 27, 328–30, 354, 359–60
Wedding With a Dowry (Diakonov, Nikolai) 304–5
When Swords Are Crossed (Pogodin, Nikolai) 213
White, Hayden 138–9

Zamiatin, Evgenii 41–2
Zaslavskii, David 117*n*, 150, 181–90, 198
Zharov, Mikhail: *A Noisy Household* 292
Zhdanov, Andrei 382–5
Zhitomirskii, Aleksandr 155–7, 159–63*n*, 161, 169–70, 172
Zhurbina, Evgeniia 57–8
Zinoviev, Grigorii 70–1, 74, 77, 100, 106–8
Žižek, Slavoj 88, 93, 136, 277
Zorkaia, Neia 27
Zoshchenko, Mikhail 18*n*, 19, 22, 37, 41–2, 56, 146, 292–3, 380–1
Zupančič, Alenka 119, 136, 145–6, 275, 336–8, 359